WARSHIPS TODAY

WARSHIPS TODAY

OVER 200 OF THE WORLD'S DEADLIEST WARSHIPS

CHRIS CHANT

Published in 2004 by Silverdale Books
an imprint of Bookmart Ltd
Registered Number 2372865
Trading as Bookmart Ltd
Blaby Road
Wigston
Leicester LE18 4SE

ISBN 1-84509-007-1

Produced by
Amber Books Ltd
Bradley's Close
74–77 White Lion Street
London N1 9PF
www.amberbooks.co.uk

Project Editor: Charlotte Judet
Design: Brian Rust

Printed and bound in Republic of South Korea

Previously published as part of the reference set *War Machine*.

Contents

Introduction

The days when a nation's power and status were measured by the number of battleships sailing under its flag are long gone, but the size of a country's navy remains an indicator of its perceived position on the world stage. The United States Navy today dwarfs that of its rivals, and one of its Nimitz-class aircraft carriers can single-handedly wield more airpower than the majority of the world's air forces. Nevertheless, other nations also possess strong navies: China, Russia, India, the United Kingdom, France, and Italy, for example.

The larger European modern navies have evolved from the fleets that contested World War II and the Cold War. The Atlantic is no longer a potential battleground, and the NATO navies do not have to protect extended supply lines from the Soviet threat. The emphasis for America and its allies has switched from 'blue water' or ocean-focused operations to fighting in the 'littoral' – in other words operations near a (usually hostile) coastline – in support of an expeditionary force, as has happened in both Afghanistan and Iraq recently. This change of emphasis has led to new weapons systems and ships being developed that are optimised to work in a much more threat-rich environment. Stealth, for so long only a preoccupation for submariners, is now becoming an important factor in ship design.

With the decline of the former Soviet navy and the rise of both China and India's fleets, the focus for naval operations is moving towards the east, to the Indian Ocean and the South China Sea and the shipping lanes that carry much of the world's manufactured goods. Piracy remains a problem in the twenty-first century, and modern navies are expected to cope with small, manoeuvrable, fast attack craft as easily as a conventional frigate or submarine. Anti-drug and anti-smuggling operations are also now a priority.

Many of the world's smaller navies such as those in South America and South East Asia use second-hand vessels from the larger nations to patrol their waters, most of them legacies of the Cold War. Richer nations such as the Gulf states buy their vessels 'off the shelf' from the shipyards of the USA or its NATO allies. Although only a few navies possess aircraft or helicopter carriers, there are a great many smaller vessels that serve as patrol craft, minesweepers, or missile boats in the world's navies.

In this book you will find an introduction to the various types of vessels that serve in the world's navies and how they operate, and a detailed directory of key classes of ship, including the aircraft and helicopters which now play such an important role in modern naval life.

A Russian Navy Kamov KA-27 'Helix' helicopter lifts off the flight deck of USS *Vella Gulf* during the annual 'Baltic Operations 2003' maritime exercise.

F-14 Tomcats formate over the 'Nimitz'-class carrier USS Eisenhower in the Mediterranean in 1988. Displacing over 95,000 tons fully loaded, the 'Nimitz' boats were designed as all-purpose carriers, incorporating the anti-submarine capability of the 'Essex'-class ASW carriers. The first three 'Nimitz' CVNs form a distinct sub-class.

The birth of the supercarrier

From 'Forrestal' to 'Nimitz'

The end of World War II saw the aircraft carrier firmly in place as the most powerful component of the modern navy, and the post-war years saw the United States pursue the most extensive carrier programme.

The landing of the first jet aircraft aboard the British carrier HMS *Ocean* late in 1945 heralded a new era for the aircraft carrier. The rapid advance in jet propulsion was to represent a major threat to that importance, however, and until the carrier could handle the increased size and speed of the new aircraft, naval aviation was to lag behind its land-based counterpart.

The post-war American carrier force was based on the 'Essex'-class carriers of World War II, together with the three large carriers of the 'Midway' class, which had been laid down as fleet carriers for wartime service. Many carriers had been laid up in reserve when the Navy was called to action in Korea.

Initially missions were flown with World War II-era machines like the F4U Corsair. However, the Navy had been experimenting with jets since the late 1940s, and the old propeller-driven aircraft were supplemented by jets like the F9F Panther. Navy aircraft proved highly effective during the war, providing close-support for United Nations troops on the ground.

Angled decks

In order to meet the requirements of jet-propelled aircraft a number of innovations were incorporated into old and new designs in the 1950s and 1960s. By far the most important of these was the angled flight deck. The high landing speeds of jet aircraft entailed comparatively long landing runs, and considerations of safety dictated that such runs be angled away from the longitudinal axis of the flight deck. The resultant change not only removed the possibility of aircraft collisions during a landing but also at a stroke allowed both the opportunity for more attempts to be made and, more importantly, the capability for the carrier to launch aircraft from its bow catapults while landings were being made on the angled deck.

First ordered in 1951, design of the 'Forrestal' class (this is the lead ship, with Skyraiders, Banshees and Furys on deck) was largely based around the Skywarrior bomber and incorporated lessons from the abortive 'United States' project. Forrestal entered service in 1956.

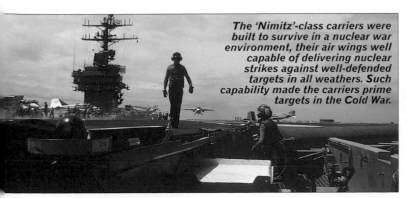

The 'Nimitz'-class carriers were built to survive in a nuclear war environment, their air wings well capable of delivering nuclear strikes against well-defended targets in all weathers. Such capability made the carriers prime targets in the Cold War.

The 'Kitty Hawk'- or 'Improved Forrestal'-class carrier USS Constellation *flanked by the replenishment vessel* Niagara Falls *and the cruiser* Leahy *in the South China Sea in January 1979.*

At the same time that the flight deck revolution occurred, it was realised that something more potent than a hydraulic catapult was needed to launch the jets.

Following trials (again aboard a British carrier, HMS *Perseus*) the solution universally adopted was the steam, or slotted cylinder catapult which drew power from the ship's boilers. It actually took up less space and was much lighter in relation to its power than its hydraulic predecessors. It is the size of the steam catapult and hence its operating capacity in terms of the load that can be accelerated safely, which today influences to a considerable degree the physical parameters and hence the cost of a carrier design.

The F-14 Tomcat weighs in at more than 33 tonnes when fully loaded, and the minimum catapult length required to accelerate such a machine to flying speed is in the order of 90 m (295 ft). To carry sev-eral examples of such long, powerful catapults requires a very big ship – which is part of the reason that the US Navy's supercarriers are the size that they are.

Deck landing aids

The problems associated with poor landing approaches to the carrier deck were also resolved by supplementing the human deck landing control officer with a mirror landing system – a visual aid that can be seen at a considerable distance by an incoming pilot, who can judge for himself whether or not his approach altitude is correct. However, the landing safety officer still has the final say on whether it is safe for an aircraft to land.

The US Navy wanted to play its part in providing America's post-war nuclear deterrent, in the face of fierce opposition from the USAF and its Strategic Air Command. But the Navy needed much larger carriers to operate nuclear-capable bombers like the AJ Savage, the A3D Skywarrior and the A2J Vigilante.

Air Force opposition brought the development of the flush-decked USS *United States* to an end, and funds allocated to its construction were transferred to strategic bomber programmes. However, many of its design features were to be used in the USS *Forrestal*, the first new carrier to be designed and laid down for the US Navy after the end of World War II. When it finally entered service, the 'Forrestal' design would introduce the hull form and deck arrangements for all subsequent US Navy carriers.

Commissioned in October 1955, the *Forrestal* was the largest warship built up to that time. Originally intended to be a smaller version of the *United States* design, with a flush deck, it was completely redesigned before construction started and emerged as the first carrier designed and built specifically for jet aircraft operations.

More than 315 m (1,033 ft) long, and with a flight deck over 76 m (250 ft) in width, the huge new carrier displaced over 75,000 tonnes at full load. *Forrestal* was followed by three sister ships, which were followed in turn by four further conventionally-powered 'Kitty Hawk'-class carriers. Each of these was built to a modified 'Forrestal' design.

Nuclear power

Even as the *Kitty Hawk* was entering service in 1961, however, the future of the American carrier was being heralded by the commissioning of the USS *Enterprise*. The world's first nuclear-powered carrier, the *Enterprise* was built to the same general layout as the 'Forrestals', but enlarged to make room for eight nuclear reactors. These gave the carrier virtually unlimited range.

The lessons learned in the operations of the *Enterprise* were incorporated into the next nuclear-powered carrier, the USS *Nimitz*, which was commissioned in 1975. The 'Nimitz' class has become the standard US Navy carrier design, with another seven ships entering service by the end of the 20th century. The latest examples displace more than 100,000 tonnes.

CVN-75: THE USN'S LATEST CARRIER

March 2003, and the USS *Harry S. Truman* (CVN-75) steams underway in the Eastern Mediterranean. *Harry S. Truman* was deployed in support of Operation Iraqi Freedom, the multi-national coalition effort to eliminate Iraq's weapons of mass destruction, and end the regime of Saddam Hussein. The carrier is the latest 'Nimitz'-class carrier to enter service, and will be followed by a further two vessels, the first of which is named USS *Ronald Reagan*. The later 'Nimitz' vessels displace up to a further 10,500 tons compared to their predecessors.

Below: An S-3 Viking prepares for take-off from the USS Enterprise, *the US Navy's first nuclear-powered carrier, with no less than eight reactors. Another notable feature was the island which originally incorporated antennas for electronically scanned main radars.*

Light carriers and V/STOL
Low-cost naval air power

After the conventional aircraft carrier became unacceptably costly and complex during the 1950s and 1960s, some navies acquired smaller ships – dedicated to the carriage of helicopters and/or V/STOL fighter/attack aircraft.

The 1950s and 1960s saw the aircraft carrier increase in size, cost and complexity, with the US Navy deploying its new nuclear-powered supercarriers, each capable of carrying up to 80 aircraft. However, the size, cost and complexity of these ships meant that few navies could afford to operate them and this led to a requirement for smaller, cheaper carriers carrying helicopters for amphibious assault operations.

Helicopter carriers

The use of aircraft carriers as bases for seaborne assaults was really pioneered by the British during their ill-starred Suez operation. The US Navy had already converted a surplus escort carrier as an experimental helicopter carrier, but Suez provided real combat experience for the concept. At Suez the British used a pair of obsolete light carriers, *Ocean* and *Theseus*, which had been intended to be used as troopships only, pointing the way forward for the development of dedicated helicopter carriers. These emerged as the US Navy 'Iwo Jima' class, which

dispensed with the usual strengthened decks, arrester gear, mirror landing aids, angled deck and steam catapults of the carrier, to concentrate on the carriage of some 24 assault helicopters, able to lift 200 Marines in a single wave.

The success of the assault carrier concept led directly to the development of dedicated ASW carriers, carrying a mix of helicopters and sometimes also some relatively 'easy' and undemanding fixed wing Grumman S-2 Trackers.

Light carriers

The British Hawker Siddeley Harrier was designed as a forward-deployable, land-based fighter bomber. However, trials in 1963 clearly demonstrated that the Harrier could operate from even very small ships (almost any ship that could embark a helicopter) and the US Navy, the Royal Navy and the Soviet navy each began separately examining the concept of a small cheap carrier, embarking STOVL aircraft and helicopters. The US Navy called this type of vessel a 'Sea Control Ship', but eventually cancelled it.

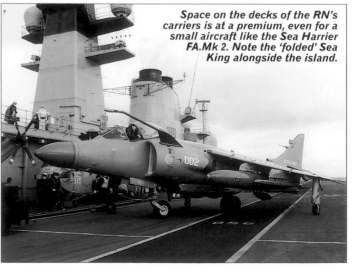

Britain's Royal Navy has operated four 'Harrier Carriers': HMS Ark Royal, Hermes, Illustrious (shown here) and Invincible. Of these, only Hermes was not laid down as a Through-Deck Cruiser, being modified for Sea Harrier operations later in its life.

Budgetary constraints and political considerations forced the RN to officially abandon plans to embark Harriers on its new 'Through Deck Cruisers'. In fact, Britain pressed on with a class of ships that was actually capable of (but not officially intended for)

embarking Harriers, and this ploy paid off when the Sea Harrier was finally ordered in 1975.

In the meantime, however, the delays in Britain had allowed the Soviets to catch up. The original Yak-36 undertook brief trials aboard the helicopter-carrier

More than any other nation, Britain has proven the concept of the light carrier in modern warfare. HMS Invincible has seen action during the Falklands War and off the Balkans. Its Sea Harriers shot down seven Argentine aircraft in 1982.

Space on the decks of the RN's carriers is at a premium, even for a small aircraft like the Sea Harrier FA.Mk 2. Note the 'folded' Sea King alongside the island.

CVF: BRITAIN'S NEXT CARRIER

On 30 September 2002, the British Government announced that 150 STOVL F-35B aircraft would be purchased to replace the country's Harrier/Sea Harrier fleet. The aircraft will operate from shore bases and from a new future aircraft carrier known as CVF. A pair of carriers is expected to be bought at a cost of £13 billion with a winning constructor from either BAE Systems (illustrated) or Thales to be announced in February 2003. The carriers will be built in such a way that they may be converted for CTOL operations at some point in the future.

Moskva, and a new class of 'Aviation Cruisers' was ordered. These were to be equipped with helicopters and a Yak-36-based multi-role fighter bomber. A service trials unit of Yak-38s deployed in December 1975 and the first operational Yak-38 squadron deployed aboard the *Kiev* in July 1976. It was initially cleared for VTOL operations only, with 'rolling take-offs' and short landings cleared from 1979. This led to some misunderstanding, with many believing that the Yak-38's configuration with separate lift jets and propulsion engines, prevented it from making rolling take-offs and landings. The Yak-38 (and the more powerful Yak-38M) remained in service until 1993, with the withdrawal of their carriers.

'Harrier carriers'

The introduction of the Sea Harrier led to another round of alterations to the aircraft-carrier. The Harrier's unique engine configuration makes it easy for it to perform rolling take-offs.

Dedicated 'Harrier Carriers' do not have to be fitted with catapults or arrester gear, making them lighter and cheaper than conventional carrier equivalents. They also feature distinctive 'ski-jump' take-off ramps, although these were initially conceived as a safety device to give conventional carrierborne

In 2002/03, 'Harrier Carriers' were being operated by India, Italy (left), Spain, Thailand and the UK (below). The US Marine Corps operates its Harriers off amphibious assault ships in support of shore operations.

aircraft a 'boost' of altitude on launch. British 'experts' did not see the benefit of a ski-jump for conventional take-off and landing (CTOL) aircraft, but realised straight-away that it could increase the payload of a Sea Harrier on launch. It was also realised that much steeper ski-jumps would be useable by STOVL aircraft, and that steeper angles would confer bigger payload/range benefits.

The potential of STOVL aircraft and ski-jumps was convincingly demonstrated in the Falklands, and this led to intensive efforts to market a 'conversion package' which could convert any civilian ship into a temporary 'Harrier Carrier'. Known as SCADS, the package incorporated a ski-jump, runway and containerised hangarage and maintenance facilities.

Although British experts rejected the ski-jump for CTOL applications, the USN felt it had advantages, but that the benefits were outweighed by the cost of rebuilding existing carriers. Nevertheless, the new French carriers are being fitted with a narrow and fairly shallow ramp which will help rotate the noses of the Aéronavale's new Rafales. In the USSR, the ski-jump was embraced with even more enthusiasm on the USSR's new genera-tion of carriers - only one of which – *Tbilisi* (later *Admiral Kuznetsov*) – entered service. The ski-jump on this Russian ship is almost as steep as that used by the Sea Harrier and is used for STOBAR (Short Take-Off But Arrested Recovery) operations, by air-craft like the Su-27K, without thrust vectoring. By using deck-mounted hold-backs to restrain an aircraft as it runs up to full power, a heavy CTOL fighter like the Su-27K can take off in a short distance from a rela-tively small, light ship by using a ski-jump.

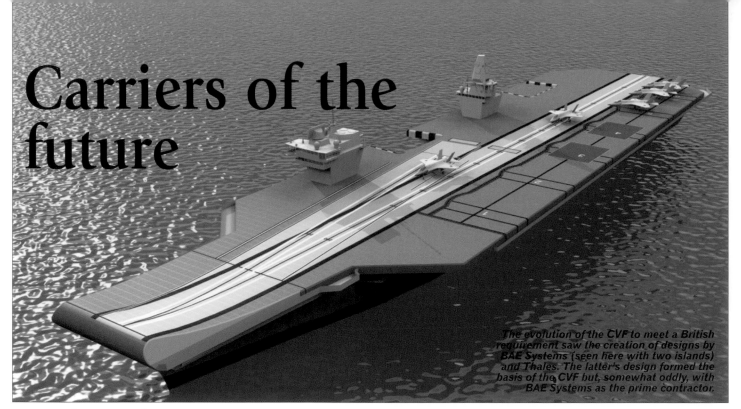

Carriers of the future

The evolution of the CVF to meet a British requirement saw the creation of designs by BAE Systems (seen here with two islands) and Thales. The latter's design formed the basis of the CVF but, somewhat oddly, with BAE Systems as the prime contractor.

Major air power at sea

At a time of changing and uncertain national imperatives, the aircraft carrier is still the most effective platform for long-range power projection, offering huge capabilities and excellent mobility.

The US Navy is committed to the development of an advanced-technology aircraft carrier for service through much of the 21st century. The service's goal is the creation of a sea-based tactical air platform that retains the warfighting relevance of the 'Nimitz' class, while allowing the US Navy to take advantage of maturing technologies to enhance capability at the same time as substantially reducing operating costs. An evolutionary progression of the current 'Nimitz' design, the new CVN-21 will have stealthier features than current carriers, but will not be a completely stealthy vessel.

The first ship is projected to be part of the fleet for at least 50 years through to 2063. In addition to the F/A-18E/F, the CVN-21 design will also integrate two emerging aircraft systems: the Joint Strike Fighter and Unmanned Combat Air Vehicle – Navy (UCAV-N). These three new aircraft systems, coupled with the navy's new Integrated Warfare System (IWS), will provide future joint force commanders with significantly enhanced strategic and operational capabilities.

CVN-21 (formerly known as CVNX-1) will feature a new-design nuclear propulsion plant incorporating the experience of three generations of submarine reactor development. The new propulsion system is necessary to reduce manning, maintenance, acquisition, and life-cycle costs. The new powerplant will be optimised to meet the large-scale electrical demands predicted for 21st century shipboard technology. A new electrical generation distribution system will also be a critical feature of the design.

Key innovative features in the new carrier will include an electromagnetic aircraft launch system that will have reduced manpower and maintenance requirements. This system will also extend aircraft life, as peak loads on the airframe will be reduced. This design utilises technol-

ogy similar to that used by experimental maglev trains. The benefits will include freeing the catapults from dependence on ship-generated steam, an increase in available energy, and a major reduction in both weight and volume. CVN-21 will have an advanced armour system to improve combat survivability. Commercial systems will be adapted for use in ship operations, habitability, mooring, and manoeuvring. An advanced weapons information management system will automate the process of inventory control, movement, and deployment of weapons from the magazine directly to the aircraft.

Royal Navy

The UK is also getting back into the 'carrier game'. The Strategic Defence Review announced plans to replace the current 'Invincible'-class

Left: An asset as valuable as an aircraft carrier must be very well defended. This MBDA image shows the Charles de Gaulle firing Aster 15 SAMs from one of the two Sylver A43 octuple launchers of the SAAM/F system.

Below: An artist's concept of a possible CVN-21 configuration. Though based ultimately on the 'Nimitz'-class carrier, the CVN-21 will introduce a number of steadily more radical features.

carriers from 2012 with two larger and more capable vessels able to operate a more powerful force. Successive operations in the Persian Gulf and off ex-Yugoslavia have demonstrated that aircraft carriers play a key role in force projection, contributing to peace support and, when necessary, military action. In these capacities the carrier offers both a coercive presence that can help contribute to conflict prevention, and also a flexible and rapidly deployable base for operations in which land-based airfields are currently unavailable or facilities ashore are still being established for use.

The three 'Invincible'-class aircraft carriers were designed for Cold War anti-submarine warfare operations in the North Atlantic. While undoubtedly effective in this role, their limited air groups mean they would be unable to fulfil the increasingly challenging demands of the new strategic

A photograph of the PCU (Pre-Commissioning Unit) Ronald Reagan (CVN-76), the US Navy's latest 'Nimitz'-class carrier, reveals the ship testing its countermeasure wash-down system to remove nuclear, biological and chemical agents.

environment. It was therefore decided to replace these vessels with two larger carriers that could each operate up to 46 aircraft, of both the fixed- and rotary-wing types.

The Future Aircraft Carrier, or CVF, will be the principal platform for the Royal Navy's and Royal Air Force's JCA (Joint Combat Aircraft), which will replace the two services' Harrier and Sea Harrier warplanes. The JCA will be capable of operating in all weathers, by day and night, to provide air defence for the carrier, as well as flying strike missions and conducting offensive support for ground forces ashore. The carrier air group will also include the Maritime Airborne Surveillance & Control (MASC) system, which will replace the capability provided by Sea King AEW helicopters. MASC will provide sensor coverage against air and surface threats, together with command and control for other air operations. The CVF will also be capable of supporting the operation of helicopters in a wide variety of roles including anti-submarine warfare, attack and support.

The STOVL variant of the F-35 JSF has been selected to fulfil the JCA role and, in order to maximise the flexibility that CVF can offer over its potential 50-year service life, the carriers will be built to an innovative adaptable design. The ships will be fitted for but not with catapults and arrester gear, and a 'ski-jump' ramp will be installed in order to facilitate operation of the STOVL F-35 aircraft. If required, post-JSF, the design will be capable of modification to operate aircraft requiring both a catapult launch and arrested recovery.

Other navies

France operates the most modern operational carrier design in the shape of the nuclear-powered *Charles de Gaulle*, a 36,600-ton vessel that entered service in 2000. A second new carrier is scheduled for service in the 2012-15 timeframe, but this will not necessarily be a repeat design. Talks are currently ongoing with the UK about the possibility of combining both nations' distinct carrier requirements.

The Russian navy remains

formally committed to aircraft carrier development on the American model. Indeed, the commander-in-chief of the Russian navy has been quoted as viewing a 'Nimitz'-class CVN as 'ideal', but impractical given today's economic realities. The Russian active carrier fleet now consists only of the *Admiral Kuznetsov*, but maintenance of the vessel is already proving to be problematical. Assembling a trained crew has provided major challenges, and the lack of a carrier facility on Russian territory is a further impediment to progress.

The only other major carrier project currently under way is in Italy. At 22,000 tons, the new 'Andrea Doria'-class unit will displace twice as much as the current 'Giuseppe Garibaldi' class of light ASW carrier, though it will be less than half the size of future British and French designs, and is a quarter the size of US Navy supercarriers. A multi-role design, the *Andrea Doria* will be able to serve as a landing ship for a force of 450 marines, a helicopter carrier, or an aircraft carrier able to operate eight STOVL fighters such as the F-35 JSF. Work on the ship began in 2001, and the vessel is due for delivery in 2007.

Left: The design studies for the UK's planned **CVF** went through a number of evolutionary forms, this being a BAE Systems study of 2002 for a relatively conventional type with a single island and a 'ski-jump'.

UCAV-N: FUTURE CARRIER AIR VEHICLE

The object of the US Navy's UCAV-N (Unmanned Combat Air Vehicle-Naval) programme is to validate the technical feasibility of creating an affordable naval unmanned combat air system to undertake the SEAD (Suppression of Enemy Air Defences), strike and surveillance roles within the context of the US's 'net-centric' command and control concept. Though optimised for carrierborne operation the UCAV-N is, for cost and interoperability reasons, to possess the maximum possible commonality with the US Air Force's land-based UCAV. The programme is looking at the whole gamut of appropriate technologies to ensure maximum operational capability in concert with low procurement and life-cycle costs, and is assessing the potential for 12 to 16 UCAV-Ns within the 'legacy force' carrier air wing.

The Royal Navy's initial SSBN, the four-ship 'Resolution' class, was built by stretching the hull of a 'Valiant'-class attack submarine for the carriage of 16 Polaris A3 missiles. Each weapon carried three 200-kT MIRVS, all aimed around the same target. Unlike their US counterparts, the Royal Navy's Polaris fleet remained in service until after the end of the Cold War.

Cold War submarine patrol

The silent threat

The shield protecting both East and West from the horrors of nuclear conflict during the years of the Cold War was to a large extent provided by constant patrols by the respective navies' submarine forces.

The nuclear-powered ballistic missile submarine, or 'SSBN' (Sub-Surface/Ballistic/ Nuclear) is beloved of Hollywood film directors. Movies such as *The Hunt for Red October*, *Crimson Tide* and *K-19* have illustrated how things can go dramatically wrong on vessels armed with unimaginable levels of destructive power. The reality, both during the Cold War and after, was invariably more mundane. These submarines, with their arsenals of long-range nuclear-tipped missiles, would quietly patrol for weeks, sometimes months on end, trying to avoid detection by other submarines, surface ships or Anti Submarine Warfare (ASW) aircraft. Their crews would conduct endless practice missile launchings, hoping that they would never need to do their job for real.

SSBNs have several advantages. The reactors provide power for vastly extended periods, unlike conventional diesel-electric engines. The air supply in the boat is continually regenerated and filtered, eliminating the need for surfacing. The only limit to the SSBN's endurance is the food supply and crew stamina.

To avoid detection, SSBNs would follow complex courses and manoeuvres to disorientate any surveillance. Sometimes these boats would be accompanied by hunter-killer submarines and surface combatants to provide a secure cordon around the vessel. Communications to and from the SSBNs were few. They normally consisted of short bursts, in the orders of one-tenth of a second, of Exceptionally Low Frequency (ELF) 'flash' radio traffic. Should they ever be detected, SSBNs were fitted with countermeasures such as decoys and acoustic homing torpedoes for self-defence.

Entry into service

The first ballistic missile submarine to enter service was the Soviet diesel-electric 'Zulu' class. These boats were constructed in the early 1950s. Initially, a single boat was converted to launch the R-11FM (SS-N-1b 'Scud-A') ballistic nuclear missile. Five boats were then converted following successful trials. Each carried two R-11FMs, later replaced with the R-13 (SS-N-4 'Sark'), with a range of 650 km (404 miles) and a 5-megaton (MT) warhead.

The 'Zulu' vessels were later followed by the diesel-electric 'Golf'-class boats. However, these boats were easy prey for the US Navy's anti-submarine force. The range of the R-13 missiles forced the 'Golfs' to operate close to the continental US. Fifteen 'Golf'-class boats entered service between 1960-62. Some 13 of the vessels were later converted to

USS Georgia enters port at New London, Connecticut, in February 1984. Unlike its Soviet contemporary, the 'Typhoon', the 'Ohio'-class SSBNs were not equipped to operate through weak spots in the polar ice.

deploy the R-21 (SS-N-5 'Sark') – a revolutionary missile for the Soviet navy in that it could be fired while the submarine was submerged, unlike previous Soviet SLBMs.

The first SSBN to enter service with the US Navy was the USS *George Washington*. This boat was effectively a stretched 'Scorpion'-class nuclear submarine. The hull was lengthened to allow for two rows of eight Polaris A1 missiles to be installed. Polaris A1 had a range of 2600 km (1,615 miles) and a single 500-kiloton (kT) warhead. The USS *George Washington* was launched on 15 November 1960, a mere three years after its keel was laid down. The rapid completion of the boat was seen as a managerial and technical triumph for Rear Admiral W. Raborn, who led the project.

Left: As the most potent Western SSBNs of the Cold War, the 'Ohio' class were originally fitted with 24 missile launch tubes for the Trident I SLBM.

Right: The sonar room of the 'Lafayette' boat USS Ulysses S. Grant in 1969. SSBNs can be fitted with very large sonar arrays, as their nuclear reactors generate so much electricity.

However, the range of the Polaris A1 meant the boats had to be based at forward locations such as Holy Loch in Scotland, Rota in Spain and Guam in the Pacific Ocean.

The seminal 'George Washington'-class nuclear-powered boats would see the introduction of several now-standard procedures for American SSBNs. For instance, each boat was served by two crews, designated 'Blue' and 'Gold', one of which was at sea, while the other was on shore, preparing to relieve the Blue crew on its next mission.

The 'George Washingtons' were followed by the 'Ethan Allen' class. Completed between 1961-63, these vessels were similar to their predecessors, but were designed specifically to serve as SSBNs.

In 1962, the Royal Navy deployed its first SSBN, after the UK signed an agreement with the US to purchase four

Polaris missile submarines. The first boat, HMS *Resolution*, was completed in 1967. The Polaris missile bodies were constructed in the US, while warheads and some command and control systems were designed and built in the UK.

Missile conversions

During the same year, the US completed the service induction of the 'Lafayette'-class SSBN. Thirty-one boats entered service. The first eight boats were fitted with the Polaris A2, the rest of the class were fitted with the Polaris A3, the most modern variant. Between 1979-83, 12 'Lafayettes' were converted to deploy the Trident C4 SLBM. The first vessel to receive the conversion, the USS *Francis Scott Key*, began its first deterrence patrol on 20 October 1979.

In 1972 the Soviets announced a new, major SSBN. Known as the 'Yankee' class, it was armed with 16 R-27 (SS-N-6 'Serb') missiles. However, the R-27, with a range of 2,400 km (1,491 miles) and 3000 km (1,864 miles) for models one and two respectively, meant that the boats would have to get close to the US coastline, and therefore closer to US anti-submarine activities, if they were to strike targets deep in the US. However, this gave the Soviets a major

advantage, as flight times of the missiles would be around four to five minutes, leaving little time for warning.

The Soviets followed the 'Yankee' class with the 'Delta' class. Most of the 'Deltas' deployed 12 R-29 (SS-N-8 'Sawfly') missiles, with a 7800-km (4,846-mile) range. Later, the 'Delta III' class would deploy the R-29R (SS-N-18 'Stingray') with a range of 8000 km (4,971 miles). The 'Deltas' were essentially designed to be a first-strike weapon. They would pierce the relatively thin ice in the Arctic and fire their missiles for a crippling nuclear strike against the US.

During the same year, the US began the development of the Trident I SLBM, based on the previous Poseidon SLBM. In 1981, Trident was deployed on the massive US 'Ohio'-class SSBNs. These boats deployed 24 missiles. The first eight boats, entering service between 1981-86, were armed with the Trident I missile. The remaining boats, completed between 1988-97 were fitted with Trident II.

The Soviet response to the 'Ohios' were the 'Typhoon'-

class SSBNs. These vessels would each deploy 20 R-39 (SS-N-20 'Sturgeon') missiles. These boats were designed to stay beneath the waves for over a year. They would be used to deliver a blow against the US once it was beginning to recover from a nuclear war. Unlike previous Soviet and American SSBNs, the missiles of the 'Typhoon' are equipped forward of the sail. Due to the long period that the vessel was expected to stay away from port, and submerged, crew areas were lavishly furnished with saunas and even a swimming pool. Six 'Typhoons' were completed between 1977-89.

While some land and air units charged with nuclear delivery belonging to the world's nuclear powers were downsized or eliminated at the end of the Cold War, the US, UK, France, Russia and China show no signs of dismantling their SSBN forces. Such vessels continue to provide a powerful message of stealthy deterrent, and an important badge of national prestige, providing future filmmakers with dramatic settings for many years to come.

US SLBM RANGE: STRATEGIC REACH

Although Poseidon could not strike as far as Polaris A3, it made up for this by carrying 10 kiloton-yield MIRVs (a maximum of 14 was possible, but outlawed under the SALT I agreement) rather than the three of its predecessor. Polaris A3 passed from US Navy service in 1981, but was retained by the Royal Navy until after the Cold War. Trident I, development of which began in 1972, was based on the Poseidon C3 missile but added a third stage for increased range.

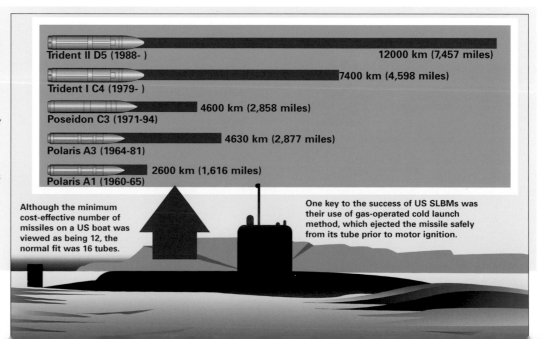

Missile	Range
Trident II D5 (1988-)	12000 km (7,457 miles)
Trident I C4 (1979-)	7400 km (4,598 miles)
Poseidon C3 (1971-94)	4600 km (2,858 miles)
Polaris A3 (1964-81)	4630 km (2,877 miles)
Polaris A1 (1960-65)	2600 km (1,616 miles)

Although the minimum cost-effective number of missiles on a US boat was viewed as being 12, the normal fit was 16 tubes.

One key to the success of US SLBMs was their use of gas-operated cold launch method, which ejected the missile safely from its tube prior to motor ignition.

Submarine sensors
Undersea warfare

The submarine sensor had a vital role in the nuclear-armed game of cat and mouse that was played out between Allied and Soviet submarines in the tense days of the Cold War.

Underwater warfare is unlike any other form of conflict. A duel between submarines is a bit like that between two men, blindfold in a darkened room. Both carry loaded revolvers, but the only clues to each other's position come from the sounds the opponent makes: the rustle of shoes on the carpet or of moving clothes, or at close range the sound of breathing.

Sound is the only sense that is of any real use under water. Light, radio and radar penetrate the ocean poorly or not at all. Sound, on the other hand, can travel great distances. The first underwater sensors developed in the early years of this century were simple hydrophones. By using an array of several such listening devices, sub-marines could be detected at distances of thousands of yards, and even the general direction of their movement might be determined.

ASDIC and sonar

During World War II, active sound systems like the British ASDIC and the American sonar were developed. They used bursts of sound, or 'pings', which produced echoes. These echoes were then detected as they bounced back off targets, in much the same way that radar uses radio waves to detect aircraft. Sonar, which was originally an acronym for SOund Navigation And Ranging, has become the generic term for any underwater use of echo-location, and has even been compared to the navigation techniques used by whales and dolphins.

The art of anti-submarine warfare would be especially useful during the Cold War in the north Atlantic. Huge

The 'Vanguard'-class SSBN boats feature a Type 2043 hull-mounted sonar system. This can be configured to act in both active and passive modes.

resources were invested by both the Western powers and the Soviets to develop increasingly sophisticated sonar systems and anti-sonar countermeasures. One such example was the US SOund SUrveillance System (SOSUS) line – a network of undersea microphones laid across the seabed at the Bering Straits. It was designed to listen for Soviet missile boats and hunter-killer submarines entering and leaving their home port of Murmansk. Once a positive 'fix' had been identified, NATO hunter-killer submarines would then follow the Soviet boat. In response, Soviet submarine commanders invented a manoeuvre dubbed the 'Crazy Ivan'. Upon discovering that it was being followed by a Western submarine, the Soviet boat would suddenly rotate 180°, doubling back on itself and driving at high speed towards its pursuer, an intensely nerve-racking experience for the Allied boat.

When operating at surface level, the 'Vanguard'-class boats use, among other systems, a Kelvin-Hughes Type 1007 I-band radar navigation system.

One of the Soviet navy's primary missions throughout the Cold War was the detection and destruction of NATO submarines, in particular ballistic missile boats (SSBNs). Hunter-killer boats were also targeted, however. The purpose behind this was twofold; not only did the Soviets want to destroy the threat to their shipping and submarines, but they also wanted to allow their own SSBNs to disperse in order to fire their missiles. The tense nature of anti-submarine combat made the north Atlantic one of the most terrifying theatres of the Cold War.

Sonar clutter

Technology has made sonar effective beyond the wildest dreams of its early operators, but the sea remains a confusing place. In spite of all the highly-advanced sensor and computerised signal processing equipment that make up a modern sonar system, the performance of that system will vary greatly depending on the conditions. For one thing, sound does not travel in straight lines under water. Much also depends upon transient ocean conditions, such as water temperature and salinity, and confusing echoes can be generated by the sea bed, storm waves,

schools of fish or pods of whales.

A basic fact of sonar operations is that the lower the sound frequency, the further it will travel. However, there is a trade-off between range and discrimination. Small, high-frequency sonars have limited range, but are useful for providing detailed information in specialist situations, such as mine-hunting or when operating under ice. Lower-frequency sonars have longer range but provide less detailed information about targets. In general, the larger the sound generator, the lower the frequency it can generate. This may go some way to explaining why modern submarines and ASW vessels are much larger than earlier vessels.

ASW destroyers and frigates usually have a large bow sonar – often indicated by a sharply-raked stern – that is used as an early-warning system, with helicopters being used to close in precisely on the contact using their own higher frequency dipping sonars.

Despite efforts to develop new submarine detection systems, sound remains the primary method of detection. Nevertheless, ASW aircraft also use an additional search technique called Magnetic Anomaly Detection.

Inset: 'Vanguard'-class submarines are fitted with a Thales CH91 attack periscope and a Thales CK51 search periscope. Both of these feature a TV camera and a normal optical channel.

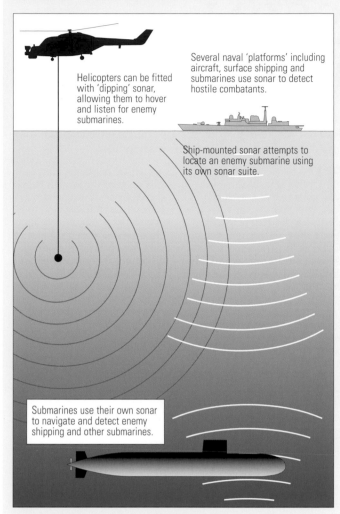

SONAR: LISTENING FOR THE ENEMY

Helicopters can be fitted with 'dipping' sonar, allowing them to hover and listen for enemy submarines.

Several naval 'platforms' including aircraft, surface shipping and submarines use sonar to detect hostile combatants.

Ship-mounted sonar attempts to locate an enemy submarine using its own sonar suite.

Submarines use their own sonar to navigate and detect enemy shipping and other submarines.

Arguably one of the most vital naval war-fighting tools ever invented, sonar is used across most naval platforms for the detection and destruction of submarines and surface shipping. During the Cold War, naval helicopters would become particularly useful for submarine detection. They were able to 'dip' a sonar sensor into the water and listen for submarines. They could be deployed on ships far away from their home ports and had the added advantage of being able to fly quickly from place to place, covering a wide area in a relatively short amount of time. The helicopter brought a quiet revolution to anti-shipping and submarine warfare.

With their huge destructive force, the 'Vanguard'-class submarines represent a powerful nuclear deterrent.

SSBNs
Death from the deep

Lurking stealthily beneath the surface of the world's oceans, nuclear-powered ballistic missile submarines carry the ultimate threat of destruction.

The history of nuclear missile submarines is interwoven with the Cold War rivalry between the USA and the USSR. After World War II, the outermost Soviet defensive line consisted of a huge force of submarines to deter or to intercept hostile task forces.

After a period of instability following Stalin's death in 1953, Nikita Khrushchev took power in February 1955. He quickly initiated a crash programme of submarine development. By August 1958, the first of the 'November' class of nuclear-powered submarines had been commissioned, and ways of giving the submarine an offensive strategic role were also being studied.

After some unsuccessful attempts with V-2 missiles towed in watertight contain-ers, the Soviets decided to install vertical launch tubes in the conning tower of the submarine itself. Between 1956 and 1958, a number of 'Zulu' class boats were modified to take two tubes, each about 2.25 m (7 ft) in diameter, in the aft part of the fin. The missiles needed to be fired from the surface, and their range was only 563 km (350 miles).

Polaris

Meanwhile, the USA had been engaged in more cautious submarine development. The first sub-launched strategic weapons were solid-fuel, low-trajectory cruise missiles. However, in an astonishing display of scientific, economic, engineering and financial muscle, the US Navy developed the Polaris system in less than four years. By 1960,

The Polaris missile brought about a revolution in strategic warfare. Developed in under four years, it was the West's primary strategic deterrent for two decades from 1960.

The mighty 'Typhoon' ballistic missile submarine – known to its Russian users as Akula or Shark – is the largest submarine ever built.

BOOMERS: UNDERWATER DETERRENT

Early submarine-launched missiles were not very accurate. However, the development of advanced guidance systems means that the current generation of missile submarines, known as 'Boomers' to the US Navy, can be used against specific targets with devastating accuracy.

01 MISSILE ALERT

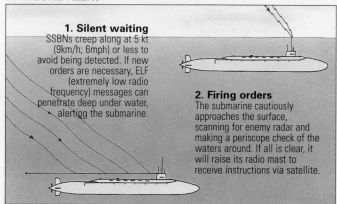

1. Silent waiting
SSBNs creep along at 5 kt (9km/h; 6mph) or less to avoid being detected. If new orders are necessary, ELF (extremely low radio frequency) messages can penetrate deep under water, alerting the submarine.

2. Firing orders
The submarine cautiously approaches the surface, scanning for enemy radar and making a periscope check of the waters around. If all is clear, it will raise its radio mast to receive instructions via satellite.

02 UNDERWATER LAUNCH

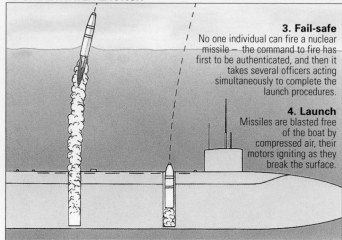

3. Fail-safe
No one individual can fire a nuclear missile – the command to fire has first to be authenticated, and then it takes several officers acting simultaneously to complete the launch procedures.

4. Launch
Missiles are blasted free of the boat by compressed air, their motors igniting as they break the surface.

03 MID-COURSE

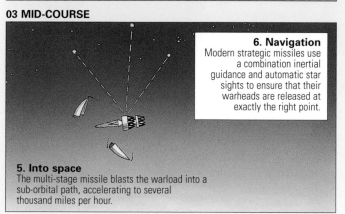

6. Navigation
Modern strategic missiles use a combination inertial guidance and automatic star sights to ensure that their warheads are released at exactly the right point.

5. Into space
The multi-stage missile blasts the warload into a sub-orbital path, accelerating to several thousand miles per hour.

04 TERMINAL MANOEUVRES

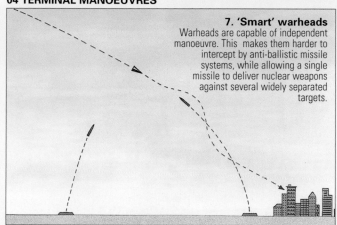

7. 'Smart' warheads
Warheads are capable of independent manoeuvre. This makes them harder to intercept by anti-ballistic missile systems, while allowing a single missile to deliver nuclear weapons against several widely separated targets.

the first of the 'George Washington' class was in service, armed with sixteen Polaris A-1 ballistic missiles: These were solid-fuelled, could be launched under water, and had a range of some 2253 km (1,400 miles). By 1965, a fleet of 41 had been commissioned.

The Soviets were unable to deploy a similar submarine until 1967, when the first of 34 'Yankee' boats was commissioned. It is believed that the Soviets based the design on stolen US plans. It was fitted with 16 SS-N-6 'Sawfly' single-stage liquid-fuel missiles in hull-mounted tubes placed aft of the conning tower.

From the beginning of the 1970s, both navies concentrated on the development of larger and larger submarines to carry even longer-range missiles. In 1980 the four Soviet 'Delta' class designs were joined by the first of the 'Typhoon' class – at 171 m (561 ft) and up to 40,000 tons, the largest submarines in the world.

Meanwhile, the Americans had replaced Polaris with Poseidon, and then in 1976 began to build the 24 missile 'Ohio' class (170.7 m/560 ft; 18,700 tons). Smaller than the Typhoon, they are much more quiet, and are even more deadly. They carry the D5 Trident 2 missile, which is as accurate as any land-based missile.

Other navies

The Royal Navy began operations with four Polaris boats of the 'Resolution' class in the late 1960s. They have been replaced by the larger 'Vanguard'-class vessels (148 m/486 ft; 15,000 tons), which carry 16 Trident 2s. The French, who withdrew from NATO in 1966, went ahead with the development of their own nuclear submarines and ballistic missiles. *Le Redoutable* (128 m/420 ft; 9,000 tons), commissioned in 1971, deployed 16 M1 missiles of a size and range similar to the Polaris A-2. The 'Triomphant' class (138 m/ 453 ft; 14,200 tons) became operational in the 1990s, and will be upgraded to the M5, comparable with the Trident 2.

Crewmen manning ballistic missile submarines spend long, boring patrols at sea – but they must be ready to launch their awesome charges at a moment's notice.

China completed one 'Xia' class boat in 1987. It carries 12 Chinese-manufactured JL-2 two-stage solid-fuel missiles, which have a range in excess of 6437 km (4,000 miles). A new missile submarine is currently under development.

With the ratification of the SALT agreements and the START process, the number of US and Soviet missile submarines has been decreased. However, it is noteworthy that even in the new world order, defence cuts have rarely extended to submarines, and these vessels continue to prowl the black depths of the world's oceans.

Seamen on the casing of a US Navy attack submarine prepare to leave harbour. Nuclear submariners like these from several nations have been waging a shadowy war of nerves beneath the waves for more than four decades. Even with the end of the Cold War, the Hunter-Killers still put to sea.

Nuclear hunter-killers
The art of underwater ambush

The 'war' waged between nuclear-powered attack submarines was that of cat-and-mouse. Concealment and stealthy approach were vital elements, but so too were quietness of operation, advanced sensors and weapons, and the skills of captains and crews.

The nuclear-powered attack submarine (SSN) can undertake 'area defence', tasking the SSN with patrol of a large swath of ocean to safeguard an area against other SSNs and ASW ships, and 'point defence', requiring the SSN to patrol a specific 'point' to protect a convoy, task force or ship.

To perform these missions, the SSN 'trails' a target boat (a 'contact') covertly or overtly. The SSN acquires its contact as the target leaves port or passes through a 'chokepoint'. If the contact believes it is being trailed, it can perform a U-turn (a tactic known to Western SSN crews as a 'Crazy Ivan'), tow a detection device to listen for trailers, or launch decoys and countermeasures to confuse the pursuer's sonar. It is important for the trailer to keep contact with the target, and itself remain undetected. This affects how close the trailer can get to its contact, and also its evasive actions to avoid countermeasures.

The second option is 'overt' trailing. This can mean illuminating the contact with regular sonar bursts. If the trailer stays close to its contact, it can be very difficult for the contact to elude its pursuer. The overtness of the trailing also simplifies the use of countermeasures by the contact, however. Once the contact determines that it is being trailed, it can release large concentrations of bubbles to mask the boat from its pursuer's sonar. The contact can also seek to jam the trailer's sonar with electronic countermeasures. Finally, the contact can ask friendly submarine and ASW forces to harass its pursuer.

During the Cold War, the US and Soviet navies developed different doctrines for their SSN forces. Soviet SSNs protected their SSBN flotillas and forward-located major surface ships. A Soviet imperative was the destruction of US SSNs before the latter entered the GIUK (Greenland-Iceland-UK) gap,

Above: The US Navy's 'Seawolf' is the ultimate hunter-killer, with a performance unlikely to be matched for decades. Built to fight the Soviets, it is far too expensive for the post-Cold War world.

Below: In the 1980s, Soviet submarine designs like this 'Akula'-class nuclear-powered attack boat closed a major part of the technological gap between the Soviet Navy and its Western foes.

Above and left: The massive Soviet submarine fleet created during the 1950s was composed of diesel-powered boats like this 'Foxtrot'. The rapid US development of nuclear powered boats like the Pogy, (left), seen here surfaced in the Arctic, meant that the Soviets had to develop their own nuclear boats more quickly.

a chokepoint for Soviet shipping between the Barents Sea and the North Atlantic. Once US SSNs were in the Barents Sea they were able to 'mix' with Soviet boats, thereby making their detection and destruction difficult. However, the chokepoints could also work to the Soviets' advantage because any boats beyond the GIUK gap could be regarded as hostile: this provided the Soviet SSNs with a 'stand-off' distance to attack Western boats. The Soviets could also attempt to 'lure' Western SSNs into the launch of a torpedo, giving away their position and facilitating attack by Soviet ASW forces.

Some US SSN exercises suggested that there was only a 50 per cent chance that a single torpedo would destroy an SSN.

Worst-case scenario

For the US, such tactics could have resulted in a 'worst-case' scenario in which their SSNs were drawn into 'dogfights' with Soviet boats. This would have removed the US boats' advantage in being quieter. A dogfight would have revealed the presence of each side's boats to the other, and fortune would not favour the quieter boat but that with the greater firepower, agility, countermeasures and damage resistance.

The priority for the US Navy's SSNs was the protection of carrier battle groups and amphibious forces, as well as seeking out Soviet SSBNs, laying minefields and attacking coastal targets with cruise missiles. To this end, of the 40-45 SSNs that the US Navy might have had available in the Atlantic at any one time during the late part of the Cold War, a dozen might have been detailed with protection of carrier battle groups, nine or ten with patrol of the GIUK chokepoint, and about 20 with the forward area patrol.

The first priority was for the US SSN fleet to deny the Soviets access to the sea from Murmansk and Petropavlovsk on the Atlantic and Pacific coasts respectively. Soviet ASW forces were aware of the US SSN strategy and concentrated their sensors around the ports, forcing US boats to patrol farther offshore. This widened the gap through which the Soviet SSNs could pass, while hampering the detection efforts of the US submarines. Moreover, the closer the US SSNs got to the Soviet chokepoints, the tighter the concentration of friendly boats. This could cause a commensurate increase in the risk of friendly fire should a shooting war have begun.

SSN OF TOMORROW: C21 SUBMARINES

The most advanced nuclear-powered designs currently being built include the US Navy's 'Virginia' class and the British 'Astute'-class boats. The prohibitive unit cost of the 'Seawolf' class and changing strategic requirements led to the US Navy defining a smaller new generation attack submarine. The 'Virginia'-class New Attack Submarine is an advanced, stealthy, multi-mission nuclear-powered vessel designed for deep ocean anti-submarine warfare and for littoral (shallow water) operations. The Royal Navy's 'Astute'-class submarine is a nuclear-powered attack submarine which is to replace the five 'Swiftsure'-class submarines, launched between 1973 and 1977. An evolutionary development of the 'Trafalgar' class, the new design will carry up to 38 tube-launched torpedoes and missiles, increasing fighting power by over 50 per cent.

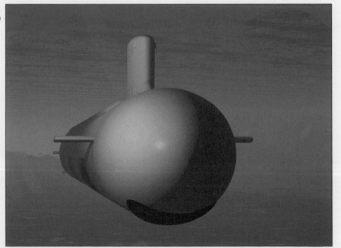

Above: Since supporting land operations with cruise missile fire has become a key submarine mission, the new 'Virginia' class is designed to operate in shallow coastal waters as well as in the deep ocean and under the ice cap.

Left: A little smaller than the US 'Virginia' class, the 'Astute' class will be armed with a mix of Tomahawk cruise missiles, Harpoon anti-ship missiles and heavyweight wire-guided torpedoes.

Surface action groups
Naval arbiters

After World War II, the battleship largely disappeared from the world's fleets. The classic surface action of ship against ship was no longer the deciding factor in oceanic warfare dominated by supercarriers and nuclear submarines.

After World War II smaller surface combatants soon became dedicated to the anti-aircraft or ASW roles. Fleets were organised into carrier battle groups, ASW groups or amphibious squadrons with ships carrying fewer weapons.

In the 1980s the battleship gained a new lease of life as the US recommissioned the four 'Iowa'-class battleships in an upgraded form, and the Soviets launched their first 'Kirov'-class nuclear 'battle-cruisers'.

While the US battleship's nine 16-in (406-mm) guns kept all of their power, it was the hull's great capacity for carrying modern weapons that was most useful. Thus long-range strike capability was provided by 32 Tomahawk cruise missiles and 16 Harpoon anti-ship missiles.

The 'Iowas' were intended to lead surface action groups, able to substitute for carriers as power projection tools. They were then replaced by new multi-role vessels. All modern US combatants have at least one medium-calibre gun, but Harpoon can destroy ships at a range of 100 km (62 miles), and Tomahawk can reach land targets more than 1000 km (621 miles) distant.

New threats

The end of the Cold War saw a radical change in the threat facing the world's only remaining superpower. At the end of the 20th century, the US Navy's force structure was centred on 12 carrier battle groups and 12 amphibious ready groups. However, the nature of sea battle has changed considerably. The USN has now to counter enemies ranging from small terrorist groups operating across national boundaries, through small navies

Above: The 'Iowa'-class battleships saw service during the 1991 Gulf War, but were retired soon after this; they required too many men to be cost effective, and most of their functions could be performed by more economical vessels able to undertake a variety of roles.

Right: Development of guided surface-to-surface missiles gave surface action groups new life. Without main guns, the Royal Navy's Type 22 'Broadsword' relied on Exocet missiles in surface combat.

Above: US Navy action groups increasingly operate with foreign vessels. This Security Council Coalition fleet, deployed in support of Enduring Freedom, includes (from left to right) HMAS Darwin ('Oliver Hazard Perry' class), USS Paul Hamilton ('Arleigh Burke') USS Fletcher ('Spruance'), HMAS Anzac and HMS Cardiff (Type 42).

Above: The USS Florida launches a Tomahawk cruise missile. The Florida is one of four 'Ohio'-class SSBNs being converted to guided missile submarine (SSGN) standard with 154 Tomahawk missiles.

Above: The attack submarine USS Toledo conducts surface operations alongside the destroyer USS Donald Cook. Toledo was among the first boats to launch Tomahawks during Operation Iraqi Freedom.

equipped with missile-armed FACs, to regional powers able to deny sea control in key areas.

The USN's Global Concept of Operations creates new force packages, improving the ability to operate in more areas around the world. This expansion of power is critical, because in place of the old 'two and a half wars' which was the yardstick for USN capability, modern lower-intensity operations can occur in four or more widely dispersed theatres simultaneously.

To increase operational flexibility, Global ConOps envisages 12 carrier strike groups, 12 expeditionary strike groups, nine strike and missile defence surface action groups, and four converted 'Ohio'-class SSBNs each carrying up to 154 Tomahawks; in all, 37 independent strike groups, able to provide a continuous and powerful presence over a greater percentage of the globe than is now possible.

Carrier strike groups will remain the core of USN warfighting strength. They will be escorted by fewer surface combatants and submarines when operating against transnational enemies offering little or no naval threat. Amphibious or expeditionary

groups will remain important. The addition of 'Ticonderoga'-class cruisers and 'Arleigh Burke'-class destroyers will add a surface action capability to amphibious forces, and enhance organic air defence, undersea warfare and strike capability required for independent operation in any low-to medium-threat situation.

Surface capability

Recent combat has shown that while the carrier battle group remains the strongest US power projection tool, the missile-armed surface action group is of growing importance. At least two units of each group will be Aegis ships with missile defence weapons, and a third ship (an Aegis combatant where possible) will provide additional striking power and defensive protection to the group. These surface action groups will also serve as independent crisis-response forces, making full use of their Tomahawks' precision-attack capability.

These components of the future fleet are designed to operate independently when involved in low-threat areas, but will have the ability to combine and form expeditionary strike forces that will maximise offensive power when necessary.

'KIROV': SOVIET BATTLECRUISER

The Soviet 'Kirov' design was a very different breed to the US Navy's reborn battleships. The 'Kirov'-class vessels carried a wide array of ASW and anti-aircraft weapons in addition to their anti-surface ship missiles. Soviet naval doctrine used to consider all surface ships to be subordinate to submarine operations, and indeed the 'Kirovs' were well suited to leading a surface force supporting friendly SSBNs and hunting out enemy submarines. But these powerful missile cruisers were equally suited to a more aggressive role, as the nucleus of a Soviet surface action group. Had the Cold War ever turned hot, it is likely that the 'Kirovs', together with 'Slava'-class cruisers and 'Sovremenny'-class destroyers, would have used their nuclear-capable long-range, supersonic missiles as part of a multi-layered air, surface and submarine attack on forward-deployed US Navy carrier battle groups.

For either a deliberate show of force or a pinpoint attack, the land-attack missile has replaced the naval gun as the weapon of choice for attacks on land targets by naval units. Here the USS Philippine Sea launches a Tomahawk missile during Operation Allied Force over Kosovo in 1999.

Below: An 'Iowa'-class battleship fires all of its nine 16-in (406-mm) main guns in a full three-turret salvo. Apparently, the flash is powerful enough to be observed on the ship's radar.

Below: A closed-circuit TV camera captures the moment that an explosion ripped through Number Two turret on the USS Iowa on 19 April 1989, killing all 47 crew in the gun turret.

Land Attack
From gun to missile

Gunboat diplomacy at the touch of a button. The battleship has played a vital role in shore bombardment, but the big guns of yesteryear have now been replaced by the lethally precise Tomahawk.

For several centuries the battleship was the dominant naval platform for land attack. Cannon, and later large-calibre naval guns, played a major role in coastal bombardment. From the days of Sir Francis Drake and the Spanish Armada in the 16th century, the battleship grew in size and sophistication to reach its zenith in World War II. However, in spite of the important role that such ships played in the maritime wars of the Pacific and the European theatres, these conflicts made the battleship obsolete.

During World War II, 32 capital ships were sunk. Of that total, only eight were destroyed by similar vessels, and the others succumbed to aircraft and submarines. The importance of these two relatively new weapons systems would act as a curtain raiser to the Cold War, where they would assume almost supreme importance in modern naval tactics.

Iowa in Korea

HMS *Vanguard*, the last British battleship, was scrapped in 1960, but the US Navy kept its four 'Iowa'-class battleships. These vessels saw active combat for a brief period, assisting shore bombardment during the Korean War. The USS *New Jersey* was pressed back into service for a brief period during the Vietnam War but was one of the first ships to be withdrawn after President Richard Nixon began to downsize the US commitment to the ongoing conflict.

The US did not totally forsake the battleship, though. Its capability for land attack was highly valued by the US Navy for, among other things, battleships could pound land positions in support of amphibious landings. In one incident, the USS *New Jersey* sailed near to the coast of Nicaragua as a show of resolve to the country's Marxist regime.

Battleship upgrade

Under the Reagan administration, the battleship gained a new lease of life. The 'Iowa'-class ships had their land attack capabilities comprehensively upgraded from 1980 onwards. While the nine 16-in (406-mm) guns were retained, the ships were adapted to carry the Tomahawk Land Attack Cruise Missile (TLAM), which entered service with the US Navy in 1986. The improved 'Iowa'-class ships could now each carry 32 such missiles in armoured box launchers. The Reagan administration's goal had been to increase the navy's fleet to 600 ships, and the reactivation and upgrading of the 'Iowa'-class ships represented an important saving, as each ship could be

Emerging in its post-refit splendour in 1981, the USS New Jersey sails in a warm July day, flanked by an escort. Retaining its guns, it was now able to fire Tomahawk cruise missiles.

Striking back at terror: a cruise missile, bound for Taliban and al-Qaeda units, is launched from a US Navy ship at the start of Operation Enduring Freedom.

upgraded for the same cost as buying an entirely new frigate.

During the 1980s, naval artillery bombardment underwent a renaissance. In 1982, the Royal Navy used its 4.5-in (114-mm) guns to destroy Argentine coastal defences before the landings in San Carlos Water in the Falklands. Guided by forward observers on the landing beaches, 25 rounds per minute pounded the shore. In excess of 8,000 shells were fired in this intense period of bombardment.

Show of force

One year later, the *New Jersey* would use its guns for the first time in anger since

the Vietnam War. It was ordered to sail from Central America to Lebanon to assist US Marines from the multinational peacekeeping force in that country. The success of the naval barrage against land targets in Lebanon was debatable; however, the *New Jersey* did give an important show of force.

Five years after its introduction, the Tomahawk missile made its operational debut during the 1991 Gulf War. During this campaign several US Navy ships, including the battleships USS *Missouri* and USS *Wisconsin*, made 297 attempted TLAM firings. Of these, 290 missiles fired successfully, and 242 hit their targets. Despite the

media reports of the TLAM's almost flawless combat performance, bomb damage assessment for the missiles was particularly difficult. Moreover, the flat, featureless terrain of the Arabian Desert presented problems for the digital maps used by the TLAMs for guidance.

TLAM deployment

Between 1991 and 1996 the US Navy increased the number of its vessels able to deploy the TLAM, and to this end, in five years, seven new vessels were built. By 1996, 70 US surface ships could deploy the Tomahawk, giving a total of 5,570 launchers, while 72 submarines could also fire the weapon for a

grand total of 696 launchers. During this year, there were over 4,000 TLAMs in the US Navy's inventory.

In the post-Cold War era, the TLAM has become the preferred method of gunboat diplomacy. In 1996, TLAMs were fired from US warships against Bosnian Serb units during Operation Deliberate Force.

The heavy reliance on the TLAM has also made the system a victim of its own success. During Operation 'Enduring Freedom' against Taliban and al-Qaeda units in Afghanistan, rumours have circulated in the US and British press regarding possible TLAM shortages.

DESERT STRIKE: SADDAM SUCCUMBS

In August 1996, Iraqi forces moved into the town of Irbil in the Kurdish autonomous region of northern Iraq, in violation of the ceasefire agreement following the 1991 Gulf War. In retaliation, the United States led an attack against the southern Iraqi air defence network, codenamed Operation Desert Strike. Illustrating their utility for land attack, TLAMs were launched by the USS *Laboon* (DDG-58) and the USS *Shiloh* (CG-67), which fired 14 cruise missiles. This was reinforced by an attack of 13 conventional air-launched cruise missiles from Boeing B-52 bombers during a 34-hour mission. On 4 September, the following day, a further 17 TLAMs were launched from the USS *Russell* (DDG-39), USS *Hewitt* (DD-966), the *Laboon,* and also from a nuclear-powered attack submarine, the USS *Jefferson City* (SSN-759). The boundary of the southern 'no-fly' zone was moved north to the 33rd parallel, and US and UK forces threatened a 'disproportionate response' if any action was taken to repair the destroyed sites. The attacks succeeded in forcing the Iraqis to withdraw from the northern areas.

Rise of the missile
Anti-ship missiles

The most widely deployed Western surface-to-surface AShM is the subsonic RGM-84 Harpoon, seen here departing the octuple Mk 16 launcher of a US Navy 'Knox'-class frigate. The launcher itself was primarily armed with ASROC, although two tubes at any time were given over to the Harpoon.

Above: The battleship USS New Jersey test launches a Tomahawk cruise missile off the coast of southern California in 1983. The conventional BGM-109B was a dedicated AShM variant with Passive Identification/Passive Direction Finding (PI/PDF) equipment in order to discriminate among potential targets.

Inheriting the role of the warship's traditional big guns, the anti-ship missile relies on high speed, saturation (i.e. launching numerous weapons at a given target) or stealth in order to counter defences.

If naval battles during World War II were characterised by battleships slugging it out at close quarters with their huge naval guns, then Cold War naval power was characterised by the advent of the anti-ship missile (AShM). AShM weapons such as Harpoon and Exocet were capable of hitting their targets – other naval vessels – from hundreds of kilometres away as opposed to even the largest naval guns which could only destroy targets at less than 55 km (34 miles). In a hypothetical naval engagement between NATO and Warsaw Pact warships, the range of their missiles made it unlikely that the two fleets would ever even see each other.

World War II did give an indication of things to come. In 1943, a prototype German Fritz-X AShM sank the Italian battleship *Roma*. However, it would not be until after the war that the development and deployment of the AShM would be pursued in earnest. Warships would become incredibly attractive targets for the designers of the early in AShM in the US, Soviet Union and Europe. These great chunks of metal moved at slow speeds on a relatively flat surface. At the same time, the vessels emitted huge amounts of electro-magnetic radiation from their air defence and surface search radars. This was ideal for the AShM, providing plenty of target 'fixes' for the missile to home in on. Although naval battles during the Cold War were relatively few and far between, the destruction wrought on HMS *Sheffield* by an (air-launched) Exocet AShM during the Falklands conflict in 1982 vividly displayed the awesome power of the AShM.

Soviet developments

One of the earliest pioneers of the AShM was the Soviet Union. Building on the expertise from captured German missile scientists, the Soviets developed the P-15 Termit (codename SS-N-2A 'Styx'). The 'Styx' was a potent missile, with a 454-kg (1000-lb) warhead, and a range of 80 km (49 miles). Its capabilities were graphically illustrated in 1967, when one of the missiles destroyed the Israeli destroyer *Eilat*. The weapon had been fired from an Egyptian fast attack boat. The other important AShM in the Soviet inventory was the P-5/P-35 family (SS-N-3 'Shaddock'). This system, with a 463 km (287 mile) range first appeared in the late 1960s, and it armed the 'Kynda'-class light cruiser, which entered service in 1962. Such high speed AShMs remained unmatched by Western navies throughout the Cold War.

In contrast to the Soviets, the US began to develop and deploy AShMs comparatively late. In 1977, the US Navy received its first dedicated surface-launched AShM; the RGM-84 Harpoon. However, Harpoon proved to be a success and was deployed across the US fleet and remains in service today. Harpoon is a sea-skimming system designed to hit its target just above the waterline. This makes missile detection more difficult and can also cause intense flooding to the vessel once the missile has exploded. The missile also has the

Left: The Royal Navy frigate HMS Richmond launches a Harpoon missile during a joint Atlantic exercise with the US Navy in 2002. The intended target was the decommissioned cruiser USS Wainwright.

Below: Developed for the Norwegian navy, the Penguin Mk 1 AShM entered service in 1972 as a ship-borne anti-invasion defence system and was the first Western 'fire and forget' missile in its class.

capacity for mid-course guidance alterations, and is guided by active radar during its terminal phase. In addition, the missile has in-built electronic counter-counter measures (ECCM) to protect against any electronic defensive measures deployed by its target. The missile was also designed with the capacity to defend against targets which are taking high-speed evasive action.

Tactical Tomahawks

US anti-ship missile research has led to one of the most successful and lethal designs of long-range missile. The BGM-109 Tomahawk cruise missile was engineered to carry either a nuclear or a conventional warhead and the range of the missile was reduced from 1111 km (690 miles) for the land attack version, to 833 km (517 miles) for the AShM variant. The anti-ship BGM-109B/E Tomahawk was deployed throughout the US Navy.

However, it has since been replaced by a more modern variant of the Harpoon.

One of the most successful European AShM systems was the French Exocet system. Displaying its abilities to devastating effect during the 1982 Falklands War, the Exocet became the standard anti-shipping missile of the Royal Navy and the French navy amongst several others. The Exocet has a two-stage rocket motor, which propels the missile at transonic speeds, and an active warhead. Like the Harpoon, the Exocet is a surface-skimming system, and has an active-radar homing warhead. Furthermore, a powerful ECCM system is fitted and the missile can engage targets in all weathers.

The Royal Navy's 'County'-class destroyers were fitted with the MM 38 Exocet system, and four launchers were carried on each vessel. HMS *Norfolk* was the first Royal Navy vessel to fire an SSM,

testing the Exocet in April 1974. The missile launchers replaced the 4.5-in (114-mm) gun of the previous vessels. The Type 12 'Leander'-class frigates were retrofitted to carry the Exocet system, also losing their forward 4.5-in gun. The Royal Navy continued their use of the Exocet missile. The MM 38 variant was deployed on the Type 22 'Broadsword'- class frigate, although the Royal Navy has since replaced these missiles with launchers for eight Harpoon Block 1C. The new Type 45 destroyers, due to enter service between 2002-05, will have provision for eight Harpoon AShM launchers.

The adoption of the AShM has led to the development of increasingly sophisticated

anti-missile tactics to be developed for surface shipping. Prevention is always better than cure in naval warfare, and at the beginning of a naval confrontation, efforts are usually made to sink hostile vessels which have major AShM capabilities. If this fails, and a missile is launched, then the target ship must try to out-range the incoming missile. This has become considerably more difficult as the speed of successive AShMs has accelerated, and their abilities to fly lower have improved. However, the increased sophistication of internal guidance systems in anti-ship missiles made this task progressively more difficult as AShM development advanced.

EXOCET: 'FIRE AND FORGET' SHIP-KILLER

Taking its name from the Latin/Greek word 'ekokottos', meaning 'flying fish', the Exocet is one of the most successful anti-ship missiles ever designed. It has been exported to 33 customers around the world since entering production. The

Mach 0.93-capable Exocet MM 40 (pictured) is the long-range surface-to-surface AShM version. The missiles are housed on ships in water-resistant containers. When launched, the missile hugs the water, making detection very difficult. The missile is guided to the target using inertial navigation. It is directed to the target using an active radio frequency homing head, before it strikes and detonates just above the target's waterline. Development of the system began in France in 1967 after the destruction of the *Eilat*, and it entered service with the French navy in 1979. The missile was designed specifically to hit large warships, and has achieved a claimed 93 per cent strike rate. During the Iran-Iraq war from 1980-88, Exocet missiles were fired on more than 100 occasions by Iraqi naval vessels and aircraft and an example severely damaged the frigate USS *Stark*. The missile has undergone the Block 2 upgrade programme between 1980-93, which introduced an improved active radar seeker and upgraded the inertial navigation and control equipment. Almost 40 years after its design, the Exocet continues to provide a potent anti-ship missile to navies around the world.

US amphibious assault

Marine Corps in action

The end of the Cold War, and the amphibious operations in the Gulf bought the amphibious operation back into sharp focus. Amphibious forces can rapidly deploy to a war-torn state, and are ideally suited to the complex nature of modern warfare.

The first major amphibious operation by the US Marines since the Korean War occurred in 1991 during Operation Desert Storm. A huge armada of ships and a massive force of amphibious troops was assembled off the coast of Kuwait. Forty-three amphibious ships, two command ships and 18,000 US Marines prepared to land on the beaches of Kuwait to assist the eviction of the Iraqis.

The Marines' show of force was designed as a grand deception, intended to convince Iraq that the Coalition would attack from the sea. However, the beaches were well defended. Any operation would have been costly despite the superior technology and tactics at the Marine's disposal.

The threat posed by the Marines caused Saddam

Hussein to divert several divisions of troops away from the Saudi border to defend Kuwait's coastline, reducing the strength of the troops who were supposed to stop the Coalition land attack.

Amphibious Squadrons

The core of American amphibious capability is the Amphibious Squadron, or PHIBRON. Eight are currently operational with the US Navy. A PHIBRON normally consists of a large Amphibious Assault Ship (LHD or LHA), an Amphibious Transport Dock (LPD) and a Dock Landing Ship (LSD). It includes a Fleet Surgical Team, a Fleet Information Warfare Center detachment, a Naval Beach Group detachment, a Search and Rescue detachment, an Explosive Ordinance Disposal detachment, a Tactical Air

Control Squadron (TACRON), and a Naval Special Warfare Task Unit.

In the past, getting Marines ashore required the use of specialist landing craft and amphibious assault craft. These are slow and relatively short-ranged, and require the launching ships to stand in relatively close to the shore – within the range of defences. The first means of giving the

amphibious force a stand-off capability was the helicopter, but while this can deliver troops inland rapidly, it cannot carry heavy equipment.

AFVs and artillery are now landed by fast air-cushioned landing craft, or LCACS. All modern US Navy amphibious ships are designed to operate with such craft, enabling an amphibious force to launch attacks from over the horizon, while still landing troops faster than would have been possible from much shorter ranges with old-style landing craft. The new generation of amphibious assault vehicle (AAV) will also be much faster on water, to match the performance of the LCACs.

Marines units

The main purpose of the PHIBRON is to provide the platform from which the Marines conduct operations. The unit in the Marines specifically groomed for the task of fighting amphibious battles is the Marine Expeditionary Unit or MEU.

A MEU is normally built around a reinforced battalion, a composite aircraft squadron, and a MEU Service Support group totalling about 2,000 personnel in all. Commanded by a colonel, the MEU is employed to fulfil routine forward deployments with fleets in the Mediterranean, the Western Pacific, and periodically, the Atlantic and Indian Oceans.

The MEU's very existence is vital because with the decline of American bases abroad, it is possible that the only US forces available to respond to worldwide crisis quickly will be the Marines. The MEU is an expeditionary intervention force with the ability to rapidly organise for combat operations in virtually any environment. There are always three MEUs forward deployed.

Each MEU is embarked on Navy ships as part of the Amphibious Ready Group (ARG) which is, in turn, a member of a carrier task force. Travelling with the Navy, each MEU is capable of reaching 75 per cent of the littoral waters of the world within five days. MEUs are constantly forward-deployed to designated 'hot' regions and

ALLIED FORCE: MEU IN ACTION

An AV-8B from HMM-266 lands on board USS *Nassau* following a strike mission over Kosovo. Embarked aboard the 'Tarawa'-class LHA USS *Nassau*, HMM-266 launched the amphibious battle group's first strikes in support of NATO Operation Allied Force. The unit was part of the 26th MEU(SOC), which comprised 2,400 troops deployed aboard *Nassau* on station in the Adriatic, and supported by one 'Austin'-class LPD (USS *Nashville*) and the 'Anchorage'-class LSD USS *Pensacola*. The MEU later supported the NATO relief operation in Albania.

are able to execute contingency missions within those regions with just six hours notice. Each MEU deploys for six months and can operate ashore for 15 days without replenishment.

The Ground Combat Element of the MEU is based on an infantry battalion, which becomes a Battalion Landing Team with the addition of tanks, artillery, engineers, amphibious vehicles, light armoured vehicles, and other combat support assets. Typically it includes 2200 troops, four MBTs, 13 AAVs and six howitzers.

Aviation component

The Aviation Combat Element is a composite squadron of both fixed- and rotary-wing aircraft with 22 helicopters, including CH-46 Sea Knights, CH-53s, AH-1 gunships, and up to eight AV-8B Harrier IIs.

The Marine Expeditionary Units are the smallest and most visible examples of the Marine-Air Ground Task Force (MAGTF) Concept.

The largest is the Marine Expeditionary Forces (MEFs). Commanded by a 3-Star General Officer, a MEF consists of one or more full Marine Aircraft Wings, one or more Force Service Support Groups and one or more com-

LAVs are among the vehicles transportable from ship to shore aboard an LCAC such as this one carried aboard the LHD USS Bonhomme Richard, seen on deployment in support of Operation Enduring Freedom.

plete Infantry Divisions. An MEF can account for anything between 20,000 to 90,000 Marines, averaging around 40,000 men and women.

In between are the Marine Expeditionary Brigades (MEBs), which are organised to respond to a full range of crises, from forcible entry to humanitarian assistance. The USMC has three numbered MEBs. A MEB deploys on 15 amphibious ships of which five are large deck ships such as LHA or LHD ships and has the capacity to sustain operations for 30 days. Rapid deployment continues to be important. In 1999, during Allied Force, the USMC deployed from the Aegean Sea to Kosovo in under four days.

A US Navy Landing Craft Utility (LCU) approaches the well deck of the USS Nassau. The floodable docking well of the 'Tarawa'-class vessel is capable of accommodating four LCU 1610 type landing craft, which in turn can carry two M1A1 MBTs or 350 troops.

Amphibious warfare

21st century assault

In the immediate post-war years, amphibious forces were somewhat neglected by western navies. Most were equipped with vessels little different from those that were used in Normandy and the Pacific

The end of the Cold War has brought about a major revolution in military affairs. Whereas before the superpowers had concentrated on developing weapons able to play their parts in an all-out nuclear exchange, the end of the 20th century has seen the rise in importance of worldwide power projection and intervention, and vessels dedicated to amphibious operations have become increasingly important.

Amphibious warfare is littoral in nature, in that it takes place in coastal waters, across the shore and immediately inland. Littoral areas are home to three-quarters of world's population, and 80 per cent of the world's capital cities are located on or near coasts.

Counter-terrorism

The end of the Cold War has seen a widespread breakdown of order, with trouble caused by rival ethnic and religious groups being predominant. One new element are the 'non-state' terrorist organisations, many of whom are believed to be pursuing

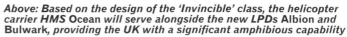

Above: Based on the design of the 'Invincible' class, the helicopter carrier HMS Ocean will serve alongside the new LPDs Albion and Bulwark, providing the UK with a significant amphibious capability

Left: The MV-22 Osprey is as fast as a conventional fixed-wing turboprop, but thanks to its tilting rotors can take off and land vertically. It is intended to replace US Navy medium helicopters.

Top: The 'Wasp' class large amphibious assault ship is a one-ship landing force. Able to operate rotorcraft and V/STOL jets, it has a docking well for LCAC hovercraft and AAV7 amphibious vehicles. USS Iwo Jima (LHD-7) commissioned in June 2001.

'FOUDRE' CLASS LSD: FLEXIBLE PAYLOADS

The French 'Foudre' class of LSD is typical of modern multi-purpose assault ships. Designed to carry up to 467 troops and a load of 1,880 tons, the well dock can accommodate either landing craft (typically one LCT and four LCMs) or, with the use of moveable decks, it can provide vehicle parking space: VAB armoured personnel carriers and P4 light vehicles are seen embarked. The flight deck can support up to four AS 532 Cougar medium transport helicopters.

or acquiring weapons of mass destruction.

The viability, planning, and conduct of amphibious operations is dependent on a number of key factors including geography, distance, allies and enemy capabilities.

Since the end of World War II the US has been involved in more than 200 military operations of all sizes. However, the closure of bases overseas has eliminated much of the United States' continuous military presence, and has made the need for an offensive amphibious capability even more important.

The likely types of conflict will determine the nature of future amphibious operations. Many experts felt that the days of large-scale, conventional operations seen in World War II were over, but the 1991 Gulf War proved otherwise. However, most modern amphibious operations have arisen out of regional crises – Grenada, the Falklands, Somalia and Afghanistan are typical.

Operational needs

There is little chance of achieving operational surprise, given current intelligence capabilities and the instant nature of modern news gathering and broadcasting. However, modern technology provides more options for landing. Invasions no longer need a beach, at least in the initial assault phase. The range of modern aircraft may offer deployment alternatives such as vertical envelopment which improves the chances of avoiding enemy resistance at the shoreline

In any case, a direct assault against a fortified beach, World War II-style, may no longer be feasible given the capabilities and widespread deployment of sophisticated modern guided weaponry.

The US Navy has tackled the problem by improving its 'over-the-horizon' capability. The use of Landing Craft, Air Cushion (LCAC) hovercraft enables an amphibious force to deliver heavy equipment at great speed, while standing well out to sea. A new generation of amphibious assault vehicles is in development, which will allow troops to be delivered to the beach and beyond at much greater speed than is currently possible with the existing AAV7.

The Bell-Boeing MV-22 Osprey will add further capability. The tiltrotor design combines the vertical flight capabilities of a helicopter with the speed and range of a fixed-wing turboprop aircraft and permits aerial refuelling and also world-wide self-deployment.

Strategic option

While peacekeeping or peace enforcement missions in places as diverse as Somalia, Liberia and the Balkans prove that crisis-response operations remain the most likely missions for amphibious forces, the planned amphibious landings against Iraq during Operation Desert Storm showed that large-scale amphibious assaults are still considered a viable military strategic option.

Expeditionary warfare will be the foundation for most peacetime military operations in the 21st century. As a result, amphibious forces must be ready to mount operations from the sea.

Developed in conjunction with the Dutch 'Rotterdam' class of LPD, the Galicia is one of two dock landing ships built for the Spanish navy. It can transport and land a Marine battalion of 600 men and carries a complement of six AB 212 or four SH-3H helicopters.

Soviet intelligence gatherers were often converted from, or based on, deep-sea trawler designs. Such vessels were not particularly comfortable for their crew, but had the endurance and seaworthiness to trail naval units through all but the very worst weather.

Cold War Soviet spyships

Intelligence gatherers

In the Cold War, the best method of obtaining information was through visual or electro-magnetic examination. This was particularly true at sea, where every detail of NATO and US operational procedure was closely observed by the AGIs of the Soviet navy.

It was a fact of military life that whenever NATO ships exercised at sea they were closely shadowed by ubiquitous Soviet 'spy' trawlers, small ships festooned with antennae and direction-finding equipment. Despite their indifferent appearance, these intelligence gatherers compared well with the US Navy's sophisticated submarines and electronic listening ships. Most of these trawlers were never used for commercial fishing, and were potentially among the most capable weapons that the USSR had at its disposal. The USSR had hundreds of them, together with larger ships ranging from frigates converted to the Elint (electronic intelligence) role to the 45,000-ton *Kosmonaut Yuri Gagarin*. The Soviets had an ever-increasing appetite for information about the West, and such ships played a major role in

the Soviets' search for military, economic and political intelligence.

Geographical factors

To understand why this was the case, one must look at the USSR's geography. Depending on one's viewpoint, the USSR was either an unfriendly nation surrounded by civilised countries, or the lone outpost of humanity continually threatened by warmongering capitalists clustered round its borders. It was considerably easier for the US to run land-based listening stations close to the USSR than the reverse. It is also true that the USSR and its satellite countries were, by and large, geographically lumped together, whereas 'the opposition' was scattered throughout that same world. The Soviets tried to maintain listening posts in client states like Vietnam, Angola and

The 'Okean'-class AGI Gidrofon shadows the USS Coral Sea in the Gulf of Tonkin during 1969. The AGI's role was to report the launch of US Navy strike aircraft packages heading towards Vietnam.

Cuba, but with few exceptions they discovered that all too often one revolution could be quickly followed by another, often leading to the embarrassment of an expulsion. The geographical problem was compounded by the emergence of the 'spy' satellite: the USSR simply did not have the land-based

tracking and communications stations to remain in constant touch with its 'spies in the sky'.

Naval ELINT

The USSR made the decision in the late 1950s to develop a sea-based Elint-gathering capability. At first the USSR used converted trawlers, typi-

SPIES IN ACTION: CARRIER SHADOWING

While few shots were fired in the Cold War, electronic warfare was as vital as any major battle in World War II. The 'Okean'-class AGI may have looked harmless, but it was an intrinsic part of a weapons system that was potentially as capable as any nuclear missile. NATO carrier activity always attracted Soviet AGIs, as evidenced by this 1974 exercise when HMS *Hermes* attracted the AGIs *Mayak* (in the foreground) and *Moma*. Royal Navy carriers were tracked again shortly after the start of the Falklands War in May 1982, when a Soviet satellite was launched and placed in orbit over the islands. It is hardly likely that any information was passed to either the UK or Argentina; this launch was purely to gain information about British offensive capabilities and Argentine weapon systems.

cally the 'Okean' class of 720 tons with a crew of 32. These trawlers (or AGIs, Auxiliary Vessel Miscellaneous Type Intelligence, to give them their NATO designation), were tasked with spying on NATO warships. Their mission went some way beyond the mere discovery of ship and weapon capabilities and tactics; they were responsible for finding out anything that would make the USSR more secure and the Soviet navy more effective. So they would observe how the British refuelled at sea or how the Americans handled night carrier landings in bad weather. Gradually, as the Elint process became more sophisticated, new ships with greater capabilities were demanded. Typical of the later Soviet AGI was the 'Balzam' class, of 4,000 tons and with a crew of 180, and the later 'Vishnya' class. Even

so, the 'Okean'-class AGI was not completely abandoned, especially for operations in coastal waters.

Roles of the AGI

The main tasks of the Soviet AGIs, of all sizes, could be said to be ASW (anti-submarine warfare); SATCOM (satellite communications, which may have involved an ASW role); military intelligence; and political and economic intelligence. ASW Elint was regarded as particularly important because of the threat posed by NATO nuclear submarines, both those firing missiles and the hunter/killers targeted against Soviet submarines. To understand how these tasks were carried out, it must be stressed that Elint went far beyond the simple interception of radio signals.

There are very few objects that do not produce some form of recognisable electro-

magnetic radiation. EM radiation is of three types: naturally occurring, artificially generated (e.g. radar) and the radiation emitted when an object is bombarded by, or enters a field of, another electro-magnetic force. Elint techniques advanced incredibly in the 1980s, and some examples illustrate the point. As noted above, nearly every object produces recognisable EM radiation. But no two objects have identical radiation patterns. This means that both surface ships and submarines have their own 'electronic' signatures: a pattern of radiation that will identify the class, if not the individual ship. These signatures can be detected by various types of radar and by magnetic listening/detection devices, either floating on the surface or lurking on the ocean floor. They can also be in an aircraft or a satellite, but the greater the distance, the greater the chance of an incorrect identification.

Similarly, a large metal object passing through the Earth's own magnetic field will produce a recognisable pattern of interference in exactly the same way that a

ship is followed by its wake.

Again, IR (infra-red) radiation can be used for the detection and identification of aircraft, ground troops, surface ships and submarines; ships in particular leave an IR 'shadow' behind them. In the Cold War, this type of IR surveillance was carried out by satellite or aircraft; if the satellite in question was too far from a Soviet-based land station it would transmit its information via an AGI, as would a spyplane. The AGI would send on the information received by retransmitting it to another satellite nearer the USSR, or by beaming it to an overflying aircraft such as the Tu-95RTs 'Bear-D'. As technology advanced, the Soviets showed a distinct preference for using satellite links.

AGIs provided the backbone of the Soviet Elint process. The deployment and tasking of AGIs was tightly controlled: they were not simply let loose on the world's oceans to gather whatever Elint they could find, but were directed at specific targets, be it the Holy Loch SSBN base or a test firing of the latest submarine-launched ballistic missile.

Left: The naval missile-range instrumentation ship **Sibir** *monitors US tests south of Midway island in the Pacific. This vessel had a deck but no hangar for operating a* **Ka-25 'Hormone'** *helicopter.*

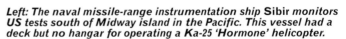

Below: The AGI trawler **Teodolit** *shadows the Royal Navy's 'Leander'-class frigate HMS* **Juno** *in the North Sea during 1979. The Soviet AGI was trailing the frigate to record as many as possible of the NATO vessel's acoustic and electronic transmissions.*

AEGIS
Fleet air defence system

The US Navy and Japan's MSDF are the only operators of the world's most sophisticated naval air defence system, a system so capable that it can shoot down incoming ballistic missiles.

In the late 1950s, the major threat perceived by the US Navy was that of saturation air and missile attack. The Soviets were expected to try to overwhelm fleet missile defences with a large number of targets – which would have to be engaged simultaneously.

The very long-range Typhon system was proposed to deal with the problem, but it was cancelled as it became clear that it was beyond then-current technology.

Nevertheless, many of the ideas and concepts generated for Typhon were to emerge in the AEGIS system. This vastly ambitious programme was initiated in 1964, with engineering development beginning in 1969. The first AEGIS-equipped ship was the cruiser USS *Ticonderoga* (CG-47), which joined the US fleet in 1983. Since then, 27 further AEGIS cruisers

have been commissioned, followed by more than 30 AEGIS-equipped destroyers of the 'Arleigh Burke' class. Additionally, four AEGIS-equipped destroyers have entered service with the Japanese Maritime Self-Defence Force. These are equipped with a lightweight development of the original AEGIS system.

AEGIS components

The major components of the AEGIS system are the missile, the launcher, the fire-control system and the radar. The Standard SM-2 missile is semi-autonomous, using inertial navigation and terminal homing, and only needing guidance if it strays off course. This means that each missile requires much less attention from the ship's radars and fire-control computers.

The huge octagonal 'billboards', high on the superstructure of AEGIS-

Top: USS Ticonderoga was the first AEGIS cruiser. In spite of early criticism – it was thought to be top heavy and too expensive – it proved to be the most capable AAW vessel ever built.

Left: The SM-2MR has a maximum speed of more than Mach 2, and can engage supersonic targets through an altitude envelope stretching from sea level to 25,000 m (over 82,000 ft).

The second AEGIS cruiser, USS Yorktown, launches a Standard SM-2MR missile. The medium-range version of the Standard has an engagement range of more than 70 km (43 miles).

The latest version of the AN/SPY-1 radar used by AEGIS ships can detect a target the size of a baseball at ranges in excess of 150 km (93 miles), and can control the intercept of more than 100 targets simultaneously.

FLEET DEFENDER: AEGIS IN ACTION

The AEGIS weapon system can be directed against targets from wave top to directly overhead, flying in all speed ranges. It enables fighters to concentrate on the outer air battle, while cruisers and destroyers handle battle group area defence.

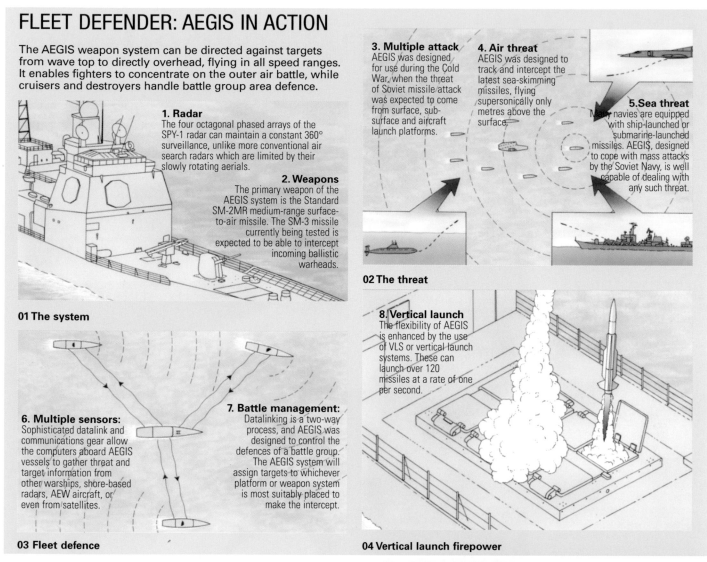

1. Radar
The four octagonal phased arrays of the SPY-1 radar can maintain a constant 360° surveillance, unlike more conventional air search radars which are limited by their slowly rotating aerials.

2. Weapons
The primary weapon of the AEGIS system is the Standard SM-2MR medium-range surface-to-air missile. The SM-3 missile currently being tested is expected to be able to intercept incoming ballistic warheads.

01 The system

3. Multiple attack
AEGIS was designed for use during the Cold War, when the threat of Soviet missile attack was expected to come from surface, sub-surface and aircraft launch platforms.

4. Air threat
AEGIS was designed to track and intercept the latest sea-skimming missiles, flying supersonically only metres above the surface.

5. Sea threat
Many navies are equipped with ship-launched or submarine-launched missiles. AEGIS, designed to cope with mass attacks by the Soviet Navy, is well capable of dealing with any such threat.

02 The threat

6. Multiple sensors:
Sophisticated datalink and communications gear allow the computers aboard AEGIS vessels to gather threat and target information from other warships, shore-based radars, AEW aircraft, or even from satellites.

7. Battle management:
Datalinking is a two-way process, and AEGIS was designed to control the defences of a battle group. The AEGIS system will assign targets to whichever platform or weapon system is most suitably placed to make the intercept.

03 Fleet defence

8. Vertical launch
The flexibility of AEGIS is enhanced by the use of VLS or vertical launch systems. These can launch over 120 missiles at a rate of one per second.

04 Vertical launch firepower

equipped ships, are the antennae for the phased array radar system. This can detect and track over 200 targets simultaneously.

Computer control

Advanced computers use radar threat data and assign the most suitable weapon to ensure the target's destruction. AEGIS can also control the air defences of a fleet, taking target information by data link directly from the sensors of other vessels or aircraft.

Tracking several hundred targets at once demands radars with highly precise beams, working in three dimensions to give bearing, height and range. Normal antennae rotate slowly compared with the crossing rate of high-speed aerial targets, and set high on ship masts they contribute greatly to destabilising top weight. The AN/SPY-1 phased arrays of the AEGIS system are very different. Set on the super-structure, each octagonal matrix consists of an array

of some 4,100 phase-shifting elements, which arc, in effect, small radar transmitters. Groups of elements can be electronically switched in turn to produce several parallel channels simultaneously, in the form of energy beams that can be shaped, swept at many times per second, and moved in any three-dimensional pattern to suit any situation.

Fleet defence

The computers manage target search, detection and tracking. They also provide target designation data for the vessel's fire-control radars, and can indicate targets for the fire-control systems of other vessels.

The reliability and rate of fire of its launcher have a great impact on the efficiency of an air defence system as a whole. The first AEGIS cruisers were equipped with twin-rail launchers, but from the sixth vessel onwards they have been fitted with Mk 41 Vertical Launch Systems

Crewmen manning the CIC (Combat Information Centre) deep within the hull of the vessel watch a comprehensive computerised radar display of the airspace for hundreds of kilometres around.

(VLSs). These need no training towards the target, do not require the complex magazine and launcher equipment of previous systems, and are easy to replenish. A Mk 41 launcher holds 61 missiles, but takes up less space than the twin-rail launcher and 44-missile magazine of the preceding Mk 26 system.

Both American and Japanese AEGIS destroyers have smaller 29-round Mk 41 launchers mounted forward, but can still engage almost 100 separate targets simultaneously. The VLS system can also fire Tomahawk cruise missiles, Harpoon anti-ship missiles and ASROC anti-submarine missiles.

Anti-submarine torpedoes
Weapons in the underwater war

Anti-submarine warfare (ASW) remains one of the key factors in the control of the sea, but it has changed considerably since the end of the Cold War. However, torpedoes remain perhaps the most potent of ASW weapons.

Existing ASW capabilities in the major naval powers were created to counter the Soviet submarine force in a global, deep-water conflict. However, the collapse of the USSR has seen a new world order arise, and the major threat to surface forces now comes from quiet diesel- or air-independent-powered boats, operating in coastal or littoral waters. The submarine is a deadly weapon, and as increasingly capable vessels are becoming available at an affordable price, defence against sub-surface attack is a priority for all seagoing nations. Further, since the Russian navy has continued to maintain nuclear submarines with global reach, the 'Cold War' threat, though numerically smaller, must still be considered.

Despite the advance of technology, ASW remains an extremely difficult mission, which rarely has simple or elegant solutions. There are three fundamental truths about ASW. Firstly, it is critically important to any strategy of sea control, power projection, and direct support to land campaigns – exactly the kinds of operations which have been prominent for much of the last decade.

Secondly, ASW is the ultimate team sport. It requires a complex combination of very different resources to work in a highly variable physical environment, which ranges from coastal shallows to the ocean dephs. It requires contributions from intelligence sources, oceanography research, complex command and control, the use of multiple sensor technologies, and a wide variety of underwater weapons.

Finally, ASW is hard. During the Falklands War, the

The Mk 46 torpedo is designed to attack high-performance submarines, and may be considered the backbone of the US Navy's ASW inventory. This lightweight torpedo is launched from triple Mk 32 Surface Vessel Torpedo Tubes (SVTTs) onboard US Navy warships. Mk 46 can also be launched by aircraft and ASROC missiles, and forms the payload of the CAPTOR mine.

Left: MILAS is typical of modern stand-off ASW weapons and can be armed with an MU 90 or Mk 46 lightweight torpedo. The long range of such systems means the launch ship can attack a submarine while outside of enemy torpedo range.

Argentine diesel boat *San Luis* operated in the vicinity of the British task force for more than a month. Despite the deployment of five nuclear attack submarines, 24-hour airborne ASW operations, and expenditures of precious time, energy, and ordnance, the British never once detected the Argentine submarine. The move to coastal operations

The Mk 46 Mod 5 torpedo, launched here from the destroyer USS Preble, has an improved shallow-water performance and is also capable of attacking surface targets.

has increased the problems. Acoustic reverberation, poor sound propagation, local ship traffic, false targets, and seabed 'clutter' all make torpedo operations more difficult in this noisy operating environment, and the need for more capable guidance and control becomes critical.

Torpedoes have replaced the depth charge as the primary ASW weapon of surface vessels. Modern torpedoes usually carry their own sonar, able to home in on the sound generated by a hostile submarine. However, they are usually guided into the vicinity of the target by wires connecting them to the launch platform. They can be delivered in a variety of ways: lightweight weapons can be fired from torpedo tubes on warships, dropped from helicopters or maritime aircraft, or can form the payload of a long-range missile. Heavyweight torpedoes are

the primary ASW weapon of submarines.

There are several new approaches under study to build more intelligent guidance and control systems for the torpedo. In addition to improved signal and tactical data processing, progress is being made in connectivity between submarines and weapons, intelligent controllers, and ultra-broadband sonar arrays. Acoustic and fibre-optic communications will improve connections between weapon and launch platform, allowing the torpedo to act as an improved sensor for the fire-control systems, giving an improved tactical picture for combat control systems. Torpedoes themselves are becoming more intelligent, using neural nets and fuzzy logic to more accurately predict a target's movements.

Developing a truly stealthy torpedo will provide more approach-and-attack options

for submarines. A stealth weapon that cannot be heard until very late in the encounter will delay the threat's detection of the torpedo and impair its ability to respond effectively with either countermeasures or return fire. This will greatly increase the probability of killing the enemy and avoiding a potentially lethal counter-attack.

Future technology

As these new torpedo technologies take shape, they promise some dramatic departures from the configuration of current weapons. Pushing the speed envelope, for example, will greatly affect torpedo performance and resulting effectiveness – the ability to kill a target before it can react provides a distinct advantage.

Anti-torpedo torpedoes will provide future ships and submarines with an additional defensive capability. Their primary mission is to destroy

incoming torpedoes that may have evaded a countermeasure field. A 6.25-in (158.7-mm) diameter self-protection weapon is currently the subject of a US Navy study for the defence of surface ships and submarines. The Advanced High Speed Underwater Munition (AHSUM) program has already demonstrated the effectiveness of such high-speed underwater 'bullets'. Fired from an underwater gun, these projectiles have successfully broken the speed of sound in water (1500 metres/ 4,921 ft per second) over short distances. Future operational systems are likely to be used as last-ditch defences, in the same way that the CIWS serves against air and missile threats above the surface.

Torpedo payloads will also see improvement in the future. Warheads will be capable of multi-mode detonation, offering both purely explosive effect and directed detonation. They will provide higher lethality and use increasingly energetic materials. This will give the torpedo more destructive power and provide the potential for weapons to be smaller and lighter, with increased range capability or room for additional sensors.

AIPS: THE QUIET ALTERNATIVE

An air-independent propulsion system (AIPS) such as that employed by the Swedish navy's 'Gotland' class, increases a non-nuclear submarine's submerged endurance to weeks rather than days, and offers a quiet alternative to battery power. On a normal diesel-electric boat the batteries require frequent recharging which means using the noisy diesel generators. AIPS-equipped boats present a new challenge to both detection equipment and torpedoes.

Above: Spearfish is the Royal Navy's primary submarine-launched heavyweight torpedo and the latest version is capable of a speed in excess of 80 kts, although this is much reduced at great depths.

Helicopter Anti-Submarine Warfare

Sensors and systems

Helicopter ASW is a complex science involving multiple sensors and well-trained operators. Here, the key sensors and techniques are described, with reference to Canadian Armed Forces operations.

Number 443 Squadron CAF operates the CH-124A as an active sonar-dipping platform. Its primary sensor is the Tethered Sonar Sub-System (TSSS) employing the Bendix AN/AQS-502 sonar (internationally known as the AN/AQS-13). This medium-frequency sonar is able to function in active, passive, or underwater communications modes. Although old, it is an adequate sonar that was intended to be used primarily in the open ocean environment. Current output is rated at 5,000 watts. Three frequencies can be emitted, and the pulse width for each frequency can be changed.

The CH-124A does not have a sonobuoy processing capability, but it can receive signals from sonobuoys on 31 different radio frequency channels. The CH-124 generally carries three types of sonobuoys.

The AN/SSQ-47B is an active sonobuoy that provides only range information when it receives an echo return from a contact; this is ascertained with the aid of a stopwatch. Crew members aurally monitor these sonobuoys to determine which are in contact. Up to four sonobuoys can be aurally monitored by the aircrew, one per crew member. At least three sonobuoys must be in contact to localise a contact and determine tracking information, elicited by triangulation methods.

The AN/SSQ-53D/E Directional Frequency Analysis and Recording (DIFAR) passive sonobuoy, and the AN/SSQ-62C Directional Command Activated Sonobuoy System (DICASS) sonobuoy can also be dispensed. Signals are processed by nearby ships

operating with the helicopter. Conversely, the CH-124B helicopter is a sonobuoy-processing platform, and does not carry a dipping sonar.

The single-frequency Litton Canada AN/APS-503 I-band multi-mode surveillance radar is also standard equipment and a rather primitive FLIR Systems 2000G FLIR is nose mounted when operational requirements dictate.

AESOP responsibilities

The Airborne Electronic Systems Operator (AESOP) is responsible for the proper use of the sonar, radar and FLIR. Contact information acquired by the sonar or radar is electronically transferred to the AN/ASN-123 Tactical Doppler. Contacts then need to be tracked by the Tactical Coordinator (TACCO) to discern what the target could be. The TACCO and AESOP stations are next to each other on the starboard side of the aircraft, directly behind the pilot and co-pilot.

The ability to properly identify a target essentially comes down to training and recognition of a contact's track and speed. A team effort is always used in identifying targets, whether it be the TACCO analysing acquired target information from the AESOP, or pilot and co-pilot assistance for verifying targets in visual range. In contrast, modern ASW helicopter sensor suites, such as that fielded on the US Navy's Sikorsky MH-60R Seahawk, are able to acquire, track, identify, and integrate by way of data fusion any sonar, radar, IFF, and ESM contacts automatically.

Effective anti-submarine warfare does not necessarily entail destroying a hostile submarine. ASW tactics do, however, require keeping a

Having been licence built abroad and manufactured in some numbers at home, Sikorsky's Sea King is one of the world's classic military helicopters. For anti-submarine warfare (ASW), it is fitted with the sensors and armament required to detect, localise, track, identify and prosecute submerged hostile submarines.

hostile submarine at a place where it cannot fire at friendly assets. This is achieved by keeping it deep and/or distant. Part of ASW helicopter tactics dictate establishing an active sonar or sonobuoy field, creating an acoustic barrier between a submarine and friendly assets. This serves to localise areas for a helicopter to search within, and also serves to cut off avenues of approach for a submarine. A submarine skipper would thus be required to conduct a risk assessment to determine whether he is willing to attack a target. ASW helicopters are very effective in creating these screens for friendly assets. This effective-

ness is greatly enhanced when CH-124s work in conjunction with fixed-wing CP-140 Aurora long-range patrol aircraft, and/or towed array equipped surface combatant vessels.

Random dipping

Random dipping is used as an effective means of searching an Area of Probability (AOP). This method is used to confuse a submarine's tactical picture, making it more difficult to formulate a firing solution on friendly assets. The AESOP may also change sonar parameters during each dip, or from one dip to the next, to further confuse any submarine in the area.

When tasked to search for a

possible contact, sonobuoys may be used as an effective means for area coverage. The benefits of dropping sonobuoys are speed, and route denial by creating an acoustic barrier. This avails the helicopter to search other areas, hopefully in cooperation with other friendly ships and aircraft.

Mission planning

Planning for a mission takes place well before the actual flight. Helicopter ASW crews onboard ship will typically brief the mission objectives, weather, threat assessment, aircraft state, water-space management, and emergency procedures. Additionally, a bathythermograph reading

supplied by the ship will also be reviewed. This reading gives a record of water temperature in relation to depth. This knowledge is essential to agitate the water sufficiently with a sonar signal in search of hostile submarines.

Water temperature varies with depth, causing invisible temperature layers. When a sonar transducer (also known as a 'ball') sends out its pulse, that pulse seeks a water layer where the sound speed refracts towards colder water. The factors affecting this propagation are temperature, salinity and pressure. Submarines use these layers to hide in, primarily because sonar pulses do not diffuse very well through adjacent

layers. To identify different temperature levels, the sonar transducer is fitted with a temperature sensor. This allows best sonar ball depths to be calculated by the AESOP for the prevailing water conditions.

To ideally search a body of water for a submarine, a sonar-dipping ASW helicopter would lower its sonar transducer into as many different temperature layers as possible. During a busy target prosecution, the crew would need to determine if and when to attempt this time-consuming procedure.

Once a submarine is located, there are a number of attack methods an ASW helicopter could use.

Attacking a submarine can be a self-initiated evolution, or can be a vectored/guided event. Torpedoes can be dropped from the helicopter in forward flight, in the hover, or while dipping. On the Ch-124A a maximum of two Alliant Techsystems Mk 46 Mod 5 fire-and-forget torpedoes can be mounted. Prior to release, various attack parameters must be set; these include torpedo search depth, seabed floor depth (for shallow water operations), and a selection of active or passive homing. To effect a successful attack, an ASW helicopter crew would always prefer to work in conjunction with other ASW assets.

INSIDE THE CH-124: CANADIAN ANTI-SUBMARINE OPERATING ENVIRONMENT

Operating with a four-person crew, two configurations of the CH-124 (A and B) are operated by the Canadian Forces. Internal stores can be carried in 30 chutes located in the aft cabin floor. Six chutes are capable of loading various sonobuoys, Mk 58 marine location markers, and Thiokol LUU-2B/B illumination flares, while 24 smaller chutes are intended for C2A1 smoke markers and electronic Sound Underwater Signalling (SUS) devices.

The TACCO and AESOP sit alongside each other at these two stations, with the AESOP furthest away in this image. Note the dated display units and switch gear of the veteran Canadian Forces ASW helicopter.

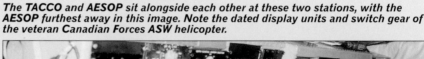

In addition to the sonobuoy chutes seen here in the cabin floor, two racks can be mounted inside the aircraft for a maximum of 18 additional sonobuoys.

Below: The CH-124A has approximately 152 m (500 ft) of cable on its sonar transducer reeling machine. A number of variables are considered in deciding how deep to lower a transducer. These variables primarily take into account target considerations, water temperature, and the time it takes to lower/raise a sonar transducer to the preferred search depth.

Underwater stand-off
Keeping the submarine at bay

The formidable strike range of submarines armed with long-range torpedoes, and later with missiles, has led to the creation of shipborne anti-submarine weapons of greater lethality and increasingly long range.

There are two ways in which ASW projectiles destroy a target. Proximity weapons, such as the depth charge, must be large enough to damage a submarine at a distance, which can be enlarged by the use of nuclear depth charges. Contact weapons can be smaller but must either be guided onto their targets or used in very large numbers to ensure a kill. A homing torpedo is an intermediate case, since its effective homing volume may rival that of a nuclear depth charge.

Development

Improvements in submarine weapon systems from the late 1950s meant that a ship carrying conventional depth charges, mortars (such as the British three-barrel Limbo with a range of 1000 m/ 1,095 yards), or simple rocket systems such as the US Navy's Weapon Alfa (firing a 25-kg/55-lb projectile to 900 m /985 yards) might not be able to get within range of a hostile submarine before the latter was able to fire its torpedoes. In the 1960s the development of submarine-launched anti-ship missiles magnified the problem. Some way had to be found to deliver an anti-submarine weapon to greater distances.

Most large modern warships carry helicopters,

usually armed with homing torpedoes, which can engage a submarine many miles from the parent ship. But the helicopter is not ideal in every case: while it can pursue a contact for long periods, it takes some time to reach an operational area from launch. The US Navy recognised the problem early, and in 1952 tested a RAT (Rocket-Assisted Torpedo). The idea was that the weapon would be launched under rocket power to the general area of the target, dropping its homing torpedo payload which would then search for the submarine.

However, the two initial RAT designs had unsatisfactory ballistic characteristics and failed to achieve the needed accuracy. A redesigned RAT-C was initiated in 1955: combined with a requirement for a rocket-boosted nuclear depth charge, the name was changed to ASROC. A solid-propellant rocket boosted the unguided weapon on a ballistic trajectory, range being determined by a timer set before launch. At the predetermined moment, the motor was separated and the payload fell into the water: a depth charge simply plunged into the water, while a homing torpedo was lowered by parachute. The payload options of the original RUR-5A ASROC were the 10-kT W44 nuclear depth charge or the Mk 44 homing torpedo. In September 1989, at the end of the Cold War, ASROC's nuclear capability was removed. By the 1990s the RUR-5A was being replaced by the RUM-139 VL-ASROC (Vertical Launch ASROC), which is the ASROC modified for launch from the Mk 41 Vertical Launch System.

Similar weapons were

The RUR-5A ASROC was a stand-off delivery system for depth charges or torpedoes.

Above: Limbo was a bulky three-barrel mortar. It was one of the last of the old-style depth charge throwers, which gave vessels the ability to attack submarines several hundred metres away.

Right: The forecastle of the 'Kiev' class carried AShMs and a gun as well as an RBU-6000 12-tube ASW rocket launcher and a single-arm launcher for nuclear-armed RPK-1 Vikhr ASW rockets.

Below: Carried by Royal Navy destroyers and ASW frigates, Ikara was a small winged vehicle with a homing torpedo carried under its body.

developed in Australia and France as the Ikara and Malafon respectively. More recently, France and Italy have developed the capable Milas system, which is faster and has a greatly increased range than its predecessors. The system combines long-range detection, high precision, and the ability to deliver an advanced homing torpedo to 35 km (22 miles) within three minutes of initiating launch.

The Soviets developed a wide range of stand-off ASW weapons in much the same categories as those of Western navies, but Soviet and current Russian systems tend to be larger, have longer range and carry much heavier loads. Soviet and Russian RBU series mortar systems can fire single rounds or salvoes out to ranges in excess of 4000 m (4,375 yards), and the latest versions can fire decoy rockets to divert homing torpedoes.

Soviet missiles

Soviet ASW missiles are also large. The RPK-2 Viyoga (SS-N-15 'Starfish') can deliver a torpedo or a nuclear depth charge to a range of 45-50 km (27-31 miles). The command-guided RPK-3 Metel (SS-N-14 'Silex') can carry a homing torpedo or a special homing warhead; in the latter case the whole missile is guided onto a target by the launch vessel's fire control. The massive RPK-6 Vodopod (SS-N-16 'Stallion') can carry a torpedo or 10/12-kT nuclear warhead to a range estimated at more than 100 km (62 miles), and can also be used against surface ships. Deployed around 1980, it has also been adapted for submarine launch as the RPK-7 Vodopei. The latest Russian ASW weapon is the RPK-9 Medvedka (SS-N-29). Similar to ASROC, this is designed for launch from smaller surface combatants. The basic variant of the system comprises two four-tube launcher modules.

SUBROC: SUBMARINE-LAUNCH ASROC

Entering service in 1965, the UUM-44A SUBROC was the submarine-launched counterpart of the RUR-5A ASROC. Fired from one of the submarine's standard torpedo tubes on the basis of data provided by the submarine's own sensors and fire-control system, the inertially guided SUBROC ignited its rocket motor when well clear of the submarine for a short horizontal distance before pitching up to emerge from the water and adopt its maximum 56-km (35-mile) course to the target area, where a 5-kT W55 nuclear depth charge was released.

Above: A 'Petya'-class escort vessel mounts a pair of RBU-6000 launchers abaft and above the main gun. The RBU is a mortar which fires salvoes of ASW rockets out to a range of six kilometres.

Modern mine warfare
Mine technology

Modern mine technology has evolved immensely in the last few decades but its purpose remains the same: denying an enemy free use of the seas and sinking his ships if possible. It also has the advantage of being relatively cheap.

It is in maritime choke-points that the mine comes into its own. Mines come in four types or, more correctly, mine detonation systems come in four types, though certain mines can have one, two or even three detonating systems. Acoustic mines are actuated by noise from water round a moving hull, propeller, and engine and life-support machinery sounds. This noise is detected by the mine's hydrophones, which gradually become covered with mud and sea growth to the point of insensitivity and/or battery rundown. Acoustic mines can be made to respond only to specific ship or submarine noise 'signatures'. As a result, it is not possible to sweep an acoustic minefield simply by generating noise on a towed array: every mine must be individually found and destroyed.

Selective explosions

Magnetic mines are activated by a change in the Earth's magnetic field caused by the proximity of a large metal conductor, such as a ship's hull. They can be programmed to explode only when a large disturbance takes place, thereby ignoring frigates and destroyers but being triggered by an aircraft carrier. Again, they have to be individually located and destroyed, although a towed array can have some success in exploding them.

Pressure mines are actuated by changes in water pressure caused by the passage of a medium/large-sized vessel. Though various sweeping techniques have been developed, it would seem that these mines, too, must be tackled individually.

The final type of mine is the contact mine. Whereas the previous three types are anchored on or close to the bottom, contact mines lurk just below the surface.

Acoustic, magnetic and pressure mines are far more effective than contact mines inasmuch as a blast close to the sea bed goes only in one direction (upward) and thus does more damage than a contact mine, whose blast is dissipated spherically. The disadvantages of the acoustic, magnetic and pressure mines are that they have to be laid in shallow water and are subject to 'nervous breakdowns'. The electronics used to actuate an acoustic, magnetic or pressure mine are fairly complicated. In those instances where a mine can be actuated by a combination of all three, or in the case of a mine that has been programmed to 'count' (i.e. ignore the first, second, third and so on) contacts so that escort vessels will again escape unharmed, the electronics have to be complex and sensitive, especially as they operate in constantly changing water and magnetic conditions. Filtering out these factors can cause a mine to 'sulk' and refuse to detonate, or to detonate at the smallest stimulus.

US Navy and Danish sailors watch as a crane lifts Mk 52 mines to the deck of the HDMS Falster at Naval Station Mayport in March 1996. Denmark and Germany are close to chokepoints and as a result are two of the principal exponents of mine warfare.

Right: The British Versatile Mine System displays many of the characteristics typical of modern mine technology. Its small size means that it can be laid by a submarine through its torpedo tubes, often in a location optimised for submarine destruction.

Below: The partially completed frigate USS Oliver Hazard Perry undergoes the structural tests essential in making any warship resistant to mine damage.

Even though the average mine is cheap, minelaying can obviously be an expensive business. Mines are therefore laid only as and when required, and with this a new

MINE SENSOR SYSTEMS: SEVERAL TRIGGERING OPTIONS

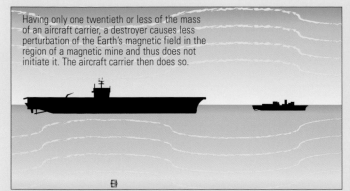

Having only one twentieth or less of the mass of an aircraft carrier, a destroyer causes less perturbation of the Earth's magnetic field in the region of a magnetic mine and thus does not initiate it. The aircraft carrier then does so.

Modern acoustic mines make use of the most advanced computer technology, and can therefore be programmed to respond only to specific acoustic 'signatures', allowing precision attacks to be made on high-value targets.

The earth has a large magnetic field whose force lines lie parallel to its surface in most locations. When a large body of metal, such as a ship's or submarine's hull, passes through the field, it produces distortions in the lines of force, and it is these distortions that a magnetic mine's sensors detect. As

their name suggests, acoustic mines respond to the noise created as a ship or submarine passes through the water. Such mines may incorporate their own listening capability, or may be controlled remotely via underwater sonar arrays such as the SOSUS in the Greenland-UK gap.

Flares are dropped by aircraft onto the surface of the sea so that the crew can assess the local wind speed and direction. This is an invaluable aid to the accurate laying of mines from the air.

type of mine actuation has been developed: remote control. In fact there is little reason to lay far in advance because laying is an easy task that can be undertaken by aircraft, helicopter, ship and submarine.

Usually aircraft are preferred, particularly when the mines are to be laid close into one's own shoreline. However,

there is one type of mine laid by submarine: the type of mine that lurks outside an enemy's harbour. A hunter-killer submarine (probably diesel-electric as it runs more quietly than a nuclear boat) slips past the defences to reach a point about 30 km (18.6 miles) from the target area before launching a mine. The US Mk 67 mobile mine,

which is a variable-influence mine converted from a Mk 37 torpedo, weighs 1069 kg (2,356 lb) with a diameter of 533 mm (21 in) and length of 3.506 m (11 ft 6 in). The Mk 67 can be set to respond to acoustic, magnetic or pressure detection of a target, and can also be set to ignore everything except the one ship or submarine type that has been targeted. If and when the mine (now on the sea bed) detects its target a rocket propels the mine upward to a point at which it can make satisfactory contact with the target's hull. At this point it explodes and, especially if it is a nuclear mine, causes devastating damage. However, it is more likely to be a CAPTOR type mine with a 43.5-kg (96-lb) conventional warhead.

Standard conversion

It should not be thought that all mines are purpose-built for the job. It is often only the triggering device that is specifically designed to work underwater. Virtually any type of standard bomb can be converted to the shallow-water mine role. A relatively recent and classic example of this has been the US DESTRUCTOR mine, which was developed as a direct result of the Vietnam War. It is essentially a 2,000-lb (907-kg) Mk 84 bomb, with magnetic and acoustic sensors added to the fuse pocket, and deployed by parachute.

During the Cold War, the US listened for Soviet movement through various chokepoints with the SOSUS (SOund SUrveillance System) system of passive listening devices. These are

hydrophones (anchored to the sea bottom) that can release their data in short-burst transmissions. Often they are backed up by cables coiled in the same area to monitor the change in the Earth's magnetic field caused by a passing ship. However, these are only passive sensor devices, meaning that a high-speed target will have moved some distance before the SOSUS's long-range 'ears' have heard it. So though it is good to know where something was a few minutes ago, destruction of that something benefits from more current information. JEZEBEL is a far-from-passive listening device and, when alerted, sends out its own sonar signals in an attempt to discover the submarine's course and speed, and if successful release a CAPTOR in its guise as a homing torpedo. The one disadvantage is that the target can detect the torpedo and take countermeasures. It is far better if the target passes over or close to the waiting CAPTOR, thereby reducing the reaction time radically.

One of the major problems with mines is the threat they constitute to friendly forces. After a time a mine is as likely to attack a 'friendly' as an 'enemy' target, and mines do not always stay where they were laid. The mine nonetheless remains an extremely effective weapon, for one very good reason: it is difficult to locate. In times of war, any surface ship or submarine commander must assume that there are mines out there waiting for them, and this limits their flexibility of operation.

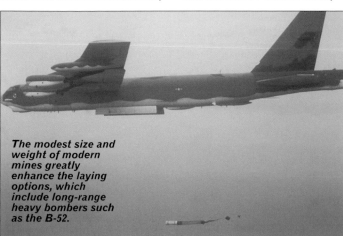

The modest size and weight of modern mines greatly enhance the laying options, which include long-range heavy bombers such as the B-52.

'Charles de Gaulle' class Nuclear-powered carrier

In September 1980, the French government approved the construction of two nuclear-powered aircraft carriers to replace its two conventionally powered 'Clemenceau'-class carriers that date back to the 1950s. However, the French CVN programme has been bedevilled by political opposition and technical problems, both with the vessel and the aircraft. The first ship of the class, **Charles de Gaulle** was laid down in April 1989 and launched in May 1994 but not commissioned until May 2001. Repeated budget cuts delayed work but so did a number of errors in its construction. Thus, even in 2003 the *Charles de Gaulle* is non-operational and still lacks a proper air group. The navalised Rafale remains delayed, leaving the carrier to operate an air group comprising 20 Super Etendards. As

Charles de Gaulle *has a pair of 75-m (246-ft) US Type C13F catapults which can launch 23-tonne aircraft. Enhanced weight capability allows the flight deck to allow AEW aircraft operations*

completed the *Charles de Gaulle* was unable to operate E-2C Hawkeye aircraft as critical dimensions were wrongly measured. Between 1999-2000, the angled flight deck was lengthened accordingly, and additional radiation shielding was also added. Prospects for a second (perhaps conventionally-powered) ship of the 'Charles de Gaulle' class remain poor; although the navy has pressed for one (to be called **Richelieu** or, possibly, *Clemenceau*), political and popular support for such an expensive investment may never be forthcoming.

The *Charles de Gaulle* is equipped with a hangar for 20-25 aircraft (around half the air group) and carries the same reactor units as the 'Le Triomphant'-class SSBN: this permits five years of continuous steaming at 25 kts before refuelling. Seakeeping behaviour is improved through the fitting of four pairs of fin stabilisers.

SPECIFICATION

Charles de Gaulle
Displacement: 40,600 tons full load
Dimensions: length 261.42 m (857 ft 8 in); beam 64.4 m (211 ft 4 in); draught 8.5 m (27 ft 10 in)
Machinery: two Type K15 reactors delivering 300 MW (402,145 shp) and two turbines delivering 56845.2 kW (76,000 shp) to two shafts
Speed: 28 kts (limited to 25 kts)
Aircraft: up to 40 aircraft, including 24 Super Etendard, two E-2C Hawkeye, 10 Rafale M, and two SA 365F Dauphin (plane-guard) or AS 322 Cougar (CSAR)

Armament: four Sylver octuple VLS launchers for Aster 15 anti-missile missiles, two Sadral PDMS sextuple launchers for Mistral SAMs, eight Giat 20-mm guns
Countermeasures: four Sagaie 10-barrel decoy launchers, LAD offboard decoys, SLAT torpedo decoys (to be fitted)
Electronics: DRBJ 11B air search radar, DRBV 26D Jupiter air search radar, DRBV 15D air/surface search radar, two DRBN 34A navigation radars, Arabel 3D fire-control radar
Complement: 1,150 plus 550 aircrew and 50 flag staff; can accommodate 800 marines

The island of the **Charles de Gaulle** *is located well forward in order to provide protection from the weather for the two 36-ton capacity aircraft lifts.*

Viraat 'Hermes'-class carrier

Flagship of the Indian fleet, Viraat has undergone a number of modifications since it was commissioned into Indian service in 1986. These include new safety features and defences, the latter including the Israeli Barak close-in missile defence system with anti-missile capability. The vessel is due to be replaced by a new 'Vikrant'-class CTOL carrier.

SPECIFICATION	
Viraat	**Armament:** two octuple VLS
Displacement: 28,700 tons full	launchers for Barak missiles, four
load	Oerlikon 20-mm guns, two 40-mm
Dimensions: length 208.8 m	Bofors guns, and four AK-230 30-mm
(685 ft); beam 27.4 m (90 ft); draught	guns
8.7 m (28 ft 6 in)	**Countermeasures:** two Corvus
Machinery: four boilers generating	chaff launchers
56673 kW (76,000 shp) to two shafts	**Electronics:** Bharat RAWL-02 Mk II
Speed: 28 kts	air search radar, Bharat RAWS
Range: 6,500 miles (10460 km) at	air/surface search radar, Bharat
14 kts	Rashmi navigation radar, Graseby
Aircraft: (normal) 12-18 Sea Harrier	Type 184M hull-mounted active
FRS.Mk 51/60, up to seven Sea King	search/attack sonar
Mk 42 or Ka-28 'Helix-A'; three	**Complement:** 1,350 including 143
Ka-31 on order	officers with the air group

Viraat is fitted with a 12° ski jump and a reinforced flight deck with armour over the magazines and machinery spaces. Capacity is provided for 30 Harriers.

HMS *Hermes* was commissioned into the Royal Navy in November 1959, having been built at Barrow-in-Furness between 1944-53. Four years after playing a crucial role in the liberation of the Falklands, *Hermes* was sold to India. Refitted, the ship was commissioned into the Indian Navy as the **Viraat** in May 1987. Refitted again from July 1999 to December 2000, *Viraat* returned to the fleet in June 2001 and is planned to remain in service until 2010, by which time a 32,000-ton CTOL carrier (which has been approved for construction) is scheduled to enter service.

Modifications since its Falklands days include the substitution of Russian AK-230 six-barrel 30-mm guns for the old Sea Cat SAM system (these may in turn be replaced by Kashtan CIWS); new fire control, search and navigation radars; new deck-landing aids; improved NBC protection; conversion of boilers to use distillate fuel; and after 2001, the IAI/Rafael Barak SAM. Like *Hermes*, *Viraat* is fitted to carry up to 750 troops and four LCVPs are carried for amphibious landings, and in addition up to 80 lightweight torpedoes can be carried in the magazine. However, *Viraat* may be retired early now that India has finally completed a deal with Russia to buy the 'Kiev'-class carrier *Admiral Gorshkov* and with it, a number of MiG-29K fighters – a $700 million refit and through-deck conversion for the *Gorshkov* is supposed to be completed by 2003. The Sea Harriers carried by the *Viraat* are scheduled for modernisation too but this may be shelved with the advent of the MiG-29Ks.

Giuseppe Garibaldi ASW carrier

Designed as a gas turbine-powered helicopter carrier, the ***Giuseppe Garibaldi*** incorporates features suiting it for the carriage and operation of V/STOL fighters. The flight deck is 173.8 m (570 ft 2 in) long and 21 m (68 ft 11 in) wide, and is fitted with a 6.5° ski-jump ramp. The hangar is 110 m (360 ft 11 in) long, 15 m (49 ft 3 in) wide and 6 m (19 ft 8 in) high, and is built to accommodate 12 SH-3D or EH 101 ASW helicopters, or 10 AV-8B aircraft and one SH-3D, although the available height permits the embarkation of CH-47C helicopters if required. A maximum air wing comprising 18 helicopters (six on deck) or 16 AV-8Bs can be embarked. Two aircraft lifts are fitted (one forward and one abaft the island), and there are six marked flight deck spaces for helicopter operations.

ASW role

The *Garibaldi* was designed specifically to provide ASW support for naval task forces and merchant convoys, and as such is fitted with full flagship facilities plus command, control and communication systems for both naval and air force operations. In emergencies it can also carry up to 600 troops for short periods. The extensive weaponry fitted also allows it to operate as an independent surface unit. The carrier carries a bow-mounted active search sonar. To permit helicopter operations in heavy weather the vessel has been fitted out with two pairs of fin stabilisers, and the aircraft maintenance facilities are sufficient not only to service the ship's own air group but also the light ASW helicopters of any escorting warships.

Commissioned in September 1985, the *Garibaldi* originally operated solely as an assault carrier with SH-3s and AB 212s embarked. After the Italian navy was given political clearance to operate fixed-winged types, AV-8Bs were acquired, although these have only been routinely embarked since December 1994. Under modernisation, the Teseo Mk 2 SSM launchers are to be removed and replaced with SATCOM domes, and Aster 15 missiles will eventually replace Aspide.

Flagship of the Italian navy, the Giuseppe Garibaldi *and its air group are one of the more powerful naval forces in the Mediterranean. As well as regular air group operations, the ship can act as an assault carrier, and has operated army CH-47Cs, AB 205s and A 129s.*

SPECIFICATION	
Giuseppe Garibaldi	torpedoes
Displacement: 10,100 tons	**Countermeasures:** various passive
standard; 13,139 full load	ESM systems, two SCLAR chaff
Dimensions: length 179 m (587 ft	launchers and one DE 1160 sonar
3 in); beam 30.4 m (99 ft 9 in);	**Electronics:** one SPS-52C long-
draught 6.7 m (22 ft)	range 3D air search radar, one
Machinery: two-shaft gas turbine	SPS-768 D-band air search radar,
(four Fiat/GE LM2 500) delivering	one SPN-728 I-band air search
59655 kW (80,000 shp)	radar, one SPS-774 air/surface
Speed: 30 kts	search radar, one SPS-702 surface
Aircraft: 12-18 helicopters or 16	search/target indication radar,
AV-8B Harrier II or combination	three SPG-74 gun fire-control
Armament: eight OTO Melara	radars, three SPG-75 SAM fire-
Teseo Mk 2 SSM launchers, two	control radars, one SPN-749(V)2
octuple Albatros launchers for	navigation radar, one SRN-15A
Aspide SAMs (48 missiles), three	TACAN system, one IPN-20
twin 40-mm Breda guns, two	combat data system
triple 324-mm (12.75-in) B-515	**Complement:** 550 normal, 825
torpedo tubes for Mk 46 ASW	maximum including air group

Garibaldi is well defended for a Western carrier, with eight Teseo Mk 2 anti-ship missile launchers and two octuple Albatros launchers for 48 Aspide SAMs.

'Kuznetsov' class Heavy aviation cruiser

The 'Kiev' class could never be considered true aircraft carriers. From the 1960s onwards, the rapidly expanding Soviet Navy began to see its lack of such a vessel to be a handicap, especially to a navy looking to spread its influence around the world.

Several abortive projects were started, including the 1973 design for a nuclear-powered aircraft carrier of 85,000 tons which would be capable of accommodating 60 to 70 aircraft. In the early 1980s, two less ambitious projects began to make serious progress, the **Project 1143.5** which was to become the **Kuznetsov** and the 75,000-ton **Project 1143.7** which, had it been built, would have been the **Ulyanovsk**. This nuclear-powered ship with twin catapults was proposed to carry the upgraded Su-27KM and Yak-44 AEW/ASW fixed-wing aircraft within its complement of 60-70 aircraft.

Propulsion

Initially, Western analysts anticipated that the ships would have a combined nuclear and steam (CONAS) propulsion plant similar to the *Kirov* battle cruiser and the *SSV-33* support/command ship. However the class was in fact conventionally propelled with oil-fired boilers.

Although superficially similar to American carriers, the 60,000-ton Soviet aircraft car-

Two starboard lifts carry the aircraft from the hangar to the flight deck. The ship was designed to operate Su-27K, MiG-29K, Yak-41 (and later the heavier and more capable Yak-43) supersonic STOVL fighters, but the only fixed wing aircraft regularly taken to sea have been the Su-27K (Su-33) and Su-25UTG, the latter being used as an unarmed trainer.

The first unit was originally named **Riga**. The name was changed to **Leonid Brezhnev**

Vastly more capable than the preceding vessels of the 'Kiev' class, the Kuznetsov is also vastly more expensive. The cash-strapped Russian navy can ill afford such a vessel, and no more are to be built in the foreseeable future.

and handed the hulk over to Ukraine. In 1998, the sale of the *Varyag* was announced – to a Macau-based entertainment company. The

The huge expanse of the Kuznetsov's flight deck is as large as that of a US Navy supercarrier, though it operates with a much smaller air wing.

rier was always intended to be subordinate to missile submarines operating in their 'bastions' in the Arctic. It is capable of engaging surface, subsurface and airborne targets. The lack of catapults precludes launching aircraft with heavy strike loads, and the air superiority orientation of the air wing is apparent.

The flight deck area is 14700 m² (158,235 sq ft) and aircraft take-off is assisted by a bow ski-jump angled at 12 degrees in lieu of steam catapults. The flight deck is equipped with arrester wires.

and then to **Tbilisi** before settling in October 1990 on **Admiral Flota Sovetskogo Soyuza Kuznetsov**, normally being shortened to **Admiral Kuznetsov**.

Abortive construction

Construction of a sister ship (**Project 1143.6**), initially named **Riga** and later **Varyag**, the second of the class, started in December 1985 at Nikolayev, and the ship was launched in November 1988. Late in 1991 the Russian Defence Ministry stopped financing the carrier,

unfinished hull was to be towed to the Far East where it would be converted into an entertainment complex and casino – though Russian media reports claim the company is a front for the Chinese navy.

Like its predecessors, the Kuznetsov is primarily an ASW platform, and as such is armed mainly with helicopters. However, the Su-27K 'Flanker' interceptor gives it a considerable counter-air capability.

'Kiev' class Aviation cruiser

The impetus behind the development of an aviation capability by the Soviet Navy was provided by the entry into service of the US Navy's Polaris missile submarines. The two 'Moskva'-class helicopter carriers were completed in the late 1960s, but they were fairly limited and notoriously unreliable. Work on an improved helicopter carrier began in 1967. The **Project 1143** vessels, which were known in the USSR as the *Krechyet* class, were much larger than the 'Moskva'-class.

Into service

The new carriers were built at the Chernomorsky yard at Nikolayev on the Black Sea. The 44,000 ton **Kiev** was the first of the class. It passed through the Bosphorus on 18 July 1976, to international protests about possible infractions of the Montreux Convention. Three more ships were later built in this class; **Minsk**, **Novorossiysk** and **Baku** (later renamed **Admiral Gorshkov**). Because of improvements which included a phased array radar, extensive electronic warfare installations, and an enlarged command and control suite, the *Baku* was sometimes considered a separate class. A fifth unit was approved in 1979, but not built.

Aviation cruisers

Classified as aviation cruisers (takticheskoye avianosny kreyser), they were much closer to conventional aircraft carriers than the 'Moskva' class. They had a large island superstructure to starboard, with an angled flight deck to port. However, unlike American carriers, the bow of the ships carried a very heavy armament fit, including the long-range, nuclear-capable P-500 Bazalt anti-ship missile, known to NATO as the SS-N-12 'Sandbox'. The air wing con-

Lacking catapults and arrester gear, the 'Kiev'-class carriers were much less capable aviation platforms than the US Navy's supercarriers.

SPECIFICATION

'Kiev' class
Type: Anti-submarine/aviation cruiser
Displacement: 36,000 tons (38,000 tons *Gorshkov*) standard; 43,500 tons (45,500 tons *Gorshkov*) full load
Dimensions: length 274 m (899 ft); beam 32.7 m (107 ft 4 in); flight deck 53 m (173 ft 10 in); max draught 12 m (39 ft 4 in)
Propulsion: eight turbo-pressurised boilers powering four steam turbines delivering 149 MW (200,000 shp) to four shafts
Speed: 32 kts
Aircraft: 12 Yakovlev Yak-38 'Forger' VTOL fighters plus up to 17 Kamov Ka-25 'Hormone' or Ka-27 'Helix' ASW helicopters
Armament: Two Shtorm (SA-N-3 'Goblet') twin SAM launchers with 72 missiles, two Osa-M (SA-N-4 'Gecko') twin SAM launchers with 40 missiles, four Kinshal (SA-N-9 'Gauntlet') eight-cell vertical

launchers with 96 missiles (*Novorossiysk* only) or 192 missiles (*Gorshkov* only), eight P-500 Bazalt (SS-N-12 'Sandbox') anti-ship missile tubes for 16 missiles, four 76-mm (3-inch) guns in two twin DP mounts (two single 100-mm/3.9-inch in *Gorshkov*), eight AK 630 six-barrel 30-mm CIWS, two RBU 6000 ASW rocket launchers, ten 533-mm (21-in) torpedo tubes
Electronics: 'Plate Steer' air search radar, 'Sky Watch 4' phased array radar (on *Gorshkov*), two 'Strut Pair' surface search radars, three 'Palm Frond' navigation radars, one 'Trap Door', one 'Kite Screech', four 'Bass Tilt' and four 'Cross Sword' fire control radars, one 'Fly Trap' and one 'Cake Stand' aircraft control and landing system, 'Horse Jaw', 'Horse Tail' and variable depth sonars, two twin chaff launchers plus full ECM/ESM and IFF suite
Complement: 1,600

First seen in the Mediterranean in 1976, the 44,000 ton 'Kiev'-class V/STOL carriers of the Soviet Navy were impressive vessels.

sisted of up to 22 Yakovlev Yak-38 'Forger' VTOL fighters and 16 Kamov Ka-25 'Hormone' or Ka-27 'Helix' helicopters. Ten of the helicopters were ASW machines, with two utility/SAR machines and four missile-guidance aircraft. None of the vessels are in service today – *Kiev*, *Minsk* and *Novorossiysk* were decommissioned in 1993 and were later sold for scrap. The *Admiral Gorshkov*, inactive since 1991, is due to be transferred to the Indian navy, following the addition of a redesigned 'Kuznetsov'-style flight deck with a 'ski-jump' built in a newly raised bow.

The 'Kievs' were hybrid carrier/cruisers, carrying a very heavy missile armament capable of engaging submarine, surface ship and airborne targets.

Principe de Asturias Light aircraft carrier

To replace the *Dédalo* (ex-'Independence'-class light aircraft carrier USS *Cabot*) from 1986, the Spanish navy placed a 29 June 1977 contract for a vessel with gas turbine propulsion. The design of the new Spanish ship, prepared by Gibbs and Cox of New York, was based on the Enal design variant of the US Navy's abortive Sea Control Ship. Originally to have been named the **Almirante Carrero Blanco** but then renamed as the **Principe de Asturias** before being launched, the new ship is analogous in many respects to the three British light aircraft carriers of the 'Invincible' class.

Slow completion

The *Principe de Asturias* was laid down on 8 October 1979 at the Ferrol yard of the Bazán company, was launched on 22 May 1982, and commissioned on

30 May 1988. The long period between the launch and the commissioning was attributable to the need for changes to the command and control system, and also to the addition of a flag bridge to facilitate the ship's use in the command role.

The *Principe de Asturias* has a flight deck measuring 175.3 m (575 ft 2 in) in length and 29 m (95 ft 2 in) in width, and this is fitted with a 12° 'ski-jump' ramp blended into the bow. Two aircraft lifts are fitted, one of them at the extreme stern, and these are used to move aircraft (both fixed- and rotary-wing) from the hangar, which has an area of 2300 m² (24,760 sq ft).

For the *Principe de Asturias'* air wing, Spain ordered the EAV-8B (VA.2) Harrier II V/STOL multi-role warplane (from early 1996, radar-equipped Harrier II Plus were delivered) and the

SH-60B Seahawk ASW helicopter. The standard aircraft complement is 24, although this can be increased to 37 in times of crisis with the aid of flight-deck parking. The standard aircraft mix is six to 12 AV-8Bs, two SH-60Bs, two to four AB 212 ASW helicopters, and six to 10 SH-3H Sea King helicopters.

Advanced electronics

The fully digital Tritan command and control system is fitted with the Link 11 and Link 14 data transmission/ reception terminals of the Naval Tactical Display System, and there is also the standard complex of air- and surface surveillance radars, aircraft and gun control radars, and counter-measures both electronic and physical. The ship also carries two LCVPs, and two pairs of stabilisers are fitted for stability in heavier seas.

Above: The Principe de Asturias *has a straight flight deck and a substantial 'ski jump' rise at the bow for the launch of heavily laden Harrier II aircraft.*

SPECIFICATION	
Principe de Asturias	**Armament:** four 12-barrel Meroka
Displacement: 16,700 tons full	20-mm CIWS
load	**Electronics:** one SPS-55 surface
Dimensions: length 195.9 m	search radar, one SPS-52 3D radar,
(642 ft 9 in); beam 24.3 m (79 ft	four Meroka fire-control radars, one
9 in); draught 9.4 m (30 ft 10 in)	SPN-3SA air control radar, one
Machinery: two General Electric	URN-22 TACAN system, one
LM 2500 gas turbines delivering	SLQ-25 Nixie towed decoy and four
34300 kW (46,000 shp) to one shaft	Mk 36 SRBOC chaff launchers
Speed: 26 kts	**Complement:** 555 plus a flag staff
Aircraft: see text	and air group of 208

The hangar of the Principe de Asturias *opens at its after end onto one of the two aircraft lifts. Spotted round the ship's two sides and the stern are the four Meroka defensive guns, each with 12 20-mm barrels.*

Chakri Naruebet Light aircraft carrier

The **Chakri Naruebet** ('The Great of the Chakri Dynasty') is the newest and most powerful warship of the Royal Thai navy, which otherwise comprises a dozen frigates and a similar number of corvettes and fast attack craft plus amphibious forces. The ship is the first aircraft carrier to be operated by a country in Southeast Asia. Built at Ferrol in Spain by the Bazán company, the vessel was laid down on 12 July 1994 and launched on 20 January 1996. Sea trials began in October 1996 and the ship spent the first months of 1997 working up with the Spanish fleet. (*Chakri Naruebet* is very similar to the Spanish *Principe de Asturias*.)

Arriving in Thailand in

August 1997 the vessel is in active service with the Third Naval Area Command and its home port is Rayong. However, the planned primary anti-aircraft armament (a Mk 41 LCHR 8-cell VLS launcher for Sea Sparrow missiles and four Vulcan Phalanx CIWS mountings) has not been installed, leaving the vessel protected by just Mistral infra-red homing missiles with a maximum range of 4000 m (4,375 yards). The *Chakri Naruebet* makes few operational sorties, and when it does put to sea it is usually to carry members of the Thai Royal family. The vessel is therefore to be regarded less as a V/STOL amphibious warfare capable carrier and more as the most expensive royal yacht afloat.

The Chakri Naruebet *was ordered to give the Thai navy the means to support the country's amphibious forces, but the country's financial problems then prevented the addition of the defensive weapons vital to survival in contested waters.*

A side view of the Chakri Naruebet reveals the considerable similarity between this major element of the Royal Thai navy and the Principe de Asturias of the Spanish navy, which was built by the same yard.

'Invincible' class Light aircraft carrier

The demise of the British fixed-wing aircraft carrier, with the cancellation of the CVA-01 fleet carrier programme in 1966, led in 1967 to a Staff Requirement for a 12,500-ton command cruiser equipped with six Sea King ASW helicopters. A redesign of this basic concept to give more deck space showed that a nine-helicopter air group was much more effective. A new specification resulted in a design that became known as the 19,500-ton 'through deck cruiser' (TDC), a term used for what was essentially a light carrier design because of the political sensitivity with which politicians viewed the possibility of a carrier resurrection at the time.

Despite this, the designers showed initiative in allowing sufficient space and facilities to be incorporated from the outset for a naval version of the RAF's Harrier V/STOL warplane. The designers were duly awarded for such foresight in May 1975 when it was announced officially that the TDC would carry the Sea Harrier. The first of the 'Invincible' class, HMS **Invincible**, which had been laid down in July 1973 at the Vickers shipyard at Barrow-in-Furness, was not delayed during building. In May 1976 the second ship, HMS **Illustrious**, was ordered, and in December 1978 the third, HMS **Indomitable**, was contracted. However as a result of public disquiet, the

Admiralty in placatory mood renamed the ship **HMS Ark Royal**. The ships were commissioned in July 1980, July 1982 and November 1985.

Gas turbines

The ships of the class are the largest gas turbine-powered warships in the world, with virtually every piece of below-deck equipment, including the engine modules, suitable for maintenance by exchange. During building both the Invincible and the Illustrious were fitted with 7° 'ski-jump' ramps, while the Ark Royal has a 15° ramp. In February 1982 it was announced that the Invincible was to be sold to Australia as a helicopter carrier to replace HMAS

Melbourne, leaving only two carriers in British service. However, the deal was cancelled after the Falklands campaign, to the relief of the Royal Navy, as it was realised by the government that three carriers ought to be available to ensure two in service at any one time. During Operation Corporate the Invincible started with an air group of eight Sea Harriers and nine Sea King ASW helicopters. However, as a result of losses and replacements this was modified to a group of 11 Sea Harriers, eight ASW Sea Kings and two Lynx helicopters configured to decoy Exocet missiles. One of the problems was that most of the extra aircraft had to be

accommodated on the deck as there was insufficient room for them in the hangar. The Illustrious was hurried through to completion in time to relieve the Invincible after the war, and went south with 10 Sea Harriers, nine ASW Sea Kings and two Sea King AEW conversions. The vessels were also fitted with two 20-mm Phalanx CIWS mountings for anti-missile defence and two single 20-mm AA guns to improve on the previous non-existent close-in air defences. The normal air group consisted of five Sea Harriers and 10 Sea Kings (eight ASW and two AEW).

TDCs in service

Since the 1980s the Royal Navy has run two ships with the third undergoing a refit. The Invincible was brought to the standard of the Ark Royal, then Illustrious followed. The Ark Royal started a two-year refit in 1999.

In recent years six RAF GR.Mk 7 Harriers have been regularly embarked for ground-attack missions under Joint Force Harrier. Illustrious has had its Sea Dart missile launcher removed to allow space for a flight extension and a new ordnance magazine. The Invincible was on station off the Adriatic in 1994 when Sea Harrier F/A.Mk 2s were first operationally deployed.

Above: The primary long-range air defence weapon installed on the carriers of the 'Invincible' class was the Sea Dart surface-to-air missile fired from a twin-arm launcher beside the forward edge of the flight deck.

Left: The 'Invincible'-class carriers carry fixed- and rotary-wing aircraft, the former comprising various Harrier and Sea Harrier V/STOL multi-role warplane marks in blends suiting the task in question.

SPECIFICATION	
'Invincible' class	**Aircraft:** see text
Displacement: 16,000 tons standard and 19,500 tons full load	**Electronics:** one Type 1022 air search radar, one Type 992R air search radar, two Type 909 Sea Dart guidance radars, two Type 1006 navigation/helicopter direction radars, one Type 184 or Type 2016 bow sonar, one Type 762 echo sounder, one Type 2008 underwater telephone, one ADAWS 5 action information data processing system, one UAA-1 Abbey Hill ESM suite, and two Corvus chaff launchers
Dimensions: length 206.6 m (677 ft); beam 27.5 m (90 ft); draught 7.3 m (24 ft)	
Propulsion: four Rolls-Royce Olympus TN1313 gas turbines delivering 83520 kW (112,000 shp) to four shafts	
Speed: 28 kts	
Armament: one twin Sea Dart SAM launcher with 22 missiles, two 20-mm Phalanx (replaced by Goalkeeper on Illustrious) CIWS, and two single 20-mm AA	**Complement:** 1,000 plus 320 air group (provision for emergency Marine Commando)

'Improved Forrestal' class Nuclear-powered carrier

USS America (CVA 66), commissioned in January 1965, first entered service with the Atlantic Fleet and made three combat deployments to Southeast Asia during 1968-73. In 1975 the vessel was modified to handle F-14 and S-3 aircraft, and in 1980 became the first carrier to receive the Phalanx CIWS. America was involved in action against Libya in 1986 and Iraq in 1991.

Built to an **'Improved Forrestal'-class** design, these four carriers in reality constitute three sub-classes that are easily distinguished from their predecessors by the fact that their island superstructures are set farther aft. In addition, two of their four aircraft elevators are forward of the island, the 'Forrestals' having only one in this location. A lattice radar mast is also carried abaft of the island.

USS *America*

The **USS America** (commissioned in January 1965) was very similar to the first two ships (**USS Kitty Hawk** and **USS Constellation**, commissioned in June 1961 and January 1962), and was built in preference to an austere-version nuclear-powered carrier. It was, however, the only US carrier of post-war construction to be fitted with a sonar system. The last unit,

the **USS** *John F. Kennedy*, was built to a revised design incorporating an underwater protection system developed originally for the nuclear carrier programme, and was commissioned in September 1968. All four were built with steam catapults and carried some 2,150 tons of aviation ordnance plus about 7.38 million litres (1.95 million US gal) of aviation fuel for their air groups. These are again similar in size and composition to those of the 'Nimitz' class. The tactical reconnaissance element in each of the air wings is usually provided by a handful of Grumman F-14 Tomcats equipped with a digital TARPS (tactical airborne reconnaissance system) pod. Replacement of the Tomcat in all its roles by the Boeing F/A-18E/F Super Hornet multirole fighter and strike aircraft is under way, although this aircraft has initially deployed on units of the 'Nimitz' class.

The ships were all fitted with full Anti-Submarine Classification and Analysis Center (ASCAC), Navigational Tactical Direction System (NTDS) and Tactical Flag Command Center (TFCC) facilities, *America* being the first carrier to be fitted with the NTDS. The ships all had the OE-82 satellite communications system, and were the first carriers able simultaneously to launch and recover aircraft easily; on previous carriers this was considered a tricky operation. Three of the ships passed through a SLEP (service life extension programme), but *America* was retired in the early 1990s without SLEPing. *Constellation* and *Kitty Hawk* were due to remain with the Pacific Fleet until 2003 and 2008, respectively. *JFK* is scheduled to remain on Atlantic Fleet strength until at least 2018.

Above: **Kitty Hawk** *refuels the 'Sumner'-class destroyers* **McKean** *and* **Harry E. Hubbard** *in 1962, a year after entering service with the US Pacific Fleet.*

USS Kitty Hawk is pictured in Apra Harbor, Guam, in April 2000 during a scheduled two-month deployment to the western Pacific. Between 1998-2001 the vessel operated as the Japan-based US carrier.

Below left: USS Constellation (foreground) and Kitty Hawk conduct joint carrier operations in the western Pacific Ocean in August 1999. Constellation was due to be retired in favour of USS Ronald Reagan in 2003, whilst Kitty Hawk will be replaced by CVN 77 in 2008.

SPECIFICATION	
USS *John F. Kennedy* **Displacement:** 81,430 tons full load **Dimensions:** length 320.6 m (1,052 ft); beam 39.60 m (130 ft); draught 11.40 m (37 ft 5 in); flightdeck width 76.80 m (252 ft) **Machinery:** four-shaft geared steam turbines delivering 209 MW (280,000 shp) **Speed:** 32 kts (59 km/h; 37 mph) **Aircraft:** air wing depends on mission; includes up to 20 F-14 Tomcat, 36 F/A-18 Hornet, four EA-6B Prowler, four E-2C Hawkeye, six S-3B Viking, two ES-3A Shadow (until 1999), four SH-60F Ocean Hawk and two HH-60H Rescue Hawk **Armament:** three octuple Mk 29 Sea Sparrow SAM launchers (no reloads), three 20-mm Vulcan Phalanx close-in weapons systems (CIWSs); two Phalanx mountings	scheduled to be replaced by Sea RAM (Rolling Airframe Missile) CIWS **Electronics:** one SPN-64(V)9 navigation radar, one SPS-49(V)5 air search radar, one SPS-48E 3D radar, one Mk 23 TAS (Target Acquisition System), one SPS-67 surface search radar, six Mk 95 fire control radars, three Mk 91 MFCS (Missile Fire Control System) directors; one SPN-41, one SPN-43A and two SPN-46 CCA (Carrier-Controlled Approach) radars, one URN-25 TACAN system, one SLQ-36 Nixie towed torpedo decoy, SLQ-32(V)4/SLY-2 ESM/ECM suite, SSTDS (Surface Ship Torpedo Defence System), four SRBOC Mk 36 chaff/flare launchers **Complement:** 2,930 (155 officers) plus 2,480 air group (320 officers)

USS *Enterprise* Nuclear-powered carrier

The use of nuclear power as the propulsion plant allows **USS** *Enterprise to carry sufficient aircraft fuel and ordnance for 12 days of sustained air operations before having to undergo replenishment.*

The world's first nuclear-powered aircraft-carrier, the *Enterprise* was laid down in 1958 and commissioned in November 1961, as what was then the largest war-ship ever built. Since exceeded in size by the 'Nimitz'-class ships, the *Enterprise* was built to a modified 'Forrestal'-class design, with its larger dimensions dictated by the powerplant of eight A2W pressurised water enriched-uranium fuelled nuclear reactors. The high cost of its construction prevented five other vessels in the naval building programme from being built.

Major refit

From January 1979 to March 1982 *Enterprise* underwent an extensive refit which included the rebuilding of its island superstructure and the fitting of new radar systems and a mast to replace the characteristic ECM dome and billboard radar antenna that had been used since it was built. *Enterprise* is equipped with four steam catapults, four deck-edge aircraft elevators and carries 2,520 tons of aviation ordnance plus 10.3 million litres (2.72 million US gal) of aircraft fuel. Like that of other US carriers the *Enterprise*'s ordnance has included 10-kT B61, 20-kT

USS Enterprise, *the US Navy's oldest active nuclear-powered carrier and a veteran of the Cuban Missile Crisis, steams in the Arabian Gulf in support of Operation Southern Watch in September 2001.*

B57, 60-kT B43, 100-kT B61, 200-kT B43, 330-kT B61, 400-kT B43, 600-kT B43 and 900-kT B61 tactical nuclear gravity bombs, 100-kT Walleye air-to-surface missiles and 10-kT B57 depth bombs, while 1.4-MT B43 and 1.2-MT B28 strategic bombs could be carried as and when required. The air group is similar in size and configuration to that carried by the 'Nimitz'-class carriers, and the *Enterprise* is fitted with the same ASCAC, NTDS and Tactical

Flag Command Center (TFCC) facilities. In addition to its OE-82 satellite system it also carries two British SCOT satellite communications antenna units for use with British fleet units and NATO. These two systems were fitted in 1976.

Enterprise is currently deployed with the Pacific Fleet and was SLEPed between 1991 and 1994. It is estimated that it will be eventually paid off in about 2014.

Above: Air traffic controllers on board **USS** *Enterprise assist in guiding strike aircraft in and out of Iraq during Operation Desert Fox in December 1998.*

USS Enterprise *(top) and* USS George Washington, *the fast combat support ship USS* Supply *(centre) and the ammunition ship USS* Mount Baker *(bottom) steam in formation in the western Mediterranean during turnover operations in 1996.*

SPECIFICATION

USS *Enterprise*
Displacement: 75,700 tons standard, 93,970 tons full load
Dimensions: length 342.30 m (1,123 ft); beam 40.50 m (133 ft); draught 10.90 m (39 ft); flightdeck width 76.80 m (252 ft)
Machinery: four-shaft geared steam turbines (eight A2W nuclear reactors) delivering 209 MW (280,000 shp)
Speed: 33 kts (60 km/h; 38 mph)
Aircraft: see 'Improved Forrestal' class
Armament: three octuple Mk 29 Sea Sparrow launchers (no reloads), three 20-mm Vulcan

Phalanx CIWS (may be replaced by Sea RAM)
Electronics: one SPN-64(V)9 navigation radar, one SPS-49(V)5 air search radar, one SPS-48E 3D radar, one Mk 23 TAS, one SPS-67 surface search radar, six Mk 95 fire control radars, three Mk 91 MFCS directors; one SPN-41, one SPN-43A and two SPN-46 CCA radars, one URN-25 TACAN system, one SLQ-36 Nixie towed torpedo decoy, SLQ-32(V)4/SLY-2 ESM/ECM suite, SSTDS, four SRBOC Mk 36 chaff/flare launchers
Complement: 3,215 (171 officers) plus 2,480 air group (358 officers)

'Nimitz' class
Nuclear-powered aircraft carrier

The first three **'Nimitz'-class** carriers were originally designed as replacements for the elderly 'Midway' class. The largest and most powerful warships ever built, they differ from the earlier nuclear-powered USS *Enterprise* in having two reactors rather than eight, with ordnance magazines between and forward of them. This increases the internal space available to allow some 2,570 tons of aviation weapons and 10.6 million litres (2.8 million US gal) of aircraft fuel to be carried. These totals are sufficient for 16 days of continuous flight operations before stocks have to be replenished. The class is also fitted with the same torpedo protection arrangement as carried by the USS *John F. Kennedy*, and is laid out with the same general arrangement and electronic fit as the JFK.

Flight deck
Four deck-edge aircraft elevators are available: two forward and one aft of the island on the starboard side and one aft on the port side. The hangar is 7.80 m (25 ft 7 in) high, and like those of other US carriers can accommodate, at most, only half of the aircraft embarked at any one time; the remainder is spotted on the flight deck in aircraft parks. The flight deck measures 333 x 77 m (1,093 x 253 ft), the angled section being 237.70 m (780 ft) long. It is fitted with four arrester wires and an arrester net for recovering aircraft. Four steam catapults are carried, two on the bow launch position and two on the angled flightdeck. With four cata-pults the carrier can launch one aircraft every 20 seconds.

Air Wing
The standard US Navy air wing at the beginning of the 21st Century includes 20 F-14D 'Bomcats' (Tomcats with a strike role), 36 F/A-18 Hornets, eight S-3A/B Vikings, four E-2C Hawkeyes, four EA-6B Prowlers, four SH-60F and two HH-60H Seahawks. Air wings can be varied according to the nature of the operation: for example, in 1994, 50 army helicopters replaced the usual air wing on the *Eisenhower* during peacekeeping operations off Haiti. There are also facilities for a Grumman C-2A Greyhound carrier on-board delivery aircraft.

A million miles
The core life of the A4W reactors fitted is, under normal usage, expected to provide a cruising distance of some 1287440 to 1609300 km (800,000 to 1,000,000 miles) and last for 13 or so years before the cores have to be replaced. Although the class is relatively new, it is planned for the 'Nimitz'-class to undergo Service Life Extension Program (SLEP) refits by 2010 in order to extend their service life by 15 years.

As the primary means of American power projection, the ships of the 'Nimitz' class have seen a considerable amount of use around the hotspots of the world. The USS *Nimitz* (CVN-68), commissioned in May 1975, was the base for the abortive Iranian hostage rescue mission in 1980. In 1981 her fighters were in action against Libya.

Transferring from the Atlantic to the Pacific in 1987, Nimitz deployed to the Persian Gulf and Asian waters on numerous occasions over the next decade. In 1998 the carrier returned to Norfolk for a two-year refuelling refit.

Eisenhower
Commissioned in October 1977, USS *Dwight D. Eisenhower* (CVN-69) serves with the Atlantic Fleet. The carrier has made eight Mediterranean deployments, and was the first US carrier to respond to the Iraqi invasion of Kuwait. In 1994, 'Ike' supported peacekeeping operations off Haiti, and in succeeding deployments supported US policy in the Persian Gulf.

Assigned to the Pacific fleet in 1982, the USS *Carl Vinson* (CVN-70) has conducted numerous deployments in the Pacific and Indian Oceans, as well as the Arabian Sea. Most recently, the Vinson has played a major part in the war in Afghanistan.

USS Eisenhower *steams in company with the guided missile cruiser* California *in the early 1980s. For a quarter of a century, the 'Nimitz'-class carriers have been the world's most powerful warships.*

SPECIFICATION	
'Nimitz' class	reloads); four 20-mm Phalanx close-in weapon systems (CIWS); two triple 32-cm (12.6-in) torpedo tubes
Displacement: 81,600 tons standard, 91,487 tons full load	
Hull dimensions: length 317 m (1,040 ft); beam 40.80 m (134 ft); draught 11.30 m (37 ft)	**Electronics:** (first three) one SPS48E 3D air-search, one SPS-49(V)5 air-search; one SPS-67V surface-search; one SPS-67(V)9 navigation; five aircraft landing aids (SPN-41, SPN-43B, SPN-44 and two SPN-46); one URN-20 TACAN system; six Mk 95 fire-control radars; one SLQ-32(V)4 ESM suite; four Mk 36 Super RBOC chaff launchers; SSTDS torpedo defensive system; SLQ-36 Nixie sonar defence system; ACDS combat data system; JMCIS combat data system; four UHF and one SHF SATCOM systems
Flightdeck dimensions: length 332.90 m (1,092 ft); width 76.80 m (252 ft)	
Machinery: two A4W/A1 G nuclear reactors powering four geared steam turbines delivering 208795 kW (280,000 shp) to four shafts	
Speed: over 35 kts (65 km/h; 40 mph)	
Aircraft: capacity for up to 90, but current USN air wings usually comprise 78-80 aircraft	
Armament: three octuple Sea Sparrow SAM launchers (no	**Complement:** 3,300 plus 3,000 air group

The USS **Carl Vinson** *displays about a third of a standard air wing on deck. Most of the strike aircraft can fight both air-to-air and air-to-ground.*

Improved 'Nimitz' class Nuclear-powered aircraft carrier

In 1981 the first of at least six **Improved 'Nimitz'-class** carriers was ordered after much discussion both within the Congress and the Pentagon. These vessels were completed with Kevlar armour over their vital areas and have improved hull protection arrangements. The Kevlar armour has been retrofitted to the earlier carriers, as have many of the advanced systems built into the newer ships.

Enlarged

Broader in the beam by about two metres, the newer carriers have a full-load displacement in excess of 102,000 tons (and may exceed 106,000 tons in some circumstances). The ship's complement of 3,184 personnel (203 officers) does not include the air wing of 2,800 aircrew (with 366 officers); and 70 flag staff (with 25 officers).

The combat data systems fitted to the improved carriers are based around the Naval Tactical and Advanced Combat Direction System (ACDS), with Links 4A, 11, 14, and 16 communication and data links. Weapons control is managed by three Mk 91 Mod 1 MFCS directors for the Sea Sparrow missile. USS *Nimitz* is being fitted with the SSDS Mk2 Mod 0 ship self-defense system, developed by Raytheon. The SSDS will provide automated self-defence against anti-ship cruise missiles (ASCMs) by integrating and co-ordinating the ship's weapon and electronic warfare systems.

Electronic war

The Raytheon AN/SLQ-32(V) electronic warfare system detects hostile radar emissions by two sets of antennae and the system analyses the pulse repetition rate, the scan mode, the scan period, and the frequency.

The massive flight deck of the USS Harry S. Truman is as large as three football fields, and provides the base for an air wing stronger than most of the world's smaller air forces. The aircraft carrier is a powerful element of US foreign policy. Bill Clinton once said that the first thing any President asked when being presented with a new crisis anywhere in the world was 'Where are the nearest carriers?'

The system identifies the threat and direction, provides a warning signal and interfaces to the ship's countermeasures systems.

The first improved 'Nimitz' was the USS *Theodore Roosevelt* (CVN-71), which commissioned in October 1986. *Roosevelt* saw extensive action in the Gulf War. USS *Abraham Lincoln* (CVN-72) was commissioned in November 1989 and her first major operation was the evacuation of American forces from the Philippines after the eruption of Mount Pinatubo. USS *George Washington* (CVN-73) was commissioned in July 1992, followed by USS *John C. Stennis* (CVN-74) in December 1995 and USS *Harry S. Truman* (CVN-75) in 1998. USS *Ronald Reagan* (CVN-76) was christened by Mrs Nancy Reagan in 2001.

The 10th and last of the class, CVN-77, will enter service in 2008. This will be a transitional design, incorporating new technology that will significantly reduce the crew requirement. It will test systems intended for a new class of carriers (CVNX) due in the following decade.

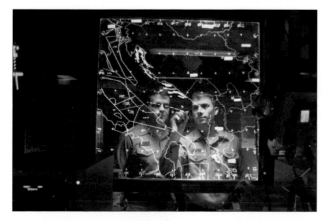

Above: Sailors man the status board in the control centre of the USS Theodore Roosevelt (CVN-71).

Right: Crewmembers aboard the USS Nimitz (CVN-68) and embarked Carrier Air Wing (CVW-11) man the rails while passing the battleship Missouri (BB-63) museum upon entering Pearl Harbour, Hawaii.

'Agosta' class Patrol submarine

Designed by the French Directorate of Naval Construction as very quiet but high-performance submarines for operations in the Mediterranean, the boats of the **'Agosta A90' class** are each armed with four bow torpedo tubes that are equipped with a pneumatically rammed rapid-reload system that can launch weapons with the minimum of noise signature. The tubes were of a completely new design which allows the submarine to fire its weapons at all speeds and at any depth down to its maximum operational limit.

The four boats in service with the French navy as its last conventionally powered submarines up to their decommissioning early in the 21st century were the **Agosta**, **Bévéziers**, **La Praya** and **Ouessant**. All were authorised in the 1970-75 naval programme as the follow-on class to the 'Daphné'-class coastal submarines. La Praya was refitted with a removable

swimmer delivery vehicle container aft of the sail to replace similar facilities that had been available aboard the *Narval*, lead boat of an obsolete class of six ocean-going submarines deleted during the 1980s.

The Spanish navy received four locally built 'Agosta'-class boats during the early 1980s, namely the **Galerna**, **Siroco**, **Mistral** and **Tramontana** using French electronics as well as French armament in the form of the L5, F17 and E18 torpedoes. In mid-1978 Pakistan purchased two units (built originally for South Africa but embargoed before delivery) as the **Hashmat** and **Hurmat**, and in 1994 ordered three more boats of the improved 'Agosta A90B' class with a number of improved features.

During the 1980s the French boats were revised with the capability to fire the SM.39 underwater-launched variant of the Exocet anti-ship missile, whereas Pakistan looked to the other

side of the Atlantic and sought to procure the UGM-84 submarine-launched version of the US Harpoon anti-ship missile.

The Agosta was the lead ship of the last class of conventionally powered submarines built for the French navy. Later in their careers, all were retrofitted to fire the SM.39 Exocet underwater-launched anti-ship missile.

Now decommissioned, the 'Agosta'-class submarines provided the French navy with a very useful capability for anti-ship operations in shallower waters. The last active French vessel in the class, Ouessant, was decommissioned in 2001.

SPECIFICATION

'Agosta A90' class
Displacement: 1,480 tons surfaced; 1,760 tons dived
Dimensions: length 67.6 m (221 ft 9 in); beam 6.8 m (22 ft 4 in); draught 5.4 m (17 ft 9 in)
Propulsion: two SEMT-Pielstick diesels delivering 2685 kW (3,600 shp) and one electric motor delivering 2200 kW (2,950 shp) to one shaft
Speed: 12.5 kts surfaced and 20.5 kts dived
Diving depth: 300 m (985 ft) operational and 500 m (1,640 ft) maximum
Torpedo tubes: four 550-mm

(21.7-in) with 533-mm (21-in) liners for 23 550-mm (21.7-in) or 533-mm (21-in) anti-submarine and anti-ship torpedoes, or 46 influence ground mines; provision for SM.39 Exocet or UGM-84 Sub-Harpoon underwater-launched anti-ship missiles on French and Pakistani units, respectively
Electronics: one DRUA 23 surface search radar, one DUUA 2A sonar, one DUUA 1D sonar, one DUUX 2A sonar, one DSUV 2H sonar, one ARUR ESM system, one ARUD ESM system, and one torpedo fire-control/action information system
Complement: 54

'Daphné' class Patrol submarine

Once they had reached the ends of their lives and also become obsolete, the 'Daphné'-class submarines were not replaced as the French navy had decided to concentrate on building only nuclear attack submarines for the future. However, the class remains in service with Pakistan (four boats), Portugal (two), South Africa (two) and Spain (four).

In 1952 plans were requested from STCAN for a second-class ocean-going submarine to complement the larger 'Narval' class. Designated the **'Daphné' class**, the boats were designed with reduced speed in order to achieve a greater diving depth and heavier armament than was possible with the contemporary 'Aréthuse' design of conventionally powered hunter-killer submarines. To reduce the crew's workload

the main armament was contained in 12 externally mounted torpedo tubes (eight forward and four aft), which eliminated the need for a torpedo room and reloads. Further crew reductions were made possible by adopting a modular replacement system for onboard maintenance. The design was based on the double-hull construction technique with the accommodation spaces split evenly fore and aft of the sail, below which

was the operations and attack centre. A total of 11 units was built for the French navy. The **Daphné**, **Diane**, **Doris**, **Eurydicé**, **Flore**, **Galatée**, **Minerve**, **Junon**, **Vénus**, **Psyché** and **Sirène** entered service between 1964 and 1970. Of these two were lost (the *Minerve* in 1968 and the *Eurydicé* in 1970) with all hands while operating in the western Mediterranean. The remaining boats all underwent an electronics and weapons

SPECIFICATION

'Daphné' class
Displacement: 869 tons surfaced; 1,043 tons dived
Dimensions: length 57.8 m (189 ft 8 in); 6.8 m (22 ft 4 in); draught 4.6 m (15 ft 1 in)
Propulsion: two SEMT-Pielstick diesel generator sets and two electric motors delivering 1940 kW (2,600 shp) to two shafts
Speed: 13.5 kts surfaced; 16 kts dived
Diving depth: 300 m (985 ft)

operational and 575 m (1,885 ft) maximum
Torpedo tubes: 12 550-mm (21.7-in) tubes (eight bow and four stern) for 12 anti-ship and anti-submarine torpedoes, or influence ground mines
Electronics: one Calypso II surface search radar, one DUUX 2 sonar, one DSUV 2 sonar, DUUA 1 and 2 sonars, and one torpedo fire-control/action information system
Complement: 54

modernisation from 1970 onwards, but have now all been retired. Another 10 were built for export, Portugal receiving the **Albacore**, **Barracuda**, **Cachalote** and **Delfim**, of which *Cachalote* was sold to

Pakistan in 1975 as the **Ghazi**. The *Albacore* and *Delfim* remained in service in 2003. Pakistan also has the **Hangor**, **Shushuk** and **Mangro**, armed with Sub-Harpoon. Ordered in 1967, South Africa took delivery of

the **Maria Van Riebeeck**, **Emily Hobhouse** and **Johanna Van der Merwe**, of which two remained in service in 2003, renamed as the **Umkhonto** and **Assegaai**. These received a weapons system upgrade (including

sonar) and features to improve habitability in 1988-90. A further four, the **Delfín**, **Tonina**, **Marsopa** and **Narval** were built under licence in Spain and were later updated similar to that which was applied to the

French boats between 1971-81. In 1971 the Pakistani submarine *Hangor* sank the Indian navy's frigate *Khukri* during the Indo-Pakistan war of that year: this was the first submarine attack since the end of World War II.

'Type 206' and 'Type 209' classes
Patrol/ocean-going submarines

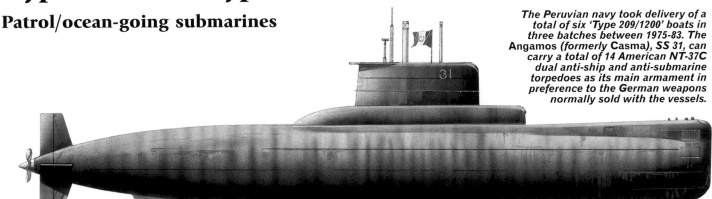

The Peruvian navy took delivery of a total of six 'Type 209/1200' boats in three batches between 1975-83. The Angamos (formerly Casma), SS 31, can carry a total of 14 American NT-37C dual anti-ship and anti-submarine torpedoes as its main armament in preference to the German weapons normally sold with the vessels.

In 1962 IKL began studies for a follow-on development of its 'Type 205' design. This new **'Type 206'** class, built of high-tensile non-magnetic steel, was to be used for coastal operations and had to conform with treaty limitations on the maximum tonnage allowed to West Germany. New safety devices for the crew were fitted, and the armament fit allowed for the carriage of wire-guided torpedoes. After final design approval had been given, construction planning took place in 1966-68, and the first orders (for an eventual total of 18 units) were placed in the following year. By 1975 all the boats, **U-13** to **U-30** were in service. Since then the class has been given extra armament in the form of two external GRP containers to carry a total of 24 ground mines in addition to their normal torpedo armament. From 1988 onwards 12 of the class were modernised with new electronics and torpedoes to form the **'Type 206A'** class. In 2003, 12 examples remained in German service.

In the mid-1960s IKL also designed for the export market a new boat that became the **'Type 209' class** in 1967. Designed specifically for the ocean-going role, the 'Type 209' can, because of its relatively short length, operate successfully in coastal waters. The 'Type 209' and its variants have proved so popular that 50 have been built or ordered by 12 export customers.

Principal variants
The six main variants of the 'Type 209' are the original **54.3-m 'Type 209/1100'** (178 ft 1 in long, 960 tons surfaced and 1,105 tons dived); **56-m 'Type 209/1200'** (183 ft 9 in long, 980 tons surfaced and 1,185 tons dived); **59.5-m 'Type 209/1300'** 195 ft 2 in long, 1,000 tons surfaced and 1,285 tons dived); **62-m 'Type 209/1400'** (203 ft 5 in long, 1,454 tons surfaced and 1,586 tons dived); **64.4-m 'Type 209/1500'** (211 ft 4 in long, 1,660 tons surfaced and 1,850 tons dived); and the smaller coastal **45-m 'Type 640'** (147 ft 7 in long, 420 tons surfaced and 600 tons dived).

The basic design of the 'Type 206' class is so versatile that customers can opt for different lengths and displacements as well as a wide assortment of electronic and armament fits. This is the German navy's U-24.

The countries which have bought these vessels are Greece (four 'Type 209/1100' and four 'Type 209/1200'), Argentina (two 'Type 209/1200'), Peru (six 'Type 209/1200'), Colombia (two 'Type 209/1200'), South Korea (nine 'Type 209/1200'), Turkey (six 'Type 209/1200' and eight 'Type 209/1400', most of which have been built locally with German help), Venezuela (two 'Type 209/1300'), Chile

(two 'Type 209/1400'), Ecuador (two 'Type 209/1300'), Indonesia (two 'Type 209/1300' plus a further four projected but unlikely to be realised), Brazil (five 'Type 209/1400'), India (four 'Type 209/1500' plus two more projected), South Africa (three 'Type 209/1400') and Israel (three 'Type 640'). Each chose its own equipment fit and crew number according to economic requirements.

During the 1982 Falklands War the Argentine navy's 'Type 209/1200'-class submarine **San Luis** made three unsuccessful torpedo attacks on vessels of the British task force, but the knowledge of the boat's presence tied up considerable British ship and aircraft resources in efforts to find the submarine.

SPECIFICATION

'Type 209/1200' class
Displacement: 1,185 tons surfaced and 1,290 tons dived
Dimensions: length 56 m (183 ft 9 in); beam 6.2 m (20 ft 4 in); draught 5.5 m (18 ft ½ in)
Propulsion: four MTU-Siemens diesel generators delivering 3730 kW (5,000 shp) and one Siemens electric motor delivering 2685 kW (3,600 shp) to one shaft
Speed: 11 kts surfaced and 21.5 kts dived
Diving depth: 300 m (985 ft)

operational and 500 m (1,640 ft) maximum
Torpedo tubes: eight 533-mm (210-in) tubes (all bow) for 14 (typically) AEG SST Mod 4 or AEG SUT anti-ship and anti-submarine torpedoes
Electronics: one Calypso surface search radar, one CSU 3 sonar, one DUUX 2C or PRS 3 sonar, one ESM system, and one Sepa Mk 3 or Sinbad M8/24 torpedo fire-control and action information system
Complement: 31-35

Above: The multiplicity of sensor and snorting masts rising from the sails of the 'Type 209' is notable. This is Tupi, a 'Type 209 Type 1400' of the Brazilian navy.

Below: The smallest of the 'Type 209' series variants is the 'Type 640'. Israel ordered three from Vickers of the UK all being commissioned in 1977.

'Enrico Toti' class Patrol submarine

The 'Enrico Toti' class was designed specifically for the shallow water areas found around the Italian coastline. Armed with four bow torpedo tubes for the wire-guided A184 heavyweight torpedo, the four vessels had a submerged dash speed of 20 kts, but could sustain 15 kts for one hour.

As the first indigenously built Italian submarine design since World War II, the **'Enrico Toti' class** had a chequered start as the plans had to be recast several times from their origins during the mid-1950s in an American-sponsored NATO project for a small anti-submarine boat. Stricken or decommissioned in the period between 1991 and 1993, the four units were the **Attilio Bagnolini**, **Enrico Toti**, **Enrico Dandolo** and **Lazzaro Mocenigo**, which entered service in 1968-69 for use in the notoriously difficult ASW conditions encoun-

*Third of the 'Enrico Toti'-class boats was the **Enrico Dandolo**, which shows off the characteristic IPD 64 active sonar system housing on the bow in this view. The crew for the relatively small boats of this class was four officers and 22 other ranks.*

tered in the central and eastern regions of the Mediterranean. For these operations the boats' relatively small size and minimum sonar cross section stood them in good stead. The main armament was originally four Kanguru anti-submarine and four anti-ship torpedoes, but then revised to six examples of the 533-mm (21-in) Whitehead Motofides A184 wire-guided dual-role anti-submarine and anti-ship

weapon with active/passive acoustic homing that features enhanced ECCM to counter decoys launched or towed by a target. With a launch weight of 1300 kg (2,866 lb), a large HE warhead and a range in the order of 20 km (12.4 miles), the electrically powered A184 would have been used by the 'Enrico Totis' at natural 'chokepoints' to attack much larger opponents such as Soviet SSNs or SSGNs.

SPECIFICATION	
'Enrico Toti' class	**Diving depth:** 180 m (591 ft)
Displacement: 535 tons surfaced; 591 tons dived	operational and 300 m (984 ft) maximum
Dimensions: length 46.2 m (151 ft 8 in); beam 4.7 m (15 ft 5 in); draught 4 m (13 ft 1 in)	**Torpedo tubes:** four 533-mm (21-in) tubes (all bow) for six A184 torpedoes, or 12 ground influence mines
Propulsion: two diesels and one electric motor delivering 1641 kW (2,200 shp) to one shaft	**Electronics:** one 3RM 20/SMG surface search radar, one IPD 64 sonar, one MD 64 sonar, torpedo
Performance: speed 14 kts surfaced and 15 kts dived; range 5550 km (3,450 miles) at 5 kts surfaced	fire-control and action information system, and ESM system
	Complement: 26

'Sauro' class Patrol submarine

During the early 1970s it became clear to the Italian navy that a new submarine type was required for defence against amphibious landings and for ASW and anti-shipping tasks in the local area. The result was the Italcantieri design for the **'Sauro' class**, whose first two units were the **Nazario Sauro** and **Carlo** Fecia di Cossato, which entered service in 1980 and 1979 respectively following major problems with their batteries. A further two units, the **Leonardo da**

*Above: The boats of the 'Sauro' class are welded from HY-80, a US-developed high-tensile steel, and thus possess a usefully greater diving depth than the earlier 'Totis'. **Nazario Sauro** decommissioned in 2001.*

*Left: **Salvatore Pelosi** is one of the sub-class of four 'Improved Sauros'. A Harpoon or Exocet capability may be added to the last two of these vessels. The current armament options are limited to the 12 Whitehead A184 torpedoes normally carried for the boats' six 533-mm (21-in) bow tubes. Alternatively, mines can be stowed.*

Leonardo da Vinci *was modernised in 1993 to receive new batteries of greater capacity, and improved habitability. Fecia di Cossato was similarly upgraded in 1990.*

Vinci and the *Guglielmo Marconi* were then for commissioning in 1981 and 1982. The class has a single pressure hull with external ballast tanks at the bow and stern, and a buoyancy tank in the sail. The pressure hull is made from the

US-developed HY-80 steel, which provides a deeper diving depth than was possible with the preceding 'Enrico Toti'-class boats. The main armament is the A184 wire-guided dual-role torpedo. The *Sauro* and *Marconi* were deleted in

2001 and 2002 respectively. In March 1983 and July 1988 two additional pairs of boats were ordered to the **'Improved Sauro' class** design, and these were delivered in 1988-89 and 1994-95 by Fincantieri as the **Salvatore Pelosi**,

Giuliano Prini, *Primo Longobardo* and *Gianfranco Gazzana Priaroggia*. The first pair have displacements of 1,476 tons surfaced and 1,662 tons dived with a length of 64.4 m (211 ft 3 in), and the second pair

have displacements of 1,653 tons surfaced and 1,862 tons dived with a length of 66.4 m (217 ft 10 in). Uprated machinery provides surfaced and dived speeds of 11 and 19 kts respectively.

'Zwaardvis' & 'Walrus' classes

Patrol submarines

Ordered in the late 1970s, the two 'Walrus'-class submarines are much improved versions of the 'Zwaardvis' design with more modern electronics, greater automation and therefore a smaller crew.

Based on the US Navy's teardrop-hulled 'Barbel' class of conventional submarine, the Dutch *Zwaardvis* and *Tijgerhaai* of the 'Zwaardvis' class were ordered in the mid-1960s. Because of the requirement to use indigenous Dutch equipment wherever possible, the design was modified to include the placement of all noise-producing machinery on a false deck with spring suspension for silent running. The two boats entered service with the Dutch navy in 1972 and were decommissioned in 1994-95. A buyer is still sought for the boats.

At the same time the need began to arise to start the design of a new class to replace the boats of the

elderly 'Dolfijn' and 'Potvis' classes. The new design evolved as the **'Walrus' class**, which was based on the basic hull form of the 'Zwaardvis' with similar dimensions and silhouette but with more automation allowing a significant reduction in the number of crew needed, more modern electronics, X-layout control surfaces and fabrication in the French MAREI high-ten-

sile steel allowing a 50 per cent increase in the maximum diving depth.

The first unit, the *Walrus*, was laid down in 1979 in Rotterdam (where all the boats were built) for commissioning in 1986 and the *Zeeleeuw* a year later for service entry in 1987. A further two, the *Dolfijn* and *Bruinvis*, were laid down in 1986 and 1988 for commissioning in 1993 and 1994.

Above: Although fitted for the Sub-Harpoon SSM, the 'Walrus' class does not carry these weapons. The lead ship of the class is illustrated.

Left: For their time the 'Zwaardvis' class of conventionally powered submarines were capable boats well suited to the demands of the Dutch navy for littoral defence. Both vessels underwent an upgrade in 1988-90.

In 1987-88 Taiwan received two **'Improved Zwaardvis'** or **'Hai Lung'-class** units *Hai*

Lung and *Hai Hu*. These are planned to carry Hsiung Feng II SSMs.

'Sjöormen' class Patrol submarine

The first of the modern type of submarines for the Swedish navy was the **'Sjöormen' class** designed in the early 1960s by Kockums, Malmö and built by that company (three units) and Karlskronavarvet (two units). The class comprised the **Sjöormen**, **Sjölejonet**, **Sjöhunden**, **Sjöbjörnen** and **Sjöhästen**. With an 'albacore' type hull for speed and a twin-deck arrangement the class was extensively used in the relatively shallow Baltic, where its excellent manoeuvrability and silent-running capabilities greatly aided the Swedish navy's ASW operations. The control surface and hydroplane arrangements were the same as those fitted to the latter Swedish submarine classes,

The five vessels of the 'Sjöormen' class were designated the Type A12 by their builders. Fitted with X-configuration stern planes for increased manoeuvrability, they carried four 533-mm (21-in) and two 400-mm (15.75-in) calibre torpedo tubes for anti-ship and ASW torpedoes respectively. Four vessels transferred to Singapore.

and it was these together with the hull design that allowed the optimum manoeuvrability characteristics to be used throughout the speed range, though they were more noticeable at the lower end: for example, a 360° turn could be achieved in five minutes within a 230-m (755-ft) diameter circle at a speed of 7 kts underwater; if the speed was increased to 15 kts the same turn would take only two and a half minutes, which meant the class could easily out-turn most of the Warsaw Pact ASW escorts encountered in the Baltic, as well as most of the NATO escorts.

Sjöbjörnen was modified and upgraded for tropical conditions 1996-97 and re-launched as **Challenger** on 26 September 1997, as one of four submarines of the **'Challenger' class** on order for the Republic of Singapore Navy. The other vessels comprise **Centurion** (ex-*Sjöormen*), **Conqueror** (ex-*Sjölejonet*) and **Chieftain** (ex-*Sjöhunden*) and together will form 171 Squadron. The weapons options for the reconditioned boats comprises a combination of FFV Type 613 anti-ship torpedoes (10 carried) and FFV Type 431 ASW torpedoes (four).

The Sjöbjörnen shows the sail-mounted hydroplanes which increased the vessel's underwater manoeuvring capabilities. The class could, at medium speeds submerged, out-turn most of the Western and Warsaw Pact ASW vessels it was likely to encounter in the Baltic.

SPECIFICATION

'Sjöormen' class
Displacement: 1,125 tons surfaced and 1,400 tons dived
Dimensions: length 51 m (167 ft 4 in); beam 6.1 m (20 ft); draught 5.8 m (19 ft)
Propulsion: four diesels delivering 1566 kW (2,100 shp) with one electric motor driving one shaft
Speed: 15 kts surfaced and 20 kts dived
Diving depth: 150 m (492 ft) operational and 250 m (820 ft) maximum

Torpedo tubes: four 533-mm (21-in) bow and two 400-mm (15.75-in) bow
Basic load: 10 Type 61 533-mm (21-in) anti-ship wire-guided torpedoes or 16 influence ground mines, plus four Type 431 anti-submarine wire-guided torpedoes
Electronics: one Terma surface search radar, one low-frequency sonar, one torpedo fire-control/action information system, and one ESM system
Complement: 18

The Sjölejonet of the 'Sjöormen' (sea serpent) class runs on the surface in the submarine's major operating area of the Baltic. In such a region speed and manoeuvrability is of greater importance than diving depth, since much of the sea is relatively shallow.

'Näcken' class Patrol submarine

Since World War II Sweden has placed considerable emphasis on the possession of a small but highly capable force of conventional submarines as a key element in the preservation of its long coastline against the incursions of other nations' surface and underwater forces for the purposes of reconnaissance and/or aggression. The Swedish navy's first post-war submarines were the six boats of the 'Hajen' class, built during the 1950s on the basis of the German Type XXI class design: the design data were derived from the *U-3503*, which its crew had scuttled off Göteborg on 8 May 1945 and which the Swedes subsequently salvaged.

From 1956 the Swedes followed with six examples of the indigenously designed 'Draken' class, and in 1961 the Swedish government approved plans for five more advanced submarines of the Type A12 or 'Sjöormen' class. This latter introduced a teardrop-shaped hull with two decks and X-configured stern planes.

'Sjöormen' successor

The Swedish navy considers the effective life of its conventional submarines to be something in the order of 10 years, and in the early 1970s raised the matter of a class to succeed the 'Sjöormen' class from a time later in the same decade. The Swedish government gave its approval to the request in 1972, and the Swedish defence ministry was therefore able to contract in March 1973 with Kockums of Malmö (two boats) and Karlskronavarvet naval dockyard (one boat) for the three **Type A14** or **'Näcken'-class** diesel-electric submarines. The boats were all laid down in 1976 and launched between April 1978 and August 1979 for commissioning between April 1980 and June 1981 as the **Näcken**, **Neptun** and **Najad**.

The Baltic, which is the primary operational theatre

Sweden's 'Näcken'-class submarines were extremely capable boats by the standards of their day, their wire-guided torpedoes providing high capability against surface ships as well as submarines. The lead unit is illustrated.

for Sweden's submarine arm, is shallow, so the diving depth of the 'Näcken'-class boats was fixed at some 150 m (500 ft). The boats were based on the same type of teardrop-shaped two-deck hull as the 'Sjöormen' class, and were completed with Kollmorgen periscopes from the US as well as the Data Saab NEDPS combined ship control and action information system.

In 1987-88 the *Näcken* was lengthened by 8 m (26 ft 3 in) to allow the installation of a neutrally buoyant section containing two liquid-oxygen tanks, two United Stirling Type V4-275 closed-cycle engines and the relevant control system, this air-independent propulsion arrangement boosting submerged endurance to 14 days and in effect making the boat a true submarine

rather than just an advanced submersible.

Danish service

From the early 1990s the boats were upgraded to a partial 'Västergötland' class standard in their electronics, but were discarded from a time later in the same decade. The sole surviving boat is the **Kronborg** of the Danish navy, which was the *Näcken* until transferred in

August 2001, after a refit by Kockums, under a lease to buy or return (in 2005).

The boat is armed with wire-guided torpedoes, the 533-mm (21-in) Type 613 passive anti-ship weapons attaining 45 kts over a range of 20 km (12.4 miles), and the 400-mm (15.75-in) Type 431 active/passive anti-submarine weapons having a speed of 25 kts over the same range.

Above: The 'Näckens' were typical diesel-electric 'submersibles', with limited submerged endurance, until the addition of air-independent propulsion in the lead boat. Neptun *and* Najad *are seen at Karlskrona.*

The submarines of the 'Näcken' class were characterised by their good fire-control system, the relevant data being derived from the passive sonar and single Kollmorgen periscope.

SPECIFICATION	
'Näcken' class (upgraded)	**Diving depth:** 150 m (492 ft)
Displacement: 1,015 tons surfaced; 1,085 tons dived	operational
Dimensions: length 57.5 m (188 ft 8 in); beam 5.7 m (18 ft 8); draught 5.5 m (18 ft)	**Torpedo tubes:** four 533-mm (21-in) and two 400-mm (15.75-in) tubes (all bow) with eight and four torpedoes respectively; up to 48 mines can be carried in an external girdle
Propulsion: one MTU 16V 652 MB80 diesel delivering 1290 kW (1,730 shp), two Stirling engines and one Jeumont Schneider electric motor delivering 1340 kW (1,800 shp) to one shaft	**Electronics:** Terma navigation radar, IPS-17 (Sesub 900C) fire-control system, AR700-S5 ESM, and Thomson-Sintra passive sonar with bow and flank arrays
Performance: speed 10 kts surfaced and 20 kts dived	**Complement:** 27

'Romeo' class

Diesel-electric submarine

The Chinese adopted the Soviet 'Romeo' class as their main submarine production type and exported the type to North Korea. Today numbers of PLAN 'Romeo' ships are decreasing, and construction ceased in 1987 in favour of the 'Ming' class.

Although it was the Soviets who built the first **'Romeo' class (Project 633)** submarines in 1958 at Gorky, as an improvement on their 'Whiskey' design, the construction coincided with the successful introduction of nuclear propulsion into Soviet submarines. As a consequence, only 20 of these diesel electric powered boats were actually completed out of the 560 boats originally planned.

Chinese production

However, the design was passed to the Chinese as part of the development of their weapons production industry, and the class was built in China from 1962, the first boats being completed at the Wuzhang shipyard under the local designation **Type 033**. Three further shipyards, located at Guangzhou (Canton), Jiangnan (Shanghai) and Huludao, then joined the programme to give a maximum yearly production rate of nine units during the early 1970s.

A total of 84 'Romeos' was constructed by the Chinese. However, it is now thought that only 31 remain in service with the People's Liberation Army Navy, with a further nine vessels in reserve. A total of four were exported to Egypt during 1982-84, and these have since been fitted with Sub Harpoon missiles. North Korea is believed to operate 22 'Romeo'-class boats, some of which were

locally built with Chinese assistance from 1976. Bulgaria operates a single Soviet-built vessel named **Slava**.

Of the original Soviet boats, all of them had been decommissioned by 1987. Two boats were loaned to Algeria in 1982-83 for a five-

year period as training boats, before Algeria's acquisition of more modern 'Kilo'-class submarines. In physical appearance both the Chinese and Soviet 'Romeos' are essentially identical, except that the Soviet boats tend to have extra sonar installations around the bow.

SPECIFICATION

Type 033 'Romeo' class
Displacement: 1,475 tons surfaced and 1,830 tons dived
Dimensions: length 76.6 m (251 ft 3 in); beam 6.7 m (22 ft); draught 5.2 m (17 ft 1 in)
Propulsion: two diesels delivering 2.94 MW (4,000 shp) with two electric motors driving two shafts
Speed: 15.2 kts surfaced and 13 kts dived
Range: 14,484 km (9,000) miles at 9 kts surfaced
Torpedo tubes: eight 533-mm

(21-in), six located in the bows and two at the stern
Basic load: 14 533-mm (21-in) anti-ship or anti-submarine torpedoes (including Yu-4 and Yu-1 weapons) or 28 mines
Electronics: one 'Snoop Plate' or 'Snoop Tray' surface search radar, one Thomson Sintra interception sonar (some vessels), one high-frequency Herkules or Tamir 5 active/passive search and attack hull-mounted sonar
Complement: 54 (10 officers)

With only a few 'Romeo' class units left in service, the Soviet navy transferred surplus vessels to Algeria, Bulgaria, Egypt and Syria. Algeria's boats were on loan and were used to train naval personnel in submarine operations. The Algerian navy have since replaced the boats with the 'Kilo'-class.

'Foxtrot' class Diesel-electric submarine

A total of up to 79 'Foxtrot'-class units were built from 1958 onwards in several subgroups. Surprisingly, even after this period of time the basic design is still being built for the export market, with new-build ships transferred to India, Libya and Cuba (three boats received between 1979-84), albeit with downgraded electronic systems.

Built in the periods 1958-68 (45 units) and 1971-74 (17 units) at Sudomekh for the Soviet Union, the **'Foxtrot' class (Project 641)** has proved to be the most suc-

cessful of the post-war Soviet conventional submarine designs, a total of 62 entering service with the Soviet navy. Two were subsequently struck off as a result

of damage sustained in accidents, one of them apparently caused by a collision with the Italian liner *Angelino Lauro* in the Bay of Naples on 10 January 1970,

after which the unit was seen later at a Soviet naval anchorage off Morocco with 8 m (26 ft 2 in) of its bow missing. All four Soviet navy fleet areas operated

'Foxtrot'-class vessels, and the Mediterranean and Indian Ocean squadrons regularly had units attached to them as part of their subsurface forces.

SPECIFICATION

'Foxtrot' class

Displacement: 1,952 tons surfaced and 2,475 tons dived
Dimensions: length 91.3 m (299 ft 5 in); beam 7.5 m (24 ft 6 in); draught 6 m (19 ft 7 in)
Propulsion: three Type 37-D diesels delivering 4.4 MW (6,000 shp) with three electric motors driving three shafts
Speed: 16 kts surfaced and 15 kts dived
Range: 32186 km (20,000) miles at 8 kts surfaced; 612 km (380 miles) at

2 kts dived
Torpedo tubes: 10 533-mm (21-in) located as six at the bows and four at the stern
Basic load: 22 533-mm (21-in) anti-ship and anti-submarine torpedoes or 32 mines
Electronics: one 'Snoop Tray' or 'Snoop Plate' surface-search radar, one 'Pike Jaw' high-frequency passive/active search and attack hull sonar, one 'Stop Light' ESM system
Complement: 75 (12 officers)

Of the 62 'Foxtrot' boats which entered service with the Soviet navy, a single boat remains in service with the Russian navy. This, the last of the class, is used for basic ASW training. Another four units were transferred to the Ukraine in 1997.

The first foreign recipient of the type was India, which took eight brand new boats between 1968 and 1975, although it now only deploys two of the vessels. India was followed by Libya, with six units received between 1976 and 1983, of which two remain operational. Poland

intended to operate two vessels, **Wilk** and **Dzik**, until 2003, while a single boat remains in the Russian navy. Export versions differed from the standard Soviet units by having export-grade electronic and weapon fits, although the eight Indian navy units (received 1968-75)

were of a very similar standard to the Soviet vessels.

Like all Soviet conventional and nuclear submarine classes, the 'Foxtrots' were fitted to carry the standard Soviet 15-kT yield anti-ship torpedo as part of its

weapons load, but liners for 400-mm (16-in) ASW torpedoes were not apparently fitted. The Soviet 'Foxtrots' were built in three distinct subclasses that differed only in the propulsion plant. The last group is thought to have

served as prototypes for the follow-on 'Tango' design. The submerged non-snorkelling endurance of the class is estimated to have been around 5 to 7 days when operating at very low speeds (2-3 kts) .

'Tango' class
Diesel-electric submarine

Production of the 'Tango' class was completed in 1982. The design succeeded the 'Foxtrot' and offered increased battery storage capacity and more advanced electronics systems. The hull was also more streamlined than that of the 'Foxtrot', making it more suitable for submerged operations.

Built as the Soviet navy's interim long-range successor to the 'Foxtrot' class in the Black Sea and Northern Fleet areas, the first unit of the **'Tango' class** (**Project 641B**) was completed at Gorky in 1972. A total of 18 were constructed in two slightly different versions, the later type being several metres longer than the first, perhaps due to the installation of ASW missile equipment. The bow sonar installations appear similar to those fitted to the latter classes of contemporary Soviet nuclear attack submarines, while the propulsion plant was the same as that tested on the last subgroup of the

'Foxtrot' design. The battery capacity was much higher than in any preceding Soviet conventional submarine class as a result of the increased pressure hull volume. This allowed an underwater endurance in excess of a week before snorkelling was required. Coupled with the new armament and sensor fit, this made the 'Tangos' ideal for use in 'ambush' operations against Western nuclear submarines at natural 'chokepoints'. Construction of this class has now stopped. However, four 'Tango'-class boats remain in service. These are operated by the Russian navy's Northern Fleet at Polyarny

and were inherited from the Soviet navy. The condition of the vessels is unknown.

The casing and fin of the long-range 'Tango'-class submarines are fitted with a continuous acoustic coating, and at least one vessel was completed with a towed sonar tube in the stern and a reel mounted in the casing forward of the fin.

SPECIFICATION

'Tango' class

Displacement: 3,100 tons surfaced and 3,800 tons dived
Dimensions: length 91 m (298 ft 6 in); beam 9.1 m (29 ft 9 in); draught 7.2 m (23 ft 6 in)
Propulsion: three diesels delivering 4.6 MW (6,256 shp) with three electric motors driving three shafts
Speed: 13 kts surfaced and 16 kts dived
Diving depth: 250 m (820 ft) operational and 300 m (984 ft) maximum

Torpedo tubes: six 533-mm (21-in) located in the bow
Basic load: 24 533-mm (21-in) anti-submarine and anti-ship torpedoes, or equivalent load of mines
Electronics: one 'Snoop Tray' surface-search radar, one medium-frequency active/passive search and attack hull-mounted sonar, one high-frequency active attack hull-mounted sonar, one 'Brick Group' or 'Squid Group' ESM system
Complement: 62 (12 officers)

The 'Tango' class prototype with its characteristic raised forecasing was first identified at the July 1973 Sevastopol Naval Review in the Black Sea. Directly ahead of the 'Tango' is a 'Whiskey Twin Cylinder' boat.

Chinese SSBNs Types 092 'Han' and 094

The Chinese navy's SSBN programme began in the 1970s but has yet to produce a functioning weapons platform. The sole Chinese SSBN, the **Changzheng 6**, is a modified 'Han'-class (NATO designation) SSN, laid down in 1978 and launched in 1981. Commissioned in 1987, the NATO designation is **'Xia' class**; to the Chinese it is the **Type 092**. Construction of both boat and intended missile system was a catalogue of disasters. The 'Xia' class is slow, noisy and its reactor unreliable. The JL-1 missile failed on its first live firings in 1985

and it took three years to achieve a successful test launch. The JL-1 (CSS-N-3) has a single 250-kT warhead and its comparatively short range of 2,150 km (1,336 miles) would force the vessel to patrol perilously close to enemy shores. In fact, the 'Xia' class has never left Chinese coastal waters and seldom put to sea before a refit that lasted from 1995 to 2000. It emerged from dockyard hands with a new coat of black paint – replacing the previous steel blue – a bow-mounted sonar, re-designed missile casing that would

allow for longer missiles and (presumably) new firing systems for a different missile, the JL-1A SLBM, which has a reported range of 2,800 km (1,740 miles).

It was reported that a second unit was constructed but lost with all hands in an accident in 1985, but Chinese secrecy remains at Cold War levels. A solitary SSBN has little strategic value but whatever plans there might have been to extend the 'Xia' class have come to nought. Even if all systems are functioning, the boat's performance is poor by modern standards. The

sole 'Xia'-class boat would not survive long in wartime against western ASW platforms. A new class of SSBN, the **Type 094**, reportedly with 16 JL-2 (CSS-N-5 'Sabbot') SLBMs (8,000-km/

4,971-mile range) is under construction with an estimated launch date of 2006. This new vessel may well be based on the hull of the new Type 093 SSN with an additional missile 'plug'.

SPECIFICATION	
'Xia' class (Type 092)	**Diving depth:** 300 m (984 ft)
Displacement: 6,500 tons dived	**Armament:** 12 JL-1A (CSS-N-3)
Dimensions: length 120 m (393 ft 6 in); beam 10 m (33 ft); draught 8 m (26 ft 2 in)	SLBMs, six 533-mm (21-in) bow tubes for Yu-3 torpedoes
Machinery: one pressurised watercooled reactor delivering 90 MW (120,643 shp) to one shaft	**Electronics:** 'Snoop Tray' surface search radar; 'Trout Cheek' hull-mounted active/passive search, Type 921A ESM
Speed: 22 kts dived	**Complement:** 140

'Le Triomphant' class New generation SSBN/SNLE

Ordered in March 1986 to replace the 'Redoutable' class, the **'Le Triomphant' class** are known to the French as SNLE-NGs (*Sous-marins Nucléares Lanceurs d'Engines-Nouvelle Génération*) or 'new generation' SSBNs. **Le Triomphant** was laid down at Cherbourg in 1989, launched in 1994 and entered service in 1997. Six boats were planned but this was reduced to four

after the end of the Cold War, and the M5 SLBM, which was proving very expensive to develop, has been abandoned. The 'Triomphant' class will be armed with the cheaper M51 missile but the two vessels currently in service carry the M45. A first submerged M45 launch was conducted by *Le Triomphant* in February 1995. Operated by two crews ('amber' and 'blue') *Le*

Triomphant is France's primary nuclear deterrent – only two of the 'L'Inflexible' M4 class are still operational and one of them is due to pay off in 2004. The 'Triomphant' class are significantly quieter than their predecessors: the primary objective of the design team was to reduce noise levels to the point that even the best acoustic sensors would struggle to detect and track the vessels.

Le Téméraire was the second of the 'Le Triomphant'-class SSBNs, launched in August 1997 and commissioned in December 1999. This boat and the name ship currently carry the M45 SLBM.

The second of the class, **Le Téméraire** was laid down in 1993, launched in 1998 and commissioned in December 1999. **Le Vigilant**, laid down in 1997, is planned to enter service in 2004. **Le Terrible** was laid down in October 2000 and is planned to join the fleet in 2010. The M45 SLBM has a maximum range of 5,300 km (3,293 miles) and each missile has six

MIRVs each carrying a 150-kT nuclear warhead. The 'Triomphant' class can launch SM39 Exocet anti-ship missiles from their torpedo tubes to attack surface targets, in addition to dual purpose L5 active/passive homing torpedoes. Between 2010-15 the class of four boats, beginning with *Le Terrible*, is to be equipped with the M51.

SPECIFICATION	
'Le Triomphant' class	**Speed:** 25 kts dived
Displacement: 12,640 tons surfaced; 14,335 tons dived	**Diving Depth:** 500 m (1,640 ft)
Dimensions: length 138 m (453 ft); beam 12.5 m (41 ft); draught 12.5 m (41 ft)	**Armament:** 16 M45 SLBMs each with six 150-kT MIRVs, four 533-mm (21-in) tubes for 18 L5 torpedoes/SM39 Exocet missiles
Machinery: one pressurised water-cooled reactor delivering 150 MW (201,072 shp), two diesels delivering 700 kW (939 shp), one pump jet propulsor, one shaft	**Electronics:** Dassault search radar, Thomson-Sintra DMUX multi-function passive bow and flank arrays, towed array passive sonar
	Complement: 111

Le Triomphant undertook its first cruise in summer 1995, while Le Téméraire began trials in April 1998. The next vessel, Le Vigilant, was due to begin trials in December 2003, and the fourth and final boat (and the first to carry the definitive M51 SLBM), Le Terrible, is scheduled to enter service in 2010.

'Le Redoutable' and 'L'Inflexible' classes SSBNs/SNLEs

First of the French strategic missile submarines was Le Redoutable, commissioned in December 1971.

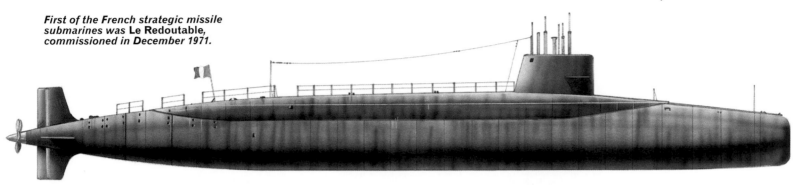

The first French SSBN (or more correctly *Sous-marin Nucléare Lanceurs d'Engine* or SNLE) **Le Redoutable** was authorised in March 1963, laid down in November 1964 and commissioned in 1971 after being employed for 2½ years on trials as the prototype for the French naval deterrent known as the *Force de Dissuasion* in official circles. This vessel and its **'Le Redoutable' class** sister ship **Le Terrible** were initially equipped with the 2400-km (1,490-mile) range two-stage solid-propellant inertially-guided M1 SLBM that had a single 500-kT nuclear warhead and a CEP of 930 m (3,050 ft). In 1974 the third unit, **Le Foudroyant**, was commissioned with the improved 3100-km (1,925-mile) range M2 SLBM with a more powerful second-stage motor but carrying the same warhead and having a similar CEP. The two previous vessels were then retrofitted with the M2 system during their normal overhauls. The fourth boat, **L'Indomptable**, was commis-

sioned into service in 1977 with the vastly improved M20 missile that had the same range and accuracy as the M2 but carried a new 1.2-MT yield hardened warhead with what is believed to be chaff-dispensing penetration aids to confuse defending radar systems. The last vessel, **Le Tonnant**, was also completed with the M20 while the three units equipped with the M2 were subsequently brought up to the same standard. From 1985 the last four units built underwent yet another modification to carry the M4 SLBM that entered service aboard **L'Inflexible**. All five boats were also converted to carry the SM39 Exocet anti-ship missile and sonars of the **'L'Inflexible' class**. After the paying off of Le Redoutable in December 1991, the remaining submarines of the class were classified as the **'L'Inflexible' class SNLE M4**. The better streamlining of the M4 conversion gave the boats a silhouette similar to that of *L'Inflexible*. The sole such boat remaining in service in

2003 was *L'Indomptable*, which received M4 missiles in 1989 and was due to decommission in late 2004. The similarly upgraded *Le Tonnant* was paid off into the reserve in 1999.

'L'Inflexible' class

Ordered in September 1978, the sole boat of the 'L'Inflexible' class, *L'Inflexible* is an intermediate design between the 'Le Redoutable' class and the 'Le Triomphant' class. *L'Inflexible* retains most of the external characteristics of the earlier class, but the internal fittings and sensors differ by taking advantage of the advances made in the propulsion system, electronics and weapons since the 'Le Redoutable'-class boats were constructed. The ratio-

Le Foudroyant *and its sister ships were designed and built in France without any help from the US, unlike the British Polaris boats, which required considerable design assistance.*

nale behind this intermediate boat lay in the fact that France required three SSBNs to be continuously available, of which two were to be on patrol. In order to achieve this the French navy had to have six submarines in service, a number one more than the 'Le Redoutable' class total.

Laid down in March 1980, *L'Inflexible* achieved operational status in April 1985 and is due to remain in service until at least 2008, or possibly until 2010. Like all French missile submarines, *L'Inflexible* has two crews, *Bleu* (blue) and *Ambre* (amber), to crew the vessel in rotation in order

to maximise the time spent on patrol between reactor-refuelling refits. French SSBNs normally undertake patrols of two months' duration, with three months as the absolute maximum. All the French SSBNs are based at Ile Longue near Brest and have special protection when transiting to and from the port.

In April 2001 *L'Inflexible* conducted a successful test launch of the M45 SLBM, containing components of the new generation M51 missile with which it is planned to equip the 'Le Triomphant'-class SSBNs.

SPECIFICATION

'L'Inflexible' class
Displacement: 8,080 tons surfaced and 8,920 tons dived
Dimensions: length 128.7 m (422 ft 3 in); beam 10.6 m (34 ft 9 in); draught 10 m (32 ft 10 in)
Propulsion: one pressurised water-cooled reactor powering two steam turbines driving one shaft
Speed: 20 kts surfaced and 25 kts dived
Diving depth: 350 m (1,150 ft) operational and 465 m (1,525 ft) maximum

Armament: 16 launch tubes for 16 M4 SLBMs (16 M45 SLBMs fitted in *I'Inflexible* in 2001), and four 533-mm (21-in) bow tubes for total of 18 L5 dual-purpose and F17 anti-ship torpedoes and SM39 Exocet anti-ship missiles
Electronics: one surface search radar, one passive ESM system, one DLT D3 torpedo and Exocet fire-control system, one DSUX 21 sonar, and one DUUX 5 underwater telephone
Complement: 135

France tries to maintain a minimum of two SNLEs on patrol at any one time, and submarines such as the Le Terrible ('Le Redoutable' class) were screened on departure and return by navy surface units, submarines and ASW aircraft in order to maintain security.

SPECIFICATION

'Le Redoutable' class
Displacement: 8,045 tons surfaced and 8,940 tons dived
Dimensions: as 'L'Inflexible' class
Propulsion: one pressurised water-cooled reactor powering two steam turbines driving one shaft
Speed: 18 kts surfaced and 25 kts dived

Diving depth: 250 m (820 ft) operational and 330 m (1,085 ft) maximum
Armament: 16 launch tubes for 16 M20 SLBMs, and four 550-mm (21.7-in) bow tubes for 18 L5 dual-purpose and F17 anti-ship torpedoes

'Delta III/IV' class
Ballistic missile submarine

At more than 16,000 tons submerged displacement, the 'Kalmar' class, known to NATO as the Delta III, were the largest submarines in the world when they entered service in 1976.

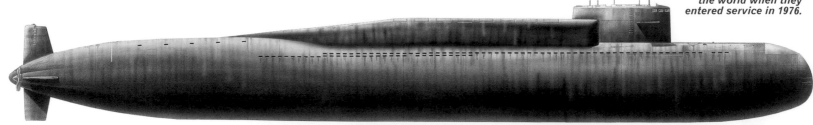

Although the Soviets were pioneers in firing missiles from submarines, their early systems were short-ranged. The 34 units of the 'Yankee' class, built between 1967 and 1974, were apparently based on stolen American plans for the 'Benjamin Franklin' class. These provided the foundation for the follow-on **'Delta'** class, an enlarged development of the 'Yankee' design. The first Deltas entered service in 1972, the original **'Delta I'** design being succeeded by the interim **'Delta II'** with 16 missiles rather than the original 12.

'Delta III'

These were followed from 1976 by the **Type 667 BDR 'Kalmar' class**, better known to NATO as the **'Delta III'**. These had a larger and longer 'turtle-back' abaft the sail. This housed R-29R missiles (NATO designation SS-N-18) the first Soviet sea-based multiple-warhead system. Fourteen submarines were built at Severodvinsk.

The 'Delta III' submarines which served in the Northern fleet formed a division and were based at Sayda and at Olyenya port. In the early 90s the ballistic missile submarines were transferred to Yagyelnaya. Pacific Fleet 'Delta IIIs' were based on Kamchatka.

Development of the **Type 667 BDRM 'Delfin'** or

'Dolphin' class, known to NATO as the **'Delta IV'**, began on 10 September 1975. The first boat, *K-51*, was commissioned into Northern fleet in December 1985. Between 1985 and 1990, seven 'Delta IVs' were constructed by the Sevmashpredpriyatiye Production Association in Severodvinsk.

The 'Delta IVs' were constructed in parallel to the 'Typhoon' class, in case the larger boats proved unsuccessful. The 'Dolphin' is a further modification of the 'Delta III', with an increased diameter pressure hull and a longer bow section. Displacement has increased by 1,200 tons and it is 12 m (39 ft) longer.

'Delta IV'

The 'Delta IV' is a strategic platform, designed to strike military and industrial installations and naval bases. The submarine carries the RSM-54 Makeyev missile (NATO designation: SS-N-23 'Skiff'). The RSM-54 is a three-stage liquid-propellant ballistic missile with a range of 8300 km (5,158 miles). The warhead consists of four to ten multiple independently targeted re-entry vehicles (MIRVs), each rated at 100 kT. The missile uses stellar inertial guidance for a CEP of 500 m (1,640 ft).

The submarine can also launch the Novator (SS-N-15 'Starfish') anti-ship missile or

Mk 40 anti-ship torpedo. 'Starfish' is armed with a 200 KT nuclear warhead and has a range of 45 km (28 miles).

The operational lifetime of these submarines was estimated to be 20–25 years, assuming normal maintenance schedules, but in the 1990s everything changed. When the START-1 treaty was signed in 1991, five 'Delta IIIs' served in the Northern and nine in the Pacific Fleet.

Russia was scheduled to dismantle one 'Yankee'-class, five 'Typhoon'-class and 25 assorted 'Delta'-class ballistic missile submarines by the year 2003.

By September 1999, US

Since 'Delta'-class boats remain a mainstay of Russia's deterrent force, they are kept in better condition than other nuclear submarines.

Bottom: Although the Russian navy is a shadow of its former self, it still maintains sufficent force to keep a minimum missile deterrent at sea at all times.

specialists had helped disassemble one 'Yankee' and six 'Deltas', while the Russians had destroyed another five ballistic missile subs on their own using US equipment.

As of June 2000, the Russian Navy claimed that it operated five 'Typhoon'-class submarines, seven 'Delta IV'-class submarines, and 13 'Delta III'-class submarines, which between them carry 2,272 nuclear warheads on 440 ballistic missiles. With

the chronic funding shortages affecting the Soviet navy, it is likely that many of these boats are of suspect seaworthiness.

However, the Russian navy reportedly believes that 12 nuclear ballistic missile submarines is the minimum necessary force structure for national security, and this force goal is likely to be maintained up until 2010 at least.

SPECIFICATION	
Type 667 'Delfin' or 'Delta IV' class **Type:** Nuclear-powered ballistic missile submarine **Displacement:** 13,500 tons surfaced, 18,200 tons submerged **Dimensions:** length 166 m (544 ft 7 in); beam 12.3 m (39 ft 6 in); draught 8.8 m (29 ft) **Machinery:** two pressurised water-cooled reactors powering two steam turbines delivering 44700 kW (60,000 shp) to two seven-bladed fixed-pitch shrouded propellers; 3 x 3200-kW (4,294-hp) turbo generators; two 800-kW (1074-hp) diesel generators; one 750-kW (1007-hp) auxiliary motor powering screw rudders bow and stern **Speed:** c.14 kts (26 km/h; 16 mph) surface; 24 kts (44 km/h; 27 mph) dived **Patrol endurance:** 90 days	**Diving depth:** 300 m (985 ft) operational and 400 m (1312 ft) max **Weapons tubes:** 16 missile and 4 x 533-mm (21-in) torpedo in bow **Weapons load:** 16 x Makeyev RSM-54 Shtil (SS-N-23 'Skiff') nuclear ballistic missiles; 18 tube-launched weapons including RPK-7 Vodopei (SS-N-16 'Stallion') ASW missiles, and Type 65K, SET-65, SAET-60M 533-mm torpedoes **Electronics:** one Snoop Tray I-band Surface Search radar; Skat-BDRM ('Shark Gill') LF active/passive sonar; 'Shark Hide' passive LF flank sonar; Pelamida passive VLF thin-line towed array sonar; 'Mouse Roar' active HF attack sonar; ESM/ECM; D/F radar warning; 'Brick Spit' optronic mast; Satellite/Inertial/Radiometric navigation; satcom plus two floating aerials for VLF/ELF radio **Complement:** 135

'Typhoon' class SSBN

The 'Typhoon' does not need to submerge or even go to sea in order to launch its payload of up to 200 nuclear warheads: during the Cold War, targets in the continental US could be attacked while the vessel was moored at its Northern Fleet home base.

The **'Typhoon'-class** (**Project 941 Akula**) boats are the largest undersea vessels ever built, and are based on a catamaran-type design that comprises two separate pressure hulls joined by a single outer covering to give increased protection against ASW weapons.

The class was built specifically for operations with the Soviet Northern Fleet in the Arctic ice pack. The reinforced sail, advanced stern fin with horizontal hydroplane fitted aft of the screws and retractable bow hydroplanes allow the submarine to break easily through spots of thin ice within the Arctic ice shelf.

'Sturgeon' SLBM

The first unit was laid down in 1977 at Severodvinsk and commissioned in 1980, achieving operational status in 1981. To arm the 'Typhoon', design of a fifth-generation SLBM, the R-39 Taifun (SS-N-20 'Sturgeon'), began in 1973. Six vessels were constructed between 1981-89, entering service to form part of the 1st Flotilla of Atomic Submarines, within the Western Theatre of the Northern Fleet, and based at Nyerpicha. Construction of a

seventh vessel was not completed.

The R-39 allowed the submarine to fire the weapon from within the Arctic Circle and still hit a target anywhere within the continental US. The 'Typhoons', were originally to be retrofitted with the improved R-39M (SS-N-28) missile.

Two vessels were decommissioned in 1997, and in 2002 only two remained in service, although it has been reported that three of the class will remain active in order to test the R-39M or the new Bulava SLBM, contravening the Co-operative Threat Reduction Program. However, the status of the R-39M, intended to arm the fourth-generation Borei-class SSBN, is uncertain.

Soviet doctrine envisaged the 'Typhoon' as a 'doomsday weapon', capable of emerging from the polar ice and launching a devastating second strike after an initial nuclear exchange. The high maintenance and manpower costs of these vessels is likely to result in their retirement in the medium term, although Russia is keen to maintain them as short term force multipliers.

SPECIFICATION

'Typhoon' class
Displacement: 23,200-24,500 tons surfaced; 33,800-48,000 tons dived
Dimensions: length 170-172 m (558-564 ft); beam 23-23.3 m (75-76 ft); draught 11-11.5 m (36-38 ft)
Propulsion: two OK-650 190-MW (254,750 shp) pressurised water-cooled reactors and two 37.3 MW (50,000 shp) steam turbines driving two shafts
Speed: 12-16 kts surfaced and 25-27 kts dived
Diving depth: 500 m (1,640 ft)
Armament: D-19 launch tubes for

20 R-39 (SS-N-20 'Sturgeon') SLBMs, two 650-mm and four 533-mm torpedo tubes for RPK-7 Vodopei (SS-N-16 'Stallion') and RPK-2 Viyoga (SS-N-15 'Starfish') or VA-111 Shkval respectively
Electronics: one surface-search radar, one ESM system, one low-frequency bow sonar, one medium-frequency torpedo fire-control sonar, VHF/SHF/UHF communications systems. One VLF towed communications buoy, and one ELF floating antenna
Complement: 150-175 (50-55 officers)

SPECIFICATION

R-39 (SS-N-20 'Sturgeon')
Type: SLBM
Dimensions: total length 16 m (52 ft 6 in); length without warhead 8.4 m (27 ft 7 in); diameter 2.4 m (7 ft 11 in)
Payload: 2550 kg (5,622 lb)

Performance: range 8300 km (5,158 miles); CEP 500 m (1,640 ft)
Warhead: up to 10 MIRVs of 200 kT each
Propulsion: three-stage solid-propellant rocket
Guidance: stellar-inertial

'Vanguard' class SSBN

Unlike its Polaris missile-armed predecessor, the 'Resolution' class, the British **'Vanguard'-class** nuclear powered ballistic missile submarine (SSBN) is a completely new design. It has, however, utilised several of the successful design features from previous SSBNs.

The 'Vanguard' class is the largest submarine type ever constructed in the UK, and the third largest type of vessel in Royal Navy service. However, it is cloaked in tight secrecy. Despite the ending of the Cold War and the downgrading of its strategic mission, details on 'Vanguard' weapon systems and patrols are still highly classified.

All four of the boats, **HMS Vanguard**, **HMS Victorious**, **HMS Vigilant** and **HMS Vengeance**, were built by Vickers Submarine Engineering Limited (now BAE Systems Marine) at its dockyard in Barrow-in-Furness, Cumbria. Such was their size that a special production facility, the Devonshire Dock Hall, had to be constructed. The boat's large hull was prompted by the Trident D5 Submarine-Launched Ballistic Missile (SLBM), of which it can deploy 16. However, the vessels patrol with a smaller complement of crew than that of the previous 'Resolution' class (132 as opposed to 149).

Transition

The first major transition from Polaris to Trident occurred in 1996, when HMS Victorious was deployed on patrol with a complement of Trident SLBMs. Trident has since become the sole component of the UK's nuclear deterrent, following the decommissioning of the WE177 tactical nuclear gravity/depth bomb in 1998, as part of the UK Strategic Defence Review. Furthermore, the 'Vanguard'-class boats had their 'readiness to fire' changed

from a matter of minutes to 'a matter of days' according to the UK Secretary of State for Defence.

The 'Vanguard'-class missile suite contains 16 tubes and is based on the 24-tube design which the US Navy deploys on its 'Ohio'-class Trident boats. The Trident missile system was built by Lockheed Martin, and is technically leased from the US. The Trident D5 is a MIRV (Multiple Independently-targeted Re-entry Vehicle) system, capable of deploying 12 warheads per missile.

Missile maintenance occurs in the US. However, the UK Atomic Weapons Establishment at Aldermaston undertakes all the design, construction, installation and maintenance of the warheads.

Deployment

Each 'Vanguard'-class submarine can carry a maximum of 192 nuclear warheads, although the Royal Navy originally insisted that each boat would carry no more than 96, deployed across eight missiles. Since the Strategic Defence Review, this has been further reduced to 48 warheads per boat, spread across four missiles. Although the Ministry of Defence refuses to comment on how many missiles are deployed when a boat is on patrol, it has indicated that the complement of Trident missiles now only carries one warhead per missile, which is probably in the sub-strategic kiloton range. A single 'Vanguard'-class boat is on deterrence patrol at any one time, and a reserve boat is also available.

New systems

As well as having a new strategic weapons system, the Vanguard also features several other new systems. These include a Rolls-Royce nuclear Pressurised Water Reactor propulsion system, and new tactical weapons fit including Tigerfish and

The 'Vanguard' class is fitted with state-of-the art periscopes for both search and attack. TV cameras and infra-red technology aid reconnaissance.

Spearfish torpedoes for short and medium defence. Tigerfish has a range of 13-29 km (8-18 miles) depending on the homing configuration, while Spearfish can hit targets up to 65 km (40 miles) away. The submarine also features a greatly improved Electronic Counter Measures (ECM) suite, and state-of-the-art attack and search periscopes. These are fitted with a TV camera and thermal imager as well as the traditional optical channel.

Right: This 'Vanguard'-class submarine is pictured being escorted out of port by a tug and a French naval Alouette III. The submarine will not return for several months.

SPECIFICATION

'Vanguard' class
Displacement: 15,900 tonnes dived
Dimensions: length 149.9 m (492 ft); beam 12.8 m (42 ft); draught 12 m (32 ft).
Machinery: (nuclear) one Rolls-Royce Pressurised Water Reactor; (conventional) two GEC turbines developing 20.5 MW (27,500 shp)
Speed: 25 kts dived
Torpedo tubes: four 21-in (533-mm) tubes
Missiles: 16 Lockheed Trident 2

(D5) 3-stage 12000-km (6,500 nm) range solid-fuel nuclear-armed missiles. Each D5 can carry 12 MIRV of 100-120-kT, sub-strategic warheads introduced in 1996
Electronics: Type 1007 I-band nav radar, Type 2054 composite multi-frequency sonar suite including Type 2046 towed array, Type 2043 hull-mounted active/passive search and Type 2082 passive intercept and ranging
Complement: 132 (14 officers)

At least one 'Vanguard'-class boat is permanently at sea, providing the UK's nuclear deterrent. The submarines now perform a sub-strategic role.

'Lafayette' class SSBN

The 'Lafayette' class followed a successful series of US strategic submarines, which had begun with the 'George Washington' class, America's first strategic nuclear submarine. The 'Ethan Allen' class submarines followed the 'George Washington' class, the vessels being constructed between 1961 and 1963. However, unlike the 'George Washington' submarines, the 'Ethan Allen' class had the advantage of being designed as SSBNs from the start.

Nevertheless, both classes faced a distinct tactical disadvantage in having to operate close to Soviet shores. This so-called 'Moscow criteria' meant that the US Navy's ballistic missile submarines had to operate close to the USSR in order to destroy targets in Moscow due to the range of their Polaris missiles. For example, Polaris A3, the model with the longest range, could still only hit targets at a maximum range of 4600 km (2,858 miles).

Underrated and underplayed, the 'Lafayette' was, for many years, backbone of the USN strategic missile submarine fleet and was a highly successful design.

An officer on the sail scans the horizon for hostile vessels and anti-submarine aircraft while his 'Lafayette'-class vessel carries out deterrence patrol.

Construction

Construction of the **USS Lafayette** began in 1963, before the first 'Ethan Allen'-class vessel had been completed. Between 1963 and 1967, a total of 31 'Lafayette'-class boats were constructed. All of the vessels were fitted with Polaris missiles, originally the Polaris A2 with a range of 2800 km (1,740 miles). However, in 1968, the **USS James Monroe** became the first submarine to receive the longer-range Polaris A3. Another four boats were planned although they were never constructed. Between 1970 and 1978, all of the vessels were converted to deploy the Poseidon SLBM system. Later on, between 1978 and 1983, 12 of these boats were converted to deploy the Trident C4 system. The first of these Trident vessels, the **USS Francis Scott Key**, began its maiden patrol on 20 October 1979.

Although the Lafayette-class began its life deploying the Polaris missile, it was converted to take the Poseidon, for which the class had originally been designed. The Lafayette-class earned its place in Cold War history as the first SLBM to be fitted with Multiple Independently-targeted Re-entry Vehicles (MIRVs). Each MIRV contained a single 50-kT warhead. However, Poseidon proved to be a troubled system, being unreliable and prone to mechanical failure. Nevertheless, it set the standard and the ensuing Trident series still equips the US Navy SSBN fleet today.

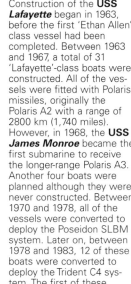

Left: This submarine is pictured preparing to dive. One of the strengths of nuclear-powered boats is the length of time for which they can remain submerged on patrol.

The 'Lafayette'-class submarines represented a formidable nuclear deterrent. This submarine displays 12 of its missile tubes. The 'Lafayette' class were the largest Western submarines completed during the 1960s.

Technically speaking, the 'Lafayette' class was divided into three separate classes, each group having only minor differences. The original 'Lafayette' class consisted of nine vessels; the modified **'James Madison' class** comprised 10 boats; and the **'Benjamin Franklin' class** was the largest, with 12 submarines. One vessel in the 'James Madison' class, the **USS Daniel Boone**, was the first ever fleet SSBN to visit Hawaii.

Modernisation

The 'Lafayette' class and its Poseidon missile system would eventually succumb to modernisation as the US Navy's 'Ohio' class came on stream deploying the Trident missile. The 'Lafayette' class would be an important platform for the Trident, with the USS *Daniel Boone* being the first boat to be converted to carry the Trident.

SPECIFICATION

'Lafayette' class
Displacement: 7250 tons standard surfaced; 8250 tons dived
Dimensions: length 129.5 m (424 ft 11 in); beam 10.1 m (33 ft); draught 9.6 m (31 ft 6 in)
Machinery: one pressurised-water cooled Westinghouse S5W reactor; two geared turbines developing 11186 kW (15,000 shp)
Speed: 20 kts surfaced; approximately 30 kts dived
Torpedo tubes: four 21-in (533-mm) Mk 65 (bow)
Missiles: first eight vessels fitted with Polaris A2 missiles, next 23 with Polaris A3 missiles, five vessels rearmed with Polaris A3 during 1968-70, vessels of class subsequently converted to carry Poseidon C3 in 16 tubes, from 1978-82 12 vessels fitted with Trident I/C4 missiles
Electronics: Mk 113 Mod 9 torpedo fire control system, WSC-3 satellite communication transceiver, Mk 2 Mod 4 Ship's Inertial Navigation System (SINS)
Complement: 140

'George Washington' class First-generation SSBN

On 28 June 1960 the **USS George Washington**, first of the eventually five-strong **'George Washington' class**, made the world's first successful test launch of a ballistic missile from a submerged submarine. The vessel launched two Polaris missiles, the second two hours after the first, while cruising off Cape Canaveral, Florida. Once the practicality of submerged launches had been demonstrated, the SSBN (nuclear-powered ballistic missile submarine) has been a key element in the concept and practice of nuclear deterrence. It is the proud boast of the SSBN fleets of the US Navy and Royal Navy that there were no fully confirmed detections of their boats by any potential enemy in some 40 years of operational patrols. The enormous difficulty in detecting and fixing the position of

an SSBN means that the US, British, French and Soviet (now Russian) nuclear forces are constantly ready to retaliate against a nuclear strike on their homelands.

'Skipjack'-class SSN

The *George Washington* was actually laid down by Electric Boat of Groton, Connecticut, as the *Scorpion*, a 'Skipjack'-class SSN, but the boat was then cut in half during construction to allow the insertion of an additional 39.64-m (130-ft) section to carry the vertical tubes required for the stowage and launch of 16 Polaris A1 ballistic missiles. These each carried a 600-kT warhead and had a range of 2200 km (1,367 miles). From the 'Skipjack' class the boats inherited the S5W reactor and six bow torpedo tubes, albeit with a reduced number of reloads.

The **USS** *Robert E. Lee is seen in November 1960. The volume of the missile compartment added to the 'Skipjack' design is readily apparent.*

Launched in June 1959, the *George Washington* sailed on its first operational patrol on 15 November 1960 as a member of Submarine Squadron 14. In 1966 the **Patrick Henry** (built by Electric Boat and launched in April 1960) was modified during a refit to carry the Polaris A3, an improved version of the Polaris A1 to deliver the 200-kT W58 warhead over the significantly greater range of 4360 km (2,709 miles) and in the process vastly enlarge the ocean areas in which the submarines could patrol but still be within range of their designated targets, and this missile soon became the core of the missile armament

carried by all of the 'George Washington'-class SSBNs.

In 1977 the **USS Abraham Lincoln** (built by Portsmouth Navy Yard and launched in March 1961) became the first SSBN to complete 50 patrols. But by this time newer SSBNs were entering service and the strategic arms limitation talks led to three of the class being converted to attack submarines. The *George Washington*, *Patrick Henry* and **USS Robert E. Lee** (built by Newport News of Norfolk, Virginia) had their Polaris missiles and associated systems (including the control room) removed in 1982, and at that stage were reclassified as SSNs even though they lacked sufficient torpedo stowage and the large bow sonars that would have made them effective in the attack submarine role. It is worth noting, though, that the 'George Washington'-class boats were quieter than the 'Skipjack' boats, though because of their

greater size somewhat slower. As it was, the Polaris missile tubes were filled with cement ballast as it had been decided that the boats were too old to warrant modification to carry the newer Poseidon C3 missile.

Final chapter

The *George Washington* was decommissioned in 1985 and scrapped in 1998. The *Robert E. Lee* was scrapped in 1991 and the *Abraham Lincoln* in 1994, while the **USS Theodore Roosevelt** (built by Mare Island Navy Yard and launched in February 1961) was decommissioned in 1981 and scrapped 1995. The *Patrick Henry* was decommissioned in 1984 and scrapped in 1997. Some consideration had been given to the revision of the boats to carry other weapons (each Polaris missile tube could carry eight cruise missiles, for instance), but nothing came of the various plans.

SPECIFICATION

'George Washington' class
Displacement: 5,959 tons surfaced; 6,709 tons dived
Dimensions: length 116 m (381 ft 8½ in); beam 10.5 m (33 ft); draught 8.1 m (26 ft 8 in)
Propulsion: one S5W pressurised water-cooled reactor powering two geared steam turbines delivering 11185 kW (15,000 shp) to one shaft

Speed: 18 kts surfaced and 25 kts dived
Diving depth: 180 m (700 ft)
Armament: 16 Polaris A1 (later Polaris A3) submarine-launched ballistic missiles (SLBMs), and six 21-in (533-mm) torpedo tubes
Electronics: BQS-4 sonar later replaced by BQR-19 sonar
Complement: 112

The USS **Theodore Roosevelt** *was the third of the 'George Washington'-class boats to be ordered but the fourth to be launched. This and the last two boats were based at Guam in the Marianas Islands.*

'Benjamin Franklin' class SSBN

The last 12 units built to the 'Lafayette' SSBN design were officially designated as the 'Benjamin Franklin' class because they were completed with quieter propulsion machinery. Six boats were converted to carry the Trident I C4 instead of the Polaris A3 SLBM.

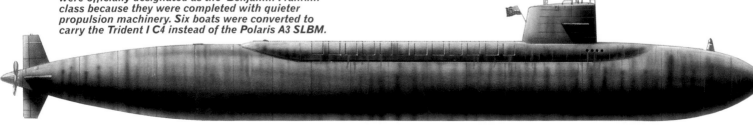

Although actually two classes, the 12 **'Benjamin Franklin'-class** and 19 'Lafayette'-class submarines were very similar in overall appearance and in many physical and operational aspects. The main difference between the two classes was that the boats of the

'Benjamin Franklin' class were built with quieter machinery outfits than those of the 'Lafayette' class. An additional four boats were proposed for the FY65 shipbuilding programme so that there would be 35 submarines in these two related classes to complete the

planned total of 45 SSBNs (including both earlier classes, the 'Ethan Allen' and 'George Washington' classes, each of five boats) required for an SSBN force of five squadrons each of nine boats. The additional boats were cancelled by Secretary of Defense Robert McNamara.

The 'Lafayette'- and 'Benjamin Franklin'-class boats had a small diesel-electric arrangement for stand-by propulsion in the event of problems with the nuclear propulsion system, snort masts, and had an auxiliary propeller. The individual submarines that comprised the

'Benjamin Franklin' class were the **USS Benjamin Franklin**, USS **Simon Bolivar**, USS **Kamehameha**, USS **George Bancroft**, USS **Lewis and Clark**, USS **James K. Polk**, USS **George C. Marshall**, USS **Henry L. Stimson**, USS **George Washington Carver**, USS

Francis Scott Key, **USS *Mariano G. Vallejo*** and **USS *Will Rogers***.

The boats were built by the Electric Boat Division of the General Dynamics Corporation (six boats), Newport News Shipbuilding (four boats), and Mare Island Navy Yard (two boats), and were laid down between April 1963 and March 1965 for launch between August 1964 and July 1966, and commissioning between October 1965 and April 1967. The boats served with the Atlantic Fleet (from New London, Connecticut; Charleston, South Carolina; King's Bay,

Georgia; and Holy Loch, Scotland) until decommissioned (or in two cases converted to SSN/special operations standard with provision for carrying, launching and recovering SEAL commando teams) between July 1992 and January 1999.

Armament

Completed with provision for the Polaris A3 SLBM, the boats were later converted to carry the altogether more capable Poseidon C3 missile with up to 14 re-entry vehicles (RVs) carrying W68 warheads and then the Trident C4 missile.

The 'Benjamin Franklin'-class boat USS Mariano G. Vallejo, *equipped with the longer-range Trident I C4 SLBMs each with eight re-entry vehicles.*

The 'Benjamin Franklin'-class SSBN USS Simon Bolivar *underway off Hampton Roads, Virginia, at the beginning of the boat's sea trials in October 1965.*

SPECIFICATION	
'Benjamin Franklin' class **Displacement:** 7,250 tons surfaced; 8,250 tons dived **Dimensions:** length 129.6 m (425 ft); beam 10.06 m (33 ft); draught 9.6 m (31 ft 6 in) **Propulsion:** one S5W pressurised water-cooled reactor powering two steam turbines delivering 11185 kW (15,000 shp) to one shaft **Speed:** 28 kts surfaced and 25 kts dived **Diving depth:** 350 m (1,150 ft) operational and 465 m (1,525 ft) maximum	**Armament:** 16 launch tubes for 16 Poseidon C3 or Trident I C4 SLBMs, and four 21-in (533-mm) tubes (all bow) for 12 Mk 48 ASW/anti-ship torpedoes **Electronics:** one BPS-11A or BPS-15 surface search radar, one ESM system, one BQR-7 sonar, one BQR-15 towed-array sonar, one BQR-19 sonar, one BQR-21 sonar, one BQS-4 sonar, and extensive communications and navigation systems **Complement:** 143

'Ohio' class SSBN

The mainstay of the American SSBN fleet, the 'Ohio' class carry the Trident II D5 SLBM that allows these submarines to operate in patrol zones close to the American coasts, where they can be protected more easily by other submarines, surface vessels and maritime patrol aircraft.

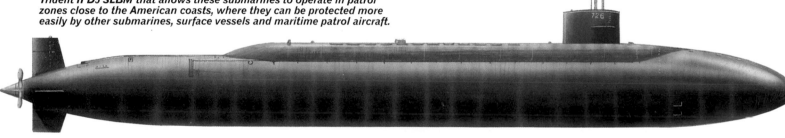

Designed in the early 1970s as successor to the 'Benjamin Franklin' and 'Lafayette' classes in the SSBN role, the lead boat of the **'Ohio' class**, the **USS *Ohio***, was contracted to the Electric Boat Division of the General Dynamics Corporation in July 1974. As the result of an unfortunate series of problems both in Washington, DC, and at the shipyard, the lead vessel did not run its first sea trials until June 1981, and was not

finally commissioned until November of that year, three years late. Production then improved, and the **USS *Louisiana***, the last of these 18 'boomers', was commissioned in September 1997. The Atlantic and Pacific Fleets have 10 and eight boats with the Trident II D5 and Trident I C4 missiles respectively; the latter are being replaced from 1996 with the D5 weapon. The Trident I carries up to eight re-entry vehicles each with

one 100-kT W76 warhead delivered over a range of up to some 7780 km (4,835 miles), while the larger Trident II carries up to a maximum of 14 but more typically eight RVs each with one 475-kT W88 warhead delivered to a classified range some hundreds of miles longer than that of the Trident I.

Each submarine carries 24 rather than the earlier standard of 16 SLBMs, is expected to have a 12-

month reactor refuelling refit every nine years, and works a patrol period of 70 days followed by 25 days spent alongside a tender or jetty readying for the next patrol. Because of their longer-range Trident missiles, the 'Ohio'-class boats have patrol areas in waters either close to the US or in the remoter parts of the world's oceans, making virtually impossible effective ASW

measures, the more so as the boats are acoustically very quiet.

Other than the *Ohio* and *Louisiana*, the 'Ohio' class boats are the **Michigan**, **Florida**, **Georgia**, **Henry M. Jackson**, **Alabama**, **Alaska**, **Nevada**, **Tennessee**, **Pennsylvania**, **West Virginia**, **Kentucky**, **Maryland**, **Nebraska**, **Rhode Island**, **Maine** and **Wyoming**.

Based on the streamlining of a fish, the clean shape and smooth contours of the 'Ohio'-class SSBN produce a boat that is fast. The shape is also designed for highly efficient and quiet cruising while underwater.

SPECIFICATION	
'Ohio' class **Displacement:** 16,764 tons surfaced; 18,750 tons dived **Dimensions:** length 170.69 m (560 ft); beam 12.8 m (42 ft); draught 11.1 m (36 ft 6 in) **Propulsion:** one S8G pressurised water-cooled natural-circulation reactor powering two geared steam turbines delivering 44735 kW (60,000 shp) to one shaft **Speed:** 20 kts surfaced and 25+ kts dived **Diving depth:** 300 m (985 ft) operational and 500 m (1,640 ft)	maximum **Armament:** 24 launch tubes for 24 Trident I C4 or Trident II D5 SLBMs, and four 21-in (533-mm) tubes (all bow) for Mk 48 anti-ship/submarines torpedoes **Electronics:** one BPS-15 surface search radar, one WLR-8(V) ESM system, one BQQ-6 bow sonar, one BQS-13 active sonar, one BQR-19 navigation sonar, one TB-16 towed-array sonar, and extensive communications and navigation systems **Complement:** 155

'Han' class
Nuclear anti-ship submarine

China began building its submarine force in the 1950s, basing its boats primarily on Soviet designs. However, with the split between Mao Tse Tung and Khrushchev, developments in the 1960s had to be carried out without outside assistance. China lacked the scientific, engineering or technological resources to match the USSR or Western navies, and development of an indigenous nuclear submarine was protracted.

The first of the **'Type 91'** class attack boats, also known as the **'Han' class**, was laid down in 1967. It was commissioned in 1974, but because of continuing problems with the nuclear reactor **Submarine 401** was probably not truly opera-

Right: Submarine 404 is a stretched and improved version of the 'Han' class. It serves as part of the North Sea Fleet at Jianggezhuang.

tional for a decade. Four more boats were commissioned through the 1980s. The last three are several metres longer, and have vertical launch tubes fitted to allow anti-ship missiles to be carried without cutting into the torpedo load.

These boats are rather noisy, even by the standards of the time they were built. Their equipment, based on Soviet designs of the 1950s, was primitive. However, the original Soviet ESM system, as well as the ineffective passive sonar, have been

Right: The 'Han' class is a key part of China's expansion plans, which aim to project power out into the Pacific beyond Japan and Taiwan.

replaced by French equipment, and the last three boats have been given an even more extensive refit.

Anti-ship
The primary function of the Han class appears to be anti-surface-ship: the boats carry a mix of straight-running and homing torpedoes, as well as the C-801 Ying-Ji (Eagle Strike) anti-ship missile. They are too noisy to be effective anti-submarine vessels, but they have the capability to strike at shipping lanes far beyond China's coastal waters.

The next-generation 'Type 93' SSN is intended to replace the 'Hans'. Being built with Russian help, the

design is reportedly based on the Soviet Victor III, which would make it the equivalent of one of the US Navy's 'Sturgeon'-class boats of the 1970s and 1980s. But although the first of the class has been under construction at the Huludao

ship yard since 1994, the programme has been considerably delayed.

As an interim measure, it is believed that the PLA Navy has been looking into the possibility of leasing or buying an 'Akula' class boat from Russia.

SPECIFICATION	
'Han' class	29 mph) dived
Type: Nuclear-powered attack submarine	**Diving depth (estimated):** 200 m (656 ft) normal and 300 m (985 ft) maximum
Displacement: 4,500 tons surfaced and 5,550 tons dived	**Torpedo tubes:** six 533-mm (21-in)
Dimensions: length 98 m (321 ft 6 in); beam 10 m (32 ft 10 in); draught 7.4 m (24 ft 2½ in)	**Basic load:** 18 weapons, usually a mix of homing and straight-running torpedoes, or up to 36 mines
Machinery: one 90-MW pressurized water reactor driving one shaft	**Electronics:** Snoop Tray surface search radar; Trout Cheek medium frequency sonar; DUUX-5 low frequency sonar; Type 921A ESM
Speed: 12 kts (22 km/h; 14 mph) surfaced and 25 kts (46 km/h;	**Complement:** 75

'Rubis' class

In 1964 the French Navy began the design of a 4,000-ton nuclear-powered attack submarine. This was cancelled in 1968, before construction started. A smaller design was then initiated, based on the hull form of the diesel-electric 'Agosta' class and with basically the same fire-control, torpedo-launching and sonar detection systems.

The resulting **'SNA72'** class built at Cherbourg is the smallest SSN type in operational service with any navy, and was made possible by the French development of a small 48-megawatt integrated reactor-heat exchanger system driving two turbo-alternators and a main electric motor. The hull depth was increased compared with the 'Agosta'

class, and has allowed the typical three-deck layout of larger SSNs to be used for the areas forward and immediately aft of the fin. The forward diving planes of the Agostas have been relocated to the fin to improve underwater manoeuvrability.

Service entry
The first boat, the **Rubis**, was laid down at Cherbourg in 1976, and was commissioned in February 1983. It was followed by three further boats, the **Saphir**, the **Casabianca**, and the **Émeraude**, which were commissioned between 1984 and 1987.

The French Navy had originally planned for two squadrons of these SSNs, one to be based at Brest to cover the SSBN base, and

Above: Currently the world's smallest front-line SSN, the 'Rubis'-class boats are essentially a heavily-modified version of the conventionally-powered 'Agosta'-class boats.

Left: France's refusal to accept American aid meant that her first nuclear attack boats entered service 20 years after their British equivalents.

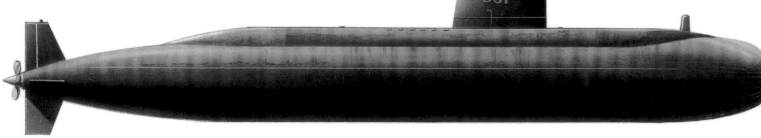

the other at Toulon. In the event, all of the boats are based at Toulon, together with the two boats of the follow-on 'Améthyste' class. All, however, operate frequently in the Atlantic.

Originally, the 'Rubis' class were tasked primarily with anti-surface warfare. Endurance, limited primarily by the amount of food which can be carried, is estimated at 45 days.

All of the boats carry versions of the F 17 and L5 torpedoes and, from the middle of the 1980s, have been equipped with the underwater-launched, encapsulated SM.39 Exocet anti-ship missile.

However, in the early 1990s, they were joined by two improved boats, the

Améthyste and the *Perle*. Built to the same basic design, but stretched by about two metres, the new boats were designed primarily as anti-submarine platforms. They have a more advanced sonar and electronic fit, and are quieter than the original boats.

Between 1989 and 1995 the early boats underwent

the Améthyste modernisation programme. Standing for AMElioration Tactique HYdrodynamique Silence Transmission Ecoute it brings them up to the standard of their successors.

A new, larger class of SSN is currently in development, and is expected to enter service some time after 2010.

Left: Although initially a little slower and noisier than contemporary British and American boats, the 'Rubis' class has evolved into a highly effective ASW platform.

SPECIFICATION

'Rubis' class
Type: Nuclear-powered attack submarine
Displacement: 2,385 tons surfaced and 2,670 tons dived
Dimensions: length 72.1 m (236 ft 6½ in); beam 7.6 m (24 ft 11 in); draught 6.4 m (21 ft)
Machinery: one 48-MW pressurized water reactor (PWR) powering two turbo-alternators driving one shaft
Speed: 18 kts (33 km/h; 21 mph) surfaced and 25 kts (46 km/h; 29 mph) dived
Diving depth: 300 m (985 ft) normal and 500 m (1, 640 ft) max maximum

Torpedo tubes: four 550-mm (21¾-in), all bow
Basic load: 10 F 17 wire-guided anti-ship and/or L5 mod.3 ASW torpedoes; four SM.39 Exocet missiles; or up to 28 TSM35 10 ground mines
Electronics: one Kelvin-Hughes surface search radar; one DMUX 20 multi-function sonar and one DSUV 62C passive towed array sonar; ARUR 13/DR 3000U ESM system
Complement: 66
Boats in class: *Rubis* (S601), *Saphir* (S602), *Casabianca* (S603), *Émeraude* (S604), *Améthyste* (S605) and *Perle* (S606)

'November' class Nuclear-powered anti-shipping submarine

The 14-vessel **Project 627** class of submarine was called the **'November'** class by NATO. They were the first operational Soviet nuclear-powered boats, built from 1958 at Severodvinsk. Contemporary with the American 'Nautilus', 'Seawolf' and 'Skate', they were built primarily for performance rather than stealth.

Armed with nuclear torpedoes, the original task of these boats was to get close enough to American ports to fire their torpedoes into the harbours. However, the role

rapidly changed, the primary function of the 'Novembers' for most of their lives being to attack carrier battle groups in the hope of getting a clear shot at the carrier itself.

Noise makers

By modern standards, the 'Novembers' were very noisy, thanks to their hull form, elderly reactor design and the many free flood holes in the casing. Retractable hydroplanes were carried just aft of the bow sonar systems, and two 406-mm (16-in) anti-escort

torpedo tubes were fitted aft.

The first of the class was the *Leninskiy Komsomol*, also known as **K3**. Becoming operational in July 1958, it was the first Soviet submarine to reach the North Pole, in July 1962. However, it also suffered two major reactor accidents in the 1960s, accidents which would become typical of the class.

The 'Novembers', along with the related 'Echo' and 'Hotel' class missile boats, were a definite radiation hazard to their crews, because of design defects and poor

shielding. It is known that several specialist hospitals were set up in the Soviet Union to treat the radiation casualties from these boats, and they acquired the nickname 'widow-makers' amongst Soviet submarine crews.

Four were lost to reactor accidents, and there were numerous incidents of machinery breakdown whilst

on operational patrol.

Most of the 'Novembers' served with the Northern Fleet, though four were transferred to the Far East in the 1960s. Surviving vessels were decommissioned between 1988 and 1992.

All survivors, except K3, which was preserved as a memorial, remain to this day as radioactive hulks in Russian ports.

SPECIFICATION

'November' class
Type: Nuclear-powered attack submarine
Displacement: 4,200 tons surfaced and 5,000 tons dived
Dimensions: length 109.7 m (359 ft 11 in); beam 9.1 m (29 ft 10 in); draught 6.7 m (22 ft)
Machinery: two liquid metal or pressurised water-cooled reactors powering two steam turbines driving two propellers
Speed: 15 kts (28 km/h; 17 mph) surface; 30 kts (55 km/h; 34 mph) dived
Diving depth: 214 m (790 ft) operational and 300 m (980 ft)
Torpedo tubes: eight 533-mm

(21-in) in bow and two 406-mm (16-in) at stern
Basic load: maximum of 20 533-mm (21-in) torpedoes; normally a mix of 14 533-mm (21-in) anti-ship or anti-submarine and six 533-mm (21-in) anti-ship 15-kiloton nuclear torpedoes, plus two 406-mm (16-in) anti-ship torpedoes
Electronics: one RLK-101 search radar; one MG-100 Arktika active sonar, one MG-10 Feniks passive sonar, one MG-13 sonar intercept receiver, one Luch mine-detector sonar; VHF/UHF communications and one underwater telephone
Complement: 24 officers, 86 men

Above: In April 1970, a 'November'-class boat got into difficulty south west of the British Isles. Crewmen are seen here escaping a fire in the reactor room. They were taken off by a Soviet support ship just before the submarine sank.

Below: As the first Soviet nuclear submarine, the 'November' class lacked the efficient 'teardrop' hull standard on later boats. However it was quite fast, and nuclear-tipped torpedoes gave it a considerable punch.

'Victor I', 'Victor II' and 'Victor III' class SSNs

Nuclear attack submarines

The **'Victor I' class** was designated by the Soviets as a PLA (podvodaya lodka atomnaya, or nuclear-powered submarine), and together with the contemporary 'Charlie I' SSGN and 'Yankee' SSBN classes formed the second generation of Soviet nuclear submarines. The **Project 671** boats, known to the Soviets as the **'Yersey' class**, were the first Soviet submarines built to the teardrop hull design for high underwater speeds. **K 38**, the first 'Victor', was completed in 1967 at the Admiralty Shipyard, Leningrad, where the last of 16 units was completed in 1974. The 'Victor Is' were the fastest pressurised-water reactor-powered SSNs afloat, even

structed at the Admiralty Shipyard in 1975.

Initially called the **'Uniform' class** by NATO, the 'Victor II' class is marked by a 6.1-m (20-ft) extension inserted into the hull forward of the sail. This was to make room for the new generation of 65-cm (25-in) heavy torpedoes together with the power equipment to handle them.

Silent Victors

In 1976 the first of the **'Victor III'** units was launched at the Admiralty Shipyard. In 1978 the Komsomolsk yard joined the production team, building two boats per year after the end of 'Delta I' class production. A total of 26 'Victor III' class boats were built

A Soviet 'Victor I' class SSN in the Malacca Straits during 1974. The personnel seen on the sail structure are sunbathing – a favourite pastime of Soviet sailors in warm climate regions.

A windfall for Western naval intelligence, this Soviet 'Victor III' class SSN got into difficulties off the North Carolina coast in November 1983. The vessel had to be towed to Cuba for repairs after becoming the most photographed submarine in the Soviet navy.

with the advent of the American 'Los Angeles' class. The enriched uranium-fuelled reactor was of the same type as installed in both the 'Charlie' and 'Yankee' class vessels.

In 1972, the first of the improved **'Victor II' class** was built at the Gorky shipyard, being produced in alternate years to the 'Charlie II' design there. Four were built there, whilst another three were con-

between 1978 and 1992. Given the Soviet designation of **Schuka**, the 'Victor IIIs' are unofficially known to the US Navy as the 'Walker' class, since many of the improvements in quieting the boats and in providing them with more effective sensors were the product of the activities of the Walker spy ring in the 1970s and 1980s.

The 'Victor III's have a 3-m (9-ft 10-in) hull extension forward of the fin and a pod mounted atop the upper rudder which deployed a brand new towed sonar array. The extension provided the extra volume for the additional electronic equipment required to process the data from the towed array and two new flank arrays.

'Clusterguard' anechoic coatings helped to decrease radiated noise levels as the

design was improved, the 'Victor III' class being described officially in US Navy circles as the equivalent to the USS 'Sturgeon' class SSN in quietness. They also have bow hydroplanes that retract into the hull at high underwater speeds or when a boat is on the surface. Like all boats after the 'Hotel' SSBN, 'Echo' SSGN and 'November' SSN classes, the 'Victor' class boats had two of their 533-mm (21-in) tubes fitted with 406-mm (16-in) ASW torpedo liners for self-defence use. Two of these weapons are carried in the place of every 533-mm (21-in) reload offloaded.

Surviving Victor I and II boats had been decommissioned by 1996, along with about a dozen of the first Victor IIIs.

'Victor I' class
Displacement: 4,100 tons surfaced and 6,085 tons dived
Dimensions: length 92.5 m (303 ft 5 in); beam 11.7 m (38 ft 5 in); draught 7.3 m (23 ft 11 in)
Machinery: two VM-4T PW reactors powering one OK-300 steam turbine delivering 22.7 MW 31,000 shp one five-blade propeller. Two two-blade 'creep' props also fitted
Speed: 12 kts surfaced and 32 kts dived
Diving depth: 320 m (1,050 ft) operational and 396 m (1,300 ft) maximum
Torpedo tubes: six 533-mm (21-in), two with 406-mm (16-in) liners, all bow
Basic load: maximum of 18

533-mm (21-in) torpedoes, but normally a mixture of eight 533-mm (21-in) anti-ship or anti-submarine, 10 406-mm (16-in) anti-submarine and two 533-mm (21-in) anti-ship 15-kiloton nuclear torpedoes, or a total of 36 AMD-1000 ground mines
Missiles: two Tsakra (SS-N-15 'Starfish') nuclear anti-submarine 15-kiloton missiles
Electronics: one MRK-50 Topol surface-search radar, one low-frequency MGK-300 Rubin active/passive bow sonar, one MG-24 Luch mine-detection sonar, one Zhaliv-P passive intercept and threat-warning ESM system, one MG-14 sonar intercept receiver, VHF/UHF communications, and one MG-29 Khost underwater telephone
Complement: 100

'Victor II' class
Displacement: 4,700 tons surfaced and 7,190 tons dived
Dimensions: length 101.8 m (334 ft); beam 10.8 m (35 ft 4 in); draught 7.3 m (23 ft 11 in)
Machinery: as for 'Victor I' class
Speed: 12 kts surfaced and 31.7 kts dived
Diving depth: as for 'Victor I' class
Torpedo tubes: as for 'Victor I' plus two 650-mm (25.6-in) bow

Basic load: as for 'Victor I' class plus six 650-mm weapons
Missiles: as for 'Victor I' class
Electronics: one low-frequency MGK-400 Rubikon active/passive bow sonar; rest as for 'Victor I' class plus one Paravan towed VLF communications buoy and one floating ELF communications antenna for Molniya-671 communication system
Complement: 110

'Victor III' class
Displacement: 5,000 tons surfaced and 7,000 tons dived
Dimensions: length 107.2 m (351 ft 6 in); beam 10.8 m (35 ft 4 in); draught 7.4 m (24 ft 2 in)
Machinery: as for 'Victor I' class
Speed: 18 kts surfaced and 30 kts dived
Diving depth: as for 'Victor I' class

Torpedo tubes: as for 'Victor II' class
Basic load: as for 'Victor II' class
Missiles: as for 'Viktor II' plus two Granat (SS-N-21 'Sampson') cruise missiles or two Vodopei (SS-N-16 'Stallion') rocket torpedoes
Electronics: as for 'Victor II' class plus one Pithon towed sonar
Complement: 115

A Soviet 'Victor III' class vessel. The pod on the top of the upper rudder is for a towed sonar array, which was the first such installation on a Soviet submarine. To match the sonar's long range, the class can carry both SS-N-15 and SS-N-16 ASW missiles.

'Akula' class Nuclear-powered attack submarine

The 'Akula' class of nuclear-powered attack submarines was designed to provide the Soviet navy with much enhanced attack submarine capability. Although officially designated Shuka-B (pike) by the Russians, it is commonly known in service as the Bars (snow leopard).

The steel-hulled submarines of the **Project 971 Shuka-B** or **'Akula' class** were easier and cheaper to build than the 'Sierras', and are essentially successors to the prolific 'Victor' class. Today, they make up about half of Russia's dwindling fleet of nuclear-powered attack submarines. The first seven boats (designated in the West as the **'Akula I' class**) were constructed between 1982-90, and are the **Puma**, **Del'fin**, **Kashalot**, **Bars**, **Kit**, **Pantera** and **Narval**. Five more (the **Volk**, **Morzh**, **Leopard**, **Tigr** and **Drakon** built between 1986-95) are classified as the **Project 971U** or **'Improved Akula'** **class**, while a 13th boat, the **Vepr** of the **Project 971M**

or **'Akula II' class**, was launched in 1995 but is still incomplete at the end of 2002. Three additional boats, the **Belgograd**, **Kuguar** and **Nerpa** launched between 1998-2000 as 'Akula II' boats, are also incomplete. At least two more were projected but were not built.

Evolutionary design

The design was approved in the early 1970s but modified in 1978-80 to carry the Granat (SS-N-21 'Sampson') land attack cruise missile. The 'Akula' marked a significant improvement in Soviet submarine design as it is far quieter than the 'Victor' and earlier SSNs. The use of commercially available Western technology to

reduce noise levels played an important role in this, eroding a long-held NATO advantage in the underwater Cold War. Sensors were also much improved, the use of digital technology enabling them to detect targets at three times the range possible in a 'Victor'.

The 'Akulas' sport a massive tear-drop shaped pod on the after fin: this houses the Skat-3 VLF passive towed array. There is an escape pod built into the fin. The 'Improved Akula' and 'Akula II' boats are fitted with six additional 533-mm (21-in) external torpedo tubes: as these cannot be reloaded from within the pressure hull, it is considered likely they are fitted with the

Tsakra (SS-N-15 'Starfish') anti-submarine missile. Additionally, the 'Akula II' boats are credited with an increased operational diving depth.

Four 'Akula I' boats were paid off in the late 1990s and are unlikely to return, and the surviving boats are divided between the Northern and Pacific Fleets.

SPECIFICATION

'Akula' class (Project 971)
Displacement: 7,500 tons surfaced and 9,100 tons submerged
Dimensions: length 111.7 m (366 ft 5½ in); beam 13.5 m (44 ft 3½ in); draught 9.6 m (31 ft 6 in)
Propulsion: one OK-650B pressurised water reactor powering a steam turbine delivering 32060 kW (43,000 shp) to one shaft
Speed: 20 kts surfaced and 35 kts submerged
Diving depth: 450 m (1,475 ft) maximum
Torpedo tubes: four 650-mm (25.6-in) and four 533-mm (21-in) tubes
Armament: 3M10 (SS-N-21 'Sampson') SLCMs, RPK-6/7 (SS-N-16 'Stallion') rocket-delivered nuclear depth charges/torpedoes,

VA-111 Shkval underwater rockets, 533-mm SET-72, TEST-71M and USET-80 torpedoes, 650-mm Type 65-76 torpedoes, or 42 mines
Electronics: (Russian designations) Chiblis surface search radar, Medvyedista-945 navigation system, Molniya-M satcom; Tsunami, Kiparis, Anis, Sintez and Kora communications, Paravan towed VLF receiver, Vspletsk combat direction system, MGK-503 Skat-3 active/passive sonar, Akula flank-array sonar, Pelamida towed-array sonar, MG-70 mine-detection sonar, Bukhta integrated ESM/ECM system, two MG-74 Korund decoys, MT 70 sonar intercept receiver, and Nikhrom-M IFF
Complement: 62 (25 officers and 26 enlisted)

Left: A notable feature of the 'Akula' class design is its highly streamlined shaping, a fact that reduces underwater noise and enhances speed.

Below: The large fairing atop the upper fin of the 'Akula' class carries the sensor array and cable for the Skat-3 'Shark Gill' active/passive towed sonar system.

'Los Angeles' class SSN

With a total of 51 boats still in service out of a total of 62 hulls completed, the 'Los Angeles' design is the most numerous nuclear-powered warship class, as well as being the second most expensive SSN type after the new 'Seawolf' class.

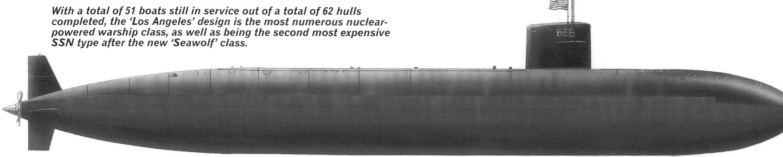

Comprising the largest number of nuclear-powered vessels built to one design, the **'Los Angeles' class** couples the speed advantage of the elderly 'Skipjack' class with the sonar and weapons capability of the 'Permit' and 'Sturgeon' classes. The significant increase in size is mainly the result of doubling the installed power available by the fitting of a new reactor design, the S6G pressurised-water reactor based on the D2G reactor fitted in the nuclear-powered cruisers of the 'Bainbridge' and 'Truxtun' classes. Reactor refuelling takes place every 10 years. The boats originally carried the BQQ-5 passive/active search and attack sonar system. From the **USS San Juan (SSN-751)** onward, the

BSY-1 system was fitted. The **USS Augusta** and the **USS Cheyenne** were both fitted with a BQG-5D wide-aperture flank array. All boats have the BQS-15 active close-range high-frequency sonar for ice detection. Other sensors include a MIDAS (Mine and Ice Detection Avoidance System) first fitted in the *San Juan*, and all the boats from this onward were fitted with sound-reducing tiles and hydroplanes relocated from the fin to the forward part of the hull.

Soviet 'Victor'?

Thanks to its electronic systems, the class has proved to be an exceptionally good ASW platform although, on one occasion on the first out-of-area 'Alpha I' deployment, the Soviet boat was easily able to outrun a trailing 'Los Angeles'-class boat off Iceland just by using its superior underwater speed. Against more conventional Soviet-designed nuclear-powered boats the success rate of detection and tracking is quite high. The advanced BQQ-5 system on one occasion acquired and held contact with two Soviet 'Victor'-class SSNs for an extended time.

The class features a very potent weapons array including the Tomahawk Tactical Land Attack Missile (TLAM) with a range between 900 and 1700 km (559 and 1,056 miles). Current versions of the missile are the TLAM-C version, which can carry a single 454-kg (1,000-lb) warhead, and the

TLAM-D which carries a sub-munition payload to 900 km. The standard unitary HE warhead can also be replaced by a 318-kg (692-lb) shaped-charge warhead. In order to overcome the problem of limited weapons stowage, all boats from the **USS Providence (SSN-719)** onward are fitted with a vertical launch system in which the launch tubes for the TLAMs are placed outside the pressure hull behind the sonar array. Although the Tomahawk is nuclear-capable, such weapons are not now deployed on a routine basis.

Furthermore, the boats can also carry the 21-in (533-m) Mk 48 active/passive homing torpedo with a wire-guidance option. This

guidance is suitable for ranges up to 50 km (31 miles) or 38 km (23 miles) in the active or passive modes respectively. The torpedo has a 267-kg (588-lb) warhead, and 26 Mk 48 weapons can be carried by a 'Los Angeles'-class boat though another load is 14 torpedoes and 12 tube-launched TLAMs. These are fired out of four tubes placed amidships in the vessel. The 'Los Angeles' class has already participated in operations in Iraq, Kosovo and Afghanistan. Furthermore, the boats have also continued their under-ice operations, and in mid-2001, the **USS Scranton (SSN-756)** surfaced through the Arctic ice cap. Eleven of the class have been retired.

Above: Full steam ahead on the USS **City of Corpus Christi** *as it heads towards the Colombian city of Cartagena. The boat's commander is seen on the right and is flanked by a navigator and an observer.*

SPECIFICATION	
'Los Angeles' class **Displacement:** 6,082 tons surfaced; 6,927 tons dived **Dimensions:** length 110.34 m (362 ft); beam 10.06 m (33 ft); draught 9.75 m (32 ft) **Propulsion:** one S6G pressurised water-cooled reactor powering two steam turbines delivering 26095 kW (35,000 shp) to one shaft **Speed:** 18 kts surfaced; 32 kts dived **Diving depth:** 450 m (1,475 ft) operational and 750 m (2,460 ft) maximum	**Torpedo tubes:** four 21-in (533-mm) tubes amidships for 26 weapons including Mk 48 torpedoes, Sub-Harpoon and Tomahawk missiles, plus (from SSN-719) 12 external tubes for Tomahawk SLCMs (TLAM-C and TLAM-D now carried) **Electronics:** one BPS-15 surface search radar, one BQQ-5 or BSY-1 passive/active search and attack low-frequency sonar, BDY-1/BQS-15 sonar array, TB-18 passive towed array and MIDAS **Complement:** 133

The USS **Birmingham (SSN-695)** *shows off an emergency surfacing drill during its sea trials. Note the large volumes of water pouring from the fin and the early fin-mounted diving planes. A normal surfacing is achieved gradually by selective blowing of ballast tanks. This boat was withdrawn in 1999.*

'Seawolf' class SSN

The boats of the **'Seawolf' class** are the most advanced but also the most expensive hunter-killer submarines in the world. The first completely new American submarine design for some 30 years, the **USS Seawolf** was laid down in 1989 as the lead boat in a class of 12. The cost of the 'Seawolf' class in 1991 was estimated at $33.6 billion (25 per cent of the naval construction budget), making it the most expensive naval building programme ever. At that time the US Navy planned an additional 17 boats. Then the 'peace dividend' resulting from the collapse of the USSR and the end of the Cold War caused US politicians to question the need for more ultra-quiet boats, and the class was capped at three units and the replacement for the 51 current 'Los Angeles'-class boats will be a much cheaper design.

The 'Seawolf' class was intended to restore the technological edge which the US Navy had enjoyed over the Soviets from 1945 until the mid-1980s, when espionage and the cynical trading practices of some US allies somewhat eroded it. The new boats were designed to operate at greater depths than existing US submarines and to operate under the polar ice cap. New welding materials have been used to join the hull subsections and the 'Seawolf' class are the first attack submarines to use HY-100 steel rather than the HY-80 used for previous boats. (HY-100 was used in experimental deep-diving submarines during the 1960s.) The most important advantage of the 'Seawolf'

class design is its exceptional quietness even at high tactical speeds. Whereas most submarines need to keep their speed down to as little as 5 kts to avoid detection by passive sonar arrays, the 'Seawolf' class are credited with being able to cruise at 20 kts and still be impossible to locate.

Sound of silence

The US Navy describes the 'Seawolf' as 10 times as quiet as an improved 'Los Angeles' and 70 times as quiet as the original 'Los Angeles' boat: a 'Seawolf' at 25 kts makes less noise than a 'Los Angeles' tied up alongside the pier! However, during their construction and subsequent trials, several problems were experienced on the *Seawolf* after acoustic panels kept falling off the boat.

With eight torpedo tubes in a double-decked torpedo room, the 'Seawolf' class are capable of dealing with multiple targets simultaneously. Now that the originally intended targets are rusting at anchor in Murmansk and Vladivostok, it is the 'Seawolf's ability to make a stealthy approach to enemy coasts that makes it so valuable. The third and last unit, the **USS Jimmy Carter**, which was commissioned in

The US Navy's 'Seawolf' class is the most expensive submarine design: the research costs for the pressurised water reactor alone are thought to have cost in excess of $1 billion. Retractable bow planes improve surfacing capabilities through thick polar ice.

The USS Seawolf, the first boat in the class, conducts 'Bravo' trials in September 1996. The 'Seawolf' class is arguably the quietest design of submarine constructed.

December 2001, incorporates a dry deck shelter, for which its hull was lengthened by 30.5 m (100 ft). The dry deck hangar is an air transportable device that can be fitted piggy-back style to carry swimmer delivery vehicles and combat swimmers. There is a combat swimmer silo too, an internal lock-out chamber that can fit up to eight swimmers and their equipment. The irony of such a submarine being named after the president who bungled the Iran hostage rescue mission is not lost on older US Navy personnel!

Armament

The class is completed by its second unit, the **USS Connecticut**, and all three of the boats can carry Tomahawk TLAM cruise missiles. The boats also have eight 26-in (660-mm) torpedo tubes. A total complement of 50 torpedoes and missiles can be carried by the boats of the 'Seawolf' class, but an alternative is up to 100 marine

mines in place of either the torpedoes or the cruise missiles. It is thought that in the future the vessels may also be fitted for the carriage, deployment and recovery of Uninhabited Underwater Vehicles (UUVs). The state of the art electronic system on the boats features a BSY-2 sonar suite with an active or passive sonar array and a wide-aperture passive flank array; TB-16 and TB-29 surveillance and tactical towed arrays are also fitted. The class features a BPS-16 navigation radar and a Raytheon Mk 2 weapons control system. A countermeasures suite includes the WLY-1 advanced torpedo decoy system.

The boats have great manoeuvrability, and additional space was built into the class for improvements in weapons development. Despite their potent weapons load, their ultra-quietness, and their robust electronics fit, the 'Seawolf' class are yet to be deployed in combat.

SPECIFICATION	
'Seawolf' class **Displacement:** 8,080 tons surfaced; 9,142 tons dived **Dimensions:** length 107.6 m (353 ft); beam 12.9 m (42 ft 4 in); draught 10.7 m (35 ft) **Propulsion:** one S6W pressurised water-cooled reactor powering steam turbines delivering 38770 kW (52,000 shp) to one pumpjet propulsor **Speed:** 18 kts surfaced; 35 kts dived	**Diving depth:** 487 m (1,600 ft) **Armament:** eight 26-in (660-mm) torpedo tubes with up to 50 Tomahawk cruise missiles; Mk 48 ADCAP torpedoes or 100 mines **Electronics:** one BPS-16 navigation radar, one BQQ-5D sonar suite with bow spherical active/passive array, TB-16 and TB-29 surveillance and tactical towed sonar arrays, and BQS-24 active close-range detection sonar **Complement:** 134

'Upholder' and 'Victoria' classes Patrol submarines

To meet the requirement for a diesel-electric submarine type to succeed the 'Oberons' in Royal Navy service, Vickers Shipbuilding and Engineering Ltd developed the **Type 2400** or **'Upholder' class**. As in most new submarine classes, the emphasis was placed on standardisation and automation to reduce manning requirements. The first of the class was ordered in 1983 and completed in June 1990, and there followed another three boats ordered in 1986 and completed in 1991-93. It had at first been planned to order 12 such boats, but this scheme was trimmed first to 10 and then nine before being curtailed at just four as part of the 'peace dividend' at the end of the Cold War in the early 1990s.

Also included in the design were advanced noise-attenuation features to reduce the radiated noise levels below those of the already very quiet 'Oberon' class. There was also a reduction in the short time required to recharge the batteries to ensure a minimum

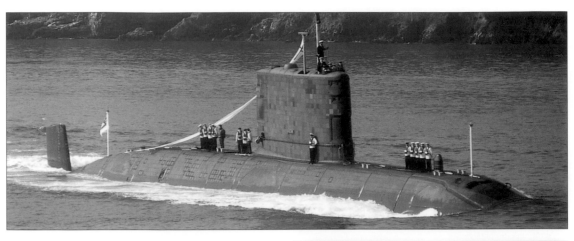

The 'Upholder' class had only a very short British career, being deemed surplus to requirements in the early 1990s and laid up before Canadian purchase.

exposure time of any part of the masts above the water. The armament fit includes a new positive discharge and fully automated weapon-handling system to avoid the stability problems at torpedo launch and the limitations that are sometimes made on the platform's speed and manoeuvrability.

HMS *Upholder*, HMS *Unseen*, HMS *Ursula* and HMS *Unicorn* were laid up in 1994, and in 1998 were bought by Canada for service from 2000 as the **'Victoria' class**. These are named HMCS *Chicoutimi*, HMCS *Victoria*, HMCS *Cornerbrook* and HMCS *Windsor* respectively.

SPECIFICATION

'Victoria' class
Displacement: 2,168 tons surfaced; 2,455 tons dived
Dimensions: length 70.3 m (230 ft 7 in); beam 7.6 m (25 ft); draught 5.5 m (17 ft 8 in)
Propulsion: two Paxman Valenta 16SZ diesels delivering 2700 kW (3,620 shp) and one GEC electric motor delivering 4025 kW (5,400 shp) to one shaft
Performance: speed 12 kts surfaced and 20 kts dived; range 14805 km (9,200 miles) at 8 kts snorting
Diving depth: 300 m (985 ft) operational and 500 m (1,640 ft)

maximum
Torpedo tubes: six 21-in (533-mm) tubes (all bow) for 18 Mk 48 Mod 4 wire-guided active/passive-homing dual-role torpedoes; provision for mines and Sub-Harpoon anti-ship missiles has been removed. Anti-aircraft capability may be added.
Electronics: one Type 1007 navigation radar, one Type 2040 passive bow sonar, one Type 2007 passive flank-array sonar, one MUSL passive towed-array sonar, one Librascope fire-control system, one AR 900 ESM system, and two SSE decoy launchers
Complement: up to 53

The single-hulled 'Upholder'-class submarines were trimmed to just four in number, and entered British service from 1990 with provision for advanced weapons such as the Spearfish torpedo and UGM-84B Sub-Harpoon anti-ship missile.

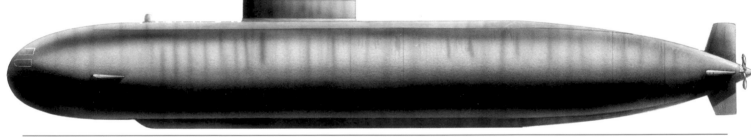

'Shishumar' class Patrol submarine

In December 1981 the Indian government reached an agreement with Howaldtswerke-Deutsche Werft, a German organisation based in Kiel, for a four-section contract covering four conventional submarines of the Type 1500 variant of the very successful boats of the Type 209 class. The four-part contract covered the construction in Germany of an initial pair of submarines of the **'Shishumar' class**, packages of equipment and components for the building of another two boats by the Mazagon Dock Ltd. of Mumbai (Bombay), the training of specialised design and construction personnel employed by Mazagon, and the provision of logistical support and consultation

services during the manufacture and early service of the boats. In 1984 it was announced that another two boats would be built at Mazagon, giving the Indian navy a total of six 'Shishumar'-class submarines, but this scheme was overtaken in the later part of the decade by changes in the thinking of the Indian navy, and in 1988 it was revealed that the arrangement with Howaldtswerke would end with the completion of the fourth boat.

The decision was reviewed 1992 and 1997, and in 1999 the Indian navy decided to move ahead with its Project 75 for the Indian construction of three submarines of the French 'Scorpène' class design.

The Type 1500 is the largest of the sub-classes derived from the basic Type 209 class, and submarines of this very successful and long-lived design are also operated by the navies of Argentina, Brazil, Chile, Colombia, Ecuador, Greece, Indonesia, Peru, South Korea, Turkey and Venezuela.

The four 'Shishumar' boats are the **Shishumar**, **Shankush**, **Shalki** and **Shankul**. Built in Germany, the first two boats were laid down in May and September 1982 for launching in December and May 1984 and completion in September and November 1986, while the last two boats, built in India, were laid down in June 1984 and September 1989 for launching in September 1989 and March 1992 and completion in February 1992 and May 1994.

The submarines are basically conventional with a single central bulkhead, their most notable operational features being the provision of an IKL-designed escape system. This latter comprises an integrated escape sphere able to accommodate the entire 40-man crew. This sphere can withstand the same pressure as the

The 'Shishumar'-class boats have given the Indian navy an effective operational capability and also invaluable experience in modern submarine thinking.

hull, has its own eight-hour air supply, and is outfitted for short term survival and communications.

Bow tubes
The eight torpedo tubes are all grouped in the bows, and provision is made for the embarkation of six reload torpedoes. The standard weapon for these tubes is a German torpedo, the AEG SUT, which is a wire-guided weapon with active/passive onboard terminal guidance. The weapon carries a 250-kg (551-lb) HE warhead, and its two primary capabilities in terms of range and speed are 28 km (17.4 miles) at 23 kts and 12 km (7.5 miles)

at 35 kts. The fifth and sixth boats were to have been completed with provision for the carriage and firing of anti-ship missiles, but the existing boats lack this facility. They do have, however, provision for the addition of external 'strap-on' carriers.

The *Shishumar* started a mid-life refit in 1999, with the other boats following in order of completion, and improvements that may be retrofitted are French Eledone sonar and an Indian action data system.

'Collins' class Patrol submarine

Needing a successor to its obsolescent 'Oberon' class diesel-electric submarines, the Royal Australian Navy decided in the first part of the 1980s to consider the full range of foreign-designed submarines that would meet the RAN's operational requirement and also be suitable for construction in an Australian yard. The decision eventually went to a Swedish design, the Type 471 designed by Kockums, and in June 1987 the Australian Submarine Corporation contracted with Kockums for six such submarines, to be built in Adelaide, South Australia, and known in Australian service as the **'Collins'-class**. The contract included an option for another two boats, but this option was not exercised.

Fabrication of the boats' initial assemblies began in June 1989, and the bows and midships sections of the first submarines were produced in Sweden and shipped to Adelaide to be mated with locally built sec-

tions. The boats were laid down between February 1990 and May 1995, launched between August 1993 and November 2001, and completed between July 1996 and a time in 2003, and are named **HMAS Collins**, **HMAS Farncomb**, **HMAS Waller**, **HMAS Dechaineux**, **HMAS Sheean** and **HMAS Rankin**.

The armament and fire-control/combat system, the latter proving very troublesome during development and initial service, are along American lines, while the sonar is basically of French and Australian origins. As noted above, the Boeing/Rockwell combat system has been plagued by problems, and only after the Raytheon CCS Mk 2 system has been installed will the boats be regarded as fully operational from about 2007. All but the *Collins*, which was retrofitted, were built with anechoic tiles on their outer surfaces, and the periscopes are British, in the form of the Pilkington (now Thales)

The 'Collins'-class submarines are based at the Royal Australian Navy's Fleet Base West (HMAS Stirling) in Western Australia, with pairs of boats making regular deployments to the east coast.

Optronics CK43 search and CH93 attack units. The tubes are all located in the bows, and are designed to fire either the Mk 48 Mod 4 heavyweight torpedo or the UGM-84B Sub-Harpoon

underwater-launched anti-ship missile, of which a combined total of 22 can be shipped. An alternative is 44 mines. The Mk 48 Mod 4 is a wire-guided dual-role weapon with active/passive homing, and can carry its 267-kg (590-lb) warhead to a range of 38 km (23.6 miles) at 55 kts or 50 km (31.1 miles) at 40 kts. The tube-launched weapons

are discharged by an air turbine pump arrangement.

Great development effort has improved the boats' reliability and quietness. The revision of the boats with a Stirling air-independent propulsion system in a lengthened hull is being considered, and a test rig has been bought from Sweden.

The RAN's six-strong class of 'Collins' boats are typical of modern submarine design, and may be retrofitted with an air-independent propulsion system (AIPS).

'Dolphin' class Patrol submarine

To replace three elderly Type 206 coastal submarines deleted in 1999-2000, the Israeli navy decided in 1988 to purchase two boats of the the **'Dolphin'** or **Type 800 class** as variants of the German Type 212 class design by IKL. On the basis of promised American FMS (Foreign Military Sales) funding, Israel contracted with the Ingalls Shipbuilding Division of the Litton Corporation as prime contractor for the boats, to be built in Germany by Howaldtswerke of Kiel with participation by Thyssen Nordseewerke of Emden.

Funding was made available in July 1989 and the contract became effective in January 1990, but in November it was cancelled because of funding pressures in the period leading up to the 1991 Gulf War. The programme was revived with German funding in April 1991, and then in July 1994 Israel exercised its option for a third boat of the same class.

The first steel for the three boats was cut in April 1992, and the boats were laid down in October 1994, April 1995 and December 1996 for completion in July 1999, November 1999 and July 2000 as the **Dolphin**, **Leviathan** and **Tekuma**.

The three boats are similar to the Type 212 class except for internal revisions to permit the incorporation of a 'wet and dry' compartment so that underwater swimmers can leave and re-enter the boat. It is also likely that the boats are fitted with the Triten anti-helicopter SAM system.

Weapons fit

Primary anti-ship and anti-submarine armament is the STN Atlas DM2A4 Seehecht wire-guided torpedo carrying a 260-kg (573-lb) warhead to a range of 13000 m (14,215 yards) in active mode at 35 kts, or to 28000 m (30,620 yards) in passive mode at 23 kts. Pending the delivery of the complete DM2A4 package from Germany, a number of NT 37E torpedoes are included in the torpedo fit. Tube-laid mines are an alternative to the 16 torpedoes, and other weapons that can also be launched are up to five UGM-84C Sub-Harpoon underwater-launched AShMs, or conventionally armed cruise missiles of Israeli design and manufacture. In addition to the six 533-mm (21-in) conventional tubes, the boats also have four 650-mm (25.6-in) tubes optimised for the launch of swimmer deliv-

The three 'Dolphin'-class submarines provide Israel with a capable cruise missile deterrent, interdiction, surveillance and also a swimmer delivery capability.

ery vehicles (SDVs) but with provision for the carriage of liners so that they can also be used as conventional torpedo tubes.

The boats are painted in blue and green for reduced visibility in the shallow water of the East Mediterranean.

SPECIFICATION	
'Dolphin' class	surfaced and 780 km (485 miles) at
Displacement: 1,640 tons	8 kts dived
surfaced; 1,900 tons dived	**Diving depth:** 350 m (1,150 ft)
Dimensions: length 57.3 m	operational
(188 ft); beam 6.8 m (22 ft 4 in);	**Torpedo tubes:** six 533-mm (21-in)
draught 6.2 m (20 ft 4 in)	and four 650-mm (25.6-in) tubes (all
Propulsion: three MTU 16V 396	bow); for weapons see text
SE 84 diesels delivering 3165 kW	**Electronics:** Elta surface search
(4,245 shp) and one Siemens	radar, CSU 90 active/passive hull
electric motor delivering 2890 kW	sonar, PRS-3 passive ranging sonar,
(3,875 shp) to one shaft	FAS-3 passive flank-array sonar,
Performance: speed 11 kts	ISUS 90-1 torpedo fire-control
snorting and 20 kts dived; range	system, and Tinmex 4CH(V) 2 ESM
14825 km (9,210 miles) at 8 kts	**Complement:** 30

'Västergötland' class Patrol submarine

In the late 1970s the Swedish navy began to consider building a class of patrol submarines to replace the 'Draken'-class boats built in the late 1950s and early 1960s, and to supplement the 'Sjöormen' classes built in the second half of the 1960s and eventually sold to Singapore as training boats in the second half of the 1990s. The result was the **'Västergötland' class**, whose design was contracted to Kockums of Malmö during April 1978.

The type was conceived with a single hull, X-type after control surfaces combining rudder and hydroplane functions, and a Pilkington Optronics CK 38 optronic search periscope enhanced with night vision capability. Four boats in the class were commissioned in the period 1987-90. They were constructed by Kockums on the basis of its own central section and bow and stern sections by Karlskrona varvet.

Operations in the acoustically tricky shallow waters of the Baltic demanded special consideration of quietening features, and the boats are also coated with an anechoic layer to reduce their reflection of active sonar pulses. The torpedo tubes are all located in the bow, and comprise six 533-mm (21-in) tubes over three 400-mm (15.75-in)

tubes. All the tubes are used for wire-guided torpedoes, the larger-diameter tubes firing swim-out FFV Type 613 passive-homing anti-ship weapons carrying a 240-kg (529-lb) warhead to a range of 20 km (12.4 miles) at 45 kts, and the smaller-diameter tubes firing FFV Type 431/451 active/passive-homing anti-submarine weapons carrying a 45-kg (99-lb) shaped-charge warhead to a range of 20 km at 25 kts.

The last two boats are being lengthened by 10 m (32 ft 10 in) to allow the incorporation of a Stirling-cycle AIPS (Air-Independent Propulsion System) providing a submerged endurance of some 14 days. The first two boats may be passed to Denmark,

which already has one 'Näcken'- class submarine from Sweden.

Above: Commissioned in January 1990, Östergötland was the last 'Västergötland' completed, and is being modernised. The first pair may be leased to Denmark.

SPECIFICATION	
'Västergötland' class	operational
Displacement: 1,070 tons	**Torpedo tubes:** six 533-mm (21-in)
surfaced; 1,143 tons dived	and three 400-mm (15.75-in) tubes
Dimensions: length 48.5 m (159 ft	(all bow) for 12 and six torpedoes
1 in); beam 6.06 m (19 ft 11 in);	respectively; 48 mines can be
draught 5.6 m (18 ft 4 in)	carried in an external girdle
Propulsion: two Hedemora	**Electronics:** Terma surface search
V12A/15-Ub diesels delivering	and navigation radar, CSU 83
1640 kW (2,200 shp) and one	active/passive hull sonar, passive
Jeumont Schneider electric motor	flank-array sonar, IPS-17 (Sesub
delivering 1350 kW (1,810 shp) to	900A) torpedo fire-control system,
one shaft	and Argo AR-700-S5 or Condor
Performance: speed 10 kts	CS 3071 ESM
surfaced and 20 kts dived	**Complement:** 28
Diving depth: 300 m (985 ft)	

Above: There are four boats in the 'Västergötland' class: Västergötland, Hälsingland, Södermanland and Östergötland.

'Kilo' class Patrol submarine

Built at Komsomolsk and two other yards, the 'Kilo' diesel-electric submarines were derived from the longer-range 'Tango' class, and despite problems with its batteries in hotter conditions has achieved respectable export sales to countries of North Africa, the Middle East and the Far East.

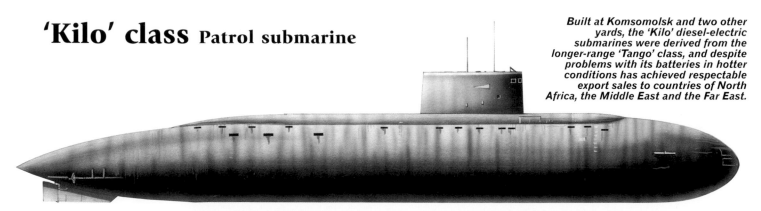

The **Project 877** or **Vashavyanka** diesel-electric submarine, better known in the West as the **'Kilo' class**, was designed in the early 1970s for the anti-submarine and anti-ship defence of Soviet naval bases, coastal installations and sea lanes, and also for the patrol and surveillance tasks. First delivered from the shipyard at Komsomolsk in eastern Siberia, but then built in the western USSR at Nizhny Novgorod and the Admiralty Yard in Leningrad (now St Petersburg), the boat is of the medium-endurance type and the first example was launched in 1979 for completion in 1982.

Soviet deletions

Some 24 'Kilos' were built for the Soviet navy, and by the first part of the 21st century the Russian navy had deleted 15 of these, leaving it with nine boats with the Northern and Pacific Fleets (three and four respectively), and single boats with the Baltic and Black Sea Fleets, the latter's boat having been modified with pumpjet propulsion.

In design the 'Kilo' class is a development of the 'Tango' class with an improved hull form. Even so, the boat can be considered only basic by comparison with contemporary Western submarines. The Soviets procured the submarine in four variants: the Project 877 baseline model,

Between 1986 and 2000 India received 10 'Kilos'. Known as the 'Sindhughosh' class, after the name of the first boat delivered, the submarines are allocated to the 11th Submarine Squadron (four boats at Vishakapatnam) and the 10th Submarine Squadron (six boats based at Mumbai). Five boats are armed with 3M54 Alfa (SS-N-27) active radar homing SLCMs with a supersonic attack phase and a range of 180 km (112 miles).

Project 877K with improved fire-control, **Project 877M** with provision for wire-guided torpedoes from two tubes, and the slightly longer **Project 4B** with uprated diesels, an electric motor turning more slowly for less noise, and an automated data system to provide fire-control data for two simultaneous interceptions. Boats have been exported to Algeria (two), China (four), India (10), Iran (three), Poland (one) and Romania (one), some of them **Type 636** submarines with improved propulsion and fire-control systems.

Above: Poland received a single 'Project 877E' class submarine, the letter suffix indicating export, in June 1986. Based at Gdynia, the submarine is named Orzel.

SPECIFICATION	
'Kilo' (Project 4B) class	**Diving depth:** 240 m (790 ft) operational
Displacement: 2,325 tons surfaced; 3,076 tons dived	**Torpedo tubes:** six 533-mm (21-in) tubes (all bow) for 18 torpedoes or 24 mines, and provision for one short-range SAM launcher
Dimensions: length 73.8 m (242 ft 2 in); beam 9.9 m (32 ft 6 in); draught 6.6 m (21 ft 8 in)	
Propulsion: two diesels delivering 2720 kW (3,650 shp) and one electric motor delivering 4400 kW (5,900 shp) to one shaft	**Electronics:** one 'Snoop Tray' radar, one 'Shark Teeth'/'Shark Fin' active/passive hull sonar, one 'Mouse Roar' active attack hull sonar, MVU-110EM or MVU-119EM torpedo fire-control system, and 'Squid Head' or 'Brick Pulp' ESM
Performance: 10 kts surfaced and 17 kts dived; range 11125 km (6,915 miles) at 8 kts snorting and 740 km (460 miles) at 3 kts dived	**Complement:** 52

With the retirement of its more maintenance-intensive vessels, the earlier 'Kilo'-class submarines have disappeared from the Russian navy's active list.

'Tupi' class Patrol submarine

S 30 is the lead boat of the 'Tupi' class of German-designed submarines. The Tupi was built in Germany, being commissioned in May 1989, and then came three Brazilian-made boats.

In 1984 Brazil contracted with Howaldtswerke-Deutsche Werft for six **'Tupi' class** submarines to the 'Type 1400' subvariant of the 'Type 209' model, the first built in Kiel and the other five in Rio de Janeiro. Financial constraints trimmed the Brazilian-built quantity to three, while the pair of **'Tikuna'-class** boats, to an improved 'Tupi' class

standard, are far behind schedule: the *Tikuna*'s commissioning date is delayed from 2000 to 2005 and work on the *Tapuia* has been suspended.

Brazil established an uranium-enrichment plant in 1988 with the announced intention of building an SSN, but this project has not proceeded beyond the design stage. The 'Tikuna'-class

boats were described as intermediate between the older SSKs and an SSN.

Brazilian torpedoes

The 'Tupi' class boats operate from Moncangue island's Base Almirante Castro e Silva across the bay from Rio. These are well armed small boats, carrying a combination of British Mk 24 Tigerfish torpedoes

and an anti-submarine torpedo developed by the IPqM (Instituto de Pesquisas da Marinha, or naval research institute). Eight torpedoes are carried in the tubes and there are eight reloads. The Tigerfish is a wire-guided torpedo capable of active homing at 35 kts to a range of 13 km (8 miles) or passive homing at 24 kts to 29.6 km (18.4 miles). The

IPqM torpedo has a swim-out launch system and travels up to 18.5 km (11.5 miles) at 45 kts.

The 'Tikuna'-class boats are larger, at 2,425 tons dived, and have a crew of 39. Designed for an endurance of 60 days, they are designed to carry MCF-01/100 acoustic-magnetic mines (produced by IPqM) instead of some torpedoes.

The **Tamoio** *was built in Brazil as the second unit of the 'Tupi' class, and was completed in December 1994 at the end of a construction effort lasting somewhat more than eight years.*

The Brazilian 'Tupi'-class submarines offer generally good capabilities, and it is planned that their torpedo armament should be upgraded in the future with the advanced Bofors 2000 torpedo.

SPECIFICATION

'Tupi' class
Boats in class: *Tupi*, *Tamoio*, *Timbira* and *Tapajo*
Displacement: 1,400 tons surfaced; 1,550 tons dived
Dimensions: length 61.2 m (200 ft 9 in); beam 6.2 m (20 ft 4 in); draught 5.5 m (18 ft)
Propulsion: four MTU 12V 493 AZ80 diesels delivering 1800 kW (2,414 shp) and one Siemens electric motor delivering 3425 kW (4,595 shp to one shaft
Performance: speed 11 kts

surfaced/snorting and 21.5 kts dived; range 15000 km (9,320 miles) at 8 kts surfaced and 740 km (460 miles) at 4 kts dived
Diving depth: 250 m (820 ft)
Armament: eight 533-mm (21-in) tubes with up to 16 Mk 24 Mod 1 or 2 Tigerfish torpedoes or IPqM anti-submarine torpedoes
Electronics: Calypso navigation radar; DR-4000 ESM, CSU 83/1 hull-mounted passive search/attack sonar
Complement: 30

'Type 212A' Patrol submarine

Since the 1980s there has been a steadily rising level of interest among the world's navies in the advantages offered by the introduction of an air-independent propulsion system to create true 'submarines' out of what are otherwise conventionally powered 'submersibles'.

Germany trialled such a system in a 'Type-205' boat adapted with an AIPS in 1988-89, and then moved forward to the creation of a highly streamlined boat designed from the outset with an AIPS, in this case using a hybrid fuel cell/battery propulsion arrangement based on Siemens PEM fuel cell technology. In 1992, ARGE 212 (a consortium of Howaldtswerke-Deutsche Werft and Thyssen Nordseewerke, supported by IKL) completed the initial design of the **'Type 212A' class**, and an initial four boats were authorised in July 1994. However, it was only in July 1998 that the first metal was cut as the programme had been slowed to allow the incorporation of changes (including improved habitability and a greater diving depth) to maximise commonality with two boats ordered by Italy.

The four German boats, which may be complemented by a further eight,

are the **U 31** to **U 34**. These are based on forward and after sections produced by HDW at Kiel and TNSW at Emden, with the boats completed alternately at the two yards. The first boat was launched in 2002, and the schedule allows thorough testing of this boat before the other three are finalised.

The design is based on a partial double hull in which the larger-diameter forward section is connected to the narrower-diameter after section (carrying the two liquid oxygen tanks and the hydrogen tankage) by a tapered section accommodating the fuel cell plant. The underwater propulsion can provide a maximum speed of 20 kts declining to 8 kts on just the fuel cells.

The two Italian boats, of which the first is to be called the **Salvatore Todaro**, are being built at Muggiano by Fincantieri, and are scheduled for completion in 2005-2006 to a standard essentially similar to that of the German boats.

Other key features of the 'Type 212A' class design are the diving planes on the conning tower, the X-configured control surfaces at the stern, and the propeller with seven scimitar-shaped blades.

Above: The U 31 under way just off the yard in which its final assembly was undertaken. The 'Type 212A'-class boats are notable for their AIPS and their streamlined exterior lines.

Right: The AIPS, created and manufactured by Siemens and HDW, offer extended underwater endurance. The attack periscopes are by Zeiss.

SPECIFICATION

'Type 212A' class
Displacement: 1,450 tons surfaced; 1,830 tons dived
Dimensions: length 55.9 m (183 ft 5 in); beam 7 m (23 ft); draught 6 m (19 ft 8 in)
Propulsion: one MTU diesel delivering 3165 kW (4,245 hp) and one electric motor delivering 2890 kW (3,875 shp) to one shaft
Performance: speed 12 kts surfaced and 20 kts dived; range 14805 km (9,200 miles) at 8 kts

surfaced
Torpedo tubes: six 21-in (533-mm) tubes (all bow) for 12 DM2A4 wire-guided torpedoes
Electronics: Type 1007 navigation radar, DBQS-40 passive ranging and intercept sonar, FAS-3 flank and passive towed-array sonar, MOA 3070 or ELAK mine-detection sonar, MSI-90U weapon-control system, FL 1800 ESM, and TAU 2000 torpedo decoy system
Complement: 27

'Type 214' Patrol submarine

Ordered by Greece and South Korea, the **'Type 214'-class** submarine is basically a development of the 'Type 209'-class design with a hull further optimised for hydrodynamic efficiency and therefore 'stealthiness', but with the 'Type 212A' class's AIPS (Air-Independent

Propulsion System) based on the Siemens PEM (Polymer Electrolyte Membrane) fuel cell technology rather than the Stirling system used in Swedish submarines. Each of the boats has two PEM cells, producing 120 kW (161 shp) per module, and this trans-

lates into a submerged endurance of 14 days.

In October 1998 the Greek government announced that the Greek navy was to procure four 'Type 214'-class submarines with the local designation **'Katsonis' class**. The first boat is being built by Howaldtswerke of Kiel for planned launch in December 2003 and commissioning in 2005, and the other three are to be completed by the Skaramanga yard of Hellenic Shipyards. The four Greek boats are the **Katsonis, Papanilolis, Pipinos** and **Matrozos**. Changes differentiating the 'Type 214' class from the 'Type 212A' class include the location of the diving planes on the forward part of the hull rather than the conning tower, more conventional control surfaces (horizontal and vertical elements rather than an X-configuration) at the stern, eight rather than six swimout rather than water ram discharge bow tubes (includ-

ing four fitted for Harpoon anti-ship missiles), a hull made of different materials for a greater diving depth, and slightly different electronics even though a similar Zeiss optronic periscope is used.

It was in December 2000 that the South Korean defence ministry selected the 'Type 214' in preference to the French 'Scorpène' design (and the Russian offer of three 'Kilo'-class boats) to meet its 'KS-II' requirement

for three submarines. The contract to build the new boats was awarded to Hyundai Heavy Industries rather than Daewoo Shipbuilding and Marine Engineering, which built South Korea's nine 'Chang Bogo' ('Type 1200' subclass of the 'Type 209' class) boats.

The boats are to be built with German technical assistance and equipment, and are scheduled for completion in 2007, 2008 and 2009.

The advent of their 'Type 214' submarines, derived from the 'Type 209' design with the AIPS developed for the 'Type 212A', will transform the submarine capabilities of the Greek and South Korean navies.

SPECIFICATION

'Type 214' class
Displacement: 1,700 tons surfaced; 1,980 tons dived
Dimensions: length 65 m (213 ft 3 in); beam 6.3 m (20 ft 8 in); draught 6 m (19 ft 8 in)
Propulsion: two MTU 16V 396 diesels delivering 6320 kW (8,475 shp) and one Siemens Permasyn electric motor delivering unspecified power to one shaft
Performance: speed 12 kts

surfaced and 20 kts dived
Diving depth: 400 m (1,315 ft)
Torpedo tubes: eight 21-in (533-mm) tubes (all bow) for 16 STN Atlas torpedoes and Harpoon anti-ship missiles
Electronics: navigation radar, bow, flank-array and towed-array sonars, ISUS 90 weapon-control system, ESM, and Circe torpedo decoy system
Complement: 27

'Uzushio' class
Diesel attack submarine

The revolutionary teardrop shape introduced by the US submarine Albacore was a major influence on the design of Japan's first truly modern submarine, the Uzushio.

The increase in Cold War tensions in the 1950s made it necessary for the US and its allies to allow former enemies Germany and Japan to rearm.

The US Navy's submarine stranglehold on the home islands was a major factor in Japan's crushing defeat during World War II. The reborn Japanese navy, originally called the Maritime Safety Agency and latterly known as the Maritime Self-Defence Force to emphasise its purely defensive nature, recognised that fact. As a result, its first priority was anti-submarine warfare.

ASW training

The best defence against submarines is often other submarines. The first MSDF boat was an ex-US 'Gato'-class vessel, followed in the late 1950s by a number of small coastal submarines. Five larger 'Oshio'-class boats followed in the late 1960s, the first Japanese fleet boats to sail since the war. They were conservative in design, and their primary function was to serve as targets for ASW training.

Commissioned between 1971 and 1978, the seven boats of the **'Uzushio'sss** class marked a great leap forwards. Influenced strongly by American designs, the boats had an Albacore-type teardrop hull for maximum hydrodynamic efficiency. The bow sonar array meant that the torpedo tubes had to be located amidships, again following US Navy practice.

Double hull

Manufactured from NS-63 high-tensile steel, the 'Uzushios' were double-hulled, and had a diving depth in excess of 200 m (656 ft). They incorporated a certain amount of automation, most notably in the provision of a kind of submarine auto-pilot, combining automatic depth and direction maintenance.

The 'Uzushios' were succeeded in production by the improved and enlarged 'Yuushio'-class, and were retired through the 1990s as they were replaced in service one for one by the 'Harushio'-class boats.

SPECIFICATION

'Uzushio' class
Type: Diesel-powered attack submarine
Displacement: 1,850 tons standard surfaced and 3,600 tons dived
Dimensions: length 72 m (236 ft 3 in); beam 9.90 m (32 ft 6 in); draught 7.50 m (24 ft 7 in)
Machinery: two Kawasaki-MAN V8/V24-30 diesels driving one shaft delivering 2685 kW (3,600 bhp) on the surface and 5369 kW (7,200 bhp) dived
Speed: 12 kts (22 km/h; 14 mph) surfaced and 20 kts (37 km/h; 23 mph) dived
Diving depth: 200 m (656 ft) normal
Torpedo tubes: six 533-mm (21-in) amidships
Basic load: 18 weapons, usually a mix of homing torpedoes
Complement: 80

The 'Uzushio'-class submarine Isoshio enters port. Commissioned in the 1970s, these boats were the foundation of Japan's modern submarine service.

'Yuushio' class
Diesel attack submarine

The 10 boats of the **'Yuushio' class** have provided the backbone of the Maritime Self-Defence Force's submarine strength since the 1980s. Essentially an enlarged version of the preceding teardrop 'Uzushio' class, the 'Yuushios' differ primarily in having a deeper diving capability. The 'Uzushios' were decommissioned in the 1990s as the new 'Harushio' class was commissioned.

Bow sonar

Of double-hull construction, these boats follow the US Navy nuclear attack submarine practice of having a bow sonar array with the torpedo tubes moved to amidships and angled outwards. The first of the class, **Yuushio** (SS573), entered service in 1980 with the **Mochishio** (SS574), **Setoshio** (SS575), **Okishio** (SS576), **Nadashio** (SS577), **Hamashio** (SS578), **Akishio** (SS579), **Takeshio** (SS580), **Yukishio** (SS581), and **Sachishio** (SS582) following at yearly intervals.

From the *Nadashio* onwards the class was fitted to carry and fire the American Sub-Harpoon anti-ship missile, a capability which was retrofitted to all of the earlier boats except for the *Yuushio* itself. All the boats carry the Type 89 dual-purpose, active-passive torpedoes which have a maximum speed of 55 kts (102 km/h; 63 mph) and a maximum reduced speed range of 50 km (31 miles).

The electronics carried are of the latest design, and include the ZQQ-5 bow sonar (a modified American BQS-4) and the ZQR-1 towed array (similar to the American BQR-15). *Yuushio* was removed from front-line service to become a training boat in 1996.

Last of the line

The last of the 'Yuushios' was commissioned in 1989. By that time, the first three boats of the follow-on 'Harushio' class had been

The second 'Yuushio'-class boat Mochishio enters the US Pacific Fleet base as it makes a courtesy visit to Pearl Harbor in the mid 1990s.

laid down, with the name-ship commissioning at the end of November 1990. *Harushio* was followed at yearly intervals by *Natsushio, Hayashio, Arashio, Wakashio, Fuyushio*, and by *Asashio* in 1997. As each entered service one of the 'Uzushio'-class boats was paid off.

The 'Harushios' follow the same basic design as the 'Yuushios', but are slightly larger in all dimensions.

More attention has been paid to reducing noise internally, and all have anechoic material applied to the outer surfaces. A stronger pressure hull means that operational diving depth has been increased to some 300 m (1,150 ft).

Asashio, the last of the class, was completed to a modified design. Increased systems automation has allowed its crew to be reduced from 74 to 71.

Sailors prepare to moor the **Mochishio** *as it approaches the dock.*

SPECIFICATION

'Yuushio' class
Displacement: 2,200 tons standard surfaced and 2,730 tons dived
Dimensions: length 76 m (249 ft 4 in); beam 9.90 m (32 ft 6 in); draught 7.50 m (24 ft 7¼ in)
Propulsion: two diesels delivering 2535 kW (3,400 hp) to one electric motor driving one shaft
Speed: 12 kts (22 km/h; 14 mph) surfaced and 20 kts (37 km/h; 23 mph) dived

Diving depth: 275 m (900 ft) operational
Torpedo tubes: six 533-mm (21-in) amidships
Basic load: 18-20 torpedoes and anti-ship missiles
Electronics: one ZPS-6 surface-search radar, one ZQQ-5 bow sonar, one SQS-36(J) sonar, one ZQR-1 towed array, one ALR 3-6 ESM suite
Complement: 75

Left: Although influenced by US Navy practice, by the time Harushio *was commissioned in 1990, Japanese submarine designs were using mainly home-built systems and equipment.*

Right: Yuushio *conducts an emergency surfacing drill. The name ship of its class has been in use as a training submarine since 1996.*

'Oyashio' class Diesel attack submarine

The **Oyashio**, commissioned in 1998, was the first of five advanced diesel-powered patrol submarines to enter service with the Japan Maritime Self-Defence Force. The new submarines are examples of the changing face of Japanese military equipment acquisition since the establishment of the Self-Defence Forces in the 1950s.

The first generation of equipment was often second hand and generally acquired from the United States. By 1960, however, Japanese industry was up and running after the devastation of World War II, and the second stage saw

American equipment or licence-built Japanese copies of American equipment installed in Japanese-built platforms.

All Japanese
From the late 1970s, an increasing proportion of JMSDF systems has been of Japanese origin. Even where those systems are based on state-of-the-art American or European designs, they have often been upgraded – at great cost – to be even more capable then the original.

The 'Oyashio' class is equipped with Japanese-designed radar and electronics. Its sonar sys-

tems are based on American designs, but have been modified to suit Japanese requirements. Outwardly, the 'Oyashios' have changed a little from preceding Japanese submarines. The revised outer casing gives them something of the look of British nuclear boats, while the fin is of a more efficient hydrodynamic shape.

The new boats share the double hulls and anechoic coating of the previous class, but have been equipped with large flank sonar arrays, which according to some sources account for the increase in displacement over the 'Harushios'.

Future engines
Kawasaki Heavy Industries have been conducting experiments in using Sterling-Cycle air-independent powerplants and fuel cells, and at one stage these were planned for the later 'Oyashios'. It is now likely that such systems, which allow boats to operate submerged for extended periods, will make their appearance in the next class of Japanese submarines.

As the 'Oyashios' are completed they will replace the older 'Yuushio' class boats. The Japanese Defense Agency expects

Oyashio *is as capable as most nuclear boats. Although slower and with less endurance, its diesel electric powerplant makes it quieter than a 'nuke'.*

that future world conditions will call for an operational total of 12 to 14 boats. Most of these will be of the 'Oyashio' class as cur-

rent building plans call for as many as 10 boats to be in service by 2007 or 2008.

Oyashio, *commissioned in 1998, is the first Japanese submarine in nearly three decades to have a significantly different hull form and fin.*

SPECIFICATION

'Oyashio' class
Displacement: 2,700 tons standard surfaced and 3,000 tons dived
Dimensions: length 81.70 m (268 ft); beam 8.90 m (29 ft 3 in); draught 7.90 m (25 ft 11 in)
Propulsion: two Kawasaki 12V25S diesels delivering 4100 kW (5,520 hp) to two Fuji electric motors driving one shaft
Speed: 12 kts (22 km/h; 14 mph) surfaced and 20 kts (37 km/h; 23 mph) dived

Diving depth: 300 m (984 ft) operational and 500 m (1,640 ft) maximum
Torpedo tubes: six 533-mm (21-in) amidships
Basic load: 20 Type 89 torpedoes and Harpoon anti-ship missiles
Electronics: one ZPS-6 surface-search radar, one Hughes-Oki ZQQ-5B bow sonar, port and starboard flank sonar arrays, one ZQR-1 (BQR-15) towed array, one ZLR 7 ESM suite
Complement: 69

'Ula' class Patrol submarine

Since the deletion of the last six of the original 15 'Kobben'-class boats in the second half of the 1990s, the Norwegian navy operates just six submarines in the form of the boats of the **'Ula' class** with diesel-electric propulsion. The boats are named **Ula, Uredd, Utvaer, Uthaug, Utstein** and **Utsira**, all but the second of these names having been used for the boats of an earlier 'Ula' class (five British 'U'-class submarines bought from the UK in 1943-46, modernised in 1955-56 and deleted in the first part of the 1960s).

The current 'Ula'-class submarines are intended primarily for coastal operations, and are therefore comparatively small in size and limited in their diving depth to some 250 m (820 ft).

German construction

The entire class was ordered from Thyssen Nordseewerke of Emden on 30 September 1982 in a joint Norwegian and West German programme known in the latter country as Project 210, but the option for another two boats of the class was not, in the event, exercised.

Although the boats were completed in the West German yard they did incorporate a measure of Norwegian structural expertise inasmuch as sections of the pressure hulls were fabricated in a Norwegian facility and then shipped to Emden for inclusion into the otherwise German-built boats. The boats were laid down between January 1987 and June 1990, launched between July 1988 and November 1991, and finally commissioned into Norwegian service in the period between April 1989 and April 1992.

Though much of the hull and all of the propulsion machinery are German, the boats were completed with a mix of French, German and Norwegian systems. The basic command and weapon control systems are Norwegian (the torpedo fire-control system being the Kongsberg MSI-90U that is being upgraded and modernised in 2000-05), while the sonars are of French and German origins. The Thomson-CSF low-frequency passive flank-array sonar is of French origin, and is based on piezoelectric polymer technology offering significantly reduced flow noise. The Atlas Elektronik CSU 83 medium-frequency active/passive intercept, search and attack sonar, however, is of German origin. Another notable feature, designed to reduce the need to incorporate apertures in the pressure hull, is the use of Calzoni Trident modular non-penetrating masts, and the periscopes use Zeiss optics.

Eventful careers

Since entering service, the 'Ula'-class submarines have been found to suffer from noise problems with their machinery, which is a major handicap in submarine operations in which sound is the primary medium for discovering submerged boats. The submarines have undergone quite interesting careers to date. The *Ula*, for example was damaged by a practice torpedo during the boat's trials in 1989, while the *Uredd* in March 1991 was damaged in a docking accident and then in February 1992 suffered a control room fire.

The Utsira was the last of the Norwegian navy's six 'Ula'-class submarines to be completed and was commissioned in April 1992.

'Götland' class Patrol submarine

Resulting from a research and preliminary design contract placed with the Kockums yard of Malmö in October 1986 for a conventionally powered submarine to replace the obsolescent boats of the 'Sjöormen' class, the design of the boats of the **A19** or **'Götland' class** was derived from that of the A17 or 'Västergötland' class. The three boats of the class, namely the **Götland, Uppland** and **Halland**, were ordered from Kockums in March 1990, but another two projected units were not in the event procured. In September of the following year, before the first boat had been laid down, the programme was temporarily suspended to allow a reworking of the design to incorporate, for the first time

Right: The 'Götland'-class boats are fairly small, but offer excellent capabilities including a sizeable load of modern torpedoes and an extended underwater cruising capability.

Below: Highly reliable boats, the 'Götlands' provide Sweden with effective coastal defence.

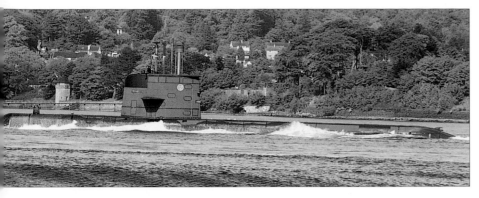

SPECIFICATION	
'Götland' class **Displacement:** 1,240 tons surfaced; 1,494 tons dived **Dimensions:** length 60.4 m (198 ft 2 in); beam 6.2 m (20 ft 4 in); draught 5.6 m (18 ft 4 in) **Propulsion:** two Hedemora V12A-15-Ub diesels delivering 4,830 kW (6,480 shp), two Kockums V4-275R Mk 2 Stirling AIPS, and one Jeumont-Schneider electric motor delivering 1350 kW (1,810 shp) to one shaft **Performance:** speed 10 kts	surfaced and 20 kts dived **Torpedo tubes:** four 533-mm (21-in) and two 400-mm (15.75-in) tubes (all bow) for 12 Tp 613 or Tp 62 wire-guided anti-ship and six Tp 432/451 wire-guided anti-submarine torpedoes **Electronics:** one Scanter navigation radar, one CSU 90-2 passive search and attack sonar with bow and flank arrays, one IPS-19 torpedo fire-control system, and one Manta S ESM system **Complement:** 25

before the start of fabrication rather than as a retrofit, an AIPS (Air-Independent Propulsion System), using liquid oxygen and diesel fuel in a helium environment, for much enhanced submerged operating capability. The design of the hull was lengthened by 7.5 m (24 ft 7 in) to allow the incorporation of two such systems with volume left for the later addition of another two systems should this prove desirable. As it is, the boats can apparently cruise at a submerged speed of 5 kts for several weeks without recourse to snorting.

The boats were laid down in 1992-1994, launched in 1995-96, and commissioned in 1996-97, the lengthening of

the hull having resulted in a 200-ton increase in displacement. Another advanced feature of the design was the installation of a periscope with optronic sensors, and this unit is the only mast that penetrates through the pressure hull. The boats' underwater signature is being further reduced by the application of anechoic coatings.

Torpedo armament
The torpedo tubes are all located in the bow, and comprise four 533-mm (21-in) tubes over two 400-mm (15.75-in) tubes. The larger units fire anti-ship torpedoes of the swim-out type in the form of the wire-guided Type 613 passive or (since 2000)

Type 62 active/passive weapons: the former carries a 240-kg (529-lb) HE warhead to 20 km (12.4 miles) at 45 kts, while the latter carries a 250-kg (551-lb) HE warhead to 50 km (31.1 miles) at a speed of 20-50 kts. Twelve Tp 47 mines can be carried in place of the heavy torpedoes, these swimming out to a predetermined position before laying themselves on the bottom. Another 48 mines can be carried by an external girdle. The smaller torpedo tubes can be tandem loaded with wire-guided Tp 432/451 active/passive ASW torpedoes, each able to carry a 45-kg (99-lb) HE warhead out to 20 km (12.4 miles) at 25 kts.

Above left: The 'Götlands' are very quiet under the water, where their detectability is reduced by silent machinery and an anechoic outer covering.

*Below: Commissioned in May 1997, the **Uppland** was the second of the three 'Götland'-class boats to be completed by the Kockums yard at Malmö.*

'Chang Bogo' class Patrol submarine

Up to the 1980s the South Korean navy, faced largely with the threat of North Korean aggression largely through the agency of conventional submarines and small surface ships, concentrated its efforts on the deployment of ex-US surface warships and the development of its overall capability to operate more advanced vessels. The process began to bear fruit toward the end of the 1980s, when a number of more advanced vessels were ordered.

Among the new types were the service's first submarines, which were of the

West German Type 209 class in its Type 1200 subvariant, which was ordered as the **'Chang Bogo' class** with a diving depth of 250 m (820 ft).

The first order placed late in 1997 covered three boats, one to be completed by Howaldtswerke of Kiel in Germany and the other two by Daewoo at Okpo in South Korea from German-supplied kits. There followed additional three-boat orders placed in October 1989 and January 1994 for boats of South Korean construction, and the entire class comprises the **Chang Bogo, Yi Chon, Choi**

Muson, Pakui, Lee Jongmu, Jeongun, Lee Sunsin, Nadaeyong and **Lee Okki**. The boats were laid down in the period between 1989 and 1997, launched in the period between 1992 and 2000, and commissioned in the period from 1993 to a final hand-over in 2001.

Turkish similarity
The South Korean boats are generally similar to Turkey's six 'Atilay'-class submarines, and emphasis is therefore placed on the installation of German sensors and weapons. Using the swim-out discharge method

(resulting in reduced noise levels) from eight 533-mm (21-in) tubes all located in the bows, the latter comprise 14 SystemTechnik Nord (STN) SUT Mod 2 torpedoes, which are wire-guided weapons with active/passive homing and the ability to carry a 260-kg (573-lb) HE warhead out to a maximum range of 28 km (17.4 miles) at 23 kts or a shorter range of 12 km (7.6 mile) at a speed of 35 kts. The boats can also carry 28 tube-laid mines in place of the torpedoes.

The older boats are being upgraded from a time early in the 21st century, and

although details are currently unclear, it is believed that the modernisation will include a hull 'stretch' to the Type 1400 length of some 62 m (203 ft 5 in) with surfaced and submerged displacements of about 1,455 and 1,585 tons respectively, provision for tube-launched UGM-84 Harpoon missiles to enhance the boats' capabilities against surface ships, and possibly the addition of a towed-array sonar for a superior capability for the detection of submerged submarines.

*The **Pakui** was completed by Daewoo on 3 February 1996, as the fourth of the South Korean navy's 'Chang Bogo'-class conventional submarines. The service plans to operate the boats as a trio attached to each of its three fleets, and further improvement of the boats may be based on an indigenous South Korean development of a US torpedo, the Northrop NP 37.*

SPECIFICATION	
'Chang Bogo' class **Displacement:** 1,100 tons surfaced; 1,285 tons dived **Dimensions:** length 56 m (183 ft 9 in); beam 6.2 m (20 ft 4 in); draught 5.5 m (18 ft) **Propulsion:** diesel-electric arrangement with four MTU 12V 396SE diesels delivering 2840 kW (3,810 shp) and driving four alternators, and one electric motor delivering 3425 kW (4,595 shp) to one shaft **Performance:** speed 11 kts	surfaced/snorting and 22 kts dived; endurance 13900 km (8,635 miles) at 8 kts surfaced **Diving depth:** 250 m (820 ft) **Torpedo tubes:** eight 533-mm (21-in) tubes (all bow) for 14 SUT Mod 2 wire-guided active/passive-homing torpedoes or 28 mines **Electronics:** one navigation radar, one CSU 83 hull-mounted passive search and attack sonar, one ISUS 83 torpedo fire-control system, and one Argo ESM system **Complement:** 33

'Tourville' class Guided missile destroyer

In 1973 the French navy commissioned the 'C 65' class destroyer *Aconit* as the prototype for a new series of escorts optimised for the anti-submarine role in the North Atlantic. The ship was 127 m (417 ft) long and had single-shaft propulsion for a speed of 27 kts. Even as the ship was being built, however, it was clear that it was too small and limited in capabilities, so the following **'F 67'** or **'Tourville'-class** destroyers featured greater dimensions for a 1,350-ton increase in standard displacement, a doubling of power delivered to two shafts, hangarage for two Westland Lynx helicopters, and an enhanced anti-ship capability through the addition of Exocet missiles.

Completed in 1974-77 at the Lorient naval dockyard, the three ships were commissioned as the **Tourville**, **Duguay-Trouin** and **de Grasse**. The first two ships were completed with three 100-mm (3.9-in) guns, but the *de Grasse* was completed with only the two forward guns as it had been decided that the ships would have a Crotale SAM installation (with 26 missiles) above the hangar.

The ships were to have been completed with the same electronic fit as the *Aconit*, but the decision was taken during the ships' construction to adopt a more modern and capable suite including the DRBV 26 air surveillance radar, the DRBV 50 (later DRBV 51B) target designation radar, and a lightweight version of the DRBC 32 fire-control radar, but the *Aconit*'s SENIT 3 tactical data system was retained.

The ships have two sets of non-retracting stabilisers, and helicopter capability is enhanced by the provision of a downhaul system on the flight platform and a SPHEX traverse system serving the double hangar. Habitability was improved over that of earlier ships, and the capability of the electronics (especially the sonar) has been upgraded, although the Malafon system was removed in the 1990s. The *Tourville* and *de Grasse* are still in service.

Like its sister ship de Grasse, the destroyer Tourville is based at Brest in north-west France as part of the French navy's forces allocated to operations in the North Atlantic.

The 'Tourville-class' destroyers (de Grasse being seen here) were designed for the oceanic anti-submarine role with the Malafon rocket-launched torpedo system and two embarked helicopters.

SPECIFICATION	
'Tourville' (F 67) class (as built)	(3.9-in) DP guns, one Crotale
Displacement: 4,580 tons	launcher for 26 R.440 short-range
standard; 5,950 tons full load	SAMs, and one launcher for 13
Dimensions: length 152.5 m (500 ft	Malafon torpedo-carrying rockets
4 in); beam 15.3 m (50 ft 2 in);	**Electronics:** one DRBV 26 air
draught 6.5 m (21 ft 4 in)	search radar, one DRBV 51B
Propulsion: geared steam turbines	air/surface search radar, two
delivering 40560 kW (54,400 shp) to	navigation radars, one DRBC 32D
two shafts	fire-control radar, one SENIT 3
Performance: speed 31 kts;	tactical data system, one DUBV 23
endurance 9250 km (5,750 miles) at	hull sonar, and one DUBV 43
18 kts	variable-depth sonar
Armament: two triple launchers for	**Aircraft:** two Lynx helicopters
MM.38 Exocet SSMs, two 100-mm	**Complement:** 282

'Hamburg' class Guided missile destroyer

In the mid-1950s West Germany was authorised to start the process of creating armed forces, prohibited after the 1945 defeat, to participate in the country's defence under the auspices of the Western European Union and later NATO. The new West German navy started to train personnel in 1956, and in 1958 received its first major warships in the form of six World War II-vintage 'Fletcher'-class destroyers, transferred from the US Navy on five-year leases under the terms of the US's Mutual Defense Assistance Program. The ships were modernised before transfer and adapted to facilitate their operation within the context of West German operational practices. The ships were finally phased out of West German service in 1968-82.

The next type of destroyer intended for service with the West German navy was a class designed and built in West Germany but featuring weapons and sensors from several European sources.

Otherwise known as **Type 101** units, these **'Hamburg'-class** destroyers were originally to have numbered 12, and were ordered in August 1957. It then emerged that the ships could not be built to the 2,500-ton limit then imposed on West German ships, but although the Western European Union raised the limit to 6,000 tons, the West Germans then opted for a class of four ships each with a standard displacement in the order of 3,350 tons.

Built in Germany
The ships were built by Stülcken of Hamburg, being laid down in 1959-61, launched in 1960-63, and commissioned in 1964-68 as the **Hamburg**, **Schleswig-Holstein**, **Bayern** and **Hessen**. The ships were conceptually akin to the definitive destroyers of World War II, and featured West German propulsion equipment including four Wahodag boilers, fired by a maximum of 600 tons of oil, supplying steam to four sets of Wahodag-geared steam turbines driving two shafts.

In their original form, the ships were wholly conventional gun-armed destroyers with the primary armament of four 100-mm (3.9-in) L/55 guns in paired superfiring turrets fore and aft. In the period 1974-77 all four of the ships were updated: the boilers were modified to burn light oil, the lattice main mast was removed, and 'X' turret was replaced by two pairs of launchers for MM.38 Exocet anti-ship missiles.

During Exercise 'Northern Wedding' in 1986, the 'Hamburg'-class destroyer Hessen refuels from the 'Cimarron'-class fleet oiler USS Platte in the Norwegian Sea.

SPECIFICATION	
'Hamburg' class (1982)	(3.9-in) guns, four twin 40-mm AA
Displacement: 3,340 tons	guns, five 533-mm (21-in) torpedo
standard; 4,330 tons full load	tubes, and two 375-mm (14.76-in)
Dimensions: length 133.7 m (438 ft	launchers for anti-submarine rockets
9 in); beam 13.4 m (44 ft); draught	**Electronics:** one LW-04 air
5.2 m (17 ft)	surveillance radar, one DA-08
Propulsion: geared steam turbines	surface search radar, one Kelvin
delivering 53685 kW (72,000 shp) to	Hughes 14/9 navigation radar, four
two shafts	WM-45 fire-control radars (100-mm
Performance: speed 36 kts;	and 40-mm guns), and one ELAC
endurance 11000 km (6,835 miles)	1BV hull-mounted sonar
at 13 kts	**Aircraft:** none
Armament: two twin launchers for	**Complement:** 284
MM.38 Exocet SSMs, three 100-mm	

Further change came in the following year, when all the ships received an enclosed bridge for better operability in adverse conditions. Later modifications included the modification of the superstructure and the funnel caps, the replacement of the five fixed tubes (three bow and two stern) for 533-mm (21-in) heavyweight anti-submarine torpedoes by two pairs of short tubes for 324-mm (12.8-in) lightweight anti-submarine torpedoes, the

replacement of the original 40-mm AA guns in four twin mountings by more modern weapons, and the steady upgrade of the electronics.

The four ships were decommissioned in 1990-94 and replaced by 'Brandenburg'-class frigates.

The Bayern was the third of the 'Hamburg'-class ships. It was completed in July 1965 and taken out of service in December 1993 before being sold for scrap.

'Lütjens' class Guided missile destroyer

Reformed after Germany's 1945 defeat only in the mid-1950s, the West German navy was initially confined to a limited capability by the obsolescence of the ships it initially operated and the limited skills of its personnel. During the late 1950s and early 1960s, however, the capabilities of the Soviet navy increased dramatically and it became reasonable to expect the West German navy to shoulder an increasing proportion of the naval burden associated with the NATO alliance's defence of Western Europe.

Limited capability

The West Germany navy's obsolescent American-supplied 'Fletcher'-class and German-built 'Hamburg'-class destroyers, supplemented by 'Köln'-class frigates also built in West Germany, were limited in operational capability, so in May 1964 West Germany and the US signed an agreement for the purchase of **Modified Charles F. Adams'-class** guided missile destroyers to be known in West German service as

Type 103A or **'Lütjens' class**-units.

After the abandonment of the initial plan for six units of the class to be built in West German yards, during April 1965 the US Navy ordered just three ships from the Bath Iron Works of the US on behalf of the West German navy, and the vessels were laid down in 1966-67, launched in 1967-69, and commissioned in 1969-70 as the *Lütjens*, *Mölders* and *Rommel*, who were respectively sea, air and land leaders of World War II lacking in any Nazi taint and therefore politically acceptable to both West Germany and NATO.

The 'Charles F. Adams'-class destroyer had been designed as a fleet escort optimised for the anti-air and anti-submarine roles with the Tartar short/medium-range SAM and RUR-5 ASROC rocket-delivered torpedo respectively: the single-arm SAM launcher was located over the after part of the ship and supported by two fire-control radars for the simultaneous engagement of

two aerial targets, while the octuple ASROC launcher was located amidships between the forward and after superstructure blocks.

Revised standard

The West German ships were based on the standard of the US Navy's later 'Charles F. Adams'-class ships modified by the adoption of two combined masts and stacks (or 'macks') with side exhausts for the propulsion arrangement's wastes in place of the US ship's separate masts and stacks.

At the end of the 1970s the ships were taken in hand by two Kiel-based organisations, the naval dockyard and Howaldtswerke, for a major upgrade to **Type 103B** standard. The upgrades to the *Lütjens*, *Mölders* and *Rommel* were completed in 1986, 1984 and 1985 respectively, and included modification of the Mk 13 launcher for the Standard medium-range SAM and Harpoon anti-ship missile, modernisation of the fire-control system with digital rather than analogue com-

puters, and heightening of the superstructure abaft the bridge with a platform for the SPG-60 and SPQ-9 fire-control radars.

From 1993 the ships received a short-range AA

capability through the addition of two launchers for RAM missiles. The *Rommel* was taken out of service in 1998, and the other two were scheduled for retirement at the end of 2003.

By the standards of the late 1960s and early 1970s, the 'Lütjens'-class destroyer offered a excellent blend of performance and capability in the anti-air and anti-submarine roles.

The Lütjens was completed as the lead ship of the Type 103 class, in its time the most capable major surface combatant class in West German naval service.

SPECIFICATION

'Lütjens' (Type 103B) class
Displacement: 3,370 tons standard; 4,500 tons full load
Dimensions: length 133.2 m (437 ft); beam 14.3 m (47 ft); draught 6.1 m (20 ft)
Propulsion: geared steam turbines delivering 52190 kW (70,000 shp) to two shafts
Performance: speed 32 kts; endurance 8350 km (5,190 miles) at 20 kts
Armament: one launcher for 40 Standard medium-range SAMs and Harpoon SSMs, two launchers for 42 RAM short-range SAMs, two 5-in (127-mm) DP guns, one octuple launcher for eight ASROC rocket-

delivered anti-submarine torpedoes, and two triple 12.8-in (324-mm) tubes for Mk 46 lightweight anti-submarine torpedoes
Electronics: one SPS-52 3D search radar, one SPS-40 air search radar, one SPS-67 surface search radar, two SPG-51 fire-control radars, one SPQ-9 and one SPG-60 fire-control radars, one SATIR 1 action information system, FL-1800S-II ESM system, Mk 36 SRBOC decoy launcher, and DSQS-21B hull sonar
Aircraft: none
Complement: 337

'Kashin' and 'Kashin (Mod)' classes DDG

The world's first major warship class with gas turbine propulsion, the 20-ship **'Kashin' class** was produced from 1963 at the Zhdanov Shipyard, Leningrad (five units 1964-66) and at the 61 Kommuna (North) Shipyard, Nikolayev (15 units 1963-73). The last unit of what was known to the Soviets as **Project 61** was the **Sderzhanny** completed to a revised **Project 61M** design designated as the **'Kashin (Mod)' class** by NATO. This involved lengthening the hull, updating the electronics, and installing four P-15M Termit SSMs, later replaced by eight Uran SSMs, AK-630 CIWS mountings and a variable-depth sonar. Five other ships (**Ognevoy**, **Obraztsovy**, **Odarenny**, **Slavny** and **Steregushchiy**) were thus modified between 1973-80.

Explosion

In 1974 the **Orel** (ex-**Otvazhny**) of the standard type foundered in the Black Sea following a catastrophic explosion. In 1981 the **Provorny** re-entered service with the Black Sea Fleet following conversion to the trials ship for the Uragan SAM system. The other units of this *bolshoy protivolodochny korabl* (large ASW ship) type were the **Komsomolets Ukrainy**, **Krasny Kavkaz**, **Krasny Krim**, **Reshitelny**, **Skory**, **Smetlivy**, **Smely** (transferred to Poland in 1988 as the **Warszawa**),

Smyshlenny, **Soobrazitelny**, **Sposobny**, **Stroigiy** and **Stroyny**. All but two of the ships had been stricken by the end of the 20th century.

Five **'Kashin II'-class** ships were built at Nikolayev and delivered to India in batches of three and two ships (1980-83 and 1986-87) as the 'Rajput' class. These are considerably different from the Soviet ships, having only a single 76-mm (3-in) gun, four Termit-R (SS-N-2d 'Styx') SSM launchers in pairs on each side of the bridge, and a helicopter flight deck and hangar aft for one Ka-28 'Helix' ASW helicopter.

The 'Kashin' class were the world's first major ships built with gas turbine propulsion. Completed between 1964 and 1973, the 20 ships were operated in two forms as the 'Kashin' class without anti-ship missiles and the 'Kashin (Mod)' class with such weapons.

SPECIFICATION

'Kashin' class
Displacement: 4,010 tons standard; 4,750 tons full load
Dimensions: length 144 m (472 ft 5 in); beam 15.8 m (51 ft 10 in); draught 4.7 m (15 ft 5 in)
Propulsion: COGAG with four DE 59 gas turbines delivering 53700 kW (72,025 shp) to two shafts
Performance: speed 32 kts; range 7400 km (4,600 miles) at 18 kts
Armament: two twin launchers for 32 Volna (SA-N-1 'Goa') SAMs except *Provorny* one single launcher for 23 Uragan (SA-N-7 'Gadfly') SAMs, two twin 76-mm (3-in) AK-726 DP guns, two 250-mm (9.84-in) RPK-8 Zapad (RBU 6000) 12-tube ASW rocket launchers, one quintuple 533-mm (21-in) ASW torpedo tube mounting (except *Provorny*), and 20-40 mines depending on type

Electronics: (*Provorny*) one 'Head Net-C' 3D radar, one 'Top Steer' 3D radar, two 'Don Kay' navigation radars, eight 'Front Dome' SA-N-7 fire-control radars, two 'Watch Dog' ECM systems, one 'High Pole-B' IFF system, two 'Owl Screech' gun fire-control radars and one high-frequency hull sonar
Electronics: (rest) eight ships one 'Big Net' air search and one 'Head Net-C' 3D radars, or four ships two 'Head Net-A' air search radars, or *Soobrazitelny* two 'Head Net-C' 3D radars; two 'Peel Group' SAM fire-control radars, two 'Don Kay' or 'Don 2' navigation radars, two 'Owl Screech' gun fire-control radars, two 'Watch Dog' ECM systems, two 'High Pole-B' IFF systems, and one high-frequency hull sonar
Aircraft: helicopter platform only
Complement: 280

The 'Kashin' class were the world's first major ships built with gas turbine propulsion. Completed between 1964 and 1973, the 20 ships were operated in two forms as the 'Kashin' class without anti-ship missiles and the 'Kashin (Mod)' class with such weapons.

SPECIFICATION

'Kashin (Mod)' class
Displacement: 4,975 tons full load
Dimensions: length 146.2 m (479 ft 8 in); beam 15.8 m (51 ft 10 in); draught 4.7 m (15 ft 5 in)
Propulsion: as 'Kashin 'class
Performance: speed 31 kts
Armament: four P-15M Termit (SS-N-2c 'Styx') SSMs later replaced by eight Uran (SS-N-25 'Switchblade') SSMs, two twin launchers for 32 Volna (SA-N-1 'Goa') SAMs, four 30-mm AK-630 CIWS mountings, two 250-mm (9.84-in) RPK-8 Zapad 12-tube ASW rocket launchers, and one quintuple 533-mm (21-in) ASW torpedo tube

mounting
Electronics: one 'Big Net' air search radar, one 'Head Net-C' 3D radar (except *Ognevoy* two 'Head Net-A' air search radars), two 'Don Kay' navigation radars, two 'Owl Screech' gun fire-control radars, two 'Bass Tilt' CIWS fire-control radars, two 'Peel Group' SAM fire-control radars, two 'Bell Shroud' and two 'Bell Squat' ECM systems, four 16-barrel chaff and IR decoy launchers, one medium-frequency hull sonar, and one low-frequency variable-depth sonar
Aircraft: helicopter platform only
Complement: 300

The ships of the 'Kashin' class were optimised for the anti-air and anti-submarine roles, the former capability being provided by a pair of two-arm missile launchers, and the latter by the combination of two 12-tube launchers for specialised rockets and a PTA-53-61 quintuple 533-mm (21-in) torpedo tube mounting.

'Daring' class Destroyer

The eight destroyers of the **'Daring' class** were the first destroyers to be built in the UK after World War II, although their design was prepared in the closing stages of that conflict. The vessels reflected the Royal Navy's experience in six long years of war, although they marked something of a departure in that they were somewhat larger and more capable than most British destroyers other than the roughly contemporary 'Battle'-class units. Although destroyers of a similar size

were created in other countries, the Admiralty decided in 1953 that they were in effect small light cruisers rather than large destroyers.

Construction

Laid down between December 1945 and July 1948 for launch between 1949 and 1952 – and completion between February 1952 and March 1954 – the ships came from seven yards and fell into two groups. **Dainty**, **Daring**, **Defender** (ex-**Dogstar**) and **Delight** (ex-**Disdain**, ex-

Ypres) had a 220-volt DC electrical system, whereas **Decoy** (ex-**Dragon**), **Diamond**, **Diana** (ex-**Druid**) and **Duchess** had the new

440-volt AC system that was to become the Royal Navy's standard.

From 1963 the ships in the class were modernised.

HMS Dainty was built by White in the period 1945-50, and the ship was finally commissioned in February 1953.

The after 21-in (533-mm) quintuple torpedo tube mounting had already been removed in 1958-59, and now the other quintuple mounting was removed, as were the radar-controlled STAAG mountings (each with two 40-mm Bofors AA guns) in the bridge wings. The Mk 6M director was replaced by an MRS3 director, and finally the four ships with the DC electrical system received a pair of more reliable Mk 5 mountings for two 40-mm Bofors guns, while the four ships with the AC electrical system received Mk 7 mountings for single 40-mm Bofors guns.

Updated destroyer

In 1963 the *Decoy* was updated with a quadruple launcher for Seacat short-range surface-to-air missiles abaft the second funnel. This system used the radar-controlled MRS8 (Medium-Range System Mk 8) fire-control system, which was a development of the earlier CRBF (Close-Range Blind Fire) system with the predictor units replaced by a computer. The firing trials were successful, but the Admiralty decided not to standardise the system for the 'Daring'-class ships and the first installation was then removed from the *Decoy*.

The *Diana* and *Daring* were revised temporarily with a streamlined after funnel casing for a short period after their completions, at the personal wish of Admiral Lord Mountbatten, and while the change certainly improved the ships' appearances it also limited the firing arcs of the after twin Bofors mounting and the ships were returned to the standard of the other six units after a few years.

The ships served in most parts of the world where there was a British naval commitment, but this was at a time when ships' capabilities were being enhanced rapidly by emergent technologies and the 'Darings', though larger than their predecessors, still lacked the deck area and volume for the introduction of new weapons and sensors.

Replacement

The *Duchess* was transferred to the Royal Australian Navy in 1964 to replace HMAS *Voyager* (name ship of a four-strong class based on the 'Daring' class), sunk in a collision with the aircraft carrier HMAS *Melbourne*, and retained its name until stricken in 1979. In 1970 the *Decoy* and *Diana* were sold to Peru, becoming the *Ferré* and *Palacios*. The ships were upgraded with a helicopter platform in 1975, and while the former is still in service the latter was stricken in 1993. The armament of the surviving ship, which has upgraded radar, comprises six 4.5-in guns, two twin 40-mm Bofors guns in radar-controlled Breda mountings and provision for up to eight MM.38 Exocet anti-ship missiles.

The *Diamond* became a harbour training ship in 1970-81, and the other British ships were stricken in the early 1970s.

'County' class Guided-missile destroyer (DDG)

HMS London *was sold to Pakistan in February 1982 as the* Babur. *The Seaslug SAM was obsolescent and in short supply, so the system was stripped from the ship, which was also revised to handle the Sea King helicopter, and the ship's light defensive armament was increased.*

The title 'destroyer' was applied to the **'County'-class** ships to obtain Treasury approval for their construction, but they were little short of guided-missile cruisers. Built around the beam-riding Seaslug, the UK's first-generation area-defence SAM system, the 'County' class was ordered in two batches. Completed in 1962-63, the four **Batch 1** ships were *Devonshire*, *Hampshire*, *London* and *Kent*. The first was sunk as a target in 1984, the third was sold to Pakistan in 1982 as the *Babur* after the Seaslug system had been removed and has now been deleted, and the other two were deleted by the British in 1979-80. Completed in 1966-70, the **Batch 2** ships were *Fife*, *Glamorgan*, *Antrim* and *Norfolk*, modernised with Exocet SSMs in place of one of their two 4.5-in (114-mm) gun mountings and the Seaslug Mk 2 SAM with limited SSM capability.

Possessing extensive command and control facilities, the *Glamorgan* and *Antrim* served in the Falklands War, the former surviving a direct hit from an MM.38 Exocet and the latter a hit from a bomb which failed to explode.

Chilean service

Due to the 1981 British defence cuts, however, the *Norfolk* had been sold to Chile as the *Capitán Prat*, while the *Fife* was undergoing a refit which kept the vessel out of the war. Later disposals saw the departure of the *Antrim*, *Glamorgan* and *Fife* to Chile as the *Almirante Cochrane*, *Almirante Latorre* and *Almirante Blanco Encalada* in 1984, 1986 and 1987. The *Latorre* was deleted in 1998, and the other three vessels now have two octuple launchers for the Israeli Barak 1 SAM in place of the obsolete Seaslug system, in addition to the quadruple Exocet launcher: the original MM.38 missiles may be replaced by improved MM.40s. The *Cochrane* and *Blanco Encalada* have their after ends revised with a hangar and an additional flight platform for two Exocet-capable NAS 332SC Cougar medium helicopters.

HMS Glamorgan *is seen prior to the refit to repair the damage suffered in the Falklands War. Second of the four 'County Batch 2'-class ships,* Glamorgan *was revised to carry the more capable Lynx HAS.Mk 2 helicopter in place of the original Wessex HAS.Mk 3.*

'Almirante Brown' class
Guided-missile destroyer

Argentina trimmed its 1978 Meko 360 order from six to four ships after deciding to order six smaller Meko 140 frigates (the locally built 'Espora' class) in 1979. All four Meko 360s are active and based at Puerto Belgrano. The vessels can also be used as flagships.

Originally to have been a class of six, with four built in Argentina, the **Meko 360** design is based on the modularised systems concept in which each of the weapons and sensor systems is carried as a separate modular unit that can be interchanged with a replacement or newer system without the usual reconstruction that otherwise accompanies the modernisation of a ship. The final agreement signed with the West German firms of Thyssen Rheinstahl and Blohm & Voss in December 1978 was for four ships to be built in West Germany. All four, the **Almirante Brown**, **La Argentina**, **Heroina** and **Sarandi**, were commissioned in 1983-84 as the **'Almirante Brown' class**.

During the Falklands War the ships were under construction, and the British Rolls-Royce Olympus and Tyne gas turbines were embargoed for a short time. In 1996 Fennec helicopters were delivered in order to improve the ASW capability and provide over the horizon SSM targeting for the 'Almirante Brown' class.

A near sister to Argentina's vessels is the Nigerian navy's **Aradu**, ordered in 1977 as the world's first warship with modular construction. This differs from the Argentine vessels in having Otomat Mk 2 SSMs, a single Lynx Mk 89 helicopter and a CODOG propulsion system. In 2003 the ship's status was uncertain.

SPECIFICATION

'Almirante Brown' class
Displacement: 2,900 tons standard; 3,360 tons full load
Dimensions: length 125.9 m (413 ft 1 in); beam 14 m (46 ft); draught 5.8 m (19 ft)
Propulsion: Rolls-Royce COGOG with two Olympus TM3B delivering 37280 kW (50,00 shp) and two Tyne RM1C delivering 7380 kW (9,900 shp) to two shafts
Speed: 30.5 kts
Armament: two quadruple launchers for MM.40 Exocet SSMs, one Albatros octuple launcher for

24 Aspide SAMs, one 127-mm (5-in) DP gun, four twin 40-mm AA guns, two 20-mm guns, and two triple 324-mm (12.75-in) ILAS 3 tubes for 18 Whitehead A 244 anti-submarine torpedoes
Electronics: one DA-08A air/surface search radar, one ZW-06 navigation radar, one STIR fire-control radar, one AEG-Telefunken ECM suite, two SCLAR and two Dagaie decoy launchers, and one DSQS-21BZ active hull sonar
Aircraft: one or two AS 555 Fennec
Complement: 200

Above: The commissioning of the destroyers of the 'Almirante Brown' class – Sarandi is illustrated with an Alouette on the flight deck – into the Argentine navy represented a significant increase in the service's overall capabilities. Almirante Brown took part in operations in the Persian Gulf in 1990.

Right: Note the forward quadruple launcher for Exocet anti-ship missiles on the port side of Heroina: the original weapons may be upgraded to MM.40 Block II standard. A second quadruple launcher is located amidships.

'Iroquois' class Guided-missile destroyer

Ordered in 1968 as anti-submarine destroyers, the four vessels of the **'Iroquois'** class comprise **Iroquois**, **Huron**, **Athabaskan** and **Algonquin** and are a revised version of the eight Tartar SAM-equipped 'Tribal' class of general-purpose frigates cancelled in 1963. They retain the same hull design, dimensions and basic characteristics of the 'Tribals' but have enhanced ASW features such as three sonars, a

The Iroquois was commissioned in July 1972 and with its three sister ships is destined to serve on into the second decade of the 21st century as the major ASW platform of the Canadian navy. The design weight limit of the 'Iroquois' class has now been reached and the initial SAM armament of navalised AIM-7E Sparrows has been replaced by SM-2MR Standard missiles. A new class will supplement them from about 2010 to extend the capabilities of the 12 'Halifax'-class frigates.

helicopter flight deck and hangarage for two licence-built CH-124A Sea King ASW helicopters: these can also carry 12.7-mm (0.5-in) machine-guns and ESM/FLIR equipment in place of ASW gear. The weapons and sensor fit was a mixed bag with an Italian 127-mm (5-in) OTO Melara Compact gun, two four-rail launchers for the US Sea Sparrow SAM system that retracted into a deckhouse in the forward superstructure, Dutch and US electronics and a British ASW mortar. The last was the ubiquitous triple-bar-relled Mk 10 Limbo weapon.

For a new class of proposed helicopter-carrying destroyers, the *Huron* tested a vertical-launch Sparrow system in 1982, but the class did not materialise, and in the TRUMP (TRibal class Update and Modernisation Project) in 1986 the ships were revised with a Mk 41 vertical-launch system (with 29 Standard SM-2MR medium/long-range SAMs in place of the Limbo installation). The electronics were also improved with more modern, capable systems, the process yielding ships with much enhanced anti-aircraft and anti-submarine capabilities. The original main gun was replaced by a 76-mm (3-in) Super Rapid weapon from the same manufacturer and is complemented by a single Mk 15 Phalanx installation.

ASW helicopters

For the embarked helicopters the ships can carry the active acoustic-homing Mk 44 and active/passive acoustic-homing Mk 46 torpedoes. The landing decks are fitted with the Beartrap system. The 'Iroquois' class are to remain in service until at least 2010.

'Luda' class Guided-missile destroyer

The first ocean-going warships built by communist China, the **'Luda I' class** or **Type 051** destroyers were derived, despite their outward similarity to the Soviet 'Kotlin' class, from the earlier Soviet 'Neustrashimy' (NATO 'Tallinn') class, of which just a single example was built. The Chinese ships have two triple launchers for HY-2 (CSS-N-2 'Seersucker') or (in *Kaifeng* only) two quadruple launchers for C-802 (CSS-N-8 'Saccade') anti-ship missiles in place of the Soviet ship's torpedo tubes, but the design of their hull and also their armament and sensors compare poorly with those of contemporary destroyers and even with those of Taiwan's refitted ex-US ships.

Some 16 of the class were completed between 1971 and 1991 by three yards (Luda, Shanghai and Dalian), and one unit was scrapped after an explosion off Zanjiang in August 1978. The ships have possessed an underway replenishment capability since the early 1980s, but have poor command and control facilities. In 1987, *Jinan* was refitted with a hangar and flight platform aft for two Z-9A helicopters, replacing the after gun mountings and the depth-charge throwers, to become the sole **'Luda II'-class** trials vessel.

China has made several attempts to obtain Western armament and electronics for these ships, but almost all of these failed. The sole exceptions are the French Crotale octuple launcher for the HQ-7 SAM (and associated radar) in *Kaifeng*, **Dalian** and **Xian**, and the Tavitac combat data system (complete with Vega fire-control system) in some ships. The sole **'Luda III'**-class ship **Zhuhai** was completed in 1991 with four twin launchers for YJ-1 (CSS-N-4 'Sardine') SSMs, two triple tubes for Mk 46 torpedoes and much French electronic gear. CY-1 ASW missiles may be fitted on the after set of missile launchers.

Zhuhai is the sole 'Luda III' and is rumoured to have received a ballistic trajectory ASW weapon known as the CY-1 for launch from the modified rear missile launcher.

'Luhu' class Guided-missile destroyer

The design of the **Type 052** or **'Luhu'-class** destroyer was originally conceived during a time of Sino-American detente, and was therefore schemed with a high proportion of US weapons and equipment. The latter included General Electric LM2500 gas turbines that were, in the event, among the little US equipment that was in fact exported to China. It is worth noting that the gun mountings are of a new enclosed type, and that full helicopter facilities (flight platform and hangar) are located over the after part of the hull with a French helicopter-handling system.

American embargo

Following the 1989 embargo on the delivery of US military equipment to China in the aftermath of the Tianenmen Square massacre, thought was given to the use in planned future units of different gas turbines, possibly of Soviet design, but in the event the class was terminated at just the original pair of ships. The second of them is powered by gas turbines purchased from the Ukraine.

Ordered in 1985 but then delayed by the greater priority afforded to the construction of ships ordered by Thailand, these ships are the *Harbin*, laid down at the Jiangnan shipyard in November 1990 and commissioned in July 1994, and the **Qingdao**, laid down at the same yard in January 1993 and commissioned in March 1996.

By Chinese standards the two 'Luhu'-class destroyers are highly capable, and feature notably compact container launchers for two types of anti-ship missile (the YJ-8A (CSS-N-4 'Sardine') and C-802 (CSS-N-8 'Saccade'), a Crotale SAM launcher over the forward superstructure, a modern 100-mm (3.9-in) gun, and modern French electronics including radars, sonars and a combat data system.

Qingdao is the second 'Luhu' destroyer and, in the absence of the US gas turbines for which it was designed, was fitted with Ukrainian gas turbines.

'Georges Leygues' & 'Cassard' classes Guided-missile destroyers

Rated as anti-submarine frigates by the French navy, the seven ships of the **'Georges Leygues' class** were built at a leisurely rate. The first three units: **Georges Leygues**, **Dupleix** and **Montcalm** were authorised in 1971 and laid down between 1974-75. They were commissioned in 1979, 1981 and 1982, respectively. Four further vessels: **Jean De Vienne**, **Primauguet**, **La Motte-Picquet** and **Latouche-Tréville** were completed and joined the fleet between 1984-90. With 30-year service lives planned, the first three vessels will be retired during 2009-12.

The first two ships of the 'Georges Leygues' class were armed with sea-skimming Exocet anti-ship missiles of the MM.38 type, while the remaining vessels have the extended-range

MM.40. Air defence is handled by a single octuple Crotale Naval launcher on all vessels, and two Simbad twin launchers for Mistral missiles may be carried in lieu of two 20-mm AA guns on the last four ships. Two Sadral sextuple SAM launchers for the Mistral SAM and two 30-mm Breda/Mauser guns were fitted to the first four ships in the class as part of an air defence upgrade.

For their primary mission of engaging submarines, the 'Georges Leygues' ships carry a comprehensive sonar fit and are armed with L5 anti-submarine torpedoes launched from two fixed tubes. With active/passive homing, these have a range of only 9 km (5.6 miles) which is uncomfortably close enough to raise concerns regarding fratricide. The ships carry two Lynx Mk 4 heli-

copters armed with Mk 46 or Mu 90 anti-submarine torpedoes, except Georges Leygues which carries no helicopters, its hangar being converted for training. The helicopters track and monitor submarine contacts.

'Cassard' class

The two units of the **'Cassard' class**, **Cassard** and **Jean Bart** were built on the same hull design as the 'Georges Leygues' class but have diesel propulsion rather than CODOG combined diesel and gas turbine propulsion. They also have completely different armament, and the French navy rates them as anti-aircraft frigates. For this role they carry forty SM-1MR Standard long-range SAMs (which also have a limited anti-ship capability). Fired from a single Mk 13 launcher, these semi-active radar-homing missiles can intercept targets at altitudes up to 18300 m (60,000 ft) to a maximum range of 46 km (29 miles) and travel at Mach 2. The Standard missiles were taken from old DDGs and will be replaced during mid-life refits by Aster 30 missiles. Their primary anti-ship weapon is the MM.40 Exocet, and the vessels carry one AS 565MA Panther helicopter, not for anti-submarine duties but for SSM targeting.

The Jean De Vienne's primary 100-mm (3.9-in) main gun armament is situated forward of the bridge, while the powerful DBRV 26A air-search radar is seen forward of the main mast.

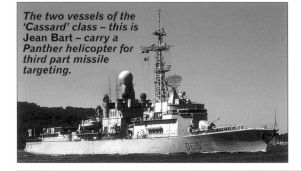
The two vessels of the 'Cassard' class – this is Jean Bart – carry a Panther helicopter for third part missile targeting.

SPECIFICATION

'Cassard' class
Displacement: 5,000 tons full load
Dimensions: length 139 m (456 ft); beam 14 m (45 ft 11 in); draught 6.5 m (21 m 3½ in)
Propulsion: four SEMT-Pialstick V280 diesels delivering 32214.2 kW (43,200 shp) to two shafts
Speed: 29 kts
Endurance: 15,186 km (9,436 miles) at 18 kts; 8,890 km (5,524 miles) at 24 kts
Complement: 244
Armament: eight MM.40 Exocet SSMs, one Mk 13 Mod 5 launcher for SM-1MR Standard SAMs (40 missiles), two Matra Sadral sextuple launchers for Mistral SAMs, one

100-mm (3.9-in) gun, and two 20-mm Oerlikon guns
Defensive systems: two 10-barrel chaff/flare launchers, Dassault LAD offboard decoys, Nixie towed torpedo decoy
Electronics: Thomson-CSF DRBJ 11B and 3D air search radar, DRBV 26C air/surface search radar, Racal DRBN 34A navigation radar, Thomson-CSF DRBC 33A fire-control radar (guns), two Raytheon SPS-51C fire-control (missiles), Thomson-Sintra DUBA 25A hull-mounted active search and attack sonar (Cassard), DUBV 24C in Jean Bart
Aircraft: one AS 565MA Panther helicopter

'Rajput' and 'Delhi' classes Guided-missile destroyers

The Indian Navy ordered five modified 'Kashin II'-class guided missile destroyers from the Soviet Union in the 1970s. Built at Nikolayev (now in Ukraine) between 1977-86, the **'Rajput' class** was commissioned between 1980-88. Their countermeasure suites were upgraded in 1993-94 but plans for further modernisation with Ukrainian assistance have now been shelved and the navy is looking to Russia for improvements instead.

Indian press reports in 2002 indicated that one of the 'Rajputs' is being fitted with the Brahmos Indo-Russian missile for its first

test-firings at sea. This 300-km (186-mile) range missile is designed to carry a nuclear warhead.

The primary anti-shipping ship weapon is the P-20M (SS-N-2D 'Styx'), a large subsonic infra-red homing missile with a range of 83 km (52 miles), it carries a 513-kg (1,131-lb) warhead. **Ranjit** and the **Ranvijay** are due to be fitted with Uran (SS-N-25 'Switchblade') missiles after refit. The ships' Volna (SA-N-1 'Goa') SAMs have a range of 31.5 km (19.6 miles) and can engage aircraft at up to 22,860 m (75,000 ft). All the 'Rajputs' are equipped with a twin 76-mm (3-in) gun for-

ward, while four twin 30-mm weapons are carried by **Rajput**, **Rana** and Ranjit, and four six-barrel 30-mm CIWS mountings are fitted to **Ranvir** and Ranvijay.

'Delhi' class

The construction of the **'Delhi' class**, the largest warships yet built in India, was delayed by the collapse of the Soviet Union and the Black Sea naval yards being taken over by the newly independent Ukraine. **Delhi** was laid down in 1987 and launched in 1991 but was not commissioned for another six years. **Mysore** was commissioned in 1999 and **Mumbai** in 2001. These are very much multinational platforms, with Russian Kashmir SAMs, Canadian sonar mountings, Dutch

With its 'Half Plate' air search radar clearly visible at the top of its main mast, Delhi lies at anchor. Eight Uran missile launchers are visible below the bridge.

radar, and French and Italian electronics systems.

Intended to serve as command ships for task forces, all three vessels have flag facilities and are designed to be able to operate in an NBC

contaminated area. The 'Delhis' sport massive blast deflectors associated with the Moskit (SS-N-22 'Sunburn') anti-shipping missiles, which they may have been intended to carry.

SPECIFICATION

'Delhi' class
Displacement: 6,700 tons full load
Dimensions: length 163 m (534 ft 10 in); beam 17 m (55 ft 10 in); draught 6.5 m (21 ft 4 in)
Propulsion: two Zorya M36E gas turbines delivering 47725 kW (64,000 shp) to two shafts
Speed: 32 kts
Endurance: 7242 km (4,500 miles) at 18 kts
Complement: 360
Armament: 16 Uran (SS-N-25 'Switchblade') SSMs, two Kashmir (SA-N-7 'Gadfly') SAM launchers, one 100-mm (3.9-in) gun, four

six-barrel 30-mm guns, five 533-mm (21-in) torpedo tubes
Defensive systems: Bharat Ajanta EW suite, TQN-2 jammer, PK-2 decoy launchers
Electronics: 'Half Plate' air/surface and Bharat/Signaal surface search radars; 'Plank Shave' (SSM), 'Front Dome' (SAM), 'Kite Screech' (100-mm) and 'Bass Tilt' (30-mm) fire-control radars, Bharat hull-mounted sonar (Delhi, Mysore), Garden Reach hull-mounted active search VDS and towed array sonar (Mumbai)
Aircraft: one Sea King or two ALH

The Rajput displays its Soviet heritage with a characteristic display of aerials and antennae. This class of ships normally deploy a single Ka-28 'Helix'.

Instead, they are armed with Uran (SS-N-25 'Switchblade'), an active radar-homing SSM with a range of 130 km (81 miles) and a 145-kg (320-lb) warhead. Four quadruple launchers are fitted, and the missiles can be launched at intervals of a few seconds.

The Kashmir SAM with which the Delhi class are equipped is the export version of the Uragan (SA-N-7 'Gadfly'). This Mach-3 semi-active homing missile has a maximum range of 25 km (15.5 miles) against aircraft and about half that against missiles. It can sustain 23 *g* manoeuvres and carries a 70-kg (154-lb) warhead. The fire-control radars can track 12 targets and illuminate and track six. There are reportedly plans to arm the 'Delhi' and 'Rajput' classes class with the Israeli Barak SAM, designed to kill sea-skimming missiles, a task for which the 'Delhis' currently carry four six-barrel 30-mm gun systems. The 'Delhi' carry a single Sea King Mk 42 or two ALH helicopters for ASW.

'Audace' class Guided-missile destroyer

Both **Ardito** and **Audace** were laid down in 1968, launched in 1971 and commissioned in 1972. Based on the previous 'Impavido' class, they are general purpose destroyers with anti-ship and anti-aircraft missiles plus anti-submarine torpedoes. They also carry a pair of torpedo-armed ASW helicopters, normally the AB 212ASW, although EH 101 operations can also be supported.

When built, the **'Audace' class** deployed two 127-mm (5-in) guns in single turrets but in both ships 'B' turret has been replaced by an octuple Selenia Albatros launcher for the semi-active radar-homing Aspide point defence missile system; long-range threats are dealt with by SM-1MR Standard SAMs launched from a single Mk 13 launcher.

Anti-ship weapon

The primary anti-ship weapon is the OTO Melara/Matra Teseo Mk 2 sea-skimming missile which has 180-km (112-mile) range, flies at a speed of Mach 0.9, and carries a 210-kg (463-lb) warhead. Four twin launchers are carried amidships, two each angled to port and starboard. Gun armament comprises a single OTO Melara 127-mm DP weapon in a forward turret; this can engage aircraft out to a range of 7 km (4.3 miles), or strike surface targets at a range of 23 km (14.3 miles). In addition, both ships are equipped with four 76-mm (3-in) OTO Melara DP weapons; *Audace* is armed with the Super Rapid version, while *Ardito* is fitted with a combination of Super Rapid and Compact guns of a similar calibre.

Ardito was modernised in 1988 and *Audace* in 1991, and stern torpedo tubes have been removed. Both ships have also added improved EW equipment, and these vessels were used for the first ship trials of the EH 101 helicopter in 1992.

Original plans for the 'Audace' class called for a total of five ships, although only two were built. Ardito carries a single 76-mm Super Rapid gun (suitable for anti-missile work) and three slower-firing 76-mm Compact weapons.

SPECIFICATION	
'Audace' class **Displacement:** 4,400 tons **Dimensions:** length 136.6 m (448 ft 2½ in); beam 14.2 m (46 ft 7 in); draught 4.6 m (15 ft 1 in) **Propulsion:** two turbines delivering 54436 kW (73,000 shp) to two shafts **Speed:** 34 kts **Endurance:** 4828 km (3,000 miles) at 20 kts **Complement:** 380 **Armament:** four twin launchers for Teseo Mk 2 SSMs, Mk 13 launcher for SM-1MR Standard SAMs (40 carried), octuple Albatros launcher for Aspide SAMs, one 127-mm (5-in)	gun, three 76-mm (3-in) Compact guns (*Ardito*), one (*Ardito*) or four (*Audace*) 76-mm Super Rapid guns, two triple 324 (12.75-in) tubes for Mk 46 ASW torpedoes **Defensive systems:** two Breda 20-barrel chaff launchers, SLQ-25 Nixie towed torpedo decoy **Electronics:** SPS-52C and SPS-768 air search radars, SPS-774 air/surface search and SPQ-2D surface search radars, SPG-76 and SPG-51 fire-control radars, CWE 610 hull-mounted active search/attack sonar **Aircraft:** two AB 212ASW or EH 101 helicopters.

'De la Penne' class Guided-missile destroyer

The guided-missile destroyers **Animoso** and **Ardimentoso** were laid down in 1986 and 1988 respectively. They were launched in 1989 and 1991 and both commissioned in 1993. The previous year the Italian navy had decided to re-name both of the ships after Italian naval heroes of World War II. *Animoso* and *Ardimentoso* were thus renamed **Luigi Durand de la Penne** and **Francesco Mimbelli** respectively.

These multi-role destroyers have served in the Adriatic during NATO operations in Bosnia and in 2000 were fitted with the OTO Melara/Matra Milas anti-submarine system, which can launch a Mk 46 or Mu 90 torpedo out to a range of 55 km (34 miles). Their primary anti-ship weapon is the Teseo Mk 2, a sea-skimmer with a range of 180 km (112 miles) and a 210-kg (463-lb) warhead. The weapons are due to be replaced by the Teseo Mk 3, with radar/IR-homing to a range of 300 km (186 miles). The ships are also fitted with one OTO Melara 127-mm (5-in) main gun mounting forward (taken from the 'B' turrets of the 'Audace' class), and three OTO Melara Super Rapid 76-mm (3-in) DP guns as secondary armament. Six 324-mm (12.75-in) torpedo tubes are fitted to deploy further Mk 46 torpedoes with a 11-km (6.8-mile) range. The ships can also deploy either AB 212ASW, SH-3D Sea King or EH 101 helicopters for stand-off ASW missions.

Air defence weapons

For the air defence role, these DDGs are armed with a total of 40 SM-1MR Standard missiles, which are launched from a single-arm launcher. The vessels may be upgraded to carry the SM-2 Standard missile. For point-defence, a single Albatros Mk 2 octuple automatic-loading launcher is used to deploy the Aspide semi-active radar-homing SAM, of which 16 are carried. Aspide has a range of 13 km (8 miles) flying at a speed of Mach 2.5.

The **Luigi Durand de la Penne** *at Sydney. These ships are protected by Kevlar armour. Note the octuple Aspide launcher forward of the bridge.*

SPECIFICATION	
'De la Penne' class **Displacement:** 4,300 tons standard; 5,400 tons full load **Dimensions:** length 147.7 m (484 ft 7 in); beam 16.1 m (52 ft 10 in); draught 8.6 m (28 ft 2½ in) **Propulsion:** CODOG; two FIAT gas turbines delivering 40267.8 kW (54,000 shp) plus two GMT diesels developing 9395.8 kW (12,600 shp) to two shafts **Speed:** 31 kts **Range:** 12964 km (8,056 miles) at 18 kts **Armament:** four or eight OTO Teseo Mk 2 (two or four twin) SSMs, one Mk 13 launcher for SM-1MR Standard SAMs, one Albatros Mk 2 SAM launcher for Aspide SAMs, one OTO Melara/Matra Milas anti-submarine missile launcher with	Mk 46 Mod 5 or Mu 90 torpedoes, two triple B-515 324-mm (12.75-in) torpedo tubes with Mk 46 torpedoes, one OTO Melara 127-mm (5-in) gun, three OTO Melara 76-mm (3-in) Super Rapid guns **Countermeasures:** two CSEE Sagaie chaff launchers, one SLQ-25 Nixie anti-torpedo system **Electronics:** SPS-52 long range air search radar, SPS-768 air search radar, SPS-774 air/surface search radar, SPS-702 surface search radar, four SPG-76 fire-control radars, two SPG-51G fire-control radars, SPN-748 navigation radar, DE 1164 low-frequency bow and variable depth sonar **Complement:** 377 **Aircraft:** two AB 212ASW, SH-3D or EH 101 helicopters

'Murasame' class Guided-missile destroyer

SPECIFICATION

'Murasame' class

Ships in class: Murasame (DD 101), Harusame (DD 102), Yuudachi (DD 103), Kirisame (DD 104), Inazuma (DD 105), Samidare (DD 106), Ikazuchi (DD 107), Akebono (DD 108) and Ariake (DD 109)

Displacement: 4,400 tons standard; 5,200 tons maximum

Dimensions: length 150.8 m (494 ft 9 in); beam 17 m (55 ft 9 in); draught 5.2 m (17 ft 1 in)

Propulsion: two General Electric LM2500 gas turbines delivering 64120 kW (86,000 shp) and two Rolls-Royce Spey SM1C gas turbines delivering 20130 kW (27,000 shp) to two shafts

Speed: 30+ kts

Armament: Mk 41 VLS for ASROC (two 8-cell modules on ships DD 101 to DD 108, four 8-cell modules on Ariake), 16-cell Mk 48 VLS for RIM-7M Sea Sparrow SAMs, eight SSM-1B Harpoon SSMs, one 76-mm (3-in) OTO Melara Compact gun, two 20-mm Phalanx Mk 15 CIWS mountings, and two 324-mm (12.75-in) Mk 32 Mod 14 triple tubes for Mk 46 Mod 5 anti-submarine torpedoes

Electronics: OPS-28 surface search radar, OPS-24 3D air search radar, OPS-2 navigation radar, two Type 2-31 fire-control radars, URN-25 TACAN radio beacon, UPX-29 AIMS Mk XII IFF, OQS-5 hull-mounted active search sonar, OQR-1 (SQR-19) TACTASS towed-array passive search sonar, four SRBOC 6-barrel fixed Mk 36 Mod 12 chaff/flare decoys, and SLQ-25 Nixie towed decoy

Aircraft: one SH-60J Seahawk

Complement: 165

In the 1991 fiscal year, the Tokyo yard of Ishikawajima Harima Heavy Industries began work on nine **'Murasame'-class** ships officially designated as guided-missile destroyers for the JMSDF (Japanese Maritime Self-Defence Force). It is debatable whether these ships are really destroyers or large frigates, but there is no argument that that they are escort ships and constitute a major component of the JMSDF. The first ship of the class, **Murasame (DD 101)** was laid down in 1993 and was commissioned in 1996.

The vessels of the 'Murasame' class are multi-purpose ships in which considerable effort was devoted in the design phase to the maximised automation of onboard systems wherever possible. This effort paid off in the reduction of the crew to 165 sailors, who thus enjoy the benefits of improved crew accommodation spaces. The ships are powered by four gas turbines for a maximum speed of 30 kts or more, and at a cruising speed of 18 kts the range is 8350 km (5,190 miles).

US weapon systems

Under contract to Lockheed Martin of the US, Mitsubishi Heavy Industries assembled and tested the primary armament for the 'Murasame'-class ships, namely the Mk 41 Vertical-Launch System (VLS). Mounted below deck in the bows of the ship, this system is capable of launching several types of missile, though only the Vertical Launch Anti-Submarine Rocket (VL ASROC) is carried in the 'Murasame' class. The first eight ships of the class were each fitted with two eight-cell modules, but in 1998 it was decided to double this capability to four modules on the ninth ship of the class, the **Ariake (DD 109)**.

A 16-cell Mk 48 VLS unit is located amidships, and this carries the RIM-7M Sea Sparrow surface-to-air missile. A 76-mm (3-in) OTO Melara Compact main gun is mounted forward of the VLS unit on the forecastle. Eight Harpoon anti-ship missiles are mounted amidships, as are six torpedo tubes, in the form of two triple units, to fire the Mk 46 Mod 5 anti-submarine torpedo. For self defence, two 20-mm Close-in Weapon Systems (CIWS) are mounted, one forward of the bridge and the other above the helicopter hangar.

With an aft landing pad and hangar, the 'Murasame'-class ships are each able to carry, house, maintain and operate a single SH-60J helicopter in the anti-submarine warfare role.

With new Japanese legislation directed against terrorism, the JMSDF has deployed ships in non-combat military support roles to the Indian Ocean. On 9 November 2001, the **Kirisame (DD 104)** was one of three JMSDF ships deployed, with the primary mission being to gather information and intelligence on routes to ferry supplies

DD 109 is the Ariake, the last and most formidably equipped of the Japanese Maritime Self-Defence Force's nine 'Murasame'-class destroyers.

into the area.

In November 2002, Japanese Self-Defence Forces participated in Exercise Keen Sword 2003 in conjunction with US military forces. A number of JMSDF ships including the Ariake, which was integrated into the USS Kitty Hawk's carrier battle group, took part in this bilateral co-operation training exercise for regional conflict.

'Hatsuyuki' class Guided-missile destroyer

This 12-strong class of destroyers was authorised at the end of the 1970s for the Japanese navy, or Japanese Maritime Self-Defence Force as it has styled itself since being re-established in the 1950s. The gas turbine-powered 'Hatsuyuki' class was created as a multi-purpose design incorporating a balanced anti-air, anti-ship and anti-submarine sensor and armament fit. The first seven ships were built with weight-saving aluminium alloy for their bridge structures and other upperworks, but later vessels used steel which led to a slight increase in displacement. The name-ship was laid down in March 1979, launched in November 1980 and commissioned in May 1982; the last of the class was laid down in 1984 and commissioned in 1987. In 1992 the **Shirayuki (DD 123)** became the first to be fitted with the 20-mm Phalanx CIWS (Close-in Weapons System): this short-ranged but fast-reacting anti-missile system was progressively fitted to the rest of the class during the 1990s. Other improvements include the Canadian Beartrap helicopter landing system and state-of-the-art ECM equipment to the last three ships of the class. The **Shimayuki (DD 133)** was converted to a training ship (**TV 35**) in 1999 and now has a lecture theatre added to the helicopter hangar.

The 'Hatsuyuki' class are capable all-round warships fitted with fin stabilisers.

SPECIFICATION

'Hatsuyuki' class

Ships in class: Hatsuyuki (DD 122), Shirayuki (DD 123), Mineyuki (DD 124), Sawayuki (DD 125), Hamayuki (DD 126), Isoyuki (DD 127), Haruyuki (DD 128), Yamayuki (DD 129), Matsuyuki (DD 130), Setoyuki (DD 131) and Asayuki (DD 132)

Displacement: 2,950 or, from DD 129, 3,050 tons standard; 3,700 or, from DD 129, 3,800 tons full load

Dimensions: length 130 m (426 ft 6 in); beam 13.6 m (44 ft 7 in); draught 4.2 m (13 ft 9 in) or, in DD 129-132, 4.4 m (14 ft 5 in)

Propulsion: COGOG with two Rolls-Royce Olympus TM3B gas turbines delivering 36535 kW (49,000 shp) and two Rolls-Royce Tyne RM1C gas turbines delivering 7380 kW (9,900 shp) to two shafts

Speed: 30 kts

Range: 12975 km (8,065 miles) at 20 kts

Armament: two quadruple Harpoon launchers, one Mk 29 Sea Sparrow SAM launcher, one Mk 112 octuple ASROC ASW torpedo launcher, one 76-mm (3-in) OTO Melara Compact gun, two Mk 15 20-mm Phalanx CIWS, two triple Type 68 324-mm (12.75-in) tubes for Mk 46 Mod 5 anti-submarine torpedoes

Electronics: OPS-14B air search radar, ORS-18 surface search radar, Type 2-12A SAM fire-control and Type 2-21/21A gun fire-control radars, OQS-4A (SQS-23) bow-mounted active search/attack sonar, OQR-1 TACTASS passive sonar in some, and Mk 36 SRBOC chaff/flare launchers

Aircraft: one SH-60J Seahawk

Complement: 195-200

The 'Hatsuyuki' destroyers, seen in the form of the Isoyuki (DD 127), are optimised for the anti-ship and anti-submarine roles with Harpoon and ASROC.

Their primary anti-ship armament is the Harpoon missile which has a range of some 130 km (80 miles): flying just above the sea, it delivers a 500-lb (227-kg) warhead at a speed of Mach 0.9. To attack submarines, the ships carry the widely used ASROC system that can drop a Mk 46 homing torpedo up to 9 km (6 miles) from the ship. The 'Hatsuyuki'-class ships do not carry a long-range anti-aircraft weapon, built as they were to engage surface and sub-surface threats under cover of the US or Japanese air forces. Their Sea Sparrow SAMs have a range of 15 km (9 miles), while the

The Asayuki (DD 132) was the penultimate unit of the 'Hatsuyuki' class, and was built by Sumitomo, one of five shipyards involved in the building programme.

CIWS is purely a point-defence system intended primarily for the engagement and destruction of anti-ship missiles.

'Asagiri' class Guided-missile destroyer

SPECIFICATION

'Asagiri' class
Ships in class: *Asagiri* (DD 151), *Yamagiri* (DD 152), *Yuugiri* (DD 153), *Amagiri* (DD 154), *Hamagiri* (DD 155), *Setogiri* (DD 156), *Sawagiri* (DD 157) and *Umigiri* (DD 158)
Displacement: 3,500 tons standard; 4,200 tons full load
Dimensions: length 137 m (449 ft 6 in), beam 14.6 m (47 ft 11 in); draught 4.5 m (14 ft 9 in)
Propulsion: COGAG with four Rolls-Royce Spey SM1A gas turbines delivering 39515 kW (53,000 shp) to two shafts
Speed: 30 kts
Armament: two quadruple Harpoon launchers, one Mk 29 Sea Sparrow SAM octuple launcher with 20 missiles, one octuple

Mk 112 launcher for ASROC ASW rockets with Mk 46 Neartip torpedoes, one 76-mm (3-in) OTO Melara Compact gun, two Mk 15 20-mm Phalanx CIWS, two Type 68 324-mm (12.75-in) triple tubes for Mk 46 ASW torpedoes
Electronics: OPS-14C (or from DD 155 OPS-24) air search radar, OPS-28C (or DD 153-154 OPS-28Y) surface search radar, Type 2-22 gun fire-control radar, Type 2-12G (or from DD 155 Type 2-12E) SAM fire-control radar, OQS-4A hull-mounted active search/attack sonar, OQR-1 towed-array sonar, two SRBOC 6-barrel chaff/flare launchers, and one SLQ-51 Nixie or Type 4 towed anti-torpedo decoy
Aircraft: one SH-60J Seahawk
Complement: 220

The eight guided-missile destroyers of the **'Asagiri' class** were laid down between 1985 and 1988, and were commissioned between 1988 and 1991. Like the destroyers of the preceding 'Hatsuyuki' class, they are intended primarily for the engagement of surface or sub-surface targets, although the ships do also carry a powerful suite of point-defence systems to defeat incoming missiles or aircraft. The ships' primary anti-ship weapon is the Harpoon medium-range surface-to-surface missile, and their main anti-submarine weapon is the

Mk 46 Mod 5 Neartip lightweight homing torpedo delivered either by the ship-launched ASROC rocket, torpedo tubes or by the ships' embarked helicopter. When first commissioned, the ships each carried one HSS-2B Sea King helicopter, but these have now been replaced by the SH-60J Seahawk.

The Asagiri (DD 151) is the name-ship of this eight-strong class of well-armed and well-equipped anti-ship and anti-submarine destroyers.

The 'Asagiri' class destroyers suffered from a serious design fault: hot gases from the funnels damaged the electronic systems on the main mast and also gave the ships a very pronounced IR signature. The main mast was therefore heightened and offset to port, the forward funnel was offset to port and the after funnel to starboard. This was undertaken on the last four as they were completing. These vessels also carry improved electronics including a data link to their helicopter, a system that was later retrofitted to the earlier ships.

Below: The original position of the main mast, just to the rear of the funnels for the large quantities of hot exhaust gases from the four gas turbines, was poor.

Above: The revision of the main mast and after funnel arrangement saw the former offset to port and the latter to starboard. Pictured is Yuugiri (DD 153).

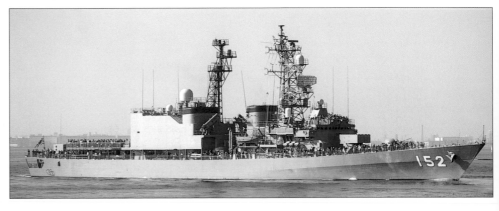

'Haruna' and 'Shirane' class
Anti-submarine warfare destroyers

Shirane as completed in the early 1980s. The two 'Shirane'-class destroyers are distinguishable from the preceding 'Harunas' by their twin 'macks' – combined radar masts and smoke stacks.

The **'Haruna' class** and follow-on improved **'Shirane' class** were the world's first destroyer-sized warships designed to carry and operate three large Sea King-sized ASW helicopters. Both ship classes were completed with strong ASW armaments, though as built they were weaker than most contemporary Western designs in both anti-air and anti-surface warfare systems.

To help rectify these shortcomings, both classes were refitted in the late 1980s and early 1990s. The destroyers had 20-mm Phalanx CIWS and Sea Sparrow missile systems added to improve anti-aircraft and anti-missile point defence.

The 'Haruna' class, comprising **Haruna** (DD 141) and **Hiei** (DD 142), were completed in 1973 and 1974. They have continuous superstructures. Their single combined radar mast and funnel (known as a 'mack') offset to port allow space for the third helicopter in the hangar.

Improved
The later 'Shirane'-class units, **Shirane** (DD 143) and **Kurama** (DD 144), were commissioned in 1980 and 1981 respectively.

They have a broken superstructure with two 'macks', one offset to port atop the main superstructure forward, and the other atop the detached hangar aft. Larger than their predecessors, they were fitted with towed-array sonars in the early 1990s.

Helicopters
For landing helicopters in bad weather, the ships are fitted with the Canadian Bear Trap haul-down system. To reduce their underwater radiated noise levels from the main propulsion machinery they are equipped with the 'Masker' bubble-generating system. This forms a continuous curtain of minute air bubbles over the parts of the hull beneath the machinery spaces, with the bubbles acting as a sound-damping layer.

Haruna was completed in 1973. Its ability to carry three helicopters made it one of the most capable ASW destroyers of its time.

SPECIFICATION

'Shirane' class
Displacement: 5,200 tons standard and 6,800 tons full load
Dimensions: length 158.8 m (521 ft); beam 17.5 m (57 ft 5 in); draught 5.3 m (17 ft 5 in)
Machinery: geared steam turbines delivering 52200 kW (70,000 shp) to two shafts
Speed: 32 kts (59 km/h; 37 mph)
Aircraft: three Mitsubishi-Sikorsky SH-60J Seahawk ASW helicopters
Armament: one octuple ASROC Mk 112 ASW missile launcher (24 missiles carrying Mk 46 NEARTIP lightweight torpedoes); two triple 324-mm (12.75-in) Type 68 ASW torpedo tubes armed with Mk 46 Mod 5 NEARTIP ASW torpedoes); two single FMC 127-mm (5-in) DP guns; one octuple Sea Sparrow SAM launcher; two 20-mm Phalanx CIWS
Electronics: one OPS-12 3D radar, one OPS-28 surface-search radar, OFS-2D navigation radar, Signaal WM-25 missile fire-control radar, two Type 72 gun fire-control radars, one ORN-6C TACAN, comprehensive ESM and countermeasures/decoy suite, OQS-101 bow-mounted sonar, SQR-18A passive towed-array sonar, and SQS-35(J) active/passive variable depth sonar

'Tachikaze' and 'Hatakaze' class Anti-air warfare destroyers

During the early 1970s, the Japanese Maritime Self-Defence Force needed to improve its medium-range area defence SAM capabilities, and thus laid down the three **'Tachikaze'-class** ships at three-yearly intervals from 1973. These vessels are the **Tachikaze** (DDG 168), **Asakaze** (DDG 169) and **Sawakaze** (DDG 170), which commissioned in 1976, 1979 and 1982 respectively.

Missile fit
Each ship carries one single-rail Mk 13 launcher for the Standard SM-1MR missile, allowing the ships to engage aircraft targets out to a range of nearly 50 km (31 miles). The altitude envelope of the SM-1MR enables aircraft and missiles to be intercepted at heights between 40 m (131 ft) and

18000 m (59,055 ft).

The two dual-purpose guns can also be used for air defence as well as for engaging surface targets, and surface attack capability was enhanced in the 1980s by the addition of Harpoon anti-ship missiles, fired from the Mk 13 launcher. All three ships received Phalanx CIWS at the same time.

These vessels were designed almost exclusively as anti-aircraft platforms. No helicopter facilities are provided, and the ASW armament is confined to ASROC missiles and Mk 46

Right: The 'Tachikaze'-class destroyer Asakaze soon after its commissioning. The first two ships serve with the 64th DesDiv at Yokosuka; Sawakaze is part of the 62nd DesDiv at Sasebo.

'Tachikaze' class
Displacement: (DDG 168 and 169) 3,850 tons standard and 4,800 tons full load; (DDG 170) 3,950 tons standard and 4,800 tons full load
Dimensions: length 1430 m (469 ft 2 in); beam 14.3 m (46 ft 11 in); draught 4.6 m (15 ft 1 in)
Machinery: geared steam turbines delivering 52200 kW (70,000 shp) to two shafts
Speed: 32 kts (59 km/h; 37 mph)
Armament: one single-rail Mk 13 launcher able to fire both Standard SM-1 MR and Harpoon missile (standard load 40 missiles); two single 127-mm (5-in) DP guns; two 20-mm (0.8-in) Phalanx CIWS

mountings; one octuple ASROC ASW missile launcher (only DDG 170 carries reloads), and two triple Type 68 324-mm (12.75-in) ASW torpedo tubes with six Mk 46 Mod 5 torpedoes
Electronics: one SPS-52B/C 3D radar, one OPS-110 air-search radar, one OPS-160 (OPS-28 in DDG 170) surface-search radar, two SPG-51C missile fire control radars, two Type 72 gun fire control radars, two SATCOM communications systems, comprehensive counter-measures suite, four Mk 36 Super RBOC chaff launchers, and one OQS-3A hull sonar
Complement: 250-270

Above: Larger than the 'Tachikazes', Hatakaze is part of the 61st DesDiv at Yokosuka. Shimakaze is based at Maizuru with the 63rd DesDiv.

self-defence torpedoes. In order to save on construction costs the class adopted the propulsion plant and machinery of the 'Haruna' class of helicopter-carrying ASW destroyers.

Soon after the last of the 'Tachikazes' was completed, work started on the first of two slightly larger air-defence destroyers of the **'Hatakaze' class**. The **Hatakaze** (DDG 171) and the **Shimakaze** (DDG 172) were commissioned in 1986 and 1988 respectively.

They have a similar armaments fit to the preceding vessels, though their increased size – the 'Hatakazes' are eight metres (26 feet) longer and

displace about 700 tons more than the 'Tachikazes' – means that they can carry two quadruple Harpoon launchers, which frees magazine space for SAMs. They also have platforms capable of accepting a single SH-60J Seahawk helicopter.

'Kongou' class Advanced anti-air warfare destroyer

For much of the last four decades, the primary focus of the Japanese Maritime Self-Defence Force has been on anti-air and anti-submarine warfare. During the 1980s and 1990s, the increasing threat from China, together with the reduction of the US military presence in the region, meant that Japan was forced to take a more active military role in Asian waters.

To meet this new role a new **'Kongou' class** of guided-missile destroyers has been commissioned. These anti-aircraft vessels are by far the most capable of their type in the region.

AEGIS system
Based loosely upon the US Navy's 'Arleigh Burke' class, the 'Kongous' have been built to mercantile instead of warship standards. However, they are slightly bigger than the American ships, and carry an improved lightweight version of the AEGIS air defence system.

AEGIS integrates weapons, radar and fire control into one highly efficient system, capable of controlling a fleet battle above and below the surface.

First proposed in the JSDF's FY 87 programme, **Kongou** (DDG 173) was commissioned in 1993. It was followed by **Kirishima** (DDG 174) in 1995, **Myouko** (DDG 175) in 1996 and **Choukai** (DDG 176) in 1998. The main external difference between these vessels and the 'Burkes' is that the 'Kongous' have a longer flush deck at the stern, making it easier to handle helicopters up to the size of the SH-60J Seahawk or larger.

The 'Kongous' are an extremely important element in the protection of Japan. Their sophisticated long-range air defence capability is seen as a national asset beyond their duty to protect the fleet. Even though National Defense Program Outline or NDPO

has called for a slimming in Japanese Self-Defence force levels, it has also called for an expansion in its counter-terrorism capabilities. To its cost, the world has learned that air defences are a vital asset in the war against the terrorists.

Above: The characteristic octagonal phased array antennae of the SPY-1 radar system identify the Kongou as an AEGIS-equipped vessel. There are four arrays, giving 360° coverage.

Below: The 'Kongous' have a longer helicopter flight deck than the closely-related 'Arleigh Burke' class, but like the American destroyers they have no permanent aircraft facilities.

'Kongou' class
Displacement: 7,250 tons standard and 9,485 tons full load
Dimensions: length 1610 m (528 ft 3 in); beam 21 m (68 ft 10 in); draught 6.2 m (20 ft 4 in)
Machinery: four General Electric LM 2500 gas turbines delivering 76210 kW (102,160 shp) to two shafts
Speed: 30 kts (55 km/h; 34 mph)
Armament: two Mk 41 VLS launchers with a total of 90 Standard SM-2MR SAMs and ASROC ASW missiles; two quad Harpoon launchers; one OTO-Melara 127-mm (5-in) compact DP

gun; two Mk 15 Phalanx; two triple HOS 302 torpedo tubes with Mk 46 Mod 5 Neartip ASW torpedoes
Electronics: one SPY-1D phased array air search 3-D system with four arrays; one OPS 28 surface search, one OPS-20 navigation radar, three SPG-62 fire-control radars; AEGIS combat data system, WSC-3 SATCOM; one SQQ-28 helicopter datalink; comprehensive ESM/ECM/counter-measures suite; one OQS 102 bow-mounted active sonar, one OQR-2 passive towed array
Complement: 307

'Kara' class
Large anti-submarine ship

Although classed by some authorities as a destroyer thanks to its primary anti-submarine mission, the powerful 'Kara' class is cruiser-sized, and carries a heavy and versatile weapons mix.

Built at the 61 Kommuna, Nikolayev North Shipyard between 1971 and 1977, the seven units of the **'Nikolayev' class** (known as the **'Kara' class** by NATO) were intended to boost the Soviet fleet's blue-water anti-submarine capability. Cruiser-sized ships, they were rated as BPKs (*Bolshoy Protivolodochnyy Korabl*, or large anti-submarine ship) by

the Soviets, and were considered as destroyers by function.

The 'Kara' is an enlarged gas turbine-powered refinement of the steam-powered 'Kresta II' design, with improved anti-aircraft and anti-submarine capability. The class was commissioned between 1973 and 1980 for service primarily in the Black Sea, as well as in the

Mediterranean and the Pacific. Extensive command and control facilities meant that the 'Karas' often acted as hunter-killer task group leaders.

A single gas-turbine exhaust funnel dominated the large superstructure. On the ship's stern was a helicopter landing pad with a hangar partially recessed below the flight deck. To stow the ASW helicopter the hanger roof hatch and doors had to be opened; the helicopter was pushed in and then lowered to the deck via an elevator.

Nuclear armed

The ship's Shtorm (SA-N-3 'Goblet') and Rastrub (SS-N-14 'Silex') ASW missiles have secondary anti-ship capabilities, the former having a 25-kiloton nuclear warhead available in place of the normal 150-kg (331-lb) HE type. At the height of the Cold War it is believed that all Soviet ships with dual-capable weapon systems had at least 25 per cent of their missiles equipped with nuclear warheads while at sea.

Nikolayev was transferred to the Ukraine after the fall of the USSR, and was scrapped in India in 1994. **Ochakov** went into reserve in the

A 'Kara'-class cruiser underway shows the incredible clutter of search, navigation and fire-control radars together with missiles and guns. This appearance is characteristic of large Soviet navy warships commissioned in the 1970s and 1980s.

Pacific in the late 1990s. **Kerch** went into refit in the late 1990s, and is the only member of the class still nominally in commission, serving as flagship of the Black Sea Fleet.

Test ship

Azov was the trials ship for the new generation SA-N-6 vertical-launch SAM and its associated 'Top Dome' fire

control radar. She remained in the Black Sea after one Shtorm and 'Headlight' fire control radar combination had been replaced by the new systems. **Petropavlovsk** is in reserve in the Pacific, and is likely to be scrapped, a fate that **Tashkent** has already met. **Vladivostok** is in reserve in the Black Sea.

SPECIFICATION	
'Kara' class **Type:** large ASW ship **Displacement:** 8,200 tons standard and 9,700 tons full load **Dimensions:** length 173 m (567 ft 7¼ in); beam 18.60 m (61 ft); draught 6.70 m (22 ft) **Propulsion:** COGAG gas turbine arrangement delivering 89485 kW (120,000 shp) to two shafts **Speed:** 34 kts **Aircraft:** one Ka-27 'Helix' ASW helicopter **Armament:** two quadruple Rastrub (SS-N-14 'Silex') ASW launchers with eight missiles, two twin Shtorm (SA-N-3 'Goblet') SAM launchers with 72 missiles (except in *Azov* which has one Shtorm system plus one Fort (SA-N-6 'Grumble') system with 24 missiles), two twin Osa-M (SA-N-4 'Gecko') SAM launchers with 40 missiles, two twin 76-mm	(3-in) DP guns, four 30-mm AK-630 six-barrel CIWS, two 12-barrel RBU 6000 ASW rocket launchers, two RBU 1000 ASW rocket launchers **Electronics:** one MR-700F Pobderezovik 'Flat Screen' 3D air search radar, one MR-310U Angara-M 'Head Net-C' 3D search radar, two 'Don Kay' or 'Palm Frond' navigation radars, two Grom 'Head Light-B' SA-N-3 and SS-N-14 fire-control radars, two MPZ-301 'Pop Group' SA-N-4 fire control radars, two 'Owl Screech' 76-mm fire-control radars, two 'Bass Tilt' CIWS fire control radars, 'High Pole-A' and 'High Pole-B' IFF; one 'Side Globe' ESM suite, one 'Bell' series or one 'Rum Tub' ECM suite, one MG-332 Titan-2T 'Bull Nose' hull mounted sonar, one MG-325 Vega 'Mare Tail' variable depth sonar **Complement:** 525

'Kirov' class
Large guided-missile cruiser

In December 1977 the Baltic Shipyard in Leningrad launched the largest warship other than aircraft carriers built by any nation since World War II. Commissioned into Soviet fleet service in 1980, **Kirov** was assigned the RKR (*Raketnyy Kreyser*, or missile cruiser) designation by the Soviets and a CGN designation by the Americans. Planned initially to find and engage enemy missile submarines, it became a much more capable warship when it was equipped with the long-range P-700 Granit anti-ship missile. In appearance and firepower *Kirov* is more like a battlecruiser than a normal missile cruiser.

Nuclear/steam

Its powerplant is unique in being a combined nuclear and steam system. Two reactors are coupled to oil-fired

boilers that superheat the steam produced in the reactor plant to increase the power output available during high-speed running.

Missile 'farm'

Most of the weapons systems are located forward of the massive superstructure. The stern is used to house machinery and a below-deck helicopter hangar, which accesses the flight deck via a lift. Up to five Kamov Ka-25 'Hormone' or Ka-27 'Helix' helicopters can be accommodated in the hangar, though a normal complement is three.

The helicopters are a mix of ASW and missile-guidance/Elint variants. The latter provide target data for the main battery of 20 Granit (SS-N-19 'Shipwreck') Mach-2.5 anti-ship cruise missiles, located below decks forward in 45° angled

The largest surface-action fighting ships built for any navy since World War II, the 'Kirov'-class battlecruisers carry heavy armament beneath the hatches on their foredeck. However, they are very expensive to crew and maintain, and have spent relatively short periods at sea.

launch tubes.

Other weapons and systems vary from ship to ship. Area air defence is provided by vertical launch Fort (SA-N-6) missiles, housed in 12 eight-round rotary launchers forward of the SS-N-19 bins. Close-in air defence is handled by a mix of Osa-M

(SA-N-4 'Gecko') missiles, 30-mm CIWS mountings and 130-mm (5-in) DP guns. The main ASW armament is a reloadable twin Rastrub (SS-N-14 'Silex') ASW missile-launcher with associated variable-depth low-frequency sonar aft and a low-frequency bow sonar.

Later ships carry 10 Vodopod (SS-N-16 'Stallion') torpedo-carrying missiles.

Flagships

The sheer size of the ships mean that they have plenty of space for a command, control and communications (C^3) outfit, and could serve

CRUISERS AND DESTROYERS

The primary 'Kirov' mission in time of war would have been to destroy US Navy carrier battle groups with Granit nuclear-tipped missiles.

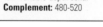

Frunze, renamed Admiral Lazarev in 1992, served with the Soviet Pacific Fleet. The comprehensive command and communications facilities it carries meant that it was often used as a fleet flagship.

as effective fleet flagships. One of their intended missions was to act as a task group command escort to the aircraft carriers being planned by the Soviet navy.

Five vessels were laid down between 1974 and 1989, but only four were completed. The first ships were named after heroes of the Bolshevik revolution, but with the end of the Communist state all have been renamed. **Admiral Ushakov** (ex-*Kirov*) was inactive through most of the 1990s following a reactor accident, and has been cannibalised to provide parts. **Admiral Lazarev** (ex-*Frunze*) has been out of service for a decade, and is destined to be scrapped. The **Admiral Nakhimov** (ex-*Kalinin*) was refitted in 1994, but did not go to sea for more than three years from 1997. The *Nakhimov* is the only 'Kirov' on the active list in late 2001. *Petr Veliky* was launched in 1989, but was not completed until 1998, and was laid up soon after completing sea trials. Lack of funds also meant that the fifth ship, the *Kuznetsov*, was scrapped before launch, the name being assigned to a carrier.

'Slava' class Missile cruiser

The Slava (now known as the Moskva) seen during the first foray into the Mediterranean in 1983. As with most large vessels, these powerful cruisers are too expensive for the cash-strapped Russian navy to keep in operation.

The first of the 'Kara' follow-on class was first seen outside the Black Sea in 1983. At first designated **BlackCom 1** by Western intelligence, and later known as the **'Krasina' class**, these powerful vessels are now known as the **'Slava' class** after the original name of the lead ship. *Slava* (now **Moskva**), was laid down at the Nikolayev Shipyard in 1976. Launched in 1979, *Slava* entered service in 1983 after extensive trials. By 1990 three of the class were in service, with a fourth under construction.

Surface action

Possibly designed as a less-expensive complement to the massive 'Kirov'-class battlecruisers, the 'Slavas' are primarily surface action vessels, designated RKR (*Raketnyy Kreyzer*, or missile cruiser). Their primary weapons are 16 P-500 Bazalt (SS-N-12 'Sandbox') anti-ship missiles, although they possess great anti-aircraft and anti-submarine capability.

Design features

The hull appears to be an improved 'Kara' type with increased beam and length to accommodate new weapon systems, the larger size also enhancing stability and allowing the radar mast height to be increased. Twin funnels are fitted, venting the exhaust from the gas turbine propulsion system.

There have been reports that the 'Slavas' were built with large quantities of flammable material, and their damage control systems were poorly designed.

Initially it was believed that at least eight and as many as 20 cruisers were planned, replacing the 'Kynda' and 'Kresta' classes as they retired. However, with the Russian navy virtually bankrupt there were no funds available for such expensive warships, and only four were laid down.

Moskva was in refit through most of the 1990s, returning to become flagship of the Black Sea Fleet. The second unit, **Marshal Ustinov**, commissioned in 1986, serves with the Northern fleet, though it has been in overhaul since the mid-1990s. **Varyag** (formerly the **Chervona Ukraina**) was commissioned into the Pacific Fleet in 1989. The fourth unit was launched in 1990 as the **Admiral Lobov**, but was transferred incomplete to the Ukrainian Navy. Renamed **Ukraina**, it was still incomplete in 2000, but if funds become available it is intended to serve as the Ukrainian fleet flagship.

The hull of Slava is dominated by the launch tubes for 16 Bazalt (SS-N-12 'Sandbox') missiles. These Mach-1.7 weapons are nuclear-capable, and have a range of more than 550 km (342 miles).

'Sovremenny' class Destroyer

The **'Sovremenny' class** (**Project 956 Sarych**) was derived from the hull of the previous 'Kresta II' cruisers, and was intended to offer a surface-strike capability and to provide other warships with protection against air and ship attack. As such, the class was seen as a specialist anti-shipping complement to the 'Udaloy' ASW cruiser.

A total of 20 vessels were constructed at Zhadanov (later North Yard), with another three cancelled or aborted (up to 28 ships may have been planned). The first, **Sovremenny**, was laid down in 1977 and commissioned in December 1980. From **Bespokoiny** (commissioned February 1992) onwards, the class was known as the **Project 956A**, which features improved weapons and EW systems. Currently, there are only four units in active Russian service (three of Project 956A type), reduced from a total of 17, with a single vessel (**Bulny**) awaiting completion.

Surface warfare

Designated by the Soviets as *eskadrenny minonosets* (destroyer), the class was initially armed with the rocket/ramjet-powered P-80 Zubr missile, replaced on the Project 956A by the longer-range P-270 Moskit. The P-80 is a sea-skimming weapon, with a low-altitude speed of Mach 2.2 (three times that of Harpoon) and a 320-kg (705-lb) or 200-kT nuclear warhead. Both weapons carry the NATO designation SS-N-22 'Sunburn'. Air defence requirements are handled by the Mach-3 Uragan (SA-N-7 'Gadfly') missile system, which has a range of 44 km (27 miles) and a maximum altitude of 15000 m (50,000 ft). A total of 44 missiles are carried for launchers mounted on the raised decks fore and aft of the two islands. Project 956A ships introduced the Yozh (SA-N-12 'Grizzly') using the same launcher.

In 2000-1, the Chinese navy received two Project 956A vessels (hulls 18 and 19), **Hangzhou** (ex-**Yekaterinburg**) and **Fuzhou** (ex-**Alexandr Nevsky**).

Although they were designed to operate in concert with one another, the 'Sovremenny' vessels are being sacrificed by the Russian navy in favour of the 'Udaloy' class, which has a more reliable propulsion system.

Comparable in size to the US Navy's 'Aegis' class, the primary weapon of the 'Sovremenny' is the Moskit anti-ship missile, for which two quadruple launchers are provided, one either side of the forward island.

The 'Sovremenny' class introduced the telescopic helicopter hangar to the Soviet navy, and was the first vessel to appear with the fully automatic twin-barrel 130-mm AK-130 gun, which is mounted fore and aft and provided with 2000 rounds. The guns can fire 35-45 rds/min to a distance of 29.5 km (18 miles).

*The remnants of the 'Sovremenny' class serve with Russia's Baltic Fleet (**N**astoychivy and Bespokoiny), Northern Fleet (Besstrashny) and Pacific Fleet (Burny).*

SPECIFICATION

Type 956 'Sovremenny' class
Displacement: 6,600 tons standard and 7,940 tons full load
Dimensions: length 156 m (511 ft 10 in); beam 17.3 m (56 ft 9 in); draught 6.5 m (21 ft 4 in)
Machinery: two GTZA-674 turbo-pressurised steam turbines delivering 73.13 MW (99,500 shp) to two shafts
Speed: 33 kts
Aircraft: one Ka-27 'Helix-A' ASW helicopter
Armament: two quadruple Zubr (SS-N-22 'Sunburn') SSM launchers (no reloads), two single Uragan (SA-N-7 'Gadfly') SAM launchers (44 missiles), two twin AK-130 130-mm (5.12-in) DP guns, four AK-630 six-barrel 30-mm CIWS mountings, two RBU-1000 ASW rocket launchers with 48 rockets, two twin 533-mm (21-in) ASW torpedo tubes and 30-50 mines

Electronics: one 'Top Plate' 3D air search radar, three 'Palm Frond' surface search radars, one 'Band Stand' SSM fire-control radar, two 'Bass Tilt' CIWS fire-control radars, one 'Kite Screech' 130-mm fire-control radar, six 'Front Dome' SAM fire-control radars, two 'Bell Shroud' and two 'Bell Squat' ECM systems, two PK-2 and eight PK-10 decoy launchers, 'Bull Horn' and 'Whale Tongue' hull sonars, two 'Light Bulb' TACAN
Complement: 296-344

'Udaloy' class ASW destroyer

'Udaloy I' vessels may be seen as Soviet equivalents to the US 'Spruance'-class destroyers, the ASW emphasis on these ships means they have limited anti-surface and anti-air capabilities. This was addressed in the design of the 'Udaloy II' class, which introduced hypersonic anti-ship missiles and combined gun/missile CIWS.

The **'Udaloy I' class** (**Project 1155 Fregat**) were considered 'large ASW ships' (*bolshoy protivolodochny korabl*). The programme was initiated in 1972, and two ships, **Udaloy** and **Vitse-Admiral Kulakov** were operational by early 1982. Based upon the 'Krivak' class, the 'Udaloy I' ships were intended as long-range ASW platforms, with an underway replenishment capability, to provide support for surface task forces. The series eventually yielded 12 vessels. Seven ships remain in service, these being maintained partly at the expense of the 'Sovremenny' class.

The 'Udaloy I' class is armed with two quadruple launchers for the Rastrub (SS-N-14 'Silex') missile. A unique twin hangar system with associated helicopter flight deck is located aft for two Ka-27 'Helix-A' ASW helicopters. Additional ASW equipment comprises a Polinom ('Horse Jaw') active/passive search/attack sonar system. For air defence, the 'Udaloy I' ships are fitted with eight six-round vertical launchers for the Klinok (SA-N-9 'Gauntlet') missile, of which 64 are carried. These can engage aerial targets at a range of up to 12 km (7.5 miles) and at altitudes as low as three metres and up to 12192 m (10-40,000 ft).

Improved 'Udaloy'

A single follow-on vessel of the **'Udaloy II'** (**Project 115.I Fregat**) class was commissioned in 1995. This design was intended to pro-

The 'Udaloy I' class are based with Russia's two principal fleets: the Northern Fleet (Severomorsk, Admiral Kharlamov and Admiral Levchenko) and the Pacific Fleet (Marshal Shaposhnikov, Admiral Panteleyev, Admiral Vinogradov and Admiral Tributs).

vide more balanced capabilities, and as such introduced two quadruple P-270 Moskit (SS-N-22 'Sunburn') anti-ship missile launchers in place of the Rastrub. For self-defence, two Kortik (CADS-N-1) combined gun/missile CIWS were added, each incorporating two six-barrel 30-mm guns and eight 9M87/9M88 (SA-N-11 'Grison') SAMs. A new twin 130-mm DP gun is also fitted, whilst ASW capability is maintained by Viyoga (SS-N-15 'Starfish') missiles. Although two more vessels were planned, only **Admiral Chabanenko** has entered Northern Fleet service.

Above right: Compared to its predecessors, the 'Krivak I' and 'Krivak II' classes, the 'Udaloy' vessels offer facilities for helicopter operations, limited sonar capabilities and improved air defence systems.

Below: The Soviet navy intended to deploy two or three brigades of seven 'Udaloy I' and 'Udaloy II' ships before follow-on vessels were cancelled in the early 1990s.

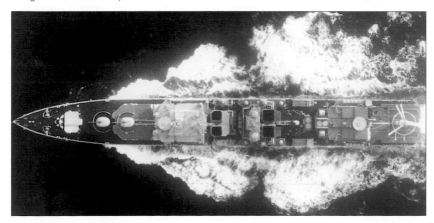

SPECIFICATION	
Type 1155 'Udaloy I' class	torpedo tubes and rails for 26 mines
Displacement: 6,700 tons standard and 8,500 tons full load	**Electronics:** one 'Strut Pair' air search radar, one 'Top Plate' 3D air search radar, three 'Palm Frond' surface search radars, two 'Eye Bowl' SS-N-14 fire-control radars, two 'Cross Sword' SA-N-9 fire-control radars, one 'Kite Screech' 100-mm fire-control radars, two 'Bass Tilt' CIWS fire-control radars, two 'Round House' TACAN, two 'Salt Pot' IFF, one 'Fly Screen-B' and two 'Fly Spike-B' aircraft landing aids, two 'Bell Squat' jammers, two 'Foot Ball-B' and two 'Wine Glass' ESM/ECM, six 'Half Cup' laser warning aids, two PK-2 and 10 PK-10 decoy launchers, one 'Horse Jaw' low-/medium-frequency bow sonar and one 'Mouse Tail' medium frequency variable-depth sonar
Dimensions: length 163.5 m (536 ft 5 in); beam 19.3 m (63 ft 4 in); draught 7.5 m (24 ft 7 in)	
Machinery: COGAG; two M62 gas turbines developing 10 MW (13,600 shp); two M8KF gas turbines developing 40.8 MW (55,500 shp)	
Speed: 29 kts	
Aircraft: two Ka-27 'Helix-A' ASW helicopters	
Armament: two quadruple Rastrub (SS-N-14 'Silex') ASW missile launchers (no reloads), eight Klinok (SA-N-9 'Gauntlet') SAM launchers (64 missiles), two 100-mm (3.9-in) DP guns, four AK-630 CIWS six-barrel 30-mm mountings, two RBU-6000 ASW rocket launchers, two quadruple 533-mm (21-in)	
	Complement: 220-249

'Alvaro de Bazán' class Frigate

In the early 1980s, the Spanish Navy identified a need to develop a multi-role frigate for escort duties. In 1983, Spain decided to participate in the future NFR-90 Frigate initiative. The NFR-90 project would see eight NATO members trying to co-develop a common ship. However, this project was eventually abandoned in 1989, given the divergence of national requirements among the participating nations. This led Spain to develop its **F-100** class of frigate. Its missions include protection of expeditionary forces, anti-submarine duties, long-range anti-aircraft defence and anti-missile protection. The vessels are also fitted with command facilities and can act as flag-ships.

Advanced design

The design of the F-100 emerged from Spain's desire to create a technologically advanced ship, which also featured a high degree of national industrial input. This would afford the Spanish navy a high degree of independence in the definition, selection and modification of the ship's weapons systems. In 1994, Spain signed an agreement with Germany and the Netherlands to co-develop the F-100. However, unlike NFR-90, this agreement only covered co-operation on the design of the ship itself, not its construction or associated weapons systems.

Four of the ships will enter service by 2006. The Spanish shipbuilder Izar will construct the entire class. The first vessel, *Alvaro de Bazán*, was launched in October 2000, and was commissioned in September 2002. The second ship, the

Almirante Don Juan de Borbón, was launched in 2002, and the remaining two vessels, *Blas de Lezo* and *Mendez Nuñez*, will be laid down by June 2003.

The ships' weapons will feature the Lockheed Martin Naval Electronics SPY-1D Aegis system. Aegis is already in service with the US Navy. It controls the detection and engagement of hostile air, surface and submarine threats. The core of the Aegis system is the AN/UYK-43/44 computer system. This co-ordinates the processing capabilities of the system, and is linked to the ship's Weapon Control System (WCS) and Command and Decision System (C&D). Using a multi-function phased array AN/SPY-1 radar, Aegis can track hundreds of targets simultaneously, whilst providing fire control tracks. Northrop Grumman Norden Systems builds the Aegis AN/SPS-67 G/H band surface search radar. Furthermore, the vessel is fitted with the Link 11 secure tactical data system for communication with other naval assets.

F-100 weapons

The F-100's weapons system is reinforced with the Boeing Harpoon anti-ship missile. The Harpoon has a range of 120 km (75 miles), a 220-kg (485 lb) warhead and active radar and thermal guidance. The surface-to-air system is the Evolved Sea Sparrow Missile (ESSM), developed by a consortium led by Raytheon. Area air defence is provided by the Raytheon Standard SM-2MR missile, which is also linked to the Aegis system. SM-2MR has a range of 70 km (43 miles) and a speed of Mach 2.5. Additionally, the vessel is fit-

ted with a 127-mm (5-in) United Defence Mk 45 gun for shore and anti-ship bombardment. Gun control is provided by the Dorna radar/electro-optic fire control system. The Dorna system includes K-band radar as well as infra-red, TV and laser range-finding. A FABA Meroka 2B weapon system forms the Close-In Weapons System (CIWS), which features two 20-mm guns. Further anti-submarine/anti-shipping capabilities are provided via two Mk 32 twin torpedo launchers for Mk 46 lightweight torpedoes.

Detection

Submarine detection is provided by a Raytheon DE 1160 active and passive sonar system. The ships also carry two anti-ship mortars. The F-100's electronic countermeasures (ECM) suite includes four Sippican Hycor Mk 36 SRBOC chaff and decoy launchers, together with an SLQ-25 Nixie acoustic torpedo countermeasures system.

The vessel was designed with a 26.4-m (86-ft 7-in) long flight deck, which can accommodate the Sikorsky SH-60B Seahawk LAMPS Mk III helicopter. The Spanish navy ordered six of the aircraft, which it designates HS.23, and the first was delivered in December 2001. The helicopters are fitted with Hellfire ASMs and FLIR. They can also deploy AN/SQQ-28

As integrated onto the F-100, the Fire Scout UAV will feature a laser designator and range-finder, and surveillance equipment. It will be able to transmit real-time information to commanders on the ship. Alvaro de Bazán is illustrated.

LAMPS III sonobuoys to aid submarine detection.

In August 2002, the Spanish Navy announced its intention to purchase the Northrop Grumman Fire Scout uninhabited rotorcraft. Fire Scout will improve the vessel's precision targeting capabilities, when guiding weapons during land attack missions.

SPECIFICATION

'Alvaro de Bazán' class
Displacement: 5,853 tons full load
Dimensions: length 146.7 m (481 ft 3 in) overall; beam 18.6 m (61 ft); draught 4.9 m (16 ft 1 in)
Machinery: combined diesel or gas turbine (CODOG); two GE LM 2500 gas turbines delivering 34.8 MW (47,328 shp) and two Bazán/Caterpillar diesels delivering 9 MW (12,240 shp) to two shafts
Speed: 28 kts
Aircraft: one SH-60B Seahawk LAMPS III; Fire Scout UAV to be added
Armament: eight Harpoon Block II

missiles, Mk 41 VLS for Standard SM-2MR (32 missiles) and Evolved Sea Sparrow (64 missiles) and one 127-mm (5-in) Mk 45 gun, one Bazán 20-mm gun, two Oerlikon 20-mm AA, two twin Mk 32 fixed launchers for 323-mm (12.75-in) torpedoes (24 Mk 46 weapons carried), two anti-ship mortars
Electronics: Lockheed Aegis Baseline 5 Phase III, Link 11/16, SATCOM, MCCIS, SPS-67 surface search radar, two SPG-62 fire-control radars, SQR-4 helicopter datalink, DE 1160 LF sonar, ATAS towed sonar
Complement: 250 (35 officers)

Type 42 class Destroyer

The **Type 42** destroyer emerged from the cancelled Type 82, which yielded a single ship – HMS *Bristol* – in the 1960s. The Type 42 was developed as an air-defence and escort ship. Outfitted with Sea Dart missiles to deter air threats, it was smaller and cheaper than the Type 82.

The Type 42 is the Royal Navy's primary air defence platform, providing full area air defence coverage for other ships. The Type 42 also has a limited anti-shipping capability. Designed with the smallest possible hull, the Type 42 placed a heavy emphasis on automation to reduce the ship's complement and crew workload. The first vessel, HMS *Sheffield*, was launched in 1971, and the entire class was com-

pleted by 1985. Two ships, *Hercules* and *Santisima Trinidad*, were built for Argentina and both were in service by 1981.

Sub-classes

There were three sub-classes within the Type 42 series. **Batch 2** ships were similar to the original **Batch 1** vessels, but contained an improved sensor suite, including the Type 1022 long-range air search radar. **Batch 3**, often referred to as the 'Manchester' class – on account of the lead ship's name – have a stretched hull. This extra space allows for additional weapons systems and increases stability in bad weather. In addition, the Sea Dart missile system and Mk 8 gun could be spaced slightly further apart to

improve their arcs of fire. To the rear, the extension allowed for extra space on the flight deck.

The Type 42 saw active service during the Falklands War in 1982. The Argentine Navy also deployed its two Type 42 vessels, and the Royal Navy's ships were painted with a large black band surrounding their hulls to assist identification. Five of the Royal Navy's Type 42 vessels took part in the conflict: HMS *Coventry*, HMS *Sheffield*, **HMS** *Cardiff*, HMS *Exeter* and **HMS** *Glasgow* all provided fleet air defence to the task force aircraft carriers. *Sheffield* was lost to an Argentine Exocet missile on 4 May 1982 and, 20 days later, HMS *Coventry* was sunk, after being hit by three bombs.

With the Type 42 continuing to perform the air defence role, a single ship of the class sails with each of the Royal Navy's three aircraft carriers on overseas deployments.

Several lessons were learnt from the Type 42's experiences in the South Atlantic. Most importantly, the Royal Navy identified the need for a CIWS to protect the vessels against low-flying aircraft and sea-skimming missiles. To this end, a 20-mm gun system was installed, together with chaff decoys. The ships were also fitted with Type 996 radar, and an improved Sea Dart fusing and control system.

The Type 42 class fared much better during the 1990-91 Gulf War, when the ships' Lynx helicopters extended radar coverage. Furthermore, the Lynx deployed the Sea Skua anti-shipping missile and, flying from HMS *Gloucester* and **HMS *Cardiff***, were successful in destroying several Iraqi small combat craft and AA batteries. HMS *Gloucester* scored a spectacular success when it detected and destroyed a hostile 'Silkworm' missile, which was targeting the battleship USS *Missouri*.

Following the end of the Gulf War, Type 42 ships have helped to enforce sea embargoes in the Gulf and the Adriatic during the war in Yugoslavia. **HMS *Southampton*** and **HMS *Liverpool*** assisted humanitarian operations in Montserrat and East Timor, while HMS *Glasgow* supported the UN peacekeeping force in East Timor.

*The Type 42, including **HMS Exeter (D 89)**, will serve with the Royal Navy until 2006, after which the eleven remaining units will be decommissioned at six monthly intervals.*

SPECIFICATION

Type 42 class (Batch 1/2)
Displacement: 3,500 tons standard; 4,100 tons full load
Dimensions: length 125 m (412 ft) overall; beam 14.3 m (47 ft); draught 5.8 m (19 ft)
Machinery: combined gas turbine or gas turbine (COGOG); two Rolls-Royce Olympus TM3B gas turbines delivering 37.3 MW (50,000 shp) and two Rolls-Royce Tyne RM1C gas turbines delivering 7.4 MW (19,900 shp) to two shafts
Speed: 29 kts
Aircraft: one Lynx HAS.Mk 3 or HMA.Mk 8

Armament: one Sea Dart twin launcher (22 missiles), one Vickers 4.5-in (114-mm) gun, two or four Oerlikon 20-mm AA, two 20-mm Vulcan Phalanx CIWS, two twin 324-mm (12.75-in) Mk 3 torpedo tubes
Electronics: Type 1022 air search radar, Type 996 air/surface search radar, Type 1007 and 1008 navigation radar, two Type 9091 fire-control radars, Type 2050 or 2016 hull-mounted sonar
Complement: 253 (24 officers)

Type 45 class Destroyer

The Royal Navy's Type 42 destroyers will eventually be replaced by the **Type 45**. The Type 45 ships will be the largest surface combatants to be operated by the Royal Navy since World War II. It is claimed that the class will provide an air defence capability 'several orders of magnitude' greater than that offered by the Type 42.

The Type 42 class was originally to be replaced by a joint Anglo-French-Italian project called 'Project Horizon'. However, this initiative was beset with delays. When the project stalled, the US Navy offered to lease to the Royal Navy five 'Ticonderoga'-class Aegis cruisers, however this offer was declined. In 1999, the Royal Navy decided to commence the development of the Type 45 class. It is expected that the first ship, **HMS *Daring***, will enter service in 2007.

Several features will be incorporated into the Type 45, which were earmarked for the ill-fated Project Horizon. These include some of the internal architecture of the ship, and the Principal Anti-Aircraft Missile System (PAAMS). PAAMS will strengthen the Type 45's air defence capability, and will incorporate the Aster 30 missile, which has a range of 80 km (50 miles). The system can intercept super-agile missiles fitted with re-attack modes, together with the full envelope of current and anticipated air threats. Furthermore, the ship can engage missile threats operating either individually or in salvos. In addition to PAAMS, it is hoped that the Type 45 will eventually deploy Tomahawk cruise missiles.

Sensor suite

While Type 45 is expected to have cheaper operating overheads than Type 42, the cost of its individual spare parts could be slightly higher, although the ships will field a smaller complement of crew and officers. The ships will feature a comprehensive suite of sensors. An S1850M radar will provide wide-area, long-range search. This will be reinforced by an MFS-7000 bow-mounted sonar. Air defence combat management will be co-ordinated by the Sampson radar system, combining surveillance and tracking roles in a single system. This can detect and track hostile aircraft or missiles while providing guidance for the ship's own weapons systems. The ship's sensors will be linked together by the Combat Management System (CMS), while communications with other vessels and satellite systems will be facilitated through the Fully-Integrated Communications System (FICS).

Ship protection is provided by the Surface Ship Torpedo Defence System. Furthermore, the ship will embark a complement of 60 Royal Marine Commandos with a supporting aircraft. The flight deck will accommodate the Royal Navy's Merlin helicopter, although the ships will initially operate with Lynx. Type 45 will feature a revolutionary WR-21 advanced gas turbine engine which will afford significant cost savings. The engines will feature an Integrated Electric Propulsion System, which eliminates the gearbox and increases fuel efficiency.

Complement

The ship's interior has been designed with 'room for growth' as a major consideration. While the ship's complement will include around 190 crew, there will be the option to increase this to 235. This will permit the accommodation of specialist personnel, which will allow for an increased range of missions, such as humanitarian relief, to be performed.

In total, six Type 45 vessels will be built. HMS *Daring* will be followed by **HMS *Dauntless*** and **HMS *Diamond*** in 2009. These original vessels will be followed by another three ships: **HMS *Dragon*, HMS *Defender*** and **HMS *Duncan***. The Navy may commission a further six ships, leading to total class of 12 units. The original production contract was placed with Marconi Electronic Systems (now BAE Systems) as the prime contractor. All of the vessels will be assembled and launched at BAE's facilities at Yarrow.

A computer graphic depicts the possible configuration of HMS Daring, the lead ship in the class, supporting the Merlin helicopter.

SPECIFICATION

Type 45 class
Displacement: 7,350 tons full load
Dimensions: length 152.4 m (462 ft 11 in) overall; beam 21.2 m (69 ft 7 in); draught 5.3 m (17 ft 5 in)
Machinery: Integrated Electric Propulsion; two Rolls-Royce WR-21 gas turbine alternators; two diesel generators; two motors
Speed: 29 kts
Aircraft: one Lynx HMA.Mk 8 or Merlin HM.Mk 1

Armament: two quadruple Harpoon launchers (optional), six A 50 vertical launchers for PAAMS (16 Aster 15 or 32 Aster 30 missiles), one Vickers 4.5-in (114-mm) gun, two 30-mm AA, two 20-mm Vulcan Phalanx CIWS
Electronics: Link 11/16/22, SATCOM, CEC, GSA 8/GPEOD weapons control, S1850M air/surface search radar, Sampson surveillance/fire-control radar, MFS-7000 bow-mounted sonar
Complement: 187 (plus 38 spare)

'Spruance' class
ASW destroyer

This illustration shows USS Comte de Grasse (DD 974) as she appeared soon after commissioning in 1978. The Kaman SH-2D LAMPS I ASW helicopter has now been replaced by two Sikorsky SH-60B LAMPS III aircraft. The SH-60R is due to replace SH-60B in service by 2012.

The 31 destroyers of the **'Spruance' class** were the first large US Navy warships to employ all gas-turbine propulsion. Marking a considerable break from traditional building techniques, the 'Spruances' were constructed by the modular assembly technique, whereby large sections of the hull are built in various parts of the shipyard, then welded together on the slipway. **USS Spruance (DD 963)** was commissioned in September 1975, construction of the class continuing into the early 1980s.

Room to grow
Much larger than previous American destroyers, they were built with future growth in mind. Their size and modular design allowed for easy installation of entire subsystems of weapons, equipment and sensors.

They were originally developed as anti-submarine (ASW) destroyers, to hunt down and destroy high speed submarines in all weathers. However, 24 ships of this class were given significant anti-ship and land attack capabilities in the 1980s with the installation of a 61-cell Vertical Launch Missile System (VLS) capable of launching Tomahawk and Harpoon missiles.

US Navy destroyers have historically been built with a planned operational life of 30 years, but the seven vessels which did not receive the Tomahawk VLS upgrade are being decommissioned after only two decades of service.

Helicopters
As completed, the class carried two Kaman SH-2D/F Seasprite LAMPS Mk I helicopters, but the primary ASW weapon system is now the SH-60B LAMPS Mk III helicopter, which extends the range of the ship's weapons and sensors well beyond the horizon. The SH-60B is being upgraded

The 'Spruances' are as large as a World War II cruiser, giving plenty of room for additional weapon systems and upgrades.

fleet-wide as the SH-60R. Secondary missions for the helicopters include gunfire spotting, over-the-horizon targeting, MEDEVAC, transport and SAR operations.

Comfort and habitability are integral elements to the ship's design, which includes amenities such as a crew lounge, ATM machine, gymnasium, classroom, and ship's store.

In 1974 the government of Iran ordered six SAM-equipped versions of the 'Spruances' for service in the Persian Gulf and Indian Ocean. However, following the revolution in that country, two were cancelled in 1979 whilst the remaining four under construction were taken over by the US Navy as the **'Kidd' class**. These are powerfully armed general-purpose destroyers, and for some time were unofficially known in the US Navy as the 'Ayatollah'-class. The four ships were commissioned as the **USS Kidd (DDG 993)**, **USS Callaghan (DDG 994)**, **USS Scott (DDG 995)** and **USS Chandler (DDG 996)**.

SPECIFICATION

'Spruance' class
Displacement: 8,200 tons full load
Dimensions: length 171.70 m (563 ft 3 in); beam 16.80 m (55 ft 2 in); draught 8.80 m (29 ft)
Machinery: four General Electric LM2500 gas turbines delivering 59655 kW (80,000 shp) to two shafts
Speed: 33 kts (60 km/h; 38 mph)
Aircraft: Two SH-60B (SH-60R) Seahawk LAMPS III helicopters
Armament: one Mk 41 vertical launch system for Tomahawk; 2 quad Harpoon launchers; 2 octuple Sea Sparrow SAM launchers (24 missiles); two Mk 15 Phalanx 20-mm CIWS; two 127-mm (5-in) DP guns; one octuple Mk 112 ASROC launcher; two triple 324-mm (12¾-in) Mk 32 ASW torpedo

tubes with Mk 46 torpedoes
Electronics: one SPS-40E air-search radar, one SPS-55 surface-search radar, one SPG-60 fire-control radar, one SPQ-9A fire-control radar, one SLQ-32(V)2 ESM suite, two Mk 36 Super RBOC chaff launchers, one SQS-53 bow sonar, one SQR-19 towed sonar
Complement: 320-350

'Kidd' class
Similar to early Spruance, except:
Armament: one twin Mk 26 Standard SM-1 ER SAM/ASROC ASW missile launchers (50 Standard, 16 ASROC and 2 test missiles)
Electronics: includes one SPS-48C 3D radar; one SPS-49 air search radar, two SPG-51D Standard fire control radars

---

'Ticonderoga' class
AEGIS air defence cruiser

Envisaged as a minimum cost, advanced area-defence platform for construction in large numbers, the **'Ticonderoga' class** has evolved over the years into what is possibly the most advanced warship ever built. The design was based on the hull of the cruiser-sized 'Spruance'-class destroyer. **USS Ticonderoga** was originally designated as a destroyer, but the design was redesignated as a cruiser in 1980 with the pennant number **CG 47**. The original number to be constructed was 28, increased by the Reagan administration to 30, and then cut back to 27 and USS Ticonderoga was commissioned in 1983. The last of the class was the USS Port Royal, which entered service in 1994.

The 'Ticonderogas' were the first surface combatant ships equipped with the AEGIS Weapons System, the most sophisticated air defence system in the world. The heart of AEGIS is the SPY-1A radar. Two paired phased array radars automatically detect and track air contacts to beyond 322 km (200 miles).

Air defence
AEGIS is designed to defeat attacking missiles by providing quick-reacting firepower and jamming resistance against any aerial threat expected to be faced by a US Navy Battle Group. The AEGIS system can control friendly aircraft as well as providing simultaneous surveillance, target-detection and target-tracking in a hemisphere over and around the ship. It also provides a uni-

Based on the hull of the 'Spruance'-class destroyer, USS Ticonderoga and her sisters were criticised for being top-heavy. However, they have served with distinction in most American naval actions since 1983.

A Tomahawk is launched against Afghanistan in October 2001. Cruise missiles give the 'Ticonderoga' class the ability to strike at targets hundreds of miles inland from the coast.

fied command and control platform for all the vessels of a battle group.

The first five ships have two twin Mk 26 missile launchers, firing Standard SM2-MR missiles. These were designed to cope with saturation attacks by high-performance aircraft as well as low-level and high-level air, surface- and sub-surface launched anti-ship missiles in heavy ECM environments.

From **USS Bunker Hill (CG 52)** onwards, the two Mk 26 launchers and their magazines have been replaced by two Mk 41 vertical launchers. The 127 VLS cells can be loaded with Standard, Harpoon, ASROC

and Tomahawk missiles, giving later vessels the ability to engage targets above, on and below the surface.

The 'Ticonderoga'-class cruisers were built to support and protect Carrier Battle Groups, Amphibious Assault Groups, and to perform interdiction and escort missions. The class has seen action in most US Navy operations of the last two decades, from the Lebanon in 1983 through to the Tomahawk bombardment of Afghanistan in 2001.

'Arleigh Burke' class
AEGIS general-purpose destroyer

The **'Arleigh Burke' class** of guided-missile destroyers was designed as a gas turbine-powered replacement for the 'Coontz'-class missile destroyers and the 'Leahy'- and 'Belknap'-classes of missile cruisers.

Originally intended to be a cheaper, less capable vessel than the 'Ticonderoga'-class cruiser, the design has evolved into an extremely capable general purpose warship, incorporating highly advanced weaponry and systems.

Stealth ship
Arleigh Burke (DDG 51) was the first large US Navy vessel designed to incorporate stealth shaping techniques to reduce radar cross-section. Originally tasked with defending

The USS Arleigh Burke (DDG 51) was named after the US Navy's most aggressive and successful World War II destroyer commander.

against Soviet aircraft, missiles and submarines, this potent destroyer is now used in high-threat areas to conduct anti-air, anti-submarine, anti-surface, and strike operations.

High-speed hull
A new hull profile significantly improves seakeeping, permitting high speeds to be maintained in difficult sea states. The hull form is characterised by considerable flare and a 'V'-shape appearance at the waterline.

Built primarily from steel, the class has aluminium masts to reduce topweight. Kevlar armour is fitted over all vital machinery and operations room spaces. Surprisingly, it was the first US warship class to be fully equipped to operate in NBC environments, with the crew confined to a protected citadel located within the hull and superstructure.

The AN/SPY-1D Phased Array Radar incorporates significant advances in the

detection capabilities of the AEGIS Weapons System, particularly in its resistance to enemy electronic countermeasures (ECM).

The AEGIS system is designed to counter all current and projected missile threats to the Navy's battle forces. A conventional, mechanically rotating radar 'sees' a target when the radar beam strikes that target once during each 360° rotation of the antenna. A separate tracking radar is then required to engage each target.

AEGIS radar
By contrast, the AEGIS system brings these functions together within one system. The four fixed arrays of the SPY-1D send out beams of electromagnetic energy in all directions simultaneously, continuously providing a search and tracking capability for hundreds of targets at the same time. The SPY-1D and the Mark 99 Fire Control System allow them

***USS** Russell (DDG 59) was the ninth of the 'Arleigh Burke' class, commissioning in May 1995. As with all ships in the class, the Russell has a full NBC protection system for the crew, and its superstructure incorporates stealthy angled surfaces.*

to guide vertically-launched Standard missiles to intercept hostile aircraft and missiles at long ranges. For point defence the ships are equipped with the Block 1 upgrade to the Phalanx CIWS.

The US Navy planned on having a force of 57 'Burke'-class destroyers in service by 2004, but Congressional budget cuts have extended the schedule to 2008. One

point of criticism of the original design was that no hangar was provided for a helicopter, although the first 28 vessels do have flight-decks capable of handling a Sikorsky SH-60 helicopter.

The improved **'Flight IIA'** variant does have a helicopter hangar, as well as an enlarged vertical launch system, a new 127-mm (5-in) gun and improved communications.

'De Zeven Provincien' class Guided-missile destroyer (DDG)

Royal Schelde of Vlissingen is building four air-defence guided-missile destroyers of the **'De Zeven Provincien' class** for the Dutch navy, the first two with a command (flagship) capability as successors to the two 'Tromp'-class frigates and the second two without this capability as successors to the two 'Jacob van Heemskerck'-class frigates. Ordered in February 1995, **De Zeven Provincien** was commissioned in April 2002, the **Tromp** in March 2003, with **De Ruyter** launched in April 2002 for commissioning in 2004 and the **Evertsen** launched in 2003 for commissioning in 2005.

The ships are the result of a tripartite programme initiated by Germany, the Netherlands and Spain. Thus Germany and Spain are building three 'Sachsen'- and four 'Alvaro de Bazán'-class frigates with much ship platform commonality with the 'De Zeven Provincien'-class ships. The design of the ship incorporates stealth features to minimise the radar, thermal, acoustic, electrical and magnetic signatures. Meanwhile compartmentalisation, insulation, redundancy in vital systems, power distribution, and structural features to channel and retain blast and fragments combine for enhanced survivability. For NBC protection the ship is subdivided into two main citadels and one sub-citadel.

Missile triad

The core of the ship's operational capability is the SEWACO XI combat data system developed by Thales Naval Nederland (originally Signaal). The shorter-range SAM system is the Evolved Sea Sparrow Missile (ESSM) developed by an international team led by Raytheon Missile Systems with semi-active radar guidance and vectoring of the rocket motor's thrust for greater range, speed and manoeuvrability. The medium-range SAM system is based on the Raytheon Standard Missile SM-2MR Block IIIA with a range of 70 km (43.5 miles), speed of Mach 2.5 and semi-active radar guidance. Both the ESSM and SM-2MR are launched from a 40-cell Mk 41 Vertical Launch System (VLS). The five octuple launchers are installed with the caps almost flush with the surface of the forecastle abaft the main gun. Expanded anti-ship capability is provided by the Harpoon missile system located on the raised deck immediately abaft the mast.

The ship's main gun is a 127-mm (5-in) Otobreda L/54 weapon, and last-ditch defence against anti-ship missiles is provided by two 30-mm Thales Naval Nederland Goalkeeper CIWS, one just forward of the mast and the other on the roof of the helicopter hangar. There are also two 20-mm Oerlikon cannon (to port and starboard of the mast). Short-range anti-submarine defence is vested in two 324-mm (12.75-in) Mk 32 twin launchers (one on each side of the ship) for 24 Mk 46 Mod 5 torpedoes. Longer-range anti-submarine operations are entrusted to a single Lynx (to be succeeded by the larger NFH 90 from 2007) helicopter stowed in a hangar just forward of the flight platform (with a DCN Samahé handling system) located over the stern.

Advanced radar

The ship's radar suite is also supplied by Thales Naval Nederland. The SMART-L system above the hangar provides 3D air search, the APAR (Active Phased Array Radar) round the mast provides air/surface search and SM-2MR fire-control capability, and the Scout LPI (Low Probability of Intercept) radar on the front of the mast provides surface search. Other key Thales elements are the Sirius long-range IR search and track system above the bridge and the Mirador optronic surface surveillance system.

The sonar system is the STN Atlas Elektronik DSQS-24C bow-mounted active search and attack equipment.

As indicated by its character as a CODOG system, the ship's propulsion system has two independent elements. The two Rolls-Royce Spey SM1C gas turbine units each provide 19495 kW (26,150 shp) for high-speed operations, while the two Stork-Wärtsilä 16V 26 ST diesel engines each provide 5070 kW (6,800 shp) for economical cruising. The two gearboxes are installed in a separate transmission room, and the ship has two propellers of the controllable-pitch type, and two rudders that also provide roll stabilisation.

Above: The mast carries four planar antennae for the APAR radar, and is flanked by satcom antennae in spherical radomes.

Right: Gas turbine and diesel gases from the CODOG machinery are vented via outward-canted funnels.

Below: Large enough to accommodate an NFH 90, the hangar carries the SMART-L radar and one of the two CIWS. F802 is lead ship of the class.

SPECIFICATION	
'De Zeven Provincien' class **Displacement:** 6,048 tons full load **Dimensions:** length 144.2 m (473 ft); beam 18.8 m (61 ft 8 in); draught 5.2 m (17 ft 1 in) **Propulsion:** CODOG with two Rolls-Royce Spey SM1C gas turbines delivering 38995 kW (52,300 shp) and two Stork-Wärtsilä 16V 26 ST diesels delivering 10140 kW (13,600 hp) to two shafts **Performance:** speed 28 kts; range 9250 km (5,750 miles) at 18 kts **Armament:** eight Harpoon anti-ship missiles, one 40-cell	Mk 41 VLS for SM-2MR and ESSM SAMs, one 127-mm (5-in) gun, two 30-mm CIWS, two 20-mm cannon, and two twin 324-mm (12.75-in) Mk 32 launchers for Mk 46 anti-submarine torpedoes **Electronics:** one SMART-L 3D radar, one APAR air/surface-search and fire-control radar, one Scout surface-search radar, one Sirius optronic director, one SEWACO XI combat data system, one Sabre ESM/ECM system, SBROC chaff launchers, and one DSQS-24C sonar **Aircraft:** one Lynx or NFH 90 helicopter **Complement:** 204

'Okpo' class Guided-missile destroyer (DDG)

The South Korean navy is in the midst of a major ship-building programme within the context of its Korean Destroyer Experimental (KDX) effort. This is a three-stage programme based on three classes: the 3,800-ton KDX-1, 5,000-ton KDX-2 and 7,000-ton or more KDX-3 for service from 1998, 2004 and 2007-08 respectively. Each class is more ambitious than its predecessor in ship size, sensors and weapons. The

KDX-1 programme yielded three destroyers of the **'Okpo' class** from which the KDX-2 and KDX-3 classes were evolved. The 'Okpo' ships marked the beginning of the South Korean navy's transformation from a coastal to oceanic force.

Design of the 'Okpo' class was a somewhat slow process: the first ship was to have been laid down in 1992 but was in fact started in 1995. The primary task is the

air-defence and anti-submarine escort of strike, anti-submarine and amphibious forces. As such, the ships of the 'Okpo' class (so named from the city in which Daewoo built the vessels) are multi-role combatants with advanced sensors and weapon systems. Originally to have comprised up to 10 units, the class was curtailed to just three units to allow concentration on the KDX-2 type. *Kwanggaeto the*

Great, *Euljimundok* and *Yangmanchun* were thus commissioned in 1998, 1999 and 2000 respectively.

The ships are equipped for offensive operations in multi-threat environments, working either independently or as part of a combat group. For this reason there is a very high degree of integration and automation in the control and weapon systems to facilitate effective operation in any aspect of modern

naval warfare.

Propulsion is entrusted to a CODOG arrangement of two gas turbines and two diesels for high combat speed combined with long cruising endurance, and as part of the integration of ship systems the propulsion control, electric plant control, damage control and fire detection consoles are located in the central control station.

The ships incorporate many items of sensor, weapon, fire-control and propulsion equipment of US and European origin. US input is evident in the Sea Sparrow short-range SAMs, Harpoon anti-ship missiles, anti-submarine torpedo system and air-search radar, while European input is seen in weapons such as the 127-mm (5-in) gun, CIWS, Super Lynx helicopters and sensors such as the surface-search and fire-control radars, and the sonar. The hangar and flight platform support two helicopters.

Above the helicopter hangar are, from forward, the SPS-49(V)5 air-search radar, one of the two STIR 180 fire-control radars, and one of the two 30-mm Goalkeeper CIWS. The Harpoon anti-ship missile launchers are abaft the funnels.

Below: The 30-mm Goalkeeper CIWS is for use against anti-ship missiles and, with Frangible Armour-Piercing Discarding Sabot ammunition, FACs.

SPECIFICATION

'Okpo' class
Displacement: 3,855 tons full load
Dimensions: length 135.4 m (444 ft 3 in); beam 14.2 m (46 ft 7 in); draught 4.2 m (13 ft 9 in)
Propulsion: CODOG; two General Electric GE LM2500 gas turbines delivering 43395 kW (58,200 shp) and two MTU 20V 956 TB92 diesels delivering 5960 kW (7,995 shp) to two shafts
Performance: speed 30 kts; range 7400 km (4,600 miles) at 18 kts
Armament: two quad launchers for Harpoon AShMs, one Mk 48 Mod 2 VLS for RIM-7P Sea Sparrow SAMs, one 127-mm (5-in) Otobreda gun,

two 30-mm Goalkeeper CIWS, and two triple 324-mm (12.75-in) Mk 32 launchers for Mk 46 ASW torpedoes
Electronics: one SPS-49(V)5 air-search, one MW-08 surface-search, one SPS-55M navigation, and two STIR 180 fire-control radars; one SSCS Mk 7 combat data system, one Argo ESM/ECM system, four Dagaie Mk 2 chaff launchers, one SLQ-25 Nixie torpedo decoy, one DSQS-21BZ hull-mounted active search sonar, and one Daewoo passive towed-array sonar
Aircraft: two Super Lynx helicopters
Complement: 170

'Wielingen' class Guided-missile frigate

The **'Wielingen' class** is the first post-war warship type to have been designed and built wholly in Belgium. The programme was approved in June 1971, the final studies being completed in July 1973. The order for the first two ships was placed in October of that year, and the

hulls were laid down in 1974. The remaining two were laid down in 1975, all four units commissioning during 1978.

Based at Zeebrugge, the three surviving ships (the **Westhinder** having been decommissioned) are the largest surface warships in the Belgian navy and form

Wielingen has no helicopter facilities, but is well armed for a small ship. First of four vessels, the Wielingen and its sisters (one now decommissioned) provide Belgium's only ocean-going escort capability.

SPECIFICATION

'Wielingen' class
Displacement: 1,880 tons standard; 2,430 tons full load
Dimensions: length 106.4 m (349 ft 1 in); beam 12.3 m (39 ft 9 in); draught 5.6 m (18 ft 5 in)
Propulsion: CODOG with one Rolls-Royce Olympus TM3B gas turbine delivering 20880 kW (28,000 shp) and two Cockerill 240 CO diesels delivering 4474 kW (6,000 shp) to two shafts
Performance: speed 26 kts; range 8350 km (5,190 miles) at 18 kts
Armament: two twin launchers for four MM.38 Exocet anti-ship missiles, one Mk 29 octuple launcher for eight RIM-7P Sea

Sparrow SAMs, one 100-mm (3.9-in) Creusot-Loire Mod 68 DP gun, one 375-mm (14.76-in) Creusot-Loire sextuple launcher for Bofors ASW rockets, and two 533-mm (21-in) launchers for 10 ECAN L5 ASW torpedoes
Electronics: one DA05 air and surface search radar, one WM25 fire-control radar, one Vigy 105 optronic director, one Scout navigation radar, one SEWACO IV tactical data system, one Argos AR 900 ESM system, two Mk 36 SRBOC chaff launchers, one SLQ-25 Nixie ASW decoy system, and one SQS-510 hull search/attack sonar
Complement: 159 (13 officers)

its only seagoing escort ship element. They are fully air conditioned and are fitted with Vosper fin stabilisers and a hull sonar. The arma-

ment and sensor fits are from a wide variety of NATO countries and were chosen to make the class as well-armed as possible for so compact a size. The combined diesel or gas turbine (CODOG) machinery outfit comprises one gas turbine

and two diesels to drive two shafts fitted with control-lable-pitch propellers. The three extant ships are the **Wielingen**, **Westdiep** and **Wandelaar**, and these will remain in operational service until the second decade of the 21st century.

Distinguished by their low superstructure and relatively massive funnel, the 'Wielingens' were the first warships designed and built in Belgium after World War II. The gun armament includes a 100-mm (3.9-in) DP weapon, but the planned Goalkeeper 30-mm CIWS mounting was cancelled.

'Niteroi' class Guided-missile frigate

Ordered in September 1970 from Vosper Thornycroft in ASW and general-purpose versions, the **'Niteroi'-class** ships were based on the company's Mk 10 frigate design and were constructed in the UK and Brazil. The four ASW ships were the **Niteroi**, **Defensora**, **Independência** and **União** fitted with the Branik missile launcher system derived specifically for Brazil from the Australian

Ikara ASW missile system for the delivery of Mk 46 torpedoes. The two general-purpose units were the **Constituição** and **Liberal** similar to the ASW variant but with a second 4.5-in (114-mm) Vickers Mk 8 DP gun mounting aft instead of the Branik system and two pairs of container-launchers for MM.38 Exocet anti-ship missiles located between the bridge and fun-

nel. Fitted with a combined diesel or gas turbine (CODOG) propulsion plant, the design is considered to offer exceptional economy in terms of manpower compared with previous warships of this size. A CAAIS action information system is fitted to allow co-ordinated surface ship ASW and surface strike operations with other vessels of the Brazilian navy, including the

aircraft carrier *São Paulo*. A major programme is updat-ing the weapons and sensors to create more capa-ble air-defence frigates.

Training vessel
In June 1981 a single ship to a modified 'Niteroi'-class design was ordered as the

Brasil for commissioning in 1985 as a training ship for the naval and merchant marine academies. Fitted only with a light anti-aircraft armament as well as class-rooms, the vessel has a hangar and landing platform aft for two Super Lynx Mk 21 helicopters.

SPECIFICATION

'Niteroi' class (modernised)
Displacement: 3,200 tons standard; 3,707 tons full load
Dimensions: length 129.2 m (423 ft 11 in); beam 13.5 m (44 ft 4 in); draught 5.5 m (18 ft 1 in)
Propulsion: CODOG arrangement with two Rolls-Royce Olympus TM3B gas turbines delivering 37935 kW (50,880 shp) and four MTU 16V 956 TB91 diesels delivering 11752 kW (15,760 shp) to two shafts
Performance: speed 30 kts; range 9815 km (6,100 miles) at 17 kts
Armament: two twin container-launchers for four MM.40 Exocet anti-ship missiles, one Branik launcher for 10 missiles carrying Mk 46 torpedo payload (ASW ships, but being removed), one Albatros launcher for Aspide SAMs replacing two triple launchers for Seacat SAMs (60 Seacat missiles), one or two 4.5-in (114-mm) Mk 8 DP guns, two 40-mm Bofors DP guns in Trinity

single CIWS mountings, one Bofors 375-mm (14.76-in) trainable twin launcher with 54 ASW rockets, two triple 324-mm (12.76-in) STWS-1 tube mountings for six Mk 46 lightweight anti-submarine torpedoes, and one rail for five depth charges (on GP ships)
Electronics: one RAN 20 S (3L) air/surface search radar replacing AWS 3, one TM 1226 surface search radar replacing ZW06, one Scanter navigation radar, two RTN 30X fire-control radars replacing RTN 10X, one EOS 450 optronic director, one CAAIS 400 action information system, one SDR-2/7 or Cutlass B-1B ESM system replacing RDL-2/3, one Cygnus or Elebra SLQ-1 jammer, one EDO 610E Mod 1 hull-mounted active sonar, and (Niteroi and Defensora) one EDO 700E variable-depth sonar
Aircraft: one Super Lynx Mk 21
Complement: 217

As built, the 'Niteroi'-class general-purpose frigate Liberal was not fitted with the Branik launcher system aft to fire the Australian Ikara rocket carrying a Mk 46 torpedo payload. Instead, this vessel carried an additional 4.5-in (114-mm) gun aft (removed in 2001 after a refit) and Exocet missile launchers amidships.

'Jiangnan' and 'Jianghu' classes Guided-missile frigates

In the late 1950s China assembled four 'Riga'-class frigates from Soviet-supplied components and known locally as the 'Chengdu' class. In 1965 the Chinese laid down the first of an enlarged and modified indigenous variant at the Jiangnan yard in Shanghai, resulting in the designation **'Jiangnan' class**. Four further units were completed at the Tung Lang yard in Guangzhou (Canton) from 1967-69.

At least one of the 'Jiangnans' took part in the combat operations against South Vietnamese naval vessels in the January 1974 occupation of the Paracel Islands. The 'Jiangnans', now deleted, had a diesel rather than geared steam turbine propulsion arrangement, and were not refitted with the SY-1 (CSS-N-1 'Scrubbrush') Chinese copy of the Soviet P-15 series (SS-N-2 'Styx') anti-shipping missile.

Following the political upheaval of the Cultural Revolution, the first new frigate design to emerge was the 'Jiangdong' class, of which two examples were constructed at the Hudong yard in Shanghai between 1970-78. The long building and commissioning times were caused by the fact that the ships were due to carry the first naval SAM system designed and made in China, and was also slow to mature. The class also introduced into service the first Chinese 100-mm (3.9-in) twin gun mounting.

Anti-ship variant

While the 'Jiangdongs' were being built, a half-sister variant for the anti-ship rather than anti-air role was planned. The first units of what

became known as the **'Jianghu I' (Type 053) class** were laid down in 1973-74 at Hudong, launched in 1975 and commissioned in 1976. The Jiangnan and Huangpu yards also joined the programme, and at least 31 units were completed including two and one transferred to Egypt and Bangladesh respectively. Developments have included one **'Jianghu II'-class** conversion with only

two HY-2 (CSS-N-2 'Safflower') anti-ship missiles and a number of Western weapons and sensors, and six new-build **'Jianghu III/IV' (Type 053HT)** units (including three for Thailand) with more advanced sensors and weapons, the latter including eight YJ-1 or C-802 (CSS-N-4 'Sardine' or CSS-N-8 'Saccade') anti-ship missiles in III and IV design configuration respectively.

SPECIFICATION

'Jianghu I' class
Displacement: 1,425 tons standard; 1,702 tons full load
Dimensions: length 103.2 m (338 ft 7 in); beam 10.8 m (35 ft 5 in); draught 3.1 m (9 ft 11 in)
Propulsion: two Type 12E 390V diesels delivering 10740 kW (14,405 shp) to two shafts
Performance: speed 26 kts; range 7400 km (4,600 miles) at 15 kts
Armament: two twin container-launchers for HY-2 (CSS-N-2 'Safflower') anti-ship missiles, two single or two twin 100-mm (3.9-in) guns, six or four twin 37-mm AA guns, two or four RBU-1200 five-barrel launchers for anti-submarine

rockets, two BMB-2 depth charge projectors, in some vessels two depth charge racks, and between 40 and 60 mines
Electronics: one Type 517 air search radar, one Type 354 'Eye Shield' or 'Rice Screen'/'Rice Shield' air/surface search radar, one Type 352 'Square Tie' surface search and fire-control radar, one 'Sun Visor'/'Wasp Head' or 'Rice Lamp' fire-control radar, one 'Fin Curve' or Don-2 navigation radar, 'Jug Pair' or 'Watch Dog' ESM system, 'Wok Don' weapons director, two Mk 33 RBOC chaff launchers, and one Type 5 hull-mounted sonar
Complement: 200

SPECIFICATION

'Jianghu III' class
as 'Jianghu I' class except:
Displacement: 1,924 full load
Armament: four twin container-launchers for eight YJ-1 (CSS-N-4 'Sardine') anti-ship missiles, two twin 100-mm (3.9-in) guns, four twin 37-mm AA guns (may be replaced by PL-8H gun/missile CIWS in some vessels), two RBU-1200 five-barrel launchers for anti-submarine rockets, two BMB-2 depth charge projectors, two depth

charge racks, and between 40 and 60 mines according to type
Electronics: one Type 517 air search radar and one Type 354 'Eye Shield' air/surface search radar, one 'Square Tie' surface search and fire-control radar, one 'Sun Visor-B'/'Wasp Head' and one 'Rice Lamp' fire-control radars, one 'Fin Curve' navigation radar, Newton ESM system, Type 981 ECM system, two 26-barrel chaff launchers, and one Type 5 hull-mounted sonar

---

The People's Republic of China has built the 'Jianghu' frigate in four versions (including five subvariants of the 'Jianghu I' with funnel and bridge changes). Egypt bought two 'Jianghu I' units with revised gun armament; these are very active in the Red Sea.

'Madina' class Guided-missile frigate

Ordered from France in October 1980 as a major part of the huge 'Sawari I' weapons supply contract, the first of four frigates of the **'Madina' (F 2000S) class** was laid down in the Lorient shipyard in 1981 and launched in 1983 for commissioning in 1985 as the **Madina**. The other three vessels are the **Hofouf**, **Abha** and **Taif**, laid down at the CNIM shipyard at Seyne-sur-Mer in 1982-83 for delivery during 1985-86.

The class is a very complex design and uses much untried state-of-the-art electronics technology, and at first was seen as too

sophisticated for so young a navy as that of Saudi Arabia. The weapon systems are predominantly French, though the anti-ship missiles are the Franco-Italian Otomat Mk 2 rather than the more usual member of the Exocet family, which indicates a long-range anti-ship role, especially as the SA 365F Dauphin 2 embarked helicopter can provide mid-course guidance.

The presence of the class in an area of particularly sensitive strategic importance to both major power blocs was of considerable interest to all the Arabian

Gulf oil states, and the 'Madinas' would have been matched only by Iraq's Italian-built 'Lupo' frigates had their delivery not been embargoed.

Class upgrade

Between 1997 and 2000, the 'Madinas' underwent an upgrade by DCN Toulon. Improvements included the addition of a Thomson-CSF TAVITAC combat data system, a helicopter handling system and the hull-

mounted active search/attack sonar with integrated Sorel VDS. Based

at Jiddah, the class spend only a few weeks at sea each year.

SPECIFICATION

'Madina' class
Displacement: 2,000 tons standard; 2,870 tons full load
Dimensions: length 115 m (377 ft 4 in); beam 12.5 m (41 ft); draught 4.9 m (16 ft 1 in)
Propulsion: four SEMT-Pielstick diesels delivering 28630 kW (38,400 shp) to two shafts
Performance: speed 30 kts; range 14825 km (9,210 miles) at 18 kts
Armament: two quadruple container-launchers for Otomat Mk 2 anti-ship missiles, one octuple launcher for 26 Crotale Naval SAMs, one 100-mm (3.9-in) DP and two twin Breda 40-mm AA guns,

four single 533-mm (21-in) tubes for ECAN F17P anti-submarine torpedoes
Electronics: one DRBV 15 air/surface search radar, one Castor II fire-control radar, one DRBC 32 SAM fire-control radar, two TM 1226 navigation radars, one TAVITAC action information system, one DR 4000 ESM system, two Dagaie chaff/flare launchers, one Diodon TSM 2630 hull-mounted sonar, and one Sorel variable-depth sonar
Aircraft: one SA 365F Dauphin 2 helicopter
Complement: 179

A 'Madina' frigate of the Saudi Arabian navy. The purchase of this sophisticated class from France is typical of the tendency of oil-rich Arab nations to buy weapons with more capacity than is necessary.

'Esmeraldas' class Guided-missile corvette (FSG)

Although strictly rated as missile corvettes rather than small light frigates, the units of the **'Esmeraldas' class** must, because of their multi-purpose capabilities, be ranked with the latter. Ordered in 1978 from the Italian firm CNR del Tirreno, the design is based on the **'Wadi M'ragh'** (now **'Assad') class** for Libya but with more powerful diesel engines, the addition of a helicopter landing platform amidships and a SAM launcher aft of the bridge. All six units of the class, the **Esmeraldas** (**CM11**), **Manabi** (**CM12**), **Los Rios** (**CM13**), **El Oro** (**CM14**), **Los Galapagos** (**CM15**) and **Loja** (**CM16**), have been in ser-

vice with the Ecuadorian navy since the first half of the 1980s as the country's primary anti-ship surface strike force.

The helicopter platform is used to operate one of the navy's Bell Model 206B light helicopters in the surface-search and air-sea-rescue roles. The vessels' anti-ship missile system is the 65-km (40-mile) range MM.40 version of the Exocet, with two banks (each of three single container-launchers, firing outward) located between the landing platform and the bridge. The SAM system is the lightweight four-round launcher version of the Italian Albatros weapon system which uses the Aspide

multi-role missile. Only self-defence ASW torpedo tubes are fitted, together with a

hull-mounted sonar set, for the conduct of anti-submarine warfare operations.

The 'Esmeraldas' class are the principal surface combatants of the Ecuadorian navy.

Below: Although more correctly classed as missile corvettes, the Ecuadorian navy's 'Esmeraldas'-class vessels have more firepower per ship than a number of light frigate classes. They are armed with six MM.40 Exocets, a quadruple Albatros SAM launcher, guns and torpedoes.

'Chikugo' class Frigate (FF)

Designed and built with structural features to reduce noise and vibration, the **'Chikugo'-class** frigates were used primarily for coastal ASW missions around the Japanese home islands. To facilitate their use in this role they were retrofitted with the SQS-35(J) variable-depth sonar from an open well offset to starboard at the stern. They were also the smallest warships in the world to carry the octuple

launcher for the ASROC ASW rocket-launcher system, though no reloads were carried: the amidships launcher was trained to the bearing and then elevated to fire a two-round salvo of the solid-fuel RUR-5A rockets with their Mk 46 parachute-retarded homing torpedo payloads out to a maximum range of 9.2 km (5.7 miles). The Japanese vessels did not carry the alternative payload of a 1-kiloton Mk 17

nuclear depth charge that was carried by some US ships. The propulsion plant comprised four Mitsubishi-Burmeister & Wain UEV30/40 diesels in DE215, 217-219, 221, 223 and 225, or four Mitsui 28VBC-38 diesels in the remainder. A Mk 51 fire-control director with no radar controlled the twin 40-mm mount aft. The hull-mounted OQS-3 sonar

was a licence-built version of the US SQS-23 set, a variant of which is used on the 'Spruance'-class ASW destroyers. The 11 vessels were the **Chikugo** (**DE215**), **Ayase** (**DE216**), **Mikumo** (**DE217**), **Tokachi** (**DE218**), **Iwase** (**DE219**), **Chitose** (**DE220**), **Niyoda** (**DE221**), **Teshio** (**DE222**), **Yoshino** (**DE223**), **Kumano** (**DE2224**) and **Noshiro** (**DE2225**).

*The **Tokachi** (**DE218**) pays a courtesy visit to Hawaii. As in all but the most recent Japanese designs, the 'Chikugo' class had significant ASW capability but little surface-to-surface or surface-to-air equipment.*

'Yubari' class
Guided-missile frigate (FFG)

Smaller than the preceding 'Chikugo' class, the 'Yubari' class is highly automated with a crew of under 100. Designed to operate under land-based air cover, the design has little AAW capability. There is capability for the retrofit of the Phalanx 20-mm close-in weapon system if required.

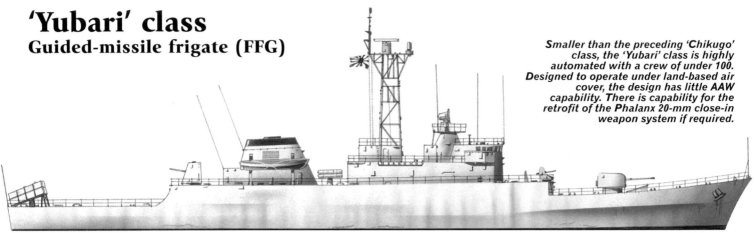

The **'Yubari'-class** frigate is basically an improved and enlarged variant of the 'Ishikari' design authorised in 1977-78. The greater length and beam have improved the seaworthiness and reduced the internal space constrictions of the earlier design. The original number of units to be built was three, but this was reduced by one when the Japanese government deleted funds from the naval budget in the early 1980s. A new three-vessel 'Improved Yubari' class was to have been constructed in the 1983-87 five-year plan, but what emerged was the six-strong 'Abukuma' class.

Although not heavily armed and having no heli-copter facilities in compari-son with contemporary Western designs, the 'Yubaris' are ideal for use in the waters around Japan, where they operate under shore-based air cover. Most of the weapons, machinery and sensors have been built under licence from foreign manufacturers. The propul-sion plant is a CODOG arrangement with a licence-built British gas turbine and a Japanese diesel. Extensive automation of the machinery reduced the crew require-ment to below 100, which is extremely good for a war-ship of this size.

The vessels which com-prise the class are the **Yubari (DE227)** and **Yubetsu (DE228)**.

*Developed from the 'Ishikari' interim design, the **Yubari** and **Yubetsu** were enlarged in both length and beam, the better to handle the armament mounted. Two quadruple Harpoon launchers give the class considerable anti-ship capability.*

SPECIFICATION

'Yubari' class
Displacement: 1,470 tons standard; 1,690 tons full load
Dimensions: length 91 m (298 ft 7 in); beam 10.8 m (35 ft 5 in); draught 3.6 m (11 ft 10 in)
Propulsion: CODOG with one Kawasaki/Rolls-Royce Olympus TM3B gas turbine delivering 21170 kW (28,390 shp) and one Mitsubishi 6DRV diesel delivering 3470 kW (4,650 shp) to two shafts
Speed: 25 kts
Armament: two quadruple launchers for eight Harpoon anti-ship missiles, one 76-mm (3-in) OTO Melara Compact gun, provision for one 20-mm Phalanx CIWS, one 14.76-in (375-mm) Bofors quadruple ASW rocket launcher, and two triple 12.75-in (324-mm) Type 68 ASW tubes with Mk 46 lightweight anti-submarine torpedoes
Electronics: one OPS 28 surface search radar, one OPS 19 navigation radar, one GFCS 1 gun fire-control radar, one NOLQ 6 ESM system, one OLT 3 ECM jammer, two Mk 36 SRBOC chaff launchers, and one OQS 1 hull sonar
Aircraft: none
Complement: 98

'Tromp' class Guided-missile frigate

SPECIFICATION

'Tromp' class
Displacement: 3,665 tons standard; 4,308 tons full load
Dimensions: length 138.4 m (454 ft 1 in); beam 14.8 m (48 ft 7 in); draught 4.6 m (15 ft 1 in)
Propulsion: COGOG with two Rolls-Royce Olympus TM313 gas turbines delivering 37285 kW (50,000 shp) and two Rolls-Royce Tyne RM1C gas turbines delivering 6115 kW (8,200 shp) to two shafts
Speed: 28 kts
Armament: two quadruple launchers for eight Harpoon anti-ship missiles, one Mk 13 Standard single-rail launcher for 40 SM-1MR SAMs, one Mk 29 octuple launcher for 60 NATO Sea Sparrow SAMs, one twin 120-mm (4.72-in) Bofors DP gun, one 30-mm Goalkeeper CIWS mounting, two 20-mm Oerlikon AA guns, and two 324-mm (12.75 in) Mk 32 triple tubes for Mk 46 anti-submarine torpedoes
Electronics: one SPS-01 3D radar, two ZW-05 surface search radars, one Decca 1226 navigation radar, one WM-25 fire-control radar, two SPG-51C SAM fire-control radars, one SEWACO I data information system, one Sphinx ESM system, two Corvus chaff launchers, one Type 162 hull sonar, and one CWE610 hull sonar
Aircraft: one SH-14B/C Lynx ASW helicopter
Complement: 306

Although designated by the Dutch navy as frigates, the **'Tromp'-class** vessels **Tromp** and **De Ruyter** were, by virtue of their armament and size, more akin to guided-missile destroyers. They were equipped with an admiral's cabin and support-ing command and control facilities to serve as the flag-ships of the two Dutch navy ASW hunter-killer groups assigned to EASTLANT con-trol during wartime. Fitted with fin stabilisers, they were excellent seaboats and weapons platforms in most types of weather. The propulsion was of the COGOG type with pairs of Rolls-Royce Olympus and Tyne gas turbines that were downrated to improve gas generator life and ease of maintenance. A full NBC citadel defence was built into the hull for operability under high-intensity warfare.

SAM defence
The primary role assigned to the ships was the provision of area SAM defence against aircraft and missiles to the hunter-killer group or convoy it may have been escorting. The ships also had secondary ASW and anti-sur-face vessel roles. The main armament was a single-rail Mk 13 Standard SM-1MR SAM launcher, backed up by an octuple NATO Sea Sparrow SAM launcher with a large reload magazine. The appearance of the vessels was characterised by the large plastic radome fitted over the forward SPS-01 3D radar.

*Replacing two cruisers in service with the Royal Netherlands navy, HNLMS **Tromp** and **De Ruyter** were among the largest and most capable of frigates afloat. Weapons fitted included Harpoon, Standard and Sea Sparrow missiles.*

'Kortenaer' and 'Jacob van Heemskerck' classes FFGs

The **'Kortenaer'**- or **'Standard'-class** frigate design was authorised in the late 1960s as the replacement for the 12 ASW destroyers of the 'Holland' and 'Friesland' classes. The propulsion plant and machinery layout was taken from the 'Tromp' design. A single pair of fin stabilisers is fitted, and as far as possible internal systems have been automated to reduce crew numbers. Eight ships were ordered in 1974, and a further four in 1976. In 1982, however, two newly completed units were purchased by Greece as the **Elli** and **Limnos**. These were replaced in the Dutch order by two vessels built to an air-defence variant design known as the **'Jacob van Heemskerck' class**. The two ships are the **Jacob van Heemskerck** and **Witte de With**, and were planned to alternate as the flagship of the Dutch navy's third ASW hunter-killer group. The helicopter facilities of these two ships have been replaced by a Mk 13 Standard SAM missile launcher. The two vessels entered service in 1986.

The 10 vessels of the ASW class were the **Kortenaer**, **Callenburgh**, **Van Kinsbergen**, **Banckert**, **Piet Hein**, **Abraham Crijnssen**, **Philips van Almonde**, **Bloys van Treslong**, **Jacob van Brakel** and **Pieter Florisz**. The **Treslong** is still in Dutch service, the **Crijnssen** and **Heyn** became the UAE's **Abu Dhabi** and **Al Emirat** in 1997-98, and the others went to Greece in 1993-2001 (without the 30-mm Goalkeeper CIWS mounting) as the **Aegeon**, **Adrias**, **Navarinon**, **Kountouriotis** and **Bouboulina**.

The Banckert was the fourth 'Kortenaer'-class frigate to enter service with the Royal Netherlands navy. The 'Kortenaers' have a well-balanced armament fit, the primary ASW weapons being two Lynx helicopters. The vessel now serves as Aegeon with the Greek navy.

SPECIFICATION

'Kortenaer' class
Displacement: 3,050 tons standard; 3,630 tons full load
Dimensions: length 130.5 m (428 ft 2 in); beam 14.6 m (47 ft 11 in); draught 4.3 m (14 ft 1 in)
Propulsion: COGOG with two Rolls-Royce Olympus TM3B gas turbines delivering 37935 kW (50,880 shp) and two Rolls-Royce Tyne RM1C gas turbines delivering 7380 kW (9,900 shp) to two shafts
Performance: speed 30 kts; range 5,405 miles (8700 km) at 16 kts
Armament: two quadruple container-launchers for Harpoon anti-ship missiles, one Mk 29 octuple launcher for 24 Sea Sparrow SAMs, one 76-mm (3-in) DP gun, one 30-mm Goalkeeper CIWS, and two twin 324-mm (12.75-in) tubes with Mk 46 ASW torpedoes
Electronics: one LW-08 air search radar, one ZW-06 navigation radar, one WM-25 and one STIR fire-control radars, one SEWACO II data information system, one Ramses ESM system, two decoy launchers, and one SQS-509 bow sonar
Aircraft: two SH-14B Lynx helicopters
Complement: 176 to 200

SPECIFICATION

'Jacob van Heemskerck' class
as 'Kortenaer' class except:
Displacement: 3,000 tons standard; 3,750 tons full load
Armament: as 'Kortenaer' class without 76-mm (3-in) DP gun but with one Mk 13 single-rail launcher with 40 Standard SM-1MR SAMs
Electronics: one LW-08 air search radar, one SMART 3D radar, one Scout surface search radar, two STIR and one STIR 180 fire-control radars, one SEWACO VI data information system, one Ramses ESM/ECM system, two Mk 36 SRBOC six-tube chaff/IR flare launchers, and one SQS-509 hull-mounted search/attack sonar
Aircraft: none
Complement: 176 plus 20 flag staff

'Oslo' class FFG

Based on the US 'Dealey'-class destroyer escorts, the **'Oslo'-class** frigates have a higher freeboard forward (to suit the sea conditions off Norway) and many European-built sub-systems. They were built under the 1960 five-year naval plan, with half the cost borne by the US. The class underwent modernisation refits in the late 1970s, these including the fitting of Penguin Mk 1 SSMs, a NATO Sea Sparrow SAM launcher and Mk 32 ASW self-defence torpedo tubes, and another from the late 1980s. Five 'Fridtjof Nansen' class have been ordered as replacements to enter service from 2005.

Norway's largest surface combatants, the 'Oslos' provide the only major ASW

The 'Oslo'-class frigates are a modification of the 'Dealey' class of destroyer escort built in the US during the 1950s. Freeboard was increased in order to improve handling in the more challenging sea conditions off Norway. This is Bergen.

force in the region. For this role they carry a forward-mounted sextuple launcher for the 120-kg (265-lb) Terne III anti-submarine rocket: once fired, the launcher is automatically trained to the vertical and reloaded within 40 seconds. For self-defence the ships have the American 11-km (6.8-mile) range Mk 46 acoustic-homing torpedo fired from the Mk 32 torpedo tubes and capable of 45 kts.

The five ships built were the **Oslo**, which sank under tow in 1994 after running aground, **Bergen**, **Trondheim**, **Stavanger** (laid up in 1999) and **Narvik**.

SPECIFICATION

'Oslo' class
Displacement: 1,650 tons standard; 1,950 tons full load
Dimensions: length 96.6 m (316 ft 11 in); beam 11.2 m (36 ft 9 in); draught 4.4 m (14 ft 5 in)
Propulsion: geared steam turbines delivering 14915 kW (20,000 shp) to one shaft
Performance: speed 25 kts; range 8350 km (5,190 miles) at 15 kts
Armament: four container-launchers for Penguin Mk 1 anti-ship missiles, one Mk 29 octuple launcher with 24 RIM-7M Sea Sparrow SAMs, one twin 3-in (76-mm) Mk 33 DP gun, one 40-mm Bofors AA gun, one sextuple Terne III ASW rocket launcher, and two triple 324-mm (12.75-in) Mk 32 tubes for Stingray ASW torpedoes. Ships have a minelaying capability.
Electronics: one AWS-9 air search radar, one TM 1226 surface search radar, one Decca navigation radar, one 9LV 218 Mk 2 and one MSI-3100 action information system, one Argo AR 700 ESM system, two chaff launchers, one TSM 2633 combined hull sonar and VDS, and one Terne III active attack sonar
Aircraft: none
Complement: 125

Displacement of the 'Oslo' class was increased by 200 tons between 1995-96, when the hulls were strengthened for VDS operations in heavy seas. Oslo, the lead-ship of the class, sank under tow south of Bergen in 1994 after an engine failure caused the vessel to run aground in heavy weather.

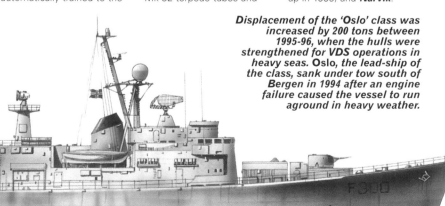

'Grisha' class Light frigate (FFL)

Built as a *malyy protivo-lodochnyy korabl'* (MPK, or small anti-submarine ship) between 1968 and 1974, the **'Grisha I' class** was built to the extent of only 16 units. These provided a more specialised ASW capability than the earlier 'Mirka' and 'Petya' classes. They were followed during 1974 and

1976 by eight **'Grisha II'-class** *pogranichnyy storozhevoy korabl'* (PSKR, or border patrol ship) units for the Maritime Border Directorate of the KGB. These differed from the 'Grisha Is' in having a second twin 57-mm AA mount substituted for the Osa-M (SA-N-4 'Gecko') SAM

launcher forward and in having no 'Pop Group' fire-control radar. In 1973-85 the **'Grisha III' class** was the Soviet navy's production model. A 'Bass Tilt' gun fire-control radar (atop a small deckhouse to port on the aft superstructure) replaced the 'Muff Cob' system on the earlier versions, whilst the space previously occupied by this radar was occupied by a single 30-mm CIWS. One 'Grisha III' was modified as the sole **'Grisha IV' class** unit in the early 1980s for trials of the Klinok (SA-N-9 'Gauntlet') SAM system. The final variant was the **'Grisha V' class** development of the 'Grisha III' with the after 57-mm twin mount replaced by a 76-mm (3-in) single mount.

Above: A 'Grisha I' unit in heavy weather shows that there is no bow sonar dome. There is a hull set and a VDS housed in the deckhouse aft beneath the hump-shaped superstructure. In the early 2000s there were only 23 'Grishas' left in Russian service.

Below: The 'Grisha II' was used solely by the maritime element of the KGB but has been retired. Exports amount to two 'Grisha IIIs' to Lithuania, and one 'Grisha V', one 'Grisha II' and two 'Grisha IIs' to Ukraine. The official name of the class is Project 1124 'Albatros'. The single 'Grisha IV' was a testbed for the SA-N-9 SAM system.

SPECIFICATION

'Grisha' classes
Displacement: 950 tons standard; 1,200 tons full load
Dimensions: length 71.2 m (233 ft 7 in); beam 9.8 m (32 ft 2 in); draught 3.7 m (12 ft 2 in)
Propulsion: CODAG with one gas turbine delivering 11185 kW (15,000 shp) and two diesels delivering 11930 kW (16,000 shp) to two shafts
Performance: speed 30 kts; range 4600 km (2,860 miles) at 14 kts
Armament: one twin launcher for 20 Osa-M (SA-N-4 'Gecko') SAMs, one twin 57-mm DP or ('Grisha V') one 76-mm (3-in) DP gun, one 30-mm CIWS mount ('Grisha III and V'), two or ('Grisha V') one 12-barrel

RBU 6000 250-mm (9.8-in) launchers for 120 ASW rockets, two twin 533-mm (21-in) tubes for anti-submarine torpedoes, two rails for 12 depth charges, and between 20 and 30 mines according to type
Electronics: one 'Strut Curve' or ('Grisha V') 'Strut Pair' or 'Half Plate Bravo' air search radar, one 'Pop Group' SAM fire-control radar, one 'Muff Cob' or ('Grisha III and V') 'Bass Tilt' gun fire-control radar, two 'Watch Dog' ECM systems, one 'High Pole-B' IFF, one 'Bull Nose' high/medium-frequency hull-mounted sonar, and one 'Elk Tail' high-frequency VDS
Aircraft: none
Complement: 60-70

'Riga' class Frigate (FF)

Built at the Kaliningrad, Nikolayev and Komsomolsk shipyards in the USSR, the 64 (including eight export) units of the **'Riga' class** were the successors to the six 'Kola'-class escorts. Designated *storozhevoy korabl'* (SKR, or patrol ship) by the Soviets, the type

proved to be an excellent coast-defence design and followed the Soviet practice in the 1950s of flush-decked hulls with a sharply raised forecastle. The 'Rigas' became one of the largest Soviet ship classes, and were exported in some numbers. In all, 17 were

transferred: two to Bulgaria, five to East Germany (of which one was retained in service as a self-propelled barracks ship), two to Finland (one modified as a minelayer) and eight to Indonesia. China built four further units in its shipyards from Soviet components, and these too have been retired. The last Soviet vessels had been taken out of service by the early 1990s.

One of the most popular pastimes practised by the Soviets in warm climates was relaxation on deck away from their spartan living conditions, as the majority of the crew of this 'Riga'-class frigate are doing.

Modifications

A few of the operational vessels were modified in the 1970s, a twin 25-mm AA gun being added each side of the funnel and a dipping sonar fitted abreast of the bridge. Before this, however,

all units were fitted with two hand-loaded 16-barrel RBU 2500 ASW rocket-launchers forward to replace the original ASW armament of a single MBU 600 'Hedgehog'

and four BMB-2 depth-charge throwers. One of the active units was also fitted with a taller stack cap and several 'Bell' ECM systems, possibly for trials.

SPECIFICATION

'Riga' class
Displacement: 1,260 tons standard; 1,510 tons full load
Dimensions: length 91.5 m (300 ft 2 in); beam 10.1 m (33 ft 2 in); draught 3.2 m (10 ft 6 in)
Propulsion: geared steam turbines delivering 14900 kW (19,985 shp) to two shafts
Performance: speed 28 kts; range 3700 km (2,300 miles) at 13 kts
Armament: three 100-mm (3.9-in) DP, two twin 37-mm AA and (some units) two twin 25-mm AA guns, two 16-barrel RBU 2500 250-mm

(9.8-in) launchers with 160 ASW rockets, two racks for 24 depth charges, one twin or triple 533-mm (21-in) tube mounting for anti-ship torpedoes, and 28 mines
Electronics: one 'Slim Net' air search radar, one 'Sun Visor-B' and one 'Wasp Head' fire-control radars, one 'Don-2' or 'Neptune' navigation radar, one 'High Pole-B' IFF, two 'Square Head' IFF, two 'Watch Dog' ECM systems, and one high-frequency hull sonar
Aircraft: none
Complement: 175

Now retired, the 'Riga' class remained in service with the Soviet navy in relatively large numbers into the 1980s for second-line duties and as training vessels.

'Petya' classes

Light frigates (FFLs)

The 'Petya II' differs from the earlier 'Petya I' in having a heavier ASW armament in the form of RBU 6000 automatic rocket launchers and additional torpedo tubes.

The 18 units of the **'Petya I' class** were constructed at the Kaliningrad and Komsomolsk shipyards between 1961 and 1964. From the latter year until 1969 both shipyards switched to building 27 units of the **'Petya II' class**, which differed from their predecessors in having an extra quintuple 406-mm (16-in) ASW torpedo tube mounting in place of the two aft ASW rocket launchers. The two forward-mounted RBU 2500 rocket launchers were also exchanged for the RBU 6000 system with automatic loading facilities. Both variants also had mine rails.

Conversion

From 1973 onwards eight 'Petya I' vessels were modified to give the **'Petya I (Mod)' class**. The conversion involved the addition of a medium-frequency variable-depth sonar system in a new raised stern deckhouse, which necessitated the removal of the mine rails. A further three were then converted as trials vessels and given the same sub-group

Left: One task sometimes undertaken by the 'Petyas' in the absence of any larger units was that of the 'tattletale'; here a 'Petya II' shadows the carrier HMS Eagle in 1975 while the latter was on an exercise.

designation: one was fitted with a larger VDS system with no deckhouse at the stern; the second had a deckhouse installed abaft the stack (following the removal of the torpedo tubes) and fitted with a complex reel/winch installation for what may have been either a towed non-acoustic ASW sensor or a towed surface-ship sonar array; the third vessel had a small box-like structure built at the stern for a towed sensor deployed from a hole in the stern. In 1978 a single unit of the 'Petya II' type was also converted into a **'Petya II (Mod)'-class** trials vessel. The conversion was along the lines of the 'Petya I (Mod)' but with a slimmer VDS deckhouse which allowed retention of the minelaying capability.

In 1984 the Soviet navy had a total of seven 'Petya I', 11 'Petya I (Mod)', including three trials vessels, 23 'Petya II' and one 'Petya II (Mod)' (for trials) in service with all four fleets. A further four 'Petya IIs' of the Soviet navy were transferred to Vietnam (three ships) and Ethiopia (one ship), and another 16 were built specifically for export with a triple 533-mm (21-in) torpedo tube mounting and RBU 2500 ASW rocket-launchers for the navies of India (12 **'Arnala'-class** ships), Vietnam (two ships) and Syria (two ships).

In the final stages of their Soviet careers, now ended, the 'Petyas' were rated as *stororzhevoy korabl'* (SKR, or patrol ship). In 2003 the only survivors were to be found in India (one ship on the verge of deletion), Syria (two, of which one may no longer be operational) and Vietnam (a single 'Petya II').

This unmodified member of the 'Petya I' class of light frigates is easily identified by the presence of the RBU 2500 ASW rocket launchers in front of the bridge and the lack of any stern superstructure for a variable-depth sonar system.

SPECIFICATION

'Petya' classes
Displacement: 950 tons standard; 1,150 tons or ('Petya II') 1,180 tons full load
Dimensions: length 81.8 m (268 ft 4 in) or ('Petya II') 82.5 m (270 ft 8 in); beam 9.1 m (29 ft 10 in); draught 2.9 m (9 ft 6 in)
Propulsion: CODAG with one diesel delivering 4000 kW (5,365 shp) and two gas turbines delivering 22370 kW (30,000 shp) to three shafts
Performance: speed 32 kts; range 5,590 miles (9000 km) at 10 kts
Armament: two ('Petya I (Mod) towed-array trials ship one) twin 76-mm (3-in) DP guns, four 16-barrel RBU 2500 250-mm (9.84-in) ASW launchers with 320 rockets or ('Petya II' and 'Petya II (Mod)' only) two 12-barrel RBU 6000 250-mm ASW launchers with

120 rockets or ('Petya I (Mod) only) two 16-barrel RBU 2500 launchers with 160 rockets, two ('Petya I (Mod)' only one) racks for 24 or 12 depth charges, one ('Petya II (Mod) two and 'Petya I (Mod)' towed-array trials ship none) 533-mm (21-in) quintuple tube mounting for five or 10 ASW torpedoes and between 20 and 30 mines (none in 'Petya I (Mod)') according to type
Electronics: one 'Slim Net' or 'Strut Curve' air search radar, one 'Hawk Screech' gun fire-control radar, one 'Don-2' navigation radar, one 'High Pole-B' and ('Petya I' only) two 'Square Head' IFF, two 'Watch Dog' ECM systems, one hull-mounted sonar, one dipping sonar, and (in some) one variable-depth sonar
Aircraft: none
Complement: 98

'Mirka' classes FFLs

Built between 1964 and 1965 at the Kaliningrad shipyard, the nine vessels of the **'Mirka I' class** were followed on the stocks during the latter half of 1965 and 1966 by nine units of the **'Mirka II' class**. They were constructed as a more specialised variation of the early 'Petya' design and were initially rated by the Soviets as *malyy protivolodochnyy korabl'* (MPK, or small anti-submarine ship). As with some other ASW-oriented ship classes, this was changed in 1978 to *stororzhevoy korabl'* (SKR, or patrol ship).

Retired vessels

The vessels of the two 'Mirka' classes, now all retired, served only with the Soviet Baltic and Black Sea Fleets. The propulsion plant was similar in concept to the combined diesel and gas turbine plant of the 'Petyas', the combination of the two different types

Black Sea Fleet 'Mirka I' and 'Mirka II' units regularly deployed to the Mediterranean squadron to provide ASW protection to higher-value surface units and the Soviet navy's many deep water anchorages in the region.

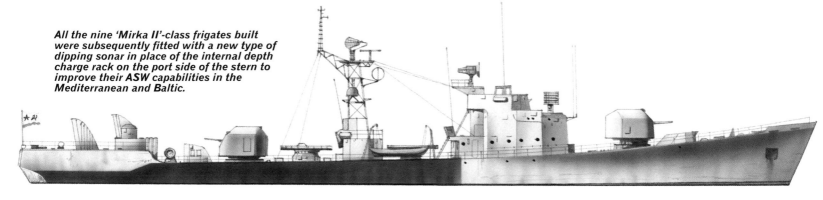

All the nine 'Mirka II'-class frigates built were subsequently fitted with a new type of dipping sonar in place of the internal depth charge rack on the port side of the stern to improve their ASW capabilities in the Mediterranean and Baltic.

of engine offering both long endurance at modest speed for routine patrolling or escort, and high speed (as well as fast acceleration) to close as rapidly as possible on the location of suspected targets in preparation for attacks on submerged submarines.

Dual-purpose guns

Both classes were characterised by a mixed armament based on four 76-mm (3-in) dual-purpose guns in a pair of two-gun mountings over the forecastle and abaft the mast. The basic difference between the two models lay in their dedicated anti-submarine armaments. In the 'Mirka I' class this comprised four 250-mm (9.84-in) 12-barrel launchers for anti-submarine rockets (two abreast of each other ahead of the bridge and two abreast of each other near the stern flanking the forward unit of the two large centreline exhaust arrangements for the gas turbines) and one quintuple mounting for anti-submarine torpedoes on the centreline abaft the lattice mast with its mass of antennae. In the 'Mirka II' class the two after rocket launchers were omitted in favour of a second quintuple mounting on the centreline in the area between the mast and the superstructure rear: both mountings carried 533-mm (21-in) electrically powered anti-submarine torpedoes. The later 'Mirka II' units had a 'Strut Curve' air search radar in place of the earlier ships' 'Slim Net' set.

Dipping sonar

Almost all the units of both classes were later fitted with a dipping sonar, either instead of the internal depth charge rack in the port side of the stern or abreast the bridge. This was intended to improve the submarine-detection capabilities in regions such as the Baltic, where oceanographic conditions for anti-submarine warfare are notoriously difficult.

The 'Mirka' light frigates remained in declining service into the early 1990s before the last units were finally deleted.

SPECIFICATION

'Mirka' classes
Displacement: 950 tons standard; 1,150 tons full load
Dimensions: 82.4 m (270 ft 4 in); beam 9.1 m (29 ft 10 in); draught 3 m (9 ft 10 in)
Propulsion: CODAG with two diesels delivering 4470 kW (5,995 shp) and two gas turbines delivering 23100 kW (30,980 shp) to two shafts
Performance: speed 35 kts; range 4600 km (2,860 miles) at 20 kts
Armament: two twin 76-mm (3-in) DP guns, four ('Mirka I') or two ('Mirka II') 250-mm (9.84-in) RBU
6000 12-barrel ASW launchers with 240 or 120 rockets, and one ('Mirka I') or two ('Mirka II') 533-mm (21-in) quintuple tube mountings for five or 10 anti-submarine torpedoes
Electronics: one 'Slim Net' or (some 'Mirka II' only) 'Strut Curve' air search radar, one 'Hawk Screech' gun fire-control radar, one 'Don-2' navigation radar, two 'High Pole-B' IFF, two 'Square Head' IFF, two 'Watch Dog' ECM systems, one hull-mounted sonar and one dipping sonar
Aircraft: none
Complement: 98

'Koni' class Frigate/guided-missile frigate

Although constructed in the USSR at the Zelenodolsk Shipyard on the Black Sea, the **'Koni' class** of *storozhevoy korabl'* (SKR, or patrol ship) was intended only for export, a mere one unit, the **Timofey Ul'yantsev**, being retained by the Soviets as a crew training ship for the personnel of the countries which bought vessels of this class. There are two distinct subclasses, the **'Koni Type II' class** differing from the **'Koni Type I' class**

in having the space between the funnel and the aft superstructure occupied by an extra deckhouse for the air-conditioning units required for service in hot climates.

The countries which took delivery of 'Koni'-class units were East Germany ('Type I' **Rostock** and **Berlin**), Yugoslavia ('Type I' **Split** now named **Beograd** and **Podgorica** now cannibalised), Algeria ('Type II' **Murat Reis**, **Ras Kellich** and **Rais Korfou**) and Cuba ('Type

The East German navy had two 'Koni Type I'-class frigates, the Rostock (141) and the Berlin (142). They differed slightly from other 'Koni'-class units in having no chaff launchers, and carried East German-built TSR333 navigation radars in place of the more usual 'Don-2' sets.

SPECIFICATION

'Koni' class
Displacement: 1,440 tons standard; 1,900 tons full load
Dimensions: length 96.4 m (316 ft 3 in); beam 12.6 m (41 ft 4 in); draught 3.5 m (11 ft 6 in)
Propulsion: CODAG with two diesels delivering 11400 kW (15,290 shp) and one gas turbine delivering 13420 kW (18,000 shp) to three shafts
Performance: speed 27 kts; range 2500 km (1,555 miles) at 14 kts
Armament: one twin launcher for 20 Osa-M (SA-N-4 'Gecko') SAMs, two twin 76-mm (3-in) DP and two
twin 30-mm AA guns, two 250-mm (9.84-in) RBU 6000 12-barrel ASW launchers with 120 rockets, two racks for 24 depth charges, and between 20 and 30 mines according to type
Electronics: one 'Strut Curve' air search radar, one 'Pop Group' SAM fire-control radar, one 'Hawk Screech' gun fire-control radar, one 'Drum Tilt' 30-mm gun fire-control radar, one 'High Pole-B' IFF, two 'Watch Dog' ECM systems, and one hull-mounted sonar
Aircraft: none
Complement: 120

II' **Mariel** plus an unnamed vessel. The Yugoslavs themselves modified their ships to carry two single aft-firing launchers for P-20 (SS-N-2c 'Styx') anti-ship missiles on each side of the rear superstructure which houses the

Osa-M (SA-N-4 'Gecko') SAM unit, and in the mid-1980s also built in their Tito Yard in Kraljevica the **'Kotor'-class** ships **Kotor** and **Novi Sad**: these have a number of structural differences from the Soviet original, different

diesel engines and the SS-N-2c missiles in forward-facing launchers abreast the forward end of the bridge superstructure. A similar ship was sold to Indonesia and a training vessel.

The 'Koni Type I'-class frigate was built in the USSR primarily for export. The 'Koni Type II' class differs in having additional superstructure, which houses air-conditioning systems for use in tropical climates.

'Krivak' classes Guided-missile frigates (FFG)

In 1970 the first gas turbine-powered **'Krivak I'-class** or **Project 1135** frigate of *bol'shoy protivolodochnyy korabl'* (BPK, or large anti-submarine ship) entered service with the Soviet navy. Built at the Zhdanov Shipyard in Leningrad, the Kaliningrad Shipyard and the Kamish-Burun Shipyard in Kerch between 1970 and 1980, 21 units of this variant were constructed. In 1975 the **'Krivak II' class**, of which 11 were built at Kaliningrad between that year and 1981, was first seen. This differed from the previous class in having single 100-mm (3.9-in) guns substituted for the twin 76-mm (3-in) turrets of the earlier version, and a larger variable-depth sonar housing at the stern. Both classes were re-rated to *storozhevoy korabl'* (SKR, or patrol ship) status in the late 1970s, possibly in view of what some Western observers considered to be the type's deficiencies in terms of size and limited endurance for ASW operations in open waters.

New and improved

The first unit of the **'Krivak III' class**, designed to remedy some of the probable defects, appeared in mid-1984. This has a hangar and flight platform for one Ka-27 helicopter in place of the after gun turrets and Osa-M (SA-N-4 'Gecko') SAM launcher, and one 100-mm gun turret in place of the forward quadruple Rastrub (SS-N-14 'Silex') launcher for ASW missiles. The variable-depth sonar remains under the flight deck at the stern, and single 30-mm AK-630 CIWS are located on each side of the hangar. The other ASW armament of the 'Krivak I/II' classes and the forward Osa-M launcher are also retained. The 'Krivak III' was built at Kamish-Burun and became the standard ASW frigate of the Soviet (now Russian) navy. A number of ships were exported.

'Krivak'-class frigates were optimised for the anti-submarine role, in time of war operating against marauding NATO submarines in Soviet coastal waters and protecting Soviet SSBNs. Note the twin 76-mm (3-in) guns in the aft turrets of this 'Krivak I' ship.

Three 'Krivak'-class frigates refuel from a 'Dubna'-class replenishment oiler. Two 'Krivak I'-class ships have been upgraded with two launchers for eight Uran (SS-N-25 'Switchblade') anti-ship missiles.

Above: The long rake of the bow of the 'Krivak' class with the anchor well forward betrays the presence of a large bow sonar dome for a 'Bull Nose' (Titan-2) medium-frequency active sonar. For under-layer searching a low-frequency VDS is fitted aft. Russia had 15 'Krivak' frigates remaining in active service in 2003.

Left: The 'Krivak I'-class frigate is distinguishable from the 'Krivak II' by its two twin 76-mm (3-in) DP gun turrets aft and a smaller housing at the stern for the VDS towed body. Other operators of the 'Krivak'-class frigate are India and Ukraine, the former having three 'Krivak III (Improved)' ships with another three or more to come, and the latter operating one 'Krivak III' ship.

The 'Krivak I'-class frigate Storozhevoy is seen in the North Atlantic, the overhead view revealing the layout of the ship's weapons and sensors. The largest item is the quadruple Rastrub (SS-N-14) ASW missile launcher.

'Nanuchka' classes Guided-missile corvettes (FSG)

Classed by the Soviets as a *malyy raketnyy korabl'* (MRK, or small rocket ship), the 17 **'Nanuchka I'-class** or **Project 1234 Ovod** units were built between 1969 and 1974 at Petrovsky, Leningrad, with a modified variant, the **'Nanuchka II' class**, following at that yard and at a Pacific coast shipyard from 1977. Appearing in 1978, the **'Nanuchka III'** is a development with one 76-mm (3-in) DP gun and one 30-mm CIWS mounting.

The 'Nanuchkas' are considered by Western observers to be coastal mis-

sile corvettes, although the fact that they are sometimes seen quite far from home waters (on deployment to such areas as the North Sea, the Mediterranean and the Pacific) tends to put them more in the light frigate category, especially when the firepower of the class is considered. The anti-ship missile carried is the Malakhit (SS-N-9 'Siren'), which can carry either a 500-kg (1,102-lb) HE or 250-kT nuclear warhead over a range of 110 km (68 miles). The SS-N-9 uses a dual active radar and passive IR terminal hom-

ing system, with third-party targeting and mid-course corrections to guide it in over-the-horizon engagements.

Export vessels
In 1977 an export version of the 'Nanuchka II' class was delivered to India with twin SS-N-2c 'Styx' SSM launchers in place of triple 'Siren' launcher systems. India received three units, two being deleted in 1999 and 2000. Algeria and Libya each received three and four ships respectively, Libya losing one in 1986 to US air attack.

A 'Nanuchka I'-class small missile ship under way. The 'Nanuchka II' class for export differs mainly in carrying SS-N-2c 'Styx' missiles, while the last Soviet operational variant, the 'Nanuchka III', has a different gun armament, with a single 76-mm gun and CIWS.

The 'Nanuchka I' class of small missile ship carries the SS-N-9 anti-ship missile as its main armament. For maximum range a third-party OTH targeting source is required. The single 'Nanuchka IV' is a trials vessel for the Yakhont (SS-N-26) missile, carried in two sextuple launchers. Twelve 'Nanuchka IIIs' remained in Russian service in 2003.

Modified Type 12 'Rothesay' class Anti-air frigate

The **Modified Type 12-** or **'Rothesay'-class** frigates were repeats of the 'Whitby'-class design, somewhat improved in their internal features, and were ordered under the 1954-55 programme to the extent of a planned 12 units. Though the 'Whitby'-class ships had been designed with a vertical funnel, the 'Rothesay' ships were completed with the slightly raked funnel that had been retrofitted in HMS *Torquay* of the 'Whitby' class, but in other respects there were but few external differences between the two classes. The 12 torpedo tubes (two twin and eight single) were later removed as superfluous to modern requirements, and only the early ships carried the two 40-mm Bofors AA guns in the high-capability STAAG Mk 2 radar-controlled automatic twin mount. In the STAAG Mk 2's place was put a large deckhouse so that the GWS.20 missile system, with the Seacat short-range SAM, could be shipped, but for some years all of the ships were fitted instead with a single 40-mm Bofors gun in a manually operated mount.

New Zealand ships

Two ships were completed for the Royal New Zealand Navy as *Otago* and *Taranaki*, but the last three hulls under British contract were cancelled and completed to the 'Leander'-class design, leaving the British class as **Rothesay**, **Londonderry**, **Brighton**, **Falmouth**, **Yarmouth**, **Rhyl**, **Lowestoft**, **Berwick** and

Plymouth, which were completed in 1960-61.

The clear superiority of the 'Leander' class then resulted in the implementation of a major upgrade for the 'Rothesays'. The most significant of the enhancements or improvement was the incorporation of a Wasp light helicopter carrying Mk 44 and later Mk 46 anti-submarine lightweight homing torpedoes. The opportunity was also taken to update the fire-control arrangements with the MRS3 system in place of the original Mk 6M system. The ships' appearance was slightly changed by a new plated foremast and the raising of the funnel, but in other respects the layout remained the same with an armament that now comprised two 4.5-in (114-mm) guns in a single mount, one

Above: Deleted in 1982, HMNZS Otago was the first of the Royal New Zealand Navy's two 'Rothesay'-class frigates.

Right: HMS Berwick was completed by Harland & Wolff in June 1961, and was finally expended as a target in 1986.

GWS.20 quadruple launcher for Seacat SAMs, two 20-mm cannon, and a single Limbo Mk 10.

Trials

In 1978 the *Falmouth* was used in trials of the quarter-deck winch gear for towed-array sonar, and in 1975-79 the *Londonderry* was reconstructed as a trials ship for the Admiralty Surface Weapons Establishment. This involved the removal of the 4.5-in

guns, altering the propulsion system to waterjets for quietness, and stepping a large, plated mizzen mast to carry the new Type 1030 STIR radar. In the autumn of 1980 the ship also received the 30-mm RARDEN cannon for trials.

The 1981 Defence Review marked the end of the class, although some lasted longer as a result of the Falklands War. The *Lowestoft* was fitted with the first Type 2031(I) towed-array sonar in 1981-82.

Seen in updated form with a Westland Wasp light anti-submarine helicopter, HMS Falmouth was completed by Swan Hunter in July 1961 as the fourth of the nine 'Rothesay'-class frigates for Royal Navy service. Evident on the quarterdeck is the three-barrel Limbo Mk 10 anti-submarine mortar.

Above: The lines and general layout mark the 'Rothesay' class as a virtually complete repeat of the 'Whitby'-class frigate and the immediate ancestor of the immensely successful 'Leander'-class frigate.

SPECIFICATION
'Rothesay' class (as built) **Displacement:** 2,150 tons standard; 2,560 tons full load **Dimensions:** length 112.7 m (370 ft); beam 12.5 m (41 ft); draught 3.9 m (17 ft) **Propulsion:** two geared steam turbines delivering 22370 kW (30,000 shp) to two shafts **Performance:** speed 29 kts; endurance 8370 km (5,200 miles) **Armament:** one twin 4.5-in (114-in) DP gun, one twin 40-mm Bofors AA gun, two twin and eight single 21-in	(533-mm) torpedo tubes, and two Limbo Mk 10 ASW mortars **Electronics:** single Type 975 surface search, Type 293 air/surface search and target indicating, Type 974 navigation, Type 262 (later Type 903) aircraft-control, Type 994 air/surface search and Type 978 navigation radars, and single Type 170 attack, Type 174/177 medium-range search and Type 162 bottom search sonars **Aircraft:** none, but see text **Complement:** 200-235

Improved Type 12 'Leander' class General-purpose frigate

A total of 26 general-purpose 'Leander'-class frigates was built for the Royal Navy in three sub-groups: eight 'Leander Batch 1', eight 'Leander Batch 2' and 10 broad-beam 'Leander Batch 3' ships. After entering service from 1963, the class underwent numerous refit and modernisation programmes that created what were in effect six separate subclasses. The five Batch 3 ships **Andromeda**, **Hermione**, **Jupiter**, **Scylla** and **Charybdis** underwent the most radical conversion, involving the addition of a GWS.25 Sea Wolf automatic point-defence missile system plus numerous new sensor systems to give the most capable of the subclasses.

Economic cutbacks

The conversion of the remaining five Batch 3 units was shelved for economic reasons. One of the five, the **Bacchante**, was sold to New Zealand in 1991, becoming **Wellington** and joining the existing 'broad-beam' **Canterbury** and the standard version **Waikato**. The remaining four Batch 3 units were **Achilles**, **Diomede**, **Apollo** and **Ariadne**, which retained their twin 4.5-in (114-mm) guns and Seacat SAM armament. The eight Batch 2 units were due to form a single Exocet-armed class, but this was changed to three different types. The first comprised **Cleopatra**, **Sirius**, **Phoebe** and **Minerva** that became the 'Leander Batch 2 Towed Array Exocet Group' as the ships

had the Type 2031(I) general-purpose surveillance and tactical towed-array sonar on the starboard side of the stern. Three of the remaining Batch 2 vessels were **Danae**, **Argonaut** and **Penelope** that constituted the original Exocet conversion group with the 4.5-in Mk 6 twin gun mount replaced by four MM.38 Exocet launchers and a third GWS.22 Seacat SAM launcher. The last Batch 2 ship, **Juno**, had its Exocet conversion halted in favour of modification as a navigation training ship.

The eight Batch 1 vessels were converted to ASW ships by the fitting of a GWS.40 Ikara ASW missile installation in place of the gun mount. To compensate for the loss in AA capability a second GWS.22 Seacat launcher was added aft atop the hangar. One vessel, **Dido**, was sold to New Zealand in 1991, becoming **Southland**, while the other seven remained in Royal Navy service as **Aurora**, **Euryalus**, **Galatea**, **Arethusa**, **Naiad**, **Ajax** and **Leander**. All the ships remaining in British service were deleted in the late 1980s and early 1990s.

Overseas exports

In addition to the vessels for the Royal Navy, a number of other nations have either purchased British-built 'Leanders' or constructed their own under licence. The former vessels are the Chilean navy's **Condell** and **Almirante Lynch**, while the

latter included the Royal Australian Navy's **Swan** and **Torrens**, the Indian navy's **Nilgiri**, **Himgiri**, **Udaygiri**, **Dunagiri**, **Taragiri** and **Vindhyagiri**, and the Dutch navy's **Van Speijk**, **Van Galen**, **Tjerk Hiddes**, **Van Nes**, **Isaac Sweers** and **Evertsen**, which became the Indonesian navy's **Ahmad Yani**, **Slamet Riyadi**, **Yos Sudarso**, **Oswald Siahaan**, **Abdul Halim Perdanakusuma** and **Karel Satsuitubun** in the later 1980s. In all cases the countries obtained ships with better armament and sensor fits than the Royal Navy vessels, apart from the final Sea Wolf conversions. The Dutch managed to double the surface-to-surface missile armament to eight by using the Harpoon, and the Indians managed to fit the last two

of their vessels to carry accompanying Sea King ASW helicopters.

As they left British service, a number of the ships were sold, the Chilean navy receiving the **Achilles** and

Ariadne as the **Ministro Zeneno** and **General Baquedano**, and the Ecuadorian navy receiving the **Penelope** and **Danae** as the **Presidente Eloy Alfar** and **Moran Valverde**.

The Isaac Sweers was completed in 1968 as the fifth of the six Dutch 'Van Speijk'-class frigates modelled on the 'Leander' class, and became the Indonesian Karel Satsuitubun.

SPECIFICATION	
'Leander' class (RN Sea Wolf conversion)	sextuple GWS.25 launcher with 30 Sea Wolf SAMs, two 20-mm AA
Displacement: 2,500 tons, later 2,790 tons standard; 2,962 tons, later 3,300 tons full load	guns, and two triple 324-mm (12.75-in) STWS-1 tubes for Mk 46 and Stingray ASW torpedoes
Dimensions: length 113.4 m (372 ft); beam 13.1 m (43 ft); draught 4.5 m (14 ft 10 in)	**Electronics:** single Type 967/978 air/surface search, Type 910 SAM-control and Type 1006 navigation radars, one CAAIS combat data
Propulsion: two geared steam turbines delivering 22370 kW (30,000 shp) to two shafts	system, one UAA-1 ESM system, two Corvus chaff launchers, one Type 2016 hull sonar and one Type
Performance: speed 27 kts; endurance 7400 km (4,600 miles) at 15 kts	2008 underwater telephone **Aircraft:** one Lynx HAS.Mk 2 ASW helicopter
Armament: four MM.38 Exocet anti-ship missile launchers, one	**Complement:** 260

Completed in 1971, HMAS Torrens was one of two 'Swan'-class frigates built in Australia to a modified 'Leander' design.

SPECIFICATION	
'Ahmad Yani' class	Simbad launchers for Mistral
Displacement: 2,255 tons standard; 2,835 tons full load	SAMs, one 76-mm (3-in) DP gun, and two triple 324-mm (12.75-in)
Dimensions: length 113.4 m (372 ft); beam 12.5 m (41 ft); draught 4.2 m (13 ft 10 in)	Mk 32 tubes for Mk 46 anti-submarine torpedoes **Electronics:** single LW-03 air
Propulsion: two geared steam turbines delivering 22370 kW (30,000 shp) to two shafts	search, DA-05 surface search, TM 1229C navigation and M-45 fire-control radars, SEWACO V data
Performance: speed 28.5 kts; endurance 8300 km (5,160 miles) at 12 kts	information system, passive ESM system, two Corvus chaff launchers, and single CWE-610 hull and
Armament: two quadruple Harpoon anti-ship missile launchers, two quadruple launchers for 32 Seacat SAMs being replaced by two twin	SQR-18A towed-array sonars **Aircraft:** one Wasp or NBO-105 helicopter **Complement:** 180

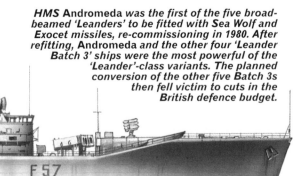

HMS Andromeda *was the first of the five broad-beamed 'Leanders' to be fitted with* **Sea Wolf** *and* **Exocet** *missiles, re-commissioning in 1980. After refitting,* **Andromeda** *and the other four 'Leander Batch 3' ships were the most powerful of the 'Leander'-class variants. The planned conversion of the other five Batch 3s then fell victim to cuts in the British defence budget.*

F 57

Type 21 'Amazon' class Guided-missile frigate

The **Type 21** or **'Amazon'-class** general-purpose frigate was a private shipbuilder's design to replace the obsolete Type 41 or 'Leopard'- and Type 61 or 'Salisbury'-class frigates. Because of numerous bureaucratic problems, private and official ship designers were not brought together on the project, resulting in a class which handled well and was much liked by crews, but lacked sufficient growth potential to take the new generation of sensor and weapon fits. Thus the vessels did not receive new equipment when refitted.

Falklands War

During the 1982 Falklands War **Avenger**, **Ardent**, **Arrow**, **Antelope** and **Alacrity** served in the main combat zone, while **Active** and **Ambuscade** assisted in supporting operations and the occasional shore bombardment. Only the lead ship, **Amazon**, missed the war as it was in the Far East. On 21 May 1982 the *Ardent* was so badly damaged in air attacks that it sank, while two days later the *Antelope* caught fire and exploded when an unexploded bomb detonated while being defused.

After the war the remaining class members were found to have severe hull cracking; indeed *Arrow* had to limp home from the Falklands

to enter emergency refit. All the ships were strengthened with steel inserts welded to the hull structure, but the future of the class remained clouded, and in 1993-94 the

six ships were sold to Pakistan as the **Tariq**, **Babur**, **Khaibar**, **Badr**, **Shajahan** and **Tippu Sultan** of the **'Tariq' class** and have been fittted with new missiles.

*The 'Oliver Hazard Perry'-class frigate USS **Rueben James** (rear) alongside Pakistan's **Shahjahan** and **Tippu Sultan**. The 'Tariq' class replace the obsolete Seacat SAM system with either the Chinese LY 60N (a copy of Aspide) or Harpoon missiles carried in place of the Exocet that was added to the Royal Navy ships.*

*Left: The ill-fated HMS **Antelope**. Type 21 frigates handle well, but lack the capacity to handle the most up-to-date weapon systems.*

*Right: HMS **Amazon** leads **Antelope** through calm sea. Royal Navy Type 21s carried four Exocet missile launchers.*

*Below: HMS **Ambuscade**. These vessels suffered severe cracking in the upper deck.*

Type 22 'Broadsword' class Guided-missile frigate

Batch 3 variants of the 'Broadsword' class are highly capable ships, although the frigate description may seem odd for a vessel with a full-load displacement of 4,800 tons and a length of 148.1 m (485 ft 10 in) with significant anti-air, surface and submarine capabilities.

Originally to have been a class of 26 to follow the 'Leanders', the **Type 22** or **'Broadsword'-class** design was conceived as an ASW type for service in the Greenland-Iceland-UK gap against modern high-performance nuclear submarines. As has happened to most modern British naval programmes, however, the 'chop' fell during defence cuts and the procurement schedule was changed somewhat. The original four **'Broadsword Batch 1'** vessels were *Broadsword*, *Battleaxe*, *Brilliant* and

Brazen. Although rated as frigates, these are in fact larger than the contemporary Type 42 destroyers, and were designated frigates for purely political reasons. The hull, with greater freeboard than that of the destroyers, is an improved Type 12 design for capability in rough weather without a significant reduction in speed. The *Brilliant* and *Broadsword* distinguished themselves in the Falklands, the former being the first to fire the Seawolf in anger.

Unfortunately, because of design shortcomings, the

Type 22s could not be fitted with the definitive Type 2031(Z) towed-array sonar at the stern, so a lengthened **'Broadsword Batch 2'** of six ships was authorised as *Boxer*, *Beaver*, *Brave*, *London*, *Sheffield* and *Coventry*. These also differ among themselves as the *Brave* has a Rolls-Royce COGAG arrangement with two Spey SM1A (later SM1C) and two Tyne RM1C gas turbines. The *Brave* was also the first Type 22 unit to have an enlarged platform to take a Sea King or Merlin ASW helicopter.

Following the ships' success in the 1982 Falklands War, a **'Broadsword Batch 3'** variant was ordered: the four units were *Cornwall*, *Cumberland*, *Campbeltown* and *Chatham*. These have the same basic hull as the Batch 2s but with eight Harpoon missiles, a single 4.5-in (114-mm) DP gun and one 30-mm Goalkeeper CIWS. All ships still in British ser-

vice now have Type 2050 rather than Type 2016 sonar.

Brazilian service

The Batch 1 ships have been sold to Brazil as the *Greenhalgh*, *Dodsworth*, *Bosisio* and *Rademaker* (with an anitional 40-mm gun added on each beam and MM.40 Exocets) and the *London*, *Boxer*, *Beaver*, *Brave* and *Coventry* were deleted in 1999-2001.

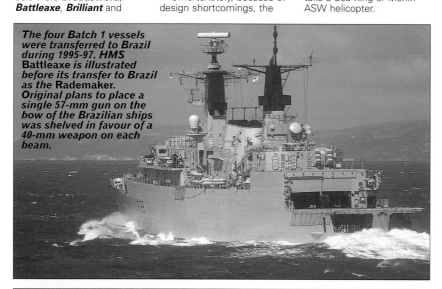

The four Batch 1 vessels were transferred to Brazil during 1995-97. HMS Battleaxe is illustrated before its transfer to Brazil as the Rademaker. Original plans to place a single 57-mm gun on the bow of the Brazilian ships was shelved in favour of a 40-mm weapon on each beam.

SPECIFICATION
'Broadsword Batch 1' class

Displacement: 3,500 tons standard; 4,400 tons full load
Dimensions: length 131.06 m (430 ft); beam 14.78 m (48 ft 6 in); draught 6.05 m (19 ft 10 in)
Propulsion: COGOG with two Rolls-Royce Olympus TM3B gas turbines delivering 40710 kW (54,600 shp) and two Rolls-Royce Tyne RM1A gas turbines delivering 7230 kW (9,700 shp) to two shafts
Performance: speed 29 kts; range 8335 km (5,180 miles) at 18 kts
Armament: four container-launchers for four MM.38 Exocet anti-ship missiles, two GWS 25 sextuple launchers for 60 Seawolf SAMs, two 40- or 30-mm AA guns,

two 20-mm AA guns, and (*Brilliant* and *Brazen*) two triple 324-mm (12.75-in) STWS Mk 1 tubes for Mk 46 and Stingray ASW torpedoes
Electronics: one Type 967/968 air/surface search radar, two Type 910 Seawolf fire-control radars, one Type 1006 navigation radar, one CAAIS combat data system, one UAA-1 ESM system, two Corvus chaff launchers, two Mk 36 SRBOC chaff launchers, one Type 2016 hull sonar, and one Type 2008 underwater telephone
Aircraft: one or two Lynx HAS.Mk 2/3 or HMA.Mk 8 ASW/anti-ship helicopters
Complement: 223 normal and 248 maximum

Below: The Batch 2 vessel HMS Boxer was retired from Royal Navy service in 1999. The 'Broadswords' were designed primarily for the ASW and are also capable of acting as OTC (Officer in Tactical Command). A single Lynx is normally embarked and additional EW equipment is added for deployments.

'Garcia' and 'Brooke' classes Frigate and Guided-missile frigate

The USS Brooke was the name ship of its class, essentially a derivative of the 'Garcia' class of ocean escort with the after 5-in (127-mm) gun replaced by a single-rail SAM launcher. The ship became the Pakistani Khaibar for a time after 1988.

Designed in the late 1950s as successors to World War II destroyers in the oceanic escort role, the **'Garcia'-class** ASW and **'Brooke'-class** AAW ships were ordered by the US Navy to the extent of 10 and six units respectively. Further production of the latter ended during Fiscal Year 1963 because of the ships' high cost and limited capability. Although they were relatively modern, the US Navy

evinced little real interest in the process of steady modernisation for the ASW ships **Garcia**, **Bradley**, **Edward McDonnell**, **Brumby**, **Davidson**, **Voge**, **Sample**, **Koelsch**, **Albert David** and **O'Callahan** (laid down at four yards between 1962 and 1964 for completion between 1964 and 1967) with new guns, Harpoon anti-ship missiles and modern ESM equipment. Over the years the ships of the class, initially

classified in USN service as destroyer escorts, were frequently used for the testing of several prototype items of systems, including the SQR-15 linear towed-array sonar which was installed in the *Garcia* and *Edward McDonnell* in place of the otherwise standard LAMPS I ASW helicopter. An automated ASW tactical data system (TDS) was carried by the *Voge* and *Koelsch*, while on the ships from the *Voge*

onward a reload magazine for the ASROC anti-submarine system was built into the superstructure, boosting the number of RUR-5A rocket-launched weapons from eight to 16.

SAM ships

The SAM ships **Brooke**, **Ramsey**, **Schofield**, **Talbot**, **Richard L. Page** and **Julius F. Furer** (built and completed by two yards in the period 1962-1967) were identical to the 'Garcias' except for the incorporation of a single-rail Mk 22 launcher, originally for 16 Tartar and later for the same number of Standard SM-1MR missiles, in place of the aft 5-in (127-mm) gun mount. From the *Talbot* onward an ASROC reload magazine was also incorpo-

rated into the forward part of the superstructure. The *Talbot* was used as the test ship for the weapons and sensor fit for the 'Oliver Hazard Perry' class, but was then returned to normal appearance. The only major modernisation of the ships was the fitting of the SLQ-32(V)2 ESM suite to replace older systems.

The ships were retired from US service in the late 1980s, four 'Garcias' being leased to Brazil as the **Pernambuco, Paraíba, Paraná** and **Pará**. Four of each class were leased to Pakistan as the **Saif, Harbah, Slqqat, Aslat, Khaibar, Hunam, Tabuk** and **Badr**, but were later returned when the US refused to renew the leases.

Left: Evident in the after part of the 'Brooke'-class USS Ramsey is the hangar for the LAMPS I light multi-role (SH-2F Seasprite) helicopter and, between the hangar and the superstructure, the Mk 22 single-arm launcher for medium-range SAMs.

Below: The USS O'Callahan was the last unit of the 'Garcia' class of oceanic escorts optimised for the anti-submarine role. The 16 'Garcia'- and 'Brooke'-class ships were complemented by a 17th unit, the experimental USS Glover with pump-jet propulsion.

SPECIFICATION

'Garcia' class
Displacement: 2,620 tons standard; 3,560 tons full load
Dimensions: length 126.3 m (414 ft 6 in); beam 13.5 m (44ft 4in); draught 4.4 m (14 ft 6 in)
Propulsion: geared steam turbines delivering 26100 kW (35,000 shp) to one shaft
Performance: speed 27.5 kts; endurance 7400 km (4,600 miles) at 20 kts
Armament: two 5-in (127-mm) Mk 30 DP guns, one octuple Mk 16 ASROC launcher with eight (first five ships) or 16 (other ships) RUR-5A

rockets, and two triple 12.75-in (324-mm) Mk 32 tubes for Mk 46 ASW torpedoes (12 reloads)
Electronics: one SPS-40 air search radar, one SPS-10 surface search radar, one SPG-35 fire-control radar, one LN66 navigation radar, one WLR-1 ECM system, one WLR-3 ECM system, one ULQ-6 ECM system, one SQS-26 bow sonar, and (*Garcia* and *McDonnell* only) one BQR-15 towed sonar
Aircraft: one SH-2F Seasprite LAMPS I helicopter (not in *Garcia* and *McDonnell*)
Complement: 239-247

'Knox' class Frigate

The USS Knox (FF-1052) was the first ship of its class. Evolved from the preceding 'Garcia' and 'Brooke' classes, the 'Knox'-class vessels were later fitted with Harpoon anti-ship missiles and the 20-mm Phalanx close-in weapon system (CIWS) for last-ditch defence against sea-skimming anti-ship missiles.

The 'Knox' class is similar to the 'Garcia' and 'Brooke' classes but with slightly larger dimensions as a result of the use of non-pressure fired boilers. The type was designed in the early 1960s, the first of these ocean escort vessels (now generally regarded as frigates) entered US Navy service in 1969, and the last units of the 46-strong class were delivered in 1974. They are specialised ASW ships and were heavily criticised for their single-shaft propulsion and gun armament of just one 5-in (127-mm) weapon.

Spanish derivative

A five-ship class based on the design but with a Mk 22 missile launcher for 13 Standard SM-1MR and three Harpoon missiles was constructed in Spain for the Spanish navy. Built with US aid, the ships are the **Baleares**, **Andalucia**, **Cataluña**, **Asturias** and **Extremadura**, which also carried two Mk 25 ASW torpedo tubes (now no longer used) as well as the two twin Mk 32 systems, for which a total of 22 Mk 44/46 and 19 Mk 37 ASW torpedoes was stored in each ship's magazines.

From 1980 onwards the American 'Knox' ships were taken in hand to receive raised bulwarks and spray strakes forward to improve their seakeeping in heavy weather. Like the 'Garcia' class, numerous 'Knox' ships have been used over the years to test individual prototype weapon and sensor systems. The first 32 ships were equipped with an octuple launcher for the Sea Sparrow SAM, but this was replaced by a 20-mm Phalanx CIWS of the type eventually fitted to all 46 ships. The port pair of the four twin cells of the ASROC launcher were retrofitted to fire the Harpoon anti-ship missile, while all of the vessels were fitted to carry the SQR-18A TACTASS towed-array sonar, in 34 of the ships replacing the SQS-35A VDS system carried in a stern well. For helicopter operations an SRN-15 TACAN is carried and the SLQ-32(V)1 ESM system was upgraded to the SLQ-32(V)2 configuration. To reduce underwater radiated noise the Prairie/Masker bubble system is used on the hull and propeller. The ASW TDS first evaluated in the 'Garcia' class was fitted as the ships were refitted. By 1986 eight units had been reassigned to the Naval Reserve Force as replacements for old World War II destroyers as these were retired.

American class

The class comprised the **Knox**, **Roark**, **Gray**, **Hepburn**, **Connole**, **Rathburne**, **Meyerkord**, **W. S. Sims**, **Lang**, **Patterson**, **Whipple**, **Reasoner**, **Lockwood**, **Stein**, **Marvin Shields**, **Francis Hammond**, **Vreeland**, **Bagley**, **Downes**, **Badger**, **Blakely**, **Robert E. Peary**, **Harold E. Holt**, **Trippe**, **Fanning**, **Ouellet**, **Joseph Hewes**, **Bowen**, **Paul**, **Aylwin**, **Elmer Montgomery**, **Cook**, **McCandless**, **Donald B. Beary**, **Brewton**, **Kirk**, **Barbey**, **Jesse L. Brown**, **Ainsworth**, **Miller**, **Thomas C. Hart**, **Capodanno**, **Pharris**, **Truett**, **Valdez** and **Moinester**.

The ships were decommissioned from US service in the early 1990s, and many of the vessels were transferred to the navies of friendly nations. At the beginning of the 21st century considerable numbers of the 'Knox'-class ships were still in extensive service with Egypt (two of four **'Damyat'-class** ships), Greece (one of three **'Epirus'-class** ships), Mexico (four **'Allende'-class** ships), Taiwan (eight out of nine **'Chin Yang'-class** ships), Thailand (two **'Phutta Yofta Chulalok'-class** ships) and Turkey (six out of nine **'Tepe'-class** ships).

Left: Seen in US Navy service, the USS Cook was completed by Avondale in December 1971 as one of the 'Knox' class of ASW frigates. In August 1995 it was recommissioned as the Taiwanese navy's Hae Yang.

The USS Pharris is seen during an exercise off the South American coast. The 46 'Knox'-class vessels were built as dedicated oceanic ASW escorts, and later in their lives were revised to improve their seakeeping qualities.

SPECIFICATION

'Knox' class

Displacement: 3,011 tons standard; 3,877 tons (first 26 ships) or 4,250 tons (last 20 ships) full load

Dimensions: length 133.5 m (438 ft); beam 14.3 m (47 ft); draught 4.6 m (15 ft)

Propulsion: geared steam turbines delivering 26100 kW (35,000 shp) to one shaft

Performance: speed 27 kts; endurance 8335 km (5,180 miles) at 20 kts

Armament: one 5-in (127-mm) Mk 42 DP gun, one 20-mm Mk 15 Phalanx CIWS replacing one octuple launcher for eight RIM-7 Sea Sparrow SAMs, one octuple Mk 16 ASROC launcher for 12 RUR-5A anti-submarine rockets and four Harpoon anti-ship missiles, and two twin 12.75-in (324-mm) Mk 32 launchers for 22 Mk 46 ASW torpedoes

Electronics: one SPS-40B air search radar, one SPS-10 surface search radar, one SPG-53 fire-control radar, one LN66 navigation radar, one ASW tactical data system, one SRN-15 TACAN, one SQS-26 bow sonar, and one SQS-35 variable-depth sonar (34 ships); all later had one SQR-18A towed-array sonar

Aircraft: one SH-2F Seasprite LAMPS I helicopter

Complement: 283

'Anzac' class Frigate

In November 1989 the Australian government contracted with Australian Marine Engineering Consolidated for the construction of 10 **'Anzac'-class** guided-missile frigates (eight and two ships for the Royal Australian and Royal New Zealand Navies respectively) based on the Meko 200

Below: Originally to have been the Arrernte, *HMAS* Arunta *is Australia's second 'Anzac'-class frigate. Capability for the Evolved Sea Sparrow SAM is retrofitted in the first two ships and built into the last six units.*

Commissioned by the Royal Australian Navy in May 1996, HMAS Anzac *was the first of its class, a capable frigate type with guided-missile frigate update capability.*

design prepared by Blohm & Voss of Germany. The design is of the modular type, allowing complete sections of the ships to be built in Newcastle in Australia and Whangerei in New Zealand for delivery to the Transfield Shipbuilding (now Tenix Defence Systems) yard at Williamstown in Australia for final assembly. The modular design also facilitates the

retrofit of updated equipment as an existing module can be removed and replaced by a new module already fitted with the new equipment, which could include a number of modern guided weapon types as well as more advanced sensors.

The 'Anzac'-class ships dif-

fer from other Meko 200 frigates mainly in their single-shaft machinery, and in response to Australian army pressure the calibre of the main gun was increased from 76 to 127 mm (3 to 5 in).

The Australian ships, due for completion between May

1996 and March 2006, are HMAS **Anzac**, **Arunta**, **Warramunga**, **Stuart**, **Parramatta**, **Ballarat**, **Toowoomba** and **Perth**, while the New Zealand ships, commissioned in July 1997 and December 1999, are HMNZS **Te Kaha** and **Te Mana**.

SPECIFICATION

'Anzac' class
Displacement: 3,600 tons full load
Dimensions: length 118 m (387 ft 2 in); beam 14.8 m (48 ft 7 in); draught 4.35 m (14 ft 3 in)
Propulsion: CODOG with one General Electric LM2500 gas turbine delivering 22495 kW (30,170 shp) and two MTU 12V 1163 TB83 diesels delivering 6590 kW (8,840 shp) to one shaft
Performance: speed 27 kts; range 11105 km (6,900 miles) at 18 kts
Armament: one 5-in (127-mm) gun, one octuple vertical-launch system for eight Sea Sparrow or Quadpack

launcher for 32 Evolved Sea Sparrow SAMs, and two triple 324-mm (12.75-in) tubes for Mk 46 anti-submarine torpedoes
Electronics: SPS-49(V)8 ANZ air search radar, 9LV 453 TIR air/ surface search radar, 9600 ARPA navigation radar, 9LV 453 fire-control radar, 9LV 453 Mk 3 combat data system, 9LV 453 optronic director, Sceptre A and PST-1720 Telegon 10 ESM, decoy launchers, SLQ-25A towed torpedo decoy, and Spherion B hull-mounted active sonar
Aircraft: one S-70B or SH-2G helicopter
Complement: 163

'Halifax' class FFG

In December 1977 the Canadian government decided to order an initial six out of a projected 20 helicopter-carrying frigates urgently needed to replace Canada's ageing force of ocean escort and anti-submarine frigates. The programme was then overtaken by a number of delays, and it was June 1983 before the contract for the first six ships was finally awarded to the St John Shipbuilding company of New Brunswick. Design of the **'Halifax'-class** ships was shared between St John and Paramax Electronics (now Loral Canada), and the building of three of the eventual 12 ships (including a second group of six ordered in December 1987) was entrusted to Marine Industries (now MIL-Davie) of Lauzon and Sorel, Quebec.

Laid down between March 1987 and April 1995 for launch between April 1988 and November 1995 and commissioning between June 1992 and September 1996, the 12 'Halifax'-class frigates are HMCS **Halifax**, **Vancouver**, **Ville de Québec**, **Toronto**, **Regina**, **Calgary**, **Montreal**, **Fredericton**, **Winnipeg**,

Right: Resulting from a much-delayed programme and then revealing a noise problem on trials, the 'Halifax' class of guided-missile frigates has matured as an excellent oceanic patrol type. This is HMCS Regina.

Below: Seen in the form of HMCS Vancouver, *the 'Halifax' class has only light gun armament (one 57-mm Bofors SAK Mk 2 mounting) but good anti-ship and anti-submarine capabilities.*

SPECIFICATION

'Halifax' class
Displacement: 4,770 tons full load
Dimensions: length 134.7 m (441 ft 1 in); beam 16.4 m (53 ft 10 in); draught 7.1 m (23 ft 2 in)
Propulsion: CODOG with two General Electric LM2500 gas turbines delivering 35412 kW (47,494 shp) and one SEMT-Pielstick 20 PA6 V 280 diesel delivering 6560 kW (8,800 shp) to two shafts
Performance: speed 29 kts; range 17620 km (10,950 miles) at 13 kts
Armament: two quadruple launchers for eight Harpoon anti-ship missiles, one Sea Sparrow SAM system, one 57-mm gun, one 20-mm Phalanx CIWS mounting, and two twin 324-mm (12.75-in) tubes for Mk 46 anti-submarine torpedoes
Electronics: SPS-49(V)5 air search radar, Sea Giraffe HC 150 air/surface search radar, Type 1007 navigation radar, two SPG-503 (STIR 1.8) fire-control radars, UYC-501 SHINPADS combat data system, Canews SLQ-501 and Ramses SLQ-503 ESM, decoy launchers, SLQ-25 towed torpedo decoy, SQS-510 hull-mounted active sonar, and SQR-501 CANTASS towed-array sonar
Aircraft: one CH-124 helicopter
Complement: 215 including 17 aircrew

Charlottetown, *St John's* and *Ottawa*.

Considerable effort was placed in the design and construction phases of the programme on the enhancement of the ships' 'stealthiness', and for this reason the gas turbines are raft-mounted and there is a Dresball IR suppression system. Even so, trials of the first ships revealed a radiated noise level higher than anticipated, mainly at higher speeds, but these problems have been overcome and the ships are now regarded as notably quiet and stable in all sea conditions.

The ships have a full capability (a hangar as well as a flight platform and an Indal RAST handling system) over the stern for one large helicopter, which is currently the CH-124A anti-submarine or CH-124B HELTAS (HELicopter Towed-Array Support) version of the obsolescent Sikorsky S-61 Sea King.

Given the importance of an advanced anti-submarine capability to Canadian maritime operations, the ships are to be revised from 2006 with an ITAPSS (Integrated Towed Active/Passive Sonar System), and self-protection against air attack is to be enhanced from 2004 by the retrofit of the Evolved Sea Sparrow SAM system in place of the current Mk 48 octuple vertical-launch system for 16 RIM-7P Sea Sparrow SAMs. The limitations of radar-based fire-control systems in the face of modern countermeasures were also reflected from 2002 by the retrofit of a Wescan 14 optronic fire-control capability.

While seven of the ships are deployed on Canada's Atlantic seaboard, the other five (in the form of the *Vancouver*, *Regina*, *Calgary*, *Winnipeg* and *Ottawa*) are based on the country's Pacific seaboard.

'Thetis' class Frigate

Requiring a successor to the 'Hvidbjørnen' class of obsolescent and relatively small frigates used for the patrol and fishery protection roles off Greenland and the Faeroe Islands as well as in the North Sea, the Danish government contracted with YARD of Glasgow in 1986 for a study to determine the parameters of the new class. The results of this study led to the award of a detailed design contract, completed in mid-1987, to Dwinger Marine Consultants. The design was of the StanFlex 3000 type offering much commonality of concept and more limited commonality of components with the earlier StanFlex300 type that had been ordered as the 'Flyvefisken' class of 14 multi-role large patrol/attack and minehunter/layer craft.

In October 1987 the Danish government ordered four examples of this **'Thetis' class** of frigate from Svenborg Vaerft. Laid down between October 1988 and January 1991 for launching between July 1989 and October 1991 and commissioning between July 1991 and November 1992, the four ships are the **Thetis**, **Triton**, **Vaedderen** and **Hvidbjørnen**. The ships are based on a hull some 30 m (100 ft) longer than that of the 'Hvidbjørnen' class for improved sea-keeping and to provide the facility for the retrofit, as and when necessary, of additional armament and/or sensors. To this extent the StanFlex concept is similar to the Meko concept pioneered by Blohm & Voss as it permits the addition of new equipment built into standard-size containers.

Features of the design include a hull strengthened to allow operation in ice up to 1 m (3ft 4in) thick, and a double skin extends to a depth of 2 m (6ft 7in) below the waterline. Some consideration was also given to making the ships moderately 'stealthy', as evidenced by the location of the anchor equipment, bollards and winches below the upper deck. The ships have a full helicopter capability (hangar as well as a flight platform), and while the type currently embarked is a Westland Lynx light helicopter, the platform has the size and strength to handle larger helicopters such as the Westland Sea King and Agusta/Westland Merlin. On each side of the hangar is accommodation for an inflatable rigid boarding craft handled by a dedicated crane.

The ships are optimised for the fishery and EEZ protection roles rather than high-intensity combat operations, and this made it feasible for the bridge and operations room to be combined as a single unit. The *Thetis* is used for seismological survey off Greenland and has a revised stern allowing the use of a towed-array sonar and a pneumatic noise gun. All four of the ships are to be upgraded with more modern air search radar and a SAM system.

*The **Thetis** is the lead ship of a Danish class of four simple frigates optimised for the fishery and **EEZ** protection role, but the design has the capability for upgrade with more capable weapons and sensors. The **Thetis** differs from its three sisters in details of her stern, which is adapted for the towing of seismological noise generators and receivers.*

SPECIFICATION

'Thetis' class
Displacement: 2,600 tons standard; 3,500 tons full load
Dimensions: length 112.5 m (369 ft 1 in); beam 14.4 m (47 ft 3 in); draught 6 m (19 ft 8 in)
Propulsion: three Burmeister & Wain diesels delivering 8050 kW (10,800 shp) to one shaft
Performance: speed 20 kts; range 15770 km (9,800 miles) at 15.5 kts
Armament: one 76-mm (3-in) gun, one or two 20-mm guns, and two depth charge rails
Electronics: AWS 6 air/surface search radar, Scanter Mil surface search radar, FR1505DA navigation radar, 9LV Mk 3 fire-control radar, 9LV 200 Mk 3 optronic director, Terma TDS combat data system, Cutlass ESM, Scorpion ECM, two Sea Gnat decoy launchers, C-Teck hull-mounted sonar, and TSM 2640 Salmon variable-depth sonar
Aircraft: one Westland Lynx Mk 91 helicopter
Complement: up to 72

'La Fayette' class Guided-missile frigate

Originally designated as *fré-gates légères* but then reclassified in 1992 as *fré-gates type La Fayette*, the **'La Fayette' class** of multi-purpose frigates was ordered in July 1988 (first three) and September 1992 (last three, of which the final unit was later cancelled). All built by the DCN at Lorient, the ships were commissioned between March 1996 and October 2001 as the **La Fayette**, **Surcouf**, **Courbet**, **Aconit** (ex-*Jauréguiberry*) and **Guépratte**.

The ships were created to perform a number of missions including crisis intervention and the seaward defence of France and its overseas territories. The ships can also be integrated into an intervention task force based on an aircraft carrier and/or amphibious ships. The multiplicity of the tasks required combined with the steady evolution of weapons and sensors to suggest a modular approach to construction in an effort to facilitate modifications and update, and also to cater for

the requirements of the export market which, by a time early in the 21st century, comprised 15 ships (three to an improved **'Arriyad' class** standard for Saudi Arabia and six each for Singapore and Taiwan, the last of the **'Kang Ding' class**).

'Stealth' features

Each ship comprises about 70 modules, two of which are large propulsion modules housing the diesel engines. Many of the modules are prefabricated off-site and assembled on the building way. The design's other new feature is the emphasis placed on electromagnetic and acoustic 'stealthing'. The engines are mounted on suspended rafts to reduce noise, the sides of the hull and the superstructures are inclined at about 10°, an inclined bulwark forward shields the single gun mounting, the masts and superstructure are coated with radar-absorbent paint, the forecastle and quarterdeck have composite radar-absorbent cladding, and

Commissioned in 1997, the Surcouf *was the second of the 'La Fayette' class of multi-role frigates to be completed. Note the 100-mm gun in raised position.*

the 'cleanliness' of the super-structure is enhanced by the concealment of the ships' boats behind amid-ships doors.

The initial armament and sensor fit is optimised for overseas patrol, but there is extensive provision for

upgrade with an anti-subma-rine capability and more modern weapons and sen-

sors, and the anti-air capabil-ity is already being improved with a new SAM system.

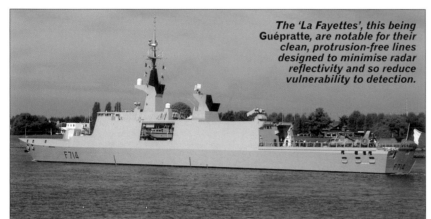

The 'La Fayettes', this being Guépratte, *are notable for their clean, protrusion-free lines designed to minimise radar reflectivity and so reduce vulnerability to detection.*

SPECIFICATION

'La Fayette' class
Displacement: 3,700 tons full load
Dimensions: length 124.2 m (407 ft 6 in); beam 15.4 m (50 ft 6 in); draught 5.9 m (19 ft 4 in)
Propulsion: CODAD with four SEMT-Pielstick 12 PA6 V 280 STC diesels delivering 15740 kW (21,110 shp) to four shafts
Performance: speed 25 kts; range 16675 km (10,360 miles) at 12 kts
Armament: two quadruple launchers for MM.40 Exocet Block 2 SSMs, one octuple Crotale Naval CN 2 launcher for VT 1 SAMs (or EDIR launcher for eight V3 SAMs on *La Fayette*) (possibly to be replaced by a SAAM vertical-launch system for 16

Aster 15 SAMs), one 100-mm (3.9-in) DP gun, and two 20-mm cannon
Electronics: one DRBV 15C Sea Tiger Mk 2 air/surface search radar, one Castor 2J gun fire-control radar, one Crotale SAM fire-control radar (possibly to be replaced by Arabel), two DRBN 34A navigation radars, one CTM radar/IR fire-control system, one TDS 90 VIGY optronic fire-control system, TAVITAC 2000 combat data system, ARBR 17 or 21 and ARBG 1 Saigon ESM systems, ARBB 33 ECM, and two Dagaie Mk 2 decoy launchers
Aircraft: one AS 565MA Panther or NH 90 helicopter
Complement: 163

'D'Estienne d'Orves' class Guided-missile frigate

Classed as an aviso, *or coastal escort, the* Commandant Blaison *was one of the later 'D'Estienne d'Orves'-class frigates to enter service. All the class have Exocet capacity, though the weapons are not always shipped. The class is now being phased out of French service, in which nine survive, including this vessel, other vessels having been sold to Argentina (three 'Drummond' class) and Turkey (six 'Buruk' class).*

Designed for coastal escort, the 17 ships of the **'D'Estienne d'Orves' class** were commissioned

between September 1976 and May 1984 as limited-capability corvettes that are now classified as light

frigates. The ships can also be used for scouting missions, training and for overseas 'flag showing'

duties, for which one officer and 17 men from the naval infantry can be accommo-dated. Since entering

service the type has been sold to the Argentine navy, whose three ships (the **Drummond**, **Guerrico** and

The 'D'Estienne d'Orves' class comprises small but useful coastal escorts. The type is being reduced in French service, six of the ships going to Turkey.

Granville) included two that had originally been ordered by South Africa but could not be delivered because of a UN arms embargo, and a third built for Argentina. The three saw service in the 1982 Falklands War, and in this campaign the *Guerrico* suffered the ignominy of being damaged by shore fire from small arms and anti-tank rocket-launchers during the Argentine seizure of

South Georgia on 3 April; this required the vessel to be dry docked for three days for repairs to the hull and armament.

Rated as *avisos* by the French, the first of the class was laid down at Lorient Naval Dockyard in 1972 and commissioned into service in 1976. Six of the ships were sold to Turkey in October 2000 and delivered by July 2002 after refit at

Brest. Two more of the 17 ships have been deleted from the French naval list, and of the remaining nine (six and three based at Brest and Toulon respectively), current plans call for their decommissioning from 2009 after a reprieve from the initial plan in which the first three would have been paid off in 1996 with the other 14 following at regular intervals up to 2004.

SPECIFICATION

'D'Estienne d'Orves' class
Ships in class: *D'Estienne d'Orves* (F781), *Amyot d'Inville* (F782), *Drogou* (F783), *Détroyat* (F784), *Jean Moulin* (F785), *Quartier Maître Anquetil* (F786), *Commandant de Pimodan* (F787), *Second Maître de Bihan* (F788), *Lieutenant de Vaisseau Le Henaff* (F789), *Lieutenant de Vaisseau Lavalle* (F790), *Commandant l'Herminier* (F791), *Premier Maître l'Her* (F792), *Commandant Blaison* (F793), *Enseigne de Vaisseau Jacoubet* (F794), *Commandant Ducuing* (F795), *Commandant Birot* (F796) and *Commandant Bouan* (F797).
Displacement: 1,175 tons standard; 1,250 tons or, later ships, 1,330 tons full load
Dimensions: length 80 m (262 ft 6 in); beam 10.3 m (33 ft 9½ in); draught 5.3 m (17 ft 4¾ in)
Propulsion: two SEMT-Pielstick 12PC2 V 400 diesels delivering 8205 kW (11,000 shp) to two shafts or, in F791, two SEMT-Pielstick 12

PA6 280 BTC diesels delivering 10740kW (14,400 shp) to two shafts
Performance: speed 23.5 kts; range 8350 km (5,190 miles) at 15 kts
Armament: (F781, F783, F786 and F787) two single launchers for MM.38 Exocet SSMs or (F792-F797) four single launchers for MM.40 Exocet SSMs, one Simbad twin launcher for Mistral short-range SAMs, one 100-mm (3.9-in) DP gun, two 20-mm AA guns, one 375-mm (14.76-in) Creusot Loire Mk 54 sextuple launcher for anti-submarine rockets (F789-F791), and four tubes for four L3 or L5 torpedoes
Electronics: one DRBV 51A air/surface search radar, one DRBC 32E gun fire-control radar, one DRBN 32 navigation radar, one Vega fire-control system, one Panda optronic director, ARBR 16 ESM, two Dagaie decoy launchers, and one DUBA 25 hull sonar
Complement: 108 with marines

'Brandenburg' class Guided-missile frigate

The **'Brandenburg' class** of guided-missile frigates, otherwise designated as the **Type 123 class**, were designed as one-for-one replacements for the four elderly destroyers of the 'Hamburg' class, which were all decommissioned in the first half of the 1990s. The new frigates were originally to have been designated as the **'Deutschland' class**, and the ships were ordered in June 1989 from four German yards on the basis of a Blohm & Voss design selected in October of the previous year. The ships are the **Brandenburg** from Blohm & Voss of Hamburg, **Schleswig-Holstein** from Howaldtswerke of Kiel, **Bayern** from Thyssen Nordseewerke of Emden, and **Mecklenburg-Vorpommern** from Bremer Vulkan/Thyssen. The ships were laid down in 1992-93, launched in 1992-95, and commissioned in 1994-96,

and currently constitute the 6th Frigate Squadron based at Wilhelmshaven.

The design is a mixture of Blohm & Voss's now well-proved MEKO system of modular construction with improved serviceability features from the Type 122 or 'Bremen' class of eight smaller guided-missile frigates, with which the 'Brandenburg' class shares the propulsion arrangement. This, because of their greater size, results in a slight loss of speed in the 'Brandenburg' vessels. The ships are of all-steel construction and incorporate current 'stealth' thinking, fin stabilisers, and provision for a task group commander and his staff. Each ship also possesses provision for one Rigid Inflatable Boat (RIB) to be used by boarding parties.

The main gun is sited on the forecastle, the two SAM systems are forward and aft on the superstruc-

Brandenburg, *lead ship of a four-strong class of general-purpose warships. The areas forward of the bridge carry the VLS for medium-range SAMs, a trainable launcher for short-range SAMs, and a 76-mm gun.*

ture, and there are two helicopters.

Pending the advent of the three 'Sachsen' (Type 124) class of air-defence frigates, the 'Brandenburgs' are Germany's most advanced surface ships.

SPECIFICATION

'Brandenburg' class
Displacement: 4,900 tons full load
Dimensions: length 138.9 m (455 ft 9 in); beam 16.7 m (54 ft 10 in); draught 6.8 m (22 ft 4 in)
Propulsion: CODOG with two General Electric LM2500SA-ML gas turbines delivering 38025 kW (51,000 shp) and two MTU 20V 956 TB92 diesels delivering 8250 kW (11,065 shp) to two shafts
Performance: speed 29 kts; range 7400 km (4,600 miles) at 18 kts
Armament: two twin launchers for MM.38 Exocet anti-ship missiles, one VLS Mk 41 for 16 NATO Sea Sparrow medium-range SAMs, two Mk 49 21-cell launchers for RAM short-range SAMs, one 76-mm (3-in) OTO Melara DP gun, two

20-mm Rheinmetall AA guns (to be replaced by two 27-mm Mauser guns), and two 324-mm (12.75-in) Mk 32 twin tubes for Mk 46 (to be replaced by Mu 90 Impact) anti-submarine torpedoes
Electronics: one LW-08 air search radar, one SMART 3D air/surface search radar, two STIR 180 fire-control radars, two Raypath navigation radars, one MWCS weapons control system with a WBA optronic director, SATIR combat data system, one FL 1800S ESM system, two SCLAR decoy launchers, one DSQS-23BZ hull-mounted active sonar, and one LFASS towed-array active sonar
Aircraft: two Lynx Mk 88 or Lynx Mk 88A helicopters
Complement: 218

'Bremen' class Guided-missile frigate

A Germanised modification of the gas turbine-powered Dutch 'Kortenaer' design, the eight-ship **'Bremen' class**, otherwise known as the **Type 122 class**, has replaced the deleted ships of two older types, namely the 'Fletcher' (Type 119) class of destroyers and the 'Köln' (Type 120) class of frigates. The hulls were mated with the propulsion plant in the five building yards, and the ships were then towed to the yard of the prime contractor, Bremer Vulkan, for the installation of the electronic and weapon systems. The first order was placed in 1977, and the ship eventually commissioned in May 1982 after government approval had been given for the construction in 1976.

The ships are fitted with fin stabilisers and the US Prairie/Masker bubble system on the hull and propellers to reduce radiated noise levels from the machinery spaces. A complete NBC defence citadel system is also fitted. Two 21-round launchers for the RAM point-defence SAM, with passive radar/infra-red terminal homing, were retrofitted atop the hangar in 1993-96. The embarked ASW helicopters are Lynx Mk 88/88A machines, which differ from the Royal Navy Lynx in having a Bendix DASQ-18 active dunking sonar for use with Mk 46 homing torpedoes and Mk 54 depth charges.

For flying in rough weather the ships are fitted with the Bear Trap landing system.

The eight ships are the **Bremen**, **Niedersachsen**, **Rheinland-Pfalz**, **Emden**, **Köln**, **Karlsruhe**, **Augsburg** and **Lübeck**. Plans call for the ships to remain in front-line service until well into the 21st century.

The Emden *was the third of the 'Bremen'-class frigates to be completed. This general-purpose ship's primary ASW weapon is a pair of Lynx helicopters.*

SPECIFICATION	
'Bremen' or Type 122 class **Displacement:** 2,900 tons standard; 3,680 tons full load **Dimensions:** length 130 m (426 ft 6 in); beam 14.5 m (47 ft 7 in); draught 6.5 m (21 ft 4 in) **Propulsion:** CODOG arrangement of two General Electric LM2500 gas turbines delivering 38478 kW (51,600 shp) and two MTU 20V TB92 diesels delivering 7755 kW (10,400 shp) to two shafts **Performance:** speed 30 kts; endurance 7400 km (4,600 miles) at 18 kts **Armament:** two quadruple launchers for eight Harpoon anti-ship missiles, one Mk 29 octuple launcher for 16 RIM-7M Sea	Sparrow SAMs, two 21-cell launchers for 42 RAM SAMs, one 76-mm (3-in) DP gun, and two twin Mk 32 324-mm (12.75-in) tubes for Mk 46 (later Mu 90) ASW torpedoes **Electronics:** one TRS-3D/32 air/surface search radar, one 3RM20 navigation radar, one WM-25/STIR radar fire-control system, one WBA optronic director, one SATIR tactical data system, one FL1800S-II ESM/ECM system, four Mk 36 SRBOC decoy launchers, one SLQ-25 Nixie towed torpedo decoy, and one DSQS-21BZ (BO) bow-mounted active sonar **Aircraft:** two Lynx Mk 88/88A ASW helicopters **Complement:** 219

Based on the Dutch 'Kortenaer'-class design, the 'Bremen' class comprises eight multi-role frigates. Forward of the bridge are the 76-mm (3-in) gun and the launcher for Sea Sparrow medium-range SAMs, abaft the bridge are the two Harpoon anti-ship missiles, and at the stern are the helicopters and two RAM point-defence SAM launchers.

'Espora' class Guided-missile frigate

As part of the Argentine navy's modernisation plans, a contract was signed in August 1979 with the West German Blohm & Voss firm for six missile-armed **Meko 140A16** ships, to be built (to a light frigate design based on the Portuguese 'Joao Coutinho' class) under licence at the AFNE shipyard in Rio Santiago, Ensenada, and known locally as the **'Espora' class**. The programme was badly affected by Argentina's 1982 Falklands defeat and subsequent economic decline, so the lead ship **Espora** was commissioned only in July 1985, a trio comprising the **Rosales**, **Spiro** and **Parker** following in 1986, 1987 and 1990, and a final pair, the **Robinson** and **Gomez**

Basically a scaled-down Meko 360 destroyer, the Meko 140 of the 'Espora' class is a light frigate optimised for the anti-ship/submarine roles. The first three ships were completed with only a platform (later enlarged to accommodate the AS 555 Fennec) for helicopter operations, while the last three were completed with a telescopic hangar of the type that is to be retrofitted to the earlier ships. The after gun mount is a Breda unit with two 40-mm Bofors guns, an identical unit being located immediately forward of the bridge behind and above the 76-mm (3-in) OTO-Melara DP gun.

Roca, in 2000 and 2002 respectively after being launched in 1985 and 1986 but not initially completed. The first three differ from the last three units in initially having only a helicopter landing platform amidships, whereas the others were completed with a telescopic hangar to allow the permanent carriage of a light helicopter. The earlier units may be retrofitted when and if finances allow.

The ships of the 'Espora' class replaced some of Argentina's obsolete ex-American destroyers of the World War II period, and though operated mainly in the offshore and fishery patrol tasks, the ships are equipped predominantly with ASW and anti-surface warfare weapon systems.

The four MM.38 Exocet container-launchers shipped aft could be replaced by eight canisters for the lighter but longer-range MM.40 Exocet anti-ship missiles which the Argentines use on their four Meko 360 destroyers of the 'Almirante Brown' class.

Though designed primarily for service in coastal operations, the class forms a potentially capable offensive force for use in future naval operations such as an admittedly extremely unlikely further attempt to take and hold the Falkland Islands.

The ships are all based at Puerto Belgrano, and the *Spiro* and *Rosales* joined the Coalition fleet during the Gulf War of 1990-91, but their primary role is nonetheless in Argentine waters.

Rosales was built by AFNE of Rio Santiago, and although launched in 1983 was commissioned only in 1986 because of financial problems. The last two ships in the class may have different EW suites.

SPECIFICATION	
'Espora' (Meko 140) class	and two triple 324-mm (12.75-in)
Displacement: 1,470 tons standard; 1,700 tons full load	ILAS 3 tubes for 12 Whitehead A 244/S ASW torpedoes
Dimensions: length 91.2 m (299 ft 2 in); beam 11.1 m (36 ft 5 in); draught 3.4 m (11 ft 2 in)	**Electronics:** one DA-05 air/surface search radar, one TM1226 navigation radar, one WM-28 fire-control radar, one
Propulsion: two SEMT-Pielstick diesels delivering 15200 kW (20,385 shp) to two shafts	Lirod 8 optronic director, one WM-22/41 fire-control system, one SEWACO action information
Performance: speed 27 kts; endurance 7400 km (4,600 miles) at 18 kts	system, one RQN-3B/TQN-2X ESM/ECM system, and one ASO-4 hull-mounted search/attack sonar
Armament: four container-launchers for MM.38 Exocet anti-ship missiles, one 76-mm (3-in) DP and two twin 40-mm AA guns,	**Aircraft:** one SA 319B Alouette III or AS 555 Fennec helicopter **Complement:** 93

'Sachsen' class Guided-missile frigate

The design of the **'Sachsen' class**, or **Type 124**, frigate is based on that of the 'Brandenburg' or Type 123 class but with enhanced 'stealth' features intended to deceive any opponent's radar and acoustic sensors. The ships were required as replacements for the German navy's ageing and indeed obsolete 'Lütjens' class of guided-missile destroyers in the air-defence role, and a memorandum of understanding was signed in 1993 between the German government and the Blohm & Voss, Royal Schelde and Bazán (now Izar) shipyards. The design that emerged is a joint German and Dutch project based on the use of a common primary anti-air warfare system using the Standard SM-2 and Evolved Sea Sparrow medium-range SAMs.

In June 1996 the German government contracted for three ships with an option on a fourth that was provisionally to have been named as the **Thüringen**, but the option for this fourth ship was not taken up. Thus the class comprises three ships,

the *Sachsen*, *Hamburg* and *Hessen*, which were built by Blohm & Voss of Hamburg, Howaldtswerke of Kiel and Thyssen Nordseewerke of Emden respectively. The ships were laid down in February 1999, September 2000 and July 2002, launched in December 1999, March 2002 and March 2003, and due for commissioning in December 2003, December 2004 and December 2005.

The primary SAM armament is carried in the Mk 41 Vertical-Launch System forward of the bridge: this carries up to 32 Standard SM-2 missiles as well as Evolved Sea Sparrows in designated cells. Local defence against air attack is entrusted to a pair of 21-cell launchers for RAM short-range SAMs, while anti-ship capability is vested in Harpoon missiles, and anti-submarine capability in two helicopters and two tube mountings for lightweight torpedoes. Mounted round the top of the superstructure are the four antennae of the Thales APAR phased-array air/surface radar.

Among the features that enhance the 'stealthiness' of the design of the 'Sachsen' class are the replacement of vertical surfaces by inward- or outward-angled surfaces wherever possible, and the omission of other angles that could reflect electromagnetic energy.

The pyramidal tower abaft the pair of outward-canted funnels carries the antenna for the SMART L 3D air search radar. The Mk 41 VLS for the primary SAMs is located flush with the deck just forward of the bridge.

SPECIFICATION	
'Sachsen' (Type 124) class	Standard SM-2 and Evolved Sea
Displacement: 5,600 tons	Sparrow SAMs, two launchers for 42
Dimensions: length 143 m (469 ft 2 in); beam 17.4 m (57 ft 1 in); draught 4.4 m (14 ft 5 in)	RAM SAMs, one 76-mm (3-in) DP gun, and two triple Mk 32 324-mm (12.75-in) tubes for Mu 90 torpedoes
Propulsion: CODAG arrangement with one gas turbine delivering 26483 kW (35,514 shp) and two diesels delivering 15009 kW (20,128 shp) to two shafts	**Electronics:** one SMART L 3D radar, one APAR air/surface search radar, one Sewaco FD action data system, one FL 1800S-II ESM/ECM system, one active attack sonar, and
Speed: 29 kts	one active towed-array sonar
Armament: two quadruple launchers for eight Harpoon anti-ship missiles, one Mk 41 VLS for 32	**Aircraft:** two NFH 90 or Lynx Mk 88A helicopters **Complement:** 255

'Lupo' and 'Maestrale' classes Guided-missile frigates (FFG)

Built and designed by CN Riuniti (now Fincantieri) naval shipbuilders, the four vessels of the **'Lupo' class** in the Italian navy were **Lupo**, **Sagittario**, **Perseo** and **Orsa**. In 2003 only the *Perseo* remained in service. The 'Lupos' were designed primarily for the convoy escort role, with a capability for anti-surface warfare using SSMs if required. The hull is based on 14 watertight compartments and has fixed-fin stabilisers. To reduce the ship's complement the machinery plant is highly automated and divided into four separate compartments housing the auxiliaries, gas turbine modules, reduction gearbox and the diesel alternator sets. A telescopic hangar is also fitted to accommodate one AB 212ASW helicopter that can double in the missile-armed surface strike role.

The 'Lupos' proved very popular in Italian navy service, and the type was exported to Venezuela, Peru and Iraq in a modified form that has a fixed-hangar structure and no reloads for the SAM launcher. The six Venezuelan ships are the **Mariscal Sucre**, **Almirante Brión**, **General Urdaneta**, **General Soublette**, **General Salom** and **Almirante Garcia**. The four Peruvian ships are the **Meliton Carvajal**, **Villavicencio**, **Montero** and **Mariategui**. The four Iraqi units were the **Hittin**, **Thi Qar**, **Al Yarmouk** and **Al Qadisiya**. These ships never reached their owners, payment problems causing the cancellation of the order in 1990, following the UN sanctions placed on Saddam Hussein's regime in retaliation for its invasion of Kuwait. All four ships were placed in Italian naval service designated as fleet patrol ships and renamed **Artigliere**, **Aviere**, **Bersagliere** and **Granatiere** respectively.

Armament

The main anti-ship weapon carried on the Italian ships is the Otomat Mk 2 missile,

which has an Italian SMA active radar-homing seeker and a sea-skimming flight profile. The original Teseo launchers have been strengthened to take two missiles each. To utilise the missile's over-the-horizon capabilities fully, the embarked helicopter is used for mid-course guidance.

'Maestrale' class

The eight-strong **'Maestrale' class** is essentially a stretched version of the 'Lupo' design with less weapons and a greater emphasis on ASW. The increase in length and beam over the earlier 'Lupos' was to provide for a fixed hangar installation and a variable-depth sonar (VDS) housing at the stern. The improvements have resulted in better seaworthiness and habitability, plus the room required to carry and operate a second light helicopter. However, to compensate for this the class carries 12 less SSMs, and because of the extra tonnage has suffered a speed reduction of around 3 kts. The Raytheon VDS operates on the same frequencies as the hull sonar set and gives the vessels a valuable below-the-thermal-layer capability for use in the very difficult ASW conditions met in the Mediterranean. To enhance the ships' ASW operations further, the

AB 212ASW helicopters carried are fitted with Bendix ASQ-13B active dunking sonars. The armament they carry is either the American Mk 46 homing torpedo or Mk 54 depth charge. The ship uses the Mk 46 torpedo as well. It is also fitted with two fixed tubes for the 25-km (15.5-mile) range Whitehead Motofides A184 533-mm (21-in) wire-guided torpedo beneath the helicopter pad aft. Capable of 36 kts, the A184 can be used against surface and sub-surface targets. In 1994, a decision was taken to modify the hull-mounted and VDS sonar to give the system better performance and a mine detection capability. A towed LF array may also be added.

Above: Perseo, the third 'Lupo' frigate to enter service with the Italian navy is seen with its forward 76-mm gun at high elevation. A total of 18 'Lupos' were built.

Below: Largely a stretched version of the preceding 'Lupo' class, Maestrale and its seven sisterships possess enhanced ASW capabilities.

SPECIFICATION

'Lupo' class (Italian navy)
Displacement: 2,208 tons standard and 2,525 tons full load
Dimensions: length 113.2 m (371 ft 4 in); beam 11.3 m (37 ft); draught 3.7 m (12 ft 1 in)
Propulsion: CODOG arrangement with two General Electric/FIAT LM 2500 gas turbines delivering 37285 kW (50,000 shp) and two GMT diesels delivering 7457 kW (10,000 shp) to two shafts
Speed: 35 kts
Armament: eight twin Teseo launchers for 16 Otomat Mk 2 SSMs, one Mk 29 octuple launcher for RIM-7M Sea Sparrow or Aspide SAMs (eight reloads), one 127-mm (5-in) DP gun, two twin 40-mm

Breda AA guns, and two triple Mk 32 324-mm (12.75-in) torpedo tubes with Mk 46 ASW torpedoes
Aircraft: one AB 212ASW helicopter
Electronics: one RAN 10S air search radar, one SPQ-2F surface search radar, one SPS-702 air search/target indication radar, one RTN 10X fire-control radar, two RTN 20X gun fire-control radars, one Mk 95 SAM fire-control radar, one SPN-748 navigation radar, one IPN 20 combat data system, active and passive ESM systems, two SCLAR 20-tube chaff launchers, one DE 1160B hull sonar, and one SLQ-25 Nixie towed torpedo decoy
Complement: 185

SPECIFICATION

'Maestrale' class
Displacement: 2,500 tons standard and 3,200 tons full load
Dimensions: length 122.7 m (402 ft 7 in); beam 12.9 m (42 ft 4 in); draught 4.6 m (15 ft 1 in)
Propulsion: CODOG arrangement with two General Electric/FIAT LM 2500 gas turbines delivering 37285 kW (50,000 shp) and two GMT diesels delivering 9395.8 kW (12,600 shp) to two shafts
Speed: 32 kts
Armament: four single Teseo launchers for four Otomat Mk 2 SSMs, one octuple Albatros launcher for 16 Aspide SAMs, one 127-mm (5-in) DP gun, two twin 40-mm Breda AA guns, two single 533-mm (21-in) B516 torpedo tubes

for A184 dual-purpose torpedoes, and two triple 324-mm (12.75-in) Mk 32 torpedo tubes for Mk 46 ASW torpedoes
Aircraft: two AB 212ASW helicopters
Electronics: one RAN 10S air and surface search radar, one SPS-702 surface search radar, one RTN 30X SAM fire-control radar, two RTN 20X gun fire-control radars, one SPN-703 navigation radar, one IPN 20 combat data system, SLR-4 and SLQ-D active and passive ESM systems, two Dagaie and two SCLAR 20-tube chaff launchers, one DE 1164 hull-mounted variable-depth sonar, and one SLQ-25 Nixie towed torpedo decoy
Complement: 232

Faster than most Western frigates of their generation (although slower than the 'Lupo' class) the 'Maestrale' vessels are comprehensively equipped with modern ASW technology including both a hull sonar and a towed variable-depth sonar. Several of these systems have been upgraded. The vessels are Maestrale, Grecale, Libeccio, Scirocco, Aliseo, Euro, Espero and Zeffiro.

'Lekiu' class Guided-missile frigate (FFG)

The **Jebat** is the flagship of the Royal Malaysian navy. It was laid down at Yarrow Shipbuilders (now BAE Systems Marine) at Glasgow in November 1994, five months after its sistership, the **Lekiu**. The **'Lekiu' class** were ordered in 1992, and although originally classified as corvettes they were subsequently upgraded to light frigates. The pair were commissioned in August 1997.

Their primary weapon is the latest MM.40 Block 2 version of the Exocet sea-skimming SSM, for which two four-cell launchers are located amidships between the radar masts. They are at a fixed elevation, one facing starboard and the other facing port. Range and bearing data are fed to the missile prior to launch and it relies on this during the inertial stage of its flight; terminal guidance is by active monopulse seeker head.

The ships' defensive system is another weapon that made its combat debut in the 1982 Falklands War: the Seawolf SAM. Travelling at Mach 2.5 it can engage incoming missiles as well as enemy aircraft. Sixteen BAE

Although **Lekiu** *(30) is the nameship of the class,* **Jebat** *(29) is the senior ship and thus took the lower pennant number. These are the largest and most capable surface vessels in Malaysian service.*

Systems vertical launchers are positioned immediately before the bridge, behind the 57-mm Bofors gun.

ASW equipment
The addition of anti-submarine torpedoes, a full sonar suite and an ASW helicopter (the ships each carry a single Super Lynx – these six aircraft replaced the elderly

Westland Wasp) make these extremely heavily armed ships for their size. Historically, attempts to cram too much weaponry on to a small hull have often led to failure under wartime conditions. Integration of the weapons systems did cause problems and the ships were eventually delivered to the Malaysian navy in 2000.

SPECIFICATION

'Lekiu' class
Displacement: 1,845 tons standard and 2,390 tons full load
Dimensions: length 105.5 m (346 ft); beam 12.8 m (42 ft); draught 3.6 m (11 ft 10 in)
Propulsion: CODAD arrangement with four MTU diesels delivering 24500 kW (33,300 shp) to four shafts
Speed: 28 kts
Armament: eight MM.40 Exocet SSMs, one 16-cell VLS for Seawolf SAMs, one 57-mm Bofors gun, two MSI 30-mm guns, and two triple

B515 324-mm (12.75-in) tubes for Stingray ASW torpedoes
Electronics: one DA08 air search radar, one Sea Giraffe surface search radar, one Racal Decca navigation radar, two Marconi 1802 fire-control radars, one Spherion hull sonar, Nautis F and Link Y combat data systems, Mentor and Scimitar ESM and ECM systems, one Sea Siren towed torpedo decoy, and two Super Barricade 12-barrel chaff launchers
Aircraft: one Super Lynx Series 300
Complement: 146

'Karel Doorman' class Guided-missile frigate (FFG)

The Royal Netherlands navy's **'Karel Doorman' class** of multi-purpose frigates were laid down between 1985-91 and commissioned between 1991-95. The names were manipulated to make the **Van Speijk** the last to complete, although it retains its original pennant number. The seven other vessels in the class are **Karel Doorman, Willem Van der Zaan, Tjerk Hiddes, Van Amstel, Abraham Van der Hulst, Van Nes** and **Van Galen**. Equipped with surface-to-surface missiles, anti-aircraft missiles and

anti-submarine torpedoes (plus an ASW helicopter) these are true multi-role warships. The design is intended to reduce the radar signature and infra-red signature and extensive NBC protection is provided for conducting operations in contaminated areas.

Frequent participants in NATO exercises, the Dutch frigates have also taken part in US Navy anti-drug operations in the Caribbean as well as missions on behalf of the UN in the Mediterranean and Adriatic. They also contributed naval units to Operation Desert

Storm in 1991. Their CODOG propulsion system helps extend range and reduces operating costs: the diesels are used for cruising, the gas turbines for high speed. Full automation and roll stabilisation is fitted.

Their primary anti-ship weapon is the Block 1C Harpoon. The vertical launch system for the Sea Sparrow SAMs is similar to that on the Greek 'Meko' and Canadian 'Halifax' classes.

Possible future modifications under discussion include the addition of low frequency active sonar to the class. From 2007 the 20

Lynx helicopters operated by the Dutch will be progressively replaced by NH 90 helicopters. The Lynx are equipped with two Mk 46 torpedoes, dipping sonar and FLIR equipment.

Modernisation
Between January 1992 and mid-1994, the class underwent a series of modernisations. This saw a new SEWACO (sensors, weapons and command systems) VIII(A) suite being installed and updated to VIII(B) standard by 1994. An APECS II electronic warfare system was also installed along with a DSBV 61 towed array. Other new systems include the IRSCAN infra-red detector fitted onto the hanger roof. Although origi-

nally fitted to the *Willem van der Zaan* for trials in 1993, this was progressively fitted across the entire class. This provides target data for the Goalkeeper 30-mm CIWS. In addition to this, the Mk 36 SRBOC launchers can disperse IR flares and chaff up to 4 km (2.4 miles). Further new equipment included an SHF satellite communications (SATCOM) system fitted along with a Scout radar positioned on the bridge roof in 1997. Four ATAS (Active Towed Array Sonar) were trialled from 1998, and have since been ordered for several vessels in the class. Numerous modifications have also been conducted to give the vessels better stealth protection.

The **Van Galen** *was the penultimate 'Karel Doorman' to enter service, in 1994. As well as being potent marine warfare platforms, these vessels were designed for peacetime roles such as drug interdiction work.*

SPECIFICATION

'Karel Doorman' class
Displacement: 3,320 tons full load
Dimensions: length 122.3 m (401 ft 3 in); beam 14.4 m (47 ft 3 in); draught 4.3 m (14 ft 1 in)
Propulsion: CODOG arrangement with two Rolls-Royce Spey gas turbines delivering 25214 kW (33,800 shp) and two Stork diesel engines delivering 7303 kW (9,790 shp) to two shafts
Speed: 30 kts (gas turbines) and 21 kts (cruising diesels)
Armament: two quadruple launchers for Harpoon SSMs, one Mk 48 VLS for 16 Sea Sparrow SAMs, one 76-mm (3-in) Mk 100 DP gun, one Goalkeeper 30-mm CIWS,

two 20-mm AA guns, two twin Mk 32 torpedo tubes for Mk 46 lightweight ASW torpedoes
Electronics: one SMART air and surface search radar, one Scout surface search radar, one LW08 air search radar, two STIR fire-control radars, one Racal Decca 1226 navigation radar, one DSBV 61 towed sonar (later ATAS), one PHS-36 hull sonar, APECS II ESM/ECM system, one SLQ-25 Nixie towed torpedo decoy, and two Mk 36 SRBOC 6-tube quad chaff launchers
Aircraft: one SH-14D Lynx ASW helicopter
Complement: 156

'Neustrashimy' class Project 1154 Guided-missile frigate

Built by Yantar at Kaliningrad and commissioned in January 1993, the **Neustrashimy** is the sole unit of the **Project 1154 Jastreb** or **'Neustrashimy' class** of guided-missile frigates that were to have been four or more in number. The second ship was launched in 1991 but the hull was later earmarked for scrapping to pay the yard's debts, and the third hull was launched incomplete in 1993 to clear space for the repair of Norwegian merchant ships, and was then apparently abandoned.

Designed as a complement to the 'Krivak'-class or Project 1135 guided-missile frigate and successor to the 'Grisha'-class or Project 1124 light frigate, the ship is based on the design of the 'Krivak III'-class vessel with slightly greater dimensions, more advanced sensors and weapons including full capability for an embarked helicopter. The design is optimised for operations against submarines and surface ships, and the escort of task forces and convoys.

The ship features a long hull with relatively great forward freeboard and an acutely raked stem reducing

Above: In the area forward of the bridge are three weapons, in the form of the 100-mm (3.9-in) gun, the four vertical launchers for SA-N-9 SAMs flush with the deck and the RBU 12000 rocket launcher.

Right: The Neustrashimy has a very elegantly configured hull, the forward end's rake, flare and freeboard helping to reduce the amount of water and spray taken over the bows in heavy weather.

the chance of damage to the bow bulb by the anchors. The flare of the sides over the ship's forward end minimises slamming and spray. The ship has bilge keels; fin stabilisers enhance seakeeping capabilities by reducing roll.

Missile armament

The ship has a missile/torpedo launch system for six Vodopod-NK (SS-N-16 'Stallion') anti-submarine missiles or torpedoes, and is equipped for (but not with) four quadruple launchers for 16 Uran (SS-N-25 'Switchblade') anti-ship cruise missiles. The Klinok air-defence system comprises four octuple vertical-launch modules for SA-N-9 'Gauntlet' SAMs just abaft the 100-mm (3.9-in) AK-100 gun. Short-range air defence is entrusted to a Kortik/Kashtan gun/missile system: this comprises a

command system and two CADS-N-1 fire units, each with two 30-mm rotary cannon (600 rounds), an octuple launcher for 9M311 (SA-N-11 'Grison') SAMs, one 'Hot Flash' fire-control radar and a 'Hot Spot' optronic director.

Submarine combat

The defence of the ship against submarine attack is entrusted to one RBU 12000 10-tube launcher installed on the raised deck immediately abaft the four Klinok missile launchers to fire anti-submarine and anti-torpedo rockets supplied from the magazine by an elevator. Longer-range offensive anti-submarine operations are entrusted to the single embarked helicopter, a Kamov Ka-27 'Helix' machine using an operating platform occupying the full width of the deck at the stern with a hangar just forward of it in the rear superstructure block.

SPECIFICATION

'Neustrashimy' class
Displacement: 3,450 tons standard; 4,250 tons full load
Dimensions: length 131.2 m (430 ft 5 in); beam 15.5 m (50 ft 10 in); draught 4.8 m (15 ft 9 in)
Propulsion: COGAG arrangement with two gas turbines delivering 36250 kW (48,620 shp) and two gas turbines delivering 18050 kW (24,210 shp) to two shafts
Performance: speed 30 kts; endurance 8350 km (5,190 miles) at 16 kts
Armament: one 100-mm (3.9-in) gun, provision for four quadruple launchers for SS-N-25 anti-ship missiles, four octuple vertical-launch systems for SA-N-9 SAMs,

two CADS-N-1 combined 30-mm cannon and SA-N-11 short-range SAM systems, six 533-mm (21-in) tubes for SS-N-16 anti-submarine missiles and/or torpedoes, one RBU 12000 anti-submarine rocket launcher, and two mine rails
Electronics: one 'Top Plate' 3D surveillance radar, two 'Palm Frond' navigation radars, one 'Cross Sword' SAM-control radar, one 'Kite Screech-B' SSM/gun-control radar, two 'Bell Crown' data-links, two 'Salt Pot' and four 'Box Bar' IFFs, eight ESM/ECM systems, and 10 chaff/decoy launchers
Aircraft: one Kamov Ka-27 helicopter
Complement: 210

The Neustrashimy's two CADS-N-1 mountings for the Kortik/Kashtan short-range air-defence system (30-mm rotary cannon and SA-N-11 short-range SAMs) are located abreast of each other on the upper part of the rear superstructure flanking the hangar for the Ka-27 helicopter.

The Type 22 Batch 3 ships have a good balance of offensive weapons and electronics, and also have the habitability and seakeeping for extended operations. The ships can also embark senior officers and their staff and then operate in the command role.

'Cornwall' class (Type 22 Batch 3) Guided-missile frigate

The Type 22 class of guided-missile frigates was one of the larger construction programmes undertaken for the Royal Navy in the last quarter of the 20th century, and amounted to 16 ships in all. First came the four 'Broadsword'- or Type 22 Batch 1-class ships, commissioned in 1979-81 and all sold to Brazil in 1995-97. Then came the six 'Boxer'-class or Type 22 Batch 2 ships commissioned in 1984-88 with a longer hull and the Type 2031Z towed-array sonar. Finally there came the four **'Cornwall'-class** or **Type 22 Batch 3** ships based on the hull and machinery of the Type 22 Batch 2 ships but with a number of operational improvements.

Conceived as a successor to the 'Leander' class, and originally to have been procured by the Netherlands as well as the UK, the Type 22 frigate was schemed for the oceanic escort role with optimisation for the anti-submarine task but with a potent short-range air-defence capability to cope with the developing threat of the sea-skimming anti-ship

missile. The Type 22 Batch 3 ships were ordered at the end of 1982 to replace ships lost in the Falklands campaign of that year, and the opportunity was taken to create an improved Type 22 Batch 2 variant with improved command facilities (including officer in tactical command and flag accommodation within provision for a maximum complement of 301 although the normal total is 250), new anti-ship missile armament, the restoration of 4.5-in (114-mm) gun armament of the type lacking from the Batch 1 and 2 ships, and the introduction of a close-in weapons system mounting for last-ditch defence against attack aircraft and missiles.

The new weapons fit required a modification of the ships' layout to accommodate the medium-calibre gun on the forecastle and the two quadruple launchers for Harpoon (rather than the earlier ships' Exocet) anti-ship missiles athwartships in the position immediately abaft the wheelhouse, and the Goalkeeper CIWS above and behind the Harpoon launchers with good forward

and lateral arcs of fire. The ships have the CACS-5 combat data system in place of the earlier vessels' CACS-1 systems, and the Mk 8 mounting for the 4.5-in gun, fitted mainly for the shore bombardment role, is controlled with the aid of two GSA 8B Sea Archer optronic directors (TV and IR imaging and laser rangefinding) side-by-side above the bridge.

The ships were also the first Royal Navy units to be completed with 30-mm RARDEN short-range anti-aircraft and anti-FAC guns in DS 30B mountings in place of the 40-mm Bofors cannon that had been standard since World War II.

Class of four

The four ships, with names beginning with C to differentiate them from the B-batch ships, were built by Yarrow (two), Cammell Laird and Swan Hunter respectively, and were completed as HMS **Cornwall**, **Cumberland**, **Campbeltown** and **Chatham** and commissioned in April 1988, June 1989, May 1989 and May 1990. Together with HMS *Sheffield*, the sole Batch 2

ship being retained by the Royal Navy, the ships constitute the 2nd Frigate Squadron based at Devonport.

Helicopter facilities

The long-range anti-submarine helicopter facilities are large enough for the carriage and operation of one Westland Sea King medium helicopter, but the standard complement is two

Westland Lynx light helicopters. The ships are also being upgraded with Type 2050 hull-mounted search and attack sonar in place of the Type 2016 equipment, improved electronic warfare systems and an enhanced Sea Wolf short-range SAM capability with improved radar, an added optronic tracker and a new fuse for better low-altitude capability.

HMS Chatham was the last of the four Type 22 Batch 3 class ships to be completed. Though categorised as frigates, these capable ships are in effect destroyers with excellent anti-submarine and anti-ship capabilities as well as a good facility for defence against air and missile attack.

Type 23 or 'Duke' class Guided-missile frigate (FFG)

Although the ships of the Type 22 or 'Broadsword', 'Boxer' and 'Cornwall' classes were clearly very effective anti-submarine warships, they were also very expensive. The Admiralty thus planned a lower-cost frigate with the Type 2031Z towed-array sonar rather than the Type 2050 hull-mounted active search/attack sonar.

The result of this process is the **Type 23** or **'Duke' class** of frigate, the development of which then came to include the Type 2050 as well as the Type 2031Z sonar, one medium rather than two light helicopters, an enhanced general-purpose capability, and a two-ended Sea Wolf SAM system. By the time the design was being finalised, the vertical-launch version of this SAM system was nearing the trials stage, and was selected in preference to the earlier GWS.25 lightweight launcher. Analysis of naval operations in the Falklands War also led to the introduction of upgraded fire precautions and enhanced damage control.

The class totals 16 ships, of which 12 and four respectively were built by Yarrow and Swan Hunter. Laid down in 1985-99, launched in 1987-2000 and commissioned in 1990-2002, the ships are the **Norfolk**, **Argyll**, **Lancaster**, **Marlborough**, **Iron Duke**, **Monmouth**, **Montrose**, **Westminster**, **Northumberland**, **Richmond**, **Somerset**, **Grafton**, **Sutherland**, **Kent**, **Portland** and **St Albans**.

Quiet operations

The Type 23 frigate is optimised for towed-array operations, so quietening of machinery was important and a unique combined diesel-electric and gas turbine (CODLAG) propulsion arrangement was selected with diesel-electric drive for quiet operations and Spey gas turbines for high speed. The CODLAG arrangement reduces gearbox noise, and the electric generators are above the waterline for a lowering of radiated noise.

Anti-noise, IR and electro-magnetic 'stealth' features were also incorporated to improve survivability, and include a flared hull with a bubble system to reduce radiated noise, and a superstructure with sloped surfaces and rounded corners.

The first ships were completed without their planned CACS-4 command system but its successor, the DNA 1 system, was retrofitted from 1995 onward and was later upgraded to DNA 5 standard. The first six ships had the UAF-1 ESM system, but later ships were completed with the UAT system that was then retrofitted to the earlier ships. All the ships have Type 675(2) or Scorpion ECM.

Upgrade programmes are to enhance the Sea Wolf system (upgraded missile fuse, improved radar and another optronic tracker), replace the Type 2031Z passive sonar with the Type 2087 active sonar, and introduce the Mk 8 Mod 1 gun, the Surface Ship Torpedo Defence system and, in seven of the ships, the CEC (Co-operative Engagement Capability) system.

Right: A key feature of the 'Duke' class is the minimisation of the ships' electro-magnetic signature through the shaping of the hull and superstructure.

Above left: HMS Grafton was built on the Clyde by Yarrow and commissioned in 1997. Evident are the 4.5-in gun and four of the eight Harpoon launchers.

Above: HMS Iron Duke, named after the Duke of Wellington. The ship's after section is dominated by the hangar and large helicopter platform.

The 'Duke'-class frigates are notably 'quiet'. Their acoustic, thermal and electro-magnetic signatures have all been reduced to the maximum degree possible.

SPECIFICATION

'Duke' (Type 23) class
Displacement: 3,500 tons standard; 4,200 tons full load
Dimensions: length 133 m (436 ft 4 in); beam 16.1 m (52 ft 10 in); draught 7.3 m (24 ft)
Propulsion: CODLAG with four 1510-kW (2,025-shp) Paxman Valenta 12CM diesel generators powering two GEC electric motors delivering 2980 kW (4,000 shp) and two Rolls-Royce Spey SM1A or, from *Westminster*, RM1C gas turbines delivering 23190 kW (31,100 shp) to two shafts
Performance: speed 28 kts; range 14485 km (9,000 miles) at 15 kts
Armament: two quadruple launchers for eight Harpoon SSMs, two GWS.26 VLS for 32 Sea Wolf SAMs, one 4.5-in (114-mm) Mk 8 DP gun, two DS 30B 30-mm AA guns, and two twin 12.75-in (324-mm) tubes for Stingray ASW torpedoes
Electronics: one Type 996(I) air/surface search radar, one Type 1008 surface search radar, one Type 1007 navigation radar, two Type 911 SAM fire-control radars, one GSA 8B/GPEOD optronic director, DNA combat data system, UAT and Type 675(2) ECM, four Sea Gnat 6-barrel decoy launchers, Type 2070 torpedo decoy, Type 2050 hull sonar and Type 2031Z towed-array sonar
Aircraft: one Lynx HMA.Mk 3/8 or Merlin HM.Mk 1 helicopter
Complement: 181

'Oliver Hazard Perry' class Guided-missile frigate (FFG)

The guided-missile frigate USS McClusky (FFG-41) manoeuvres at slow speed while training near San Diego, California. The original single hangar configuration was altered to two adjacent hangars. The two SH-60B LAMPS III helicopters normally deployed can carry AGM-119B Penguin anti-ship missiles in order to boost the ships' limited ASuW capabilities.

At its peak numerically the largest warship class in the modern US Navy, the **'Oliver Hazard Perry' class** was designed to succeed the 'Knox' class of ocean escort frigates, and was therefore optimised for the anti-air warfare role with anti-submarine and anti-ship warfare as its secondary tactical tasks.

The class was criticised for the same failings as the 'Knox' class, namely a single propeller and a single main 'weapon' (one Mk 13 missile launcher). On the other side of the coin the ship benefits from a major degree of redundancy: the Mk 92 fire-control system has two channels (two guidance radars physically well separated from each other), and there are two extending 242-kW (325-shp) motor/propeller units to bring the ship home at 6 kts if it loses its main power. Although the hull sonar is the SQS-56 short-range unit, the primary anti-submarine sonar is the SQR-19 towed-array sonar.

Combat system

The Dutch Mk 92 fire-control system is part of a combat system well adapted to the task of defeating attacks by 'pop-up' weapons. The Italian 76-mm (3-in) gun was selected as superior to the US Navy's standard 5-in (127-mm) L/54 gun in the medium/short-range air-defence role.

Because of cost considerations many of the early ships were not revised for the carriage of two LAMPS III multi-role helicopters in place of the original pair of LAMPS I machines. The ships have aluminium armour over their magazines, steel over the machinery, and Kevlar plastic armour over their vital electronic and command facilities.

The magazine for the Mk 13 launcher can take only Standard SAM and Harpoon anti-ship missiles, so the shipboard ASW capability is vested in Mk 46 torpedoes and LAMPS helicopters.

Many of the older ships have been transferred to US allies or are reserved for such transfer (seven including one for cannibalisation to Turkey, four to Egypt and one each to Bahrain and Poland, with further transfers to Poland and Turkey made in 2002, and only 33 of the class survived in US Navy service at the beginning of the 21st century.

At its peak, the class consisted of the *Oliver Hazard Perry, McInerney, Wadsworth, Duncan, Clark, George Philip, Samuel Eliot Morrison, John H. Sides, Estocin, Clifton Sprague, John A. Moore, Antrim, Flatley, Fahrion,* *Lewis B. Puller, Jack Williams, Copeland, Gallery, Mahlon S. Tisdale, Boone, Stephen W. Groves, Reid, Stark, John L. Hall, Jarrett, Aubrey Fitch, Underwood, Crommelin, Curts, Doyle, Halyburton, McClusky, Klakring, Thach, De Wert, Rentz, Nicholas, Vandegrift, Robert G. Bradley, Taylor, Gary, Carr, Hawes, Ford, Elrod, Simpson, Reuben James, Samuel B. Roberts, Kauffman, Rodney M. Davis* and *Ingraham*

Further ships are Australia's six **'Adelaide'-class** units *Adelaide, Canberra, Sydney, Darwin, Melbourne* and *Newcastle* (the last two built in Australia); Spain's six locally built **'Santa Maria'-class** units *Santa María, Victoria, Numancia, Reina Sofía (ex-América), Navarra* and *Canarias*; and Taiwan's eight locally built **'Cheng Kung'-class** units *Cheng Kung, Cheng Ho, Chi Kuang, Yueh Fei, Tzu-I, Pan Chao, Chang Chien* and *Tien Tan*.

SPECIFICATION

'Oliver Hazard Perry' class
Displacement: 2,769 tons standard; 3,638-4,100 tons full load
Dimensions: length 135.6 m (445 ft) in LAMPS I ships or 138.1 m (453 ft) in LAMPS III ships; beam 13.7 m (45 ft); draught 4.5 m (14 ft 10 in)
Propulsion: two General Electric LM2500 gas turbines delivering 29830 kW (40,000 shp) to one shaft
Performance: speed 29 kts; range 8370 km (5,200 miles) at 20 kts
Armament: one Mk 13 single-rail launcher for 36 Standard SM-1MR surface-to-air and four Harpoon anti-ship missiles, one 76-mm (3-in) Mk 75 DP gun, one 20-mm Mk 15

Phalanx CIWS, and two triple 12.75-in (324-mm) Mk 32 ASW tubes for 24 Mk 46 or Mk 50 ASW torpedoes
Electronics: one SPS-49(V)4 or 5 air search radar, one SPS-55 surface search radar, one STIR fire-control radar, one Mk 92 fire-control system, one URN-25 TACAN, one SLQ-32(V)2 ESM system, two Mk 36 SRBOC 6-barrel chaff launchers, one SQS-56 hull sonar, and (from *Underwood*) one SQR-19 towed-array sonar
Aircraft: two SH-2F Seasprite LAMPS I or SH-60B Sea Hawk LAMPS III helicopters
Complement: 176-200

Though the object of much criticism, the 'Oliver Hazard Perry' class has proved very successful despite the steady growth of displacement, equipment and complement, and in service has also been revealed as notably sturdy. The lead ship of the class is illustrated.

'Ouragan' class Landing Ship Dock (TCD/LSD)

The **'Ouragan' class** of dock landing ship is used both for amphibious warfare and logistic transport by the French navy. They are fitted with a well dock some 120 m (393 ft 8½ in) in length that has a stern gate measuring 14 m (45 ft 11 in) by 5.5 m (18 ft). The well dock can accommodate two 670-ton full load EDIC LCTs (carrying 11 light tanks, or 11 trucks or five LVTs) or 18 LCM6s (carrying 30 tons of cargo or vehicles). Above the well deck is a 36-m (79.4-ft) long six-section removable helicopter deck capable of operating one SA 321G Super Frelon heavy-lift helicopter or three SA 319B Alouette III utility helicopters. If required, a 90-m (295-ft 4-in) long temporary deck can also be fitted to stow cargo or vehicles, but its use reduces the number of landing craft carried as half the well deck is taken up. If used with this extra deck as a logistic transport then the total cargo capacity of the vessel becomes some 1,500 tons. This can comprise either 18 Super Frelon or 80 Alouette III helicopters, or 120 AMX-10s or 84 light amphibious vehicles or 340 light utility vehicles or 12 50-ton barges. A typical load may comprise one 380-ton CDIC LCT, four 56-ton CTMs,

10 AMX-10RC armoured cars and 21 further vehicles or a total of 150 to 170 vehicles (without landing craft). There is a permanent helicopter deck for up to four Super Frelons or 10 Alouette IIIs located next to the starboard bridge area. Two 35-ton capacity cranes handle the heavy equipment carried. Each of the two ships also has command and control facilities to operate as amphibious force flagships. They also carry an extensive range of repair and maintenance workshops to support the units embarked. Troop accommodation is provided for 349 men under normal conditions, although 470 can be carried for short distances. Three LCVPs are carried as deck cargo.

Nuclear test role

The **Orage** (**L 9022**) was allotted to the French Pacific nuclear experimental centre as the logistic transport to and from France. It was also the centre's floating headquarters, using a modular facility within the well deck area. In 1993, both vessels received two twin Simbad launchers for Mistral SAMs and new search radars.
Both the **Orage** and **Ouragan** (**L 9021**) have had service life extensions and are due to be replaced in

2005/6 when the two new 20,000-ton 'Mistral'-class LHDs are due.

Used for both amphibious warfare and as a logistic transport, Ouragan is capable of deploying and supporting half a battalion of marines (349 troops). In addition, a typical helicopter load comprises three or four Super Frelon or 10 Alouette III, although the former is today rarely carried and the Super Puma or Cougar (for CSAR operations) are more likely to be deployed.

Below: The Orage has an enclosed flag bridge; it has served as a floating headquarters for France's nuclear test mission in the South Pacific.

SPECIFICATION	
Names: *Ouragan* (L 9021) and *Orage* (L 9022)	**Troops:** 349 (14 officers plus 335 enlisted men) normal, 470 overload
Commissioned: L9021 1 June 1965; L9022 1 April 1968	**Cargo:** 1,500 tons as logistic transport; two LCTs, or up to 8 CTMs or 18 LCM6s; plus 3 LCVP
Displacement: 5,800 tons light; 8,500 tons full load	**Armament:** two Matra Simbad twin launchers for Mistral SAMs, four single 40-mm Bofors guns (two later replaced by Breda/Mauser 30-mm guns)
Dimensions: length 149 m (488 ft 10 in); beam 23 m (75 ft 6 in); draught 5.4 m (17 ft 8½ in)	
Propulsion: two diesels delivering 6413 kW (8,600 shp) to two shafts	**Electronics:** one DRBN 32 navigation radar, one DRBV 51A air/surface search radar, one SQS-17 sonar (L 9021)
Speed: 17 kts	
Complement: 211 (10 officers plus 201 enlisted men)	

'Foudre' class Landing Ship Dock (TCD/LSD)

For many years the French navy's amphibious capability was based on two LSDs dating back to the 1960s, *Ouragan* and *Orage*. Unlike the British defence establishment, the French recognised the limitations of its ageing LSDs and ordered a new TCD (Transport de Chalands de Débarquement)/LSD in 1984. The **Foudre** (**L 9011**) was laid down at Brest in 1986, launched in 1988 and commissioned in 1990. A sistership was authorised in 1994: the **Siroco** (**L 9012**) was laid down that year, launched in 1996 and commissioned in 1998.
The **'Foudre' class** are designed to carry a mecha-

Foudre has a 1450-m² (15,608 sq ft) flight deck, with two landing spots, one of which is fitted with a landing grid and a helicopter landing system.

nised battalion of France's Rapid Action Force (FAN), the model for the new professional army that replaces the conscript force of the 20th century. The vessels can also act as logistics support ships. A typical load for these vessels consists of one CDIC (Chaland de Débarquement d'Infanterie et de Chars) – a 380-ton LCT of which the French built a pair to operate with the 'Foudre' class; four CTMs (Chalands de Transport de Matériel) – 56-ton LCMs; ten AMX-10RC armoured cars, and up to 50 other vehicles. Without the landing craft embarked, the 'Foudre' class can carry up to 200 vehicles. The well dock measures 122 by 14 m (400 ft 4 in by 45 ft 11 in) and can accept a 400-ton ship. Cranes of 52-ton (*Foudre*) or 38-ton (*Siroco*) capacity assist in handling heavy equipment.

In terms of personnel, the 'Foudre' class can accommodate 467 troops (plus 1,880 tons load) or as many as 1,600 troops for an emergency situation. With 700 personnel embarked, the 'Foudre'-class LSD has an endurance of 30 days.

Both vessels carry comprehensive command and control facilities and medical

provision includes two operating theatres and 47 beds. *Siroco* is designed to accommodate a modular field hospital.

Helicopter operations

There are two landing spots on the 1450-m² (15,608 sq ft) flight deck plus one on the removable rolling cover above the well deck. They can operate a pair of Super Frelons or four AS 332F Super Puma helicopters. The landing deck on *Siroco* is extended aft as far as the lift, to give an increased area of 1740 m² (18,730 sq ft).

Foudre has been scheduled to receive the same

anti-aircraft gun armament as the *Siroco* since the late 1990s but the work has yet to take place. Air defence against close-in threats and sea-skimming missiles is handled by a pair of Matra Simbad lightweight twin launchers for Mistral IR-homing missiles; these are located on either side of the bridge. Without the three Breda/Mauser 30-mm guns as fitted to *Siroco*, *Foudre* relies on a single 40-mm Bofors gun forward of the bridge, and two GIAT 20F2 20-mm guns; both ships are also armed with two 12.7-mm (0.5-mm) machine-guns. In 1997, a Sagem

optronic fire-control system was fitted to both vessels. A Dassault Electronique ESM/ECM system is also due to be fitted. The two

ships are based at Toulon and assigned to the FAN; *Siroco* was deployed to East Timor for operations in 1999.

SPECIFICATION	
Names: *Foudre* (L 9011), *Siroco* (L 9012)	**Cargo:** two CDIC or 10 CTM or one EDIC/CDIC and 4 CTMs plus 1800 tons load
Commissioned: L 9011 7 December 1990; L 9012 21 December 1998	**Armament:** two Matra Simbad launchers for Mistral SAMs; *Foudre* has one 40-mm Bofors gun and two 20-mm AA guns, *Siroco* has three 30-mm Breda/Mauser AA guns
Displacement: 12,400 tons full load; 17,200 tons flooded	
Dimensions: length 168 m (551 ft 2½ in); beam 23.5 m (77 ft 1 in); draught 5.2 m (17 ft), 9.2 m (30 ft 2½ in) flooded	**Electronics:** one DRBV 21A Mars air/surface search radar, one Racal Decca 2459 surface search radar, one Racal Decca RM 1229 navigation radar, one Sagem VIGU-105 gun fire control system, Syracuse SATCOM combat data system
Propulsion: two SEMT-Pielstick V400 diesels delivering 15511 kW (20,800 shp) to two shafts	
Speed: 21 kts	
Complement: 215 (17 officers)	
Troops: 467	

Twin Simbad launchers for the Mistral IR-homing SAM provide the 'Foudre' class with air defence out to a range of 4 km (2.5 miles).

'San Giorgio' class Amphibious Transport Dock (LPD)

Capable of operating three SH-3D Sea King or EH 101 Merlin or five AB 212 helicopters from a carrier-type flight deck, the **'San Giorgio' class** LPDs each carry a battalion of Italian infantry. **San Giorgio** (**L 9892**) and **San Marco** (**L 9893**) have bow doors for amphibious landings but **San Giusto** (**L 9894**) does not. All three can ship two LCMs in the stern docking well. The *San Giorgio* and *San Marco* were laid down in 1985 and 1986 respectively while the slightly larger *San Giusto* was not ordered until 1991. The first two ships were launched in 1987 and commissioned in 1987 and 1988. The *San Giusto*, launched in 1993 (late due to industrial unrest) and finally commissioned in 1994, is some 300 tons heavier as a result of a

longer island and increased accommodation. *San Marco* was funded by the Italian Ministry of Civil Protection and, although run by the Italian navy, is specially fitted for disaster relief operations.

Modernisation

From 1999, the ships' original 20-mm guns were replaced by 25-mm Breda Oerlikon weapons, while the *San Giorgio* has had its 76-mm (3-in) gun removed, and its LCVP installation relocated from davits to a port side sponson. The vessel has also had its flight deck lengthened to allow simultaneous operations of two EH 101s and two AB 212s. The bow doors are also being removed, and similar modifications are to be undertaken for the *San Marco*.

Four landing spots are

provided, and a 30-ton lift and two 40-ton travelling cranes are used for transporting the 64.6-ton LCMs.

A typical load would include a battalion of 400 personnel, plus 30-36 APCs or 30 medium tanks. A total of

two (on davits) or three (on port side sponson) LCVPs can be carried.

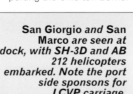

San Marco, with medium trucks carried on the deck. The stern docking well, which can accept two LCMs, measures 20.5 by 7 m (67 ft 3 in by 23 ft). The 'San Giorgio'-class LPDs are based at Brindisi and are assigned to the Third Naval Division.

San Giorgio and San Marco are seen at dock, with SH-3D and AB 212 helicopters embarked. Note the port side sponsons for LCVP carriage.

SPECIFICATION	
'San Giorgio' class	shafts
Names: *San Giorgio* (L 9892), *San Marco* (L 9893), *San Giusto* (L 9894)	**Speed:** 21 kts
	Complement: 163; (*San Giusto*) 196
Commissioned: L 9892 9 October 1987; L 9893 18 March 1988; L 9894 9 April 1994	**Troops:** 400
	Cargo: up to 36 APCs or 30 medium tanks plus two LCMs in docking well and two or three LCVPs; one LCPL
Displacement: 7,665 tons full load; (*San Giusto*) 7,950 tons	
Dimensions: length 133.3 m (437 ft 4 in), (*San Giusto*) 137 m (449 ft 6 in); beam 20.5 m (67 ft 3 in); draught 5.3 m (17 ft 5 in)	**Armament:** one OTO Melara 76-mm (3-in) gun, two Oerlikon 25-mm guns
	Electronics: one SPS-72 surface search radar, one SPN-748 navigation radar, one SPG-70 fire control radar
Propulsion: two diesels delivering 12527.8 kW (16,800 shp) to two	

'Oosumi' class Amphibious transport dock/landing ship tank

The so-called LPD/LSTs of the Japanese 'Oosumi' class look remarkably like aircraft carriers, the first to fly the rising sun naval emblem since 1945. With their stern docking wells and flight deck, the ships strongly resemble scaled-down US-type LHAs rather than the tank landing ships they purport to be. If this sounds like anachronistic paranoia, Japan's ability to maintain secrecy over its naval projects was an enduring feature of the first half of the 20th century.

The **Oosumi** was approved in 1990 but not laid down until December 1995 in Mitsui's Tamano yard. Those of the initial drawings that were released showed a ship half the size of the one actually completed and resembling the Italian 'San Giorgio' class. Launched in 1996 and commissioned in 1998, it was followed by the **Shimokita** from the same yard, and a third unit, the **Kunisaki** is currently under construction at Hitachi's Maizuru yard, with a fourth

unit planned.

Designed for the movement of a full battalion of marines together with a tank company, the 'Oosumi' class accords fully

with the recent Japanese power-projection operations into the Indian Ocean as well as around the Pacific. Each ship's defensive armament is limited to a pair of

Phalanx CIWS systems with a six-barrel rotary cannon, but the ships operate within a naval task force whose other ships provide primary protection.

SPECIFICATION

'Oosumi' class
Displacement: 8,900 tons standard
Dimensions: length 178 m (584 ft); beam 25.8 m (84 ft 8 in); draught 6 m (19 ft 8 in)
Propulsion: two Mitsui diesels delivering 20580 kW (27,600 shp) to two shafts
Performance: speed 22 kts

Armament: two Phalanx CIWS
Electronics: OPS-14C air search, OPS-28D surface search, and OPS-20 navigation radars
Military lift: 330 troops, 10 Type 90 tanks or 1,400 tons of cargo, and two LCACs
Aircraft: platform for two CH-47J Chinook helicopters
Complement: 135

The Shimokita is the second of a planned four 'Oosumi'-class ships, which combine LPD and LST capabilities in a single hull with a stern docking well.

'Rotterdam' & 'Galicia' classes Amphibious transport dock

This collaborative venture between Dutch and Spanish shipbuilders is known to the Dutch navy as the 'Rotterdam' class and by the Spanish navy as the 'Galicia' class. The **Rotterdam** and **Galicia** were both laid down in 1996, and were commis-

sioned in 1997 and 1998 respectively. The **Castilla** was laid down in 1997 and commissioned in 2000. It is planned that a second Dutch ship, the **Johan de Witt**, should enter service in 2007.

The ships of the class are designed to carry a battalion

of marines and all its associated combat and support vehicles. Carrying a large docking well in the stern, the ships can operate their landing craft and helicopters in varying degrees of bad weather conditions. They carry extensive medical facilities including a treatment

room, operating theatre and medical laboratory, and have already been used to help out during humanitarian emergencies. In addition to land forces and their kit, the ships are designed to carry additional naval ordnance (including up to 30 torpedoes) in their magazines to

support a task force operating at some distance from home ports.

The defensive armament differs between the Spanish and Dutch ships, each carrying indigenous CIWS mountings in the form of the Meroka and Goalkeeper, in addition to 20-mm cannon.

The Rotterdam was built at the Royal Schelde yard at Vlissingen, and provides capabilities for the delivery of a full battalion of marines with all necessary kit.

SPECIFICATION

'Rotterdam'/'Galicia' class
Displacement: 12,750 tons standard; 16,750 tons ('Rotterdam') or 13,815 ('Galicia') full load
Dimensions: length 166 m (544 ft 7 in) ('Rotterdam') and 160 m (524 ft 11 in) ('Galicia'); beam 25 m (82 ft); draught 5.9 m (19 ft 4 in)
Propulsion: four diesel generators delivering current to two electric motors delivering 12170 kW (16,320 shp) to two shafts
Performance: speed 19 kts; range

11125 km (6,910 miles) at 12 kts
Armament: ('Rotterdam') two 30-mm Goalkeeper CIWS and four 20-mm cannon, and ('Galicia') two 20-mm Meroka CIWS
Electronics: DA-08 air/surface and Scout surface search radars
Military lift: 611 troops, 33 tanks or 170 APCs, and 6 LCVPs or 4 LCUs or LCMs
Aircraft: six NH 90 or four EH 101 helicopters
Complement: 113

The 'Rotterdam' and 'Galicia' classes provide a large area over the stern for the operation of helicopters above the dock from which landing craft operate. The Johan de Witt has a stronger helicopter deck than the Rotterdam on a hull that is longer and wider.

'Ivan Rogov' class Amphibious transport dock

Given the designation *bol'shoy desantnyy korabl'* (BDK, or large landing craft) by the Soviets, the **Ivan Rogov** was launched in 1976 at the Kaliningrad shipyard. The vessel entered service in 1978 as the largest amphibious warfare ship built by the Soviets. A second unit, the **Aleksandr Nikolayev**, was laid down in 1979 and completed in 1983, and the third unit, laid down in 1985 and completed in 1990, is the **Mitrofan Moskalenko**. A fourth unit was not completed, and the first two were decommissioned in 1996 and 1997, one of them for possible overhaul and sale to Indonesia.

The ship can carry a reinforced Naval Infantry battalion landing team with all its APCs and other vehicles plus 10 PT-76 light amphibious tanks. An alternative load is a Naval Infantry tank battalion. The vessels were unique in Soviet amphibious ship design as they had both a well dock and a helicopter flight deck and hangar. This allowed the ship to perform not only the traditional role of over-the-beach

assault by use of bow doors and ramp, but also the stand-off assault role using a mixture of helicopters, landing craft, air-cushion vehicles (ACVs) and amphibious vehicles.

Accessibility

The bow doors and internal ramp position provide access to a vehicle parking deck located in the lower forward part of the ship. Further vehicles can be accommodated in the midships area of the upper deck, access to this being by hydraulically operated ramps that lead from the bow doors and the docking well. The vehicle deck itself leads directly into the floodable well which is some 79 m (259 ft 2 in) long with a stern door some 13 m (42 ft 8 in) across. The well can accom-

modate either two pre-loaded 'Lebed'-class ACVs and a 145-ton full load 'Ondatra'-class LCM, or three 'Gus'-class troop-carrying ACVs.

Two helicopter landing spots are provided, one forward and one aft above the well dock, each with its own flight control station. Both spots have access to the massive block superstructure, in which a hangar could accommodate five Kamov Ka-25 'Hormone-C' utility helicopters, later replaced by four Ka-29 helicopters.

Accommodation for the embarked Naval Infantry is located within the superstructure block, which also includes vehicle and helicopter workshops. To starboard, immediately in front of the block, is a tall

deck house on top of which is mounted a 122-mm (4.8-in) rocket-launcher system with two 20-round packs of launcher tubes, one to each side of a pedestal mounting that trains them in azimuth and elevation. The rockets are used to provide a saturation shore bombardment capability for the assault units. A twin 76.2-mm (3-in) DP gun turret is located on the forecastle, and a pop-up two-rail launcher bin units for SA-N-4

SAMs and four 30-mm CIWS mountings are mounted on top of the main superstructure block to provide an air-defence capability. Extensive command, control and surveillance equipment is fitted for amphibious force flagship duties.

The two Pacific Fleet units have paid off, leaving only the *Mitrofan Moskalenko* in service with the Northern Fleet from the base at Severomorsk.

SPECIFICATION

'Ivan Rogov' class
Displacement: 8,260 tons standard; 14,060 tons full load
Dimensions: length 157.5 m (516 ft 9 in); beam 24.5 m (80 ft 6 in); draught 6.5 m (21 ft 4 in)
Propulsion: two gas turbines delivering 29820 kW (39,995 shp) to two shafts
Performance: speed 19 kts; range 13900 km (8,635 miles) at 14 kts
Armament: one twin launcher for 20 SA-N-4 'Gecko' SAMs, one twin 76.2-mm (3-in) DP gun, four 30-mm ADG-630 CIWS mountings, two SA-N-5 quadruple launchers, and two 122-mm (4.8-in) rocket launchers
Electronics: one 'Top Plate-A' 3D

radar, two 'Don Kay' or 'Palm Frond' navigation radars, two 'Squeeze Box' optronic directors, one 'Owl Screech' 76.2-mm gun fire-control radar, one 'Pop Group' SA-N-4 missile fire-control radar, two 'Bass Tilt' CIWS fire-control radars, one 'Salt Pole-B' IFF system, three 'Bell Shroud' ESM systems, two 'Bell Squat' ECM systems, 20 decoy launchers, and one 'Mouse Tail' VDS
Military lift: 522 troops, typically 20 MBTs or an equivalent volume of APCs and trucks, 2,500 tons of freight, and three ACVs or six LCMs
Aircraft: four Ka-29 'Helix' helicopters
Complement: 239

'Albion' class LPD

The Royal Navy's two assault ships, HMS *Fearless* and HMS *Intrepid*, laid down in 1962, were due for deletion in 1981 as part of the Conservative government's decision to end the Royal Marines' amphibious capability. This ruling played a major role in the Argentine decision of the following year to invade the Falklands Islands. The two ships were reprieved and played a vital role in the liberation of the islands. It was another 10 years before a decision was taken to authorise replacements for what were, by the 1991 Gulf War, very elderly ships. Even then, the two **'Albion'-class** LPDs were not laid down until 1998 and 2000 respectively, by which time the *Intrepid* had been cannibalised to keep the

Fearless operational. Even then, the fire in the ship's engine room during November 2000 as the *Fearless* was operating off Sierra Leone, riven by civil war, demonstrated the dangers in relying on a 40-year old ship. Keeping it in service was estimated to require another £2 million, so the *Fearless* was paid off in March 2002.

The £429 million replacement programme was accelerated after the events of 11 September 2001, and the requirement was altered to demand the capability for the mounting of more than one amphibious operation at a time. **HMS Albion** was launched in March 2001, but its in-service date of March 2002 slipped by a year. **HMS Bulwark** was launched in

November 2001, but workers on it were transferred to accelerate the completion of the *Albion*.

Much larger and more capable LPDs than the ships they are replacing, the 'Albion'-class units are part of a wider modernisation of the British amphibious capability. They will serve alongside the new helicopter carrier HMS *Ocean* and the four 'Bay'-class landing ships (logistic) planned to replace the 'Sir Bedivere'-class LSLs. The extensive command and control systems aboard the 'Albion' class represent a great leap forward for the Royal Navy and Marines.

One feature worthy of note is the diesel-electric propulsion system, the first to be used by a British surface warship. This requires only two-thirds the engineering complement of the older LPDs and, in overall terms, automation and new technology have reduced the

The two 'Albion'-class assault ships were built by BAE Systems (formerly Vickers) at Barrow-in-Furness, and were somewhat delayed by lack of skilled workers.

manning requirement from 550 to 325. The four new LCU Mk 10 'ro-ro' landing

craft operated by each 'Albion' are capable of carrying a Challenger 2 MBT.

HMS Albion and HMS Bulwark are Royal Navy ships that provide the Royal Marines with a quantum leap forward in their amphibious assault capabilities.

SPECIFICATION

'Albion' class
Displacement: 19,560 tons full load; 21,500 tons docked down
Dimensions: length 176 m (577 ft 5 in); beam 29.9 m (98 ft 1 in); draught 6.7 m (22 ft)
Propulsion: diesel generators powering two electric motors driving two shafts
Performance: speed 20 kts; range 14825 km (9,210 miles) at 14 kts
Armament: two 30-mm Goalkeeper CIWS mountings and

two twin 20-mm AA guns
Electronics: one Type 996 air/surface-search, one surface search and two navigation radars, ADAWS 2000 combat data system, UAT-1/4 ESM system and eight Sea Gnat decoy launchers
Military lift: 305 or overload 710 troops, six Challenger 2 tanks or 30 APCs, four LCUs and four LCVPs
Aircraft: two/three medium helicopters
Complement: 325

The USS Belleau Wood photographed in 1987. The vessel was still equipped with a Mk 45 gun in the starboard bow position. The fully automatic 5-in weapon could fire once every three seconds, putting a 30-kg (66-lb) shell out to a range of 24000 m (78,740 ft). Primarily intended for shore bombardment, the guns could also be used against aircraft.

'Tarawa'-class amphibious assault ships

The 'Tarawa'-class LHA ships were intended to combine the capabilities of the helicopter carrier (LPH), the amphibious transport dock (LPD), the command ship (LCC) and the amphibious cargo ship (LKA) in a single hull. The class was originally to have numbered nine, but as a result of the end of the Vietnam War and budgetary constraints, the eventual number built was five. The Ingalls shipyard built them by means of its multi-ship construction technique between 1971 and 1978.

The ship's sides are vertical for some two-thirds of their length in order to maximize the internal space available for cargo. An 82-m (268-ft) long by 24 m (78-ft) wide hangar with a 6.1-m (20-ft) overhead is located above a similarly sized well deck set into the stern. The hangar is served by an 18182-kg (40,085-lb) capacity side lift to port and a larger 36364-kg (80,170-lb) capacity centre-line lift at the stern. The docking well, vehicle deck, cargo holds and hangar deck are connected by a series of five elevators capable of carrying 1000-kg (2,205-lb) palletised loads. The three forward elevators serve the vehicle deck and use a conveyor belt system, while the aft two elevators (located at the other end of the belt) serve both the well deck, where an overhead cargo-carrying monorail system takes the pallets onto the landing craft, and the hangar deck. An angled ramp from the hangar deck leads to the flight deck to allow direct loading of helicopters.

Vehicle accomodation

Forward of the docking well (and connected to it and the flight deck by ramps) are the vehicle decks. These normally accommodate 160 tracked vehicles, artillery pieces and trucks together with 40 AAV7A1 amphibious assault personnel carriers. The well deck can accommodate up to four LCUs or two LCUs and two LCM 8s or 17 LCM 6s. The four LCUs and eight of the AAV7A1s can be launched simultaneously from the well deck. The vessels normally carry two LCM 6s and two LCPLs stowed on deck for launch by a large deck crane. The aircraft hangar has the capacity for 26 CH-46E Sea Knight or 19 CH-53D Sea Stallion/CH-53E Super Stallion helicopters, although the normal air group embarked tends to be either 12 CH-46Es, six CH-53D/Es, four AH-1W Super Cobra gunships and two UH-1N Twin Huey utility helicopters; or six CH-46Es, nine CH-53D/Es, four AH-1Ws and two UH-1Ns. Both the AV-8 Harrier series and the OV-10 Bronco fixed-wing aircraft have also been operated, the former being a V/STOL close-support fighter and the latter a STOL observation/attack aircraft. A 464.5 m² (5,000 sq ft) training and acclimatisation room is fitted for the 1,900-man reinforced US Marine battalion carried to exercise in a controlled environment.

To act as an amphibious squadron flagship, the LHA is fitted with the Tactical Amphibious Warfare Data System (TAWDS) to provide command and control over the group's aircraft. weapons, sensors and landing craft. The same satellite communications system and data links as fitted to the LCCs are carried. Two of the LHAs are assigned to the Atlantic fleets while the other three are with the Pacific fleets.

The USS Saipan *is seen in comapny with the amphibious transport dock (LPD) ship USS* Ponce *(top) and the underway replenishment oiler USNS* Patuxent *(centre) during a simultaneous underway replenishment in September 2002.*

The main function of an assault ship is to get troops ashore in the shortest possible time, with assault troops riding into battle within amphibious assault vehicles. Here an AAV7A1 Amphibious Assault Vehicle from the USS Nassau advances onto the beach during a mock invasion of Newfoundland. In the post Cold War era, such realistic training exercises improve the skills that may be called upon during a NATO-led peacekeeping support operation. The AAV is the heart of the Marine assault, 'Tarawa'-class vessels carrying up to 40 examples.

Below right: A US Navy LCAC (Landing Craft Air Cushion) of Assault Craft Unit Five delivers troops and cargo to the USS Peleliu during an amphibious exercise off the coast of Southern California.

Below left: Mainstay of the USMC's heavylift capability, a CH-53E Super Stallion lands on the deck of the USS Nassau off the coast of Nova Scotia. In service with five active duty units, the three-engined CH-53E variant is capable of externally lifting any USMC tactical jet or an LAV.

'GATOR NAVY': US AMPHIBIOUS ASSAULT

The five 'Tarawa'-class vessels form an important component of the US Navy's assault fleet, or 'Gator Navy'. Although these ships are now ageing, to date only a single additional 'Wasp'-class ship has been ordered to replace the USS Tarawa. The latter may replace the USS Inchon in the specialist mine warfare role. Nocturnal operations are illustrated aboard the USS Nassau during the Combined Joint Task Force Exercise '96, with a CH-46 preparing for a night launch (below right) and a USMC LAV (Light Armored Vehicle) backing onto a US Navy landing craft prior to amphibious operations from the ship's well deck (right). The 'Tarawa' class have also been active in military campaigns. Pictured below is an AV-8B taxiing aboard the USS Tarawa in the Persian Gulf in support of Operation Southern Watch, enforcing the No-Fly Zone over southern Iraq in December 1998.

'Whidbey Island' and 'Harpers Ferry' class Landing ships

Based on the 'Anchorage' class, the **'Whidbey Island' class** were conceived as replacements for the 'Thomaston'-class LSDs. The first 'Whidbey Island' vessel was laid down in 1981. In 1988 the class was enlarged from 8 to 12 units, the last four forming a sub-class (the **'Harpers Ferry'-class LSD-CVs** or Landing Ship Dock-Cargo Variant ships) with an enhanced cargo capacity. The **LSD 41** (Landing Ship Dock-41) programme replaced the eight ageing LSD 28-class ships which reached the end of their service lives during the 1980s.

Enter the hovercraft

The 'Whidbey Island' class were designed from the outset to operate LCAC (Landing Craft Air Cushion) hovercraft. These carry a 60-ton payload and travel at speeds in excess of 40 kts in calm conditions, enabling amphibious assaults to be made over greater distances and against a wide variety of beaches. The well deck mea-

sures 134.1 m (440 ft) by 15.2 m (50 ft). It can accommodate four hovercraft, which is more than any other amphibious assault vessel.

The most obvious visual differences between the sub-classes are that the LSD-CVs have only one crane and that the forward Phalanx CIWS is mounted atop the bridge on LSD 41-48 but below and forward of the superstructure on the 'Harpers Ferry' class.

Ship self defence

USS *Whidbey Island* trialled the QRCC (Quick Reaction Combat Capability) system from June 1993. The combination of RIM-116A missiles, Phalanx CIWS and AN/SLQ-32 EW system was accorded a higher priority after the Iraqi Exocet attack against the USS *Stark* on 17 May 1987. Now designated the SSDS (Ship Self Defense System) it has been installed on all 'Whidbey Island'-class ships.

The 'Whidbey Island'-class ships are intended to land a

battalion of US Marines via four LCAC hovercraft, 21 LCMs (Landing Craft Medium) or three LCUs (Landing Craft Utilities). Alternatively, the troops can be landed in 64 AAV7A1 amphibious tracked armoured personnel carriers. The LSD-CV cargo variants deploy fewer landing craft: two hovercraft, nine LCMs or one

LCU. In addition to the anti-aircraft and anti-missile guns and missiles carried for active defence, extensive passive measures are available. A powerful ESM suite is complemented by chaff rockets capable of 'seducing' incoming missiles and AN/SLQ-49 chaff buoys that are effective for several hours in moderate sea conditions, producing a

radar signature greater than that of the ship. The Nixie decoy system has a similar effect on torpedoes trying to target the ship.

The first two units cost over $300 million. The last four averaged $150 million per ship. 1996 figures quoted the annual operating cost of one of these vessels at approximately $20 million.

As well as having generous freight space, the 'Whidbey Island'-class LSDs also feature a potent self defence weapons system. This is LSD 44, the USS Gunston Hill.

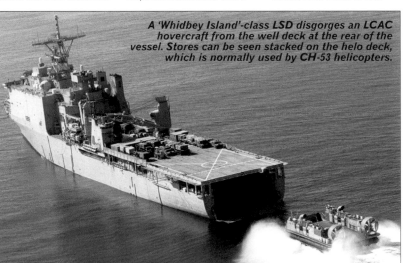

A 'Whidbey Island'-class LSD disgorges an LCAC hovercraft from the well deck at the rear of the vessel. Stores can be seen stacked on the helo deck, which is normally used by CH-53 helicopters.

SPECIFICATION

'Whidbey Island' class
Displacement: 15,726 tons full load (LSD 41-48); 16,740 tons (LSD 49-52)
Dimensions: length 185.8 m (609 ft 6 in); beam 25.6 m (84 ft); draught 6.3 m (20 ft 6 in)
Propulsion: four diesel engines delivering 24608 kW (33,000 shp) to two shafts
Speed: 22 kts
Range: 8,000 nm (14816 km; 9,206 miles) at 18 kts (33 km/h; 20 mph)
Complement: 22 officers and 391 enlisted personnel
Troops: 402 but surge capacity is 627
Cargo: 141.6 m³ (5,000 cu ft) available for general cargo plus 1161 m² (12,500 sq ft) for vehicles (including four pre-loaded

hovercraft in the well deck); LSD 49-52 have 1914 m³ (67,600 cu ft) space for cargo plus 1877 m² (20,200 sq ft) for motor transport but only two or three hovercraft
Armament: two General Dynamics 20-mm six-barrelled Vulcan Phalanx Mk 15 guns; two 25-mm Mk 38 guns; eight or more 0.5-in (12.7-mm) machine-guns
Countermeasures: four Loral Hycor SRBOC six-barrelled Mk 36 launchers, AN/SLQ-25 Nixie acoustic torpedo decoy, AN/SLQ-49 chaff buoys, AN/SLQ-32 radar warning/jammer/deception system
Electronics: AN/SPS-67 surface search radar, AN/SPS-49 air search radar, AN/SPS-64 navigation radar
Aircraft: two CH-53 Sea Stallions (platform only)

'Wasp' class Amphibious assault ship

The **'Wasp'-class** ships are the largest amphibious assault vessels in the world, providing the US Navy with an unrivalled ability to attack hostile shores around the world. They are the first ships specifically designed to operate both the AV-8B Harrier II and a complement of LCAC hovercraft. The last three of the class to be completed have cost an average of $750 million each. The US plans for a 12-strong ARG (Amphibious Ready Group) to be deployed by 2010, when the

first 'Tarawa'-class vessel will be 35-years-old.

The 'Wasp' class is a follow-on from the 'Tarawa' class and its ships share the same basic hull and engineering plant. However, the bridge is two decks lower than the LHAs (Landing Helicopter Amphibious) and the command, control and communications centres are inside the hull where they less easy to disable. To facilitate landing and recovery operations, the ships can ballast some 15,000 tons of sea water for trimming.

The USS Wasp (LHD 1) alongside the underway replenishment (UNREP) vessel USNS Supply during a deployment in support of Operation Enduring Freedom. Wasp's airwing includes AV-8B and CH-53 aircraft.

In addition to deploying a powerful air component, the 'Wasp'-class vessels can operate three LCAC hovercraft (pictured) or 12 LCM landing craft.

Capable of embarking a 2,000-strong MEU (Marine Expeditionary Unit), the 'Wasp' class can land its troops on the beach using its own landing craft, or deliver them inland via helicopters (a manoeuvre known as 'vertical envelopment'). Each 'Wasp' class can accommodate up to three LCACs or twelve LCMs in the 81 m x 15.2 m (267 x 50 ft) well deck. In total, 61 AAVs (Amphibious Assault Vehicles – the AAV7A1) can be shipped aboard, 40 stowed in the well deck and 21 in the upper vehicle storage area.

The flight deck has nine landing spots for helicopters and up to 42 CH-46 Sea Knights can be operated; the class can also deploy AH-1 SeaCobra attack helicopters or other transports such as the CH-53E Super Stallion, UH-1N Twin Huey or the multi-purpose SH-60B Seahawk. The 'Wasp' class can operate six to eight AV-8B Harrier IIs in the combat role, but can support up to 20. There are two aircraft elevators, one amidships on the port side, the other to starboard, abaft the 'island'. When the ships pass through the Panama Canal these lifts have to be folded inboard.

Air wing
The composition of the air group depends on the mission. The 'Wasp' class can function as aircraft carriers, operating 20 AV-8Bs in the sea control role, plus six ASW helicopters. For amphibious assault, a typical group consists of six AV-8Bs, four AH-1W attack helicopters, 12 CH-46 Sea Knights, nine CH-53 Sea Stallions or Super Stallions and four UH-1N Twin Hueys. Alternatively, it can also operate 42 CH-46s.

The 'Wasp'-class ships are designed to carry a balanced force of combat vehicles, including five M1 Abrams main battle tanks, 25 AAV7A1 armoured personnel carriers, eight M198 155-mm self-propelled guns, 68 lorries and a dozen or so other support vehicles. They can transport and land ashore all manner of equipment and vehicles. Monorail trains moving at up to 183 m (600 ft) per minute deliver cargo from the storage areas to the well deck, which opens to the sea through gates in the stern.

Each ship also features a 600-bed hospital with six operating theatres, so reducing an amphibious task force's dependence on medical facilities ashore.

The 'Wasp' class has been replacing the older LHAs since the mid-1990s. **USS Bataan** was built by pre-outfitting and modular construction techniques. Subassemblies were brought together to produce five hull and superstructure modules. These modules were then joined together on land. The result of this construction technique was that the ship was three-quarters complete on launch. *Bataan* is the first amphibious assault ship designed from the outset to accommodate female personnel, both in the crew and Marine contingent. Full accommodation for up to 450 female officers, enlisted personnel and troops is provided on the vessel.

'San Antonio' class Amphibious transport docks

The 12 ships of the **LPD 17** or **'San Antonio'** (**Landing Platform Dock**) **class** will eventually replace three classes of amphibious assault vessel: LPD 4s, LSD 36s and LSTs, as well as the LKA (already retired in 2002) – a total of 41 vessels in all. This will not only modernise an increasingly elderly amphibious assault fleet but deliver significant savings in life-cycle costs and personnel numbers. However, costs of the first three vessels are substantially over-budget: the LPD 17 class will cost more than $800 million against an estimate of $617 million. This is despite numerous cost-saving measures including the decision to adopt a commercial surface search radar (AN/SPS-73). The design process exploited virtual reality computer programmes, enabling many internal layouts to be tested without prototypes being built. Input from over 2,500 serving personnel is intended to produce a vessel truly designed for the men and women who will live onboard.

Mobility triad
Approved in 1993, construction of the LPD 17 was delayed by legal disputes over the award of contracts but the first of the class, **San Antonio**, was due to join the fleet by 2003.

The US Marine Corps has developed the concept of the 'mobility triad' and the LPD 17 class is the first assault ship designed from the outset to accommodate all three modes of transport: the MV-22 Osprey tiltrotor aircraft, the LCAC hovercraft and the AAV amphibious APC. It is thus capable of landing troops some 173 nm (320 km; 200 miles) inland, making 'littoral operations' far greater in scope than ever previously imagined. Two LCAC hovercraft or one LCU are embarked along with 14 AAVs. The well deck and stern layout are similar to that of the 'Wasp' class but the superstructure is angled to reduce radar signature. A 24-bed hospital is included with two operating theatres and a casualty overflow capacity of 100 persons. Defensive weapons systems will include the SSDS which will be fitted as construction of the vessels is completed.

The LPD 17 class ships deploy up to four CH-46 Sea Knight helicopters simultaneously or two MV-22 Ospreys. Four MV-22s can be spotted on deck and one more in the hanger. Alternatively the hanger can accommodate one CH-53E, two CH-46s or two UH-1s. With double the vehicle storage space of the old LPD 4 class, the LPD 17 class is also designed for maximum survivability, the combination of reduced radar profile and advanced computer systems to coordinate defensive weaponry is intended to allow the ship to operate alone if required, although it would normally be part of an amphibious ready group. *San Antonio* is the first US warship to be equipped with a fibre-optic Shipboard Wide Area Network (SWAN) that connects all ship systems, sensors and weapons, providing integrated real-time data to its combat command centre.

On 7 September 2002, about one year after the attack on the World Trade Center, Secretary of the Navy, Gordon England, announced that the fifth ship of the class would be named *New York*.

The LPD 17-class vessels have been designed with low-observable characteristics. An MV-22 Osprey can be seen on the flight deck in this artist's impression.

'Attack' class Large patrol craft (PC)

Given the very long coastline for which Australia is responsible (Papua New Guinea and the island groups off it, as well as Australia proper), the country decided that adequate patrol of this responsibility had to be entrusted to a combination of maritime patrol aircraft (the P-2 Neptune, for example, followed by the P-3 Orion, supplemented by smaller machines such as the Nomad Missionmaster series) and large patrol craft. Only thus, it was believed, could the security of Australia and its northern dependencies be assured against direct attack and encroachment on their economic zones.

New order

In November 1965, the Australian authorities ordered a class of 20 large patrol craft as the **'Attack' class**, of which five were to be allocated to Papua New Guinea and the other 15 used around Australia itself. Five of the craft were built by Evans Deakin and the other 15 craft by the Maryborough-located Walker's yard. The 20 craft were **Acute**, **Adroit**, **Advance**, **Aitape**, **Samarai**, **Archer**, **Ardent**, **Arrow**, **Assail**, **Attack**, **Aware**, **Ladava**, **Lae**, **Madang**, **Bandolier**, **Barbette**, **Barricade**, **Bombard**, **Buccaneer** and **Bayonet**, of

which the five named for New Guinea towns (*Aitape*, *Samarai*, *Ladava*, *Lae* and *Madang*) were allocated to New Guinea. When Papua New Guinea became independent in 1975, Australia transferred these five craft to the new nation's defence force. Four of the craft were stricken for cannibalisation from 1981, allowing the *Madang* to be retained in service into the second half of the 1990s.

Production run

The first of the craft to be completed, in 1967, was the *Attack*, and the rest of the class followed at short intervals. However, experience soon revealed that the 'Attack'-class craft were too small for the task demanded of them, and from the late 1970s the 'Attack' class craft were superseded by the 20 considerably larger craft of the 'Fremantle' class to a design by Brooke Marine, a British company. In a December 1974 hurricane the *Arrow* sank at its moorings, but the badly damaged *Attack* was saved and repaired.

Phasing the 'Attack'-class craft from Australian service had started before that time, however, for in 1973-74 the *Bandolier* and *Archer* were sold to Indonesia as the **Sibarau** and **Siliman**. The Indonesian **'Sibarau' class**

HMAS Attack was the lead craft of a 20-strong class that had only a short Australian career. In 1985 the Attack became the Sikuda of the Indonesian navy.

was increased to eight craft by 1986 as a result of further transfers from Australia, the later craft being the **Sigalu**, **Silea**, **Siribua**, **Siada**, **Sikuda** and **Sigurot**. In 1982-83 Indonesia built two other units of the class as near

copies of the Australian originals. These last two have not been seen for some time, but

the eight ex-Australian craft are in service in the early years of the 21st century.

SPECIFICATION	
'Sibarau' class	at 13 kts
Displacement: 146 tons full load	**Armament:** one 40-mm Bofors
Dimensions: length 32.8 m (107 ft 6 in); beam 6.1 m (20 ft); draught 2.2 m (7 ft 4 in)	gun, and one 12.7-mm (0.5-in) machine-gun
	Electronics: one Decca 916
Propulsion: two Paxman 16YJCM diesels delivering 2985 kW (4,000 shp) to two shafts	surface search and navigation radar, and one Telegon VIII ESM system
Performance: maximum speed 21 kts; range 1930 km (1,200 miles)	**Complement:** 19

'Fremantle' class Large patrol craft (PC)

Soon after they had entered service, it became evident to the Royal Australian Navy that the patrol craft of the 'Attack' class were too small for truly effective service, and in September 1977 it was announced that the 20 'Attack'-class units were to be replaced from the late 1970s by the same number of **'Fremantle' class** craft.

Brooke Marine design

The new type was based on the PCF-420 design by Brooke Marine of Lowestoft in the UK, where the lead unit was built for commissioning in March 1980. The other 14 (out of a planned 19) craft were built in Australia by the Cairns yard of North Queensland Engineers and Agents for commissioning between March 1981 and December 1984. The whole class comprised **Fremantle**, **Warrnambool**, **Townsville**, **Wollongong**, **Launceston**, **Whyalla**, **Ipswich**, **Cessnock**, **Bendigo**, **Gawler**, **Geraldton**, **Dubbo**, **Geelong**, **Gladstone** and **Bunbury**. The **Ballarat**, **Mildura**, **Armidale**, **Bundaberg** and **Pirie** were planned but not built.

HMAS Launceston was completed as the fifth patrol craft of the 'Fremantle' class, and is based at Darwin as part of the forces shielding the north of Australia from illegal immigration, and also checking the illegal economic exploitation of northern Australian waters.

SPECIFICATION	
'Fremantle' class	at 30 kts
Displacement: 245 tons full load	**Armament:** one 40-mm Bofors gun,
Dimensions: length 41.8 m	one 81-mm (3.2-in) mortar, and
(137 ft 1 in); beam 7.1 m (23 ft 4 in);	three 0.5-in (12.7-mm) machine-
draught 1.8 m (6 ft)	guns
Propulsion: two MTU 16V 538	**Electronics:** one Kelvin Hughes
TB91 diesels delivering 4580 kW	Type 1006 navigation radar, and one
(6,140 shp) to two shafts	AWA Defence Industries Type 133
Performance: maximum speed	PRISM ESM system
30 kts; range 2335 km (1,450 miles)	**Complement:** 24

The pennant number 217 identifies this patrol craft of the 'Fremantle' class as HMAS Bunbury, the last of the class. The unit was commissioned on 15 December 1984 and is used for patrols of Australia's huge coastline. Some 12 of the class are based in the north (five at Cairns and seven at Darwin) with two at Sydney and one at Fremantle.

The craft were designed for a 15-year service life, but this was later extended to 19 years and has since been extended once more by refits and updates which included, in 1994-95, the addition of an ESM system. As completed, the craft had a centreline shaft for low-speed cruising on the power of a Dorman 12-cylinder cruising diesel, but this has been removed: the centre-line shaft provided a speed of 8 kts and a range of 5,500 miles (8850 km).

Enhanced Bofors gun

The armament is centred on a 40-mm L/60 Bofors gun, itself of some age but still useful as it is fitted on the AN 4-40 mounting designed and manufactured by the Australian Government Ordnance Factory, and providing enhanced accuracy, especially in heavy weather. The gun has a rate of fire of 120 rounds per minute and a maximum range of 10 km (6.2 miles) in the surface-to-surface role. The armament also includes an 81-mm (3.2-in) mortar and provision for up to three 0.5-in (12.7-mm) Browning M2 machine-guns.

It was planned that the 'Fremantle' class should be replaced by 2003 on a one-to-one basis by a new class of 15 patrol craft. However, the units of the new 'Armidale' class will be delivered only from the second half of 2004 at the earliest, forcing the retention in operational service of many of the elderly 'Fremantle'-class units long past the time it was originally envisaged they would have been retired.

'Huchuan' and 'Shanghai' classes

Fast attack craft (gun and torpedo)

Fast disappearing from Chinese service by 2003, the 'Huchuan I' class of torpedo-armed fast attack hydrofoils (PHT) was for over 25 year China's most important coastal anti-ship weapon. The forward set of hydrofoils is retracted when the craft is hullborne. Some 32 examples of the 'Huchuan' were exported to Albania

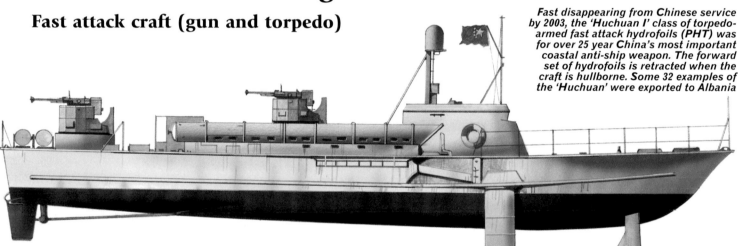

For many years the Chinese navy relied on vessels supplied by the USSR or built locally to Soviet designs. In 1959 the first prototypes of what became the major construction programme in the build-up of the Chinese coastal forces were seen. These were large patrol craft of the **'Shanghai'** (or **Type 062) class**, of which more than 350 were completed beginning in 1961, in five subvariants of which one is still in production for the export market. A relatively unsophisticated design, the 'Shanghai' class once constituted the bulk of China's coastal patrol strength in the forms of the **'Shanghai I' class** with a length of 35.1 m (115 ft 2 in) and twin 57-mm and 37-mm guns forward and aft, the **'Shanghai II'**, **'Shanghai III'** or **'Haizhui' (Type 062/1)**, **'Shanghai IV'** and **'Shanghai V' classes** with greater lengths, different bridge designs and different armaments. By 2003, all of the 'Shanghai I' craft had been removed from Chinese service, although some 98 of the later variants remained in use. Some of these 'Shanghais' are reportedly fitted with RBU-1200 ASW mortars while others may have adopted a minesweeping role.

'Shanghais' for export

Large numbers have also been exported to Albania (six), Bangladesh (eight in 1980-82), Cameroon, Congo (three), Egypt (four in 1984), Guinea (six), North Korea (12), Pakistan (12), Sri Lanka (five in 1972 and three in 1991), Sierra Leone, Tanzania (seven in 1970-71 and two in 1992), Tunisia (two in 1977), North Vietnam (eight in May 1966) and Romania, in the last of which the type was built locally in three variants. The last is particularly intriguing as Romania was at the time a member of the Soviet Warsaw Pact alliance.

Around 1966 the first of an indigenously designed and built hydrofoil fast attack craft (torpedo) was seen, Constructed by the Hudong yard in Shanghai, this **'Huchuan'** (or **Type 025/026) class** was subsequently identified in two versions. The first is the **'Huchuan I' class** with a pair of 14.5-mm (0.57-in) machine-guns on a mounting amidships with a second twin mounting aft of it, while the bridge is placed forward of the torpedo tube mouths. The second is the **'Huchuan II' class** with the bridge placed farther aft, in line with the tubes, and the amidships mounting moved to the forecastle. The hull is of all-metal construction and the forward pair of foils can be withdrawn into recesses in the hull when the craft is hullborne. There were once some 140 in Chinese service, exports were made to Albania, Pakistan, Bangladesh, Tanzania and Romania, where local construction was also undertaken.

SPECIFICATION	
'Shanghai II' class	at 16.5 kts
Displacement: 134 tons full load	**Armament:** two twin 37-mm or, in
Dimensions: length 38.8 m (127 ft	some, 57-mm AA and two twin
4 in); beam 5.4 m (17 ft 9 in);	25-mm AA guns, plus provision for
draught 1.7 m (5 ft 7 in)	eight depth charges and 10 mines
Propulsion: two L-12V-180 diesels	**Electronics:** one 'Pot Head' or
delivering 1800 kW (2,415 shp) and	'Skin Head' surface search radar,
two 12-D-6 delivering 1360 kW	one 'High Pole' IFF, and provision
(1,825 shp) to four shafts	for hull-mounted active or variable-
Performance: maximum speed	depth sonar
30 kts; range 1300 km (810 miles)	**Complement:** 38

SPECIFICATION	
'Huchuan' class	**Performance:** maximum speed
Displacement: 45.8 tons full load	50 kts; range 925 km (575 miles) at
Dimensions: length 21.8 m (71 ft	30 kts
6 in); beam 6.3 m (20 ft 8 in)	**Armament:** two 533-mm (21-in)
foilborne; draught 3.6 m (11 ft	torpedo tubes and two twin
10 in) hullborne	14.5-mm (0.57-in) machine-guns
Propulsion: three M50 diesels	**Electronics:** one 'Skin Head' or
delivering 2460 kW (3,300 hp) to	Type 753 surface search radar
three shafts	**Complement:** 16

'Jaguar' and 'Zobel'

West Germany's first fast attack craft were three ex-World War II S-boats and six new-build 'Silbermöwe' class FAC(G)s delivered in the mid-1950s. These served to start the process of building a West German FAC capability, but were obsolescent in their concept and succeeded from the later 1950s by the 40 craft of the **'Jaguar' class**, initially designated as the **Schnellboot 55** by its designer, Lürssen of Vegesack, and then as the **TNC 42 class**. In West German service the boats were divided into the **Type 140** and **Type 141** variants, which comprised 30 and 10 craft with Mercedes-Benz and Maybach diesel engines respectively. The craft of the 'Jaguar' class were the *Iltis*, *Jaguar*, *Leopard*, *Luchs*, *Wolf*, *Tiger*, *Panther*, *Löwe*, *Fuchs*, *Marder*, *Seeadler*, *Albatros*, *Kondor*, *Greif*, *Falke*, *Geier*, *Bussard*, *Habicht*, *Sperber*, *Kormoran*, *Weihe*, *Kranich*, *Alk*, *Storch*, *Pelikan*, *Haher*, *Elster*, *Reiher*, *Pinguin* and *Dommel*.

The 'Jaguar'-class units were built by Lürssen and Kröger to the extent of 32

Gepard, of the Type 142 'Zobel' class of torpedo boats. These converted Type 140/141 vessels were reconditioned and re-armed with AEG-Telefunken Seal wire-guided torpedoes.

and eight craft respectively, and reflected the current state of the art in FAC thinking far more effectively than the 'Silbermöwe' class, for while the earlier craft were fitted only with gun armament (two 20-mm weapons later replaced by one 40-mm Bofors gun), the later craft had a combination of two 40-mm Bofors guns and four heavyweight torpedoes launched from four tubes. There was also provision for minelaying using tracks fixed to the deck, although the use of this capability demanded the removal of the two after torpedo tubes.

The craft were deemed obsolete in the mid-1970s. Ten each were handed over to Greece and Turkey in the middle of the decade, one was given to France as a target, one became a museum exhibit, and the others were sold out of the

service for scrap.

Ten more boats were built by Lürssen and Kröger (seven and three respectively) as the Mercedes-engined **'Zobel' class** or **Type 142** in the early 1960s with a modified superstructure, bridge and masts. These were the *Zobel*, *Wiesel*, *Dachs*, *Hermelin*, *Nerz*, *Puma*, *Gepard*, *Hyäne*, *Frettchen* and *Ozelot*. Obsolescent in the mid-1980s, six were transferred to Turkey.

SPECIFICATION

'Jaguar' class (Type 140/141)
Displacement: 183.6 tons (Type 140) or 194.6 tons (Type 141) standard; 210 tons (Type 140) or 221 tons (Type 141) tons full load
Dimensions: length 42.6 m (139 ft 10 in); beam 7.1 m (23 ft 4 in); draught 2.3 m (7 ft 6 in) for Type 140 and 2.4 m (8 ft) for Type 141
Propulsion: four Mercedes-Benz diesels (Type 140) or Maybach diesels (Type 141) in each case

delivering 8940 kW (12,000 shp) to four shafts
Performance: speed 43 kts; endurance 1850 km (1,150 miles) at 32 kts declining to 925 km (575 miles) at 39 kts
Armament: two 40-mm Bofors DP guns and four 533-mm (21-in) tubes for four torpedoes
Electronics: one surface search and navigation radar
Complement: 39

'Achimota' class Fast attack craft (gun) FAC(G)

Reviving its experience as the premier creator of S-boats for the German navy in World War II, Lürssen of Vegesack has been the most important single force in the Western design and manufacture of fast attack craft since the later 1950s. The company has produced many FACs for German and other European service, but has also helped many navies in Africa, Asia, the Middle East and South America to develop effective coastal defence or coastal patrol capabilities, perhaps as a stepping stone to the creation of larger and more capable forces.

One of the keys to Lürssen's success has been the creation of a relatively limited number of basic hull designs in different lengths

and displacements, to which can be added the propulsion, weapon and sensor outfits specified by any particular customer. One such hull is that of the **PB 57 class**, which can also be produced as the FPB 57 class for customers wanting a fast attack rather than just patrol capability. Thus the West German navy ordered the FPB 57 model as its Type 143 replacement for the Types 140, 141 and 142, with a four-shaft propulsion arrangement and two armament variations (in each case four anti-ship missiles combined with two 76-mm/3-in DP guns and two 533-mm/21-in torpedo tubes in the Type 143A and two 76-mm guns but no torpedo tubes in the Type 143B, later upgraded by the replacement of the after

gun by a RIM-116 RAM SAM launcher).

Ghanaian order
Ghana has lesser ambitions, and opted for the PB 57 design for its two **'Achimota'-class** fast patrol craft. The two craft were ordered in 1977 and both built in Vegesack by Lürssen for commissioning in March 1981 as the **Achimota** and **Yohaga**. The two craft are used mainly in the fishery protection role, and for this the speed of 30 kts offered by their comparatively low-powered three-shaft propulsion arrangement is more than adequate. The gun armament is typical of such craft, but their electronic sophistication is modest. In keeping with their offshore role over

extended patrols, the craft have a relatively high manning level.

The *Yohaga* was extensively refitted by Swan Hunter on the Tyne up to May 1989, and the *Achimota* underwent a similar refit at CMN's yard at Cherbourg up to August 1992.

There are four other operators of FPB 57-class craft: Indonesia has four units operating in the patrol role; Kuwait received two in the FAC(M) task, losing one in 1991; Nigeria has three large patrol craft that are probably not operational; and Turkey has eight FAC(M)s. Spain developed its 'Lazaga' class from the same basic hull.

SPECIFICATION

'Achimota' class
Displacement: 389 tons full load
Dimensions: length 58.1 m (190 ft 7 in); beam 7.6 m (25 ft); draught 2.8 m (9 ft 2 in)
Propulsion: three MTU 16V 538 TB91 diesels delivering 6870 kW (9,215 shp) to three shafts
Performance: speed 30 kts; endurance 9600 km (5,965 miles) at 12 kts declining to 6100 km

(3,790 miles) at 16 kts
Armament: one 76-mm (3-in) OTO-Melara Compact DP gun and one 40-mm Bofors AA gun
Electronics: one Canopus A surface search and fire-control radar, one TM 1226C navigation radar, and one LIOD optronic director
Complement: 55

The Ghanaian navy's PB 57 type patrol vessel Achimota is typical of the employment by developing nations of an advanced hull in a low-powered form, with limited armament and sensor capability, for tasks such as fishery protection and offshore patrol.

'Al Manama' class FSG

Bahrain's two 'Al Manama'-class guided-missile corvettes pack much capability into a relatively small hull. Limited power results in modest speed but good range.

One step up the size ladder in Lürssen's basic design offerings from the FPB/PB 57 type is the **FPB 62 class**, which has the size to allow the combination of armament and sensor capabilities that makes it sensible to categorise many of these vessels as light corvettes rather than fast attack craft. There are currently three nations who operate class FPB 62 units, namely Bahrain, Singapore and the United Arab Emirates.

Bahrain ordered its two

FPB 62 corvettes in February 1984, and these were built by Lürssen as the **'Al Manama'-class** units **Al Manama** and **Al Muharraq**, completed in December 1987 and February 1988 respectively.

A particular feature of the design is the provision of full flight and hangarage facilities for a light helicopter, which is raised to the flight platform by a lift. The ships' size makes the 'Al Manama' class units effective FAC(M) flotilla leaders, the heli-

copters being able to provide long-range targeting data for the Exocet MM.40 anti-ship missiles.

The design is based on a steel hull with an aluminium alloy superstructure, and although it was planned that the vessels should operate Aérospatiale AS 365F Dauphin 2 helicopters each carrying four AS.15TT light anti-ship missiles, unarmed Eurocopter BO 105 helicopters were procured. A planned update will add a short-range SAM launcher.

SPECIFICATION	
'Al Manama' class	twin Breda 40-mm DP gun, and two
Displacement: 632 tons full load	twin launchers for four MM.40
Dimensions: length 63 m (206 ft	Exocet anti-ship missiles
9 in); beam 9.3 m (30 ft 6 in);	**Electronics:** one Sea Giraffe 50HC
draught 2.9 m (9 ft 5 in)	air/surface search radar, one Decca
Propulsion: four MTU 20V 538	1226 navigation radar, one 9LV 331
TB92 diesels delivering 9560 kW	fire-control radar, one optronic
(12,820 shp) to four shafts	director, one optical director, one
Performance: speed 32 kts;	Cutlass/Cygnus ESM/ECM system,
endurance 7400 km (4,600 miles) at	and one Dagaie decoy launcher
16 kts	**Aircraft:** one Eurocopter BO 105
Armament: one 76-mm (3-in)	helicopter
OTO-Melara Compact DP gun, one	**Complement:** 43

'Turunmaa' and 'Ruissalo' classes FS and PC

Ordered in February 1965 and built in Helsinki by Wärtsilä, the **'Turunmaa'-class** corvettes **Turunmaa** and **Karjala** were commissioned in 1969 as the largest major surface combatants to have been constructed in Finland since the end of World War II. The ships were designed largely for coastal operations with a high capability for the control of fast attack craft flotillas.

The ships were flush-docked and fitted with Vosper

Right: With their low silhouettes, lacking any funnel, the 'Turunmaa'-class corvettes had a highly distinctive appearance. This vessel is the Karjala.

Below: The 'Ruissalo'-class patrol craft were unremarkable but proved effective and were deleted only at the end of the 20th century. The Raisio is illustrated.

Thornycroft fin stabilisation equipment, and the engine exhausts were trunked to outlets on each side of the quarterdeck, from where the two plumes met about 15 m (49 ft) abaft the stern. The armament was standard for such vessels at the time, a notable feature being the incorporation of the RBU

1200 five-barrel launchers for anti-submarine rockets inside the main-deck superstructure at a point abaft the pennant number. Both the ships were refitted at Wärtsilä's Turku facility, re-entering service in 1986 with new radar, electronic warfare equipment and sonar, and were deleted in 2000 and 2001, the *Karjala*

being a museum ship.

The three **'Ruissalo'-class** large patrol craft, **Ruissalo**, **Raisio** and **Röytta**, were built at Turku by Laivateollisuus and commissioned in August/October 1959. With a length of 32 m (108 ft 11 in) and full-load displacement of 130 tons, the craft were slightly enlarged half-sisters

of the two 'Rihtniemi'-class patrol craft, and were powered by two MTU diesels for a speed of 17 kts. The armament was centred on one 40-mm Bofors gun and one 20-mm gun (replaced from 1976 by two twin 23-mm guns) and two RBU 1200 launchers. The last two units were deleted in 2000.

SPECIFICATION	
'Turunmaa' class	14 kts
Displacement: 650 tons standard;	**Armament:** one 120-mm (4.72-in)
770 tons full load	Bofors gun, two 40-mm Bofors DP
Dimensions: length 74 m (243 ft	guns, two twin 23-mm AA guns,
1 in); beam 7.8 m (25 ft 7 in);	two five-barrel RBU 1200 anti-
draught 2.4 m (7 ft 11 in)	submarine rocket launchers, and
Propulsion: CODOG arrangement	two depth charge throwers
with one Rolls-Royce Olympus	**Electronics:** one WM-22 search
TM3B gas turbine delivering	radar, one navigation radar, one 9LV
12,065 kW (16,180 shp) and three	200 Mk 2 fire-control radar, one
MTU diesels delivering 3015 kW	EOS-400 optronic director, one ESM
(4,045 hp) to three shafts	system, one Barricade decoy
Performance: speed 35 kts;	launcher, and one sonar
endurance 4600 km (2,860 miles) at	**Complement:** 70

'Intrepida' class PCF/PCFG

Ordered from Lürssen of Vegesack as the first two of a planned four units whose second two units were omitted for financial reasons, the PCFs of the **'Intrepida' class**, *Intrepida* and *Indomita* were launched in December 1973 and April 1974 and commissioned into the Argentine navy in July and December 1974 respectively. The two craft were built to a gun- and torpedo-armed standard which differed slightly from that of Lürssen's standard FAC design, the **TNC 45 class**, notably in their slightly greater length and beam.

As completed, the craft carried a useful coast-defence armament by the standards of the day. The gun armament was one 76-mm (3-in) Compact gun on the forecastle as well as two 40-mm Bofors L/70 guns in single mountings abaft the superstructure. The torpedo armament comprised two tubes for 533-mm (21-in) AEG SST-4 wire-guided heavyweight torpedoes with active/passive homing for the delivery of a 250-kg (551-lb) warhead over a range of 28 km (17.4 miles) at 23 kts. There were also two 20-mm cannon and two 81-mm (3.2-in) launchers for illuminants.

In 1998 the *Intrepida* was converted to PCFG standard by the replacement of the forward of the two Bofors guns by two container/launchers for MM.38 Exocet anti-ship missiles, but there are no indications that the *Indomita* is to be upgraded to this standard.

Both of the craft are painted in a brown and green camouflage scheme, and their outlines can be broken by the addition of camouflage netting for enhanced concealment along the Argentine coastline.

Above: The camouflage finish of Argentina's 'Intrepida'-class PCFs is optimised for coastal operations, generally in the south of the country.

Below: Intrepida is modified to a missile-armed configuration with two Exocet anti-ship missiles in place of the forward of the two 40-mm Bofors guns.

Below: In its basic form the 'Intrepida'-class PCF (fast patrol craft) carries the primary armament of one 76-mm (3-in) gun and two 533-mm (21-in) torpedoes backed by two 40-mm guns.

SPECIFICATION	
'Intrepida' class (PCF)	**Armament:** one 76-mm (3-in), two 40-mm and two 20-mm guns, and two 533-mm (21-in) torpedo tubes.
Displacement: 268 tons full load	**Electronics:** one Decca 626 surface search and navigation radar, one WM-22 optronic director, one M11 torpedo fire-control system, and one RDL-1 ESM system
Dimensions: length 44.9 m (147 ft 4 in); beam 7.4 m (24 ft 3 in); draught 2.3 m (7 ft 6 in)	
Propulsion: four MTU 16V 538 TB90 diesels delivering 8940 kW (11,990 shp) to four shafts	
Performance: speed 38 kts; range 2700 km (1,680 miles) at 20 kts	**Complement:** 39

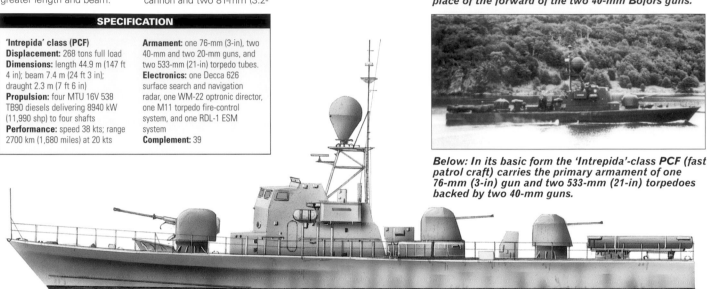

'Hayabusa' class Patrol ship (PG)

Despite the fact that is has a very lengthy coastline for a homeland centred on a small number of large islands and a considerably larger number of small islands, Japan has in historical terms paid little real attention to the concept of coast defence. Instead it prefers the idea of seaward defence as the means of preventing an enemy from reaching the Japanese coast with a view to landing an invasion force. However, a number of fast patrol craft were operated from the late 1950s to the early 1990s, when two new types were adopted for the patrol forces of the Japanese navy. The first of these is the 'PG 01' class of three missile-armed hydrofoils, and the second is the **'Hayabusa' class**. The Japanese classify this latter, of which pairs were ordered in the 1999, 2000 and 2001 financial years, as patrol craft, general.

Single-hulled craft built at Mitsubishi's Shimonoseki yard, the first two craft were commissioned in March 2002 as the *Hayabusa* and *Wakataka*, with the other pairs scheduled for commissioning in 2003 and 2004.

Three turbines

The craft are of unusual appearance, largely as a result of their propulsion arrangement of three General Electric LM2500 gas turbines. These are located in the after part of the hull, where a very blocky deckhouse with three exhausts above it reveals the presence of the engines. On the forecastle of each of the craft is the 76-mm (3-in) Compact gun in a low-observability gunhouse. To the rear of this is the main superstructure carrying the antennae for most of the electronic systems, and abaft the propulsion system's deckhouse are the two pairs of launchers for the four Mitsubishi SSM-1B anti-ship missiles. The SSM-1B is a surface-to-surface weapon introduced in 1990. The missile weighs some 660 kg (1,455 lb), has cruise propulsion by a small turbojet for a maximum range of 150 km (93 miles), and uses active radar terminal guidance for the accurate delivery of its high explosive warhead.

The 'Hayabusa' class of gun/missile-armed fast attack craft is designed for the protection of Japan's extensive coastline, their high speed allowing the craft to reach an operational area with minimum delay. The name ship of the class is illustrated.

SPECIFICATION	
'Hayabusa' class	OTO-Melara Compact DP gun, two 0.5-in (12.7-mm) machine-guns, and four SSM-1B long-range anti-ship missiles
Displacement: 200 tons full load	
Dimensions: length 50.1 m (164 ft 4 in); beam 8.4 m (27 ft 7 in); draught 4.2 m (13 ft 9 in)	
Propulsion: three General Electric LM2500 gas turbines delivering 12080 kW (16,200 shp) to three waterjets	**Electronics:** one surface search radar, one navigation radar, one Type 2-31 fire-control radar, one ESM/ECM system, and decoy launchers
Performance: speed 44 kts	
Armament: one 76-mm (3-in)	**Complement:** 18 plus provision for three staff

'Dabur' class Coastal patrol craft (PC)

Thirty-four patrol craft of the **'Dabur' class** were built in the period 1973-77 for the Israeli navy. Twelve of these were constructed in the US by Sewart Seacraft, and the other 22 in Israel by the RAMTA division of Israel Aircraft Industries. The design is based on an aluminium alloy hull, and the craft are designed for overland transport between operational theatres. Thus the Israeli boats were based on both of Israel's coasts, namely the eastern end of the Mediterranean Sea and the northern end of the Gulf of Aqaba. Used to intercept Arab raiders, their armament has been supplemented by rocket launchers but their top speed is insufficient to deal with more modern speedboats. Eight were re-engined to achieve a speed of up to

30 kts, and many have been sold now in line with the commissioning of the 'Super Dvora'-class PCFs.

Israel's sales of 'Dabur'-class patrol boats began in 1978 with the delivery of four boats to the military junta in Argentina ('**Baradero' class**, deployed in support of UN Central American peacekeeping force in 1991-92) and four to the Nicaraguan dictator General Somoza (one lost to gunfire in 1985). Later sales were made to Sri Lanka (six, two lost to Tamil forces in 1995-96), Chile (10 **'Grumete Diaz' class**), Fiji (four **'Vai' class**) and Nicaragua (three more delivered in 1996). Five given by Israel to the Lebanese Christian militia in 1976 were taken back as Israel ended its occupation of southern Lebanon.

The 'Dabur'-class craft can be fitted with two 324-mm (12.75-in) tubes on the forecastle for Honeywell Mk 46 lightweight anti-submarine torpedoes. These carry a 44-kg (97-lb) warhead to a a range of 11 km (6.8 miles) at 40 kts.

The 'Dabur'-class coastal PCs (patrol craft) are useful assets for the limited coast defence role, but only when the opposition lacks high-speed craft. This the Israeli navy learned from experience, and as a result procured the larger and faster craft of the 'Super Dvora' class, allowing it to sell its surplus 'Daburs' to other navies. The 84-mm (3.3-in) Carl Gustav portable rocket launcher can be carried by the Israeli boats for anti-terrorist duties.

SPECIFICATION	
'Dabur' class	825 km (515 miles) at 13 kts
Displacement: 39 tons full load	**Armament:** two 324-mm (12.75-in)
Dimensions: length 19.8 m (64 ft 11 in); beam 5.5 m (18 ft); draught 1.8 m (6 ft)	tubes for Mk 46 anti-submarine torpedoes, two 20-mm cannon, two 0.5-in (12.7-mm) machine-guns, and
Propulsion: two General Motors 12V-71TA diesels delivering 625 kW (840 shp) to two shafts	two racks for depth charges **Electronics:** surface search radar, Elop optronic director, and sonar
Performance: speed 19 kts; range	**Complement:** 6 to 9

'Chon Buri' class FAC(G)

Ordered from the Italian CN Breda yard at Mestre, outside Venice, in 1979 (first pair) and 1981, the **'Chon Buri' class** are gun-armed MV400-type fast patrol vessels based on a steel hull with an alloy superstructure. The craft are the **Chon Buri**, **Songkhla** and **Phuket**, which were laid down in August, September and December 1981, launched in November and September 1982 and February 1983, and commissioned in February and July 1983 and January 1984 respectively.

Though completed to a

useful FAC(G) standard capable of 30 kts, the craft are large enough in terms of displacement, available deck area and electronic sophistication for comparatively easy adaptation to a FAC(M) standard should the situation in which Thailand finds itself ever demand a missile capability.

Corvette dimensions

In terms of their size and armament the craft are little short of small corvettes. The armament is based on two 76-mm (3-in) OTO-Melara Compact DP guns located

on the centreline fore and aft, and complemented for anti-aircraft and short-range anti-FAC capability by two 40-mm Bofors L/70 guns in a single Breda twin mounting above the after deckhouse. The OTO-Melara gun fires a 6-kg (13.2-lb) shell to 16 km (9.9 miles) at the rate of 85 rounds per minute. For self defence, the 'Chon Buri' craft carry four Hycor Mk 135 decoy launchers.

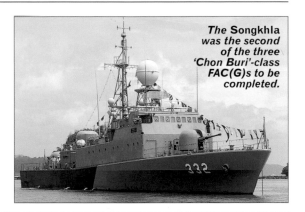

The Songkhla was the second of the three 'Chon Buri'-class FAC(G)s to be completed.

There is little remarkable about the 'Chon Buri'-class FAC(G)s of the Thai navy, which finds the vessels to be limited but nonetheless capable assets for the coastal defence role.

SPECIFICATION	
'Chon Buri' class	**Armament:** two 76-mm (3-in)
Displacement: 450 tons full load	OTO-Melara Compact guns, and one
Dimensions: length 60.4 m (198 ft); beam 8.8 m (29 ft); draught 1.95 m (6 ft)	twin 40-mm Breda AA gun **Electronics:** one ZW-06 surface search radar, one W-22/61 fire-
Propulsion: three MTU 20V 539 TB92 diesels delivering 9540 kW (12,795 shp) to three shafts	control radar, one Lirod 8 optronic director, one Newton ESM system, and four Hycor Mk 135 chaff
Performance: speed 30 kts; range 4600 km (2,860 miles) at 18 kts	launchers **Complement:** 41

'Azteca' class Large patrol craft (PC)

Mexico has long coasts on the Pacific Ocean and the Gulf of Mexico, each requiring a major patrol 'effort' in an attempt effort to check smuggling, especially of narcotics. Mexico contracted with a British company, TT Boat Designs of the Isle of Wight, for the design of the **'Azteca' class** of large patrol craft, and in March 1973 placed an order for the craft with Associated British Machine Tool Makers Ltd, which subcontracted the work for the first 20 craft to three British yards, namely Ailsa Shipbuilding, Scott & Sons and Lamont for 11, five and four units respectively.

Another 10 vessels were built in Mexico by Veracruz (seven) and Salina Cruz (three). The British-built craft were commissioned in the period between November 1974 and December 1976, while the Mexican-built craft were commissioned between June 1976 and June 1982.

The class was renamed and renumbered in 1991, and now comprises the **Andrés Quintana Roo, Matias de Cordova, Manuel Ramos Arizpe, Jose Maria Izazaga, Juan Bautista Morales, Ignacio López Rayón, Manuel Crescencio Rejon, Juan**

Antonio de la Fuente, Leon Guzman, Ignacio Ramirez, Ignacio Mariscal, Heriberto Jara Corona, Jose Maria Mata, Colima, Jose Joaquin Fernandez de Lizardi, Francisco J. Mugica, Pastor Rouaix, Jose Maria del Castillo Velasco, Luis Manuel Rojas, Jose Natividad Macias, Ignacio Zaragoza, Tamaulipas, Yucatan, Tabasco, Veracruz, Campeche, Puebla, Margarita Maza de Juarez, Leona Vicario and **Josefa Ortiz de Dominguez.**

The 'Azteca' class has not been notably successful in service as a result of main-

The pennant number identifies this 'Azteca'-class patrol craft as the Huichol, which in 2001 became the Heriberto Jara Corona (PC 212).

tenance problems. During 1987 the first 21 craft were modernised using parts and equipment supplied by the Marine Division of ABMTM,

which also supervised the programme. The effort included refurbishment of the engines and the addition of air conditioning.

There is nothing remarkable about the 'Azteca' class of large patrol craft, which are therefore basically akin to similar craft operated in many other parts of the world. This is the lead unit, Azteca, that in the 2001 wholesale revision of the Mexican navy's pennant numbering received the revised pennant number PC 201 and was also renamed as the Andrés Quintana Roo.

SPECIFICATION

'Azteca' class
Displacement: 148 tons full load
Dimensions: length 34.4 m (112 ft 9 in); beam 8.7 m (28 ft 4 in); draught 2.2 m (7 ft 3 in)
Propulsion: two Ruston Paxman Ventura 12YJCM diesels delivering 2240 kW (3,005 shp) to two shafts
Performance: speed 24 kts;

endurance 2850 km (1,770 miles) at 14 kts
Armament: one 40-mm Bofors DP gun and one Oerlikon 20-mm gun or 7.62-mm (0.3-in) machine-gun
Electronics: one Kelvin Hughes surface search and navigation radar
Complement: 24

'Tjeld' ('Nasty') class FAC(T/G)

In 1958 the Westermoens Baatbyggeri of Mandal in Norway completed the **Nasty** as the wooden-hulled prototype of a motor torpedo boat, a type later recategorised as a FAC(T). One year earlier the Norwegian navy had ordered from the same yard an initial series of 12 production-standard craft as the **'Tjeld' class**, whose units were commissioned in 1960-62 on the basis of a mahogany-built hull as the **Tjeld, Skarv, Teist, Jo, Lom, Stegg, Hauk, Falk, Ravn, Gribb, Geir** and **Erle.** In 1963-66 these first craft were complemented by another eight units, ordered in 1962 and placed in service as the **Skrei, Hai, Sel,**

Capable of a speed of 45 kts, the 'Tjeld' class of fast attack torpedo boats (pictured) was derived from the 'Nasty' class delivered to Greece, Turkey, West Germany and the US Navy.

Hval, Laks, Knurr, Delfin and **Lyr** to increase the 'Tjeld' class to a total of 20 craft. These were perfectly conventional units by the standard of their day, with provision for operation as a motor torpedo boat with a 40-mm Bofors gun on the forecastle, a 20-mm cannon above the stern and two 533-mm (21-in) torpedo tubes on each beam, or as a motor gun boat with two 40-mm guns and two

533-mm torpedo tubes.

Too small for ready upgrade to FAC(M) standard as anti-ship missiles became standard weapons for FACs, the craft did not enjoy a long operational career. The *Skarv* was stricken in 1978, to be followed by the *Teist, Lom, Jo, Hauk, Falk* and *Sel* in 1979, when the other 13 units of the class were placed in reserve for limited use in the training role. By 1982 only eight of the class were still in existence, and

the last of these had disappeared by 1995.

Another 22 basically similar **'Nasty'** craft were built by Westermoens as six for Greece, 14 for the US (where another six were produced) and two for West Germany. Delivered in 1967 the Greek units were the **Andromeda, Iniohos, Kastor, Kyknos, Pigasos** and **Toxotis** with two 40-mm guns and four tubes. The *Iniohos* was deleted in 1972 and the other five

placed in reserve in 1983. All but the *Kastor* were then re-engined with MTU diesels in 1988 and re-entered service. Delivered in 1962-68, the unnamed US Navy craft were used for 'unconventional operations', and saw much service in the Vietnam War. The West German **Type 152** craft, delivered in the early 1960s, were the **Hugin** and **Munin**, which were transferred to Turkey in 1964 as the **Dogan** and **Marti**, discarded in 1973.

SPECIFICATION

'Tjeld' class
Displacement: 70 tons standard; 76 tons full load
Dimensions: length 24.5 m (80 ft 4 in); beam 7.5 m (24 ft 6 in); draught 2.1 m (6 ft 9 in)
Propulsion: two Napier Deltic 18-cylinder turbocharged diesels delivering 4620 kW (6,200 shp) to two shafts

Performance: speed 45 kts; endurance 3000 km (1,865 miles) at 25 kts declining to 825 km (515 miles) at 40 kts
Armament: one 40-mm Bofors DP gun, one 20-mm gun and four 533-mm (21-in) tubes for four torpedoes
Electronics: one surface search and navigation radar
Complement: 22

'P4', 'P6', 'Shershen', 'Mol' and 'Turya' classes FAC/H(T)

By comparison with the 'P6'-class MTB with a wooden semi-planing hull, the 'Shershen' class had a metal hull of the round-bilge type, and paved the way for torpedo-armed subvariants such as the 'Mol' class FAC(T) and 'Turya'-class FAH(T).

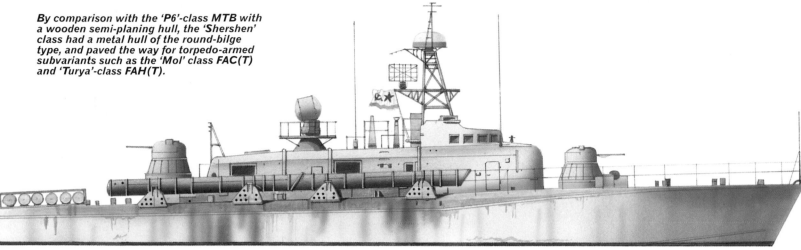

The **'P4' class** was the second Soviet torpedo boat series of the period after World War II. Built with aluminum hulls to the extent of some 350 craft between 1946 and the mid-1950s, the small size of this **Project 123 Komsomolets** type restricted its employment to inshore waters. The 'P4'-class units have long been absent from Soviet (now Russian) service, although the class survived among some 16 export recipients for a longer time, and is indeed still in North Korean service in 2003.

The successor to the 'P4' was the wooden-hulled **'P6' class**, of which some 622 **Project 183** units were built in 1953-60. This was the standard Soviet torpedo attack craft until the mid-1970s. The basic hulls were also converted to other types, such as the **'Komar'-**

class craft fitted with anti-ship missiles (about 100), the **'MO-VI' class** of patrol craft (50), the **'P8'** and **'P10'-class** experimental torpedo attack craft (20), and as target and KGB border surveillance patrol craft. Large numbers were also exported, some remaining in service in Cuba, Egypt and North Korea.

The largest conventional torpedo attack craft built was the **'Shershen' class**, of which 123 were built in 1962-74 to the **Project 206** design based on a scaled-down 'Osa I'-class hull with the same powerplant but equipped with four 533-mm (21-in) tubes for long-range anti-ship torpedoes instead of missiles. Fitted with an NBC citadel, the craft was intended to work with the 'Osa' FAC(M)s in mixed brigades of coastal craft. The **'Mol' class** (Project 206E) is

a modified version for export. Based on the standard 'Osa I' hull, this carries torpedoes of shorter range than those embarked on Soviet craft. The Soviets built some 85 'Shershen' and seven 'Mol' craft, but the only surviving examples of the 'Shershen' class are later transfers to Croatia, Egypt and Vietnam.

In 1971 the 'Shershen' class was joined in production by the **'Turya' class** (**Project 206M Shtorm**) of

torpedo-armed fast attack hydrofoil. This has the hull and machinery of the 'Osa II' class with a single foil system forward. The role was usually stated to be anti-ship attack, but the four 533-mm tubes could also carry anti-submarine torpedoes allowing the use of the craft as fast-reaction ASW units for coast defence in conjunction with shore-based ASW aircraft (fixed- and rotary-wing) and other small ASW surface units. For

these operations they also carry dipping sonar, which is particularly useful in the Baltic and Pacific areas for searching below thermal layers. Production for the Soviet navy stopped in 1979 after the delivery of some 30 units, but a further 19 **Project 206ME** craft were later built without the sonar but with provision only for anti-ship torpedoes. These were delivered to Cuba, Ethiopia, Kampuchea, the Seychelles and Vietnam.

Right: The 'Shershen' class FAC(T), which is still in limited service, carries four 533-mm (21-in) torpedoes and two remotely-controlled twin 30-mm cannon.

Below: The 'P4' class MTB reflected the USSR's experience of coastal operations in World War II, and although fast was notably small and compact.

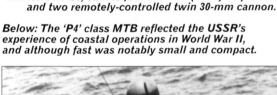

SPECIFICATION	
'P4' class	13 kts
Displacement: 22 tons standard; 25 tons full load	**Armament:** two 457-mm (18-in) tubes for two anti-ship torpedoes,
Dimensions: length 22 m (72 ft 2 in); beam 4.7 m (15 ft 5 in); draught 1.5 m (4 ft 11 in)	one twin 12.7-mm or 14.5-mm (0.5-in or 0.57-in) heavy machine-gun, and between four and eight
Propulsion: two M-503 diesels delivering 1790 kW (2,400 shp) to two shafts	depth charges
Performance: speed 42 kts; endurance 740 km (460 miles) at	**Electronics:** one 'Skin Head' surface search radar, one 'High Pole-A' IFF and one 'Dead Duck' IFF
	Complement: 12

SPECIFICATION	
'Turya' class	14 kts
Displacement: 250 tons full load	**Armament:** two 533-mm (21-in) tubes for two torpedoes, one twin
Dimensions: length 39.6 m (129 ft 9 in); beam 7.6 m (24 ft 9 in); draught 1.8 m (6 ft 7 in)	57-mm (2.24-in) DP gun, one twin 25-mm AA gun and depth charges
Propulsion: three M-503, M-503A or M-504 diesels delivering 11175 kW (14,990 shp) to three shafts	**Electronics:** one 'Pot Drum' surface search radar, one 'Muff Cob' fire-control radar, two IFF, and one 'Foal Tail' variable-depth sonar
Performance: speed 40+ kts; endurance 2700 km (1,680 miles) at	**Complement:** 30

'Flyvefisken' class Large patrol/attack and mine warfare craft

The **'Flyvefisken' class** are true multi-role warships able to operate as large patrol/attack craft or mine-hunters/minelayers. With GRP sandwich hulls and CODAG propulsion, they can be modified for their different missions within 48 hours.

The name-ship was commissioned in December 1989 as part of a seven-boat batch contracted in July 1985. A second batch of six vessels was ordered from Danyard in June 1990 and the last of the class was authorised in 1993. Two more planned vessels were later cancelled. In Danish service, the 'Flyvefiskens' replaced the 'Daphne' class of seaward defence vessels, the 'Søløven' class of fast attack torpedo craft and the 'Sund' mine countermeasures (MCM) class.

In the attack role, the primary weapon of the

*The **Skaden** of the 'Flyvefisken' class alongside the German navy's **'Gepard'**-class fast attack missile craft **Dachs**. Note the Skaden's Harpoon tubes.*

'Flyvefiskens' is the Harpoon anti-ship missile. Since 2001, the addition of the Harpoon Block II with GPS has added a land-attack capability to the vessels. The 76-mm (3-in) Super Rapid gun is dual purpose, able to elevate to 85° to engage aerial targets. However, the boats' anti-aircraft defences have now been enhanced by the addition of Sea Sparrow radar-homing missiles: these are carried for the attack, MCM and minelaying roles. The six SAMs were initially launched from three Mk 48 Mod 3 twin launchers, but a dual pack with 12 weapons was fitted in their place from 2002. To attack surface targets, the class can also carry FFV Type 613 wire-guided passive-homing torpedoes, or (since 2001) Eurotorp Mu 90 Impact torpedoes, from two 533-mm (21-in) tubes.

'Flyvefisken' roles

The torpedo tubes and mine rails are detachable. The boats have four positions into which different weapons can be fitted: all can be outfitted for the patrol role if required. The number of outfits for the various different

duties comprises 10 for the attack role, five for the MCM role, 14 for the minelaying role and four for the ASW role. However, the 'Flyvefiskens' can also be equipped for some non-military tasks, for instance pollution control and hydrographic survey.

'Robot' vessel

In the MCM role, the 'Flyvefiskens' operate a tethered underwater vehicle for classification, and control a surface 'robot' vessel that is equipped with a Reson Seabat 6012 sonar, TV camera and a mine disposal charge. These Double Eagle remote operated vehicles (ROVs) are based on the 'Hugin' class of torpedo recovery vessel (TRV) with a 30-ton displacement and the hull length extended to 17.7 m (58 ft).

In 2001, a prototype vessel underwent a major C³I upgrade, known as C-Flex, which is planned to be added to a further five vessels following weapons integration in 2003. The remaining eight vessels may be similarly upgraded at a later date.

In addition to their basic armament, the 'Flyvefiskens' can carry four depth charges or up to 60 mines when fitted for the minelaying role.

Above: For self defence, the vessels of the 'Flyvefisken' class are equipped with a pair of 130-mm (5.1-in) Sea Gnat DL-6T six-barrel chaff and infra-red flare launchers and a Racal Sygnus jammer.

Below: The design of 'Flyvefiskens' allows various roles to be undertaken using the same hull. Four positions can accept 'plug in' armament and equipment modules in various combinations.

SPECIFICATION

'Flyvefisken' class
Names: *Flyvefisken* (P550), *Hajen* (P551), *Havkatten* (P552), *Laxen* (P553), *Makrelen* (P554), *Støren* (P555), *Svaerdfisken* (P556), *Glenten* (P557), *Gribben* (P558), *Lommen* (P559), *Ravnen* (P560), *Skaden* (P561), *Viben* (P562), *Søløven* (P563)
Displacement: 480 tons full load
Dimensions: length 54 m (177 ft 2 in); beam 9 m (29 ft 6 in); draught 2.5 m (8 ft 2 in)
Propulsion: CODAG; one GE LM 500 gas turbine delivering 4064 kW (5,450 shp) to central shaft and two MTU 16V 396 TB94 diesels delivering 4325 kW (5,800 shp) to two outer shafts
Performance: maximum speed 30 kts or 20 kts on diesels alone; range 3862 km (2,400 miles) at

18 kts
Armament: eight Harpoon SSMs, three Mk 48 Mod 3 twin Sea Sparrow SAM launchers (but see text), one OTO-Melara 76-mm (3-in) Super Rapid gun, two 12.7-mm (0.5-in) machine guns, two 533-mm (21-in) torpedo tubes (for torpedo types see text), up to 60 mines (minelaying role only)
Electronics: AWS 6 (P550-556) or TRS-3D (P557-563) air/surface search radar, Scanter surface search radar, Furuno navigation radar, 9LV 200 fire-control radar, TSM 2640 Salmon variable-depth sonar, CTS-36/39 hull-mounted sonar, Terma/Celsius Tech and Link 11 tactical data systems, 9LV Mk 3 weapons control system
Complement: 19-29

'Cyclone class' Patrol Coastal Ship (PCF)

The United States Navy operates only a small fleet of coastal patrol craft, the majority of which is made up of small security and assault craft and rigid inflatable boats (RIBs): the 'stealthy' Norwegian patrol craft *Skjold* was loaned for a period of evaluation in 2002.

Based on the British Vosper Thorneycroft patrol boats of the 'Ramadan' class, the 13-strong **'Cyclone' class** are designed for coastal patrol work, and form the most capable element of the US Navy's patrol forces. A contract for eight such craft was awarded in August 1990, followed by a further five in July 1991. Commissioned between 1993 and 1996, the 'Cyclones' have been deployed as far as the Mediterranean but they have been frequently used to

Employed principally for homeland security operations, the 'Cyclones' come under the tactical command of the USCG, but remain under the control of the US Navy. USS Chinook is seen conducting a patrol off the US coast during Operation Enduring Freedom.

patrol Caribbean waters as part of the multi-billion dollar campaign to reduce the flow of narcotics from Latin America to the US. The **USS Cyclone** was decommissioned in 2000 and handed over to the US Coast Guard.

Unlike the 'Ramadans', the 'Cyclone' class carry 25 mm (1 in) of armour plate on parts of the superstructure in expectation that they will come under small arms fire. Able to operate in up to Sea State 5, they are also designed to loiter at low speed. Both characteristics can be equally useful for landing special forces teams and they are designed to accommodate an additional eight personnel, comprising Marines, Navy SEALs or other specialists. A swimmer launch platform is fitted at the stern.

All the vessels are currently assigned to NSW (Naval Special Warfare) with nine operating from Little

Left: A crewmember aboard USS Chinook scans the horizon for hostile shipping. The vessel was deployed to the Arabian Gulf in March 2003.

Creek and four from the Naval Amphibious Base at Coronado.

The 'Cyclone' class has an anti-aircraft capability in the form of a stabilised sextuple mounting for FIM-92 Stinger SAMs. Further shoulder-launched Stingers can also be launched from onboard. Gun armament includes a single 25-mm Bushmaster cannon fitted fore and aft and eight machine-guns. The latter can be exchanged for 40-mm (1.57-in) grenade launchers.

Improved equipment

The final vessel in the class, **USS Tornado**, differs in that it has been fitted with advanced ESM, a rocket launcher, improved communications equipment and a Mk 96 stabilised weapon platform. *Tornado*, plus a further four 'Cyclone' craft, are modified to incorporate a semi-dry well, a boat ramp and a stern gate to allow the launch and recovery of a fully loaded RIB whilst underway. These changes replace the crane and ship's boat originally fitted on the aft deck.

The 'Cyclones' normally carry two SEAL raiding craft for special operations infiltration or narcotics interdiction and a single RIB. USS Firebolt (PC-10) displays the splinter camouflage paint scheme common to this class of PCF.

USS Chinook in the Arabian Gulf during Operation Iraqi Freedom in 2003. When deployed overseas, the 'Cyclones' can be operated in pairs with a 12-man maintenance team located in two small trucks ashore.

SPECIFICATION
'Cyclone' class

Names: *Cyclone* (PC-1), *Tempest* (PC-2), *Hurricane* (PC-3), *Monsoon* (PC-4), *Typhoon* (PC-5), *Sirocco* (PC-6), *Squall* (PC-7), *Zephyr* (PC-8), *Chinook* (PC-9), *Firebolt* (PC-10), *Whirlwind* (PC-11), *Thunderbolt* (PC-12), *Shamal* (PC-13), *Tornado* (PC-14)
Displacement: 334 tons or (PC-2, -8, -13 and -14) 360 tons full load
Dimensions: length 51.9 m (170 ft 4 in) or (PC-2, -8, -13 and -14) 54.6 m (179 ft 1 in); beam 7.9 m (25.9 ft); draught 2.4 m (7 ft 11 in)
Propulsion: four Paxman Valenta 16RP200CM diesels delivering 9992 kW (13,400 shp) to four shafts
Performance: maximum speed 35 kts; range 4023 km (2,500 miles) at 12 kts
Armament: one 25-mm Mk 38 and one Mk 96 Bushmaster cannon, four 0.5-in (12.7-mm) and four 0.3-in (7.62-mm) machine-guns, two Mk 19 40-mm (1.57-in) grenade launchers
Electronics: two RASCAR surface search radars, SPS-64 navigation radar, Wesmar hull-mounted sonar, VISTAR IM 405 weapons control system, APR-39 ESM system
Complement: 28 plus 8 (see text)

'Nyayo' class Kenyan fast attack craft (missile)

The Kenyan navy ordered two missile-armed fast attack craft from Vosper Thornycroft in September 1984. Launched in 1986 and 1987 respectively for commissioning July and September of the latter year, the **Nyayo** and **Umoja** sailed together from the UK to Mombasa in August 1988. These **Vosper Thornycroft 56.7-m craft** are essentially similar to the four 'Dhofar'-class craft operated by Oman.

Today the **'Nyayo' class** form Squadron 86 of the Kenyan navy. The primary armament of these FAC(M)s is the OTO Melara/Matra Otomat Mk 2 surface-to-surface missile, which is an active radar-homing weapon used in the anti-ship role with a 210-kg (463-lb) HE warhead. Travelling at Mach 0.9, the Otomat Mk 2 has a maximum range of 160 km (99 miles) and for the last 4000 m (4,375 yards) of its flight skims the surface of the sea to present the most difficult target possible to the intended target's anti-missile systems. A first live firing from a 'Nyayo'-class vessel was undertaken in February 1989.

The gun armament comprises a single OTO Melara 76-mm (3-in) DP weapon, which is capable of engaging surface targets out to a range of 16 km (10 miles), or airborne targets out to 12 km (7.4 miles). This main element of the gun armament is complemented by a secondary element based on two Oerlikon 30-mm DP cannon in a GCM-AO2 power-operated twin mounting carried aft, and two 20-mm Oerlikon AA cannon on single A41A mountings.

Electronic defence is provided by a Racal Cutlass ESM system integrated with a Racal Cygnus jammer and two Wallop Barricade 18-barrel launchers for Stockade and Palisade rockets. The fire-control system is based on the CAAIS action data automation system based on a Ferranti computer.

Both craft are now awaiting a proposed refit.

Above: The 'Nyayo'-class FAC(M)s are the Kenyan navy's primary means of protecting the country's coastline, and are well-balanced craft in terms of their missile and gun armaments.

The two FAC(M)s of the Kenyan 'Nyayo' class are little different from their half-sisters of the Omani 'Dhofar' class in terms of their hulls and propulsion arrangements, but carry different armament and electronic fits.

SPECIFICATION

'Nyayo' class
Craft in class: Nyayo and Umoja
Displacement: 310 tons standard; 400 tons full load
Dimensions: length 56.7 m (186 ft); beam 8.2 m (26 ft 11 in); draught 2.4 m (7 ft 11 in)
Machinery: four Paxman Valenta 18 RP 200 CM diesels delivering 13570 kW (18,200 shp) to four shafts
Performance: speed 40 kts; range 3700 km (2,300 miles) at 18 kts

Armament: two twin launchers for Otomat Mk 2 SSMs, one 76-mm (3-in) OTO Melara Compact gun, two Oerlikon 30-mm guns, and two Oerlikon 20-mm guns
Electronics: one AWS-4 surface search radar, one AC 1226 navigation radar, one ST802 fire-control RWR, one Cutlass RWR, one Cygnus ECM, and two Barricade decoy launchers
Complement: 40

'Dhofar' class Omani fast attack craft (missile)

The Omani navy ordered one **Vosper Thornycroft 56.7-m** fast attack craft during 1980, another order in January 1981 added a further two craft, and a final order in January 1986 completed the navy's requirement with a fourth unit. The craft are very similar to those of the Kenyan navy's 'Nyayo' class, but are armed with the French Aérospatiale MM.40 Exocet sea-skimming anti-ship missile, of Falklands War fame in its air-launched version, rather than the Franco-Italian Otomat system of the Kenyan craft. Eight of the missiles are carried in three of the boats, the exception being the first-of-class **Dhofar**, which carries only six missiles and has a modified electronics fit.

The Omani vessels also have a somewhat different electronic fit based on the AWS-6 air and surface search radar and 9LV 307 fire-control system in all except the Dhofar, which has the AWS-4 and Sea Archer equipments. All of the craft have basically the same navigation radar, and also the same countermeasures suite with the Racal Cutlass radar warning receiver, Scorpion radar jammer and Wallop Barricade triple launchers for flare and chaff rockets.

The craft were all built by Vosper Thornycroft in the UK, and the initial vessel was the Dhofar launched in October 1981 for commissioning in August 1982. The second and third craft were commissioned in December 1983 and January 1984, while the last unit was launched in March 1988 and was commissioned in March 1989. The four craft constitute a substantial proportion of the Omani navy, which also operates two corvettes armed with Exocet missiles and three French-built patrol craft armed with anti-submarine torpedoes, all ordered after the 'Dhofar' class.

SPECIFICATION

'Dhofar' class
Craft in class: Dhofar, Al Sharqiyah, Al Bat'nah and Mussandam
Displacement: 311 tons standard; 394 tons full load
Dimensions: length 56.7 m (186 ft); beam 8.2 m (26 ft 11 in); draught 2.4 m (7 ft 11 in)
Machinery: four Paxman Valenta 18 RP 200 CM diesels delivering 13570 kW (18,200 shp) to four shafts
Performance: speed 38 kts; range

2700 km (2,300 miles) at 18 kts
Armament: six (Dhofar) or eight MM.40 Exocet SSMs, one 76-mm (3-in) OTO Melara Compact gun, two 40-mm Bofors guns in a Breda Compact twin mounting, and two 0.5-in (12.7-mm) machine-guns
Electronics: one AWS-4 or AWS-6 air/surface search radar, one AC 1226 navigation radar, 9LV 307 fire-control radar, Cutlass RWR, Scorpion jammer and two Barricade decoy launchers
Complement: 45

The Dhofar differs from the three later craft in having six rather than eight Exocet anti-ship missiles, and a slightly different radar and fire-control system. Note the medium and light guns.

'Velarde' class Peruvian fast attack craft (missile)

In 1976 Peru ordered six fast attack craft (missile) of the **PR 72P type** from SFCN of France, which delivered two (*Okba* and *Triki*) and one (*Njambur*) related craft of the PR 72M and PR 72S types to France and Senegal respectively: these are smaller than the Peruvian craft and lack missile armament. SFCN subcontracted the construction of the hulls for three of the Peruvian craft to Lorient Naval Yard, and built the other three at its own Villeneuve-la-Garonne facility, where fitting out was undertaken.

The first two craft were commissioned in July 1980, and the other four followed in November of the same year, and then February, June and September of the following year. Possessing a full-load displacement of more than 500 tons, the craft of the **'Velarde' class** are classified by the Peruvian navy as corvettes. Their primary weapon system is the Aérospatiale MM.40 Exocet anti-ship missile, which has a maximum range of 28.5 miles (46 km), delivering its 165-kg (364-lb) HE warhead in a sea-skim-

ming attack profile using active radar homing in the final stage of the attack: these missiles are carried in pairs of container-launchers abaft the superstructure to fire obliquely ahead to port and starboard.

The gun armament is based on one 76-mm (3-in) OTO Melara Compact weapon on the forecastle and two 40-mm Bofors guns in a Breda twin mounting at the stern, and these weapons provide a very use-

*The **Herrera** was completed as the fourth unit of the 'Velarde' class of missile-armed FACs that provide Peru with a potent coastal anti-ship capability.*

ful anti-aircraft and anti-ship capability. This is complemented by a MPG-86 launcher for the Russian-supplied 9M39 Igla (SA-N-10 'Gimlet') SAM which can be mounted on the stern of some of the 'Velarde' class.

SPECIFICATION	
'Velarde' class	**Performance:** speed 37 kts; range
Craft in class: *Velarde, Santillana,*	4625 km (2,875 miles) at 16 kts
De Los Heros, Herrera, Larrea and	**Armament:** four MM.40 Exocet
Sanchez Carrillon	SSMs, one 76-mm (3-in) OTO
Displacement: 470 tons standard;	Melara Compact gun, two 40-mm
560 tons full load	Breda Compact guns, and two
Dimensions: length 64 m (210 ft);	0.5-in (12.7-mm) machine-guns
beam 8.35 m (27 ft 5 in); draught	**Electronics:** one Triton surface
2.6 m (8 ft 6 in)	search radar, one Decca AC 1226
Propulsion: four SACM/AGO 240	navigation radar, and one Castor II
V16 M7 diesel engines delivering	radar and Panda optical director in
16400 kW (21,995 shp) to four	the Vega fire-control system
shafts	**Complement:** 36 with 46 possible

'Fearless' class Singapore fast attack craft (missile)

In 1995 STEC Marine (Singapore Technologies Marine Ltd.) laid down the first of 12 fast attack craft that have now replaced the six British-designed 'Type A' and 'Type B' FAC(G)s and the six German-designed FPB-45 FAC(M)s operated by the island republic's navy in the patrol role since the early 1970s.

Resulting from a 1993 plan to revitalise the navy with more modern and capable vessels, the original concept was to have the first six of the 12 craft fitted for the anti-submarine warfare role with an armament centred on Whitehead light-weight anti-submarine

homing torpedoes and equipped with sonar, and the second group of six equipped for the surface warfare role with the Israel Aircraft Industries Gabriel Mk 2 anti-ship missile with a 100-kg (220-lb) HE warhead and a range between 6 and 36 km (3.7 and 22.4 miles). The ASW craft are fitted with waterjet propulsion in addition to their diesels.

All of the boats also possess gun armament in the form of a 76-mm (3-in) gun on the forecastle, and for short-range air defence there is a Simbad twin launcher for Mistral SAMs on all except the **Brave**, which is equipped with a towed-array sonar. The **Sovereignty** has a deck crane and is intended to support special forces. The 12 craft were commissioned in the period between the first quarter of 1996 and May 1999.

The 'Fearless' class FAC is based on a round-bilge hull of steel construction with a super-structure of marine-grade aluminium alloy.

SPECIFICATION	
'Fearless' class	**Armament:** one Simbad twin
Craft in class: *Fearless, Brave,*	launcher for Mistral SAMs and six
Courageous, Gallant, Daring,	Whitehead 324-mm (12.75-in) tubes
Dauntless, Resilience, Unity,	for A244 active/passive homing
Sovereignty, Justice, Freedom and	torpedoes (first six vessels), one
Independence	76-mm (3-in) OTO Melara Super
Displacement: 500 tons full load	Rapid gun, and four 12.7-mm
Dimensions: length 55 m (180 ft	(0.5-in) machine-guns
5 in); beam 8.6 m (28 ft 2½ in);	**Electronics:** one EL/M 2228(X)
draught 2.7 m (8 ft 11 in)	surface search and fire-control
Propulsion: two MTU 12V 595	radar, one Kelvin Hughes 1007
TE90 diesel engines delivering	navigation radar, one TSM 2362
6480 kW (8,690 shp) to two	Gudgeon active hull sonar, and two
waterjets	Shield III sextuple chaff launchers
Performance: speed 20 kts	**Complement:** 32

Left: Mounted on the forecastle is a 76-mm (3-in) OTO Melara Super Rapid gun mounting able to fire a 6-kg (13.2-lb) shell to a maximum range of 16000 m (17,500 yards) at the rate of 120 rounds per minute. There are also four 12.7-mm (0.5-in) machine-guns.

'Combattante I' class FAC(G/M)

Otherwise known by the local designation **'Um Almaradim' class**, the **'Combattante I' class** of gun-armed fast attack/patrol craft are the newest vessels in the Kuwaiti navy as the service rebuilds itself after its temporary destruction in the first Gulf War that followed the Iraqi invasion and occupation of Kuwait in 1990.

Ordered from the CMN yard in the northern French port city of Cherbourg in March 1995, the eight craft are named **Um Almaradim, Ouha, Failaka, Masdan, Al-Ahmadi, Alfahaheel, Al-Yarmouk** and **Garoh**, which are names of earlier Kuwaiti patrol craft. The vessels were launched between February 1997 and June 1999, and were commissioned between July 1998 and June 2000. The training of the vessels' crews, of which 10 are planned for the eight units, was undertaken in France, and the first four vessels reached Kuwait in August 1999, with the second four

following in mid-2000. Pending the ordering and completion of a class of offshore patrol vessels, for which there is a requirement to a size about twice the size of the 'Combattante I'-class craft and with an armament of anti-ship missiles, these are arguably the most effective but not quite the largest vessels in the Kuwaiti navy.

There is little remarkable about the design, which is typical of vessels of this type for service in the confined waters of the Persian Gulf, but the design is nonetheless notable for the size and height of the mast carrying the antennae for the primary electronic equipment.

Simple armament

The basic armament comprises one Otobreda 40-mm gun in a single mounting forward, one GIAT M621 20-mm cannon and two 0.5-in (12.7-mm) machine-guns. The 40-mm gun is an L/70 DP weapon firing a 0.96-kg (2.12-lb) shell to a range of

Its eight 'Combattante I'-class patrol vessels offer the navy of Kuwait an ideal means of patrolling the nation's waters, but the craft have only limited offensive power.

12500 m (13,670 yards) at the rate of 120 rounds per minute. The last two units were each completed with two twin launchers for Sea Skua short-range anti-ship missiles, and this capability is being retrofitted to the first six craft. There is provision in the design for a sextuple launcher for Mistral short-range SAMs, and for Dagaie decoy launchers.

SPECIFICATION	
'Combattante I' class	Sea Skua anti-ship missiles, one
Displacement: 245 tons full load	40-mm DP gun, and one 20-mm gun
Dimensions: length 42 m (137 ft 9 in); beam 8.2 m (26 ft 11 in); draught 1.9 m (6 ft 3 in)	**Electronics:** one MRR 3D air/surface search radar, one Seaspray Mk 3 fire-control radar,
Propulsion: two MTU 16V 538 TB93 diesels delivering 3000 kW (4,025 hp) to two waterjets	one 20V90 navigation radar, one Najir Mk 2 optronic director, one TAVITAC NT combat data system,
Performance: speed 30 kts	and one DR 3000 S1 ESM system
Armament: two twin launchers for	**Complement:** 29

'Combattante II' & 'Combattante III' classes FAC(M)

The **'Combattante II' class** is based on a Lürssen design and, together with its larger **'Combattante III' class** version, has proved very popular. The hull and superstructure are of steel and light alloy respectively, and the versatility in the design allows the operator country to choose its own electronics and weapon fits, although French electronics and weapons were generally proposed by the builder and have been well favoured. The standard gun is the 76-mm (3-in) OTO-Melara (now Otobreda) Compact DP weapon. At present the following countries ordered 'Combattante II'-class units: Greece (four **'Anninos' class** delivered in 1971-72 with

MM.38 Exocets), Iran (12 **'Kaman' class** delivered in 1977-81 with Harpoon SSMs), Libya (10 delivered in 1982-83 with Otomat SSMs, of which one was sunk and another two are inactive) and Malaysia (four **'Perdana' class** delivered in 1972-73 with MM.38s). The Iranian craft saw extensive service in the Iran/Iraq war of the 1980s, at least two having been lost to AM.39 air-launched Exocets from Aerospatialé Super Frelon helicopters flown by the Iraqi air force.

Both the 'Combattante II'- and the larger steel-hulled 'Combattante III'-class vessels have good habitability, the latter type having been designed for longer

endurance and to act as command ships for smaller craft. The 'Combattante III' has been adopted by Greece (four **'Laskos' class** delivered in 1977-81 with MM.38s plus six locally built with cheaper machinery, electronics and missile fit of Penguin Mk 2 anti-ship missiles), Nigeria (three **'Combattante IIIB' or 'Siri' class** delivered in 1981 with MM.38s), Qatar (three **'Combattante IIIM' or 'Damsah' class** delivered in 1982-83 with MM.40s) and Tunisia (three 'Combattante IIIM' or **'La Galité' class** delivered in 1985 with MM.40s).

Typical class characteristics are given in the accompanying specifica-

tions, and the builder for both versions was CMN of Cherbourg in northern France. The Greek 'Combattante III'-class units of the first type differ from the rest in having two rearward firing 533-mm (21-in)

torpedo tubes for German SST4 wire-guided anti-ship torpedoes with active/passive acoustic homing, a warhead of 260-kg (573-lb) weight and maximum range of about 20000 m (21,870 yards).

SPECIFICATION	
'Combattante II' or 'Kaman' class	15 kts
Displacement: 249 tons standard; 275 tons full load	**Armament:** one or two twin launchers for C-802 anti-ship missiles or four launchers for Harpoon anti-ship missiles, one
Dimensions: length 47 m (154 ft 2 in); beam 7.1 m (23 ft 4 in); draught 1.9 m (6 ft 3 in)	76-mm (3-in) DP gun and one 40-mm AA gun
Propulsion: four MTU 16V 538 TB91 diesels delivering 9160 kW (12,285 hp) to four shafts	**Electronics:** one WM-28 surface search/fire-control radar, one Decca 1226 navigation radar, and one
Performance: speed 36 kts; endurance 3700 km (2,300 miles) at	Dalia/Aligator ESM/ECM system **Complement:** 31

The Gorz was the first of Iran's 'Kaman'-class FACs to carry the Harpoon anti-ship missile (four missiles in two twin launchers, as depicted here), but now carries Standard SM-1 missiles from deleted 'Sumner'-class destroyers.

SPECIFICATION

'Combattante III' or 'Laskos' class
Displacement: 359 tons standard; 425 tons full load
Dimensions: length 56.15 m (184 ft 3 in); beam 8 m (26 ft 3 in); draught 2.1 m (6 ft 11 in)
Propulsion: (Type 1) four MTU 20V 538 TB92 diesels delivering 12720 kW (17,060 hp) or (Type 2) four MTU 20V 538 TB91 diesels delivering 11460 kW (15,370 hp), in each case to four shafts
Performance: speed (Type 1) 36.5 kts and (Type 2) 32.5 kts; endurance 5000 km (3,105 miles) at 15 kts
Armament: (Type 1) four launchers for MM.38 Exocet anti-ship

missiles, two 76-mm (3-in) OTO-Melara DP guns, two twin 30-mm AA guns, and two 533-mm (21-in) torpedo tubes, and (Type 2) six launchers for Penguin Mk 2 anti-ship missiles, two 76-mm (3-in) DP guns, and two twin 30-mm AA guns
Electronics: one Triton surface search radar, one Decca 1226C navigation radar, one Castor II and one Pollux fire-control radars, one Vega I or II (Type 1) or PFCS-2 (Type 2) weapon-control system, two Panda optical directors, one DR 2000S ESM system and Wegmann chaff launchers
Complement: 42

Above: The first 'Combattante III' Type 2 FAC for the Greek navy was the Simeoforos Kavaloudis, built in Greece with a lower-powered propulsion arrangement than the Type 1 units and equipped with Penguin missiles.

Below: The Greek navy's 'Combattante III' Type 1 FAC has two 76-mm (3-in) guns and MM.38 Exocet anti-ship missiles.

'Tiger' class (Type 148) FAC(M)

The **'Tiger' class** or **Type 148** FAC(M) is a development of the 'Combattante II'-class vessel (itself derived from a German design by Lürssen) built largely in France by Chantiers Mécaniques de Normandie (CMN) of Cherbourg, although some six of the steel hulls were subcontracted to Lürssen even though the hulls were then towed to France for fitting out.

The order for the 20 craft was placed in December 1970 following a Franco-German agreement of October of the same year, the German navy's requirement being for a class of later and more modern units, fitted with heavier guns and

anti-ship missiles, to replace the 'Jaguar' class or Type 140 craft armed with light guns and four 533-mm (21-in) torpedo tubes.

The craft were launched between 1972 and 1975, and entered service with the names **S 41** to **S 60**, but in 1981 were renamed as the **Tiger**, **Iltis**, **Luchs**, **Marder**, **Leopard**, **Fuchs**, **Jaguar**, **Löwe**, **Wolf**, **Panther**, **Haher**, **Storch**, **Pelikan**, **Elster**, **Alk**, **Dommel**, **Weihe**, **Pinguin**, **Reiher** and **Kranich**. This perpetuated

the names of the retired 'Jaguar'-class craft, of which most had been transferred to Greece and Turkey.

During a mid-life update, the craft were revised with more modern radar (Triton search and Castor fire-control systems) and also received a Racal ESM system, and in this form constituted the German navy's 5th Squadron based on the tender *Main*, located at Olpenitz. The service began to dispose of the craft in the early 1990s, and by

2002 had reduced its strength to just three units, which are scheduled for retirement by mid-2004. There was still a measure of useful life in the vessels, and most of the class have been transferred to Greece or sold to Chile.

Greece has six of the craft as its **'Votsis' class**. Transferred in pairs in 1993, 1995 and 2000, the craft are the **Ypoploiarchos Votsis**, **Antiploiarchos Pezopoulos**, **Plotarchis Vlahavas**, **Plotarchis Maridakis**,

Ypoploiarchos Tournas and **Plotarchis Sapikos**. The craft were updated with new electronic warfare systems after their transfer, and the last two units had Harpoon rather than Exocet anti-ship missiles.

Chile has four of the class in service as its **'Riquelme' class**, which have the names **Riquelme**, **Orella**, **Serrano** and **Uribe**. The first two units were delivered to Chile by ship in 1997, and another four followed in 1998, all of them being damaged in a storm during the passage, two of them being repaired and the other two retained for cannibalisation. The EW systems and missiles were removed before the same, Chile then acquiring its own Exocet missiles but no EW system. In 2000 the craft, which operate in the Beagle Channel, were fitted with new engines in the form of MTU 16V 396 diesels delivering 9700 kW (13,010 hp) for a speed of 31 kts.

Right: A 'Tiger' class or Type 148 craft is seen in its definitive form as operated by the German navy with 76- and 40-mm guns and missile launchers amidships.

Left: One of the last three units remaining in German service at the beginning of the 21st century, the Weihe is representative of FAC thinking of the 1970s, and is thus obsolescent.

SPECIFICATION

'Tiger' class or Type 148
Displacement: 265 tons full load
Dimensions: length 47 m (154 ft 2 in); beam 7 m (23 ft); draught 2.7 m (8 ft 10 in)
Propulsion: four MTU 16V 538 TB90 diesels delivering 8940 kW (11,990 hp) to four shafts
Performance: speed 36 kts
Armament: two twin launchers for MM.38 Exocet anti-ship missiles, one 76-mm (3-in)

OTO-Melara Compact DP gun, and one 40-mm Bofors AA gun
Electronics: one Triton air/surface search radar, one 3RM20 navigation radar, one Castor fire-control radar, one Panda optical director, one Vega weapons control system, one PALIS combat data system, one Octopus ESM/ECM system, and decoy launchers
Complement: 30

'Gepard' and 'Albatros' classes PCFGs

West Germany (now just Germany since the reunification of East and West Germany) has long relied on submarines and fast attack craft (FACs), the latter now generally known as fast patrol craft (PCFs) for the protection of its coast, and has become pre-eminent in the world of FAC/PCF design and manufacture.

In the mid-1960s the West German navy saw the need for a successor to the Type 141 and 142 FACs in the

Dachs (P6127) is a member of the 'Gepard' class. The related 'Albatros' class are also based at Warnemünde and form the 2nd Squadron with the tender Donau. Both Type 143 subclasses are based on wooden hulls.

short and medium term respectively, and decided to adopt two Type 143 variants of a composite hull design by Lürssen. The 10 craft of the Type 143 class were ordered from AEG-Telefunken in July 1972, and the craft were built by Kröger (three) and Lürssen (seven) for completion in 1976-77 as the S61 to S70, which were later renamed as the **Albatros, Falke, Geier, Bussard, Sperber, Greif, Kondor, Seeadler, Habicht** and **Kormoran**. Possessing a full-load displacement of 397.5 tons, these craft are armed with two 76-mm (3-in) OTO-Melara Compact guns, two 533-mm (21-in) Seal wire-guided torpedoes, and four MM.38 Exocet anti-ship missiles.

With the advent of the Type 143A or 'Gepard' class, delivered in 1982-84

The Hyäne (P6130) was completed as the last unit of the 'Gepard' class, which constitutes the 7th Squadron based on the tender Elbe at Warnemünde.

without provision for torpedo tubes, the Type 143 became the Type 143B or 'Albatros' class. Originally the S71 to S80, the craft of the Type 143A class are now named **Gepard, Puma, Hermelin,** **Nerz, Zobel, Frettchen, Dachs, Ozelot, Wiesel** and **Hyäne.** From 1994 the craft were updated electronically and with a SAM launcher in place of the after 76-mm Compact gun.

SPECIFICATION

'Gepard' (Type 143A) class
Displacement: 391 tons full load
Dimensions: length 57.6 m (189 ft); beam 7.8 m (25 ft 7 in); draught 2.6 m (8 ft 6 in)
Propulsion: four MTU MA 16V 956 SB80 diesels delivering 9840 kW (13,195 shp) to four shafts
Performance: speed 40 kts; endurance 4800 km (2,985 miles) at 16 kts declining to 1125 km (690 miles) at 33 kts
Armament: one 76-mm (3-in) OTO-Melara Compact DP gun, two twin launchers for four MM.38

Exocet anti-ship missiles, one 21-cell launcher for RIM-116 RAM short-range SAMs, and provision for mines
Electronics: one WM27 surface search and gun fire-control radar, one SMA 3 RM 20 navigation radar, one Thales-updated AEG AGIS combat data system, one STN Atlas WBA optronic director, one FL 1800 Mk 2 ESM system, and Hot Dog/Silver Dog flare/chaff dispenser
Complement: 34

Geier (P6113) of the 'Albatros' class. Note the aft 76-mm Compact gun, retained on this vessel instead of the 21-cell RAM launcher.

'Ban Yas' and 'Mubarraz' classes PCFGs

The most advanced missile-armed FACs operated by the navy of the United Arab Emirates, until the advent of the six 'Baynuyah'-class craft, are the eight units of the closely related **'Ban Yas' class** and **'Mubarraz' class** based on the Lürssen TNC 45 design.

The older of the two is the 'Ban Yas' class, whose six units are the **Ban Yas, Marban, Rodqm, Shaheen, Sagar** and **Tarif,**

commissioned in 1980-81 after construction by Lürssen at Vegesack to a 1977 order with a propulsion arrangement of four MTU 16V diesels delivering 10160 kW (13,625 shp) to four shafts for a speed of 40 kts. Based on the MM.40 variant of the Exocet anti-ship missile, the armament is basically similar to that of the 'Mubarraz'-class units except for the shipping of a

40-mm Breda twin mounting rather than a Sadral SAM launcher for Mistral infra-red homing weapons (the latter being first export version of this system).

The 'Mubarraz' class units **Mubarraz** and **Makasib** were completed in 1990 by Lürssen of Bremen to a modified TNC 38 design with a two-engined propulsion arrangement.

The Mubarraz is lead unit of a two-craft class based on the 'Ban Yas' class, but with twin-shaft propulsion.

SPECIFICATION

'Mubarraz' class
Displacement: 260 tons full load
Dimensions: length 44.9 m (147 ft 4 in); beam 7 m (23 ft); draught 2.2 m (7 ft 3 in)
Propulsion: two MTU 20V 538 TB93 diesels delivering 7000 kW (9,390 hp) to two shafts
Performance: speed 40 kts; endurance 925 km (575 miles) at 38 kts
Armament: one 76-mm (3-in) OTO-Melara Super Rapid DP gun, two

20-mm cannon, two twin launchers for four MM.40 Exocet anti-ship missiles, and one Sadral sextuple launcher for Mistral short-range SAMs
Electronics: one Sea Giraffe 50HC air/surface search radar, one Decca 1226 navigation radar, one Bofors 9LV 223 fire-control radar, one Najir optronic director, one Cutlass/Cygnus ESM/ECM system, and two Dagaie chaff/flare launchers
Complement: 40

Seen at speed, the Ban Yas is the lead unit of a six-strong class providing the United Arab Emirates with an effective coastal patrol and anti-ship capability.

'Sea Wolf' class PCFG

With much of her trade dependent on shipping moving in and out of the congested waters between Malaysia and the Indonesian archipelago, which is also a chokepoint for shipping movements between the Indian Ocean and East China Sea, Malaysia maintains a small but highly capable naval establishment.

Although smaller than the 12 units of the 'Fearless' class of offshore patrol vessels, which carry no missile armament and are more optimised for the anti-submarine role with a modest speed and launchers for lightweight torpedoes, the six craft of the **'Sea Wolf' class** constitute a powerful

*The **Sea Wolf** is the lead vessel of a six-strong class, and was commissioned in 1972 after construction in West Germany by Lürssen at Vegesack.*

offensive capability in combination with the six corvettes of the 'Victory' class. Based on the yard's FPB 45 design and built by Lürssen of Vegesack (first two units) and Singapore SBEC, the craft are the **Sea Wolf, Sea Lion, Sea Dragon, Sea Tiger, Sea Hawk** and **Sea Scorpion.** The craft were commissioned in 1972-76 with the first examples of the Gabriel anti-ship missile

released for export by Israel.

The missile armament is concentrated on the after part of each unit, the deck area forward of the superstructure being reserved for the primary gun armament, which is a Swedish type, the Bofors SAK-57 mounting car-

rying a single 57-mm L/70 DP gun, which fires a 2.4-kg (5.3-lb) shell to a maximum range of 17 km (10.6 miles).

From 1988 the craft were taken in hand for a rolling upgrade programme concerned mainly with the missile armament and electronics. The main change in

the missile fit was the replacement of the triple Gabriel launcher by two twin launchers for the longer-range Harpoon anti-ship missile, but the Bofors 40-mm AA gun was replaced by a Simbad SAM launcher. The craft are dated, and are to be retired from 2005.

*The **Sea Tiger** was the fourth 'Sea Wolf'-class FAC, and the second of those built by Singapore Shipbuilding and Engineering. Note the mixed missile outfit.*

SPECIFICATION	
'Sea Wolf' class	SAK-57 DP gun, two twin launchers
Displacement: 226 tons standard; 254 tons full load	for four Harpoon anti-ship missiles, four (or more usually two)
Dimensions: length 44.9 m (147 ft 4 in); beam 7 m (23 ft); draught 2.5 m (8 ft 2 in)	launchers for Gabriel I anti-ship missiles, and one Simbad twin launcher for Mistral short-range
Propulsion: four MTU 16V 538 TB92 diesels delivering 10160 kW (13,625 shp) to four shafts	SAMs **Electronics:** one Decca surface search/navigation radar, WM28/5
Performance: speed 35 kts; endurance 3350 km (2,080 miles) at 15 kts declining to 1750 km (1,085 miles) at 30 kts	fire-control radar, one Elbit MSIS optronic director, one RQN-3B (INS-3) ESM/ECM system, and two Hycor flare/chaff launchers
Armament: one 57-mm Bofors	**Complement:** 41

'Victory' class FSG

The most significant assets of the navy operated by the island republic of Singapore are the six missile corvettes of the **'Victory' class**. The subject of an order placed in June 1986, the vessels are variants of Lürssen's MGB 62 design ordered by Bahrain and the UAE. In common with other

*Below: The **Valour** was completed as the second of the 'Victory'-class missile corvettes for the navy of the Republic of Singapore. The **Barak SAM** launchers are located on either side of the **VDS** installation.*

Lürssen craft ordered by Singapore, the contract specified that while a certain number was to be built in West Germany (in this instance only the lead vessel), the rest of the class would be built locally by a company now known as Singapore Shipbuilding and Marine.

The class was completed in two trios, the first three being commissioned on 18 August 1990 and the second trio in 25 May 1991. The vessels are the **Victory, Valour, Vigilance, Valiant, Vigour** and **Vengeance,** which constitute Squadron 188 of the Singapore navy.

It is believed that in overall terms the craft have not been wholly successful, largely as a result of their excessive topweight. This stemmed from the use of a very substantial enclosed mast structure to accommodate the extensive electronic warfare suite, which is composed mainly of Israeli systems.

Coventional layout

The ships are conventionally laid out, with the main gun forward, the anti-ship missile launchers abaft the superstructure, the launchers for lightweight anti-submarine torpedoes

on the beams just forward of the after funnel and, as a retrofit, two octuple vertical-launch systems for IAI/Rafael Barak I SAMs by the stern abeam of the vari-

able-depth sonar installation. A roll stabilisation system was retrofitted in an effort to improve the vessels' seakeeping qualities.

SPECIFICATION	
'Victory' class	Harpoon anti-ship missiles, two
Displacement: 595 tons full load	octuple launchers for Barak I
Dimensions: length 62.4 m (204 ft 9 in); beam 8.5 m (27 ft 11 in); draught 3.1 m (10 ft 2 in)	SAMs, and two triple B 515 324-mm (12.75-in) tubes for A 244S anti-submarine torpedoes
Propulsion: four MTU 16V 538 TB92 diesels delivering 11200 kW (15,020 shp) to four shafts	**Electronics:** one Sea Giraffe 150HC surface search radar, one Type 1007 navigation radar, two
Performance: speed 35 kts; endurance 7400 km (4,600 miles) at 18 kts	EL/M-2221(X) fire-control radars, one MSIS optronic director, one Elbit combat data system, Elisra
Armament: one 76-mm (3-in) OTO-Melara Super Rapid DP gun, two quadruple launchers for	and Rafael EW systems, and chaff/flare launchers **Complement:** 49

*The **Valiant** reveals the forward layout of the 'Victory'-class FSG, and also the height and cross-section of the mast structure with its mass of antennae.*

'Dvora' class Fast attack craft (gun/missile)

Israeli **'Dvora'-class** coastal craft are now in service all over the world. The basic 'Dvora' design, a 21.6-m (71-ft) diesel-powered aluminium alloy hulled boat with a top speed of 45 kts is no longer in service with Israel. Six were supplied to Sri Lanka (of which three were in service in 2003, two having been lost to Tamil forces in 1995-96) and two to Taiwan where the design was developed by the Sun Yat Sen Scientific Research Institute. Taiwan manufactured numerous examples of what they called the **'Hai Ou' class**. In 2003, 58 such craft were in service with Taiwan, although not all were operational. Two modified examples, possibly based on Israeli-built boats, were later sold to Paraguay (**Capitán Ortiz** and **Teniente Robles**). The 'Hai Ou' are armed with Taiwanese SSMs: the Hsiung Feng 1 weapon carries a 75-kg (165-lb) warhead to a maximum range of 36 km (22 miles) at a speed of Mach 0.7. The vessels also regularly carry shoulder-launched missiles and a 20-mm cannon has been added at the stern. The Taiwanese boats are no longer capable of their designed top speed and a maximum of 30 kts is probably nearer the mark.

Israel operates 13 **'Super**

Dvora'-class boats today, comprising nine of the original **'Super Dvora Mk 1'** type and four of the slightly larger **'Super Dvora Mk 2'**. These improved 54-ton craft have been exported to Sri Lanka (the current fleet includes four 'Super Dvora Mk 1', after two were lost to Tamil guerrillas in 1993-95, and five 'Super Dvora Mk 2', one having been sunk in action in 1995), Eritrea (four Mk 1 based at Massawa, although a total of six may have been ordered), Slovenia (one Mk 2 delivered in 1996 and based at Isola) and India (which ordered some 17 Mk 2s, although to date only two have been delivered).

'Dvora' armament

Armament fits are as varied as Israel's customer base. Israeli boats sometimes ship Hellfire SSMs with an 8-km (4.9-mile) range or an 84-mm (3.3-in) rocket launcher in

The 'Super Dvora' is notably compact with a low profile superstructure. Gun mountings are located forward of the bridge and in the port aft position. 20-mm Oerlikon or 25-mm Bushmaster cannon can be mounted by the Israeli craft.

addition to their gun armament of two Oerlikon 20-mm cannon or two Bushmaster 25-mm cannon or three Rafael Typhoon 12.7-mm (0.5-in) machine-guns in addition to two 7.62-mm (0.3-in)

or 12.7-mm machine-guns. Eritrean 'Super Dvoras' carry Russian twin 23-mm cannon and a pair of 12.7-mm machine guns; Indian examples ship a single Oerlikon 20-mm cannon plus two

12.7-mm machine guns; Sri Lankan boats have two Oerlikon 20-mm cannon and two 12.7-mm machine-guns; while the Slovenians content themselves with just a pair of 12.7-mm machine-guns.

SPECIFICATION	
'Super Dvora' class	**Maximum speed:** 36 kts (Mk 1);
Displacement: 54 tons	46 kts (Mk 2)
Dimensions: length 21.6 m (70 ft	**Range:** 1931 km (1,200 miles) at
10 in); beam 5.5 m (18 ft); draught	17 kts
1.8 m (5 ft 11 in)	**Complement:** 10
Propulsion: two shaft, (Mk 1) two	**Armament:** see text
Detroit 16V-92TA diesels delivering	**Electronics:** Raytheon surface
1029.1 kW (1,380 shp) or (Mk 2) two	search (Israel, Eritrea); Koden
MTU 12V 396 TE94 diesels	surface search (India, Slovenia, Sri
delivering 3113.3 kW (4175 shp)	Lanka, Mk 2); Decca 926 (Sri Lanka)

SPECIFICATION	
'Hai Ou' class	**Armament:** two Hsiung Feng 1
Displacement: 47 tons	SSMs, one CS Type 75 20-mm gun,
Dimensions: length 21.6 m (70 ft	two 12.7-mm guns; shoulder-
10 in); beam 5.5 m (18 ft); draught	launched SAMs often embarked
1 m (3 ft 4 in)	**Electronics:** Marconi LN66 search
Propulsion: two MTU 12V 331	radar, RCA R76 fire-control radar
TC82 diesels delivering 1942.5 kW	**Complement:** 10
(2,605 shp) to two shafts	
Maximum speed: 45 kts (as	
designed)	

'Saar 1/2/3' and 'Aliya' classes Fast attack craft (gun/missile)

After the USSR, and hastened in its plans by the loss of the *Eilat* to an Egyptian missile attack in 1967, the Israeli navy was the first of the 'European' powers to realise the importance of the missile craft. The first class that Israel ordered was the **'Saar' class**, built by the French CMN shipyard in Cherbourg between 1967 and 1969 to a West German Lürssen design with steel hulls and light alloy superstructures. The first six units were originally built as the **'Saar 1' class** with an all-gun armament of three single 40-mm AA guns. The second six were constructed as the **'Saar 2' class** with a single 76-mm (3-in) OTO Melara gun forward, two single 12.7-mm (0.5-in) heavy machine-guns and two triple mountings for the Gabriel Mk 1 SSM. Subsequently all the 'Saars' were modified to carry new armament. Four of the original 'Saar 1' were modified as ASW units with EDO 780 variable-depth sonar aft and two to four Mk 32 tubes for 324-mm (12.75-in) Mk 46 11-km (6.8-mile) range active/passive acoustic-homing ASW torpedoes. The gun fit was two single 40-mm AA and

two single 12.7-mm (0.5-in) heavy machine-guns. The remaining two units were given the same gun armament plus one triple and two single launchers for Gabriel Mk 1 and Mk 2 missiles. They were then redesignated 'Saar 2' class, while the original six 'Saar 2' craft were re-equipped with a pair of Harpoon SSM launchers in place of one of the triple Gabriel mountings and redesignated the **'Saar 3' class**. The remaining Gabriel launcher was later equipped to fire Mk 1 and Mk 2 SSMs.

'Aliya' class

Following the testing of the 'Reshef'-class *Nitzhon* with a temporary helicopter landing pad aft, and to meet a requirement for a missile craft group leader, the **'Aliya'** (or **'Saar 4.5'**) **class** was designed and built. Using the successful 'Reshef'-class hull as the basis, the 'Aliyas' have a helicopter hangar and landing platform aft for a Bell Model 206 ASW and target-spotting helicopter. The latter is particularly useful for over-the-horizon targeting of the Harpoon SSMs carried on one quadruple or two twin launchers. The other arma-

ment is four single Gabriel Mk 2 SSMs, a twin 30-mm AA gun mounting, two single 20-mm AA guns and four single 12.7-mm (0.5-in) machine-guns. Israel currently operates two 'Aliyas', and these are now equipped with Mk 15 Phalanx 20-mm CIWS. The helicopter platforms on the remaining craft have given way to aft davits for the operation of special forces boats.

An Israeli 'Saar 2', with a torpedo boat to the rear, in heavy seas. Built in France to a West German design, these craft were armed with Israeli Gabriel missiles.

SPECIFICATION	
'Aliya' class	**Propulsion:** four Maybach (MTU)
Names: *Aliya, Geoula, Romat,*	diesels delivering 10440 kW
Keshmet, Nirit	(14,000 shp) to four shafts
Displacement: 498 tons full load	**Maximum speed:** 31 kts
Dimensions: length 61.7 m (202 ft	**Complement:** 53
5 in); beam 7.6 m (24 ft 11 in);	**Armament:** see text
draught 2.4 m (7 ft 11 in)	**Electronics:** as 'Reshef' class

'Reshef' and 'Hetz' classes Fast attack craft (missile)

An Israeli 'Reshef'-class missile boat. Equipped with a variety of missile types, the vessels of this class are among the most capable missile boats in service. Two Israeli vessels were transferred to Chilean service in the 1979-81, and were subsequently joined by two more acquired in 1997.

For long-range missions in the Mediterranean and the Red Sea Israel required a new fast patrol craft design, so the locally designed and built **'Reshef'** (or **'Saar 4'**) class of steel-hulled craft was produced. The first two of these, **Reshef** (built and commissioned in 1973) and **Keshet**, were involved in the 1973 Arab-Israeli War.

These craft have air-conditioned quarters, a combat operations centre, and Italian- and Israeli-built ESM/ECM systems. A total of 10 was constructed (four subsequently being transferred to Chile where they formed part of the three-ship **'Casma' class** in 2003), whilst three others were built in Israel for South Africa with another six built at Durban under licence. The Israeli 'Reshefs' carry an armament formed from the following: twin or quadruple Harpoon SSM launchers (the missiles have Israeli homing systems), four to six Gabriel Mk 2 SSMs, one or two single OTO Melara Compact 76-mm (3-in) DP guns or one 76-mm DP and one 40-mm AA gun (later replaced by two Mk 15 Phalanx 20-mm CIWS) plus, in all craft, two single 20-mm AA cannon and two or three twin 12.7-mm (0.5-in) heavy machine-guns. A variable-depth sonar is fitted in some craft. 'Reshef'-class units have also been transferred to Sri Lanka, which received two vessels, **Nandimithra** and **Suranimala** in 2000. Only two of the five 'Reshef' class (**Nitzhon** and **Atsmout**) remain in service with Israel.

Armament fits vary between the other navies. The Chilean and Sri Lankan boats retain the Gabriel system but the South African examples ship a licence-built Gabriel Mk 2 known as the Skerpioen. All export boats carry one or two Compact guns although the South Africans may replace one 76-mm turret with twin 35-mm Vektor cannon. The Chilean and Sri Lankan boats have two Oerlikon 20-mm cannon in addition to the 76-mm Compact guns. Israeli boats meanwhile bristle with chaff/flare launchers, with up to six 24-tube decoy launchers; Chilean and South African boats carry four Rafael or ACDS decoy launchers, but the Sri Lankans carry none.

Electronics fits are different among export craft too. South African boats, known as the **'Warrior' class**, have Elta EL/M 2208 air/surface search radar; Israeli, Chilean and Sri Lankan boats carry Thomson-CSF TH-D 1040 air/surface search radar. Chilean boats have Raytheon 20X navigation radar. The 'Saar 4' class have Selenia Orion RTN-10X fire-control radar except for some Chilean units.

'Hetz' class

The very similar **'Hetz' class** or **'Saar 4.5' class** is only operated by Israel: there are six of these, built or converted at intervals since 1975, the last not being commissioned until 1998. The 'Hetz' boats are also armed with a combination of Harpoon and Gabriel Mk 2 missiles. The latter is a semi-active radar homing missile with a range of 36 km (22.4 miles); it carries a 75-kg (165-lb) warhead and travels at Mach 0.7, and it can carry a TV camera to transmit the target image back to the firing ship over the horizon. The 'Hetz' is also armed with the Vulcan Phalanx CIWS in addition to the Barak SAM (only operational in one of the class).

Left and above: Formerly know as the 'Minister' class, the South African 'Warrior' class comprises nine vessels of the 'Saar 4' class, armed with licence-built Gabriel missiles, some of which were built locally at Durban. P 1562 (left) was one of four vessels in reserve in 2003 and unlikely to return to sea.

Top: The primary armament of the 'Reshef' class comprises the Gabriel missile in its Mk 1 and Mk 2 forms (the Mk 3 variant was cancelled) and the American Harpoon. Note the six Gabriel launchers on this vessel, which is not fitted with Harpoon.

SPECIFICATION

'Hetz' class
Names: *Romat, Keshet, Hetz (ex-Nirit), Kidon, Tarshish, Yaffo*
Displacement: 488 tons
Dimensions: length 61.7 m (202 ft 5 in); beam 7.6 m (24 ft 11 in); draught 2.5 m (8 ft 2½ in)
Propulsion: four MTU/Bazan diesels delivering 11185.5 kW (15,000 shp) to four shafts
Maximum speed: 31 kts
Range: 1,500 miles at 30 kts; 3,000 miles at 17 kts
Armament: four Harpoon SSMs, six Gabriel Mk 2 SSMs, one 16- or 32-cell vertical launcher for Barak SAMs, one 76-mm (3-in) Compact gun, one 20-mm Mk 15 Vulcan Phalanx CIWS, two Oerlikon 20-mm cannon, two or four 12.7-mm (0.5-in) machine-guns
Electronics: Thomson-CSF TH-D 1040 Neptune air/surface search radar, Elta EL/M fire-control radar, one 72-barrel chaff/flare launcher
Complement: 53

SPECIFICATION

'Reshef' class
Names: *Reshef, Kidon, Tarshish, Yaffo, Nitzhon, Komemiut, Atsmout, Moledt, Romah, Keshet*
Displacement: 450 tons full load
Dimensions: length 58 m (190 ft 4 in); beam 7.8 m (25 ft 7 in); draught 2.4 m (7 ft 11 in)
Propulsion: four MTU/Bazan diesels delivering 15,000 shp to four shafts
Maximum speed: 32 kts
Range: 1,650 miles at 30 kts
Complement: 45
Armament: (see text)
Electronics: one Thomson-CSF TH-D 1040 Neptune air/surface search radar, one Selenia Orion RTN-10X ECM system, chaff/flare launchers and (some craft) ELAC sonar
Complement: 45

'Sparviero' class

Fast attack hydrofoil

Together with the US Navy, Italy was unique among NATO navies in having missile-armed hydrofoils as part of its operational surface fleet. The prototype of the **'Sparviero' class** was based on the Boeing Tucumcari design and assessed in detail by Alinavi. Built between 1971-74, the original craft was followed by six others between 1980-83. They used the Boeing jetfoil system, with one foil forward and two aft.

Power for the foilborne mode came from a gas turbine driving a waterjet system, while hullborne power came from a single diesel. The hull was made entirely of aluminium, and it was found that the craft had a relatively short range and limited armament for combat operations. However, the Italian navy was willing to accept this as Italy is surrounded by restricted waters ideal for such craft.

The six later vessels had a more modern surface search radar than the **Sparviero**, and also carried the later 150-km (93-mile) range Teseo Mk 2 SSM variant of

the Otomat Mk 1, though use of this extra range capability required a helicopter for mid-course guidance and targeting. The radar was fitted with an IFF interrogator unit, and the gun armament was a single OTO-Melara 76-mm (3-in) DP gun forward. Italy's last 'Sparviero'-class vessel was retired from service in 1999.

Below: Italy's seven 'Sparviero'-class vessels were named Sparviero, Nibbio, Falcone, Astore, Grifone, Gheppio *(pictured) and* Condore.

Japan's Maritime Self-Defence Force is the final operator of the 'Sparviero' class, with three licence-built PG 01 craft in service. These are armed with four Mitsubishi SSM-1B missiles and a 20-mm Sea Vulcan gun.

'Helsinki' and 'Rauma' classes Fast attack craft

The Finnish navy is a small coastal defence force with some 2,000 personnel. Not all vessels are manned at any one time. Fast attack craft (FAC) of the **'Helsinki' class** and its derivative, the **'Rauma' class**,form the main striking force although two corvettes dating from the 1960s remain on the strength.

The 'Helsinki'-class FACs are 300-ton vessels designed around their Swedish Saab RBS 15 anti-ship missiles; their primary role is to attack enemy surface ships but they have a limited anti-submarine capability. Like their Swedish equivalents, the Finnish FACs wear a tank-like camouflage of greens and greys, as they are intended to lie up in coastal waters where they can be easily concealed. The hull and superstructure are

built of light alloy and the armament fit can be altered depending on role; the standard arrangement offers modest anti-aircraft defence plus depth-charge rails.

Anti-ship missile

The RBS 15 missile fitted on the 'Helsinki' class carries a 150-kg (331-lb) high explosive blast fragmentation warhead. The tank of paraffin-based fuel behind the warhead adds to the incendiary effect if the missile strikes its target well within its maximum range of 70 km (43.5 miles). The total weight of the missile, including its rocket boosters is 780 kg (1,720 lb) and, as was demonstrated during the Falklands War and in the attack on the USS *Stark*, a single hit from a weapon of this type can be sufficient to disable or even sink a modern destroyer.

Accelerated by a three-second burst from its boosters, the missile is powered by a turbojet and makes the first part of its flight at an altitude intended to clear offshore islands. It can be off-set by up to 90 degrees before its own active radar searches for the target and guides it on collision course.

The four 'Helsinki' boats formed the basis for the 'Rauma' class of which the first was commissioned in 1990 with another five in service by 1998. These are slightly smaller but visually similar vessels with a reduced crew of only 19. They normally carry six rather than eight missiles of the RBS 15SF type.

Above: Missile racks on the 'Helsinki' class can be replaced by mine rails, and the vessel's light armament can be altered to suit the intended role.

Below: Developed from the 'Helsinki', the 'Rauma' class has a secondary ASW capability and is fitted with four Saab 9-tube mortars and a depth charge rail.

'Storm' class Fast attack craft

One of the smaller classes of FAC, the 100-ton **'Storm' class** formerly operated by the Norwegian navy were primarily armed with the Penguin Mk 1 anti-ship missile. Developed in Norway, this weapon is unusual in relying on heat-seeking rather than radar to guide itself to the target – an advantage in that it does not

emit a telltale radar signal, but a less reliable method of placing the missile on the right trajectory. Its range is only about 20 km (12.4 miles). However, its 125-kg (276-lb) semi-armour piercing warhead packs a useful punch and it has been widely exported since its service entry in the 1970s.

With their modest dimen-

sions and crew of only 19, the 'Storm' class cannot take on air, surface and sub-surface threats. The 76-mm (3-in) gun is not dual purpose and it has only a 40-mm Bofors gun for AA defence, has no sonar and carries no anti-submarine weapons: its sole function was to attack enemy surface

Hvass (P 972) pictured in 1998, following the removal of its missile armament. The 76-mm Bofors gun was for surface fire only and had a 13-km (8-mile) range.

ships with a volley of Penguin missiles and hope to dodge any retaliatory strike by concealment among the Norwegian fjords and islands. There were originally 19 boats in the class

but these were all retired from Norwegian service by 2000. Since then non missile-armed vessels have been transferred to Estonia (one), Latvia (three) and Lithuania (three).

'Hauk' class Fast attack craft

The **'Hauk' class** now provide the majority of Norway's fast attack craft fleet. Ordered in June 1975, they differ from the 'Storm' class in that they carry torpedoes, improving their ability to attack enemy surface ships. Their primary weapon remains up to six of the relatively short-range IR-homing Penguin surface-to-surface missile. This is the Mk 2 Mod 5 version with a range of 27 km (16.8 miles) and a speed of Mach 0.8. These are not always shipped by the navy today, leaving the 'Hauk' class to engage with its FFV Type 613 passive-homing torpedoes, which have a range of 27 km

(16.8 miles) travelling at 45 kts, and carry a 240-kg (529-lb) warhead.

AA armament

The anti-aircraft weapons fit of the 'Hauk' class originally comprised a 40-mm Bofors dual purpose gun and a 20-mm gun, but the latter was replaced from 1994 by a Simbad twin SAM launcher for the IR homing Matra Sadral. This has a range of

4 km (2.5 miles). The single 40-mm Bofors fires at a rate of 300 rounds per minute and has a range of 12 km (7.5 miles). A further upgrade will keep these vessels in service until 2015 or until they have been replaced by the 'Skjold'-class FAC which incorporates 'stealth' features. A wave-piercing bow, tested on *Tjeld*, may eventually be added to other ships in the 'Hauk' class.

Right: Tjeld (P 989) is the only vessel in the class to have been fitted with an experimental wave-piercing bow designed to improve hydrodynamic performance.

Below: Upgrades have given 'Hauk'-class vessels the SENIT 2000 combat data system. This includes a new navigation radar and communications equipment.

'Snögg' and 'Hugin' classes Fast attack craft

The Royal Norwegian Navy has always operated light strike craft, from the second half of the 19th century, when the steam torpedo boat represented the state of the art. The network of islands and deep fjords are ideal for hit and run tactics, and a modern series of fast attack craft (FAC) continues to exploit Norway's geographical advantages.

Highly regarded
In the early 1970s four **'Snögg' class** FACs were built by Westermoens Båtbyggeri at Mandal in southern Norway. They were armed with a combination of Swedish Tp 61 high-speed anti-ship torpedoes and Norwegian Penguin short-range sea-skimming missiles. The design was based closely on the previous 'Storm' class, but with

Hugin was the lead ship of a class of 16 missile craft built for Sweden. Based on the Norwegian 'Hauk' class, they were less effective than had been expected.

anti-ship missiles and torpedoes rather than a heavy gun armament. A further fourteen 'Hauk' class were ordered in 1975 to the same design, but with more modern armament. This series of FACs was highly regarded, and the fact that fourteen are still in service today and undergoing further modernisation speaks for itself.

Full modernisation
In appearance they are conventional, with a light gun forward, single 533-mm (21-in) torpedo tubes flanking the bridge, a short lattice

mast and a long quarterdeck with room for up to six Penguin missiles in box-launchers and a 20-mm (0.79-in) gun (now replaced by a French Simbad twin short-range air defence missile-launcher). Two-shaft diesel engines give them a smooth-water speed of 35 knots. By the end of 2003 all

Twenty 'Storm' class gunboats were built for the Norwegian Navy in the 1960s. They were armed with Penguin missiles in the 1970s

Based on the hull of the 'Storm' class, the six boats of the 'Snögg' class were completed with four Penguin missiles, four torpedo tubes plus one 40-mm (1.58-in) and one 20-mm (0.79-in) gun. They were followed by 19 examples of the similar 'Hauk' class, fourteen of which are still in service.

will have undergone full modernisation, with the SENIT 2000 combat management system, optronic fire control and improved communications. An experimental wave-piercing bow has been fitted to the *Tjeld*, and if it proves successful it may be retrofitted to her sister ships.

Swedish variants
A modified version, the prototype *Jagaren*, was ordered by the Royal Swedish Navy in 1970 as an

experiment in co-operation between the two navies. After three years of trials an order was placed for sixteen **'Hugin' class** from Norway's Bergens Mekaniske Verksteder shipyard. Their service with the Royal Swedish Navy was not very satisfactory, and today only eight remain active. Swedish FAC philosophy demands much heavier armament than the 'Hugin' design could carry, so the smaller design had little to offer the Royal Swedish Navy.

SPECIFICATION	
'Hauk' class	Penguin Mk 2 surface-to-surface
Displacement: 120 tonnes (standard), 160 tonnes (full load)	missiles, Sadral air defence missiles on twin Simbad launcher, one 40mm (1.58-in) L/70 Bofors gun,
Dimensions: length 36.5 m (119 ft 9 in; beam 6.2 m (20 ft 4 in); draught 1.8 m (5 ft 11 in)	two Tp 613 53mm torpedo tubes
Propulsion: two-shaft MTU 16V538 TB92 diesels, 6820 bhp	**Electronics:** SENIT 2000 combat system; argo intercept system; decoy-Launchers, VIGY-20 optronic
Speed: 32 kts	director
Range: 440 nm at 30 kts	**Complement:** six officers,
Armament: (2002): up to six	18 ratings

'Spica' and 'Willemoes' classes Fast attack craft

In 1961 funds were approved for the Royal Swedish Navy for the construction of six 41-metre (134 ft 6 in) torpedo-armed fast attack craft (FACs). All were named after stars or constellations, and the first, **HSwMS Spica**, was laid down in 1964. They were a great advance on contemporary FACs, being driven by triple Bristol Proteus gas turbines and armed with a rapid-firing Bofors 57-mm (2.24-in) gun and four 533-mm (21-in) anti-ship torpedoes. The **'Spica' class** proved a great success, being ideal for hit-and-run tactics in the Swedish Archipelago, and ten years later the first of twelve **'Spica IIs'** was laid down. Apart from a slightly longer 42-metre (137 ft 10 in) hull, the only change was a more

advanced fire control system. They were named after Swedish towns, and were more correctly known as the **'Norrköping' class**

Danish variants
The design was adopted by the Royal Danish Navy for ten **'Willemoes' class**, but they differed in being armed with an Italian OTO Melara 76-mm (3-in) Compact gun, but they had the same Tp 61 series heavyweight torpedoes and fire control as the 'Norrköping' class. They also differed slightly in appearance, with the superstructure further aft.

As a NATO member Denmark was eligible for US military aid, and each of the 'Willemoes' class was soon modified to accept eight Harpoon anti-ship missiles in two quadruple groups of

canisters. These were sited aft to allow the efflux to vent clear of the ship, but in service the ships have various combinations of torpedoes and missiles. The Swedish Defence Ministry made a similar decision, but developed an indigenous weapon,

Saab's RBS 15, rather than Harpoon. The ships were converted in 1982-84, sacrificing four torpedo-tubes to provide deck space.

The original 'Spica' class were not modernised as funds were not available, and were taken out of ser-

The 'Spica II' class entered service with the Swedish Navy between 1973 and 1976. In the 1980s they were modified to carry RBS-15 anti-ship missiles mounted at the stern, replacing the original torpedo tubes.

vice in the 1990s, but the
'Spica II' group are currently
undergoing a mid-life refit.
This involves re-engining,
new fire control and combat
system, and strengthening
anti-submarine and air
defence capabilities.
By the end of the 1990s
only six 'Spicas' remained in
service, the rest being in
reserve and likely to be
scrapped soon. None of the
'Willemoes' class were
modernised, however, and
all ten were taken out of
service in 1999-2000.

Below: The 57-mm (2.24-in) Mk.2 Bofors gun carried by the 'Spicas' can fire at 220 rounds per minute to a range of 17 km (10.56 miles).

Above: Modified variants of the 'Spica' class, the Danish 'Willemoes' class was completed with a 76-mm (3-in) OTO-Melara Compact gun, Harpoon anti-ship missiles and 533-mm (21-in) torpedo tubes. Commissioned in the 1970s, the end of the Cold War saw the ten vessels of the class placed in reserve in the last years of the 1990s.

SPECIFICATION

'Spica I' class (as built)
Displacement: 200 tonnes (standard), 235 tonnes (full load)
Dimensions: length 41.0 m (134 ft 6 in); beam 7.1 m (23 ft 3½ in); draught 1.6 m (5 ft 3 in)
Propulsion: 3-shaft Proteus gas turbines, 12,750 shp
Speed: 40 kts
Range: 500 nm at full speed
Armament: six 533-mm (21-in)
torpedo tubes; one 57-mm (2.24-in) L/70 dual-purpose gun; four heavy machine guns; four Saab RBS-15 active radar-homing anti-ship missiles were added to the 'Spica IIs' in the 1980s: surviving vessels now carry eight.
Electronics: M22 fire control and combat system
Complement: 30 officers and ratings

'Stockholm' and 'Visby' classes Missile corvettes

Designated the 'Spica III' class during the design-stage, the two **'Stockholm' class** corvettes bore little resemblance to the original FACs. In fact they reflected the Royal Swedish Navy's admission that the 'Spica' hull was not big enough to achieve a flexible balance of offensive and defensive capabilities

By lengthening and widening the hull it was possible to provide space for anti-submarine weapons, anti-ship missiles and torpedoes. The ships were never intended to mount all these weapons simultaneously, but could switch missions rapidly. Up to eight RBS 15 missiles could be mounted for anti-ship missions, while underwater grenade-launchers, four 400-mm (15.75-in) lightweight anti-submarine torpedoes, and a light variable-depth sonar could be shipped. Like all Swedish surface combatants, rails were fitted for laying mines.

Speed and economy
The powerplant selected was combined diesel and gas turbine (CODAG), with Allison light gas turbines for top speed and MTU diesels for cruising. They are undergoing a major upgrade, with new AlliedSignal TF50A gas turbine and more powerful MTU diesels. The opportunity is also being taken to remodel the superstructure to reduce its radar cross-section, i.e. incorporating

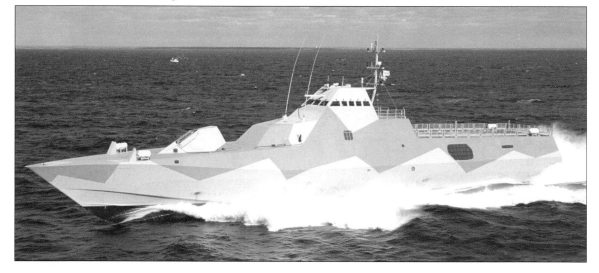

'stealth' features. When this is completed they will bear little resemblance to the original design.
Four larger **'Göteborg' class** corvettes were built in 1987-1993 with similar characteristics. They are also undergoing a major modernisation on the lines of the 'Stockholm' class. With the end of the Cold War has come a new role of international peacekeeping, and to this end all six corvettes have been refitted to provide more range and better accommodation to allow them to operate outside the Baltic. This includes air-conditioning for hot climates.
The latest Swedish corvette design is completely new, with no relationship to earlier craft. The **'Visby'** design is among one of the world's first operational stealth warships, with a structure that minimises optical and infra-red signatures, above water acoustic and hydro-acoustic signatures, underwater electrical potential and magnetic signatures, pressure signature, radar cross section and actively emitted signals.
Made from carbon fibre/vinyl/PVC laminates, the first four ships of the 'Visby' class are configured for Mine Countermeasures (MCM) and Anti-Submarine Warfare (ASW). The fifth of the class will be optimised for surface action.

Capable of reaching a speed of 35 knots at full power, the Visby class has a normal operating speed of 15 knots for maximum range and endurance. Helicopters can operate from the upper deck.

SPECIFICATION

Stockholm and Malmö (2002)
Displacement: 310 tonnes (standard), 335 tonnes (full load)
Dimensions: length 50 m (164 ft); beam 7.5 m (24 ft 8 in); draught 2.1 m (6 ft 10½ in)
Propulsion: 3 shafts; GM/Allison 570-KF gas turbines, 6540 shp; 2 MTU 16V 396 TB93, 4200 bhp
Speed: 32 kts (gas turbine), 20 (diesel)
Range: 500 nm at full speed
Armament: 8 Saab RBS 15 Mk 2 surface-to-surface missiles; two
533-mm (21-in) torpedo tubes; one 57-mm (2.24-in) L/70 Mk 2 dual-purpose gun; one 40mm (1.58-in) L/70 gun; four 400-mm (15.75-in) lightweight torpedo tubes; four Saab 601 9-tube anti-sub mortars
Electronics: 9LV 300 gunfire control; Maril combat system; Sea Giraffe 50HC air/surface search radar; Simrad SA 950 hull sonar; TSM6242 Salmon variable-depth sonar
Complement: seven officers, 27 officers and ratings

'Komar' class
Fast attack craft

Based on a standard torpedo boat hull, the 'Komar'-class fast missile craft was the herald of a revolution in small-craft fighting ability.

The **'Komar' class** of missile craft (Soviet designation **RKA**, or ***raketnyy katar***) was built between 1959 and 1961. Heralding an entirely new concept in coastal forces, the first of the 'Komars' were converted from newly completed 'P6' motor torpedo boat hulls. About 100 were built of the wooden-hulled design.

The 'Komar' carries a pair of single fixed forward-firing open-ended missile-launcher bins aimed at about 1.5° outboard and elevated at about 12°, on each side of the deck aft.

The missiles carried are the specially designed SS-N-2A 'Styx', a liquid-fuel rocket-engined type with a solid-fuel jettisonable booster motor. The 6.3-m (20-ft 8-in) long SS-N-2A has fixed wings, and is fitted with an autopilot and an I-band active-radar terminal-homing seeker.

The high-explosive warhead weighs 500 kg (1,102 lb) and the missile's maximum range is 46 km (29 miles). To decrease the load placed on the bow of the modified 'P' design hull, the single 25-mm (0.985-in) gun mount and the bridge were moved aft. Wedge-shaped sponsons were also fitted at deck level aft, as the missile installation was wider than the boat itself. Struts were fitted to protect the launchers from spray.

No 'Komars' remain in service with the Soviet navy, but several still serve in other navies. The Chinese manufactured a steel-hulled variant, the **'Hegu' class** with two 25-mm AA mountings, and many remain in service or in reserve.

The 'Komar' was the world's first missile boat to be used in action, when in October 1967 two Egyptian boats sank the Israeli destroyer *Eilat*. In April 1972 a North Vietnamese 'Komar' launched a 'Styx' SSM at three American warships bombarding coastal targets in North Vietnam.

The USS *Sterett*, a guided-missile cruiser, engaged the missile with a Terrier SAM and shot it down, this being the first time an anti-ship missile was destroyed by another missile in combat.

SPECIFICATION

'Komar' class
Displacement: 80 tons full load
Dimensions: length 26.8 m (88 ft); beam 6.4 m (21 ft); draught 1.8 m (6 ft)
Propulsion: four diesels delivering 3580 kW (4,800 hp) to four shafts
Maximum speed: 40 kts (74 km/h; 46 mph)

Armament: two SS-N-2A 'Styx' SSM launchers and one twin 25-mm (0.985-in) AA gun
Electronics: one 'Square Tie' search radar, one 'High Pole-A' IFF and one 'Dead Duck' IFF
Complement: 11
Operators: have included Algeria, China, Cuba, Egypt, North Korea

'Osa' class Fast attack craft

From 1961 through to 1966, the steel-hulled **'Osa I' class** was built as a replacement for the 'Komars'. Much larger than its predecessor, the design carried four completely enclosed launcher bins for the SS-N-2A, two on each side of the superstructure and arranged so that the aft launchers, elevated to 15°, fire over the forward pair which are elevated to 12°.

From 1966 to 1970 the **'Osa II' class** was produced for the Soviet Navy, and then subsequently for export. This version has four cylindrical launcher/containers for the SS-N-2B 'Styx', which differs from the SS-N-2A variant in having infra-red terminal homing and folding wings.

The 'Osa' class has an NBC citadel for nuclear and chemical warfare environments. Many of the 'Osa II' boats were later fitted with quadruple launchers for the SA-N-5 SAM system – the navalised version of the SA-7 'Grail' man-portable infra-red homing missile.

At their peak there were over 120 'Osa I' and 'Osa II' class craft in service with the four Soviet fleets, but what few boats remain in Soviet hands are no longer operational. 'Osa I' has seen combat service with four navies: those of Egypt (1973), India (1971), Iraq (Iran/Iraq and Gulf Wars) and Syria (1973). The 'Osa II' has seen combat with Iraq.

The type has been exported widely, and the Chinese also produced over 100 of their own variant, known as the **'Huang Feng' class**. Chinese boats have been exported to North Korea, Pakistan, Bangladesh, Iran, and the Yemen.

Right: Soviet offensive tactics called for 'Osa IIs' like these to operate in squadron or brigade strength (24 boats), launching mass missile attacks on coastal convoys and hostile amphibious forces.

Below: Egypt operated eight 'Osa I' boats. Most had been upgraded with western equipment by the time they reached the end of their service.

SPECIFICATION

'Osa I' class
Displacement: 210 tons full load (245 tons 'Osa II')
Dimensions: length 39 m (128 ft); beam 7.7 m (25 ft 4 in); draught 1.8 m (5 ft 11 in)
Propulsion: three diesels delivering 8950 kW (12,000 hp) to three shafts (11190 kW/15,000 hp in 'Osa II')
Speed: 38 kts (70 km/h; 44 mph)/ 40 kts (74 km/h; 46 mph) 'Osa II'
Complement: 30
Armament: four SS-N-2A 'Styx' SSM launchers and two twin 30-mm AA guns ('Osa I'); four SS-N-2B

'Styx' SSM launchers, one quad SA-N-5 SAM launcher and two twin 30-mm AA guns ('Osa II')
Electronics: one 'Square Tie' search radar, one 'High Pole-B' IFF, one 'Drum Tilt' fire-control radar and two 'Square Head' IFF interrogators
Operators: have included: Algeria, Angola, Bulgaria, China, Cuba, East Germany, Egypt, Ethiopia, India, Iraq, Finland, Libya, North Korea, North Yemen, Poland, Romania, Somalia, South Yemen, Syria, USSR, Yugoslavia, Vietnam

'Matka' class Fast attack craft

In 1978 the first of the 'Osa' replacement class was seen. This was the **'Matka' class**, which utilised the 'Osa' hull but had a single hydrofoil system similar to that of the 'Turya' class of torpedo boats, intended to increase speed and to improve seaworthiness.

The missile armament was reduced to two single cylindrical container-launchers for the much improved SS-N-2C variants of the 'Styx', this having a 74-km (46-mile) range and the choice of either infra-red or active radar terminal homing. The gun armament was considerably enhanced, with a new model of single-barrel 76-mm (3-in) dual-purpose turret forward and an ADG6-30 Gatling-type close-in defence system aft.

Large numbers of 'Matkas' were planned at a construction rate of three per year, but production ended in 1983 to make room for the much larger 'Tarantul' class. By the end of the 1990s, most Russian boats had been placed in reserve, with two remaining active as missile and systems trials boats.

SPECIFICATION	
'Matka' class	**Armament:** two SS-N-2C 'Styx'
Displacement: 260 tons full load	SSM launchers, one 76-mm (3-in)
Dimensions: length 40 m (131 ft	dual purpose gun and one ADG6-30
2 in); beam 7.7 m (25 ft 4 in) for the	AA 'Gatling' gun
hull and 12.0 m (39 ft 5 in) for the	**Electronics:** one 'Cheese Cake'
foil; hull draught 1.9 m (6 ft 2 in)	search radar, one 'Bass Tilt'
Propulsion: three diesels	fire-control radar, one 'High Pole-B'
delivering 11190 kW (15,000 hp) to	IFF and one 'Square Head' IFF
three shafts	interrogator
Speed: 42 kts (77 km/h; 48 mph)	**Complement:** 30

'Tarantul' class Large fast attack craft

Built at Petrovsky, Leningrad, the first **'Tarantul I'-class** unit was completed in 1978. At first, western analysts thought that it was designated *a malyy raketnyy korabl* (**MRK**, or small rocket ship), which is usually translated in western terms as a missile corvette. However, it later became clear that its real classification was *raketnyy kater*, or missile cutter and that it should be considered a large fast attack craft.

In order to rectify some initial shortcomings of the design, later units in the initial building programme were fitted with updated electronics, becoming known as the **'Tarantul II' class**. In 1981 the first **'Tarantul III'** was completed. This carried two twin over-and-under container/ launchers for the SS-N-22 'Sunburn' missile in place of the original SS-N-2D 'Styx' system. The Mach-2.5 seaskimming 'Sunburn' has active radar-homing, and has a range in excess of 110 km (62 miles) against the 80 km (50 miles) range of the 'Styx'.

The 'Tarantuls' deploy a modified version of the Soviet navy's small ship armament of a fully automatic 76-mm (3-in) DP gun, capable of 120 rounds per minute, and two 30-mm 6-barrel Gatling gun mounts.

Most of the 'Tarantul Is' have been sold abroad – to Poland, East Germany, India, the Yemen and Romania. One of the former East German boats was acquired by the US Navy, while India has built seven more boats in addition to the five

One Soviet-built 'Tarantul I'-class missile corvette has undergone testing and evaluation by the US Navy. It was acquired from the Federal German navy in November 1991. Originally named Rudolf Egelhofer *in the East German navy, the ship was renamed* Hiddensee *after the reunification of Germany.*

delivered by the USSR.

Only a handful of 'Tarantul Is' were still active with the Russian Navy in the Baltic in the late 1990s, but a dozen 'Tarantul IIs' and more than 20 'Tarantul IIIs' were in commission into the 21st century. Their operational status is uncertain, however, and many are thought to be unserviceable.

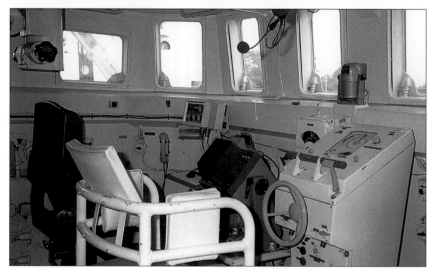

Right: The bridge of the USNS Hiddensee, seen while undergoing tests at the US Navy's Sea Systems Command.

Below: Carrying vastly more capable 'Sunburn' anti-ship missiles, the 'Tarantul III' remains in Russian service.

SPECIFICATION	
'Tarantul III' class	**Armament:** two twin container/
Displacement: 385 tons standard	launchers for four SS-N-22
and 455 tons full load	'Sunburn' anti-ship missiles, one
Dimensions: length 56.1 m	quadruple launcher for 16 SA-N-5
(184 ft); beam 11.5 m (37 ft 8 in);	'Grail' SAMs, one 76-mm (3-in) DP
draught 2.5 m (8 ft 2 in)	and two 6-barrel 30-mm CIWS guns
Propulsion: CODOG on two shafts,	**Electronics:** one 'Plank Shave'
with two Nikolayev Type DR 77 gas	surface-search radar, 'Light Bulb'
turbines delivering 11.77 MW	targeting data system, 'Hood Wink'
(16,000 hp) for performance or two	optronic director, Kivach III
CM 504 diesels delivering	navigation radar, 'Bass Tilt' gun
5.88 MW (8,000 hp) for cruising.	fire-control radar, 'High Pole-B' and
Speed: 36 kts (66 km/h; 76 mph)	'Square Head' IFF, 'Foal Tail' sonar,
Range: 400 miles (644 km) at 36	four passive ECM systems, and four
kts or 1,650 miles (2655 km) at 14	PK-10 ten-barrel chaff launchers
kts (26 km/h; 16 mph)	**Complement:** 34

Vosper vessels
'Ramadan', 'Waspada' and 'Qahir' classes

As seen in the 1980s, the Waspada *is the lead craft of a class whose other two units are the* Pejuang *and* Seteria. *The craft are each powered by two MTU 20V 538 TB91 diesels delivering 5720 kW (7,670 shp) to two shafts for a maximum speed of 32 kts. Improvements in 1998-2000 included Type 1007 radar and a Radamec 2500 optronic director.*

In 1977 Egypt contracted with the British shipbuilder Vosper Thornycroft for six missile craft to complement its ageing force of six 'Osa I'-, four 'Komar'- and six 'October'-class craft, of which the last is a locally built variant of the 'Komar' with two Otomat SSMs. Vosper came up with a design that was designated as the **'Ramadan' class** by the Egyptians. The first was launched in 1979 and the last in 1980, and all were in service by 1982. Designed to face Israeli missile craft classes on equal terms, the boats have an operations room equipped with a Marconi Sapphire fire-control system with two radar and TV weapons directors. Two alternative optical fire-control directors are also carried. A Racal electronic warfare suite (Cutlass ESM and Cygnus ECM systems) is

also fitted. The main gun armament comprises a single 76-mm (3-in) DP gun forward. This gun is effective out to 7000 m (7,655 yards) for AA fire and 15000 m (16,405 yards) in the surface-to-surface role. Aft is a twin 40-mm Breda AA mounting, while the missile armament comprises four launchers for Otomat Mk 1 SSMs. To back the 'Ramadans', the older missile boats have gradually been modernised.

Brunei order
The three 206-ton units of the **'Waspada' class** were built for Brunei by Vosper (Singapore) in 1977-79 and modernised in the late 1980s. The type's primary armament is two MM.38 Exocet SSMs. Though now eclipsed by Brunei's procurement of three 'Brunei'-class missile corvettes, they are nevertheless significant units

in local waters. They received upgraded electronics in 1998-2000 to keep them combat-capable.

Larger craft for Oman
Vosper Thornycroft was contracted in April 1992 by Oman to supply two 1,450-ton **'Qahir'-class** corvettes. The **Qahir al Amwaj** was accepted in 1996 and commissioned after working up in the UK, and the **Al Mua'zzar** followed in 1997. With an overall length of 83.7 m (274.6 ft), the design is based on that of the Mk 9

corvette but with new stealth features including a hull and superstructure designed to minimise radar cross section: avoiding sharp angles, the superstructure incorporates a measure of radar-absorbent materials.

Each armed with eight MM.40 Exocet missiles backed by a 76-mm (3-in) gun, a Crotale NG octuple launcher for 16 SAMs, and possibly two triple 12.75-in (324-mm) tubes for anti-submarine torpedoes, the ships are the most powerful units in the Omani navy. The ships have a stern platform

for Super Lynx helicopters, are good sea boats capable of 28 kts, and have mainly Thales Nederland (formerly Signaal) electronics including the TACTICOS combat data system that automatically evaluates threats and prioritises weapon assignment. On the mast is the MW-08 air/surface search radar, and other equipment includes the STING fire-control radar and an optronic sensor array comprising TV and IR cameras and a laser rangefinder. Targets can be acquired at up to 36 km (22.5 miles).

SPECIFICATION	
'Ramadan' class	**Performance:** speed 40 kts; range 2975 km (1,850 miles) at 18 kts
Displacement: 307 tons full load	**Armament:** see text
Dimensions: length 52 m (170 ft 7 in); beam 7.6 m (25 ft); draught 2 m (6 ft 7 in)	**Electronics:** S 820 search radar, S 810 navigation radar, two ST 802 fire-control radars, Sapphire fire-control system and ECM suite
Propulsion: four MTU 20V 538 TB91 diesels delivering 13400 kW (17,970 shp) to four shafts.	**Complement:** 30

Lead craft of a class whose other units are the Khyber, El Kadessaya, El Yarmouk, Badr *and* Hettein, *the* Ramadan *was commissioned in July 1981. In 2001 a contract was signed for the upgrade of these craft in 2002-07 with renovated S 820 and ST 802 radars, Mk 2 rather than Mk 1 Otomat anti-ship missiles, and the NAUTIS 3 combat data system in place of the original CAAIS.*

Above: Its two 'Qahir'-class multi-role guided-missile corvettes provide the Omani navy with a very considerable capability by local standards. The helicopter platform over the stern can support a machine up to the size of the Eurocopter Super Puma.

Brooke Marine craft 'Kebir', 'Mamba' and 'Madaraka' classes

El Mourakef was completed in 1983 and was one of the original pair of British-built 'Kebir'-class FAC(G)s. The two units were completed with a 76-mm (3-in) OTO-Melara compact gun forward and also two 14.5-mm (0.57-in) machine-guns on a twin mounting, while later craft were completed to a less capable standard with two mountings (forward and aft), each carrying two 25-mm Soviet cannon.

In 1981 the Algerian government ordered from Brooke Marine of the UK the first two fast attack craft (gun) of a planned 15 **'Kebir'-class** units. Based on the company standard 37.5-m (123-ft) hull, the craft were supplied to the purchaser in 1982 without armament and sailed for Algeria in September 1982 and June 1983 respectively. After that, the Algerians themselves assembled and/or built additional units at the ECRN yard at Mers-el-Kebir with the assistance of another British company, Vosper Thornycroft. Of these additional units, seven were completed in the 1980s and a final pair in 1997-98. The class thus comprises the *El Yadekh*, *El Mourakeb*, *El Kechef*, *El Moutarid*, *El Rassed*, *El Djari*, *El Saher*, *El Moukadem*, *El Mayher* and two others.

The first two craft each received the primary armament of one 76-mm (3-in) OTO-Melara gun, while the others received two twin 25-mm DP guns, the latter firing a 0.34-kg (0.75-lb) projectile to a range of 3000 m (3,280 yards) at the rate of 270 rounds per minute. The class, six of whose units have been transferred to the

Algerian coast guard service, possess only a very limited electronic capability, namely a single surface search and navigation radar supported, in just the first two British-built craft, by a Lawrence Scott optronic director for the 76-mm gun.

The original Algerian plan called for a class of 15 craft, but it is highly unlikely that the last four units will ever be built.

Barbadian half-sister

Brooke Marine supplied another unit of the same basic type to Barbados. The *Trident* was commissioned in 1981 and modernised in the Bender Shipyard during 1990. Intended solely for the patrol task, the *Trident* is armed with only a pair of 0.5-in (12.7-mm) machine-guns, and has a maximum speed of 29 kts on the 3730 kW (5,000 shp) delivered to two shafts by a pair of Paxman Valenta 12CM diesels. The vessel's range is 5630 km (3,500 miles) at 12 kts.

Kenyan craft

Laid down in 1972 and launched in 1973, the 160-ton *Mamba* was commissioned into the Kenyan navy in 1974 and deleted in

2000. As part of an extensive modernisation in 1982, it received Israeli Gabriel anti-ship missiles and new electronics; it returned to the UK in 1989 for another comprehensive overhaul and was shipped back to Kenya in 1990 with the similar but slightly smaller 145-ton *Madaraka*, the lead unit of a three-strong class based on the Brooke Marine 32.6-m (107-ft) hull and also including the *Jamhuri* and *Harambee*.

These large patrol craft of the **'Madaraka' class** had been ordered from Brooke Marine in May 1973. All three craft were commissioned in June 1975, and a few years later were each upgraded with more capable anti-ship weapons in the form of four Gabriel Mk 2 missiles as part of an upgrade of Kenyan navy vessels with Israeli weapons. The three craft were successively returned to the UK for refitting at Brooke Marine's Portchester facility in 1989-90, 1991-92 and 1993-94 respectively. However, after a protracted period of inactivity and lack of operational capability, the three craft were finally deleted in 1999 (*Jamhuri* and *Harambee*) and 2000 (*Madaraka*).

SPECIFICATION

'Kebir' class
Displacement: 166 tons standard; 200 tons full load
Dimensions: length 37.5 m (123 ft); beam 6.9 m (22 ft 7 in); draught 1.7 m (5 ft 7 in)
Propulsion: two MTU 12V 538 TB92 diesels delivering 3800 kW (5,095 shp) to two shafts
Performance: speed 27 kts; range 6115 km (3,800 miles) at 12 kts

Armament: one 76-mm (3-in) OTO-Melara Compact or two twin Soviet 25-mm L/60 guns and, in the first five units, one twin 14.5-mm (0.57-in) Soviet machine-gun
Electronics: Racal Decca 1226 surface search radar and, in first two units, one Lawrence Scott optronic director
Complement: 27

SPECIFICATION

'Mamba' class
Displacement: 125 tons standard; 160 tons full load
Dimensions: length 37.5 m (123 ft), beam 6.9 m (22 ft 7 in), draught 1.6 m (5 ft 2 in)
Propulsion: two Paxman Ventura 17YJCM diesels delivering 2980 kW (4,000 shp) to two shafts

Performance: speed 25 kts; range 5550 km (3,450 miles) at 13 kts
Armament: four Gabriel Mk 2 SSMs, and two 40-mm Bofors AA guns
Electronics: one Decca RM 916 surface search radar, and Selenia RTN 10X fire-control system
Complement: 25

SPECIFICATION

'Madaraka' class
Displacement: 120 tons standard; 145 tons full load
Dimensions: length 32.6 m (107 ft); beam 6.1 m (20 ft) draught 1.7 m (5 ft 7 in)
Propulsion: two Paxman Valenta 16RP 200M diesels delivering 4025 kW (5,400 shp) to two shafts

Performance: speed 25 kts; range 4265 km (2,650 miles) at 12 kts
Armament: four Gabriel Mk 2 SSMs, and two 30-mm Oerlikon AA cannon
Electronics: one RM-916 surface search radar and one Selenia RTN 10X fire-control system
Complement: 21

In its original 1975 form as depicted here, the Madaraka was a simple large patrol craft with armament limited to 30-mm Oerlikon cannon in mountings fore and aft of the superstructure. Four Israeli Gabriel Mk 2 anti-ship missiles were added in a modernisation of 1981-82.

'Falster' class Minelayer

Because of the strategic nature of Denmark's position across the entrance and exit to the Baltic Sea, the Danish navy has invested part of its defensive capabilities in minelayers. The larger of the two types currently in use is the NATO-designed **'Falster' class**, originally of four ships. Named after Danish islands, the **Falster**, **Fyen**, **Møen** and **Sjaelland** were ordered in 1960-62 and launched in 1962-63. They have a flush-decked steel hull with a raking stem and a prominent knuckle forward, a full stern through which four mine laying tracks are run to lay the mines, and the type of structural strengthening of the hull that permits the ships to operate in ice.

There was also a near-sistership, the **Nusret** launched in Denmark in 1964, that served with the Turkish navy as a minelayer until the vessel was deleted in 2001.

The *Falster* and *Sjaelland* were deleted in 2000, and in peacetime the two surviving ships are generally used on other duties, with the *Møen* converted to a midshipman training ship with specialist ECM gear aboard, and the *Fyen* converted first in 1976 as a depot ship for Denmark's

small fleet of conventional submarines and torpedo/missile boats, and later for midshipman training. In wartime both units would revert to the minelaying role with only minimal internal changes. When the *Møen* is unavailable for training duties the *Fyen* is used instead. The class can lay both moored and ground mine types.

Modernisation

The two ships have been somewhat modernised with the Terma TDS command and control system and, for improved self-defence capability in the face of low-level air attack provision for three twin launchers for Stinger short-range SAMs in place of the 20-mm Oerlikon cannon that are generally shipped. In 1997-98, more advanced electronics were added in the form of new radars (9 GR 608 air/surface search, NWS-2 surface search, Terma Pilot navigation and CGS-1 fire-control) and two Sea Gnat DL-6T six-barrel launchers for chaff and IR flare decoys.

The ships' offensive capability was also enhanced by a programme, undertaken in collaboration with Germany, to update the country's stocks of moored and bottom mines.

Møen **underway. Denmark is a small country in a strategically vital position, and to extract maximum value from the two surviving 'Falster' vessels, operates them for training and support roles when they are not needed for operational tasks. Four tracks are fitted so that up to 400 mines can be laid over the stern.**

SPECIFICATION	
'Falster' class (as built)	Mk 33 DP guns, four 20-mm AA
Displacement: 1,800 tons	guns, and up to 400 mines
standard; 1,900 tons full load	**Electronics:** one CWS-2
Dimensions: length 77 m (252 ft	air/surface search radar, one
6 in); beam 12.5 m (41 ft); draught	MWS-1 tactical radar, one NWS-2
4 m (13 ft)	navigation radar, one WM-46 fire-
Propulsion: two diesels delivering	control system, two 57-mm
3580 kW (4,800 shp) to two shafts	(2.24-in) multi-barrel decoy
Performance: speed 17 kts	launchers, and (*Møen*) ECM system
Armament: two twin 3-in (76-mm)	**Complement:** 120

Denmark has long been in a position to control access to the Baltic Sea, and the 'Falster' class of minelayers stood ready to block the channels connecting the North Sea and the Baltic. The Møen is fitted as a training ship and the Fyen as a depot vessel, but both can quickly revert to their designed role.

'Circé' class Minehunter

The French admiralty ordered the first of the **'Circé' class** of minehunters in 1968, and the eventual five units of the class were the **Cybèle**, **Calliope**, **Clio**, **Circé** and **Cérès**, these being commissioned into service during 1972-73. The class was designed solely for the hunting and destruction of ground and moored mines laid to depths of about 60 m (200 ft). To locate the mines a DUBM 20 minehunting sonar is carried and, once located, the mines are either destroyed by the six-strong detachment of divers (together with Gemini dinghies) or one of the two remotely controlled PAP 104

submersibles that are capable of 6 kts. These each weigh 700 kg (1,543 lb), are 2.7 m (8 ft 10 in) long and 1.1 m (3 ft 7 in) in diameter. Following the initial detection, they are lowered over the side aft by a large hydraulic winch mounted on the centreline. The PAP is then guided towards the contact via a 500-m (1,640-ft) cable. Once in the mine's vicinity, the TV camera in the nose is used for positive identification of the target as a mine and a 100-kg (220-lb) HE disposal charge is released next to it. The PAP is then guided back to the mother ship, recovered aboard and the charge detonated by an ultrasonic

Circé **was built in the early 1970s and was one of five vessels that were constructed solely for the minehunting role. As such, they carry no conventional minesweeping equipment such as sweeps.**

signal. To aid in the plotting and classification processes involved during a hunt, an EVEC automatic plotting table is fitted in the sonar and operations control room, which is located in the superstructure forward of the bridge.

To reduce the magnetic and acoustic signatures of the vessels their hulls were constructed in a sandwich of wood and foam, the outer skin being covered by a thin film of GRP. The deckhead and superstructure are a composite of wood and glassfibre resin. All the propulsion systems can be operated from the bridge or a sound-proofed control room located above the main deck.

In September 1997 France sold the five 'Circé' minehunters to Turkey, where the vessels form the **'Edincik' class** after being refitted with the more capable Mintac minehunting system including the improved DUBM 20B sonar.

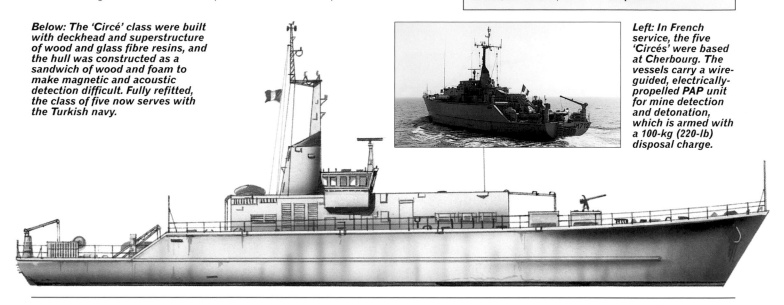

Below: The 'Circé' class were built with deckhead and superstructure of wood and glass fibre resins, and the hull was constructed as a sandwich of wood and foam to make magnetic and acoustic detection difficult. Fully refitted, the class of five now serves with the Turkish navy.

Left: In French service, the five 'Circés' were based at Cherbourg. The vessels carry a wire-guided, electrically-propelled PAP unit for mine detection and detonation, which is armed with a 100-kg (220-lb) disposal charge.

Tripartite type Coastal minehunter

A collaborative venture, the **Tripartite type** minehunter design was created by Belgium, France and the Netherlands. Belgium received 10 units of the **'Flower' class** in 1985-91, but in 1993 sold three to France. France had 10 units of the **'Éridan' class** that entered service in 1984-88, and after one had been sold in 1992 to Pakistan, which built a further two vessels of the **'Munsif' class**, ordered a replacement completed in 1996. The Netherlands took 15 examples of the **'Alkmaar' class** in 1984-89, but deleted three in 2000. The Dutch also supplied Indonesia with two vessels of the **'Pulau Rengat' class**.

Design

The design has the hull, decks and partitions made out of some 180 tons of a glass weave/polyester resin (GRP) compound, and the propulsion is essentially the same as that fitted to the French 'Circé' class. A DUBM 21A minehunting sonar, smaller and more advanced than the DUBM 20A fitted to the 'Circés', is carried as a retractable hull system to detect and classify ground and moored mines down to a depth of 80 m (260 ft). The 'Eridans' also have a position for a second sonar control centre on the upper deck aft to provide facilities for the DUBM 41 towed side-scan sonar system. The European classes also carry one light mechanical drag sweep to deal with moored mines.

The Dutch 'Alkmaar' class are undergoing a major modernisation programme, adding an improved hull-mounted sonar and propelled variable-depth sonar.

Left: Myosotis was one of seven 'Flower'-class MHCs in service with Belgium in 2003. This vessel is modified as an ammunition transport.

Below: The Tripartite type minehunters carry DUBM 21A minehunting sonar, an improved version of the DUBM 20A carried by the French 'Circé' class. This can detect and identify mines down to a depth of 80 m (260 ft).

'Lerici' and 'Gaeta' classes MHC/MSC

Italy ordered the four **'Lerici'-class** coastal mine hunter/minesweeper (MHC/MSC) vessels in January 1978 from Intermarine at Sarzana. Delayed for a while until a bridge under which they had to pass had been rebuilt, they are constructed of shock-resistant heavy GRP materials, and are equipped to carry an indigenous remotely operated MIN 77 minehunting submersible as well as six divers with CAM mine destructor charges. The sonar used is a licence-built version of the US 'Squeaky Fourteen' (SQQ-14) system, modified into a VDS lowered from a centreline well.

Capable of 5 kts, the MIN system consists of a 1300 kg (2,866 lb) GRP vehicle fitted with a sonar and an underwater TV camera. For destruction of ground mines an 85 kg (187 lb) HE charge

is carried, while moored mines are allowed to float to the surface for destruction by gunfire, by the cutting of their mooring chains with a small HE charge. Operations with the MIN are possible up to 250 m (820 ft) away from the mother ship at depths down to 150 m (490 ft).

The four vessels are the **Lerici**, **Sapri**, **Milazzo** and **Vieste**. A further eight to the improved **'Gaeta' class** design, with 2.5 m (8 ft 2 in) more length, a reduced magnetic signature and the MIN Mk 2 (Pluto Gigas) ROV, were delivered in 1992-96 as the **Gaeta**, **Termoli**, **Alghero**, **Numana**, **Crotone**, **Viareggio**, **Chioggia** and **Rimini**.

In 1985 the Malaysian navy commissioned four vessels of the original design as the **Mahamiru**, **Jerai**, **Ledang** and **Kinabula**, while the Nigerian navy commis-

Termoli *is seen in service with the Italian navy. Launched between the early 1980s and mid-1990s, a total of 12 of these GRP-hulled ships is in Italian service, with another six built for Australia, four for Malaysia, two for Nigeria, two for Thailand and 12 (to a modified design) for the US Navy.*

sioned the **Ohue** and **Maraba** in 1987-88. The Malaysian craft are fitted with French Ibis minehunting sonar and two PAP 104 mine disposal systems, while the Nigerian units are of the

standard type except for the smaller Pluto ROV of the 'Gaetas'. Thailand has the **Lat Ya** and **Tha Din Daeng**, commissioned in 1999, as revised 'Saeta'-class units with two MTU diesel

engines and the German MWS 80-6 minehunting system with Pluto ROVs. All these carry an Oropesa wire sweep to deal with moored mines.

SPECIFICATION	
'Lerici' class	1105 kW (1,480 shp) to three low-speed propellers
Displacement: 620 tons full load	**Speed:** 15 kts
Dimensions: length 50 m (164 ft); beam 9.9 m (32 ft 6 in); draught 2.6 m (8 ft 6 in)	**Armament:** one 25-mm gun
	Electronics: one SPN-728(V)3 navigation radar, radio navigation system, SQQ-14(IT) minehunting sonar, and one MIN 77 ROV
Propulsion: one Fincantieri GMT diesel delivering 1480 kW (1,985 shp) to one shaft, and three Isotta-Fraschini diesels delivering	**Complement:** 47

The 'Lerici'-class mine countermeasures vessels were completed to carry the Italian MIN 77 minehunting submersible and six divers, who fix CAM mine destructor charges. Originally equipped with 20-mm guns, these were superseded by 25-mm weapons after 1999.

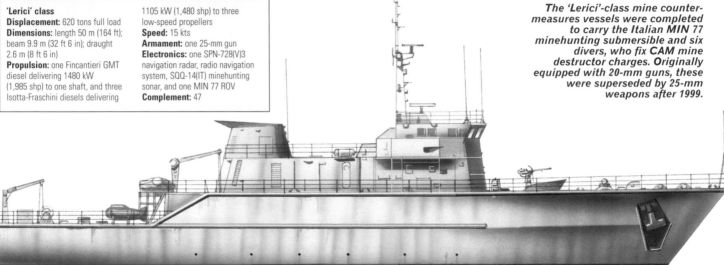

'Osprey' class Coastal minehunter (MHC)

In the mid-1980s the US Navy came to the belated realisation that its coastal mine-countermeasures capability had decayed to an unacceptable level, and decided to order a new **'Osprey' class** of minehunters based closely on the design of the Italian 'Lerici' class. The Department of Defence placed a design contract with Intermarine of Italy in August 1986, and a contract for the lead vessel followed in May 1987. Intermarine then purchased the Sayler Marine Corporation of Savannah, Georgia, to become Intermarine USA. This yard built eight of the 12 vessels, the other four being built by Avondale of Gulfport. There were plans for eight examples of a lengthened version, based generally on

The 12 'Osprey'-class vessels are limited to the coastal minehunter role with the SLQ-48 system. The system's orange-painted ROV is evident on the fantail of this unit, the USS Cardinal, built by Intermarine from 1996 and commissioned in October 1997.

the 'Gaeta' class of improved 'Lericis', but after considerable delays these plans were then dropped.

The US opted for a much

modified engine installation with two engines in place of the Italian ships' single engine, and problems associated with this change

greatly delayed the whole programme, which was also adversely affected by design and equipment modifications that eventually added

110 tons to the displacement. The two Italian diesel engines are mounted on GRP cradles inside acoustic enclosures, and drive Voith

The basic similarity of the American 'Osprey' class to the Italian 'Lerici' class is evident in this view of the USS Oriole, which was built by Intermarine USA and commissioned in September 1995.

SPECIFICATION

'Osprey' class
Displacement: 959 tons full load
Dimensions: length 57.2 m (187 ft 8 in); beam 11 m (35 ft 11 in); draught 2.9 m (9 ft 6 in)
Propulsion: two Isotta-Fraschini ID 36 SS 8V AM diesels delivering 1195 kW (1,600 shp) to two shafts, and three Isotta-Fraschini ID 36 diesel generators delivering 984 kW (1,321 shp) to two low-speed electric motors
Performance: speed 12 kts; endurance 2780 km (1,730 miles) at

12 kts
Armament: two 0.5-in (12.7-mm) machine-guns
Electronics: one SPS-64(V) or SPS-67 surface search radar, one R41XX navigation radar, one SYQ-13 combat data system, one SYQ-109 combat data system, one USQ-119(V) NTCS-A, one SLQ-48 mine neutralisation system with one ROV, one DGN-4 degaussing system, and one SQQ-32(V)3 active variable-depth minehunting sonar
Complement: 51

cycloidal propellers whose use obviates the need for forward thrusters for station keeping. The ships have an integrated combat and machinery control system for more effective operation in the minehunting role.

A single-role type limited to the minehunting or mine-sweeping task at any one time, and thus with no capability for the embarkation of any mechanical minesweeping equipment when the minehunting gear is carried, the 'Osprey'-class ship is based on a monocoque GRP hull whose high strength removed any need for frames. This hull includes a forward-mounted centreline well for the variable-depth minehunting sonar, which is used in association with the Alliant Techsystems SLQ-48 mine-neutralisation system, based on a ROV with 1065 m (3,500 ft) of cable. From 2005 the Integrated Combat Weapons System Block 1 is to be retrofitted to upgrade the existing systems, which include the SYQ-13 and SYQ-109 combat data systems, and the USQ-119(V) NTCS-A.

All of the vessels are operated by the Naval Reserve Force, and were commissioned between November 1993 and March 1999 as the *Osprey*, *Heron*, *Pelican*, *Robin*, *Oriole*, *Kingfisher*, *Cormorant*, *Black Hawk*, *Falcon*, *Cardinal*, *Raven* and *Shrike*. All of these except the *Cardinal* and *Raven*, which are based in Bahrain, are homeported in the continental US.

'Huon' class Coastal minehunter (MHC)

From the time of the USSR's collapse as a super-power, with the end of the Cold War as an inevitable consequence, Australia sensibly realised that there would be a destabilisation of the current world order and thus a rise of the potential for regional conflict. The associated problems of how the Australian Defence Forces should be restructured and re-equipped to cope with these new types of threat were addressed at an early stage in the Force Structure Review of 1991. One of the review's recommendations was that the Australian navy should acquire a force of coastal minehunters of an existing type already well proved in service.

Faced with a need to operate in deeper and more exposed waters than was possible with the two small inshore minehunters then in service, the Australian navy decided to order a variant of the Italian 'Gaeta'-class minehunter, which also offered a higher transit speed and greater on-station endurance than the current vessels. In August 1994 a contract was signed for Australian Defence Industries to build six 'Huon'-class minehunters at its yard in Newcastle, New South Wales. The hull of the first vessel was built by Intermarine in its Italian yard at Sarzana and then shipped to Australia for completion, while the other five were built wholly in Australia for an overall Australian programme content of about 69 per cent.

The six vessels, all named for Australian rivers and based at HMAS *Waterhen* in Sydney, are the *Huon*, *Hawkesbury*, *Norman*, *Gascoyne*, *Diamantina* and *Yarra*, which were commissioned during the period 1999-2002.

The vessels are of monocoque (frameless) GRP construction, and among their equipment is a recompression chamber for the six-man diving team, a rigid inflatable boat, an inflatable diving boat, a minehunting/sweeping system based on two Bofors SUTEC Double Eagle Mk 2 mine-disposal vehicles with

DAMDIC charges and a double Oropesa mechanical sweep able to tow the Australian Mini-Dyad influence sweep.

SPECIFICATION

'Huon' class
Displacement: 720 tons full load
Dimensions: length 2.5 m (172 ft 3 in); beam 9.9 m (32 ft 6 in); draught 3 m (9 ft 10 in)
Propulsion: one Fincantieri GMT diesel delivering 1480 kW (1,986 shp) to one shaft, and three Isotta-Fraschini 1300 diesels delivering 1060 kW (1,440 shp) to three electro-hydraulic low-speed motors
Performance: speed 14 kts; endurance 2960 km (1,840 miles) at

12 kts
Armament: one 30-mm MSI DS 30B gun
Electronics: one Kelvin Hughes 1007 navigation radar, one Radamec optronic surveillance system, one Nautis 2M combat data system, one Prism ESM system, two Super Barricade chaff launchers, two Double Eagle Mk 2 ROVs, and one Type 2093 variable-depth mine search and classification sonar
Complement: 38

HMAS Diamantina was completed in the spring of 2002 as the fifth of the Royal Australian Navy's six 'Huon'-class coastal minehunters.

'Lindau' class Coastal minesweeper/minehunter (MSC/MHC)

The **'Lindau'** or **Type 320 class** of 18 coastal minesweepers were the first naval vessels built in West Germany after World War II. Constructed to a NATO standard design adapted for West Germany, they have a wooden hull and a superstructure of non-magnetic materials. In 1968-69 the **Fulda** was converted to a minehunter of the **Type 331A class**, the **Flensburg** following in 1970-71. This proved so successful that in 1976-79 a further 10 vessels were modified to a similar standard but without the retractable Scholtel propeller system for low-speed manoeuvring. These **Type 331B** minehunters were the **Lindau**, **Tübingen**, **Minden**, **Koblenz**, **Göttingen**, **Cuxhaven**, **Weilheim**, **Marburg**, **Völklingen** and **Wetzlar**. The vessels of neither subclass carried any mechanical sweep gear, but instead embarked six divers, a hydraulic crane and two French PAP 104 remotely controlled submersibles to work with the Type 193M minehunting sonar.

In 1979-83 the remaining six 'Lindaus', namely the **Schleswig**, **Paderborn**, **Düren**, **Konstanz**, **Wolfsburg** and **Ulm**, were converted as **Type 351** drone minesweeper control vessels each fitted to control up to three F-1 Troika magnetic/acoustic/mechanical minesweeper drones as well as carrying the SGD-21 Oropesa mechanical sweep and an acoustic generator system. The 18 Seehund drones, each 25 m (81 ft 9 in) long with provision for a three-man passage crew, were in a pool from which the units were drawn as required. All 18 units of the 'Lindau' subclasses were allocated to the West German navy's North Sea mine countermeasures squadron.

'Lindau' exports

None of the vessels remained in German service after 2000, but Type 331 transfers included two (**Wambola** and **Sulev**) to Estonia in 2000, one (**Ayety**) to Georgia in 1997 as a patrol craft, one (**Nemejs**) to Latvia in 1999 and two (**Süduvis** and **Kursis**) to Lithuania in 1999-2000, and in 2001 South Africa gained two Type 351s (**Kapa** and **Thekwini**).

Düren, a Type 351 Troika control ship. As such it could guide up to three minesweeping drones, as well as retaining its moored and acoustic sweeping systems.

Paderborn was one of the six Type 351 control ship conversions. For passage to a sweep area the Troika minesweeper drones carried a crew of three which were taken off for operations.

Like all the other units of its class, the Koblenz was built by Burmeister of Bremen. The vessel was launched in May 1957, became a Type 331B coastal minehunter in June 1978, and in 1999 was transferred to the Lithuanian naval service as the Süduvis, together with Kursis (ex-Marburg).

SPECIFICATIONS

Type 331A/B class	Type 351 class
Displacement: 388 tons standard; 463 tons full load	**Displacement:** 388 tons standard; 488 tons full load
Dimensions: length 47.1 m (154 ft 6 in); beam 8.3 m (27 ft 3 in); draught 3 m (9 ft 10 in)	**Dimensions:** length 47.1 m (154 ft 6 in); beam 8.3 m (27 ft 3 in); draught 2.8 m (9 ft 2 in)
Propulsion: two diesels delivering 2980 kW (4,000 shp) to two shafts	**Propulsion:** two diesels delivering 2980 kW (4,000 shp) to two shafts
Performance: speed 17 kts; range 1575 km (980 miles) at 16.5 kts	**Performance:** speed 16.5 kts
Armament: one 40-mm AA gun	**Armament:** one 40-mm Bofors AA gun
Electronics: one TSR/N or Kelvin Hughes 14/9 navigation radar, one Type 193M (Type 331A) or DSQS-11 (Type 331B) minehunting sonar, and two PAP 104 mine-disposal systems	**Electronics:** one TSR/N, Kelvin Hughes 14/9 or SPS-64 navigation radar, one drone-control radio system, and one DSQS-11 minehunting sonar
Complement: 46	**Complement:** 44

Launched in February 1957, Lindau was the first German-built vessel to join the German navy after World War II. To reduce vulnerability to mines with magnetic fuses, the hull was made of wood laminated with plastic glue, and the engines were made of non-magnetic materials. The vessel was later converted to Type 331B coastal minehunter (MHC) standard.

'Hameln' and 'Frankenthal' classes MSC/MHC

By the early 1980s the West German navy had appreciated the fact that its force of minesweeping and minehunting vessels was approaching the stage of 'block obsolescence', and that the type in most urgent need of replacement was the 'Schütze' class of 30 fast inshore minesweepers. The German defence ministry contracted in July 1985 with STN Systemtechnik Nord as the prime contractor for what was eventually to total 22 fast coastal minesweepers and minehunters built by Abeking & Rasmussen (seven), Krögerwerft (six) and Lürssenwerft (nine).

The first of these vessels were the 10 coastal minesweepers of the **'Hameln'** or **Type 343 class** delivered in 1989-91 after construction to a design with a semi-buried forecastle and a structure based on a non-magnetic steel first developed for use in submarines. The armament was two 40-mm AA guns located on the forecastle and on a platform at the after end of the superstructure, and controlled by means of a WM20/2 fire-control system stripped from 'Zöbel'-class FACs as they were decommissioned.

In 2000-01, these 10 vessels were adapted into five minesweepers of the **'Ensdorf'** or **Type 352 class** (**Hameln**, **Pegnitz**, **Siegburg**, **Ensdorf** and **Auerbach**) and five minehunters of the **'Kulmbach'** (**Type 333**) **class** (**Überherrn**, **Laboe**, **Kulmbach**, **Passau** and **Herten**). The former each have a double Oropesa system for mechanical sweeping as well as the ability to control four Seehund remotely controlled minesweeping drones and a Sea Fox C remotely operated vehicle for mine disposal, while the latter each have eight to 10 Sea Fox I remotely operated disposable vehicles for mine inspection and up to 30 Sea Fox C mine disposal vehicles.

The half-sister to the 'Hameln' class, optimised from its initiation for the minehunter role, is the **'Frankenthal'** or **Type 322 class** whose 12 units, completed in 1992-98, are the **Frankenthal**, **Weiden**, **Rottweil**, **Bad Bevensen**, **Bad Rappenau**, **Grömitz**, **Datteln**, **Dillingen**, **Homburg**, **Sulzbach-Rosenburg**, **Fulda** and **Weilheim**. The vessels have only the forecastle-mounted 40-mm gun, which is being replaced by a 27-mm cannon, and no WM20/2 fire-control system, and carry two Nord Pinguin-B3 drones equipped with sonar and a TV camera in addition to two explosive anti-mine charges.

In 1999 Turkey ordered six similar vessels, the first from Abeking & Rasmussen and the other five from Pendik Naval Shipyard in Istanbul. The Turkish units, commissioned from 2003, have different engines and two PAP 104 anti-mine drones.

*M1063 is the **Bad Bevensen** coastal minehunter of the 'Frankenthal' class, built by Lürssenwerft and commissioned in December 1993. Principal equipment is two Pinguin-B3 drones with countermining charges.*

The vessels of the 'Frankenthal' class have only one Bofors 40-mm gun (being replaced by a Mauser 27-mm cannon), and no WM20/2 fire-control system. This is Rottweil.

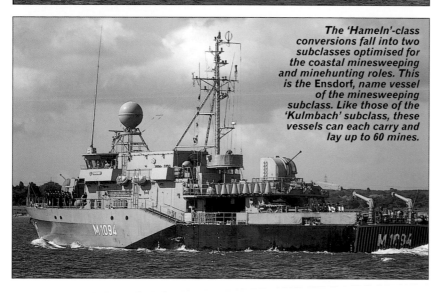

The 'Hameln'-class conversions fall into two subclasses optimised for the coastal minesweeping and minehunting roles. This is the Ensdorf, name vessel of the minesweeping subclass. Like those of the 'Kulmbach' subclass, these vessels can each carry and lay up to 60 mines.

Above: A striking feature of the vessels built as the 'Hameln' class is the egg-shaped radome above the bridge for the WM20/2 fire-control system's radar. M1099 is the Herten, completed by Krögerwerft in 1989.

SPECIFICATIONS

Type 332 'Frankenthal' class
Displacement: 650 tons full load
Dimensions: length 54.4 m (178 ft 6 in); beam 9.2 m (30 ft 2 in); draught 2.5 m (8 ft 2 in)
Propulsion: two diesels delivering 4150 kW (5,565 shp) to two shafts
Performance: speed 18 kts
Armament: one 40-mm AA gun being replaced by one 27-mm cannon, two Fliegerfaust 2 quad launchers for eight Stinger SAMs
Electronics: one SPS-64 navigation radar, one DSQS-11M minehunting sonar, MWS 80-4 combat data system, and two Pinguin-B3 mine-disposal systems
Complement: 37

Type 333 'Kulmbach' class
as Type 332 class except:
Displacement: 635 tons full load
Propulsion: two diesels delivering 4580 kW (6,145 shp) to two shafts
Armament: two 40-mm AA guns being replaced by 27-mm cannon, two Fliegerfaust 2 quad launchers for eight Stinger SAMs, and provision for 60 mines
Electronics: one SPS-64 navigation radar, one WM20/2 fire-control system, DR 2000 ESM, two Silver Dog chaff launchers, one DSQS-11M minehunting sonar, and Sea Fox mine-hunting/disposal system
Complement: 60

'Kondor II' class Ocean minesweeper (MSO)

Classified as high-seas or ocean minesweepers by the East German navy, the units of the **'Kondor II' class** were built between 1971 and 1978 at the Peenewerft shipyard, Wolgast, to replace the obsolete 'Habicht' and 'Krake' classes of minesweepers/minelayers. Twenty-four units were in service in the minesweep-

ing role during the 1980s, with several fitted with a large deckhouse abaft the main towed sweep reel to house a minehunting operations centre. A further three were used as training ships with the Walter Steffens Naval School, whilst another three served as trials ships to test new minesweeping techniques and equipment.

A further unit was extensively modified in 1978 to serve as the hydrographic survey ship **Karl Friedrich Gauss**, and the last unit was modified after launching with an enlarged superstructure to act as the state yacht **Ostseeland 1**.

Nineteen of the earlier vessels of the **'Kondor I' class**, which were classed

as coastal minesweepers, were transferred to the Grenze Brigade Küste (GBK, or coastal border guard) as patrol boats. However, they retained their sweeping gear and would have reverted to the minesweeper role on the outbreak of hostilities. A number of these continued in service with the unified German coast guard

(Küstenwache).

The 'Kondor II' MSO craft were sold off in the 1990s. Four went to Uruguay (one of which was later lost in a collision), two went to Latvia, and nine were transferred to Indonesia. 'Kondor I' craft were sold to Cape Verde (one), Malta (three) and Tunisia (six); all these vessels serve as patrol craft.

SPECIFICATION

'Kondor II' class
Displacement: 310 tons standard and 400 tons full load
Dimensions: length 55 m (180 ft 5 in); beam 7 m (23 ft); draught 2 m (6 ft 8 in)
Propulsion: two diesels delivering 2983 kW (4,000 shp) to two shafts

Speed: 21 kts
Armament: two or three twin 25-mm AA guns
Electronics: one TSR33 navigation radar, and several precision radio and sonar systems
Complement: 40

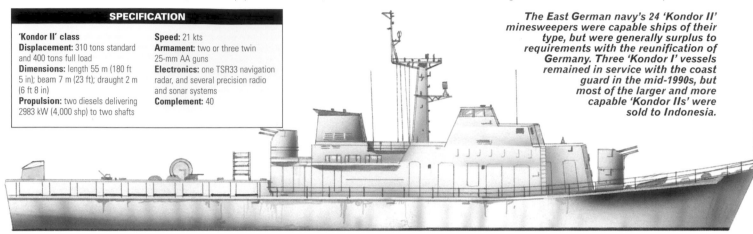

'Oksøy' and 'Alta' classes Minehunter/minesweeper (MHC/MSC)

The **'Oksøy'** and **'Alta'** classes are related mine warfare vessels, designed and built in Norway. Ordered from Kvaerner in November 1989, the four 'Oksøys', commissioned in 1994-95, are minehunters while the 'Altas' were commissioned in 1996-97 as minesweepers.

The vessels are catamarans constructed from a Fibre Reinforced Plastics (FRP) sandwich. As they move through the water an air cushion is created by the surface effect between the two hulls, reducing resistance and thus improving its speed. The catamaran design helps give the vessels a reasonably high transit speed to their chosen area of operations; it also gives a usefully low magnetic and acoustic signature and lessens the shock effect of exploding mines.

The minesweepers carry a conventional Oropesa mechanical sweep, an Agate air gun, Elma magnetic sweepers and transducer kit.

They can also be fitted with anti-mine mini-torpedoes.

The minehunters are equipped with a pair of Pluto remotely controlled mine killing vehicles. These are stored in the hangar area aft and launched by two hydraulic cranes. The cables connecting them to the mothership include a datalink to feed back images from the submersible's camera and search and scanning sonars. The camera can be switched from black and white low-light mode to colour. The submersible can travel at up to 4 kts and all its transmissions can be recorded for subsequent analysis.

Hull-mounted sonar

The minesweepers also carry an SA 950 hull-mounted sonar. This active sonar scans at high frequency (95 kHz) to detect both moored and bottom mines. The minehunters have hull-mounted TSM 2023 sonars. This sonar can detect and classify mines and covers

As with most modern minesweepers, the 'Oksøy' and 'Alta' classes are built from plastics, which greatly reduces the risk of activating magnetic mines. Måløy (M342) is a minehunter of the 'Oksøy' class.

a bearing of 90°; the system is fully steerable through 360°. In 2001, the minehunter **Karmøy** began testing the Hugin Autonomous Underwater Vehicle (AUV), designed to conduct route survey and forward mine reconnaissance.

The 'Oksøy' and 'Alta' classes are powered by diesel engines but for fine manoeuvring during minehunting operations they are equipped with two Kvaerner Eureka waterjets.

One vessel has been lost: the minesweeper **Orkla** caught fire off the Norwegian coast and was destroyed in 2002. In addition, one 'Alta'-class minesweeper is due to be converted to operate as a clearance diver support vessel.

SPECIFICATION

'Oksøy' and 'Alta' classes
Names: Oksøy (M340), Karmøy (M341), Måløy (M342), Hinnøy (M343), Alta (M350), Otra (M351), Rauma (M352), Orkla (M353), Glomma (M354)
Displacement: 375 tons
Dimensions: length 55.2 m (181 ft); beam 13.6 m (44 ft 8 in); draught 2.5 m (8 ft 3 in)
Propulsion: two MTU diesels delivering 2760 kW (3,700 shp) to two shafts, two Kvaerner Eureka waterjets

Speed: 20 kts
Armament: one twin Sadral launcher for Mistral SAMs, one or two 20-mm guns, and two 12.7-mm (0.5-in) machine guns
Electronics: two Decca navigation radars, TSM 2023N hull-mounted sonar (MHC) or SA 950 hull-mounted sonar (MSC), two Pluto submersibles (MHC) or Agate acoustic and Elma magnetic sweep (MSC)
Complement: 38 (MHC) or 32 (MSC)

Norway's mine warfare craft are a cross between air-cushion vehicles and true catamarans. Air passing between the twin hulls creates a surface effect on which the main structure of the vessel rides.

'Segura' class Coastal minehunter (MHC)

Four minehunters of the **'Segura' class** are operated by the Spanish navy. Built by Izar (formerly Bazán) at their Cartegena yard, the name-ship was commissioned in November 1998; **Sella** followed in 1999, **Tambre** in February 2000 and **Turia** in September 2000. Two additional units were ordered in 2001 with an option on two more. The **Duero** and **Tajo** were under construction as of April 2003.

The 'Segura' class are intended to detect and deal with mines to a depth of 200 m (656 ft) for bottom mines and 300 m (984 ft) for moored mines. The hull is a single skin of GRP with stiffening elements in the transverse and base frames. A layer of vinylester resin serves to protect the outer layer of the vessel.

Sound deadening

As with all modern mine warfare vessels, the hull is designed to withstand the shock of an underwater explosion but the intention is to avoid setting a mine off through the maximum use of low magnetic materials. Even the electric motors are built with this in mind and have compensated stray fields. The machinery spaces are positioned between watertight bulkheads in the stern. The diesel generator is topside to reduce noise levels below the waterline.

The afterdeck features a launch and recovery area for a remote-controlled mine disposal vehicle plus two cranes. A closed hangar serves as a storage area and to provide support facilities for divers as well as to store two inflatable boats with silent outboard engines. The 'Segura'-class vessels include a decompression chamber for the divers.

The ROV is the Gayrobot Pluto Plus, which can locate, classify and destroy all known types of sea mine to a maximum depth of 300 m (984 ft). This will be supplemented in future by a new system from Kongsberg, the

Below: The 'Seguras' form the 1st MCM Squadron, based at Cartagena alongside a number of ex-US Navy coastal minesweepers.

'mine sniper': this 30-kg (66-lb) one-shot anti-mine device is a remotely controlled semi-submersible with a maximum range of 4000 m (4,374 ft).

The 'Segura' class employ AN/SQQ-32 variable depth sonar. This is used primarily to hunt mines which it can

detect and classify, but it can function as a side scan sonar. The towed section can be lowered to a maximum depth of 200 m (656 ft) or can operate from the hull.

The ships have an MTU-Bazán diesel engine for cruising between opera-

tions, but rely on a silent-running electric motor for propulsion during minehunting. Two independent cycloidal propellers provide steering and propulsion in both cruising and minehunting modes. Twin bow thrusters assist in fine manoeuvring.

Above: Based on the British 'Sandown' class designed by Vosper Thornycroft and modified to meet Spanish requirements, the 'Segura' class may eventually total 12 vessels. The lead ship in the class is pictured.

SPECIFICATION

'Segura' class
Names: Segura (M51), Sella (M52), Tambre (M53), Turia (M54)
Displacement: 530 tons full load
Dimensions: length 54 m (177 ft); beam 10.7 m (35 ft); draught 2.2 m (7 ft 3 in)
Propulsion: two MTU-Izar diesels delivering 1136 kW (1,523 shp) to two shafts; two electric motors for

mine hunting plus side thrusters
Speed: 14 kts; 7 kts for mine hunting
Armament: one 20-mm cannon
Electronics: one Kelvin-Hughes 1007 navigation radar, one SQQ-32 mine detection VDS, FABA/Inisel MCM system, two Pluto ROVs, and one Nautis combat data system
Complement: 40

'Landsort' class Coastal minehunter (MHC)

The Swedish minehunters of the **'Landsort' class** were ordered in 1981. Seven vessels were commissioned between 1984 and 1992 and then four more units of the **'Bedok' class** were built for Singapore between 1993 and 1995. Of the latter, Bedok was completed in Sweden but the rest of the class were prefabricated in Sweden and then shipped to Singapore for assembly and fitting out by Singapore Shipbuilding.

The 'Landsort' class incorporate the usual countermeasures employed by modern minehunters to avoid becoming a victim of the weapons they are built to detect and destroy. In the first place, the hulls are built to withstand the shock from a nearby underwater explosion. They emit little noise so as not to detonate an acoustic mine; their magnetic signature is minimal so as not to trigger a magnetic influence mine. The hull is

made from a special GRP developed by the Swedish navy and Karlskronavarvet; it is robust, easily repaired and both fire and shock resistant. It also helps absorb noise and only needs regular painting for maintenance.

Each of the 'Landsorts' mounts a single 40-mm Bofors gun on the upper deck. This can engage surface and aerial targets, but it can also be used to destroy mines floating on the surface. The 'Landsorts' also

carry four Saab Elma or Saab 601 ASW mortars, each with nine launch tubes. Built from non-magnetic materials, they fire 4.2-kg (9.2-lb) shaped charges to a range of 400 m (1,312 ft) and 1200 m (3,937 ft) respectively.

Minehunting gear

Each of the 'Landsort'-class minehunters carries a pair of Sutec Sea Eagle or Double Eagle remote-controlled submersibles capable of diving to 350 m (1,148 ft). The

'Bedok' class are equipped with the widely-used French-built PAP 104 Mk V ROVs.

The Swedish minehunters are also fitted to operate two SAM-class MCM drones. These are 20-ton remote-controlled catamarans that are used to sweep for magnetic and acoustic mines and were also used by the US Navy in the Persian Gulf after the 1991 Gulf War. The SAM II drones are 56-ton air cushion MCM drones currently under development.

The seven 'Landsort'-class minehunters of the Royal Swedish navy are optimised for operations in the difficult sonar conditions of the Baltic.

SPECIFICATION

'Landsort' class
Names: Landsort (M71), Arholma (M72), Koster (M73), Kullen (M74), Vinga (M75), Ven (M76), Ulvön (M77)
Displacement: 360 tons full load
Dimensions: length 47.5 m (155 ft 10 in); beam 9.6 m (31 ft 6 in); draught 2.2 m (7 ft 4 in)
Machinery: four Saab-Scania DSI 14 diesels delivering 1187 kW (1,592 shp) to two shafts
Speed: 15 kts
Armament: one Saab MANPADS, one Bofors Sea Trinity CIWS (Vinga) or one Bofors 40-mm gun (others),

two 7.62-mm (0.3-in) machine-guns, four Saab Elma or Saab 601 nine-tube anti-submarine mortars, and two Philax decoy launchers with four magazines each containing 36 IR/chaff grenades
Electronics: one Terma navigation radar, one TSM-2022 hull-mounted minehunting sonar, one Matilda ESM system, one 9LV 100 optronic director, one 9 MJ 400 minehunting system, two Sea Eagle or Double Eagle ROVs, and two SAM drones (see text)
Complement: 29

'Vanya I' and 'Vanya II' classes Coastal minesweepers

In series production 1960-73, the **'Vanya I'-class** minesweeper, known as the **Project 257D** and **Project 257M** in its wood- and steel-hulled variants respectively, was designated a *bazory tralshchik* (BT, or base minesweeper) design which could double as a mine-hunter. Some 69 'Vanya I' units remained in Soviet service in the mid-1980s but have since disappeared, while in the early 1970s six others (two of them scrapped in 1995) were transferred to the Bulgarian navy and two (now deleted) to the Syrian navy. One other unit was converted in 1974 to a pure minehunter configuration for research and development purposes. Its superstructure was extended forward, it had a twin 25-mm AA gun in place of the normal 30-mm mount, a lattice mast with 'Don Kay' navigation radar at the amidships break point, and two diver boats on the quarterdeck.

In 1976 three **'Vanya II'-class** or **Project 699B** units were built with a 1-m (3.3-ft) longer hull, higher-powered diesels, a more extensive fantail work area and heavier davits aft, and a 'Don Kay' rather than 'Don 2' navigation radar. This subvariant was used for guidance of up

to three 'Ilyusha'-class radio-controlled inshore mine-sweeper drones. The 'Ilyushas' displaced some 85 tons full load and were 26.4 m (86.6 ft) long, and

were believed to carry both normal sweep gear and a linear explosive mine-disposal system for laying over the stern. For transit purposes they carried a crew of 10.

Designated a bazory tralshchik (base minesweeper) by the Soviets, the 'Vanya' class was in series construction from the early 1960s to the early 1970s. It was the most numerous of the Soviet coastal minesweeper types, but largely disappeared from service in the late 1980s and early 1990s.

SPECIFICATION

'Vanya' classes
Displacement: 200 tons standard; 245 tons or ('Vanya II') 260 tons full load
Dimensions: length 40 m (131 ft 3 in) or ('Vanya II') 41 m (134 ft 6 in); beam 7.3 m (24 ft); draught 1.8 m (5 ft 11 in)
Propulsion: two diesels delivering 1640 kW (2,200 hp) or ('Vanya II')

two diesels delivering 3730 kW (5,003 hp) to two shafts
Performance: speed 16 kts
Armament: one twin 30-mm AA gun, and 8-16 mines
Electronics: one 'Don 2' or 'Don Kay' navigation radar, one 'Dead Duck' IFF, one 'High Pole-B' IFF, and one minehunting sonar
Complement: 30

'Yurka' class Ocean minesweeper

The 'Yurka' class's 'Drum Tilt' fire-control radar is carried at the top of the mainmast above the IFF systems and the navigation radar. Surprisingly, for an ocean mine-sweeper, the class lacks any ASW systems, which are fitted to earlier and later classes. Notable in this overhead view is the funnel's width.

Built in 1963-72 with a steel hull, the **'Yurka'-class** or **Project 266 Rubin** minesweeper was the smaller predecessor of the 'Natya' design without the latter's ASW weapons and stern ramp. Similarly designated *morskoy tralshchik* (MT, or seagoing mine-sweeper), the 'Yurkas' are now out of Russian service, but were fitted to sweep only acoustic and magnetic mines, using gear similar to that of Western minesweepers. Some 50 units were com-

pleted, of which two were transferred to the navy of Vietnam in 1979. Four other ships were built for the Egyptian navy, which received them in 1969, to a more austere configuration lacking the 'Drum Tilt' fire-control radar of the Soviet ships but with additional side scuttles for better beneath-decks air flow for service in hot climates.

The broad funnel indicated that the diesel engines were installed in a side-by-side arrangement in the engine room, and the

The 'Yurka' class was typical of Soviet thinking about ocean minesweeping from the late 1950s, with the whole of the ship's after end devoted to the task of sweeping any mines found by the 'Stag Ear' hull-mounted classification sonar.

The metal-hulled 'Yurka' class of ocean mine-sweepers was fitted for magnetic and acoustic sweeping operations. To improve their self-defence capabilities the units of the class were later retrofitted with SA-N-5 'Grail' SAM launchers.

SPECIFICATION	
'Yurka' class	**Performance:** speed 17 kts
Displacement: 460 tons standard; 540 tons full load	**Armament:** two twin 30-mm AA guns, and up to 10 mines
Dimensions: length 52.4 m (170 ft 11 in); beam 9.4 m (30 ft 10 in); draught 2.6 m (8 ft 6 in)	**Electronics:** one 'Don 2' navigation radar, one 'Drum Tilt' AA fire-control radar, two 'Square Head' IFF, one 'High Pole-B' IFF, and one 'Stag Ear' minehunting sonar
Propulsion: two M-503 diesels delivering 4000 kW (5,365 hp) to two shafts	**Complement:** 45

funnel was a useful aid in distinguishing the 'Yurkas' from the 'Natyas'. Several units were retrofitted with the standard light forces AA armament update package of two quadruple launchers (with reloads) for SA-N-5 'Grail' short-range SAMs. The class also continued the Soviet tradition of fitting its mine-counter-measures units with mine rails for the laying of defensive minefields in coastal and deep-sea anchorages. The minehunting sonar was the 'Stag Ear' variant of the 'Tamir' high-frequency active set modified for short-range classification of mine-like objects.

'Natya I' and 'Natya II' classes Ocean minesweepers

First reported in 1970, the steel/aluminium-hulled **'Natya I' class** or **Project 266M Akvamaren** was designated a *morskoy tralshchik* (MT, or seagoing mine-sweeper) by the Soviets and is the successor to the 'Yurka' class. The vessels were built at Kolpino and Khabarovsk in 1969-82, and the initial standard included two rigid davits aft, changed in the later craft to hydraulically operated articulated davits to handle the sweep gear and towed MCM bodies over the stern ramp. The 'Natya Is' are also equipped with two five-barrel RBU 1200 ASW rocket launchers to provide a coastal ASW escort capability, and most units were also retrofitted with two quadruple launchers for SA-N-5/8 'Grail'/'Gremlin' SAMs just abaft the lattice mast, while others have had a second navigation radar added atop the pilothouse.

In 1980, a single **'Natya II' class** aluminium-hulled variant was completed with a lengthened superstructure and the transom cut away amidships to take a 1.5-m (5-ft) sheath. This was a research and development vessel.

The 'Natya I' was also produced in modest numbers for the export market in a slightly more austere version. Some 23 were built for Ethiopia (one in 1991), India

(12 in 1978-88), Libya (eight in 1981-86), Syria (one in 1985) and Yemen (one in 1991). The Russians operate their surviving 10 units

Despite their waning numbers, the 'Natya'-class minesweepers provide the Russian navy with its only significant oceanic mine counter-measures capability. In the early 2000s the nine surviving 'Natya I'-class ships were complemented by a new dedicated minehunting vessel built at St Petersburg and probably based on the sole 'Natya II'-class unit deleted in 1998.

mainly in home waters, but vessels of this class have also been seen in the Mediterranean and Indian Ocean, and off West Africa.

SPECIFICATION	
'Natya I' class	and two twin 25-mm AA guns, two 250-mm (9.84-in) RBU 1200 five-barrel ASW rocket launchers, 62 depth charges, and up to 10 mines
Displacement: 650 tons standard; 804 tons full load	
Dimensions: length 61 m (200 ft 2 in); beam 10.2 m (33 ft 6 in); draught 3 m (9 ft 10 in)	**Electronics:** one 'Don 2' or 'Low Trough' navigation radar, one 'Drum Tilt' AA fire-control radar, two 'Square Head' IFF, one 'High Pole-B' IFF, one MG 79/89 active mine-hunting sonar, and MCM including one or two GKT-2 contact sweeps, one AT-2 acoustic sweep, and one TEM-3 magnetic sweep
Propulsion: two M-504 diesels delivering 3730 kW (5,003 hp) to two shafts	
Performance: speed 16 kts	
Armament: in most units two quadruple launchers for 18 SA-N-5/8 'Grail'/'Gremlin' SAMs, two twin or two six-barrel 30-mm AA	
	Complement: 67

The 'Natyas' numbered in the 600, 700, 800 and 900 series were allocated to the Baltic, Pacific, Northern and Black Sea Fleets respectively. In the first years of the 21st century, these fleets had two, three, four and no ships respectively.

'Sonya' class Coastal minesweeper/minehunter (MSC/MHC)

Built at Vladivostok and Leningrad for commissioning between 1973 and 1995, the **'Sonya' class** or **Project 1260 Yakhut** units are designated as *bazovy tralschik* (BT, or base minesweeper) vessels by the Russians and used in coastal areas and the approaches to major ports. Construction is believed to have totalled some 72 units, of which 16 were still in Russian service at the start of the 21st century, with many of the others in reserve. **Project 1265** export craft are operated by Azerbaijan (three), Bulgaria (four), Cuba (two out of four), Ethiopia (one), Syria (one), Ukraine (two) and Vietnam (four).

The hull is of wood sheathed with fibreglass to prevent attack by marine organisms. This hull was adopted after a three-ship prototype design, the

In production at three or four units per year up to the early 1990s, the 'Sonya' class of base minesweeper has also been exported in small numbers. There have been no conversions as yet to minesweeping research and development units, as with other classes.

'Zhenya' class, was tried with an all-GRP hull in the late 1960s. The experiment did not work, possibly as a result of problems in building so large a GRP structure.

Several of the surviving units have been enhanced defensively by the retrofit of a single quadruple launcher for SA-N-5 'Grail' short-range SAMs abaft the ship's boat on the starboard side. The sweep gear appears to be of the standard type for

mechanical, acoustic and magnetic mine operations, and is lifted in and out of the water by a hydraulically operated articulated davit on the stern. The elderly 25-mm gun mount aft is carried by the class for destroying swept floating mines as it is easier to use and more accurate for this work than the 30-mm turret forward.

SPECIFICATION

'Sonya' class
Displacement: 380 tons standard; 450 tons full load
Dimensions: length 48 m (157 ft 6 in); beam 8.8 m (28 ft 10 in); draught 2 m (6 ft 8 in)
Propulsion: two diesels delivering 1790 kW (2,400 shp) to two shafts
Performance: speed 15 kts

Armament: one quadruple launcher for eight SA-N-5 'Grail' SAMs, one twin 30-mm AA gun and one twin 25-mm AA gun
Electronics: one 'Don 2', 'Kivach' or 'Nadaya' radar, two 'Square Head' IFF, one 'High Pole-B' IFF, and one MG 69/79 minehunting sonar
Complement: 43

The 'Sonya'-class minesweeper is broadly equivalent to the Royal Navy's 'Hunt' class, being intended for operations in coastal areas and the approaches to major ports, both naval and mercantile. The vessels have a wooden hull sheathed with fibreglass.

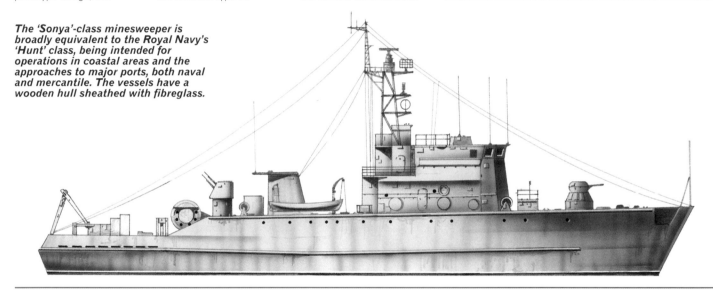

'Alesha' class Minelayer (ML)

Designated *zagraditel minnyy* (ZM, or minelayer) by the Soviets, the **Project 317** ships, known to NATO as the **'Alesha' class**, were completed in 1967-69 and

before their deletion in the later 1990s could serve as minelayers, defensive netlayers, MCW tenders and mine warfare command and control centres. The four

sets of mine rail tracks fitted ran from the amidships superstructure aft to a stern ramp arrangement that could also be used to haul large objects aboard. Two

cranes were fitted forward, with another two amidships. On the second and third units of the class the forward cranes were replaced by two kingposts and

booms. The names of the ships were **Pripyut**, **Sukhona** and **V'chegda**, and all three units were completed at an unrevealed Black Sea shipyard.

NATO allotted the reporting name 'Alesha' to the class of three substantial minelayers, built in the late 1960s in the Black Sea. The ships were each able to carry and lay up to 300 mines, these ranging from moored to ground influence types.

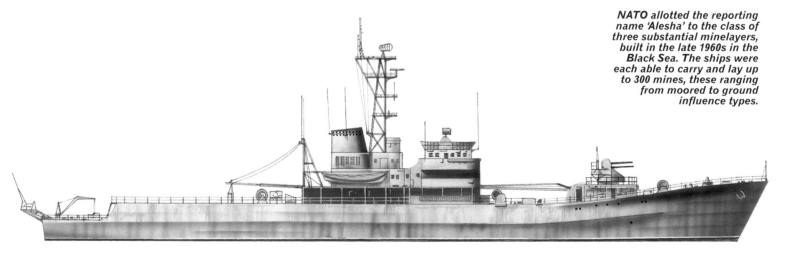

The number of mines carried varied up to a maximum of 300 according to type, but it is known that apart from the conventional moored buoyant types such as the M08 contact and the KRAB influence mines, the 'Aleshas' could also lay the MZ26 moored contact sweep obstructor and the AMD-500 and AMD-1000 ground influence mines.

The main minelaying effort of the Soviet navy shifted from the mid-1980s from surface ships toward submarines (both nuclear and conventional) complemented by maritime reconnaissance/patrol aircraft and bombers, so it is not surprising that large and therefore vulnerable single-role mine warfare ships, such as the 'Alesha'-class units with their limited defensive capabilities, were pulled out of service at a time when shrinking budgets and manpower resources were also affecting the strength of what had by that time become the Russian rather than the Soviet navy.

SPECIFICATION	
'Alesha' class	
Displacement: 2,900 tons standard; 3,500 tons full load	**Armament:** one quadruple 57-mm AA gun, and up to 300 mines
Dimensions: length 97 m (318 ft 3 in); beam 14 m (45 ft 11 in); draught 5.4 m (17 ft 9 in)	**Electronics:** one 'Strut Curve' air search radar, one 'Don 2' navigation radar, one 'Muff Cob' 57-mm fire-control radar, and one 'High Pole-B' IFF system
Propulsion: four diesels delivering 5966 kW (8,000 shp) to two shafts	**Complement:** 190
Performance: speed 17 kts	

'Hunt' class Coastal minesweeper/minehunter (MSC/MHC)

At the same time in the early 1970s that the first GRP-built minehunter, HMS *Wilton*, was being built on the lines of the 'Ton' class, the British began work on a new generation of mine-countermeasures vessels capable of undertaking both minesweeping and mine-hunting operations. The result was the **'Hunt' class**, named after various hunt meetings around the UK. These emerged as what were for their time the largest and costliest GRP-hulled ships in the world. Every effort was made to minimise the design's magnetic signature and to cut radiated noise levels underwater, while maintaining a capability for deep-sea passages to any part of the world.

In service

Eleven are now in service with the Royal Navy, namely **Brecon**, **Ledbury**, **Cattistock**, **Cottesmore**, **Brocklesbury**, **Middleton**, **Dulverton**, **Chiddingfold**, **Atherstone**, **Hurworth** and **Quorn**. Two others, **Bicester** and **Berkeley**, were sold to Greece in July 2000 and February 2001, becoming the **Europe** and **Kallisto** respectively.

For minehunting each of the ships carries a team of divers and two French-built PAP 104 unmanned submersible mine-disposal systems, the latter replaced in some units by more modern PAP 105 systems

The 'Hunt'-class units were built as the world's largest and most expensive GRP-hulled ships, and have minimal acoustic and magnetic signatures. HMS Ledbury and Brecon swept Argentine mines off Port Stanley in the Falklands.

bought in 1988-89. These operate in conjunction with the Type 2059 PAP-tracking sonar. The ships also carry the Type 193M minehunting and Mil Cross mine avoidance hull-mounted sonar systems. For conventional sweeping the ships have a Sperry Osborn TA6 acoustic system, an MM Mk 11 magnetic loop system and the M Mk 3 Mod 2 Oropesa wire sweep. All the hunting and sweeping manoeuvres

are controlled by a CAAIS DBA 4 action information data system using high-precision navigation aids. The *Brecon* and *Ledbury* were used after the 1982 Falklands War to sweep Argentine minefields off Port Stanley, and in 1985-2003 others saw service in the Suez Canal and Persian Gulf. The *Brecon*, *Cottesmore* and *Dulverton* are Northern Ireland patrol ships.

SPECIFICATION	
'Hunt' class	
Displacement: 615 tons standard; 750 tons full load	**Electronics:** one navigation radar, one CAAIS action information system, one Matilda UAR-1 ESM system, one Type 193M minehunting sonar, one Mil Cross mine-avoidance sonar, one Type 2059 PAP-tracking sonar, and two PAP 104/105 mine-disposal systems
Dimensions: length 60 m (197 ft); beam 10 m (32 ft 3 in); draught 3.4 m (11 ft 2 in)	
Propulsion: two Ruston-Paxman diesels delivering 2834 kW (3,800 shp) to two shafts	
Performance: speed 17 kts	
Armament: one 40-mm Bofors AA gun and two 20-mm cannon	**Complement:** 45

The 'Hunt'-class mine countermeasures vessel HMS Ledbury, constructed from glass-reinforced plastic (GRP), and its sister ships can dispose of mines in three ways: by conventional sweeping with cutter; by acoustic or magnetic sweeps; and by hunting with a sonar and then using clearance divers or mine disposal vehicles to destroy them.

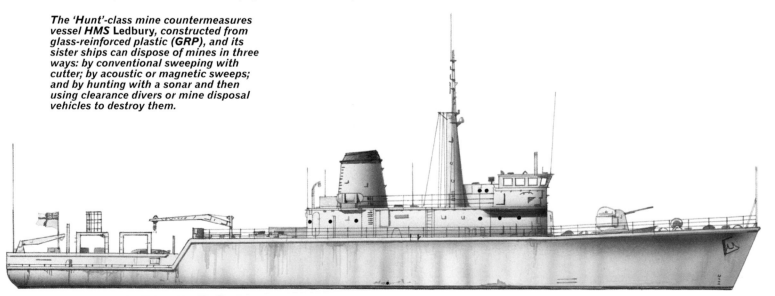

'River' class Coastal minesweeper/patrol craft (MSC/PC)

Based on a commercial North Sea oil rig supply ship design by Richards, the **'River' class** of fleet minesweepers replaced the obsolete and tired 'Ton' class of coastal minesweepers assigned to the Royal Navy Reserve. The first four were **Waveney, Carron, Dovey** and **Helford**, which entered service in 1984. Ordered in batches of four, six and two, the class was completed by **Humber, Blackwater, Itchen, Helmsdale, Orwell, Ribble, Spey** and **Arun**.

Equipment fit

All were completed with the BAJ-Vickers Mk 9 Extra-Deep Armed Team Sweep (EDATS) gear, with which two vessels work together,

HMS Dovey was third of the 'River' class to be commissioned. In peacetime the class was allocated to the various RNR divisions, except for one reserved for trial purposes such as the testing of new deep-sweeping technology.

towing between them a sweep wire with special depth-keeping gear allowing the cutting equipment to follow the contours of the sea-bed closely at very great depths. Explosive charges are attached at 91.4 m (300 ft) intervals to assist the mechanical cutters when breaking mooring chains.

The need for such a system was generated by the Soviets' acquisition of mines of the rising and underwater electrical potential types, which can be laid in deep

water on the continental shelf and rise regions. The deep-sweep concept was first tested in 1977-78, when the Royal Navy briefly chartered six commercial trawlers for the 'Highland Fling' series of minesweeping exercises. Two more trawlers were then chartered late in 1978 to develop the idea to EDATS standard.

The last ship left British service in 2000, and transfers were made to Bangladesh (**Shapla, Shaikat, Surovi** and **Shaibal**) during 1994; Brazil (**Bracui, Benevente, Bocaina** and **Babotonga** in the patrol role) during 1985-86; and Guyana (**Essequibo** in the officer training and patrol roles) during 2001.

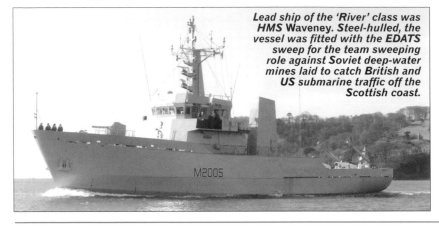

Lead ship of the 'River' class was HMS Waveney. Steel-hulled, the vessel was fitted with the EDATS sweep for the team sweeping role against Soviet deep-water mines laid to catch British and US submarine traffic off the Scottish coast.

SPECIFICATION	
'River' class	7,410 km (4,600 miles) at 10 kts
Displacement: 890 tons deep load	**Armament:** two 0.3-in (7.62-mm)
Dimensions: length 47.5 m	machine-guns and provision for one
(156 ft); beam 10.5 m (34 ft 6 in);	40-mm Bofors AA gun
draught 3.1 m (10 ft 4 in)	**Electronics:** two Decca TM 1226
Propulsion: two Ruston 6RKCM	navigation radars, one Decca QM14
diesels delivering 2267 kW	navigation system, one Decca
(3,040 shp) to two shafts	Hi-Fix navigation system, and sonar
Performance: speed 14 kts; range	**Complement:** 30

'Sandown' class Coastal minehunter (MHC/SRMH)

The Royal Navy's Mine Counter-Measures Flotilla is divided into the 1st to 3rd Squadrons based at Portsmouth (first two) and Faslane (last). Designed as a single-role minehunter (SRMH) type to hunt and destroy mines and therefore cheaper to build and operate than the multi-role 'Hunt'-class mine countermeasures type that it complements, the **'Sandown' class** was approved in 1984. The first unit of the class, designed by Vosper Thornycroft, was ordered in 1985, with orders for four more following in 1987. A final seven, which were to have been ordered in 1990, were only ordered in 1994 after two delays for politically inspired 'economic' reasons.

All the ships were built by the VT Group, as Vosper Thornycroft had become, at Woolston and commissioned between June 1989 and mid-2002. The last ships have larger-diameter main propellers, carry an improved

two-man decompression chamber for the safer operation of diver teams, and were completed with a larger crane, retrofitted to the earlier units, for the handling of the mine-disposal system's vehicles.

GRP hull

The 'Sandown'-class ships are able to hunt and destroy mines in deep and exposed waters. The hull is made from GRP (Glass Reinforced Plastics), and every effort was made to minimise the magnetic signature of these ships: even the buckets on board are made of non-magnetic materials. In addition to conventional sweeping gear that trails through the water, detonating mines, the 'Sandown'-class ships use a

The 'Sandown'-class ships were completed as single-role minehunters, which reduced their cost greatly even though they came out at some £40 million each, allowing three to be built for the price of two 'Hunts'.

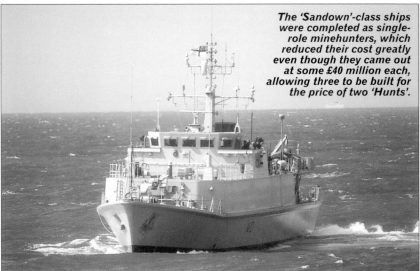

HMS Walney was commissioned in February 1993 as the third unit of the eventually 11-strong 'Sandown' class of single-role minehunters.

The equipment for the hunting and destroying of mines is concentrated in the after part of the 'Sandown'-class ships, here represented by HMS Bridport.

'Sandown' class
Displacement: 450 tons standard; 484 tons full load
Dimensions: length 52.5 m (172 ft 3 in); beam 10.5 m (34 ft 4¾ in); draught 2.3 m (7 ft 6 in)
Propulsion: two Paxman Valenta 6RP200E/M diesels delivering 1136 kW (1,523 shp) to two shafts
Performance: speed 13 kts; range 4665 km (2,900 miles) at 12 kts
Armament: one 30-mm cannon, and one Remote Control Mine

Disposal System (RCMDS) Mk 2 with two PAP 104 Mk 5 remotely controlled vehicles each with two wire cutters and one 100-kg (220-lb) high explosive charge
Electronics: one Kelvin Hughes Type 1007 navigation radar, one Nautis M action information system, and Type 2093 variable-depth sonar with five arrays
Complement: 34 plus six spare berths

very low-frequency/very high-frequency sonar (the Type 2093 variable-depth system with five arrays and deployed from a well in the hull) to locate mines, and can then deploy two remotely controlled PAP 104 Mod 5 (RCMDS 2) submersibles to destroy the mines with HE

charges. Launch and recovery of the RCMDS is undertaken by a Gemini crane.

The 11 ships of the 'Sandown' class are **Sandown**, **Inverness**, **Walney**, **Bridport**, **Penzance**, **Pembroke**, **Grimsby**, **Bangor**, **Ramsey**, **Blyth** and

Shoreham. Each ship is able to manoeuvre with great precision thanks to bow thrusters and vectored thrust units.

Between 1991-97 three units were also supplied to Saudi Arabia in response to an order placed in November 1988. The ships are named

Al Jawf, **Shaqra** and **Al Kharj**, and ship twin 30-mm guns in an Emerlec mounting instead of the single weapon of the British vessels, but are otherwise virtually identical.

Spanish development

In 1989 Spain signed a technology transfer agreement that allowed the construction of a modified version of the 'Sandown'-class design in Spain by Bázan (now Izar) of Cartagena. An initial four of a possible 12 ships were ordered in 1993 and deliv-

ered in 1999-2000. Another two units were ordered in 2001 for delivery in 2003-04.

HMS **Cromer** was decommissioned in 2001 after only 10 years in service, and from 2002 was converted into a dedicated static training vessel for Britannia Royal Naval College at Dartmouth. Once transformed into a floating classroom, the vessel will be re-named **Hindostan**, the name of the college's training vessels since 1864.

'Avenger' class Mine countermeasures vessel (MCM/MSO/MHO)

To replace the US Navy's ageing 'Aggressive'- and 'Acme'-class ocean minesweepers (MSO), the design of a new type of MCM vessel was begun in 1970. This eventually evolved into the **'Avenger' class**, of which 21 were originally planned for construction over a 10/15-year period. However, cutbacks and a lack of understanding of mine warfare in senior US

naval and political circles trimmed the total to 14, of which the first, USS **Avenger**, was commissioned in September 1987. There followed **Defender**, **Sentry**, **Champion**, **Guardian**, **Devastator**, **Patriot**, **Scout**, **Pioneer**, **Warrior**, **Gladiator**, **Ardent**, **Dextrous** and **Chief** up to November 1994.

The hull is of laminated oak, fir and cedar as these

materials have low magnetic signatures, while the superstructure is basically wood with a GRP covering to protect it from the elements.

A minehunting sonar is fitted for use with a remotely controlled MNS (Mine Neutralization System) to sweep ground mines and deep-moored mines down to 185 m (600 ft) with the aid of the retrofitted SQQ-32 variable-depth minehunting

sonar. For conventional minesweeping tasks A Mk 4 and A Mk 6 acoustic sweeps, M Mk 5, M Mk 6 and M Mk 7 magnetic sweeps and an Oropesa No. 1 wire sweep are shipped. The single MNS vehicle is controlled from an automated combat information centre which plots mine locations with the assistance of the SSN-2 precision navigation system. Satellite

communications are also carried.

The 'Avengers' were to have been complemented by the 'Cardinal' class of hovercraft minehunters, of which 17 were planned with the SQQ-30 minehunting sonar and mechanical, magnetic and acoustic sweeps. The class was cancelled and replaced by the conventional 'Osprey' class based on the Italian 'Lerici' design.

The USS Sentry was completed in September 1989 as the third 'Avenger'-class minesweeping vessel. Sentry is one of 11 units completed by Peterson Builders Inc., the other three units of the class being constructed by the Marinette Marine Corporation.

'Avenger' class
Displacement: 1,312 tons full load
Dimensions: length 68.4 m (224 ft 4 in); beam 11.9 m (38 ft 10 in); draught 3.7 m (11 ft 3 in)
Propulsion: four Waukesha L-1616 or (last nine) Isotta-Fraschini ID 36 diesels delivering 1940/1700 kW (2,600/2,280 shp) to two shafts
Performance: speed 13.5 kts;

range 4625 km (2,875 miles) at 10 kts
Armament: two 0.5-in (12.7-mm) machine-guns and two ROVs
Electronics: one SPS-55 surface search radar, one SPS-73 navigation radar, one SSN-2(V) navigation system, one Nautis M action information system, and one SQQ-32(V)3 minehunting sonar
Complement: 81

Below: The 'Avenger' class of minehunters offers a high level of operational capabilities, but sustained oceanic operations would stretch the US Navy's total of only 14 of these effective mine countermeasures (MCM) vessels, each carrying two SLQ-48 systems, with the Honeywell ROV (Remotely Operated Vehicle) carrying a cutter and demolition charge.

'Protecteur' class Replenishment fleet oiler (AOR)

The Canadian navy's 'Protecteur'-class ships can carry diesel and aviation fuel in addition to fuel oil. Unusually, they also carry four LCVPs, and can accommodate up to 50 troops for commando operations. For deployment to the Persian Gulf in 1991, the 76-mm gun was remounted, two Phalanx and two Bofors guns were fitted, and four Plessey chaff launchers and ESM equipment added.

In design the **'Protecteur' class** is an improvement on that of the prototype HMCS *Provider*. The two ships have been given the US AOR (replenishment fleet oiler) designation, and have four replenishment-at-sea stations, one elevator aft of the navigation bridge, two 15-ton capacity cranes on the aft deck, and a large helicopter hangar and flight deck at the stern. The cargo capacity is 14,590 tons of fuel oil, 600 tons of diesel, 400 tons of aviation fuel, 1,250 tons of munitions and 1,048 tons of dry cargo, spares and refrigerated provisions. The aircraft hangar/flight deck area can be used either for spare task group ASW helicopters or for military vehicles and bulk equipment for sealift operations. If required **HMCS Protecteur** and **HMCS Preserver** can also serve as limited-capacity amphibious assault transports with room for 50 or more troops serving in the commando role, and four LCVPs are carried as part of each ship's boat complement. The armament was centred on a twin 76-mm (3-in) Mk 33 DP gun mounting in the bows, but this was removed as the positioning proved precarious, mountings having been washed away on several occasions. The hull-mounted sonar has also been removed from both ships.

The *Preserver* (with the Atlantic Fleet) completed a mid-life refit in 1982, and the *Protecteur* (Pacific Fleet) underwent a similar refit later in the decade. Both ships were laid down in October 1967, and commissioned in August 1969 and July 1970 respectively.

SPECIFICATION	
'Protecteur' class	13900 km (8,640 miles) at 11.5 kts
Displacement: 8,380 tons light; 24,700 tons full load	**Armament:** two 20-mm Mk 15 Phalanx CIWS, but see text
Dimensions: length 171.9 m (564 ft); beam 23.2 m (76 ft); draught 9.1 m (30 ft)	**Electronics:** one SPS-502 surface search radar, two Decca navigation radars, one SLQ-504 ESM
Propulsion: geared steam turbine delivering 15660 kW (21,000 shp) to one shaft	**Aircraft:** three CH-124A/B Sea King helicopters
Performance: speed 21 kts; range	**Complement:** 365 plus 57 passengers

The Canadian naval replenishment ship HMCS Protecteur is equipped to carry up to three licence-built CH-124A or CH-124B Sea King ASW helicopters. These can be used as spare aircraft by an ASW hunter/killer task group as well as being able to provide vertical replenishment of ammunition, dry stores and fuel to the ships of the group.

Chinese support ships 'Fuqing', 'Nanyun', 'Dajiang' and 'Shichang' classes

Though in historical terms the navy of the People's Republic of China has, since its establishment in 1949, concentrated its naval capability on the defence of China's long coast, in recent years there has been a greater emphasis on the projection of Chinese naval power over longer distances. This has seen the introduction of a number of 'blue water' warship classes, and these can be operated effectively only with the support of a force of larger auxiliaries such as oilers and underway replenishment ships.

The **Taicang**, **Fengcang** and **Hongcang** (the last in mercantile service since 1989), of the **'Fuqing' class**, were completed at Dalian late in 1979 as the Chinese navy's first underway replenishment ships. The ships have standard and full-load displacements of 7,500 and 21,750 tons, and are each powered by a 11185-kW (15,000-hp) Sulzer diesel for a speed of 18 kts and a range of 33350 km (20,725 miles) at 14 kts. The ships each have a complement of 130, and typically carry 10,550 tons of fuel oil, 1,000 tons of diesel fuel, 200 tons of feed water, 200 tons of drinking water and dry supplies: these are transferred by two liquid and one dry replenishment stations on each side. The ships, of which a fourth example was sold to Pakistan in 1987 as the **Nasr**, have a helicopter platform aft, and are fitted for but not with four twin 37-mm (1.46-in) AA gun mountings. Of the two ships currently in service, one is attached to the North Sea Fleet and the other to the East Sea Fleet.

The Chinese navy's most

The pennant number 575 identifies this ship as the 'Fuqing'-class replenishment ship Taicang. The two units surviving in Chinese service are still useful, but are limited by their lack of a hangar for an embarked helicopter, even though they have a flight platform for helicopter operations.

SPECIFICATION

'Nanyun' class
Displacement: 37,000 tons full load
Dimensions: length 178.9 m (586 ft 11 in); beam 25.3 m (83 ft); draught 11 m (38 ft 1 in)
Propulsion: one Burmeister &

Wain diesel delivering 8650 kW (11,600 shp) to one shaft
Performance: speed 16 kts
Electronics: one surface search radar, and navigation radars
Aircraft: one Z-8 helicopter
Complement: 125

Something comparatively new in Chinese service is the helicopter training ship, here represented by the 10,000-ton Shichang that entered service in 1997 with provision for two Z-9A helicopters and 200 trainees as well as the deck area for the transport of 300 standard containers.

modern support ship is the **Nancang** of the **'Nanyun' class** that is also known at times as the **'Fusu' class**. One of a class of 11 ships built by Kherson in the Ukraine, the *Nangcang* was laid down in 1989 and sailed to Dalian in 1993 to complete its fitting out to a standard slightly superior to that of the Indian navy's **Jyoti** in terms of helicopter capability. Completed in June 1996, the ship is allocated to the South Sea Fleet, and has underway replenishment rigs on both sides as well as a stern refuelling capability for 9,630 tons of fuel oil. The

ship supported the out-of-area deployment of the 'Luhai'-class guided-missile destroyer *Shenzhen* to European waters in 2000-01.

The Chinese navy also operates numerous submarines, which are supported by four ships (three support and rescue ships, one attached to each of the Chinese navy's fleets, and one submarine tender attached to the East Sea Fleet).

Submarine support

The rescue ships are the **Changxingdao**, **Chongmingdao** and **Yongxingdao** of the **'Dajiang' class** with a

full-load displacement of 11,975 tons and each carrying one DSRV on the forward well deck abaft a handling crane. They can also carry a pair of Z-8 helicopters. Two similar ships operate in the research role.

The tender is the **Dhazi** with a 5,600-ton full-load displacement. The ship carries 500 tons of diesel fuel plus stores and torpedoes.

The single vessel of the **'Shichang' class**, commissioned in 1997, serves as

China's first aircrew training ship (ATS), although it is officially classed as a 'defence mobilisation vessel' and can also be used for shipping freight, navigation training or as a hospital ship.

'Durance' class Underway replenishment tanker

Produced for several navies, the **'Durance' class** of underway replenishment tanker is classified in its basic form as a *Pétrolier Ravitailleur d'Escadre* (PRE, or squadron replenishment tanker) by the French navy. The ships each possess two port and two starboard solid/liquid cargo underway replenishment positions, one on each beam having a heavy transfer capability. A stern refuelling position is also provided so that up to three ships may be refuelled simultaneously. Vertical replenishment (vertrep) operations and the transfer of men are carried out by the embarked light helicopter, which was originally an SA 319B Alouette III but is now generally a SA 365F Dauphin or Lynx Mk 4(FN).

Built by the naval dockyard at Brest, as were two others of the ships, the **Meuse** was commissioned in November 1980 and can carry 5,000 tons of fuel oil, 3,200 tons of diesel, 1,800 tons of TR5 aviation fuel, 130 tons of fresh water, 150 tons of munitions, 170 tons of victuals and 50 tons of fleet spares, while the other three units, namely the **Var**, **Marne** and **Somme** (commissioned in January 1983, January 1987 and March 1990 respectively, the first two from Brest and the last from la Seyne) can each carry 5,090 tons of fuel oil, 3,310 tons of diesel, 1,090 tons of TR5, 260 tons of fresh water, 180 tons of munitions and 15 tons of fleet spares.

The *Var*, *Marne* and *Somme* are classified as *Bâtiments de Commandement et de Ravitaillement* (BCRs, or command and

replenishment ships): they have accommodation for a 'maritime zone staff' or the 'commander of a logistic formation' as well as a commando unit of 45 men or, under austere conditions, some 250 men.

For this the forward superstructure is extended aft by 8 m (26 ft 3 in), the boats are stowed differently, and a crane is located between the gantries. In 1996-99 the ships were provided with an upgraded air-defence capability by addition of an ESM system, the replacement of their original complement of 20-mm and 40-mm guns by 30-mm weapons, and the addition of two twin Simbad launchers for Mistral short-range SAMs.

'Durance' exports

The original ship, the **Durance** commissioned in December 1976, was bought by the Argentine navy in July 1999 after having been in French reserve for two years, entering service as the **Patagonia** after a short refit.

A modified unit, **HMAS Success** with a full-load displacement of 17,933 tons, was built in Australia for the RAN and commissioned in February 1986. Squirrel, Seahawk or Sea King helicopters can be carried.

Two more ships, the **Boraida** and **Yunbou**, were built in France for the Saudi Arabian navy and commissioned in February 1984 and August 1985 respectively. The Saudi ships differ from the French vessels most significantly in having only a single replenishment position on each beam, and both were upgraded at Toulon in the later 1990s.

Above: The Somme was the last of France's 'Durance' class of underway replenishment tankers to be completed.

Top: The Var is one of three 'Durance' ships fitted as a BCR flagship with different accommodation and a SATCOM capability.

SPECIFICATION

'Durance' class
Displacement: 7,600 tons light; 17,900 tons full load
Dimensions: length 157.3 m (516 ft 1 in); beam 21.2 m (69 ft 6 in); draught 10.8 m (35 ft 5 in)
Propulsion: two SEMT-Pielstick 16 PC2.5 V 400 diesels delivering 15500 kW (20,790 shp) to two shafts

Performance: speed 19 kts; range 16675 km (10,360 miles) at 15 kts
Armament: two Simbad twin launchers for Mistral SAMs, and three 30-mm AA guns
Electronics: two Decca 1226 navigation radars, two SATCOM in BCR ships, and ESM
Aircraft: see text
Complement: 164 plus 29

'Rhein' and 'Elbe' classes Depot ship and tender (ARL)

Originally totalling 13 vessels, the **'Rhein' class** of depot ships was subdivided into three groups: the **Type 401** for missile and torpedo attack craft, the **Type 402** for mine countermeasures vessels, and the **Type 403** for submarines. Each group differed in overall length, machinery fit and cargo capacity. The ships were built by a number of north German yards for launch between 1959 and 1963, and the last of them left German service in 1995.

The Type 401 units, with pure diesel propulsion rather than the diesel-electric propulsion of the other two subclasses, were the **Rhein**, **Elbe**, **Weser**, **Main**, **Ruhr**, **Neckar**, **Werra** and **Donau**; the Type 402 ships were the **Isar**, **Saar** and **Mosel**; and the Type 403 units were the **Lahn** and **Lech**. The ships were all commissioned in the first half of the 1960s, and for some years after 1968 five of the ships were laid up in reserve because of an acute manpower shortage.

'Rhein' transfers

Two of the ships, the *Ruhr* and *Isar*, were transferred to Turkey in 1976 and 1982 respectively as the **Cezayirli Gaza Hasan Pasa** and the **Sokulla Mehmet Pasa**, while a third unit, the *Weser*, was transferred to Greece in 1976 as the **Aegeon**. The Turkish navy still operates two 'Rhein'-class ships in the training role, but while these have the names of the original two ships, they are in fact the *Elbe* and *Donau* transferred from Germany in 1993 and 1995 respectively as replacements for the two original ships.

The two Type 403 submarine tenders, *Lahn* and *Lech*, did not carry the two characteristic single 100-mm (3.9-in) guns of the rest of the class, which allowed these other 11 units to operate as 'second-class' frigates in times of emergency, but instead had 200 tons of stores and spares, 200 tons of fuel and 40 spare torpedoes for the submarines they supported. The last three Type 401 units, namely the *Neckar*, *Werra*

The Werra was the second of the two 'Elbe'-class ships built by the Flensburger Schiffbau, and commissioned in 1993. A large crane is located among the containers for the movement of heavy items.

and *Donau*, also functioned as training vessels when required. All 13 ships were equipped with mine rails to serve as minelayers in wartime. The Type 401 was distinguishable from the Type 402 by having a single crane to port, while the latter units had two cranes side-by-side farther aft.

After considering the conversion of existing 'Darss'-class ships for the task but then rejecting the concept for its higher life-cycle costs, the German government in November 1990 released the funding

required for the replacement of the 'Rhein'-class ships by six 'Elbe'-class tenders, commissioned in 1993-94 as the **Type 404** units **Elbe**, **Mosel**, **Rhein**, **Werra**, **Main** and **Donau**. These are very versatile units with containers for maintenance and repairs, spare parts and supplies needed by fast attack craft and minesweepers. In 1996-97 the ships were upgraded by the provision of a helicopter refuelling capability. A platform at the rear of the ships can support a single Sea King, and Stinger SAM launchers can be fitted.

The Donau was one of two 'Elbe'-class ships built by Lürssen/Krügerwerft, and was commissioned in 1994. The bulk of the equipment and stores needed for FACs and submarines is carried in deck containers.

SPECIFICATION	
'Rhein' class	(11,400-12,000 shp) to two shafts
Displacement: (Type 401) 2,370 tons standard and 3,000 tons full load; (Type 402) 2,330 tons standard and 2,940 tons full load; (Type 403) 2,400 tons standard and 2,956 tons full load	**Performance:** speed 20.5 kts; range 4600 km (2,860 miles) at 16 kts
	Armament: two 100-mm (3.9-in) DP guns (not *Rhein* and *Lech*), four single (except two twin in *Rhein* and *Lech*) 40-mm AA guns, and up to 70 mines
Dimensions: length (Type 401) 98.2 m (322 ft 2 in), (Type 402) 98.5 m (323 ft 4 in) and (Type 403) 98.6 m (323 ft 6 in); beam 11.83 m (38 ft 10 in); draught 5.2 m (17 ft 2 in)	
	Electronics: one DA-02 air/surface search radar, two WM-45 fire-control radars, one Kelvin Hughes 14/9 navigation radar, and one hull sonar
Propulsion: six MTU diesels delivering 8490-8940 kW	**Complement:** (Type 401) 122, (Type 402) 99 and (Type 403) 114

SPECIFICATION	
'Elbe' class	3700 km (2,300 miles) at 15 kts
Displacement: 3,586 tons full load	**Armament:** two 20- or 27-mm cannon, and two Fliegerfaust 2 quadruple launchers for Stinger short-range SAMs
Dimensions: length 100.5 m (329 ft 9 in); beam 15.5 m (50 ft 10 in); draught 4.1 m (13 ft 6 in)	
	Electronics: one navigation radar
Propulsion: one Deutz MWM 8V 12M 628 diesel delivering 2485 kW (3,335 shp) to one shaft	**Aircraft:** platform for Sea King
	Complement: 40 plus provision for 12 squadron staff and up to 38 maintenance personnel
Performance: speed 15 kts; range	

The 'Rhein'-class depot ships were designed for operations in the waters of the Baltic and North Sea. Serving as tenders for submarine and fast attack craft flotillas, the Type 401 and Type 402 vessels had armament making it possible for them to operate in place of frigates or as training ships.

'Lüneburg' class Support ship (ARL)

Commissioned between 1966 and 1968, these old **Type 701** support ships of the eight-strong **'Lüneburg' class** have been modified for new purposes or sold off by the German navy. The **Lüneburg** and **Nienburg** were transferred to Colombia as the **Cartagena de Indias** in 1997 and **Buenaventura** in 1998 respectively; based at Cartagena, the two ships support patrol craft. The **Coburg** and **Saarburg** were sold to Greece in 1991 and 1994 respectively, becoming the **Axios** and **Aliakmon**: after initial service as standard support ships, from 1999 the two vessels were converted by Hellenic Shipyards as fleet oilers.

Of the remaining German vessels, the **Freiburg** and the **Meersburg**, like the now-deleted **Coburg** and **Glücksburg**, were both lengthened by 10.3 m (33 ft 10 in) in 1975-76 to allow the carriage of Exocet anti-ship missiles (and their maintenance equipment) for the support of fast attack craft and converted destroyer classes. *Freiburg* alone was extended by a further 4 m (13 ft 1 in) during 1984 and is now based at Wilhelmshaven, supporting the 'Bremen'-class frigates of the 2nd and 4th Frigate Squadrons, a task in which it carries nine spare Harpoon anti-ship missiles as well as the facilities to maintain these important weapons.

The **Meersburg** is a submarine tender based at Kiel in support of the boats of the 1st Submarine Squadron. Until 2001, the *Glücksburg* remained in service as a specialist support ship for fast attack craft based at the North German port of Wilhelmshaven.

Above: Germany's two surviving 'Lüneburgs' have been modernised to support missile-armed FACs and destroyers. For self-defence, the ships are fitted with Bofors guns and two Breda SCLAR chaff launchers

Left: Freiburg was commissioned in May 1968 after being built by Blohm & Voss, and is due to be replaced by the more capable Frankfurt am Main of the 20,240-ton 'Berlin' class of combat support ships.

SPECIFICATION

'Lüneburg' class
Displacement: 3,483 tons or (*Freiburg*) 3,900 tons full load
Dimensions: length 114.3 m (375 ft) or (*Freiburg*) 118.3 m (388 ft 1 in); beam 13.2 m (43 ft 4 in); draught 4.2 m (13 ft 9 in)
Propulsion: two MTU 16V 538 TB90 diesels delivering 4470 kW
(6,000 shp) to two shafts
Performance: speed 17 kts; range 5900 km (3,665 miles) at 14 kts
Armament: two or four (one or two twin) 40-mm Bofors guns
Electronics: navigation radar
Cargo capacity: 1,100 tons
Complement: 71

'Stromboli' class Replenishment tanker (AOR)

The two 'Stromboli'-class vessels are small but nonetheless useful replenishment tankers, and can provide ships of the Italian navy with several types of fuel as well as essential stores.

Commissioned in 1975 and 1978 respectively, the **'Stromboli'-class** small AORs, **Stromboli** and **Vesuvio**, are expected to remain in service until 2010, when they will be replaced by new vessels of the 'Etna' class. A third ship of the class, the **Agnadeen**, was built for Iraq but has been sequestered in the Egyptian port of Alexandria since 1986: ownership of the ship reverted to Fincantieri in 1996, and it may yet be sold rather than scrapped.

The 'Stromboli' class can replenish one ship on each beam simultaneously via constant-tension rigs that can transfer fuel oil at a rate of 650 m³ (22,955 cu ft) per hour or diesel at 480 m³ (16,950 cu ft) per hour. Stern refuelling is also possible when working in heavy seas.

A limited self-defence capability was part of the design: the ships were intended to ship a pair of 40-mm Breda AA guns plus a 76-mm (3-in) OTO-Melara DP gun. However, the Breda guns were not fitted. When the ships served in the 1991 Gulf War they were fitted with two pairs of 20-mm Oerlikon cannon.

The Stromboli is the lead unit of its two-strong class. Both ships were built by Fincantieri, the Stromboli at Riva Trigoso and the Vesuvio at Muggiano. The two ships have different midships crane arrangements.

SPECIFICATION

'Stromboli' class
Displacement: 3,556 tons light; 8,706 tons full load
Dimensions: length 129 m (423 ft 3 in); beam 18 m (59 ft 1 in); draught 6.5 m (21 ft 4 in)
Propulsion: two GMT C428 SS diesels delivering 8350 kW (11,200 shp) to one shaft
Performance: speed 19.5 kts; range 9400 km (5,840 miles) at
18 kts
Armament: see text
Electronics: SPQ-2 surface search radar and SPG-70 fire control radar
Aircraft: platform only for SH-3D/H Sea King, AB 212 or EH 101 helicopter
Cargo capacity: 1,370 tons of fuel oil, 2,830 tons of diesel, 480 tons of JP5, and 200 tons of stores
Complement: 124

'Towada' & 'Sagami' classes AOE/AOR

Japan's Maritime Self-Defence Force operates three **'Towada'-class** fast combat support ship/replenishment oiler ships to support its maritime operations. The name ship was ordered in 1984, built by Hitachi at Maizuru, and commissioned in 1987. Two sister ships, **Tokiwa** and **Hamana**, were commissioned in 1990. The ships each have two stations for replenishment at sea on each side: one of these is for fuel only, and the other for the transfer of fuel or stores. The vessels have a cargo capacity of 5,700 tons.

'Sagami' class
The fourth fleet support ship operated by the JMSDF today is the **Sagami**. Laid down in 1977, this fast combat support ship/ replenishment oiler has a hull of the merchant ship type and is capable of replenishing from two fuel stations on each side. The ship has a cargo capacity of 5,000 tons, and is fitted with two twin chaff launchers; the 'Towada' class similarly carry no normal armament though two chaff launchers can be fitted.

Right: The fast combat support ship USS Seattle (nearer camera) receives fuel from the Tokiwa in order to supply the USS John F. Kennedy battle group during Operation Enduring Freedom.

Below: The amphibious assault ship USS Essex and the Sasebo-based Sagami participate in a replenishment at sea in 2002 – the first time a RAS had been conducted between the Essex and a JMSDF ship.

SPECIFICATION	
'Towada' class	to two shafts
Displacement: 8,150 tons standard; 15,850 tons full load	**Performance:** speed 22 kts
Dimensions: length 167 m (547 ft 11 in); beam 22 m (72 ft 2 in); draught 8.2 m (26 ft 11 in)	**Armament:** none, but see text
	Electronics: one OPS-18-1 surface search radar
Propulsion: two Mitsui diesels delivering 17859.5 kW (23,950 shp)	**Aircraft:** platform for one SH-3 size helicopter
	Complement: 140

'Poolster' & 'Amsterdam' classes AOR

Essentially a fast combat support ship design, the *Poolster* is also capable of taking part in ASW warfare operations with a hunter-killer group by operating and supporting up to five ASW helicopters with weapons and other supplies. The *Poolster* was commissioned in 1964, and has a cargo capacity of 10,300 tons, of which 8,000 tons is devoted to liquid fuel products with the rest comprising fresh water, munitions, fleet spares and other stores. If required, the ship can also carry 300 marines for short distances as an assault transport. The ship was sold to Pakistan in 1994, and became the *Moawin*. In the early 1970s an **'Improved**

Above: The latest addition to the Dutch navy's underway replenishment capacity is the Amsterdam, whose crew of 160 includes up to 24 aircrew for three helicopters.

Capable of carrying fresh water and various dry stores in addition to liquid fuel products, the ships of the 'Poolster' classes can transfer stores by means of one sliding stay transfer point and two fuelling stations per side.

The replacement for the **Poolster** *in Dutch service is the* **Amsterdam**, *created in a joint Dutch and Spanish programme to mercantile building standards, but with military features such as NBC damage control.*

SPECIFICATION	
'Poolster' class **Displacement:** 16,836 or ('Improved Poolster') 17,357 tons full load **Dimensions:** length 169.6 m (556 ft 5 in) or ('Improved Poolster') 171.1 m (561 ft 4 in); beam 20.3 m (66 ft 7 in); draught 8.2 m (26 ft 11 in) **Propulsion:** steam turbines delivering 16405 kW (22,000 shp) or ('Improved Poolster') diesels delivering 15660 kW (21,000 shp), in each case to one shaft	**Performance:** speed 21 kts **Armament:** two 40-mm or ('Improved Poolster') two 20-mm AA guns, and depth charges **Electronics:** one ZW-04 air search radar, one Kelvin Hughes 14/9 navigation radar, one CWE-610 hull sonar or ('Improved Poolster') two Decca 1226 navigation radars; and (both ships) one ESM suite and two Corvus chaff launchers **Aircraft:** up to five SH-14 Lynx helicopters **Complement:** 185

Poolster'-class unit was built as the **Zuiderkruis** and commissioned in 1975. This also has two fuelling stations per side amidships and one constant-tension sliding-stay solid cargo transfer point per side forward. The ship's cargo capacity is 9,000 tons of liquid fuel products, 400 tons of TR5 aviation fuel, 200 tons of fresh water, plus munitions, spare parts and other stores. To replace the *Poolster* and later the *Zuiderkruis*, two **'Amsterdam'-class** vessels were projected in the later 1980s. Only one ship has thus far been commissioned, in September 1995, as the **Amsterdam** with a full-load displacement of 17,040 tons, length of 166 m (544 ft 7 in) and a speed of 20 kts on two 8950-kW (12,003-shp) diesels. The ship has four abeam and one astern refuelling stations for 6,815 tons of diesel fuel and 1,660 tons of aviation fuel. The ship can carry 290 tons of solid supplies, has a platform and hangar for three helicopters and carries armament. The design was created by Spain, which has operated the similar **Patiño** since 1995.

'Outeniqua' and 'Drakensberg' classes AP and AOR

The South African navy's combat support ship **Outeniqua** was in fact built at the Kherson Shipyard in Ukraine, launched in September 1991 and first commissioned as the *Aleksandr Sledzyuk* before becoming the mercantile *Juvent* in April 1992 and then being sold to South Africa, which commissioned the ship in July 1993. The vessel was built as an Arctic supply unit with a strengthened hull and a bow optimised for 2 kts progress through ice up to 1 m (3 ft 3 in) thick.

Modifications

In 1994 the ship was taken in hand for a refit suiting it better to the South African navy's requirement. This refit involved the modification of the helicopter platform to accommodate the South African Oryx rebuild of the Puma medium helicopter, replenishment at sea equipment and light armament.

Further improvements were made in 1996 and 1997, and in 1998 a full helicopter handling system was added.

The ship's primary task is the support of land operations through the delivery of vehicles and other equipment, while secondary taskings include Antarctic support, underway replenishment, relief operations and SAR. Improvements to enhance these operational tasks were made in 2000. The ship's lift capability is 600 troops and 10 vehicles, and operations between the ship and shore are entrusted to four Delta 80 LCUs. The ship is also fitted with four heavy cranes to facilitate the transfer of heavier equipment items between the ship and shore facilities.

Whereas the *Outeniqua* is a combat support ship, the slightly older **Drakensberg** is a fleet replenishment ship. Built in Durban by Sandock Austral and launched in April

The first naval vessel designed wholly in South Africa, the **Drakensberg** *is a fleet replenishment ship that also offers very useful capabilities in a number of secondary roles, including disaster relief.*

1986 for commissioning into the South African navy in November of the following year, the *Drakensberg* remains the largest vessel yet to have been built in South Africa and also the first naval vessel wholly designed in that country. Though optimised for the replenishment role, the ship has secondary taskings in patrol, surveillance, disaster relief and SAR operations, and in addition to two Delta 80 LCUs carries two rigid inflatable boats, two diving support boats and two Oryx medium-lift helicopters. The last operate from two platforms, one each at the bow and stern.

The *Drakensberg* has a full-load displacement of 12,500 tons on a length of 147 m (482 ft 3 in) with a beam of 19.5 m (64 ft) and draught of 7.9 m (25 ft 11 in), and the ship is powered by two 6100-kW (8,180-shp) diesels geared to drive one shaft for a speed of 20 kts or more; the endurance is 14800 km (9,195 miles) at 15 kts. The ship has a complement of 96 including 10 officers and up to 10 aircrew, and has 22 spare berths as well as provision for the carriage of modest numbers of troops over short distances.

The *Drakensberg*'s primary replenishment task is made possible by its cargo capacity, which includes 5,500 tons of fuel and 750 tons of dry stores. Handling of the dry stores and LCUs is entrusted to a single large crane ahead of the superstructure. Self-defence is entrusted to the light armament of four 20-mm cannon and six 12.7-mm (0.5-in) machine-guns.

The odd appearance of the **Outeniqua** *is explained by its design for the Arctic supply role. Most of the living spaces are in the tall forward superstructure.*

SPECIFICATION	
'Outeniqua' class **Displacement:** 21,025 tons full load **Dimensions:** length 166.3 m (545 ft 8 in); beam 22.6 m (74 ft 2 in); draught 9 m (29 ft 6 in) **Propulsion:** one diesel delivering 13060 kW (17,516 shp) to one shaft **Performance:** speed 17 kts	**Armament:** two 20-mm cannon and provision for up to six 12.7-mm (0.5-in) machine-guns **Electronics:** two Racal navigation radars **Aircraft:** two Oryx helicopters **Complement:** 126 including aircrew

'Berezina' class Replenishment oiler (AOR)

Completed in 1977 at the 61 Kommuna Shipyard in Leningrad, the **Berezina** was unique in the Soviet navy as its largest and most capable replenishment ship, and was designed from the outset to supply petroleum products, munitions, fresh water, stores and provisions. Surprisingly, only one unit was built and it was thought that the vessel might have been a prototype (preceding a further class) built to gain operational experience by testing and evaluating the replenishment-at-sea concept for eventual use with the (abortive) conventional fixed-wing aircraft carrier force. The *Berezina* could transfer fuel simultaneously to ships on each beam

amidships and astern, while special provision was made for replenishing submarines. Four 10-ton capacity cranes were carried for loading stores and servicing ships moored alongside. Solid-cargo transfer underway was accomplished by two sliding-stay constant-tension transfer rigs on each side. VERTREP operations were carried out by two Ka-25PS 'Hormone-C' utility helicopters with loads being slung beneath them. The cargo capacity was estimated at 16,000 tons of petroleum products, 500 tons of fresh water and 2,000 tons of munitions, spares and victuals. The large crew carried was thought to include two or three spare crews for sub-

marines. The *Berezina* had the Soviet designation *Voyennyy Transport* (VTR) or military transport.

The ship was well furnished with defences, with one twin launcher for Osa-M (SA-N-4 'Gecko') anti-aircraft missiles. Four twin 57-mm guns were also fitted. These had an 85° elevation and could fire 120 rounds per minute to a distance of 6 km (3.7 miles). An additional four 30-mm six-barrel CIWS were also fitted which could fire 3,000 rounds per minute to a range of 2 km (1.24 miles). The Ka-25 helicopters shipped could also retain their ASW capability if required and the RBU 1000 could dispense torpedo decoys.

Berezina refuels a 'Kiev'-class carrier and a guided-missile cruiser. Berezina was constructed for the carrier support role and tested the concept for a new generation of replenishment vessels that were to have been built for the fixed-wing carrier programme.

SPECIFICATION

'Berezina' class (Project 1859)
Displacement: 35,000 tons full load
Dimensions: length 212 m (695 ft 6 in); beam 26 m (85 ft 4 in); draught 11.8 m (38 ft 8 in)
Propulsion: two shaft diesels delivering 35421 kW (47,500 shp)
Speed: 22 kts
Armament: one twin Osa-M (SA-N-4 'Gecko') SAM launcher (18 missiles), two twin 57-mm AA and four 30-mm AK-630 guns and two

RBU 1000 ASW rocket launchers
Aircraft: two Ka-25PS 'Hormone C' helicopters
Electronics: two 'Don Kay' navigation radars, two 'Don-2' navigation radars, one 'Strut Curve' air/surface search radar, one 'Muff Cob' gun fire-control radar, one 'Pop Group' SAM fire-control radar, two 'Bass Tilt' CIWS fire-control radars, one hull sonar, one 'High Pole-A' IFF, two twin PK 16 chaff launchers
Complement: 315 (plus 216 spare)

'Boris Chilikin' class Replenishment oiler (AOR)

The **'Boris Chilikin' class** is the naval version of the 'Velikiy Oktyabr' merchant tanker design, which was built for the Soviet merchant fleet and for export. The class comprises the first Soviet navy purpose-built underway replenishment ships capable of supplying both liquid fuels and solids. The designed cargo capacity is 13,000 tons of diesel and fuel oil, 500 tons of fresh water, 400 tons of provisions, 400 tons of stores and spares and 400 tons of munitions. The earlier units can supply the solids on constant-tension rigs to both sides forward, whilst the later units can supply them only to starboard, with liquids to port at the equivalent stations. All

An early 'Boris Chilikin' fitted with two twin 57-mm AA guns. The last two units completed were configured as merchant vessels without armament.

six vessels (**Boris Chilikin**, **Boris Butoma**, **Dnestr**, **Genrich Gasanov**, **Ivan Bubnov** and **Vladimir Kolechitsky**) can supply liquids to each side amidships and astern. The first four ships were completed with two twin 57-mm AA mountings, a 'Muff Cob' fire-control radar and a 'Strut Curve' air search radar. All these systems were subsequently removed, the last two units being completed in standard merchant ship configuration. Since the dissolution of the

USSR many of the vessels have become merchant ships. The Soviet type designation is *Voyennyy Tanker* (VT) or military tanker. The *Dnestr* has since been renamed as the **Sergey Osipov**, while *Boris Chilikin* transferred to Ukraine in 1997 as the **Makivka**.

Boris Chilikin *refuels two 'Kashin' destroyers. The capacity to refuel such warships underway greatly increased the Soviet navy's mobility.*

SPECIFICATION	
'Boris Chilikin' class (Project 1559V)	delivering 7159 kW (9,600 shp)
Displacement: 23,450 tons full load	**Speed:** 17 kts
	Armament: see text
Dimensions: length 162.1 m (531 ft 6 in); beam 21.4 m (70 ft 2 in); draught 10.3 m (37 ft 10 in)	**Electronics:** two 'Palm Frond' navigation radars, 'High Pole-B' IFF, and see text
Propulsion: one shaft diesel	**Complement:** 75 (without armament)

'Ugra' class Submarine tender (AS)

Built in the period 1963-72 at Nikolayev, the **'Ugra' class** is an enlarged version of the 'Don'-class submarine tender design with a larger forward superstructure that stretches aft to a shorter funnel. Designated *Plavuuchaya Baza* (PB, or floating base) by the Soviets, all were fitted with one 10-ton and two 6-ton capacity cranes. Since the ships were built many modifications were made so that the class can be divided into three sub-groups. One unit, the **Ivan Kolyshkin** was fitted with a hangar for a single Ka-25PS 'Hormone-C' utility helicopter whilst the remain-

der only had a helicopter landing pad. Several, including the **Volga** and **Ivan Kucherenko** incorporated a larger aft lattice mast topped by a twin 'Vee Cone' communications antenna. The design allowed for extensive engineering workshops and could provide logistic support for a submarine flotilla (of between eight and 12 boats that moored alongside) by providing diesel fuel, fresh water, provisions, spares, torpedo reloads and fresh crews. The 'Ugras' were also frequently used as Soviet navy task group flagships. The sixth unit was completed to a modified

design and sold to the Indian navy as the **Amba** (and armed with four 76-mm/3-in guns) to support India's flotilla of 'Foxtrot' submarines. The 'Ugra' class proper consisted

of a total of seven ships, comprising the three mentioned above and the **Ivan Vakhrameev**, the **Tobol**, the **Lentra** and one of unknown name. Two other vessels, the

Borodino and the **Gangut** were completed as '**Ugra II'-class** naval training ships for the Soviet navy. Apart from *Amba*, the vessels were all out of service by 2001.

Apart from being submarine depot ships, the 'Ugra' vessels could also serve as command and control ships for task groups.

Above: The heavy AA armament of the 'Ugra'-class submarine depot ships can be seen here with all four twin 57-mm guns at high elevation.

SPECIFICATION	
'Ugra' class (Project 1886.2)	**Aircraft:** provision for a helicopter on a landing pad, except *Ivan Kolyshkin* which had a hangar for one Ka-25PS 'Hormone-C' light helicopter
Displacement: 6,750 tons standard and 9,650 tons full load	
Dimensions: length 141 m (462 ft 7 in); beam 17.6 m (57 ft 9 in); draught 7 m (23 ft)	**Electronics:** two 'Don-2' navigation radars, one 'Strut Curve' air/surface search radar, two 'Muff Cob' gun fire-control radars, two 'Watch Dog' ECM systems, one 'High Pole-B' IFF system, and two 'Square Head' IFF systems
Propulsion: diesel electric, with four diesels delivering 5965.6 kW (8,000 shp) to two shafts	
Speed: 17 kts	
Armament: two quadruple Strela-2M (SA-N-5 'Grail') SAM launchers with 16 missiles and four twin 57-mm AA guns	**Complement:** 245

Below: An enlarged development of the 'Don' class, 'Ugra'-class submarine support ships could provide base facilities for a flotilla of eight to 12 submarines. Two vessels served as training ships.

'Ol' and 'Wave' classes Large fleet tankers (AO)

Each manned by a crew of 87, the three **'Ol'-class** large fleet tankers **Olwen**, **Olna** and **Olmeda** were the largest and fastest ships of the Royal Fleet Auxiliary Service when they entered service in 1965-66. Air-conditioned and strengthened for a limited ice navigation capability, the ships were designed for underway replenishment both alongside and, for fuel only, astern. The ships could also carry up to four Sea King medium-lift helicopters (three in a hangar to port of the funnel) and one plus spares or vehicles in the equivalent hangar to star-

board of the funnel for vertical replenishment. Displacing 36,000 tons full load and capable of 19 kts, the ships as completed carried 18,400 tons of fuel oil and 1,720 tons of diesel fuel (the proportions later being changed), 130 tons of lubricating oil, 3,730 tons of Avcat and 280 tons of Mogas. The last two of the ships to remain in service were the *Olwen* and *Olna*, which were deleted in 2001.

The latest ships to enter British service as fleet tankers are the **'Wave'-class** ships **Wave Knight** and **Wave Ruler**, built by BAE Systems for service from

Wave Ruler was launched at BAE Systems' Govan yard in February 2001, but the completion of the ship was delayed by continued problems with the construction.

2002. These ships each have a single embarked helicopter, a Merlin HM.Mk 1 in a dedicated hangar, and have three rigs and one crane for underway replenishment from a capacity of 16000 m³ (565,030 cu ft) of liquids, 500 m³ (17,657 cu ft) of solids and eight 6.1-m (20-ft) refrigerated containers.

Left: RFA Olna (A123) was the second of the three 'Ol'-class ships, and was the second of two ships built by Hawthorne Leslie of Hebburn. The ship was launched in July 1965 and completed in April 1966.

SPECIFICATION	
'Wave' class	**Armament:** two 30-mm AA guns,
Displacement: 30,300 tons full load	four 0.3-in (7.62-mm) machine-guns, and fitted for but
Dimensions: length 181.7 m (596 ft); beam 26.9 m (88 ft); draught 10 m (32 ft 10 in)	not with two 20-mm Phalanx CIWS mountings
Propulsion: four Wärtsilä 12V 32E/GECLM diesel generators delivering current to two GECLM electric motors delivering 14195 kW (19,040 shp) to two shafts	**Electronics:** one surface search radar, one Type 1007 navigation radar, Type 1017 IFF, and one decoy-launching system
Performance: speed 18 kts; endurance 18505 km (11,500 miles) at 15 kts	**Aircraft:** one Merlin HM.Mk 1 helicopter
	Complement: 80 plus 22 aircrew

'Appleleaf' and 'Rover' classes AOT and AOL

In the first part of the 1970s the Hudson Fuel and Shipping Co. ordered from Cammell Laird of Birkenhead four tankers, but then cancelled the order that was then completed by the yard to keep its facilities in production. The Royal Fleet Auxiliary Service then chartered and finally bought the ships as its **'Appleleaf'-class** support tankers (AOT) **Appleleaf**, **Brambleleaf**, **Bayleaf** and **Orangeleaf**, which were commissioned between 1970-84. The *Orangeleaf* underwent a major refit in the mid-1980s to gain a full replenishment at sea capability and additional accommodation, and while three of the ships are still in British service, the *Appleleaf* was leased to the Royal Australian Navy in September 1989 as **HMAS Westralia** and bought by that service in 1994. The ship has two beam replenishment stations, an astern refuelling capability, two 5-ton derricks and two 3-ton cranes to handle 20,000 tons of diesel, 3,000 tons of aviation fuel and 1,500 tons of water. The British ships carry 22000 m³ (236,815 cu ft) of diesel and 3800 m³ (134,195 cu ft) of aviation fuel and, unlike the

Above: The support tankers of the Royal Fleet Auxiliary Service's 'Appleleaf' class are now somewhat elderly and are limited in their underway replenishment capabilities by the availability of only two abeam replenishment rigs on each vessel.

Right: The 'Rover'-class small fleet tankers offer only modest capability, but are faster than the 'Appleleaf'-class ships and also have a helicopter operating platform.

Australian ship, lack a heli-copter platform.

'Rover' class

Somewhat smaller are the 'Rover'-class small fleet tankers (AOL). Five of these ships, with a full-load dis-placement of 11,522 tons, were built by Swan Hunter at Hebburn on the River Tyne and commissioned in 1969-74 as the **Green Rover**, **Grey Rover**, **Blue Rover**, **Gold Rover** and **Black Rover**. The second, fourth and fifth of these are

still in British service, while the first and third were sold to Indonesia and Portugal in 1992 and 1993 respectively, becoming the **Arun** and **Bérrio** respectively.

With an overall length of 140.6 m (461 ft) and a speed of 19 kts on the 11,450 kW (15,360 shp) delivered to one shaft by two SEMT-Pielstick diesels, the ships each have a com-plement of between 48 and 55, are fitted with a stern platform (accessed by a stores lift) for the operation

of one Sea King helicopter in the vertical replenish-ment role, are armed with two 20-mm Oerlikon can-non and two medium machine-guns, and have a towed torpedo decoy as well as four chaff/flare launchers. The ships are intended for the underway replenishment of warships with fuel, fresh water, dry cargo and refrigerated stores, and the cargo capacity includes 6,600 tons of fuel.

SPECIFICATION

'Leaf' class
Displacement: 37,747-40,870 tons full load
Dimensions: length 170.7 m (560 ft); beam 25.9 m (85 ft); draught 11 m (36 ft 1 in)
Propulsion: two SEMT-Pielstick 14 PC2.2 V 400 diesels delivering 10440 kW (14,000 shp) to one shaft
Performance: speed 15.5-16.3 kts
Armament: two 20-mm AA guns and four 0.3-in (7.62-mm) machine-guns or, in Westralia, RBS 70 SAMs operated by an army

detachment, four 12.7-mm (0.5-in) machine-guns and, for retrofit, provision for one 20-mm Phalanx CIWS mounting
Electronics: one Decca 1226 navigation radar, one Decca 1229 navigation radar, and two Corvus or Shield decoy launchers
Aircraft: none except in Westralia, which has provision for one VERTREP helicopter on a platform aft
Complement: 56

'Fort' classes Fleet replenishment ships (AOR)

The Royal Fleet Auxiliary Service operates four fleet replenishment ships of two different 'Fort' classes. The older of the two is the **'Fort Grange' class**, comprising the **Fort Rosalie** and **Fort Austin**, which were built by Scott-Lithgow at Greenock and commissioned in 1978 and 1979. The ships are 183.9 m (603 ft) long and possess a full-load displace-ment of 23,384 tons, and their propulsion arrangement of one Sulzer RND90 diesel delivers 17300 kW (23,205 shp) to one shaft for a speed of 12 kts. Like sev-eral other ships of the same type, the vessels have lateral thrusters (in this instance at bow and stern) to facilitate docking and also station keeping during underway replenishment.

On-board equipment

The ships carry 3,500 tons of armament, naval and vict-ualling stores in four holds with a capacity of 12800 m³ (452,025 cu ft), and these stores can be moved with the aid of six beam cranes (three of 10-ton lift and the other three of 5-ton lift). The after part of each ship is devoted to a helicopter plat-form and hangar with the capacity for four Sea King machines, although only one helicopter is generally embarked. A helicopter can also use the roof of the hangar as a landing platform in an emergency. The ships carry light armament (two

20-mm cannon) and two Corvus or Shield decoy launchers, and each has a complement of 114 supple-mented by 45 naval aircrew and 36 civilian supply staff.

Increased capability

More modern, having been built by Harland & Wolff/Cammell Laird and Swan Hunter for commis-sioning in 1994 and 1993 are the **Fort Victoria** and **Fort George** of the **'Fort Victoria' class**. The ships were ordered in 1986-87 as the first of a proposed six ships to provide Royal Navy

forces at sea with a high level of support through the combination of high speed, provision for up to five Sea Kings or a smaller number of Merlin helicopters (including an operating platform with two spots and an emer-gency capability for handling Harrier and Sea Harrier STOVL warplanes), and extensive capability for the storage and handling of fleet supplies.

The completion of the Fort Victoria was delayed by a fire at Harland & Wolff's yard as it was being built, and it was completed by Cammell Laird

after the completion of initial sea trials. The plan to order six of the class was steadily trimmed back to just the two ships that were in fact com-pleted.

The ships each have provi-sion for the carriage of up to 12505 m³ (441,610 cu ft) of liquids and 6234 m³ (220,150 cu ft) of solids, and these can be transferred to other ships at sea by VERTREP helicopter or alter-natively by four dual-purpose abeam replenishment rigs for the simultaneous move-ment of liquids and solids: underway replenishment

operations are controlled from a special quadrilateral command facility located in the centre of the replenish-ment rigs. There is also an astern refuelling capability, and the ships additionally possess a helicopter repair facility optimised for the Merlin that is replacing the Sea King in service with the Royal Navy.

The operational value of the ships is reflected in an initial plan to retrofit the GWS.26 vertical-launch sys-tem for Sea Wolf SAMs, but this scheme was terminated in favour of two CIWS.

*The **Fort Victoria** was delayed by a yard fire as it was being built, but became fully operational in 1994 and provides the Royal Navy with good replenishment capability for long-endurance missions.*

Left: The two 'Fort Grange'-class fleet replenishment ships are more limited than the 'Fort Victoria' vessels, but are still useful for the support of smaller Royal Navy forces on long deployments.

SPECIFICATION

'Fort Victoria' class
Displacement: 36,580 tons full load
Dimensions: length 203.5 m (667 ft 9 in); beam 30.4 m (99 ft 9 in); draught 9.8 m (32 ft)
Propulsion: two Crossley SEMT-Pielstick 16 PC2.2 V 400 diesels delivering 17820 kW (23,900 shp) to two shafts
Performance: speed 20 kts
Armament: two 30-mm DS 30B AA guns and two 20-mm Mk 15 Phalanx CIWS mountings

Electronics: one Type 996 3D search radar, one Kelvin Hughes 1007 navigation radar, one NUCLEUS helicopter control radar, one UAT ESM system, SCOT 1D combat data system, four Shield or Sea Gnat decoy launchers, and one Type 182 towed torpedo decoy
Aircraft: up to five Sea King or a smaller number of Merlin helicopters
Complement: 134 (95 RFA, 15 RN and 24 civilian stores specialists) plus 154 RN aircrew

'Samuel Gompers' and 'Yellowstone' classes AD

The ships of the **'Samuel Gompers' class** were the US Navy's first destroyer tenders (AD) designed after World War II specifically to support surface combatants armed with guided missiles and with nuclear or gas turbine propulsion. The two ships were similar in layout to the two 'L. Y. Spear'-class submarine tenders, and were completed with a landing platform and hangar for DASH ASW drones. In the **USS Samuel Gompers** the hangar was later converted to a boat repair shop. The class was followed by the modified **'Yellowstone' class** of four ships, which offered the same facilities and, like the two earlier ships, could simultaneously service up to six ships moored alongside. Each of the 'Yellowstones' carried two 30-ton and two 3.5-ton capacity travelling cranes, whereas the two units of the earlier class each had only the latter. The newer design also had the additional capability of carrying and overhauling spare LM2500 gas turbine engines for the 'Ticonderoga', 'Spruance', 'Kidd' and 'Oliver Hazard Perry' classes of surface combatants. Two further units of the 'Yellowstone' class were to have been ordered to meet the growth of the gas turbine propulsion in the US Navy's surface forces, but were not in fact ordered.

The *Samuel Gompers* was commissioned in 1968, followed by the **USS Puget Sound** commissioning during the following year. The four 'Yellowstone'-class ships were the **Yellowstone**, **Acadia**, **Cape Cod** and **Shenandoah**, which were commissioned at yearly intervals from 1980 to 1983. All six ships were decommissioned in 1994-96.

The USS Samuel Gompers was the first of six generally similar tenders that provided for worldwide service by gas turbine-powered US warships.

'Kilauea' class Ammunition ship (AE)

The **'Kilauea' class** of ammunition ship (AE) is easily recognised by its superstructure arrangement forward of the aft helicopter platform. The eight ships, all commissioned between 1968 and 1972, were designed for the rapid underway transfer of missiles and other munitions to the units of a battle group by alongside replenishment or helicopter VERTREP. For the latter they have a hangar 15.24 m (50 ft) long and 4.72-5.33 m (15 ft 6 in-17 ft 6 in) wide built into the aft superstructure for the two H-46D Sea Knight embarked helicopters. These are the US Navy's standard

VERTREP machines, and can carry either 1361 kg (3,000 lb) of cargo internally or up to 4536 kg (10,000 lb) as a slung external load. All the vessels have fin stabilisers, and with the exception of the **USNS Kilauea** have the Mk 36 Super RBOC chaff rocket launcher system fitted. In 1980 the *Kilauea* was transferred to the civilian-manned Military Sealift Command with the other ships following up to 1998. The total cargo capacity is assessed to be around 6,500 tons of munitions including facilities for the transport and servicing, up to the early 1990s, of nuclear weapons such as

Of the seven surviving 'Kilauea'-class ships, three are in Atlantic Fleet reserve, and the other four are allocated in pairs to the Atlantic and Pacific Fleets. This is Shasta of the Pacific Fleet.

missile warheads and aircraft bombs for use by a carrier battle group.

The other units were the **Butte**, **Santa Barbara**, **Mount Hood**, **Flint**, **Shasta**, **Mount Baker** and **Kiska**. Another four units were planned, and as of 2003 the *Mount Hood* had been deleted, and the three oldest ships were in reserve.

The 'Kilauea'-class ammunition ship, here exemplified by the name vessel, has seven operational replenishment rigs, four to port and three to starboard. The stern is devoted to helicopter operations.

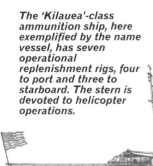

'Sirius' class Combat stores ship (AFS)

The **Sirius**, **Spica** and **Saturn**, which together constitute the **'Sirius' class** of combat stores ships (AFS), are something of an oddity in the naval strength of the US, even though they are not in any way first-line warships, as they were designed and built in the UK. All built by Swan Hunter & Wigham Richardson at Wallsend-on-Tyne, the ships were initially the *Lyness*, *Tarbatness* and *Stromness*, commissioned into the Royal Fleet Auxiliary Service in 1966-67 as combat stores replenishment ships for the Royal Navy's surface forces.

During the Iranian hostage crisis of 1979-80, the US Navy was operating two carrier battle groups in the Indian Ocean, and therefore had an immediate requirement for additional replenishment ships pending the implementation of its longer-term plans for a force of nine combat stores ships to support a navy of more than 600 surface combatants. The US Navy initially

leased the first two of the British ships in 1981 and then bought all three of the vessels between March 1982 and October 1983. The ships entered US Navy service in January 1981, November 1981 and September 1984 respectively, and as of 2003 were still active with the Naval Fleet Auxiliary Force of the largely civilian-manned Military Sealift Command: the Sirius and Saturn are active with the Atlantic Fleet, while the Spica is active with the Pacific Fleet.

In US service the ships have been modernised with improved communications, automatic data processing and underway replenishment facilities, and starting with the Sirius in 1983-84 the ships were revised to include a VERTREP capability by the addition over the stern of a substantial helicopter platform to allow the embarkation of two CH/UH-46 Sea Knight twin-rotor helicopters. The helicopter facility of the

Sirius was later improved by the addition of a large two-door hangar with a flight operations control facility above the centreline of its rear edge.

The ships have eight abeam replenishment rigs, four of them for liquids and the other four (two heavy and two medium cranes) for solids. The cargo capacity of each of the ships is 8,313 m³ (293,570 cu ft) of solid cargo and 3921 m³ (138,470 cu ft) of frozen cargo. All of the ships were refitted in 1992-96 to improve still further their communications, underway replenishment and cargo-handling capabilities.

Other AFS assets

In the first part of the 21st century, the only other combat stores ships available for the support of US Navy operations were the three surviving vessels of the once seven-strong 'Mars' class, namely the *Niagara Falls*, *Concord* and *San Jose*. The units deleted were the

USNS **Spica** *is operational with the Pacific Fleet, and is seen here replenishing by helicopter the aircraft carrier* **John F. Kennedy** *in the Mediterranean.*

Mars, Sylvania, White Plains and *San Diego*. All built by National Steel and Shipbuilding of San Diego for commissioning in 1963-70, these ships have an overall length of 177.25 m (581 ft 3 in), a full-load displacement of 16,500

tons and a speed of 20 kts on the 16405 kW (22,000 shp) delivered by a geared steam turbine to a single shaft. The ships each carry two CH/UH-46 helicopters, and their cargo capacity is 2,625 tons of dry stores and 1,300 tons of frozen stores.

A Sea Knight helicopter is seen with a slung load over the stern platform of USNS **Saturn**, *one of two 'Sirius'-class units operational with the Atlantic Fleet.*

SPECIFICATION	
'Sirius' class	endurance 22240 km (13,820 miles) at 16 kts
Displacement: 9,010 tons light; 16,792 tons full load	**Electronics:** two Raytheon navigation radars, and one URN-25 TACAN
Dimensions: length 159.7 m (524 ft); beam 22 m (72 ft); draught 6.7 m (22 ft)	**Aircraft:** two CH/UH-46D Sea Knight or commercial helicopters
Propulsion: one Wallsend-Sulzer 8RD76 diesel delivering 8590 kW (11,520 shp) to one shaft	**Complement:** 127-130 civilian and 43-45 navy altering with time to 108-119 civilian and 29-49 navy
Performance: speed 18 kts;	

'Supply' class Fast combat support ship (AOE)

The United States operates four fast combat support ships of the **'Supply' class** in the form of the **Supply**, **Rainier**, **Arctic** and **Bridge**, of which the first has been stripped of armament and transferred to the Military Sealift Command, with the other three ships to follow by mid-2004. Intended to sup-

port a carrier battle group, the design was based on that of the 'Sacramento' class of four AOEs and in keeping with its carrier battle group tasking was optimised for a notably high speed through the incorporation of a propulsion arrangement in which two shafts are turned by four potent gas turbines of

the LM2500 type already in widespread service with a number of US Navy surface combatants.

All of the ships were built by the National Steel and Shipbuilding Company's yard in San Diego, California, and were commissioned between February 1994 and August 1996 to a standard

that included significant capability for self-defence against short-range air and missile attack with missiles, guns and decoy launchers, three CH/UH-46D helicopters for the VERTREP role from two helicopter spits, six abeam underway replenishment positions, and four 10-ton capacity cargo booms. Each

ship has a large cargo-carrying capability, including 156,000 barrels of fuel, 1,800 tons of assorted ammunition, 400 tons of refrigerated goods, 250 tons of miscellaneous items, and 75710 litres (20,000 US gal) of fresh water.

The Atlantic and Pacific Fleets each have two ships.

A Sea Knight helicopter moves off with a slung load of ammunition as the USNS **Supply** *transfers fuel via two of its abeam replenishment positions.*

SPECIFICATION	
'Supply' class	launcher for Sea Sparrow SAMs, two 20-mm Mk 15 Phalanx CIWS mountings and two 25-mm AA guns
Displacement: 19,700 tons light; 49,000 tons full load	
Dimensions: length 229.7 m (753 ft 9 in); beam 32.6 m (107 ft); draught 11.6 m (38 ft)	**Electronics:** one Mk 23 air search radar, one SPS-67 air/surface search radar, one SPS-64(V)9 navigation radar, two Mk 95 fire-control radars used with two Mk 91 weapons control systems, URN-25 TACAN, one SLQ-32(V)3 ESM, and four Mk 36 SRBOC decoy launchers
Propulsion: four General Electric LM2500 gas turbines delivering 78290 kW (105,000 shp) to two shafts	
Performance: speed 30 kts; endurance 11105 km (6,900 miles) at 22 kts	**Aircraft:** three CH/UH-46D Sea Knight helicopters
Armament: one Mk 29 octuple	**Complement:** 531 plus 136 spare

'Wichita' class Replenishment oiler (AOR)

A smaller and less expensive derivative of the 'Sacramento' design, the **'Wichita' class** of replenishment fleet oiler provided for the rapid replenishment at sea of surface combatant ships with petroleum, munitions, a limited amount of provisions and fleet freight. All except the **USS Roanoke** were completed between 1969 and 1976 without hangars flanking the stack, but these were retrofitted to allow the embarkation of two H-46 Sea Knight helicopters for VERTREP operations.

Cargo capacity

The cargo capacity was 160,000 barrels of liquid fuels, 600 tons of munitions, 200 tons of dry stores and spares, and 100 tons of refrigerated goods. There were four constant tension stations for liquid cargo and two for solid cargo transfer to port, with three and two respectively to starboard. Although relatively modern, the class had to undergo a

USS Kalamazoo could carry more than 9,000 tons of cargo in addition to 160,000 barrels of oil. The ship was fitted with a hangar on each side of the stack to enable the operation of two H-46 helicopters.

Service Life Extension Program (SLEP) refit cycle in the late 1980s to ensure the US Navy's replenishment-at-sea capabilities into the next century. The seven units of the class were the **USS Wichita**, **USS Milwaukee**, **USS Kansas City**, **USS Savannah**, **USS Wabash**,

USS **Kalamazoo** and *Roanoke*. Despite their SLEP, *Wichita* was eventually retired from US Navy service in 1993; *Milwaukee*, *Kansas City* and *Wabash* were retired in 1994, *Savannah* and *Roanoke* in 1995, and *Kalamazoo* followed in 1996.

SPECIFICATION

'Wichita' class
Displacement: 12,500 tons light (*Roanoke* 13,000 tons light) and 38,100 tons full load
Dimensions: length 200.9 m (659 ft); beam 29.3 m (96 ft 1 in); draught 10.2 m (33 ft 6 in)
Propulsion: two shaft geared steam turbines delivering 23862 kW (32,000 shp)
Speed: 20 kts
Armament: one Mk 29 octuple Sea Sparrow SAM launcher with eight missiles (not on *Wichita*), and two

Mk 15 Phalanx 20-mm CIWS mountings
Aircraft: provision for two H-46E Sea Knight VERTREP helicopters
Electronics: one SPS-10F surface search radar, one SPS-58 and (all except *Wichita*) one Mk 23 TAS air search radar, two Mk 76 fire-control radars (except *Wichita*), one LN 66 navigation radar, one SLQ-32(V)3 ESM suite, one Mk 36 SRBOC chaff launcher, and URN-25 or SRN-15 TACAN
Complement: 454

USS Roanoke differed from the previous six 'Wichitas' in that it was built with the two helicopter hangars, one on each side of the stack, rather than having them retrofitted later on during an upgrade programme for the fleet.

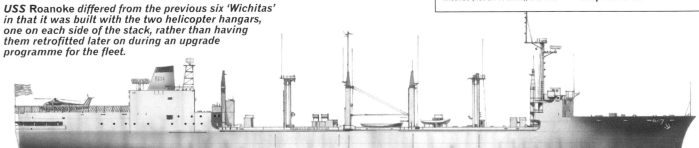

'Sacramento' class Fast combat support ship (AOE)

The **'Sacramento' class** of fast combat support ship (AOE) are the world's largest 'one-stop' underway replenishment ships. They are specifically tasked to provide a carrier battle group with the fuel, munitions and victuals it requires to continue sustained operations, combining the capabilities of the AF (store ship), AO (replenishment oiler), AE (ammunition ship)

and AK (cargo ship) single-role replenishment ships in one hull design. The cargo capacity is 177,000 barrels of liquid fuels, 2,150 tons of munitions, 250 tons of dry stores, 250 tons of refrigerated stores, and 250 tons of fleet freight and spares. Because of their immense individual cost only four of a planned five ships were built, the smaller and less expensive 'Wichita' class of

AOR being developed to supplement them. A large helicopter flight deck and hangar are fitted for two or three H-46E Sea Knight VERTREP helicopters.

FAST cargo handling

The vessels feature the Fast Automated Shuttle Transfer (FAST) system for the handling of cargo. This system uses cranes to move matériel around the

main decks. Fuel is distributed via the Standard Tensioned Replenishment Alongside Method (STREAM) which is connected to large turbines which act as pumps. This system can transfer fuel at a rate of 12491 litres (3,000 Imp gal) per minute. Elevators also assist the transfer of matériel from the cargo holds to the main deck for transfer to other

vessels during replenishment. A fleet of 33 fork-lift trucks also assists the movements of cargo around the decks and in the holds, and ensures that cargo is stored to optimise available space on the vessel.

The four units (commissioned in 1964, 1967, 1969 and 1970 respectively) are the **USS Sacramento**, **USS Camden**, **USS Seattle** and **USS Detroit**.

The fast combat support ship USS Sacramento conducts an underway replenishment (UNREP) with the 'Oliver Hazard Perry'-class frigate USS Ingraham.

SPECIFICATION

'Sacramento' class
Displacement: 19,200 tons light and 53,600 tons full load
Dimensions: length 241.6 m (792 ft 8 in); beam 32.6 m (107 ft); draught 12 m (39 ft 5 in)
Propulsion: two shaft geared steam turbines delivering 74,570 kW (100,000 shp)
Speed: 28 kts
Armament: one Mk 29 octuple SAM launcher with eight Sea Sparrow missiles, and two 20-mm Mk 15 Phalanx CIWS mountings

Aircraft: one to three H-46E Sea Knight helicopters
Electronics: one SPS-10F surface search radar, one SPS-64(V)9 navigation radar, two Mk 95 fire-control radars, one SPS-40E and one SPS-58A (*Sacramento* and *Camden*) or one SPS-58A (*Detroit*) or one Mk 23 (*Seattle*) air search radars, one SLQ-32(V)3 ESM suite, one URN-25 TACAN, one Mk 36 SRBOC chaff launcher, one SLQ-25 Nixie towed torpedo decoy
Complement: 601

'Cimarron' class Oiler (AO)

Originally to have been a class of 15 ships, the **'Cimarron' class** of fleet oilers was built to the extent of only five units because of their limited cargo capacity of 72,000 barrels of fuel oil and 48,000 barrels of JP5 aviation fuel. The cargo was sufficient to provide two complete refuellings of a fossil-fuelled carrier battle group including six to eight accompanying escorts.

Petroleum products
Each 'Cimarron' had four constant-tension replenishment stations to port and three to starboard. These could transfer up to

The 'Cimarron' class was reduced in size to five ships from a planned 15 as their cargo capacity was considered inadequate for the task of replenishing carrier battle groups. USS Platte (AO-186) was the last of the class to be completed and was retired in 1999.

408000 litres (89,750 Imp gal) of fuel oil and 245000 litres (53,894 Imp gal) of JP5 per hour whilst underway at 15 kts. A helicopter VERTREP platform was fitted aft, but no helicopter support facilities were provided.

The five 'Cimarron'-class units were the **USS Cimarron**, **USS Monongahela**, **USS Merrimack**, **USS**

Willamette and **USS Platte**. By 1992 the vessels had been 'jumboised' with the addition of new 32.9-m (108-ft) hull sections, increasing their capacities to a total of 183,000 barrels of fuel oil each. All of these ships have now been withdrawn from service. The *Merrimack* and *Cimarron* were removed from the fleet list in 1998 and were followed by the other three vessels in 1999.

SPECIFICATION	
'Cimarron' class (Jumboised)	Phalanx CIWS mountings
Displacement: 8,210 tons light and 37,870 tons full load	**Aircraft:** provision for one helicopter on a landing pad
Dimensions: length 216 m (708 ft 6 in); beam 26.8 m (88 ft); draught 10.7 m (35 ft)	**Electronics:** one SPS-64(V)9 navigation radar, one SPS-55 or SPS-10E surface search radar, one
Propulsion: one shaft geared steam turbine delivering 17897 kW (24,000 shp)	SLQ-32(V)1 ESM suite, one Mk 36 SRBOC chaff launcher, one SLQ-25 Nixie towed torpedo decoy
Speed: 19 kts	**Complement:** 135
Armament: two 20-mm Mk 15	

'Henry J. Kaiser' class Oiler (AO)

The **Henry J. Kaiser** was laid down in 1984 as the first of a planned 18 oilers for the US Navy. The first three were delivered in 1987 and they enabled the Navy to retire the ageing 1950s oilers of the 'Neosho' class and the surviving 1940s relics, the 'Mispillion' class.

The **'Kaiser' class** had an unhappy construction history. The lead ship suffered from vibration at high speed and other teething problems. Two of the class, **Benjamin Isherwood** and **Henry Eckford**, were under construction at Penn Ship when the yard filed for bankruptcy. The work was transferred to Tampa but that contract was cancelled in 1993 after running late; the incomplete hulls of both ships were eventually decommissioned in 1997 and 1998 respectively.

The last three vessels, **Patuxent**, **Laramie** and **Rappahannock**, were

Although vital for the US Navy fleet, the auxiliary fleet is staffed chiefly by civilian naval reservists. Ships such as the 'Henry J. Kaisers' allow the fleet to be practically self-sufficient.

delayed by the decision to fit them with double hulls in compliance with the 1990 Oil Pollution Act. This also reduced their cargo capacity by 17 per cent.

The 'Kaiser' class can refuel two ships at a time, pumping 3406860 litres (749,430 Imp gal) of diesel or 2044116 litres

(449,658 Imp gal) of aviation fuel per hour. They can also carry quantities of fresh or frozen provisions; the dry cargo area is 687.4 m² (7,400 sq ft) and can accommodate up to 128 pallets of chilled food. The normal cargo capacity allows for 180,000 barrels of fuel oil or aviation fuel, reduced to

159,000 barrels in the last three (double hulled) ships.

Civilian crews
Operated by the Military Sealift Command, most of the ships' crew are civilians, working to Navy instructions. The remaining vessels in the class are **Joshua Humphreys**, **John Lenthall**,

Andrew J. Higgins, **Walter S. Diehl**, **John Ericsson**, **Leroy Grumman**, **Kanawha**, **Pecos**, **Big Horn**, **Tippecanoe**, **Guadalupe** and **Yukon**. *Joshua Humphreys* and *Andrew J. Higgins* were laid up in mid-1996, leaving 14 ships in service at the beginning of the 21st century.

The refuelling hose from the Military Sealift Command 'Henry J. Kaiser'-class fleet oiler USNS Tippecanoe is guided aboard the command ship USS Blue Ridge (LCC-19) during a replenishment at sea (RAS) in the South China Sea in 2003.

SPECIFICATION	
'Henry J. Kaiser' class	**Armament:** none, but mountings
Displacement: 40,700 tons (42,000 tons for last three ships) full load	allow one Vulcan 20-mm CIWS to be fitted
Dimensions: length 206.5 m (677 ft 6 in); beam 29.7 m (97 ft 6 in); draught 10.9 m (36 ft)	**Aircraft:** platform for one VERTREP helicopter of H-46 Sea Knight size
Propulsion: two diesels delivering 25679 kW (34,422 shp) to two shafts	**Electronics:** two Raytheon navigation radars, one SLQ-25 Nixie towed torpedo decoy
Speed: 20 kts	**Complement:** 103

'Yuan Wang' class Space event ship (AGM/AGI)

First seen during the May 1980 ICBM test series in the central Pacific, the **'Yuan Wang' class** of satellite- and missile-tracking ships is an important part of China's space technology and missile-testing programme and as such operates as both missile range instrumentation ships (AGM) and intelligence collection ships (AGI). The four vessels, the **Yuan Wang 1** to **Yuan Wang 4**, were built by the Jiangnan yard in Shanghai and commissioned

in 1979 (first two), April 1995 and late 1996. For their tracking and monitoring duties they carry a large parabolic tracking antenna amidships, two log-periodic HF antennae (fore and aft) shaped like fish spines, two small missile-tracking radars and several precision theodolite optical tracking director stations. There are also several additional positions available for the retrofit of later equipment. For vertical replenishment and personnel

transfer there is a large helicopter deck located aft, but this lacks hangar facilities. A helicopter type known to use the deck is the Super Frelon or Z-8. A bow thruster and retractable fin stabilisers are fitted for station keeping and stability in rough seas.

To support these vessels the Chinese Academy of Sciences also has a fleet of research ships sailing under the name 'Xiang Yang Hong' (East is Red) and individual numbers. These vessels can

undertake several roles including general oceanographic, upper atmosphere, missile and satellite research as well as hydrometeorology.

The third and fourth 'Yuan Wangs' differ from their predecessors mainly in details of

their structure, their construction being evidence of the momentum toward the launch of manned spacecraft. Such vessels will then assume the communications relay role. The 'Yuan Wangs' are with the East Sea Fleet.

The 'Yuan Wang' class was first observed during the 1980 Chinese ICBM tests in the central Pacific. They have a large helicopter landing platform aft, but no hangar for the Super Frelon or Z-8 heavy-lift helicopters normally embarked.

SPECIFICATION	
'Yuan Wang' class	
Displacement: 17,100 tons standard; 18,400 tons full load	delivering 12975 kW (17,400 shp) to one shaft
Dimensions: length 186 m (610 ft 3 in); beam 22.6 m (74 ft 2 in); draught 7.5 m (24 ft 7 in)	**Performance:** speed 20 kts
	Electronics: radar
	Aircraft: helicopter landing deck
Propulsion: one Sulzer diesel	**Complement:** 470

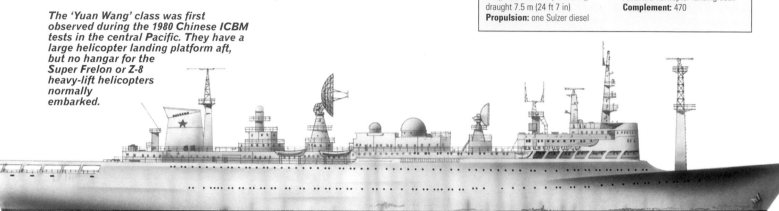

French AGMs *Henri Poincaré* and *Monge*

The **Henri Poincaré** was the sole ship of its type and until deletion in the 1990s was the flagship of Force M, the French naval test and measurement group, which takes measurements and conducts experiments as requested by the navy or any other organisation, civil or military. The *Poincaré*'s primary role was to monitor and measure the trajectory of the IRBMs and SLBMs fired from the experimental station at Landes or from missile-carrying submarines in order to compute their flight characteristics, especially in the re-entry and impact stages. During such tests the *Poincaré* also served as the range safety and command ship by assisting the flag officer-in-

charge in controlling the naval and air elements in the test zone, particularly in the descent and recovery phases.

Tracking systems

Built originally as an Italian tanker, the *Poincaré* was reconstructed at Brest in 1964-67, a second major refit following between 1979 and 1980 to update electronic systems. These included one Savoie and two Gascogne tracking radars, a fully automatic tracking station, celestial position-fixing equipment, a cinecamera-equipped theodolite, IR tracking systems, Transit navigational and Syracuse satellite communications systems, meteorological and oceanographic equipment, a

Successor to the Henri Poincaré, the Monge is a thoroughly modern AGM characterised by full facilities (platform and hangars) for two or more helicopters as well as a mass of missile tracking and telemetry reception equipment.

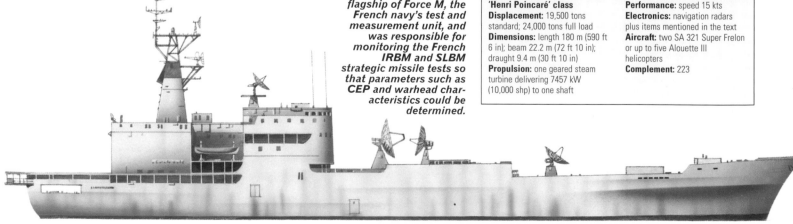

Below: The Henri Poincaré was the flagship of Force M, the French navy's test and measurement unit, and was responsible for monitoring the French IRBM and SLBM strategic missile tests so that parameters such as CEP and warhead characteristics could be determined.

SPECIFICATION	
'Henri Poincaré' class	**Performance:** speed 15 kts
Displacement: 19,500 tons standard; 24,000 tons full load	**Electronics:** navigation radars plus items mentioned in the text
Dimensions: length 180 m (590 ft 6 in); beam 22.2 m (72 ft 10 in); draught 9.4 m (30 ft 10 in)	**Aircraft:** two SA 321 Super Frelon or up to five Alouette III helicopters
Propulsion: one geared steam turbine delivering 7457 kW (10,000 shp) to one shaft	**Complement:** 223

data collection and collation system, and hull-mounted sonar. For the vertical replenishment and communications tasks *Poincaré* had a hangar and flight deck aft for either two SA 321 Super Frelon heavy-lift or up to five Alouette III light communications/utility helicopters.

Much of the *Poincaré's* task has been undertaken by the *Monge* since its completion in 1992. With a crew of 120 naval personnel and up to 100 civilian and military technicians, the *Monge* is notably well equipped. The vessel has DRBV 15C air search and two navigation radars, and its mission equipment includes Stratus, Gascogne, Armor (two), Savoie and Antarès (two)

missile-tracking radars, laser radar, an optronic tracking unit and 14 telemetry antennae. Real-time communication with mainland France is provide by a Syracuse satellite communications system. The vessel is flagship of the Trials Squadron and is also used for space surveillance by the French Space Agency.

SPECIFICATION

'Monge' class
Displacement: 21,040 tons full load
Dimensions: length 229.6 m (753 ft 4 in); beam 24.8 m (81 ft 5 in); draught 7.7 m (25 ft 4 in)
Propulsion: two SEMT-Pielstick diesels delivering 7755.3 kW (10,400 shp) to one shaft

Performance: speed 15 kts; range 24140 km (15,000 miles) at 15 kts
Electronics: see text
Aircraft: two SA 321 Super Frelon or Alouette III helicopters
Armament: two 20-mm Giat F2 cannon, and two 12.7-mm (0.5-in) machine-guns
Complement: 220 (10 officers)

'Nawigator', 'Baltyk' and 'Piast' classes
Intelligence and salvage vessels

The Polish navy uses two highly modified 'Moma'-class survey ships, the Hydrograf *and* Nawigator, *in the intelligence role in the Baltic, initially to monitor Danish, West German, Norwegian and Swedish naval exercises and shore installations for the Warsaw Pact. Both were based at Gdynia in 2003.*

The two vessels that comprise the **'Nawigator' class** (the **Nawigator** and **Hydrograf** commissioned in 1975 and 1976 respectively) and the 1,887-ton salvage vessels of the **'Piast' class** (**Piast** and **Lech**) are based on the Soviet 'Moma'-class

survey ship. The 'Nawigator' and 'Piast' classes mount a conspicuous lattice mainmast, the 'Nawigators' being distinguished by the addition of two large radomes, one immediately abaft the bridge above the main superstructure and the other atop the

aft superstructure. The *Hydrograf* differs slightly from *Nawigator* in having a much longer forecastle that is one deck higher. The *Nawigator* has two twin 25-mm guns, and both have two Fasta-4M launchers for Strela-2M (SA-N-5 'Grail') short-range SAMs. Both masts are fitted with a variety of DF and signal-intercept antennae, but it is believed that no real-time analysis capability is carried. Thus all the data obtained have to be recorded for eventual analysis at a shore station fitted with the necessary computerised equipment. In the days of the Warsaw Pact all the information derived from the

processing was then fed into the Soviet intelligence network for future use.

There was a second intelligence type, the 1,200-ton **Baltyk** (**'B10' class**) a converted trawler which also served in the AGI role with the Polish navy. Both the 'Nawigator' class units were quoted as navigational training ships, but like others were betrayed as to their real role by their considerable quantities of electronic gear and associated antennae.

The 'Piast'-class vessels have an ice-strengthened hull and both towing and firefighting capabilities as well as hospital facilities. The ships carry a three-man diving bell for operations down to 100 m (330 ft),and a decompression chamber. In 1997-98 a remotely operated vehicle was added, and the ships are fitted for but not with armament.

One other 'Piast'-class ship, the **Vangardia**, is also operated by Uruguay.

Like the 'Nawigator' class of AGI, the 'Piast'-class salvage vessel is based on the Soviet 'Moma'-class survey ship. Note the absence of radomes, the one lattice mast and the conspicuous diving bell together with its launching apparatus on the port side.

SPECIFICATION

'Nawigator' class
Displacement: 1,260 tons standard; 1,677 tons full load
Dimensions: length 73.3 m (240 ft 6 in); beam 10.8 m (35 ft 5 in); draught 3.9 m (12 ft 10 in)
Propulsion: two Zgoda-Sulzer 6TD48 diesels delivering 2460 kW (3,300 shp) to two shafts

Performance: speed 17 kts
Armament: twn twin 25-mm AA guns (*Nawigator*), and two quadruple launchers for Strela-2M (SA-N-5 'Grail') SAMs
Electronics: two SRN 7453 Nogat navigation radars plus Elint and Sigint systems
Complement: 87

'Okean' class Intelligence collection ship (AGI)

Built in East Germany from 1959 to the mid-1960s, the **'Okean' class** of 15 converted side trawlers was the largest and hence the most observed class of Soviet AGIs. All now deleted, they were designated *gigrograficheskoye sudno* (GS, or survey ship) in the Soviet navy, and retained their trawler tripod mast forward and a pole mast well aft. These were festooned with the various aerials and antennae that characterised their role. It was vessels of this class (together with the eight larger trawler units of the 'Mayak' class and the four ex-whalers of the 'Mirnyy' class) that were regularly seen off the Western nuclear submarine bases monitoring the comings and goings of SSBNs in transit.

There were many variations within the class. One modified subgroup of four (the **Linza**, **Lotlin**, **Reduktor** and **Zond**)

The 'Okean'-class spyship **Linza** *shadows the amphibious warfare ship HMS* **Fearless***. The 'Okeans' were the most numerous of the Soviet AGIs, with the antenna outfits varying considerably between the units of the class in order that they could perform different roles.*

had the port side superstructure enclosed and the starboard side open; these ships also had additional accommodation on the well-deck.

Defensive weapons

The **Alidada**, **Ampermetr**, **Barometr**, **Gidrofon** and *Reduktor* had no quadruple pedestal installation for SA-N-5 SAMs, while a self-defence capability of this type was added to the **Barograf**, **Deflektor**, **Ekholot**,

Krenometr, *Linza, Lotlin,* **Repiter**, **Teodolit**, **Traverz** and *Zond*. The *Barograf* also had two twin 14.5-mm (0.57-in) heavy machine-gun mountings to supplement the small arms

The 'Okean'-class AGI **Gidrofon***. Most of the class were eventually fitted with two positions for quadruple 'Grail' SAM launchers and 16 missiles. The* **Barograf** *was also fitted with two twin 14.5-mm (0.57-in) heavy machine-guns for protection in unfriendly areas such as the African and Chinese coasts.*

carried by the crew.

The 'Okean'-class units were replaced by conversions of the 'Al'pinist'-class stern trawlers built at the Leninskaya Kuznitsa Shipyard at Kiev and at the Volgograd Shipyard: it is believed that

only Kiev-built vessels were used for spyship conversions, with the former fish hold adapted to provide extensive volume for electronics and/or additional accommodation for the specialist personnel to operate the electronics.

SPECIFICATION	
'Okean' class	**Performance:** speed 13 kts
Displacement: 650 tons standard; 760 tons full load	**Armament:** two quadruple launchers for Strela-2M (SA-N-5 'Grail') SAMs, but see text
Dimensions: length 51 m (167 ft 4 in); beam 8.8 m (28 ft 10 in); draught 3.7 m (12 ft 2 in)	**Electronics:** one or two 'Don Kay' navigation radars and various Elint and Sigint systems
Propulsion: one diesel delivering 403 kW (540 shp) to one shaft	**Complement:** 70

'Bal'zam' class Intelligence collection ship (AGI)

Designated by the Soviets as *Sudno Svyazyy* (SSV, or communications vessel) the ships of the **'Bal'zam' class** were the first military vessels purpose-built for intelligence

collection and processing. The force eventually numbered four such ships built by the Yantar yard in Kaliningrad, but by the beginning of the 21st century only one was

left in service. The ships carried an array of intercept and direction-finding antennae that fed raw intelligence information into the onboard data analysis and processing

equipment located within the extensive superstructure. The result was then sent via the two satellite transmitting and receiving antennae located beneath the spherical

radomes, either to shore stations or to the flagships of surface action battle groups for immediate action. For the extended sea periods which they served, the ships were

There were four 'Bal'zam'-class AGIs in service with the Soviet navy in the 1980s. Designated as Sudno Svyazyy (SSV, or communications vessel) they were in their time the world's best equipped intelligence-gathering ships.

equipped to refuel under way and to transfer solid cargo and personnel via constant-tension transfer rigs on each side of the after mast. The class was also the first Soviet AGI type to be defensively armed, the lead ship appearing in service during 1980

with two quadruple Strela-2M (SA-N-5 'Grail') SAM launchers and a 30-mm AK-630 six-barrel CIWS. No radar fire-control systems were fitted (presumably to prevent interference with the electronic equipment already carried), so the weapons instead

relied on a remote 'Kolonka' pedestal director.

Eavesdropping

The 'Bal'zams' were commonly seen at sea during the 1980s and early 1990s, monitoring major NATO naval exercises in the North

Atlantic and also American carrier battle groups. Surprisingly, the class was one of the few modern ship designs fitted with major masts. The sole unit left in

service with the Russian navy in 2003 was the **Belomore**, based with the Northern Fleet. The Russian designation for the vessel is **'Asia'** (or **Project 1826**) **class**.

SPECIFICATION	
'Bal'zam' class	launchers for Strela-2M (SA-N-5 'Grail') SAMs, and one 30-mm AK-630 CIWS
Displacement: 4,000 tons standard; 4,500 tons full load	
Dimensions: length 105 m (344 ft 6 in); beam 15.5 m (50 ft 10 in); draught 5 m (16 ft 5 in)	**Electronics:** single 'Palm Frond' and 'Don Kay' surface search and navigation radars, Elint and Sigint systems, two satellite transmit-and-receive systems, intelligence analysis centre, and provision for 'Lamb Tail'/'Mouse Tail' VDS
Propulsion: two diesels delivering 13400 kW (17,970 shp) to two shafts	
Performance: speed 20 kts; range 13000 km (8,080 miles) at 16 kts	
Armament: two quadruple	**Complement:** 200

SSV-516 was the lead ship of a class of very large AGIs given the NATO code name 'Bal'zam'. Armed with two quadruple SA-N-5 'Grail' SAM launchers and a 30-mm CIWS, the class also had elaborate underway replenishment facilities and real-time satellite transmitter and receiver installations beneath the two large dome installations.

'Primor'ye' class Intelligence collection ship (AGI)

Although its units resembled small passenger liners in appearance, the **'Primor'ye' class** of AGI was the first commercially based intelligence-gathering design to have an onboard analysis capability. Based on the hull of the highly successful 'Mayakovskyy' series of stern trawler-factory ships, the six vessels were the **Kavkaz**, **Krym**, **Primor'ye**, **Zabaykalye**, **Zakarpatye** and **Zaporozhye**, of which the *Kavkaz* and *Krym* were the only two units still in Russian service at the beginning of the 21st century. They have a distinctive superstructure with box-like structures fore and aft (to house electronic

The Zakarpatye shows the multitude of arrays and antennae that are required by an AGI. Those on the foremast are primarily of the direction-finding type so as to pinpoint the origin of an electronic transmission.

processing equipment) and three main masts (for the associated aerials and antennae). The two surviving units retain the trawler kingpost aft, while all six vessels differed among themselves in minor details of superstructure and antennae outfits. Most were refitted with platforms to carry one or two

quadruple launchers for SA-N-5 'Grail' SAMs for local air defence, while as an interim measure they previously carried the shoulder-launched SA-7 'Grail' (Strela-2) SAM that had been

issued to the Soviet naval infantry. The 'Primor'ye'-class ships were often seen off both coasts of the US, especially during the missile tests off Florida by American and British SSBNs. They also regularly accompanied major NATO exercises and American aircraft carriers, but lacked the modern real-time data transmission facilities possessed by the later 'Bal'zam' class.

SPECIFICATION	
'Primor'ye' class	**Armament:** one or two quadruple launchers for eight or 16 Strela-2M (SA-N-5 'Grail') SAMs, and machine-guns and small arms
Displacement: 2,600 tons standard; 3,700 tons full load	
Dimensions: length 84.7 m (277 ft 10 in); beam 14 m (46 ft); draught 7 m (23 ft)	**Electronics:** two 'Nadaya' surface search radars, two 'Don Kay' navigation radars, various Elint and Sigint systems, and one real-time intelligence-analysis centre
Propulsion: two diesels delivering 3000 kW (4,025 shp); two shafts	
Performance: speed 12 kts; range 18500 km (11,495 miles) at 10 kts	**Complement:** 120

In 2003, the two surviving examples of the 'Primor'ye' (Project 394B) class – originally comprising six units – were the Kavkaz and Krym, based at Sevastopol in the Crimea as part of the Black Sea Fleet. During the Cold War, ships of the class regularly shadowed NATO naval exercises and US space events and missile tests to gather electronic and photographic intelligence.

Dassault Rafale M/N Next-generation naval fighter

Rafale M1, the first navalised production aircraft, maintains 80 per cent structural and systems commonality with the single-seat Rafale C. The initial software standard permits air defence missions against multiple targets, and in 2002 added IR-guided MICA AAMs, and a datalink for communication with the E-2C.

The ACX, later Rafale A, demonstrator flew several hundred test sorties, including touch-and-go deck-landings on the French carrier *Clemenceau*. As such, it proved the basic suitability of the new fighter design for carrier operations, paving the way for the **Rafale M** dedicated multi-role naval fighter.

Naval Rafale

Originally known as the **ACM** (**Avion de Combat Marine**), the first Rafale M prototype made its initial flight on 12 December 1991. The main changes differentiating the Rafale M from its land-based counterparts weigh some 750 kg (1,653 lb) and include major reinforcement of the Messier-Bugatti landing gear (whose nosewheel unit also became the first in France to require attachment of a take-off catapult bar) plus provision of a 'jump-strut' for automatic unstick rotation.

Other changes include 13 rather than 14 hardpoints, and a maximum take-off weight reduced by 2000 kg (4,409 lb) to 19500 kg (42,989 lb). The Aéronavale's initial requirement for 86 single-seat Rafale Ms is unlikely to be satisfied.

Budget cuts have forced the total buy down to 60 aircraft. In addition, having studied aircraft performance during the 1991 Gulf War and the conflict over Kosovo, the Aéronavale has decided that it requires a mix of Rafale M and two-seat **Rafale N** aircraft. In May 2001, Flottille 12F was formed with four Rafale Ms. These early aircraft are equipped to **Standard F1**, optimised for the air-to-air role, and employ some systems of the definitive aircraft.

Later standards include **Standard F2**, for delivery from 2004, with improved air-to-surface capability. This will include Scalp, a jam-resistant passive optronic surveillance and imaging system with a laser rangefinder or an Optronique Secteur Frontale IR search-and-track system mounted forward of the cockpit and supplementing the radar for passive multi-target identification and tracking, and the MIDS datalink. The definitive multi-role **Standard F3**, with improved radar able to undertake simultaneous air search and terrain following should be in service by 2010. Rafale N is due to fly for the first time in 2005, for delivery in 2007.

The second naval prototype, M02, is shown here launching from FNS Foch with a typical air-to-air load of MICA and Magic 2 missiles.

In the closing stages of Operation Enduring Freedom during 2002, Rafales flew operationally from *Charles de Gaulle*, but saw no combat. Rafale M procurement continued with an order for a further 13 machines in early 2003, at which time the final M/N mix had not yet been announced.

SPECIFICATION

Dassault Rafale M
Type: single-seat carrierborne multi-role warplane
Powerplant: two SNECMA M88-2 turbofan engines each rated at 75 kN (16,861 lb st) with afterburning
Performance: maximum speed 2125 km/h (1,321 mph) 'clean' at 11000 m (36,090 ft); maximum climb rate at sea level 18290 m (60,000 ft) per minute; service ceiling 16765 m (55,000 ft); combat radius on a low-level penetration mission with 12 250-kg (551-lb) bombs, four MICA AAMs and three

drop tanks 1055 km (655 miles)
Weights: empty equipped 9800 kg (21,605 lb); normal take-off 16500 kg (36,376 lb)
Dimensions: wing span 10.9 m (35 ft 9 in) with tip-mounted AAMs; length 15.3 m (50 ft 2¼ in); height 5.34 m (17 ft 6¼ in); wing area 46 m² (495.16 sq ft)
Armament: one 30-mm GIAT/DEFA M791 fixed forward-firing cannon in the starboard side of the forward fuselage, plus up to 6000 kg (13,228 lb) of disposable stores

During Operation Enduring Freedom, the Aéronavale's first Rafale Ms took the opportunity for a little 'cross-deck' practice. Here John C. Stennis experiences a Rafale fly-by on 14 March 2002.

Dassault Super Etendard

Multi-role and attack carrierborne fighter

The Super Etendard was developed from the 1950s-vintage Etendard IV. A new nav/attack system was installed, but the thirsty SNECMA Atar engine was retained. Despite the aircraft's increased weight, the Super Etendard's new wing does give improved handling.

A French naval requirement of the early 1970s for 100 new carrierborne strike/attack fighters (for which procurement of the navalised SEPECAT Jaguar M was originally planned) eventually resulted in a 1973 contract to Dassault-Breguet for 60 examples of a development of its current Etendard IV warplane. The upgraded **Super Etendard** (super standard) was planned with the powerplant of one 49.03-kN (11,023-lb st) SNECMA Atar 8K-50 turbojet and some 90 per cent airframe commonality with the Etendard IV. A new wing leading-edge profile and redesigned flaps ensured a mainly unchanged carrier deck performance despite the Super Etendard's heavier operating weights.

Greater capability

To widen its anti-ship attack and air-to-air capabilities, the Super Etendard also featured a new ETNA nav/attack system and an Agave monopulse search and fire-control radar, an SKN602 INS, Crouzet 66 air data computer (and associated Crouzet 97 navigation display and armament system), and a HUD. A retractable inflight-refuelling probe was fitted forward of the cockpit.

Three Etendard IVM airframes were converted as prototypes, flying from 29 October 1974. Production of 71 Super Etendards was then undertaken, the first of them flying on 24 November 1977. The new type began to replace Etendard IVs and some Vought F-8E(FN) Crusader interceptors from June 1978.

Falklands hero

By the time the Falklands War started in April 1982, the Argentine navy (the sole Super Etendard export customer) had received the first five of 14 aircraft on order to equip its air arm's 2ª Escuadrilla, together with five Aérospatiale AM39 Exocet anti-ship missiles. These aircraft made their operational debut on 4 May 1982, sinking HMS *Sheffield* off the Falklands, followed on 25 May by the destruction of the supply ship *Atlantic Conveyor*. The squadron suffered no wartime losses. In October 1983, the Iraqi air force leased five Super Etendards and bought a substantial number of AM39 missiles for use against Iranian tankers in the Iran/Iraq war, scoring many successes. One of the aircraft was lost

to an accident, however.

A mid-1980s upgrade programme was planned to extend the long-range and anti-ship attack capabilities of the Aéronavale's surviving force of nearly 60 Super Etendards (some 53 of which had already been modified to launch the ASMP stand-off nuclear missile). The main changes were: modernisation of the avionics, a revised cockpit with new instrumentation and HOTAS controls, and the new Anemone radar – incorporating track-while-scan, air-to-surface ranging, ground mapping and search functions. New systems

In service the Super Etendard has proved to be a useful type. This pair is taking fuel from a US Navy KA-6D Intruder. Note that the Super Etendards have the post-1984 camouflage scheme.

included a wide-angle HUD with TV or IR imaging, Sherloc RWR and a VCN65 ECM display together with the Barem jammer pod, a more modern INS, a weapons and air data computer with more processing capacity, and provision for night-vision goggles. Airframe changes, combined with on-going systems upgrades, will help to extend the Super Etendard's service life to about 2011.

The prototype of the

upgraded **Super Etendard Modernisé** first flew on 5 October 1990, Dassault modifying two more for operational development.

Following disbandment of Flottille 14F in July 1991, pending its eventual re-equipment as the Aéronavale's first Rafale M unit, its Super Etendards were used to replace the last 11 Etendard IVP reconnaissance aircraft equipping Escadrille 59S at Hyères. The Super Etendards were used for the operational conversion of French naval pilots after deck-landing training in Aérospatiale Zéphyr aircraft at the same base. Flottilles 11F and 17F comprise the Aéronavale's remaining front-line Super Etendard squadrons in mid 2003, flying Modernisé aircraft, and will operate the machines until they are replaced by Rafale Ms.

SPECIFICATION

Dassault Super Etendard
Type: single-seat carrier-based attack aircraft
Powerplant: one 49.05-kN (11,023-lb) thrust SNECMA Atar 8K-50 turbojet
Performance: maximum speed 'clean' at sea level 1380 km/h (857 mph); maximum climb rate at sea level 6000 m (19,685 ft) per minute; service ceiling 13700 m (44,950 ft); radius on a hi-lo-hi

mission with one AM39 and two drop tanks 850 km (528 miles)
Weights: empty equipped 6500 kg (14,330 lb); maximum take-off 12000 kg (26,455 lb)
Dimensions: wing span 9.6 m (31 ft 6 in); length 14.31 m (46 ft 11½ in); height 3.86 m (12 ft 8 in); wing area 28.4 m² (305.71 sq ft)
Armament: two 30-mm DEFA cannon plus up to 2100 kg (4,630 lb) of disposable ordnance

The Super Etendard gained fame during the Falklands campaign when Argentinian Super Etendards sank two British ships with Exocet missiles.

Sukhoi Su-27K (Su-33) 'Flanker-D' Naval Su-27

'Red 64' was assigned to the 1st Squadron of the Severomorsk Regiment, AV-MF, and was one of those aircraft deployed aboard **Admiral Kuznetsov** *for its first operational cruise in 1996.*

Development of a navalised, shipborne version of the Su-27 was launched in the early 1980s at the same time as the Soviet carrier programme. The aircraft was seen as a single-role fleet air defence aircraft, which would form one element in a mixed air wing alongside a new AWACS platform and the MiG-29K multi-role strike fighter. As such, the **Su-27K 'Flanker-D'** was developed from the basic Su-27, not the multi-role Su-27M.

Several Su-27s tested different aspects of the intended Su-27K production configuration, including canards for approach handling tests and an arrester hook. Three Su-27 prototypes and an early Su-27UB were used for early take-off trials from a dummy carrier deck. The first 'deck' take-off was made from the dummy deck at Saki on 28 August 1982. The dummy deck was subsequently rebuilt to incorporate a ski-ramp identical to that fitted to the first Soviet carrier, *Tbilisi*, and intended to reduce the take-off run.

Su-27K prototypes

The three modified Su-27s were followed by a batch of **T10K** (Su-27K) prototypes, each of which differed slightly from the others. The first Su-27K prototype made its maiden flight on 17 August 1987. All of the T10Ks featured twin nosewheels, wing and tailplane folding, and double-slotted trailing-edge flaps.

The Su-27K prototypes were also all fitted with abbreviated 'tail stings' and square-section arrester hooks; none had brake 'chutes. Later prototypes

also had an extra pair of inboard underwing weapons pylons, raising the total number to 12, including the wingtip stations.

Carrier landing trials began on 1 November 1989, when Victor Pugachev landed the second Su-27K aboard *Tbilisi*, becoming the first Russian pilot to land a conventional aircraft aboard the carrier. The second prototype was the first full-standard Su-27K.

Russian naval pilots began carrier operations on 26 September 1991. Service trials were highly successful and led to State Acceptance Trials, which were successfully passed in 1994.

Carrier fleet?

Had the Soviet Union's ambitious plan to build four aircraft-carriers reached fruition, perhaps as many as 72 production Su-27Ks would have been required simply for their air wings. However, the end of the Cold War led to a massive down-scaling of the USSR's carrier programme. With the *Admiral Kuznetsov* (formerly *Tbilisi*, and before that *Brezhnev*) the only carrier left for service with the Russian navy, both the AEW aircraft and MiG-29K programmes were abandoned.

If only one fixed-wing type was to be procured for the new carrier, logic would have dictated that it should be the multi-role MiG-29K. However, the political influence of Sukhoi's chief designer, Mikhail Simonov, was such that the Sukhoi was selected for production and service, and the Russian navy was forced to accept the aircraft's (and thus the carrier's) more limited role.

The Su-27K does enjoy some significant advantages over the MiG-29K, primarily exceptional range performance. Before entering service, the production Su-27K was redesignated **Su-33** by the OKB, but the aircraft remains a navalised version of the basic IA-PVO interceptor, with the same basic 'Slot Back' radar and with only a very limited ground-attack capability. It is uncertain whether the AV-MF regularly uses the Su-33 designation.

First cruise

Kuznetsov's first truly operational deployment took place in early 1996, when it spent two months in the Mediterranean. The ship's

Service introduction of the Su-27K made it eligible for a separate ASCC/NATO reporting name suffix, and the aircraft is now understood to have been known as 'Flanker-D'. The reporting name saw little use, however, since the aircraft's correct designation (and the OKB's Su-33 designation) became widely known and used.

complement included the Su-27K-equipped 1st Squadron of the Severomorsk Regiment. Although 24 Su-27Ks have been built, *Kuznetsov's* complement for this first cruise included just seven production Su-27K aircraft.

Since that first cruise, which revealed a number of operational deficiencies in the ship/aircraft combination, Russian defence spending has been further cut. Only a handful of

cruises has therefore occurred, but Su-27K pilots have trained in inflight-refuelling with Il-78 tankers, and live weapons training with AAMs has been accomplished.

With the advent of the two-seat **Su-27KUB**, the Russian navy potentially has a formidable new asset. Originally considered to be a naval Su-32FN/Su-34 derivative by the West, the aircraft combines a two-seat side-by-side cockpit with a conical nose profile. Designed as a trainer, the Su-27KUB also has great potential as an ECM, reconnaissance or AEW platform. However, even if funding allows, it is likely to be many years before such developments could take effect.

An Su-27K runs up to full power on **Admiral Kuznetsov.** *Early in the Russian carrier programme, it was decided that the development of a steam catapult would not be possible within the timescale set for the first of the new carriers, and that they would be fitted with ski ramps instead. The Su-27K makes unassisted take-offs, using a combination of restrainers and take-off ramps.*

Mikoyan MiG-29K A carrierborne 'Fulcrum'

Wearing calibration markings enabling it to be accurately tracked during carrier trials work, the first MiG-29K is illustrated here in its standard MiG-29 camouflage finish.

The **MiG-29K** project was launched to provide a multi-role strike fighter to complement the Su-27K interceptor on the carriers intended to enter Soviet navy service during the 1990s. However, in the event only the Su-27K was procured for service.

Trials with the hooked **MiG-29KVP** proved that the MiG-29 could be operated safely from a ski-jump, and that arrested landings were possible at operationally useful weights. However, it was decided that the ideal carrierborne MiG-29 would require both additional wing area and additional thrust. Further, improved high-lift devices might produce a useful reduction in approach speed, without unacceptably raising the angle of attack on touch-down.

Since a new variant of the MiG-29 would be required, Mikoyan adapted it from the new multi-role MiG-29M, with its lightweight airframe, multi-mode/multi-role radar and PGM capability.

Uprated engines

There was a degree of cross-fertilisation between the MiG-29M and the MiG-29K, with the uprated RD-33K engines developed for the carrier aircraft eventually being adopted for the -29M, too. The new engine gave 92.17 kN (20,725 lb st) thrust for a limited period, useful on launch and in the event of a missed approach

or go-around. It also had FADEC (full-authority digital engine control) and was made of advanced materials.

New wing

The quintessence of the MiG-29K lay in its new wing, designed with power-folding at roughly one-third span. The wing was fitted with broader-chord double-slotted trailing-edge flaps, and featured the extended-span ailerons of the MiG-29M, though they were modified to droop (as flaperons) at low speed. The tip was moved further outboard, and increased in chord and depth, housing new ECM systems. The leading edge was of reduced sweep-back, giving only slightly greater chord at the root. The leading-edge flaps were redesigned.

In addition to the new wing, the MiG-29K introduced a new, strengthened, long-stroke undercarriage, and had a tailhook. The MiG-29K prototypes also introduced a neat, fully-retractable inflight-refuelling probe below the forward edge of the port side of the cockpit windscreen.

Production MiG-29Ks would have had a fully automatic carrier landing system, in addition to the Uzel beacon homing system. The prototypes used a system derived from that fitted to the Yak-38. This was sufficient to guarantee that the aircraft would touch down

The first MiG-29K, Bort '311', is seen during trials aboard Tbilisi. These included landing aboard with R-73 and R-77 missiles, the main air-to-air weapons of the type. The aircraft bore the brunt of the carrier trials, carrying photo-calibration marks on the nose. The extended and bulged wingtips housed electronic warfare equipment.

within a 6-m (20-ft) circle on the deck, within tight airspeed and vertical speed limits – not quite enough to guarantee getting a wire, and not quite enough to guarantee being on the deck centreline point.

Carrier trials

Commonality with the MiG-29M meant that only two prototypes of the MiG-29K would be required, to prove the carrier-specific items. The first prototype was flown on 23 June 1988, and was subsequently used for extensive trials aboard Tbilisi from 1 November 1989. The second prototype was used mainly for sys-

tems trials, and made only six carrier landings.

The end of the Cold War and the break-up of the USSR led to the abandonment of Tbilisi's planned sister ships. Tbilisi itself became Admiral Kuznetsov, while the procurement of two separate fighter aircraft types for its air wing seemed unmanageably extravagant, and it became obvious that a competition

was emerging between the Su-27K and MiG-29K.

The Su-27K emerged victorious from this competition, but all was not lost for the MiG-29K. In 2000, India purchased the carrier Admiral Gorshkov from Russia. Requiring a multi-role fighter to equip the carrier, the country has ordered 46 MiG-29Ks, for delivery after 2003.

While the first MiG-29K was finished in a standard light-grey scheme, the second aircraft, Bort '312', sported this slate-grey paint. Additional markings were MiG and MAPO (Moscow Aircraft Production Organisation) badges, and the St Andrew's Cross ensign of the Russian navy. The aircraft was still active in 1998.

British Aerospace Sea Harrier FRS.Mk 1

STOVL naval fighter

The FRS designation reflected the Sea Harrier's triple capability as a fleet defence fighter, reconnaissance platform and strike/attack aircraft. This Sea Harrier FRS.Mk 1 carries the markings of the squadron commander of No. 801 Sqn, FAA. After the Falklands War, twin AIM-9 rails were added to the Sea Harrier's outer pylons.

The **BAe Sea Harrier** was developed from the RAF's Harrier close support and reconnaissance warplane, the world's first and, at that time, only operational short take-off and vertical landing (STOVL) aircraft. The Sea Harrier fortuitously filled the gap left by the phase-out of the Fleet Air Arm's Phantoms and the 1979 decommissioning of HMS *Ark Royal*, the last conventional aircraft carrier in service with the Royal Navy. The advent of the Sea Harrier happily coincided with the introduction of a new generation of 20,000-ton light carriers intended primarily for the anti-submarine role. These three ships were intended to embark only helicopters, and

the Sea Harrier was instrumental in retaining some fixed-wing strike capability when the FAA was otherwise destined to become an all-helicopter force. Concurrent with the RN's receipt of HMS *Invincible*, dubbed a 'through-deck cruiser' rather than an aircraft carrier to get it past UK Treasury scrutiny, the Sea Harrier became one of the most important types ever procured by the FAA. The 1982 Falklands War then proved the prudency of the decision to adopt the Sea Harrier.

Harrier at sea

Although a Harrier, in its original P.1127 form, had landed on *Ark Royal* as early as 8 February 1963, the

Royal Navy initially had little interest in the programme. Naval interest gradually increased, however, spurred by the knowledge that no other fixed-wing aircraft could be ordered, and in May 1975 an initial order for 24 **Sea Harrier FRS.Mk 1** single-seat warplanes and one **Harrier T.Mk 4A** two-seat trainer was placed, followed by a further order for 10 more Sea Harrier FRS.Mk 1s in May 1978.

The main differences between the RAF's Harrier GR.Mk 3 and the Sea Harrier FRS.Mk 1 were the latter's front fuselage contours, with a painted radome covering a Ferranti Blue Fox radar. The cockpit was raised by 0.25 m (10 in) and the canopy was revised to give

the pilot better fields of vision. An improved Pegasus Mk 104 turbofan was fitted. An autopilot was added, as was a revised nav/attack system and a new HUD. Magnesium was deleted from all airframe areas likely to be exposed to corrosion from salt water.

Into service, into war

Embarking aboard HMS *Hermes* in June 1981, No. 800 Sqn was joined by No. 801 Sqn. Both units were subsequently deployed as part of the RN's fixed-wing air assets during the Falklands conflict, in which the Sea Harrier served with distinction. Particularly significant during the war was the supply from the USA of AIM-9L Sidewinder short-range

AAMs. Scoring 22 confirmed victories, the Sea Harrier force lost six aircraft, all of them to causes other than aerial combat.

Contributing greatly to the weapons load with which Sea Harriers were launched was the 'ski jump', a ramp fitted to carrier bows. Following the South Atlantic operation, 14 Sea Harrier FRS.Mk 1s were ordered as attrition replacements and, in 1984, nine more single-seaters as well as three **Harrier T.Mk 4(N)** trainers were added.

In 1979, the Indian navy ordered the first of its 23 **Sea Harrier FRS.Mk 51** and six **Harrier T.Mk 60** machines, to become the only export operator. The survivors remained in service in late 2002.

SPECIFICATION

BAe Sea Harrier FRS.Mk 1
Type: single-seat carrierborne STOVL fighter, reconnaissance and strike/attack warplane
Powerplant: one Rolls-Royce Pegasus Mk 104 vectored-thrust turbofan engine rated at 96 kN (21,500 lb st)
Performance: maximum speed more than 1185 km/h (736 mph) at low altitude; initial climb rate about 15240 m (50,000 ft) per minute; service ceiling 15545 m (51,000 ft);

radius 750 km (460 miles) on a hi-hi-hi interception mission
Weights: empty 6374 kg (14,052 lb); maximum take-off 11884 kg (26,200 lb)
Dimensions: wing span 7.7 m (25 ft 3 in); length 14.5 m (47 ft 7 in); height 3.71 m (12 ft 2 in); wing area 18.68 m² (202.10 sq ft)
Armament: up to a maximum of 3629 kg (8,000 lb) or normal 2268 kg (5,000 lb) of disposable stores for STO or VTO respectively

BAe's Sea Harrier entered FAA service with colourful markings applied over its Extra Dark Sea Grey/white colour scheme. The aircraft were repainted in more sombre tones on their way to the South Atlantic.

British Aerospace Sea Harrier FA.Mk 2 Upgraded 'Shar'

In refining the Sea Harrier as a more capable interceptor while retaining its reconnaissance and strike/attack capability, BAe made some significant changes to the airframe. The company received a contract in January 1985 for the project definition phase of the programme, which included two conversions of the Sea Harrier FRS.Mk 1 to the standard that was known as the **Sea Harrier FRS.Mk 2** up to May 1994, when it was changed to **Sea Harrier F/A.Mk 2** and then to **FA.Mk 2** in 1995.

In 1984 it had been reported that the Ministry of Defence planned to award a contract to BAe and Ferranti to cover a mid-life update of the entire Sea Harrier fleet, but these plans were substantially revised in 1985 to cover an upgrade of 30 airframes with Blue Vixen radar, an improved RWR, JTIDS and provision for the AIM-120 AMRAAM. The original BAe proposal also covered the installation of wing-tip Sidewinder rails. These additions, along with several aerodynamic refinements, were eventually cut

from the project, but a kinked wing leading edge and wing fence remained.

The FA.Mk 2 greatly improves the capabilities of the basic Sea Harrier, or 'Shar'. Nevertheless, the type is due for retirement in the period 2004-06.

A revised radome was needed to house the Blue Vixen radar, giving the Sea Harrier FA.Mk 2's nose a more elongated appearance than that of its predecessor. This aircraft carries the markings of No. 899 Sqn, FAA.

The first of two prototype conversions flew on 19 September 1988. Despite the addition of an extra equipment bay and a recontoured nose to house the Blue Vixen radar, the Sea Harrier FA.Mk 2 is actually shorter overall due to the elimination of the nose-mounted pitot tube of the earlier variant.

Additional stores

No increase in wing span was found to be necessary to carry additional stores, including a pair of 190-Imp gal (864-litre) drop tanks plus AIM-120s (or ALARM anti-radar missiles) on each of the outer pylons, although ferry tips are available to increase span to 9.04 m (29 ft 8 in). The cockpit of the Sea Harrier FA.Mk 2 introduced new multi-function CRT displays and HOTAS controls to reduce pilot workload, and the type is powered by the Pegasus Mk 106 turbofan, a navalised version of the Mk 105 fitted to the AV-8B, with no magnesium in its construction.

On 7 December 1988 a contract was awarded for the conversion of 31 Sea Harrier FRS.Mk 1s to the Mk 2 standard. On 6 March 1990 the MoD revealed its intent to order at least 10 new-build Sea Harrier FRS.Mk 2s to augment the conversions, attrition having reduced the RN's Sea Harrier fleet to 39 aircraft. In January 1994 this intent was confirmed as an order for 18 Sea Harrier FRS.Mk 2s and an additional eight conversions, for a total of 57 Sea Harrier FA.Mk 2s.

In order to enhance pilot conversion training, a new two-seat **Harrier T.Mk 8** trainer was created, the four such aircraft supplementing the three surviving Harrier T.Mk 4Ns from 1996. Essentially a reconfigured T.Mk 4N, the Harrier T.Mk 8 duplicates the Sea Harrier FA.Mk 2's systems except for the radar.

SPECIFICATION
BAe Sea Harrier FA.Mk 2
Type: single-seat carrierborne STOVL fighter and attack warplane
Powerplant: one Rolls-Royce Pegasus Mk 106 vectored-thrust turbofan engine rated at 96 kN (21,500 lb st)
Performance: maximum level speed 1144 km/h (711 mph) at sea level; initial climb rate about 15240 m (50,000 ft) per minute; service ceiling about 15545 m (51,000 ft); radius 750 km (460 miles) on a hi-hi-hi interception mission
Weights: empty 6374 kg (14,052 lb); maximum take-off 11884 kg (26,200 lb)
Dimensions: wing span 7.7 m (25 ft 3 in); length 14.17 m (46 ft 6 in); height 3.71 m (12 ft 2 in); wing area 18.68 m² (202.10 sq ft)
Armament: up to a maximum of 3629 kg (8,000 lb) or normal 2268 kg (5,000 lb) of disposable stores for STO or VTO respectively

McDonnell Douglas/BAe Harrier II CAS aircraft

Italy's pair of TAV-8B aircraft apparently cost $25 million each. This machine wears the markings of 1 Gruppo Aereo of the Marina Militare, based at Grottaglie.

With the AV-8A Harrier already in service, the USMC eventually backed the development of the advanced **AV-8B Harrier II**, which was intended to carry a larger warload and to provide better range/endurance characteristics.

The new design was based around a larger wing of supercritical section, and was also schemed with more carbon fibre in other airframe areas and a completely revised cockpit, with HOTAS controls and a higher seating position for the pilot. First flown on 9 November 1978, fitted to an AV-8A (which became the first of two **YAV-8B** service test aircraft), the new wing had six hardpoints.

Into production

The USMC took delivery of the first production aircraft during 1983, later aircraft introducing more powerful engines. A total of 286 aircraft was built, including six

As fitted to the Harrier II Plus, the APG-65 radar uses an antenna cropped by 5 cm (2 in) to fit the AV-8B's fuselage cross-section.

attrition replacements ordered after Desert Storm. Several two-seat **TAV-8B** aircraft were also built.

From the 167th airframe, all USMC AV-8Bs were provided with a night-attack capability with the installation of a FLIR, an improved HUD, an HDD and a colour moving map. The terms **Night Attack Harrier II** or **Night Attack AV-8B** are sometimes applied unofficially to these aircraft. The 205th AV-8B off the production line was the first fully equipped **AV-8B Harrier II Plus**. It made its maiden flight on 22 September 1992. Equipped with the APG-65 radar, the Harrier II Plus has a revised FLIR fairing, but is otherwise externally identical to late AV-8Bs. APG-65 gives compatibility with AIM-7 and AIM-120 AAMs. It also allows the use of the AGM-84 Harpoon AShM. The last 24 USMC aircraft were built as II Pluses, while many more were converted.

Spain and Italy have also purchased the AV-8B. With the commissioning of the carrier *Principe de Asturias* in 1989, the Spanish navy embarked 12 **EAV-8B** (**VA.2 Matador II**) aircraft. It also ordered 13 (later reduced to eight) Harrier II Pluses in November 1992 and the surviving EAV-8Bs are being upgraded to this standard. A two-seat **TAV-8B** was ordered in March 1992.

In May 1989, Italy ordered two TAV-8Bs from the USMC. Its first batch of three ex-USMC Harrier II Plus aircraft was ordered in July 1991, followed by a further 13 in November 1992.

SPECIFICATION
McDonnell Douglas/BAe AV-8B Harrier II Plus
Type: single-seat STOVL multi-role warplane
Powerplant: one Rolls-Royce F402-RR-408A (Pegasus 11-61) vectored-thrust turbofan rated at 106 kN (23,800-lb st)
Performance: maximum level speed 'clean' at sea level 1065 km/h (662 mph); service ceiling over 15240 m (50,000 ft); time on station for a CAP at a 185-km 115-mile) radius 2 hours 42 minutes
Weights: empty operating 6740 kg (14,860 lb); maximum take-off 14061 kg (31,000 lb) after short take-off
Dimensions: wing span 9.25 m (30 ft 4 in); length 14.55 m (47 ft 9 in); height 3.55 m (11 ft 7¾); wing area 22.61 m² (243.40 sq ft) including LERXes
Armament: up to 6003 kg (13,235 lb) of stores usually including two 25-mm GAU-12 cannon in underfuselage pods

Boeing F/A-18 A/B/C/D Hornet
Carrier attack fighter

The US Navy's VFA-87 swopped its A-7 Corsair II attack jets for F/A-18Cs in July 1987. The unit further upgraded to the night-attack F/A-18C, as shown here, in 1992.

Mk 83 AIR (Air Inflatable Retard) bombs fall away from a US Marine Corps F/A-18D. The use of IR-decoy flares acts as a defence against IR-homing SAMs.

SPECIFICATION

Boeing F/A-18C Hornet
Type: single-seat carrierborne and land-based fighter and strike/attack warplane
Powerplant: two General Electric F404-GE-402 turbofan engines each rated at 78.73 kN (17,700 lb st) with afterburning
Performance: maximum speed more than 1915 km/h (1,190 mph) or Mach 1.80 at high altitude; initial climb rate 13715 m (45,000 ft) per minute, combat ceiling about 15740 m (50,000 ft), radius more than 740 km (460 miles) on a fighter mission or

1065 km (662 miles) for an attack mission
Weights: empty 10810 kg (23,832 lb); maximum take-off 15234 kg (33,585 lb) for a fighter mission or 21888 kg (48,753 lb) for an attack mission
Dimensions: wing span 11.43 m (37 ft 6 in) without tip-mounted missiles; length 17.07 m (56 ft); height 4.66 m (15 ft 3½ in); wing area 37.16 m2 (400 sq ft)
Armament: one internal 20-mm M61A1 Vulcan six-barrel cannon, plus up to 7031 kg (15,500 lb) of ordnance

The world's premier naval fighter originated as a derivative of the **Northrop YF-17** that was pitted successfully against the General Dynamics YF-16 in the USN's Air Combat Fighter programme of 1976. The first of 11 trials Hornets made its maiden flight on 18 November 1978.

Production of the initial **F/A-18A Hornet** single-seater eventually totalled 371 aircraft, the first US Navy squadron receiving its aircraft in 1983. Two

examples of the **TF-18A**, later redesignated F/A-18B, featured in the original contract. Procurement of the **F/A-18B** for the USN and USMC ended with the 40th example, and this version has never been employed by front-line forces.

The F/A-18 offers much greater weapons delivery accuracy than its predecessors, and is a genuinely multi-role aircraft, with remarkable dogfighting ability. The F/A-18 made its combat debut during the El

Dorado Canyon action against Libya in April 1986 and was heavily committed to action during Operation Desert Storm in 1991. The F/A-18A was superseded by the **F/A-18C**, which remained the principal single-seat production model up to 1999, some 347 having been ordered for US service.

The first F/A-18C made its maiden flight on 3 September 1986. This

introduced compatibility with the AIM-120 AMRAAM and the IIR version of the AGM-65 Maverick missile, as well as improved avionics – which from 1994 included the improved APG-73 variant of the Hornet's original APG-65 radar – and a new NACES ejection seat.

Night attack

After 137 baseline F/A-18Cs had been delivered, production switched to a night attack version with equipment including GEC Cat's Eye pilot's night vision goggles compatibility, an AAR-50 TINS (Thermal Imaging Navigation System) pod, Kaiser AVQ-28 raster HUD, externally carried AAS-38 FLIR (Forward-Looking Infra-Red) targeting pod, and colour multi-function displays. The first 'night-attack' Hornet was delivered on 1 November 1989. In addition, some 31 baseline two-seat **F/A-18D** trainers were built before 109 exam-

ples of the F/A-18D counterpart to the night-attack F/A-18C were produced. The night-attack version of the F/A-18D replaced the Grumman A-6 Intruder with the USMC's all-weather attack squadrons. Originally dubbed **F/A-18D+**, the aircraft features 'uncoupled' cockpits, usually with no control column in the rear cockpit but two sidestick weapons controllers. Marine Corps F/A-18Ds served with distinction during combat operations including Desert Storm in 1991 and Allied Force in 1999.

Export sales

The Hornet's versatility has led to substantial export sales. Canada was the first foreign customer, taking delivery of 98 single-seat **CF-188A** and 40 two-seat **CF-188B** aircraft, while Australia followed with an order for 57 **AF-18A** and 18 **ATF-18A** trainers. Spain purchased 60 **EF-18A** and 12 **EF-18B** machines (local designation **C.15** and **CE.15** respectively) and later acquired 24 former US Navy F/A-18As from late 1995. Kuwait received 32 **KAF-18C** warplanes and eight **KAF-18D** machines, while Switzerland took 26 F/A-18Cs and eight F/A-18Ds. Finland procured a fleet of 57 F/A-18Cs and seven F/A-18Ds, while Malaysia is unique in buying only the F/A-18D, of which eight were ordered.

Canada's much-depleted CF-188 fleet is involved in anti-narcotics work, as well as the air defence of Canada.

Setting out on an Enduring Freedom mission, this F/A-18C carries a pair of JDAM (Joint Direct Attack Munition) weapons with Mk 84 warheads. Note the use of four drop tanks – the Hornet has always been plagued by lack of range and has relied heavily on RAF tanker support for Enduring Freedom strikes.

Boeing F/A-18E/F Super Hornet

Boeing is supplying the Super Hornet to replace the US Navy's F-14 Tomcats, many of its Hornets and, perhaps, the EA-6B.

The first of McDonnell Douglas's (Boeing from 1997) Hornet upgrade concepts to reach fruition is the **F/A-18E Super Hornet**. The first F/A-18E made its maiden flight in November 1995 and the first aircraft was formally accepted into service with VFA-122 on 15 January 1999.

New avionics

The avionics upgrade is centred on the Raytheon APG-73 radar as already fitted to late versions of the F/A-18C. The IDECM (integrated defensive electronic countermeasures) system has three major elements: an ALR-67(V)3 RWR, ALQ-214 radio-frequency countermeasures system and ALE-55 fibre-optic towed decoy system; the last two are still under development, so the F/A-18E is initially being operated with the ALE-50 towed decoy system. The cockpit of the F/A-18E is similar to that of the F/A-18C with the exception of a larger flat-panel display in place of the current three HDDs (head-down displays).

A bigger bug

The enlarged airframe incorporates measures to reduce radar cross section and includes a fuselage lengthened by 0.86 m (2 ft 10 in), an enlarged wing characterised by a thicker section and two more hardpoints, enlarged LERXes, and horizontal and vertical tail surfaces. The Super Hornet also has a structure extensively redesigned to reduce weight and cost without sacrifice of strength. The Super Hornet also features a new quadruplex digital 'fly-by-wire' control system without the Hornet's mechanical back-up system.

Boeing has flown an F/A-18F in a configuration representing that which may be adopted by the Growler. This includes ALQ-99 jamming pods as carried by the EA-6B; the original concept of developing an all-new system for the EA-18 seems to have been abandoned.

The **F/A-18F Super Hornet** is the two-seat development of the F/A-18E, with the rear cockpit equipped with the same displays as the front cockpit and otherwise configured for alternative combat or training roles. The USN had originally planned to procure 1,000 Super Hornets, but in 1997 the total was reduced to 548. Any delay in the service debut of the F-35 to a time later than 2008-10, however, will see the number of Super Hornets rise to 748. An F/A-18F electronic combat variant has been proposed as a replacement for the Grumman EA-6B Prowler. This will be capable of active jamming as well as lethal SEAD and is known in service as the **EA-18 Growler**.

An F/A-18F (upper) and F/A-18C cavort during testing. The Super Hornet is most easily distinguished from the Hornet by means of its square intakes and enlarged LERXes (Leading Edge Root Extensions).

SPECIFICATION

Boeing F/A-18E Super Hornet
Type: single-seat carrierborne and land-based multi-role fighter, attack and maritime air superiority warplane
Powerplant: two General Electric F414-GE-400 turbofan engines each rated at 97.86 kN (22,000 lb st) with afterburning
Performance: maximum speed more than 1915 km/h (1,190 mph) or Mach 1.80 at high altitude; service ceiling about 15240 m (50,000 ft); radius 1095 km (681 miles) on a hi-hi-hi interdiction mission with four 454-kg (1,000-lb) bombs, two AIM-9 Sidewinder AAMs and two drop tanks; 1901 km (560 miles) on a hi-lo-hi interdiction mission with the same stores, or 278 km (173 miles) on a 135-minute maritime air superiority mission with six AAMs and three drop tanks
Weights: empty 13864 kg (30,564 lb); maximum take-off 29937 kg (66,000 lb)
Dimensions: wing span 13.62 m (44 ft 8½ in) including tip-mounted AAMs; length 18.31 m (60 ft 1¼ in); height 4.88 m (16 ft); wing area 46.45 m² (500 sq ft)
Armament: one 20-mm M61A2 Vulcan rotary six-barrel cannon with 570 rounds, plus up to 8051 kg (17,750 lb) of disposable stores, including the 10/20-kiloton B57 and 100/500-kiloton B61 freefall nuclear weapons, AIM-120 AMRAAM, AIM7 Sparrow and AIM-9 Sidewinder AAMs, AGM-88 HARM, AGM-65 Maverick ASM, AGM-84 Harpoon anti-ship missile, AGM-62 Walleye optronically-guided glide bomb, Paveway LGBs, Mk 80 series bombs, Rockeye and CBU-series cluster bombs, BLU-series napalm bombs and LAU-series multiple launchers for 2.75-in (70-mm) air-to-surface unguided rockets

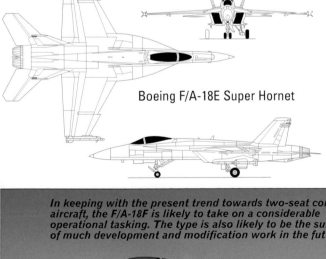

Boeing F/A-18E Super Hornet

In keeping with the present trend towards two-seat combat aircraft, the F/A-18F is likely to take on a considerable operational tasking. The type is also likely to be the subject of much development and modification work in the future.

Grumman F-14 Tomcat Swing-wing naval fighter

From May 1995, VF-2 re-equipped with F-14D Tomcats. This aircraft is depicted with a typical air-to-air load of four under-fuselage Phoenix long-range AAMs, and two each of the Sparrow and Sidewinder short-range missiles.

Designed as a successor to the F-4 Phantom II in the fleet air defence role for the US Navy, the **Grumman F-14 Tomcat** was originally conceived to engage and destroy targets at extreme range, before they could pose a threat to the carrier battle group. The **F-14A Tomcat** remains a formidable warplane, even though the original F-14A has been in service for almost 30 years. Production of the F-14A for the US Navy eventually totalled 556 examples, while 80 broadly similar machines were purchased by Iran before the downfall of the Shah. Of the latter, only 79 were actually delivered (one being diverted to the USN). The F-14 continues to be the Navy's primary air defence aircraft although with the introduction of the F/A-18E/F Super Hornet into service from late 1999, the days of the F-14 have been increasingly numbered.

Weapons system

The key to the F-14's effectiveness lies in its advanced avionics suite, the Hughes AWG-9 fire control system representing the most capable long-range interceptor radar in service, with the ability to detect, track and engage targets at ranges in excess of 160 km (100 miles). Early aircraft also had an infra-red search and track (IRST) system, replacing this during production (and by retrofit) with a long-range video camera known as TCS. The armament options allow the aircraft to engage targets over a huge range from

close up to extreme BVR (beyond visual range).

The AIM-54 Phoenix remains the longest-ranged air-to-air missile in Western service at the beginning of the 21st century and in tests it has demonstrated the ability to detect and kill targets at unparalleled distances. In the medium-range arena, Tomcat employs the AIM-7 Sparrow, not having been upgraded for compatibility with the AIM-120 AMRAAM. For short-range, close-in engagements, the F-14 carries the well-proven AIM-9 Sidewinder. Finally, there is a single M61A1

Vulcan 20-mm Gatling-type rotary cannon in the lower port fuselage with 675 rounds of ammunition.

Tomcat development

Development was initiated in the late 1960s, following the cancellation of the ill-fated F-111B naval fighter, which initially left the Navy in the unenviable position of having no new fighter in prospect. Grumman had already invested a considerable amount of effort in the navalised F-111B, and used this experience in designing a new variable-geometry fighter (the **G-303**) which was duly selected by the

Carrying a quartet of Mk 83 freefall bombs on its underfuselage stations, this F-14A is about to fly a practice strike. The aircraft hails from VF-211 'Checkmates', a unit based aboard USS John C. Stennis between January and July 2002 for the Tomcat's last cruise aboard the vessel.

Navy in January 1969. Grumman's use of a variable-geometry wing allowed excellent high-speed performance to be combined with docile low-speed handling characteristics for operations around the carrier, and a high degree of agility. A dozen **YF-14A** development aircraft were ordered, with the first making its maiden flight on 21 December 1970.

The programme made

reasonably swift progress, culminating in deliveries to the Navy from October 1972, with the first operational cruise in 1974. Production continued into the 1980s and a total of 26 front-line and four second-line squadrons was eventually equipped with the F-14A Tomcat.

Although generally successful, the F-14 has suffered many difficulties

VX-9 'Vampires' is a test unit involved in developing all aspects of the F-14's air-to-air role. This F-14D has been finished in the black scheme traditionally worn by VX-4 aircraft and continued when VX-4 and VX-5 were combined into VX-9. The aircraft was photographed in 2002 during Operation Cope Snapper.

since entering fleet service. Many were engine-related, the TF30 turbofan proving something of an Achilles heel. Fan blade losses caused several crashes before improved quality control and steel containment cases alleviated the worst consequences of engine failure. In addition, the engine was prone to compressor stall, especially during air combat manoeuvring training, and the aircraft's vicious departure characteristics (especially with one engine out) resulted in many further losses. Many problems were solved when the revised TF30-P-414A version of the powerplant was adopted as standard.

Other missions

In addition to fleet air defence tasks, F-14As are also used for reconnaissance missions, using the Tactical Air Reconnaissance Pod System (TARPS), and it is usual for three TARPS-capable aircraft to be assigned to each carrier air wing. New digital TARPS pods have replaced the original wet-film units. More recently, the F-14A has also acquired a secondary air-to-ground role, capitalising on a modest attack capability that was built in from the outset, but never utilised. The **F-14A 'Bombcat'** initially carried only conventional 'iron' bombs, but has now had the LANTIRN pod integrated for use with laser-guided bombs.

Engine problems have plagued the F-14 throughout its career. Later TF30 models solved the worst of these problems, but re-engining with the F110 has transformed the Tomcat's performance.

Continuing problems with the TF30 engine of the F-14A were a key factor in the development of re-engined and upgraded variants of the Tomcat. One of the original prototype airframes was fitted with two F401-PW-400s and employed for an abbreviated test programme as the **F-14B** as early as 1973-74. Technical problems and financial difficulties forced the abandonment of the programme, and the aircraft was placed into storage, re-emerging as the **F-14B Super Tomcat** with F101DFE (Derivative Fighter Engine) turbofans. This engine was developed into the General Electric F110-GE-400 turbofan, which was selected to power improved production Tomcat variants. It was decided to produce two distinct new Tomcats, one designated **F-14A+** (primarily by conversion of existing F-14As) with the new engine, and another, designated **F-14D**, with the new engine and improved digital avionics. The F-14A+ was originally regarded as an interim type, all examples of which would eventually be converted to full F-14D Tomcat standard.

'Bs' and 'Ds'

Subsequently, the F-14A+ was formally redesignated as the **F-14B**, 38 new-build examples being joined by 32 F-14A rebuilds in equipping half-a-dozen deployable squadrons starting in 1988. These incorporated some avionics changes, including a modernised fire control system, new radios, upgraded RWRs (radar warning receivers), and various cockpit changes. F-14Bs were

These F-14s were photographed late in 2001 preparing for the type's last departure from USS Enterprise. Note the over-sweep position of the wings.

the first re-engined Tomcats to enter fleet service.

Two modified F-14As flew as F-14D prototypes and the first F-14D to be built as such made its maiden flight on 9 February 1990. The F-14D also added digital avionics, with digital radar processing and displays (adding these to standard AWG-9 hardware under the redesignation APG-71), and a side-by-side undernose TCS/IRST sensor pod. Other improvements introduced by the F-14D include OBOGS (on-board oxygen-generating system), NACES (Naval Aircrew Escape System) ejection seats, and AN/ALR-67 radar warning receiver equipment. Like the F-14A, the F-14D has a full ground attack capability. However, a subsequent US Department of Defense

decision to cease funding the F-14D effectively halted the Navy's drive to upgrade its force of Tomcats. In consequence, the service has received only 37 new-build F-14Ds, while plans to upgrade approximately 400 existing F-14As to a similar standard were cancelled.

F-14D deliveries to the Navy began in 1990, when training squadron VF-124 accepted its first F-14D at Miramar. The type has been used in Operation Southern Watch over Iraq, including an unsuccessful Phoenix shot against a pair of MiG-23s. The F-14 performed well on attack missions during Operation Enduring Freedom. The F-14 is slowly being retired; the last F-14D is due to leave the fleet in 2008.

SPECIFICATION

Grumman F-14A Tomcat
Type: two-seat carrierborne fleet air defence fighter and interceptor, with ground attack capability
Powerplant: two Pratt & Whitney TF30-P-412A/414A turbofans each rated at 92.97 kN (20,900 lb st) with afterburning
Performance: maximum level speed 'clean' at high altitude 2485 km/h (1,544 mph); maximum rate of climb at sea level more than 9145 m (30,000 ft) per minute; service ceiling more than 15240 m (50,000 ft); radius on a combat air patrol with six AIM-7 Sparrows and four AIM-9 Sidewinders 1233 km (766 miles)
Weights: empty 18191 kg (40,104 lb) with -414A engines; maximum take-off 32098 kg (70,764 lb) with six Phoenix
Dimensions: wing span 19.54 m

(64 ft 1½ in) spread, 11.65 m (38 ft 2½ in) swept and 10.15 m (33 ft 3½ in) overswept; length 19.1 m (62 ft 8 in); height 4.88 m (16 ft); wing area 52.49 m² (565 sq ft)
Armament: standard armament consists of an internal M61A1 Vulcan 20-mm six-barrelled cannon and an AIM-9M Sidewinder on the shoulder launch rail of each wing glove pylon. The main launch rail of each glove pylon can accommodate either an AIM-7M Sparrow or an AIM-54C Phoenix. Four further AIM-7M or AIM-54C missiles can be carried under the fuselage between the engine trunks. 1011-litre (267-US gal) fuel tanks can be carried under the intakes, while 1,000-lb (454-kg) Mk 83 or 2,000-lb (907-kg) Mk 84 GP bombs or other free-fall weaponry can also be carried

Northrop Grumman E-2 Hawkeye Carrier- and land-based

AEW&C aircraft

This E-2C Hawkeye is from the US Navy's VAW-126 'Seahawks', and is illustrated as it appeared when operating from USS Kennedy during the late 1990s.

Since entering service in 1964, the **E-2 Hawkeye** has protected US Navy carrier battle groups and acted as an airborne controller for their aircraft. One of very few types designed specifically for the AEW role, it was first flown in prototype form as long ago as October 1960. As a consequence of its ability to operate from aircraft carriers, the basic **Hawkeye** is extremely compact. A total of 59 production **E-2A** machines was delivered from January 1964; 51 were updated to **E-2B** standard, before production switched to the improved **E-2C**.

E-2C Hawkeye

The first E-2C flew on 23 September 1972 and Grumman had built 139 for the US Navy when the line closed in 1994. However, low-rate production began again in 2000.

External changes to the E-2 have been minor but its systems have been progressively updated. The E-2C was initially equipped with APS-125 search radar, but this was replaced by the AN/APS-139 in **Group I** aircraft from 1988 and the AN/APS-145 in the latest **Group II E-2C**. The latter radar allows a low-flying, fighter-sized aircraft to be detected at up to 407 km (253 miles) away with the E-2C flying at its operational altitude. A passive detection system gives warning of hostile emitters at ranges up to twice the radar detection range. After almost 30 years in service, the E-2C is still an evolving design, and Northrop Grumman developed the even more capable **E-2C Group II Plus** or **Hawkeye 2000**; the last of 21 such new-build machines was scheduled for completion in 2003. Subsequent to Hawkeye 2000, Northrop Grumman has begun development of the **Advanced Hawkeye**. This features all new systems and should reach initial operational capability with the USN in 2011. The Navy plans to buy 75 of the aircraft.

E-2Cs have been exported to Egypt, France, Israel, Japan, Singapore and Taiwan. Many customers are upgrading their E-2s to Hawkeye 2000 standards.

SPECIFICATION	
Northrop Grumman E-2C Hawkeye (Group I configuration onwards) **Type:** carrierborne AEW aircraft **Powerplant:** two Allison T56-A-427 turboprops each rated at 3803 kW (5,100 ehp) **Performance:** maximum level speed 626 km/h (389 mph); maximum cruising speed at optimum altitude 602 km/h (374 mph); maximum rate of climb at sea level over 767 m (2,515 ft) per minute; service ceiling 11275 m (37,000 ft); unrefuelled time on	station at 320 km (200 miles) from base 4 hours 24 minutes; endurance with maximum fuel 6 hours 15 minutes **Weights:** empty 18363 kg (40,484 lb), maximum take-off 24687 kg (54,426 lb) **Dimensions:** wing span 24.56 m (80 ft 7 in); folded width 8.94 m (29 ft 4 in); rotodome diameter 7.32 m (24 ft); length 17.54 m (57 ft 6¾ in); height 5.58 m (18 ft 3¾ in); wing area 65.03 m² (700 sq ft)

Hawkeye 2000 (illustrated) represented a major increase in the capabilities of the E-2 design. Advanced Hawkeye will look very similar.

Lockheed Martin F-35B and F-35C Future tactical fighters

On 26 October 2001, the US government announced that Lockheed Martin had won the JSF (Joint Strike Fighter) competition in the face of stiff opposition from Boeing. The JSF requirement was set out to provide a largely common air frame to fulfil three distinct niches: a CTOL aircraft for the USAF, a carrier-capable aircraft for the US Navy and a STOVL machine for the USMC.

X-35 in detail

Lockheed Martin's **X-35** demonstrators will form the basis of the operational **F-35** fighters, with the first F-35 flight planned for 2005 and the **F-35C** due to enter US Navy service around 2012. F-35C will have a longer-span wing than the other initial variants, with provision for folding. The aircraft will also be fitted with an arrester hook and strengthened landing gear, these and other modifications making it heavier than the CTOL F-35A. All F-35s will primarily carry their armament internally, in bays along the fuselage sides. Stealth was a major consideration in the design and the aircraft has

Pictured in the hover, the X-35B demonstrates the large doors in its upper fuselage. These open to feed air to the lift fan.

been carefully shaped to avoid producing large radar-reflecting surfaces. Apertures, doors and other panels generally have serrated edges, similar to those seen on the F-117.

UK involvement
From an early stage, the UK has been a full partner in the JSF programme. Like the USMC, the UK has opted for the STOVL **F-35B**. All of the F-35 models will initially be powered by the Pratt & Whitney F135 turbofan, delivering around 178 kN (40,000 lb) of thrust with afterburning and exhausting through a vectoring nozzle. On the F-35B, a lift fan, developed by Rolls-Royce and mounted horizontally in the forward fuselage, is dri-

X-35C is immediately recognisable as a naval fighter demonstrator, thanks to the prominent arrester hook mounted beneath its rear fuselage.

ven by the main engine via a gearbox to provide the major part of the thrust needed in

vertical manoeuvres. The UK will base its F-35Bs on two new BAE Systems/Thales

aircraft carriers which are due to enter service in 2012 and 2015.

Export orders for F-35C are unlikely, but F-35B may find a limited market.

Lockheed S-3 Viking Multi-role naval aircraft

The **S-3B Viking** carries out the US Navy's carrier-based sea control mission. The S-3 was originally designed in the early 1970s with a sophisticated ASW sensor suite. The initial **S-3A** variant was replaced in the early 1990s by the S-3B. This incorporates anti-surface warfare upgrades such as the APS-137 inverse synthetic aperture radar and AGM-84 AShM capability. With the demise of the Soviet Union and the increasing dominance of littoral warfare, there has been decreased emphasis on the Viking's ASW role and more emphasis on anti-surface warfare and land-attack missions. Each carrier air wing

With its home base at Oceana, Virginia, this S-3A is seen as deployed onboard the nuclear carrier USS Nimitz with VS-24, air wing CV-8. Many S-3As were refitted with new weapons systems, including provision for Harpoon missiles, and redesignated as S-3B machines.

includes one sea control (VS) squadron equipped with S-3Bs. VS squadrons perform

ASW, anti-shipping, mine-laying, surveillance and tanking missions for the carrier bat-

tle group. This latter mission is accomplished thanks to the D-704 'buddy-buddy' refuelling store, which incorporates a retractable hose for compatibility with the Navy's probe-equipped combat aircraft. Several upgrades have been applied to the Viking, including the addition of GPS, Carrier Aircraft Inertial Navigation System II, new tactical displays, computer memory, SATCOM equipment and improved radios. Several S-3Bs have been involved in anti-drug trafficking duties, using camera systems, FLIR and hand-held sensors. The S-3B is planned for replacement from 2015 by a variant of the Common Support Aircraft,

but may be retired on an accelerated schedule.

Shadow
Sixteen S-3A airframes were converted to **ES 3A Shadow** standard during the early 1990s, with a variety of electronic surveillance and intercept equipment to locate and identify hostile emitters and communications stations. In mid-1998, the Navy made the decision to withdraw the ES-3A from service without replacement. The aircraft's mission avionics suite, becoming obsolescent in the age of interconnectivity in the 'electronic battlefield', was deemed as too expensive to upgrade.

As a force multiplier, the S-3B Viking is a crucial US Navy asset. It is ultimately likely to lose its inflight-refuelling role to the F/A-18E/F.

As a multi-role support type, the Viking continues to have an important front-line role. This Hornet was receiving fuel during an Iraqi Freedom mission.

SPECIFICATION
Lockheed S-3A Viking **Type:** four-crew carrierborne ASW warplane **Powerplant:** two General Electric TF34-GE-2 turbofan engines each rated at 41.26 kN (9,275 lb st) **Performance:** maximum speed 814 km/h (506 mph) at sea level; initial climb rate more than 1280 m (4,200 ft) per minute; service ceiling more than 10670 m (35,000 ft); radius 853 km (530 miles) with typical weapons load and a loiter of 4 hours 30 minutes **Weights:** empty 12088 kg	(26,650 lb); maximum take-off 23832 kg (52,540 lb) **Dimensions:** wing span 20.93 m (68 ft 8 in); length 16.26 m (53 ft 4 in); height 6.63 m (22 ft 9 in); wing area 55.56 m² (598 sq ft) **Armament:** up to 3175 kg (7,000 lb) of disposable stores, including B57 or Mk 80-series bombs, Mk 53 mines, Mk 54 depth bombs, Mk 46 or Mk 53 Barracuda torpedoes, six Mk 20 Mod 2 Rockeye cluster bombs or LAU-10A/A, LAU-61/A, LAU-68/A or LAU-69/A rocket launchers

Aérospatiale Dauphin, HH-65A Dolphin and Eurocopter Panther Multi-role naval helicopters

Left: The SA 365 Dauphin is employed by French naval aviation units for shipboard duties, including small ships ASW/utility work, as well as land-based SAR. This is an example from Flotille 23S, a former ship-based 'Pédro' unit.

Below: This AS 565SB has the type's maximum load of four AS.15TT anti-ship missiles, as well as anti-ship radar with its antenna in a radome beneath the helicopter's nose.

The first version of the **Aérospatiale Dauphin** developed for naval warfare was based on the twin-engined **Dauphin 2** and built for the US Coast Guard. This **SA 366G** or **HH-65A Dolphin** was built for the SAR role. Subsequently, Aérospatiale developed the versatile **AS 365F** from the the AS 365N, intended primarily for the anti-ship role.

Three SA 365Fs were acquired by the Aéronavale for plane-guard duties. The helicopters now service the nuclear-powered aircraft carrier Charles de Gaulle.

The type is also available in SAR configuration, as well as with a more advanced ASW capability.

Eurocopter Panther
The first order for the type was placed by Saudi Arabia, which received 24 examples in two subvariants now designated in the **Eurocopter AS 565 Panther** military series as the **AS 565SC**

(four for the SAR role, later redesignated **AS 565MB**) and the **AS 565SA** (20 anti-ship helicopters, later redesignated **AS 565SB**). Other small export orders were received, Israel designating its AS 565SAs **Atalef**, or bat.

Eurocopter offers two naval variants of the AS 565: the unarmed **AS 565MA** (replaced from 1997 by the **AS 565MB**) for the SAR and sea surveillance roles, and the **AS 565SB** for the ASW as well as anti-ship roles.

SPECIFICATION	
Eurocopter AS 565SA Panther	maximum take-off 4250 kg
Type: two-seat light naval utility	(9,370 lb)
helicopter optimised for the anti-	**Dimensions:** main rotor diameter
ship and anti-submarine roles	11.94 m (39 ft 2 in); length 13.68 m
Powerplant: two Turboméca Arriel	(44 ft 10¾ in) with rotor turning;
1M1 turboshaft engines each rated	height 3.98 m (13 ft ¾ in); main
at 558 kW (749 shp)	rotor disc area 111.97 m²
Performance: maximum cruising	(1,205.26 sq ft)
speed 274 km/h (170 mph) at sea	**Armament:** up to 600 kg (1,323 lb)
level; initial climb rate 420 m	of disposable stores, generally
(1,378 ft) per minute; service ceiling	comprising four AS.15TT light anti-
4575 m (15,010 ft); hovering ceiling	ship missiles or two Mk 46
2600 m (8,530 ft) in ground effect	lightweight ASW torpedoes
and 1860 m (6,100 ft) out of ground	**Payload:** up to 10 passengers or
effect; radius 250 km (155 miles)	1700 kg (3,748 lb) of freight in the
with four AShMs	cabin, or 1600 kg (3,527 lb) of
Weights: empty 2240 kg (4,938 lb);	freight carried as a slung load

Aérospatiale SA 321 Super Frelon SAR and transport helo

To meet a French armed services requirement for a medium transport helicopter, Sud-Aviation flew the prototype **SE.3200 Frelon** (hornet) on 10 June 1959. Powered by three Turmo IIIB turboshafts, the SE.3200 had large external fuel tanks that left the interior clear for a max imum 28 troops, and a swing-tail fuselage to simplify cargo loading. However, development was terminated in favour of a larger and more capable helicopter designed in conjunction with Sikorsky and Fiat. What was to become Western

Europe's largest production helicopter emerged with a rotor system of Sikorsky design, and with a water-tight hull suitable for amphibious operation. Two military prototypes of the Super Frelon were built, the **SA 3210-01** troop transport, and the **SA 3210-02** maritime version for the Aéronavale on 28 May 1963.

France's SA 321 Super Frelons are retained in service for SAR and heavylift transport, for which their long-range capability proves useful.

40013

Four pre-production aircraft were built under the new designation **SA 321 Super Frelon**. These were followed in October 1965 by production **SA 321G** ASW helicopters for the Aéronavale. Apart from ship-based ASW missions, the SA 321G also carried out sanitisation patrols in support of 'Rédoutable'-class ballistic missile submarines. Some were modified with nose-mounted targeting radar for Exocet AShMs. Five **SA 321Ga** freighters, originally used in support of the Pacific nuclear test cen-

Delivery of 16 SA 321Ja Super Frelons to the Chinese navy took place between 1975 and 1977 and was expanded with licence-built Changhe Z-8s.

tre, were transferred to assault support duties. In 2003, the surviving Aéronavale Super Frelons are assigned to transport duties including commando transport, VertRep and SAR.

Exports
Six radar-equipped **SA 321GM** helicopters were delivered to Libya in 1980-81. The SA 321G was also modified for air force and army service. Designated

SA 321H, a total of 16 was delivered from 1977 to the Iraqi air force with radar and Exocets. These aircraft were used in the Iran-Iraq conflict and the 1991 Gulf War, in which at least one example was destroyed.

The **SA 321Ja** was a higher weight version of the commercial SA 321J, of which the People's Republic of China navy received 16 aircraft fitted with targeting radar. Non-amphibious mili-

tary export versions included 12 **SA 321K** transports for Israel, 16 similar **SA 321L** transports for South Africa and eight **SA 321M** SAR/transports for Libya.

When French production ended in 1983 a total of 99

Super Frelons had been built, but production continued in China under licence-agreement as the **Changhe Z-8**. Eight Israeli aircraft were re-engined with T58 engines and later sold to Argentina.

Westland Lynx Multi-role naval helicopter

Germany's Lynx Mk 88 fleet is being upgraded to the Mk 88A 'Super Lynx' standard shown.

The first Lynx prototype flew on 21 March 1971, and the Royal Navy's **Lynx HAS.Mk 2** was the first production variant to fly, in February 1976. It was equipped for a wide range of shipboard missions including ASW, SAR, ASV, recce, troop transport, fire support, communication and

fleet liaison, and VertRep.

The basic Lynx has one of the world's most advanced flight control systems and comprehensive navaids, systems which served it well during over 3,000 hours of combat operations off the Falklands in 1982. During this campaign the Sea Skua

AShM was also brought into action for the first time.

The RN received the first of 23 upgraded **Lynx HAS.Mk 3** aircraft in March 1982, and converted its HAS.Mk 2s to this standard. Among the improved systems were Gem 41-1 engines. The **Lynx**

HAS.Mk 3ICE designation covers a few downgraded aircraft for utility work on the Antarctic patrol vessel HMS *Endurance*. Subsequently, seven HAS.Mk 3s were procured with secure speech facility and other upgrades as **HAS.Mk 3S** machines. Eighteen aircraft were upgraded to **Lynx HAS.Mk 3GM (Gulf Mod)** standard with improved cooling, and carried IR jammers and ALQ-167 ECM pods during Desert Storm. The final RN version added a central tactical system and a

flotation bag (**Lynx HAS.Mk 3CTS**). The definitive upgraded aircraft is the **Lynx HMA.Mk 8**, or export **Super Lynx**.

Super Lynx
Most of the RN's Lynxes, plus the survivors of 26 French navy **Lynx HAS.Mk 2(FN)** helicopters, received new high-efficiency composite British Experimental Rotor Programme (BERP) main rotor blades.

The definitive Mk 8 has BERP blades and a reverse-direction tail rotor to improve yaw control at higher take-off weights. Other changes include a nose-mounted Sea Owl passive identification thermal imager turret, MAD, INS and GPS systems, Orange Crop ESM and a Yellow Veil jamming pod.

Many Mk 8 features are incorporated in the export Super Lynx, which has found several buyers for new or upgraded machines.

France's HAS.Mk 2(FN) machines (illustrated) have been upgraded to Mk 4(FN) standard, but will be retired from 2004/05.

269 MARINE

EH Industries EH 101/Merlin ASW helicopter

This pre-production Merlin HM.Mk 1 was initially used for trials with the Type 23 frigate HMS Norfolk. It then moved onto sonobuoy drop trials and was fitted with full Merlin avionics.

The **EH 101** has its roots in the Westland WG.34 design that was adopted in late 1978 to meet the UK's Naval Staff Requirement 6646 for a replacement for the Westland Sea King. Work on the WG.34 was cancelled before a prototype had been completed, however, opening the way for revision of the design to meet Italian navy as well as Royal Navy requirements. European Helicopter Industries Ltd was given a formal go-ahead to develop the new aircraft in 1984.

The EH 101 is a three-engined helicopter with a five-bladed main rotor. Much use is made of composites throughout, although the fuselage itself is mainly of aluminium alloy. Systems and equipment vary with role and customer. For the Royal Navy,

which calls its initial variant of the EH 101 the **Merlin HM.Mk 1**, IBM is the prime contractor in association with Westland and provides equipment as well as overall management and integration. Armament on the Merlin comprises four Marconi Stingray torpedoes, and there are also two sonobuoy dispensers.

Merlin HM.Mk 1

The initial Royal Navy requirement for 50 Merlins to operate from Type 23-class frigates, 'Invincible'-class aircraft carriers, ships of the Royal Fleet Auxiliary and other ships or land bases has been reduced to 44, with delivery starting late in 1998 rather than in 1996, as hoped. These British helicopters are each powered by RTM 322

turboshafts, whereas the Italian helicopters (16 on order, out of a requirement for 36) each have the alternative powerplant of three 1278-kW (1,714-shp) General Electric T700-GE-T6A turboshafts, assembled in Italy. Earlier CT7 commercial variants of the General Electric engine were used to power the prototypes, the first of which was a Westland-built machine that achieved its maiden flight on 9 October 1987. A similar Agusta-built basic model flew in Italy on 26 November 1987. Next to fly in Italy, on 26 April 1989, was a prototype of the Italian ASW version, followed in the UK by a basic ASW version on 15 June and then the definitive Merlin prototype on 24 October of that year.

The second prototype was lost in an accident on 21 January 1993, resulting in a suspension of all flight-testing until 24 June that year. The RTM 322 engines were first flown in the fourth prototype during July 1993, and subsequently fitted to the fifth prototype.

Merlin HM.Mk 1 equipment includes GEC Ferranti Blue Kestrel 360° search radar, GEC Avionics AQS-903 processing and display system, Racal Orange Reaper ESM and Ferranti/Thomson-CSF dipping sonar.

Merlin HM.Mk 1 options include the Exocet, Harpoon, Sea Eagle and Marte Mk 2 AShMs, as well as the Stingray torpedo (as here).

Canada ordered 35 of the naval version as the **CH-148 Petrel**, to meet its New Shipborne Aircraft requirement for a Sea King replacement. Assembled and fitted out by IMP Group Ltd in Canada, these EH 101s were to have been powered by 1432-kW (1,920-shp) CT7-6A1 turboshaft engines. The deal was hard-fought, subject to constant scrutiny and not unimportant to the chances of the EH 101's long-term success. Deliveries were scheduled to begin early in 1998, although an increasingly bitter argument over the costs versus acquisition of less complex aircraft saw the EH 101 become a campaign

issue in the Canadian elections of 1993. The pro-EH 101 Conservative government was ousted in favour of a Liberal administration which, true to its election pledge, cancelled the entire programme. Then, in January 1998, the Canadian government placed a new order for 15 examples of the revised AW320 Cormorant version for the SAR role, for delivery between 2000 and 2003.

Further development of the EH 101 could result in variants including an airborne early warning version of the type, which might be required by both the Italian navy and the Royal Navy.

SPECIFICATION

EH Industries Merlin HM.Mk 1
Type: one/two-crew shipborne and land-based anti-submarine and utility helicopter
Powerplant: three Rolls-Royce/Turboméca RTM 322-01 turboshaft engines each rated at 1724 kW (2,312 shp)
Performance: cruising speed 278 km (173 mph) at optimum altitude; hovering ceiling 3810 m (12,500 ft) in ground effect; range 1056 km (656 miles)
Weights: empty 10500 kg (23,149 lb); maximum take-off 14600 kg (32,188 lb)

Dimensions: main rotor diameter 18.59 m (61 ft); length 22.81 m (74 ft 10 in) with the rotors turning; height 6.65 m (21 ft 10 in) with the rotors turning; main rotor disc area 271.51 m² (2,922.60 sq ft)
Armament: up to 960 kg (2,116 lb) of disposable stores carried on the lower sides of the fuselage, and generally comprising four homing torpedoes
Payload: up to 45 troops, or up to 16 litters plus a medical team, or up to 3660 kg (12,000 lb) of freight carried internally or as a slung load

NH Industries NH90 ASW/ASV helicopter

In 1985 five European nations signed a memorandum of understanding covering a 'NATO helicopter for the '90s', or **NH 90**. The UK dropped out of the programme in 1987, leaving France, Germany, Italy and the Netherlands in the project by means of NH Industries, established in 1992 to control the programme.

Two initial versions were planned, the **NH 90 NFH (NATO Frigate Helicopter)** for the autonomous ASW and anti-surface vessel roles with ASW torpedoes or AShMs and 360° search radar under the cabin as key elements in a fully integrated mission system, and the NH 90 TTH.

The NH 90 has a four-bladed main rotor and its powerplant of two turboshaft engines is installed to the rear of the main rotor and gearbox. The landing gear is fully retractable and the flightdeck is laid out for operation by a crew of two.

NH 90 NFH
NH 90 NFH is being developed under Agusta leadership, and its advanced mission suite includes radar, dipping sonar, FLIR, MAD, an ESM system and an ECM system, with weapons carried on two lateral hardpoints. Power is provided either by two RTM 322-01/9s or two General Electric T700-T6Es.

Development of the NH 90 was suspended in May 1994 but then resumed in July of the same year after a short but rigorous effort to reduce cost escalation, and the first of five flying and one ground-test prototypes was the French-assembled PT 1 that first took to the air on 18 December 1995 with RTM 322 engines. The PT 2 second prototype was also assembled in France and first flew on 19 March 1997 as the initial machine with a fly-by-wire control system (initially analogue but later the definitive digital type). The third, fourth and fifth prototypes were assembled in France, Germany and Italy, respectively.

The overall helicopter totals required were trimmed from the original 726 to 647 in July 1996 and then to 642 in 1998 and the number of naval helicopters now likely to be acquired includes 27 for the Aéronavale (which may also acquire 27 TTH aircraft to replace its Super Frelons), 38 for Germany, 56 for Italy, and 20 for the Netherlands. NH Industries has also secured export orders from Norway, while Sweden hopes for large export sales. There have been considerable delays in the signature of the production contract for the NH 90, which was originally scheduled for 1997 but finally took place in March 2000, when an initial 244 helicopters were ordered for the armed forces of the four partner nations. The first NH 90s seem likely to enter service in the period 2004-2007.

NH90 NFH is scheduled to enter French service in 2004-05, Italian service in 2005, German service in 2007 and operational Dutch service from 2007.

SPECIFICATION	
NH Industries NH 90 NFH **Type:** three/four-crew shipborne ASW/surface ship helicopter **Powerplant:** two RTM 322-01/9 turboshaft engines each rated at 1566 kW (2,100 shp) or two General Electric/Alfa Romeo T700-T6E turboshaft engines each rated at 1521 kW (2,040 shp) **Performance:** (estimated) maximum cruising speed 291 km/h (181 mph); initial climb rate 660 m (2,165 ft) per minute; hovering ceiling 3300 m (10,820 ft) in ground effect, or 2600 m (8,540 ft) out of	ground effect; radius 90 km (56 miles) for a loiter of 3 hours 18 minutes **Weights:** empty 6428 kg (14,171 lb); maximum take-off 10000 kg (22,046 lb) **Dimensions:** main rotor diameter 16.30 m (53 ft 5½ in); length 19.56 m (64 ft 2 in) with the rotors turning; height 5.44 m (17 ft 10 in) with the rotors turning; main rotor disc area 208.67 m² (2,246.18 sq ft) **Armament:** up to 1400 kg (3,086 lb) of disposable stores carried on two lateral hardpoints

Westland Wasp Multi-role naval helicopter

Though its development can be traced back to the **Saro P.531**, first flown in 1958, the **Westland Wasp HAS.Mk 1** emerged in October 1962 as a highly specialised machine for flying missions from small ships, such as frigates and destroyers with limited deck pad area. The missions were ASW and general utility, but the Wasp was not sufficiently powerful to carry a full kit of ASW sensors as well as weapons, and thus in this role relied on the sensors of its parent vessel and other friendly naval forces. In the ASV role the Wasp was autonomous, and though it had no radar, it could steer the AS12 wire-guided missile under visual conditions over ranges up to 8 km (5 miles). Other duties included SAR, liaison, VIP ferrying, casevac, ice reconnaissance and photography/ survey. The stalky quadricycle landing gear had wheels that castored so that, while the machine could be rotated on deck, it could not roll in any direction even in a rough sea. Sprag (locking) brakes were fitted to arrest all movement. Provision was made for various hauldown systems such as Beartrap to facilitate alighting on small pads in severe weather.

Wasp service
Deliveries to the Royal Navy began in 1963, and a few were flown in Operation Corporate in the South Atlantic right at the end of their active lives when most had been replaced in RN service by the Lynx. Wasp HAS.Mk 1s operated from eight ships in that campaign, all assigned to No. 829 Squadron, FAA. Most were used in reconnaissance and utility missions, though several operated in the casevac role. Three, two from HMS *Endurance* and one from the frigate HMS *Plymouth*, engaged the Argentine submarine *Santa Fe* and holed its conning tower with AS12s which passed clean through before exploding. Other Wasps served with the Australian, Brazilian, New Zealand and South African navies. In late 2003 the Wasp remained a front-line type with Indonesia and Malaysia, although the later was retiring its aircraft in favour of Fennecs.

The Westland Wasp took a long time to see action. In service with the Royal Navy for nearly 20 years, Wasps were very active during the Falklands War, just in the twilight of their careers.

SPECIFICATION	
Westland Wasp HAS.Mk 1 **Type:** light multi-role ship-based helicopter **Powerplant:** one 529-kW (710-shp) Rolls-Royce Nimbus 503 turboshaft **Performance:** maximum speed with weapons 193 km/h (120 mph); cruising speed 177 km/h (110 mph); range 435 km (270 miles)	**Weights:** empty 1566 kg (3,452 lb); maximum take-off 2495 kg (5,500 lb) **Dimensions:** main rotor diameter 9.83 m (32 ft 3 in); length overall 12.29 m (40 ft 4 in); height 3.56 m (11 ft 8 in); main rotor disc area 75.90 m² (816.86 sq ft) **Armament:** two Mk 44 AS torpedoes or two AS12 AShMs

Mil Mi-14 'Haze' Naval helicopter family

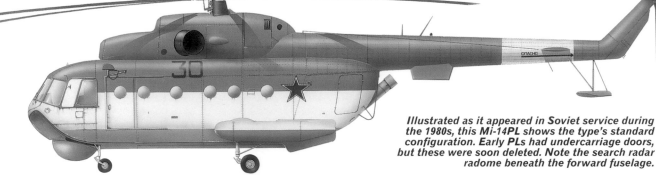

Illustrated as it appeared in Soviet service during the 1980s, this Mi-14PL shows the type's standard configuration. Early PLs had undercarriage doors, but these were soon deleted. Note the search radar radome beneath the forward fuselage.

In order to produce a replacement for the large numbers of Mi-4 'Hounds' in Soviet naval service, a version of the Mi-8 'Hip' with a boat-like hull was developed as the **Mi-14 'Haze'**. The prototype of the series, designated **V-14**, flew for the first time in 1973, to be followed by the initial production **Mi-14PL 'Haze-A'** ASW helicopter.

Improvements incorporated during production included more powerful engines and the switching of the tail rotor from the starboard to the port side for increased controllability.

New variants

The latest 'Haze-A' aircraft have revised equipment which includes a repositioned MAD system and are designated **Mi-14PLM**.

From 1983, trials were carried out with the **Mi-14BT 'Haze-B'** minesweeper. The helicopter has various airframe changes for its role and as primary equipment uses a towed mine sled. Although Mi-14BTs have been used on international mine-clearing operations, few were built. Russian forces prefer to use surface minesweepers, while some of the six BTs delivered to East Germany passed to the Luftwaffe as SAR helicopters, before emerging as civilian water bombers.

The final production 'Haze' variant was the **Mi-14PS 'Haze-C'** SAR helicopter. Built primarily for the AV-MF, 'Haze-C' was also exported to Poland.

A few non-standard Mi-14 versions and designations have also appeared. **Mi-14PL 'Strike'** was a variant proposed for attack missions with AS-7 'Kerry' ASMS. **Mi-14PW** is the Polish designation for the Mi-14PL, while the **Mi-14PX** is one Polish Mi-14PL stripped of ASW gear and used for SAR training. Other Mi-14s have been converted for civilian use.

The Mi-14BT lacks a towed MAD 'bird', the aft fuselage instead housing mine countermeasures towing equipment. Only 25-30 examples were built, including a pair for Bulgaria's Naval Air Arm (illustrated).

SPECIFICATION

Mil Mi-14PL 'Haze-A'
Type: ASW helicopter
Powerplant: two Klimov (Isotov) TV3-117A turboshafts each rated at 1268 kW (1,700 shp) in early helicopters; or two TV3-117MT turboshafts each rated at 1434 kW (1,923 shp) in late helicopters
Performance: maximum level speed 'clean' at optimum altitude 230 km/h (143 mph); maximum cruising speed at optimum altitude 215 km/h (133 mph); initial rate of climb 468 m (1,535 ft) per minute; service ceiling 4000 m (13,123 ft);
range 925 km (575 miles) with standard fuel
Weights: empty 8902 kg (19,625 lb); maximum take-off 14000 kg (30,864 lb)
Dimensions: rotor diameter, each 21.29 m (69 ft 10¼ in); length overall, rotors turning 25.32 m (83 ft 1 in); height 6.93 m (22 ft 9 in); main rotor disc area 356 m² (3,832.08 sq ft)
Armament: one AT-1 or APR-2 torpedo, or one 'Skat' nuclear depth bomb, or eight depth charges

The boat hull of the 'Haze' allows operations in Sea States 3-4, or for planing at up to 60 km/h (37 mph). Note the sponson-mounted flotation bags and tail float of this Russian navy Mi-14PS.

Kamov Ka-25 'Hormone' Naval helicopter family

Designed to meet a 1957 Soviet navy requirement for a new shipborne ASW helicopter, the first member of the Ka-20/25 family was the **Ka-20 'Harp'**, which initially flew during 1960. The production **Ka-25BSh 'Hormone-A'** was of near identical size and appearance, but was fitted with operational equipment and uprated GTD-3F turboshaft engines (from 1973 these were replaced by GTD-3BMs). It entered service in 1967.

Although the lower part of the fuselage is sealed and watertight, the Ka-25 is not intended for amphibious operations, and flotation bags are often fitted to the undercarriage for use in the event of an emergency landing on the water. The cabin is adequate for the job, but is not tall enough to allow the crew to stand upright. Progressive additions of new equipment have made the interior more cluttered.

Primary sensors for the ASW mission are the I/J-band radar (ASCC/NATO 'Big Bulge'), OKA-2 dipping sonar, a downward-looking 'Tie Rod' electro-optical sensor in the tailboom and a MAD sensor, either in a recess in the rear part of the cabin or in a fairing sometimes fitted below the central of the three tailfins. A box-like sonobuoy launcher can also be scabbed on to the starboard side of the rear fuselage. Dye-markers or smoke floats can also be carried externally. Comprehensive avionics,

SPECIFICATION

Kamov Ka-25BSh 'Hormone-A'
Type: ASW helicopter
Powerplant: two OMKB 'Mars' (Glushenkov) GTD-3F turboshafts each rated at 671 kW (898 shp) in early helicopters, or two GTD-3BM turboshafts each rated at 738 kW (900 shp) in late helicopters
Performance: maximum level speed 'clean' at optimum altitude 209 km/h (130 mph); normal cruising speed at optimum altitude 193 km/h (120 mph); service ceiling 3350 m (10,990 ft);
range 400 km (249 miles) with standard fuel
Weights: empty 4765 kg (10,505 lb); maximum take-off 7500 kg (16,534 lb)
Dimensions: rotor diameter, each 15.74 m (52 ft 7¾ in); fuselage length 9.75 m (32 ft); overall 5.37 m (17 ft 7½ in); main rotor disc area 389.15 m² (4,188.93 sq ft)
Armament: provision for torpedoes, conventional or nuclear depth charges and other stores up to a maximum of 1900 kg (4,190 lb)

This Ka-25BSh 'Hormone-A' (displaying the flag of the Soviet navy) is bereft of flotation gear, fuel tanks and all the usual ASW equipment. In this configuration, the Ka-25 could carry a useful load of freight or 12 passengers, enabling it to perform an important secondary ship-to-shore transport role.

defensive and navigation systems are also fitted as standard.

Armament is not normally carried, although the helicopter can be fitted with a long 'coffin-like' weapons bay which runs along the belly from the radome back to the tailboom, and small bombs or depth charges can be carried on tiny pylons just aft of the nosewheels. The underfuselage bay can carry a variety of weapons, including nuclear depth charges.

When wire-guided torpedoes are carried, a wire reel is mounted on the port side of the forward fuselage.

It has been estimated that some 260 of the 450 or so Ka-25s produced were 'Hormone-As', but only a handful remains in Russian and Ukrainian service, mostly fulfiling secondary roles. Small numbers of Ka-25BShs were exported to India, Syria, Vietnam and former Yugoslavia, and most of these aircraft remained in use in mid-2003.

'Hormone' variants
The second Ka-25 variant identified in the West was given the NATO reporting name **'Hormone-B'**, and is designated **Ka-25K**. This variant is externally identifiable by its bulbous (instead of flat-bottomed) undernose radome and small datalink radome under the rear fuselage. Ka-25K was used for acquiring targets and providing mid-course missile guidance, for ship- and submarine-launched missiles.

On the 'Hormone-B' only, the four undercarriage units are retractable and can be lifted out of the scanning pattern of the radar.

The final version of the military Ka-25 is the **Ka-25PS 'Hormone-C'**. A dedicated SAR and transport helicopter, the Ka-25PS can carry a practical load of freight or up to 12 passengers, making it a useful ship-to-ship or ship-to-shore transport and vertrep platform. A quadruple Yagi antenna ('Home Guard') fitted to many aircraft is reportedly used for homing on to the personal locator beacons carried by aircrew. Most Ka-25PSs also have searchlights, and a 300-kg (660-lb) capacity rescue winch. Ka-25PS has largely been replaced by Ka-27.

Kamov Ka-27, Ka-29 and Ka-31 'Helix'
Naval helicopter family

Ka-29TB is a formidable assault and attack helicopter. It mounts a sizeable weapons load on braced fuselage outriggers.

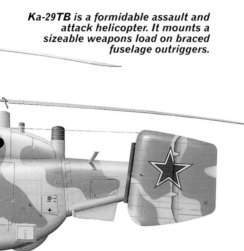

Work on the **Ka-27** family began in 1969. The Ka-27 retains Kamov's well-proven contra-rotating co-axial rotor configuration, and has dimensions similar to those of the Ka-25.

With more than double the power of the Ka-25, the Ka-27 is a considerably heavier helicopter with a larger fuselage, but nevertheless offers increased performance with much-improved avionics and more modern flight-control system.

The first production variant was the **Ka-27PL 'Helix-A'** basic ASW version, which entered service in 1982. The Ka-27PL's fuselage is sealed over its lower portions for buoyancy, while extra flotation equipment can be fitted in boxes on the lower part of the centre fuselage. Ka-27 is extremely stable and easy to fly, and automatic height hold, automatic transition to and from the hover and autohover are possible in all weather conditions. Ka-27PL has all the usual ASW and ESM equipment, including dipping sonar and sonobuoys as well as Osminog (octopus) search radar.

SAR and planeguard
The main SAR and planeguard Ka-27 variant is the radar-equipped **Ka-27PS 'Helix-D'**. This usually carries external fuel tanks and flotation gear, and has a hydraulically-operated, 300-kg (661-lb) capacity rescue winch.

Ka-28 'Helix-A' is the export version of the Ka-27PL ordered by China, India, Vietnam and Yugoslavia and with a revised avionics suite.

Assault and transport
The **Ka-29TB** (*Transportno Boyevoya*) is a dedicated assault transport derivative of the Ka-27/32 family, intended especially for the support of Russian navy amphibious operations and featuring a substantially changed airframe. The first example was seen by Western eyes on the assault ship *Ivan Rogov* in 1987, the type having entered service in 1985, and the **Ka-29TB** was initially assumed to be the Ka-27B, resulting in the allocation of the NATO reporting designation **'Helix-B'**. Many of the new variants went unnoticed, and the Ka-29TB was initially thought to be a minimum-change version of the basic Ka-27PL without radar. In fact the Ka-29TB features an entirely new, much widened forward fuselage, with a flight deck seating three members of the crew side-by-side, one of these crew members acting as a gunner to aim the various types of air-to-surface unguided rocket carried on the four hardpoints of the helicopter's pair of strut-braced lateral pylons, and the trainable machine-gun hidden behind an articulated door on the starboard side of the nose. In addition, the two-piece curved windscreen of the Ka-27 has given way to a five-piece unit.

An air data boom projects from the port side of the nose, which also carries an EO sensor to starboard and a missile guidance/illuminating and TFR pod to port.

The basic Ka-29TB served as the basis for the **Ka-31**, which was originally known as the **Ka-29RLD** (*Radiolokatsyonnogo Dozora*, or radar picket helicopter). This AEW type first flew in 1988, and was first seen during carrier trials aboard *Kuznetsov*. All four landing gear units are retractable, making space for the movement of the E-801E Oko (eye) surveillance radar's antenna, which is a large rectangular planar array that rests flat under the fuselage when inactive.

SPECIFICATION

Kamov Ka-27PL 'Helix-A'
Type: three-crew shipborne anti-submarine and utility helicopter
Powerplant: two Klimov (Isotov) TV3-117V turboshaft engines each rated at 1633 kW (2,190 shp)
Performance: maximum speed 250 km/h (155 mph) at optimum altitude; cruising speed 230 km/h (143 mph) at optimum altitude; service ceiling 5000 m (16,404 ft); hovering ceiling 3500 m (11,483 ft) out of ground effect; range 800 km (497 miles) with auxiliary fuel
Weights: empty 6100 kg

(13,448 lb); maximum take-off 12600 kg (27,778 lb)
Dimensions: rotor diameter, each 15.9 m (52 ft 2 in); length, excluding rotors 11.27 m (37 ft 11¾ in); height to top of rotor head 5.45 m (17 ft 10½ in); rotor disc area, each 198.5 m² (2,136.6 sq ft)
Armament: up to 200 kg (441 lb) of disposable stores, generally comprising four APR-2E homing torpedoes or four groups of S3V guided anti-submarine bombs
Payload: up to 5000 kg (11,023 lb) of freight

Boeing Vertol H-46 Sea Knight Assault and transport helo

Shortly after the formation of the Vertol Aircraft Corporation in March 1956, the company initiated a design study for a twin-turbine commercial transport helicopter and in the event, the US armed forces showed an interest in the type's procurement.

Early Army interest

Allocated the designation **Vertol Model 107**, a prototype was flown for the first time on 22 April 1958. The first of the armed forces wishing to evaluate the new helicopter was the US Army which, in July 1958, ordered 10 slightly modified aircraft under the designation **YHC-1A**. The first of these

flew for the first time on 27 August 1959. By that time the US Army had come to favour a larger and more powerful helicopter, which Vertol had developed from the Model 107, and reduced its order to only three YCH-1A (later **YCH-46C**) machines. The company subsequently equipped the third of these with 783-kW (1,050-shp) T58-GE-6 turboshafts and rotors of increased diameter, and, with a commercial interior, this aircraft first flew as the **Model 107-II** on 25 October 1960. By that time Vertol had become a division of the Boeing company.

When the USMC showed an interest in this helicopter,

one was modified as the **Model 107M** with two T58-GE-8s and this was successful in winning a contract for the **HRB-1** (changed to **CH-46A** in 1962) production model, which was named **Sea Knight**. Since then, Sea Knights have been used extensively by the USMC and the USN. The former uses them for troop transport, the latter mainly in the vertical replenishment role.

Production variants

The first of 160 CH-46As entered full USMC service early in 1965. Since then, a number of versions has been built, these including 266 examples of the **CH-46D** for the USMC to a

standard generally similar to that of the CH-46A except for its 1044-kW (1,400-shp) T58-GE-10 engines; 174 examples of the **CH-46F** for the USMC to a standard generally similar to that of the CH-46D but with additional avionics; 14 examples of the **UH-46A**, similar to the CH-46A, for the USN; and 10 examples of the **UH-46D** for the USN to a standard virtually identical to that of the CH-46D. The USMC updated 273 of its older Sea Knights to the **CH-46E** standard with 1394-kW (1,870-shp) T58-GE-16 turboshafts and other improvements including structural strengthening and glassfibre rotor blades.

Foreign service

Six utility helicopters, almost identical to the CH-46A, were delivered to the RCAF in 1963 under the designation **CH-113 Labrador**, and 12 similar aircraft were built

for the Canadian Army during 1964-65, these being designated **CH-113A Voyageur**. In the Canadian Armed Forces' SARCUP (Search And Rescue Capability Upgrade Project), Boeing of Canada was later contracted to modify six CH-113s and five CH-13As to an improved SAR standard by mid-1984. In 1962-63 Boeing Vertol supplied Model 107-II helicopters to the Swedish air force for SAR, and to the Swedish navy for ASW and minesweeping duties; both of these versions received the local designation **Hkp 4A**.

In 1965 Kawasaki in Japan acquired the worldwide sales rights for the Model 107-II, and built the type up to about 1990 in several versions with the basic designation **Kawasaki-Vertol KV 107-II**. The type is now being retired from Japanese service.

Photographed in June 2003, this US Navy CH-46D is seen replenishing USS Sacramento from USS Carl Vinson in the Philippine Sea. The CH-46 is now long overdue for replacement.

SPECIFICATION

Boeing Vertol CH-46A Sea Knight
Type: two/three-crew twin-rotor transport helicopter
Powerplant: two General Electric T58-GE-8B turboshaft engines each rated at 932 kW (1,250 shp)
Performance: maximum speed 249 km/h (155 mph) at sea level; cruising speed 243 km/h (151 mph) at 1525 m (5,000 ft); initial climb rate 439 m (1,440 ft) per minute; service ceiling 4265 m (14,000 ft); hovering ceiling 2765 m (9,070 ft) in ground effect and 1707 m (5,600 ft) out of ground effect;

range 426 km (265 miles) with maximum internal payload
Weights: empty 5627 kg (12,406 lb); maximum take-off 9707 kg (21,400 lb)
Dimensions: rotor diameter, each 15.24 m (50 ft); length overall, rotors turning 25.4 m (83 ft 4 in); height 5.09 m (16 ft 8¼ in); rotor disc area, total 364.82 m² (3,926.99 sq ft)
Payload: up to 25 troops, or 1814 kg (4,000 lb) of freight carried internally or 2871 kg (6,330 lb) of freight carried externally

Bell Boeing V-22 Osprey Tiltrotor assault transport

In the early 1980s Bell Helicopter Textron and Boeing Vertol began collaboration to develop a larger derivative of

the XV-15 tilt-rotor demonstrator for the Joint Services Advanced Vertical Lift Aircraft programme. Combining the

vertical lift capabilities of a helicopter with the fast-cruise forward flight efficiencies of a fixed-wing turboprop, the

resulting **V-22 Osprey** was awarded full-scale development in 1985. The engines, mounted in wingtip nacelles,

can be swivelled through 97.5° and drive three-bladed proprotors through interconnected drive shafts. For

SPECIFICATION

Bell Boeing MV-22A Osprey
Type: three/four-crew land-based and shipborne multi-mission tilt-rotor transport
Powerplant: two Allison T406-AD-400 turboshaft engines each rated at 4586 kW (6,150 shp)
Performance: (estimated) maximum cruising speed 185 km/h (115 mph) at sea level in helicopter mode and 582 km/h (361 mph) at optimum altitude in aircraft mode; initial climb rate 707 m (2,320 ft) per minute; service ceiling 7925 m (26,000 ft); hovering ceiling 4330 m (14,200 ft) out-of-ground effect; range 935 km (592 miles) in amphibious assault role
Weights: (estimated) empty 15032 kg (33,140 lb); maximum take-off 21546 kg (47,500 lb) for

VTO and 27443 kg (60,500 lb) for STO
Dimensions: width overall 25.55 m (83 ft 10 in); wing span 14.02 m (46 ft) excluding nacelles; proprotor diameter, each 11.58 m (38 ft); length 17.47 m (57 ft 4 in) excluding probe; height 6.63 m (21 ft 9 in) with nacelles vertical; wing area 35.49 m² (382 sq ft); proprotor disc area, total 210.72 m² (2,268.23 sq ft)
Armament: probably one or two 0.5-in (12.7-mm) trainable multi-barrel rotary machine-guns
Payload: up to 24 troops, or 12 litters plus medical attendants or 9072 kg (20,000 lb) of freight carried internally, or 6804 kg (15,000 lb) of freight carried externally

On 29 May 2002, Osprey flight testing was resumed after being halted in December 2000 owing to safety concerns. A USMC test aircraft is illustrated.

Right: Aircraft number 10, one of the Engineering and Manufacturing Development (EMD) MV-22 Ospreys, performs shipboard tests onboard the amphibious assault ship USS Saipan during early 1999.

shipboard stowage, the mainplanes pivot centrally to rotate along the fuselage top, the proprotor blades folding in parallel. Initial requirements called for 913 Ospreys, comprising 522 **MV-22A** assault aircraft for the USMC and US Army; 80 USAF CV-22As; and 50 USN **HV-22A** aircraft for combat SAR, special ops and fleet logistic support. The USN also foresaw a need for **SV-22A** ASW machines. Flight tests started on 19 March 1989, but a series of accidents, financial and political reviews, and allegations of malpractice have resulted in a much revised programme.

Osprey status

During mid-2003, the Osprey programme was due to realise 360 **MV-22B** machines for the USMC and 48 **HV-22B** tiltrotors for the USN. The first production Ospreys were delivered in 1999 and the type should become operational with the USMC in 2004.

Kaman SH-2 Seasprite Multi-role naval helicopter

The **H-2 Seasprite** was conceived in response to a 1956 USN requirement for a high-speed, all-weather, long-range SAR, liaison and utility helicopter. The first of four **YHU2K-1** (from 1962 **YUH-2A**) service test prototypes made its maiden flight on 2 July 1959, and the type entered production as the **HU2K-1** (**UH-2A**). Later variants were progressively improved and updated, gaining a second engine (for a greater safety margin for ship-based operations), dual mainwheels and a four-bladed tail rotor. Manufacture stopped after the delivery of the last **UH-2B**. The helicopter was first used in the ASW role in October 1970, when the USN selected the **SH-2D** as an interim **LAMPS I** (**Light Airborne Multi-Purpose System Mk I**) platform.

ASW was just one of the tasks assigned to US Navy Seasprites, like this SH-2F.

LAMPS I

The SH-2D introduced an undernose Litton LN-66 search radar radome, an ASQ-81 MAD on the starboard fuselage pylon and a removable sonobuoy rack in the port side of the fuselage. Twenty were produced as conversions from **HH-2D** armed-SAR standard, entering service in 1972.

Deliveries of the definitive **SH-2F**, which also bore the LAMPS I designation, began in May 1973. The primary role of the SH-2F was the generation of a major extension of the protected area provided by the outer defensive screen of a carrier battle group. It introduced T58-GE-8F engines, an improved main rotor, and strengthened landing gear including a tailwheel relocated farther forward. The SH-2F also featured an improved Marconi LN-66HP surface search radar, ASQ-81(V)2 towed MAD bird and a tactical navigation and communications system. Some 88 machines were converted from earlier variants, and 16 SH-2Ds were also modified.

New production

The Seasprite was reinstated in production during 1981, when the USN placed an order for the first of an eventual 60 new-build SH-2Fs. From 1987 some 16 SH-2Fs received a package of modifications to allow them to operate in the Persian Gulf. During the 1991 Gulf War, the SH-2F tested the ML-30 Magic Lantern laser sub-surface mine detector.

Continued development of the Seasprite resulted in the appearance of the **SH-2G Super Seasprite**. The prototype **YSH-2G** first flew on 2 April 1985, as an SH-2F conversion with T700 engines. The new type entered service in 1991, but the end of the Cold War reduced the USN's requirement to 23 machines and the Seasprite has left US Navy service. Kaman has sold rebuilt surplus SH-2Fs to Egypt, which received **SH-2G(E)** helicopters from October 1997. In June 1997 the Royal Australian Navy and Royal New Zealand Navy ordered a total of 15 SH-2Gs rebuilt to an improved standard from SH-2F airframes. The rebuilt **SH-2G(NZ)** helicopters for New Zealand entered service in 2001, while the **SH-2G(A)** machines for Australia have been delayed by avionics problems and will not become operational until 2004.

Kaman SH-2G Super Seasprite
Type: three-crew shipborne ASW, missile defence, SAR and utility helicopter
Powerplant: two General Electric T700-GE-401/401C turboshaft engines each rated at 1285 kW (1,723 shp)
Performance: maximum speed 256 km/h (159 mph) at sea level; cruising speed 222 km/h (138 mph) at optimum altitude; initial climb rate 762 m (2,500 ft) per minute; service ceiling 7285 m (23,900 ft); hovering ceiling 6340 m (20,800 ft) in ground effect and 5485 m (18,000 ft) out of ground effect; radius 65 km (40 miles) for a patrol of 2 hours 10 minutes with one torpedo

Weights: empty 3483 kg (7,680 lb); maximum take-off 6123 kg (13,500 lb)
Dimensions: main rotor diameter 13.51 m (44 ft 4 in); length overall 16.08 m (52 ft 9 in) with rotors turning; height 4.58 m (15 ft ½ in) with rotors turning; main rotor disc area 143.41 m² (1,543.66 sq ft)
Armament: provision for two 0.3-in (7.62-mm) M60 trainable lateral-firing machine-guns on optional pintle mounts in the cabin doors, plus up to 726 kg (1,600 lb) of disposable stores
Payload: (with sonobuoy system removed) provision for up to four passengers, or two litters, or 1814 kg (4,000 lb) of freight carried as a slung load

Australia and New Zealand (illustrated) bought their Seasprites to equip their new 'Anzac'-class multi-role frigates. Australia may purchase further SH-2G(A)s.

Sikorsky S-61/H-3 Sea King ASW and multi-role helicopter

One of the most important helicopter families yet developed, and once a mainstay of the Western world's shipborne anti-submarine forces, the **Sikorsky SH-3 Sea King** series began life as the **HSS-2** anti-submarine helicopter for the US Navy. The prototype of this helicopter first flew on 11 March 1959, and the aircraft, which has the company designation **Sikorsky S-61**, was the first which could carry all the sensors and weapons needed for ASW missions without external help (though the US Navy policy developed to regard the aircraft as an extension of the ASW surface vessel from which it operates, so that helicopter-carried sensors detect the hostile submarine before the warship is called in for the kill).

Sea King features
New features included an amphibious boat hull with retractable tailwheel landing gear, twin turboshaft engines (for power, lightness, reliability and single-engine flight capability) above the cabin and an unobstructed tactical compartment for two sonar operators whose sensors included a dipping sonobuoy lowered through a keel hatch. Above the extensive avionic systems was an attitude-hold autopilot and a

sonar coupler which maintained exact height and station in conjunction with a radar altimeter and Doppler radar. Over 1,100 **H-3** type helicopters were built, the ASW models being SH-3s in four basic models.

ASW variants
The **SH-3A** was the original model with 933-kW (1,260-shp) T58-GE-8B turboshafts, the **SH-3D** is the upgraded version; the **SH-3G** is the utility version; and the **SH-3H** is the multi-role model fitted with dipping sonar and MAD gear for ASW and search radar for the detection of incoming anti-ship missiles. Single examples of the SH-3D and SH-3G, plus 50 SH-3Hs remained in US Navy service in mid-2003.

Licence-production
Agusta has built the Sea King under licence in Italy as the **AS-61/ASH-3**, some variants being equipped with Marte anti-ship missiles. Mitsubishi built 55 Sea Kings in three versions, all retaining the original HSS-2

The US Navy produced its 150-strong SH-3H (illustrated) fleet by converting earlier SH-3A, SH-3D and SH-3G aircraft. Even a pair of ex-USAF CH-53Bs was consumed.

Italy will replace its ASH-3D (illustrated) and ASH-3H helicopters with the EH 101. The Sea Kings are flown from the Italian navy's larger vessels and the aircraft-carrier Garibaldi.

US Navy squadron HC-2 remained a Sea King operator in 2003. Its UH-3H utility helicopters were produced by conversion from SH-3H standard.

designation, for the JMSDF. By far the most important overseas manufacturer, however, has been Westland in the UK. Westland-built aircraft are powered by Rolls-Royce H.1400 Gnome-series engines and have much UK-sourced equipment. The initial **Sea King HAS.Mk 1** made its first flight on 7 May 1969 and was little more than a re-engined SH-3D. Subsequent ASW variants for the Royal Navy have included the **HAS.Mk 2**, **HAS.Mk 5** and **HAS.Mk 6**. To fill the massive gap that became apparent in the RN's airborne AEW coverage during the Falklands War, the **Sea King AEW.Mk 2A** was pro-

duced by conversion from HAS.Mk 2 standard. Later, HAS.Mk 5 aircraft were converted to **AEW.Mk 5** and **AEW.Mk 7** standard. **Sea King HAR.Mk 3** and **Mk 3A** SAR helicopters have been built for the RAF and many Westland Sea Kings, including the **Sea King International**, have been

built for export.

Sikorsky exported its Sea Kings to many countries, including Canada, where the aircraft is designated **CH-124**. Specialised US SH-3 variants included the **RH-3** minesweeper, while the **VH-3** executive transport remains in service.

SPECIFICATION	
Sikorsky SH-3D Sea King	9752 kg (21,500 lb)
Type: ASW helicopter	**Dimensions:** main rotor diameter
Powerplant: two 1044-kW	18.9 m (62 ft); fuselage length
(1,400-shp) General Electric T58-10	16.69 m (54 ft 9 in); height 5.13 m
turboshafts	(16 ft 10 in); main rotor disc area
Performance: maximum speed	280.5 m² (3,019.10 sq ft)
267 km/h (166 mph); range with	**Armament:** external hardpoints for
maximum fuel and 10 per cent	a total of 381 kg (840 lb) of
reserves 1005 km (625 miles)	weapons, normally comprising two
Weights: empty 5382 kg	Mk 46 torpedoes
(11,865 lb); maximum take-off	

Sikorsky S-70/H-60 Seahawk ASW and multi-role helicopter

A derivative of the US Army's UH-60 Black Hawk, the **Sikorsky SH-60B Seahawk** (originally produced under the company designation **S-70L**, later **S-70B**) won the US Navy's LAMPS (Light Airborne Multi-Purpose System) III competition in September 1977. A complex and extremely expensive machine, the SH-60B was

designed for two main missions: ASW and ASST (anti-ship surveillance and targeting). The ASST mission involved the aerial detection

Mitsubishi has built SH-60Js (illustrated) and UH-60Js for the JMSDF. In 2003 SH-60Js were still being funded and a KAI upgrade programme is underway.

of incoming sea-skimming AShMs, and the provision of radar-derived data for similar weapons launched from US warships. Secondary missions included SAR, medevac and vertrep (vertical replenishment). The basic airframe differs from that of the UH-60 in being marinised, with a sealed tail-boom, having its tailwheel moved and inflatable bags for emergency buoyancy fitted, and having an electrically-folding main rotor and pneumatically-folding tail (including upward-hinged tailplanes). Other modifications are greater fuel capacity and the removal of cockpit armour for the pilot and co-pilot. The type is also fitted with haul-down equipment to facilitate recovery

onto small platforms on pitching and rolling ships in heavy seas. Under the nose is the large APS-124 radar and on the left side of the fuselage is a large vertical panel with tubes for launching sonobuoys.

On the right of the rear

SPECIFICATION

Sikorsky SH-60B Seahawk
Type: multi-role shipboard helicopter
Powerplant: (aircraft delivered from 1988) two 1417-kW (1,900-shp) General Electric T700-GE-401C turboshafts
Performance: dash speed at 1525 m (5,000 ft) 234 km/h (145 mph); operational radius 92.5 km (57.5 miles) for a 3-hour loiter

Weights: (for the ASW mission) empty 6191 kg (13,648 lb); mission take-off 9182 kg (20,244 lb)
Dimensions: main rotor diameter 16.36 m (53 ft 8 in); fuselage length 15.26 m (50 ft ¾ in); height overall, rotors turning 5.18 m (17 ft); main rotor disc area 210.05 m² (2,262.03 sq ft)
Armament: normally two Mk 46 torpedoes, or Penguin AShMs

Easily identified by the two windows in its portside cabin door, this HH-60H is shown performing a vertrep mission.

fuselage is a pylon for a towed MAD 'bird'. The first prototype flew on 12 December 1979 and a total of 181 was built for the USN.

Subsequent variants for US Navy service have included the **SH-60F Ocean Hawk**, equipped with dipping sonar for inner-zone ASW cover around aircraft-carriers; the **HH-60H Rescue Hawk** for ship-borne SAR, plane guard and special forces missions and the **MH-60R** multi-mission helicopter. The latter were to be produced by conversion from SH-60B/F/HH-60H helicopters, but 243 new-build helicopters will now be bought for delivery from 2005. They will join 237

The many roles now tackled by the SH-60 family are shown here by an HH-60H taking off for a plane guard sortie.

MH-60S utility aircraft which combine much of the UH-60's airframe with SH-60 systems and began replacing Boeing-Vertol CH-46 Sea Knights in February 2002. Other, non-navy, versions

include the US Coast Guard's **HH-60J Jayhawk**, while naval variants have been widely exported and built under licence in Australia and Japan.

Sikorsky S-80/MH-53 Sea Dragon Mine-sweeping helicopter

An MH-53E from HM-14 'Vanguards' prepares for take-off. The aircraft was deployed to Bahrain in support of Operation Enduring Freedom.

Though the original Sikorsky S-65 production models, have only two engines, the **S-80/H-53E** has three engines each of 3266 kW (4,380 shp) and is the most powerful helicopter ever built outside Russia. Of the early versions, the CH-53A and more powerful CH-53D were transports for the US Marines Corps. All CH-53As were delivered with provisions for towed mine-sweeping equipment, but the US Navy decided that a dedicated mine-countermeasures version would need more power and additional modifications. Accordingly, 15 CH-53As were transferred to the US Navy as **RH-53A** mine-sweeping machines with 2927-kW (3,925-shp) T64-GE-413 turboshafts, and equipment for towing the EDO Mk 105 hydrofoil anti-mine sled.

Still more power
The RH-53As were used to explore the possibilities of these new mine-sweeping techniques, which had previously been tried only with machines of inadequate power, pending the arrival of 30 **RH-53D Sea Dragon** purpose-built machines. Equipped with drop tanks and, later, inflight-refuelling probes, the RH-53Ds were soon re-engined with 3266-kW (4,380-shp) T64-GE-415 turboshafts. The aircraft were delivered to the US Navy from the summer of 1973 and about 19 remained in US Navy service in early 2003, but were being replaced by MH-53Es. Six RH-53Ds were delivered to the Imperial Iranian Navy.

The CH-53E was developed to meet a 1973 demand for an upgraded heavy-lift transport for the US Navy and US Marine Corps. From it was developed the **MH-53E Sea Dragon**. This definitive MCM (mine countermeasures) version has enormously enlarged side sponsons for an extra 3785 litres (833 Imp gal) of fuel, for extended sweeping missions with the engines at sustained high power. The first prototype MH-53E made its initial flight on 23 December 1981 and

around 44 remained in service in 2003.

The **MH-53J** has been sold to the JMSDF.

SPECIFICATION

Sikorsky MH-53E Sea Dragon
Type: shipboard minesweeping helicopter
Powerplant: three 3266-kW (4,380-shp) General Electric T64-GE-416 turboshafts
Performance: maximum speed 315 km/h (196 mph); cruising speed at sea level 278 km/h (173 mph); maximum self-ferry range 2074 km (1,289 miles)
Weights: empty 16482 kg (36,336 lb); maximum take-off with

internal payload 31640 kg (69,750 lb); maximum take-off with external payload 33340 kg (73,500 lb)
Dimensions: main rotor diameter 24.08 m (79 ft); length overall, rotors turning 30.19 m (99 ft ½ in); height to top of main rotor head 5.32 m (17 ft 5½ in); main rotor disc area 455.38 m² (4,901.7 sq ft)
Armament: provision for window-mounted 0.5-in (12.7-mm) or 0.3-in (7.62-mm) guns

Chinese naval SAMs HQ-61, HQ-7 and HQ-9 systems

The Chinese People's Liberation Army Navy (PLAN) has historically neglected outfitting its ships with adequate air defence systems. This is a result partially of the fact that the PLAN has traditionally been a littoral force, operating within or close to Chinese territorial waters where land-based aircraft can control and prosecute on behalf of naval air defence. However, this lack of air-defence capability has been addressed in modest terms on the newer and/or larger ships the Chinese government has procured or built.

The sole 'Luhai'-class destroyer is the **Shenzen**, *whose primary air-defence capability is vested in an octuple HQ-7 launcher for the FM-80 short-range SAM, located just abaft the 100-mm (3.9-in) twin gun turret.*

Traditionally, surface-to-air missiles aboard PLAN ships were purchased from the former USSR. SAMs are fitted on the 'Sovremenny', 'Luhai', 'Luhu', and 'Luda I and II' classes of destroyers; and on the 'Jiangwei I and II' classes of frigate.

The 'Sovremenny'-class ship is equipped with two SAM launchers for the Russian Shtil (SA-N-7 'Gadfly'), or Yezh (SA-N-12 'Grizzly') semi-active radar/IR-guided intermediate-range missiles. The SA-N-12 is an improved version of the SA-N-7. Both missiles have a speed of Mach 3, and a range of approximately 25 km (16 miles).

Six-cell SAM launcher

The 'Jiangwei I'-class ship is fitted with a six-cell **HQ-61** launcher carrying **RF-61** (**CSA-N-2**) SAMs using semi-active radar guidance and possessing a range of 10 km (6.2 miles). The launcher requires manual reloading, which makes it less capable of handling high-threat environments and multi-aircraft attacks. Although less advanced, the CSA-N-2 is similar in appearance to the NATO RIM-7 Sea Sparrow.

The 'Jiangwei II', 'Luhai', 'Luda I/II' and 'Luhu' classes are fitted with a single eight-cell **HQ-7** (Crotale) launcher for the **FM-80** (**CSA-N-4**) short-range tactical SAM. This indigenous missile is standard on PLAN ships. The 85-kg (187-lb) weapon has a range of 12-15 km (7-9 miles), and employs wireless command control that is resistant to jamming. The missile uses semi-active radar with optical or IR homing systems.

Recent evidence indicates that the new Type 052B ship is to be fitted with SA-N-12 medium-range SAMs; and the new Type 052C ship will be equipped with the indigenous **HQ-9** long-range vertical-launch SAM system. The associated **FT-2000** missile has a maximum range of 100 km (62 miles) and is similar to the Russian Rif (SA-N-6 'Grumble') naval SAM.

SPECIFICATIONS

HQ-7 (FM-80)
Type: point-defence missile
Dimensions: length 3 m (9 ft 10 in); diameter 0.156 m (6.14 in); span 0.55 m (1 ft 9⅔ in)
Weight: total round 84.5 kg (186.3 lb); warhead not available proximity-fused HE-fragmentation
Performance: maximum speed Mach 2.3; range 0.5-12 km (0.3-7.5 miles) against helicopters and non-manoeuvring targets; altitude limits 30-5000 m (100-16,405 ft)

HQ-9 (FT-200)
Type: long-range area-defence missile
Dimensions: length 6.8 m (22 ft 3¾ in); diameter 0.47 m (18½ in)
Weights: total round 1300 kg (2,866 lb); warhead not available proximity-fused HE-fragmentation
Performance: maximum speed not available but in high supersonic range; range limits 12-100 km (7.5-62.1 miles); altitude limits 3000-20000 m (9,845-65,615 ft)

The 'Jiangwei I' class carries the HQ-61 sextuple launcher for CSA-N-4 short-range SAMs. These missiles have the local designation RF-61.

Naval Crotale Point-defence missile

Derived from the ground-launched Crotale system, the **Naval Crotale** variant was designed as a self-defence missile for use by ships against medium-altitude, low-altitude and sea-skimming attacks by aircraft, helicopters and missiles. It can also be used against surface targets in an emergency. The standard **Naval Crotale 8S** version comprises a turret assembly with two co-axial units (one with eight ready-to-fire **R.440N** missiles in their container-launchers and the other supporting the fire-control radar and IR tracking systems), a shelter housing the electronic data-processing cabinets, and an operator's console in the combat operation centre for supervising the system and sending the fire orders. A newer version, the **Modular Naval Crotale**, is available with either an eight-missile **Modular Naval Crotale** (**8MS**) or a four-missile **Modular Naval Crotale** (**4MS**) launcher turret for installation on ships down to a displacement of 500 tons.

SPECIFICATION

Naval Crotale (R.440)
Dimensions: length 2.89 m (9 ft 5¾ in); diameter 0.15 m (6 in); span 0.53 m (1 ft 8⅞ in)
Weights: total round 85 kg (187 lb); warhead 15-kg (33-lb) proximity-fused HE-fragmentation
Performance: maximum speed Mach 2.3; range 0.7-13 km (0.43-8.08 miles) against helicopters and non-manoeuvring targets, or 0.7-8.5 km (0.43-5.28 miles) against manoeuvring targets, or 0.7-6.5 km (0.43-4.04 miles) against sea-skimming targets; altitude limits 4-5000 m (13-16,405 ft)

The destroyer **Georges Leygues** *is seen tied up alongside the wharf in Beirut. The eight-round Crotale launcher and its associated radar systems are prominent at the top of the photograph.*

Right: The 'La Fayette' class of frigate is armed with the Naval Crotale CN2 system (the octuple launcher seen here loaded) using the latest VT-1 missiles.

Below: An R.440N missile streaks away from its eight-round Naval Crotale launcher before being gathered into the guidance radar's beam.

In all cases the target acquisition and tracking is performed by the radar of the Naval Crotale system itself after it has been designated by the ship's sensors. Missile guidance is performed by an improved line-of-sight unit. For sea-skimming targets both the missile and target are tracked by a differential IR technique. Once in the vicinity of the target the warhead is detonated by a proximity fuse with a built-in time delay so that the prefragmented splinters formed by the detonation are concentrated to impact in the most vulnerable zone of the target. A total of 18 reload rounds is normally carried for the eight-round launchers. In the French navy the Naval Crotale system has been used for the destroyers of the 'Georges Leygues' and 'Tourville' class and the 'La Fayette' class of frigate, while the Saudi Arabian navy has bought the Modular Naval Crotale 8MS system for the four 'Madina'-class frigates constructed in France and delivered in the mid-1980s.

The latest versions of the system, operational on the 'La Fayette' and Omani 'Qahir'-class ships, are the **Naval Crotale CN2** and **Naval Crotale NG** with 24 and 16 missiles respectively.

The missile is the American-designed **VT-1** which, like the original R.440N, uses command to line-of-sight guidance with semi-active radar and IR homing, and carries its 14-kg (30.9-lb) proximity-fused warhead to a range of 13 km (8.1 miles) at a speed of Mach 3.5.

Masurca Medium-range area-defence missile

Developed in the mid-1950s, the **Masurca** is a medium-range, solid-propellant area-defence naval SAM wholly designed and built in France for employment by task force and carrier escorts. Only three French ships were ever equipped with the missile and its associated radar systems, namely the cruiser *Colbert* and the missile destroyers *Duquesne* and *Suffren*, of which only the last survived more than one year into the 21st century. Each vessel was fitted with a 3D surveillance radar, a weapon-direction system, two independent fire-control radars and a twin-arm launcher fed from a 48-round magazine. Two types of guidance were developed for the definitive production version: the **Masurca Mk 2 Mod 2** used a beam-riding command to line-of-sight technique and the **Masurca Mk 2 Mod 3** introduced a semi-active radar seeker. Only the latter system remains in service, the former having been phased out in 1975.

A solid-propellant booster unit is fitted, and in under 5 seconds this accelerates the missile to a speed of about Mach 3, at which point the booster drops away and the sustainer motor takes over. During flight the missile follows a trajectory which is determined by proportional navigation as it keeps its antenna pointed at the target illuminated by one of the two DRBR 51 fire-control radars. During the mid-1980s the Masurca system was upgraded for increased reliability and an improved engagement envelope so that it could be used into the 1990s and indeed 2000s.

Right: The Masurca has strong conceptual affinities with the US Standard Missile, and is a two-stage weapon.

Left: Originally a relatively primitive beam-riding missile, the Masurca was then turned, as the result of continuous development, into what was for the time a sophisticated SARH missile with a range of 50 km (31 miles).

SPECIFICATION	
Masurca Mk 2 Mod 3	**Weights:** missile 950 kg (2,094 lb);
Dimensions: length of missile 5.38 m (17 ft 8 in) and of booster 3.32 m (10 ft 11 in); diameter of missile 0.406 m (1 ft 4 in) and of booster 0.57 m (1 ft 10 in); span of missile 0.77 m (2 ft 6 in) and of booster 1.5 m (4 ft 11 in)	booster 1148 kg (2,531 lb); warhead 100-kg (220-lb) proximity-fused HE-fragmentation
	Performance: maximum speed Mach 3; range 50 km (31 miles); altitude limits 30-23000 m (100-75,460 ft)

Aster Medium-range/anti-missile missile

The **Aster 15** and **Aster 30** constitute a family of missiles designed by Eurosam GIE, a joint venture between MBDA Missile Systems and Thales. These highly agile solid-propellant missiles are designed to provide point defence, area defence and naval fleet area defence against multi-directional co-ordinated attacks by subsonic or supersonic missiles, aircraft and UAVs.

The Aster 15 and 30 are vertically launched and have much commonality. The missiles are modular in design, and differ in their booster stage. Aster 15 has a 30-km (18.6-mile) range with a speed of 1000 m (3,281 ft)

per second, while Aster 30 has a 120-km (74.6-mile) range and a speed of 1400 m (4,593 ft) per second. The terminal dart is common to both missiles, and it is the size of their boosters that provides the two variants with their different range and also their speed capabilities.

The missiles are guided through the continuous update of the target position via automatic up-link from the fire-control radar. Once it has burned out, the booster stage separates from the terminal dart and falls away.

Once free of the booster, the terminal dart uses an active seeker in the final

phase of flight, and manoeuvres using the patented PIF-PAF system. This system combines conventional aerodynamic control surfaces with direct thrust vector control allowing for manoeuvres which can reach 60-*g*.

Naval application

Aster is the primary weapon fielded by the Principal Anti-Air Missile System (PAAMS) ship-defence system. PAAMS is intended to provide medium-range air defence and anti-missile protection for high-value units, such as aircraft carriers, in the vicinity of the escort. The Aster PAAMS uses the modular Sylver vertical launcher, in which each module contains eight cells. The Sylver A43 module carries only the Aster 15 missile, while the A50 can carry both types of missiles. Aster PAAMS will equip the Royal Navy's Type 45 destroyers, the French navy's 'Horizon'-class frigates, and the Italian navy's future 'Orizzonte'-class missile frigates.

The Principal Anti-Air Missile System (PAAMS) with the Aster missile was developed under the trilateral Horizon air defence frigate project. Despite the UK's withdrawal from Horizon, the Royal Navy will adopt the PAAMS and Aster for the Type 45 class of destroyer.

An Aster SAM starts to tilt onto its intended interception course after a vertical test launch from a warship. The booster stage is jettisoned once it is exhausted.

Below: Attached to its booster, the terminal stage of the Aster SAM reveals a strong French influence in its structural design, and is manoeuvred by aerodynamic and direct-thrust elements.

SPECIFICATION	
Aster 15	**Launch weight:** 310 kg (683 lb)
Type: medium-range/anti-missile SAM	**Performance:** range 30 km (18.6 miles)
Dimensions: length 4.2 m (13 ft 9.33 in); diameter 0.18 m (7 in)	**Warhead:** HE focused fragmentation

Aspide Point-defence missile

The **Aspide** missile is manufactured by MBDA Missile Systems (formerly Alenia Marconi Systems). Based on an American air-to-air missile, the AIM-7 Sparrow in its AIM-7E variant, the Aspide has both air-to-air and surface-to-air capability. The **Aspide 2000** is the most recent version of the missile produced.

The Aspide looks almost identical to the AIM-7 Sparrow in its external features, but there are several differences in the internal electronics. The Aspide uses a monopulse seeker with semi-active radar homing guidance. The missile can fly at Mach 2.5, has a range of 14 km (8.6 miles), and is fit-

ted with a 32-kg (70.5-lb) HE blast/fragmentation warhead.

The Aspide missile in its surface-to-air configuration can be used with the sea-based Albatros launcher, and also with the ground-based Spada and Skyguard launchers.

The Albatros system provides point and limited area air defence against aircraft, missiles and UAVs. The system can operate with a standard eight-cell missile

The close resemblance of the Aspide to the AIM-7 Sparrow AAM is clearly evident in this missile departing an Albatros system's launcher.

launcher or a lightweight four-cell launcher. The Albatros system can also fire the NATO Sea Sparrow missile. The Albatros system is commonly configured with the NA-30 fire-control system based on the Orion/RTN-30X tracking radar, but other fire-control systems can be integrated.

About 65 Albatros systems have been made, and are fielded by several navies. For example, Italy's aircraft-carrier *Giuseppe Garibaldi* has two eight-cell Albatros launchers loaded with Aspide missiles, of which 48 are carried in the ship's magazines.

Improvements in the Aspide 2000 include an enhanced single-stage solid-propellant motor, which enhances speed, lateral

acceleration and range. The Aspide 2000 is able to engage aircraft at ranges that allow most of these targets to be engaged before they release their weapons. The range for the Aspide 2000 is 25 km (15.5 miles), and the missile can operate in dense ECM environments. Existing Aspide missiles can be retrofitted to the Aspide 2000 standard at depot level maintenance facilities. The Aspide 2000 can be used by all current systems operating the Aspide missile.

Below: The Aspide missile's cropped-delta rear fins are fixed, control of the missile in the air being exercised by movement of the mid-body delta wings.

High acceleration is important to get the Aspide missile to an interception as far as possible from the ship that may be the object of the aircraft's attack.

SPECIFICATION	
Aspide 2000	**Launch weight:** 220 kg (485 lb)
Type: point-defence SAM	**Performance:** range 25 km
Dimensions: length 3.7 m (12 ft	(15.5 miles)
1.67 in); diameter 0.234 m (9.2 in)	**Warhead:** HE blast/fragmentation

Mistral Short-range surface-to-air missile

The **Mistral** missile is built by MBDA Missile Systems. Mistral is a short-range surface-to-air missile intended for use against low-altitude targets. Effective for day and night engagements, the Mistral is capable of intercepting and destroying UAV, aircraft and missile targets.

The Mistral is a very versatile weapon, and has been

mated with a number of launchers and platforms, a fact that has considerably enhanced its worldwide market appeal. The **Mistral 2** is the most recent version of the missile to have been placed in production.

The Mistral is a fire-and-forget weapon using a sensitive onboard passive IR seeker, and optimum target intercep-

tion is facilitated by the use of impact and laser proximity fuses to trigger a very effective 3-kg (6.6-lb) HE blast/fragmentation warhead containing high-density tungsten balls.

There are many naval applications for the Mistral. Both the missile and the launcher configurations include the Stabilised Integrated Gun

Missile Array (SIGMA), Tetral, Simbad and Sadral systems.

Gun/missile system

MBDA and MSI-Defence Systems collaborate to produce the dual-role SIGMA. This deck-mounted system embodies modular design, and combines a three-round Mistral launcher with a 25-mm or 30-mm cannon. The fusion of these two weapon types allows the system to be employed against air and surface targets.

The Simbad is a deck-mounted launcher with two ready-to-fire Mistral missiles. When loaded the total system weighs 250 kg (551 lb), and is manually operated by an aimer/operator. It has a

thermal camera providing a night engagement capability.

The Tetral system complements other SAM systems on larger vessels, and can serve as a primary air-defence system on smaller vessels. The 600-kg (1,323-lb) Tetral has a thermal imager and a stabilised launcher with four missiles, and is integrated into the ship's fire-control system for single-shot or salvo launch.

The 1080-kg (2,381-lb) Sadral is an autonomous system with a thermal imaging camera and six Mistrals on a gyro-stabilised launcher. The system is operated by the ship's fire-control system, and has fully automatic engagement capability.

The Mistral has an arrangement of pop-out fixed fins at its rear, and is controlled by a cruciform arrangement of rectangular pop-out fins just behind the seeker/guidance section.

SPECIFICATION	
Mistral 2	Mach 2.5; maximum range 6 km
Type: short-range SAM	(3.73 miles); maximum engagement
Dimensions: length 1.86 m (6 ft	altitude 3000 m (9,845 ft)
1.25 in); diameter 0.09 m (3.54 in);	**Warhead:** 3-kg (6.6-lb) HE
fin span 0.18 m (7.1 in)	blast/fragmentation type with
Launch weight: 18.7 kg (41.23 lb)	a filling of tungsten balls
Performance: maximum speed	

SA-N-1 'Goa' Medium-range area-defence missile system

The **SA-N-1a 'Goa'** (**Volna**) system, using the **V-600** two-stage solid-propellant missile, entered Soviet naval service in 1961 and was the first naval SAM fitted on a large scale in Soviet surface combatants.

Effective missile

It was derived from the ground-launched SA-3 'Goa' (S-125 Neva), and in its time was an effective missile at low to medium altitudes, and in the surface-to-surface role out to the radar horizon. It is a medium-range area-defence weapon that is fired from a twin-arm launcher which is rotated to the 90° vertical position for reloading from an under-deck 16-round magazine. The booster stage's four rectangular fins are folded until the missile leaves the launcher. The HE-fragmentation warhead

A 'Kashin'-class destroyer launches a 'Goa' missile. The engagement envelope of this pioneering weapon is between 6 and 25 km (3.7 and 15.5 miles) in range and 100 and 25000 m (330 and 82,020 ft) in altitude. The HE warhead has a lethal radius of 12.5 m (41 ft).

has a 12.5-m (41-ft) lethal radius at low levels against targets the size of the F-4 Phantom. Guidance is by radio command, possibly

with IR terminal guidance, although the later uprated versions of the 'Peel Group' naval fire-control radar was converted for semi-active terminal homing within the **SA-N-3b 'Goa'** system using the **V-601 Volna-M** missile. The 'Goa' was also delivered to India and Poland.

SPECIFICATION	
SA-N-1 'Goa' (V-600/V-601)	(2,086 lb) for V-600 and 950 kg
Dimensions: length 6.7 m (21 ft 11¾ in); diameter of missile 0.46 m (1 ft 6 in) and of booster 0.701 m (2 ft 3⅜ in); span of missile 1.5 m (4 ft 11 in)	(2,094 lb) for V-601; warhead 60-kg (132-lb) HE
	Performance: maximum speed Mach 3; range limits 6-25 km (3.7-15.5 miles); altitude limits 100-25000 m (330-82,020 ft)
Weights: total round 946 kg	

Above: *This twin-rail launcher of the SA-N-1 system on a 'Kashin'-class destroyer carries two V-600 surface-to-air missiles. The launcher is roll-stabilised to provide a steady launch platform in rough seas. Single and twin launchers were installed in many classes.*

The V-600/V-601 missile was designed by the Isayev Design Bureau. The booster burns for 2.6 seconds, and the sustainer for 18.7 seconds, the missile being guided by movement of its forward fins.

SA-N-3 'Goblet' Medium-range area-defence missile system

The **SA-N-3a 'Goblet'** (**Shtorm**) system entered service with ships of the Soviet navy in 1967 as the medium-range low/medium-altitude area-defence follow-on to the SA-N-1 'Goa' system. Providing significantly enhanced anti-air warfare capabilities, the SA-N-3 can also be used in the surface-to-surface role out to the radar horizon. Unlike other Soviet naval SAMs of the period, the **V-611** two-stage solid-pro-

pellant missile has no land-based equivalent, and was not derived from the SA-6 'Gainful' as was often

The twin-rail launcher of the 'Kresta'-class cruisers was once thought capable of firing the SS-N-14 anti-submarine missile as well as the SA-N-3. The system was also installed on the 'Kiev'-, 'Kara'- and 'Moskva'-class ships.

claimed. The SA-N-3 is normally fitted with an HE-fragmentation warhead, but there have been persistent reports of a low-yield nuclear alternative. The missile is fired from a twin-arm launcher, the launcher arms rotating to the vertical for reloading from an underdeck magazine holding 22, 24 or 36 missiles depending on the size of the ship. The mis-

sile's guidance is of the radio command type via the 'Head Light' fire-control radar, which has been installed on 'Kresta II'- and 'Kara'-class missile cruisers as well as on the 'Moskva' and 'Kiev' classes of aviation ships. There is also an **SA-N-3b** upgraded system offering a range increased to 55 km (34.2 miles) using the **V-611M** missile.

The 'Kiev'-class aviation ships carried two twin-arm launchers for the SA-N-3 (72 missiles in all): one forward of the island on the centreline between the after pair of SS-N-12 launchers, and the other immediately abaft the island.

SPECIFICATION

SA-N-3 'Goblet' (V-611)
Dimensions: length 6.4 m (21 ft); diameter 0.7 m (2 ft 3⅔ in); span 1.7 m (5 ft 6¾ in)
Weights: total round not known; warhead 150-kg (331-lb) HE-

fragmentation
Performance: maximum speed Mach 2.8; range 6-30 km (3.7-18.6 miles) for SA-N-3a or 6-55 km (3.7-34.2 miles) for SA-N-3b; altitude limits 90-24500 m (295-80,380 ft)

SA-N-4 'Gecko' Point-defence missile system

The **SA-N-4 'Gecko' (Osa-M)** system, using the **9M33M** single-stage solid-propellant missile, entered service in the early 1970s as the Soviet navy's point-defence missile system for service on both large and small surface combatants as the secondary/tertiary or pri-

mary air-defence weapon respectively. Based on the Soviet army's SA-8 system, the SA-N-4 naval variant is based on the use of a fully retractable twin-arm launcher supplied with missiles from a 20-round under-deck magazine. Notable for its high accelera-

tion, which was further improved in the second variant of the missile that entered service in 1980, the missile has a 19-kg (41.9-lb) HE-fragmentation warhead with impact and proximity fuses for a low-altitude lethal radius of about 5 m (16 ft 5 in), and can be used out to

its maximum range as a surface-to-surface missile in an emergency.

Semi-active guidance
The missile's guidance is of the semi-active radar type via the individual 'Pop Group' fire-control radar system associated with each launcher, and there is also provision for the use, under adverse electronic conditions such as very low

altitude operation or enemy countermeasures, of an alternative optronic and/or low-light-level TV system.

Unlike many later-generation Soviet naval SAMs, the 'Gecko' has been widely exported to a number of Soviet client states as part of the armament outfit for export versions of the 'Nanuchka'-class missile corvettes and 'Koni'-class light frigates.

SPECIFICATION

SA-N-4 'Gecko' (9M33M)
Dimensions: length 3.158 m (10 ft 4⅓ in); diameter 0.21 m (8¼ in); span 0.64 m (2 ft 1¼ in)
Weights: total round 170 kg (375 lb); warhead 19 kg (41.9 lb)

HE-fragmentation
Performance: maximum speed Mach 2.4; range limits 1.5-15 km (0.93-9.32 miles); altitude limits 10-12000 m (33-39,370 ft)

Left: Based on a missile offering high acceleration and a capable guidance system, the SA-N-4 gives light warships a good short-range air-defence capability.

Below: The 'Krivak I'-class frigate carries two Zif 122 launchers for 'Gecko' missiles, their positions being marked by the white circular covers fore and aft.

SA-N-6 'Grumble' Long-range surface-to-air missile

The S-300PMU (SA-10 'Grumble') series was designed by the Grushin and Rospletin Design Bureau, with the land-based version entering service in 1980. The missile system was designed to provide a mobile air defence system for the army and to provide a missile shield over cities and industrial installations. A sea-going version was also designed as a replacement to the V-611 Shtorm (SA-N-3 'Goblet') and was designated as the **S-300F Fort** in Soviet service (**Rif** for export models), and is known in the West as the **SA-N-6 'Grumble'**. This was intended to provide Soviet naval task groups with an advanced air defence capability similar to that of the American AEGIS fleet air defence system.

Rotary launcher

In naval service, the missiles are housed in a B-303A eight-round rotary magazine. The missiles are launched vertically from the ship, and a weapon can be launched once every three seconds. The 'Kirov' battlecruisers can each carry 96 missiles while the 'Slava' cruisers carry 64 each. The weapon is guided by semi-active radar homing with target illumination being provided by the ship's 'Top Dome' radar system. The missile is ejected from its launch tube to an altitude of 20-25 m (65-82 ft) before the rocket motor ignites. This accelerates the missile to Mach 3, which can give rise to stresses of 100 g. Once in flight, the missile's navigation is controlled by deflector

vanes and ailerons. The missile has a homing range of 100 km (62 miles). The SA-N-6 is thought to contain a 90 kg (176-lb) conventional warhead, but there is speculation that this could be substituted for a nuclear warhead if necessary.

The potent 'Top Dome' radar fire-control system allows the missile system to track up to nine targets, and independently fire at six targets, assigning one or two missiles to each contact. These can include targets with a small radar cross-section such as cruise missiles – a favourite weapon for anti-shipping warfare. This capability, it is claimed, can even extend to attacks against tactical ballistic missiles and possibly, according to some sources, strategic missiles. The 'Top Dome' radar works by illuminating the target, this illumination is then transmitted to the missile's onboard passive reflector, which then directs the missile towards the target. This information is transmitted to the missile via an ECM-resistant communications link. The missile is able to hit targets at altitudes of 25000 to 30000 m (82,020 to 98,424 ft). The guaranteed effective range of the missile is stated as 90 km (55 miles).

In April 2002 China signed an agreement with the Russian export company Rosoboronexport for the delivery of two S-300F systems. The sale was interesting as it appeared to represent a shift from the more traditional Chinese practice of purchasing complete integrated weapons systems to instead buying subsystems. It is not known which ships these missile systems will be fitted to, although the systems may be installed for air defence

The 'Kirov'-class cruiser has the vertical-launch system for the SA-N-6 'Grumble' missiles located beneath 12 hatches within the flush deck forward of the main superstructure, and ahead of the VLS for the SS-N-19 'Shipwreck' anti-ship missiles.

protection on two Chinese cruisers which it is thought could be launched in 2005.

The improved **S-300FM Rif-M** export version introduces the more capable **48N6E** missile in place of the original **5V55** as used within the baseline S-300F Rif system.

SPECIFICATION	
S-300F (SA-N-6 'Grumble')	**Performance:** range 100 km (62 miles); maximum altitude between 25000-30000 m (82,020-98,424 ft); minimum engagement altitude 5 m (16 ft)
Type: long-range area-defence missile	
Dimensions: length 7 m (22 ft); diameter 450 mm (18 in)	
Launch weight: 333-420 kg (734-881 lb) depending on variant	**Warhead:** 90-kg (176-lb) HE and possible optional nuclear

---

SA-N-7 'Gadfly' and SA-N-12 'Grizzly' Medium-range SAMs

Uragan and **Yezh** are the Russian designations for the **SA-N-7 'Gadfly'** and **SA-N-12 'Grizzly'** respectively. These systems are medium-range naval surface-to-air weapons, and can perhaps be considered Russia's equivalent to the US Navy's Standard missile.

The prototype version of the SA-N-7 was tested in 1974 aboard the 'Kashin'-class destroyer *Provorny*. The 'Gadfly' system entered operational service with the first 'Sovremenny'-class destroyer in 1980.

Targets are located using the 'Top Plate' 3D search

radar. Acquired contacts are then passed to the 3R90 H/I-band target-illuminating radar, which is linked to the 'Front Dome' fire-control radar. A supplemental TV-optical sight is also fitted, and can be used in dense ECM environments, and during radar silence. The MS-196 handling/launching system is fitted aboard ships

The forward launcher system for the 'Gadfly' is located ahead of the bridge and behind the forward gun armament on early 'Sovremenny'-class destroyers.

The rear SA-N-7 launcher on the initial batch of 'Sovremenny' destroyers is located behind the small raised flight deck for the ship's Ka-27 ASW helicopter.

using the 'Gadfly'.

Fired by a single rail launcher, 'Gadfly' is capable of engaging targets up to 30 km (18 miles) away, and at altitudes up to 22000 m (72,178 ft).

The 'Gadfly' system uses the **9M38M** surface-to-air missile derived from the land-based SA-11 'Gadfly'. This missile uses a solid-propellant motor, carries a 70-kg (154-lb) HE warhead, and is fitted with a radio proximity fuse. The missile uses iner-

tial guidance for the majority of its flight time, and semi-active radar guidance for terminal homing. The 'Front Dome' radar illuminates the target until it is within range of the missile's onboard semi-active radar. From a 'cold' start, the system has a reaction time of three minutes. The missile can be operated autonomously or as part of an integrated command and control system, and up to 48 missiles can be carried by each 'Sovremenny' vessel. However, the system is thought to be notably labour intensive, requiring 19 crew and taking up some 37 m² (398 sq ft) of space on each vessel so equipped.

India has purchased the SA-N-7 'Gadfly' for service aboard its 'Delhi'-class destroyers while China also uses the system on its own 'Sovremenny'-class destroyers.

Single-shot kill

The effectiveness of the single-shot kill capability for the 'Gadfly' is claimed to be 60-90 per cent against aircraft, 30-70 per cent against helicopters and around 40 per cent against cruise missile targets. The system is also highly resistant to ECM jamming. Once in flight, the missile can also conduct manoeuvres of up to 23 *g*.

The SA-N-12 'Grizzly' is very similar to the SA-N-7, to the extent that it is considered almost visually identical.

Derived from the land-based SA-17 'Grizzly' system, the ship-based SA-N-12 system retains the MS-196 launcher/handling system, the 3R90 radar, and the 'Front Dome' radar of the original SA-N-7, but instead fires an improved development of the 9M38M missile. This has modified guidance and improved acceleration. The 'Grizzly' system is fitted aboard the Russian 'Sovremenny' ships from *Bespokoiny* onwards.

SPECIFICATION	
Yezh (SA-N-12 'Grizzly')	**Launch weight:** 710 kg (1,565 lb)
Type: medium-range area-defence missile	**Performance:** range 3-30 km (1.8-18.6 miles); maximum altitude 22000 m (72,178 ft)
Dimensions: length 5.55 m (18 ft 2¼ in); diameter 400 mm (15.7 in); span 0.86 m (33.8 in)	**Warhead:** 70-kg (254-lb) HE

Sea Slug Medium-/long-range area-defence SAM

Sea Slug saw action for the first time in the Falklands, being used by HMS Glamorgan and (seen here during the campaign) HMS Antrim. Although much improved at low level, the essentially 1950s missile could not measure up to the low-level targets of the 1980s.

Although the Royal Navy had used unguided anti-aircraft rockets in the early years of World War II, preliminary investigation into the production of guided missiles remained as studies. It was not until 1962, with the commissioning of HMS *Devonshire*, the first of the 'County' class of guided-missile destroyers that the UK went to sea with an effective air-defence missile system.

The **Sea Slug**, result of a rather protracted development programme lasting from 1949 to 1962, was a large missile designed to counter the classic 1950s threat of high-flying bombers travelling at high subsonic speeds. Fired from a twin launcher, the missile com-

prised a cylindrical body with mid-set rectangular cruciform wings, tail-mounted rectangular cruciform control surfaces and an ICI solid-fuel rocket sustainer aided by four blunt-nosed solid-propellant boosters wrapped around the nose.

The Sea Slug was a beam-riding missile, targets first being detected by long-range Type 965 surveillance radar and Type 277 height-finding radar. Target co-ordinates were fed into the Type 901 missile tracking and illuminating radar, which launched the missile when the target was in range, gathered it into the centre of the pencil radar beam, and passed coded guidance instructions along the beam. The 135-kg (297-lb) warhead had both DA (direct

action, or impact) and proximity fuses, and the missile had a secondary surface-to-surface capacity.

Improved version

The **Sea Slug Mk 2** was announced in 1961, but once again development was slow. Nevertheless, though few external changes were made, the update considerably enhanced performance in terms of speed, range, resistance to ECM and guidance accuracy. Upgraded electronics gave the Sea Slug Mk 2 better capabilities against low-flying and surface targets than its predecessor. The new missile was fitted to the second group of four 'County'-class destroyers, plans to retrofit the first four coming to

nothing.

Sea Slug went to war for the first time 20 years after its service introduction, the Mk 2-armed destroyers HMS *Glamorgan* and HMS *Antrim* playing an important part in the South Atlantic campaign of 1982, although more modern missiles obviously achieved more against the Argentine air force's low level attacks.

The last systems remaining operational were the Mk 2s aboard HMS *Fife* and *Glamorgan*, and the Chilean *Prat* (ex-HMS *Norfolk*) and *Almirante Cochrane* (ex-*Antrim*). Those on the Chilean ships were replaced by the Israeli Barak system. Pakistan's *Babur* (ex-*London*) was initially fitted with Sea Slug Mk 1 but the system was later removed.

SPECIFICATION	
Sea Slug	(4,400 lb)
Type: medium-/long-range shipborne area-defence SAM	**Performance:** range (Mk 1) 45 km (28 miles) or (Mk 2) 68 km (36 miles); maximum altitude at least 15240 m (50,000 ft)
Dimensions: length (Mk 1) 5.99 m (19 ft 8 in) or (Mk 2) 6.1 m (20 ft); diameter 409 mm (16.1 in); span 1.45 m (4 ft 9 in)	**Warhead:** 135-kg (297-lb) HE with impact and proximity fuses
Launch weight: 1,996 kg	

Sea Cat Point-defence missile

Designed and built by Short Brothers in the late 1950s, the **Sea Cat** was the first shipborne SAM system designed for close-range air defence in place of rapid-firing guns such as the 40-mm Bofors weapon. The first guided trials took place in 1960, the initial shipboard trials following onboard HMS *Decoy* in 1961. A series of full-scale shipboard trials before service acceptance was then undertaken in 1962 aboard the same ship, the missile system becoming known as the **Guided Weapon System (GWS) Mk 20** in the Royal Navy. The Sea Cat had a dual-thrust motor, four fixed fins, hydraulically-driven wings and a continuous-rod blast warhead with both delayed-action contact and proximity fuses. The missile was guided by radio command and could also be integrated with almost any type of sighting and fire-control system, as the continual improvement and updating programme in the Royal Navy eventually proved with the introduction into service of the **GWS Mk 21** (using the Type 262 fire-control radar of the 40-mm Bofors and fitted on 'Tribal' class) and **GWS Mk 22** (modified MRS-3 director, 'County' and 'Leander' classes) versions with different radars to give darkfire capabilities. The **GWS Mk 24** on the 'Amazon' class used the WSA-4 fire-control system.

The system remained in service with the Royal Navy until the mid-1990s. The launcher which was used most often with the missile was a quadruple hand-loaded version, although some of the countries to which the missile was exported used a lightweight triple unit. Since it entered production in the 1960s, 16 navies bought the missile, but it was not until the 1982 Falklands War that it was used in combat. There it proved to be a useful 'scare' defence, but the weapon gave a lacklustre performance against modern high-performance and manoeuvring targets.

Exocet threat

During the conflict in the South Atlantic, the missile proved too slow to engage targets crossing over the ship's line of fire. In one incident a Sea Cat missile was fired against an Exocet missile although it proved to be too slow, and it was still within its minimum range (the warhead not being armed), causing it to narrowly miss the Exocet.

One of the weaknesses of the missile was that it had to be manually tracked by the missile operator. The operator would acquire the target in his binocular viewfinder. The missile would then be launched and steering commands would be transmitted to the missile by the operator. The missile was steered by the operator's thumb moving a joystick. The commands were then transmitted via a UHF or VLF radio link. A flare mounted at the rear of the missile allowed the operator to track the weapon. However, this system had one major weakness in that only a single missile could be controlled at any one time.

The missile sold well, and operators of the Sea Cat comprised Argentina, Australia, Brazil, Chile, India, Iran, Libya, Malaysia, the Netherlands, New Zealand, Nigeria, Sweden, Thailand, the UK, Venezuela and West Germany. In Australian naval service, the missile was fitted to all of the force's frigates of the Type 12 class, and was credited with bringing the Royal Australian Navy into the 'missile age'.

Developed in the late 1950s, Sea Cat entered service as the Royal Navy's primary short-range air defence system in the early 1960s, replacing systems such as the 40-mm Bofors AA gun.

Above: Seen aboard the 'County'-class missile destroyer HMS Antrim in the South Atlantic, Sea Cat first saw action in the battles around the Falkland Islands. The missile's performance was disappointing and it was less than effective against high-speed targets, although several Argentine aircraft were believed to have been destroyed by the system.

Launched from the standard four-round launcher, Sea Cat was effective to about 5.5 km (3.4 miles) and was capable of a speed of Mach 1. Interceptions could be made at altitudes between 30 and 915 m (100-3000 ft). Sea Cat would see service with some 16 navies, including both sides involved in the Falklands War.

SPECIFICATION

Sea Cat
Type: point-defence missile
Dimensions: length 1.48 m (4 ft 10.3 in); diameter 0.1905 m (7.5 in); span 0.65 m (2 ft 1.6 in)
Weights: total round 68 kg (149.9 lb); HE fragmentation warhead about 10 kg (22 lb)
Performance: maximum speed Mach 1; range 5.5 km (3.4 miles); altitude limits 30-915 m (100-3,000 ft)

Sea Dart Medium-range area-defence missile

The **Sea Dart** (or **Guided Weapon System Mk 30** to give it its Royal Navy title) was designed by British Aerospace in the 1960s as a third-generation area-defence naval SAM capable of engaging targets such as aircraft and missiles at both very high and, under certain circumstances, very low altitudes. The system was used operationally during the 1982 Falklands War, being officially credited with eight kills. However, more recent evidence suggests that the number was actually five: a Puma helicopter, a Learjet

Designed to give the Royal Navy a third-generation area SAM able to intercept both aircraft and missiles, the Sea Dart gave valiant service during the 1982 Falklands War and was credited with destroying eight enemy aircraft.

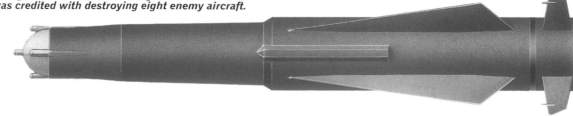

35A reconnaissance aircraft, a Canberra B.Mk 62 light bomber and two A-4C Skyhawk light attack aircraft.

The last aircraft was shot down outside the missile's official engagement envelope at very low level. The launcher is a twin-rail unit and is coupled with two Type 909 target tracking and illuminator radars on the Type 42 (20 missiles) destroyers, and formerly on the 'Invincible'-class aircraft carriers (20 missiles) and on the since retired HMS *Bristol* (40 missiles). The last vessel was the sole destroyer of the Type 82 class built. In addition, Sea Dart can be used out to 25-30 km (15.5-18.6 miles) against surface targets if required.

Argentine service

The system was also sold to Argentina for its two Type 42 destroyers, and this probably explains the relative lack of kills by the system during the war as the Argentines already knew its performance capabilities. By the early 21st century, the Sea Dart systems on Argentine ships were non-operational. Guidance is of the semi-active homing type with associated proportional navigation. A Rolls-Royce Odin ramjet engine powers the missile in flight after a solid-propellant booster unit has brought it up to the velocity required for the main engine to take over. The use of Kerosene as a fuel for the missile allows it to be stored on ships for prolonged periods with only a minimum of

In addition to arming Royal Navy destroyers of the Type 42 and 82 classes, Sea Dart was mounted on the three carriers of the 'Invincible' class. It was also used on Argentina's Type 42 ships.

maintenance and it is claimed that the missile can be handled with the equivalent ease of naval gun ammunition. An automated loader also allows a high rate of fire to be achieved for the missile.

In the 1981 defence cuts an improved **Sea Dart Mk 2** was cancelled: this was designed to combat Soviet cruise missiles by going into a terminal dive from high altitude, and this largely politically-driven economic cut left a serious gap in Royal Navy fleet defences during the late 1980s and early 1990s. A **Lightweight Sea Dart** system was also developed for ships down to 300 tons displacement: this was designed to make use of deck-mounted container-launchers with simplified

radars and fire-control units. The People's Republic of China planned to purchase this system as part of a modification package for its 'Luda'-class destroyers, although the deal was scuppered because of funding problems.

SPECIFICATION	
Sea Dart	**Weights:** total round 550 kg
Type: medium-range area-defence missile	(1,213 lb); HE-FRAG warhead
	Performance: maximum speed
Dimensions: length 4.36 m (14 ft 3.65 in); diameter 0.42 m (1 ft 4.54 in); span 0.91 m (2 ft 11.83 in)	Mach 3+; range 65 km (40.4 miles); altitude limits 30-18290 m (100-60,000 ft)

Sea Wolf Point-defence missile

Conceived in 1962 and designed by British Aerospace, the **Sea Wolf** was originally developed as the replacement for the widely-fitted Sea Cat SAM system. Unfortunately, in the **Guided Weapon System Mk 25 Mod 0** devised for the Royal Navy, the weapons package proved so large that it could be fitted on warships only down to a size of around 2,500 tons. In fact it was the room required to fit two complete manually-reloaded GWS Mk 25 systems with their attendant 30-round magazines and six-round trainable launchers that helped to finalise the dimensions and displacement of the frigates of the Type 22 class in excess of the Sea Dart-equipped

The Sea Wolf missile is 1.9 m (6 ft 2.8 in) long and weighs 82 kg (180.4 lb). Much like the Sea Dart, the Sea Wolf can be treated as a round of ammunition.

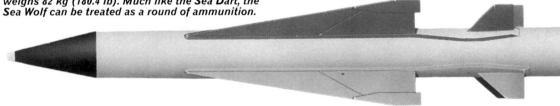

destroyers of the Type 42 class.

Sea Wolf is a fully automatic point-defence system with radio command to line of sight guidance coupled with radar differential or low-light TV tracking. The missile's manoeuvrability and speed allows it to engage small Mach 2 anti-ship missiles and

aircraft targets under severe weather conditions and sea states down to low altitudes.

Carrier protection

During the Falklands War two frigates of the Type 22 class, HMS *Brilliant* and HMS *Broadsword*, together with the converted 'Leander'-class frigate HMS *Andromeda* with only one launcher, used the missile operationally, one of the Type 22s acting as the close-range air-defence ship or 'goalkeeper' to the carriers. The first combat use was from HMS *Brilliant* on 12 May 1982 when the ship engaged a flight of four A-4 Skyhawks, shooting down two and forcing a third to crash as it evaded a missile. The official list credits the Sea Wolf with five kills, although later evidence suggests it was only the three described above,

A Sea Wolf missile is launched from a Type 22 frigate. The missile is highly effective, but with ancillary radar, launch and command systems the Sea Wolf system is rather heavy, and to operate two launchers effectively the Type 22 frigates have to be larger than Type 42 destroyers.

plus a possible fourth. What actually came out of the war was that the system required a number of software upgrades to increase its reliability: on several occasions the computers associated with target-tracking broke lock because they were unable to differentiate between targets flying close together.

The modifications culminated in a successful trial whereby a Sea Wolf engaged and destroyed a sea-skimming MM.38 Exocet anti-ship missile.

To further improve the missile's capabilities and range, a vertical-launch capability, first demonstrated in 1968 from HMS *Loch Fada* when it was considered to be of low priority, was installed on the Royal Navy's Type 23 'Duke'-class frigates as the **GWS Mk 26**. VLS Seawolf systems are also fitted on Malaysia's 'Lekiu' frigates. Several light-

weight systems have also been developed, the **GWS Mk 25 Mod 3** version being retrofitted to various RN ship classes to increase their self-defence capability. Another variant which surprisingly the Royal Navy did not follow up was the conversion of the standard four-round Sea Cat launcher to take Sea Wolf container-launchers (together with the fitting of appropriate electronics and radars). Such a programme for the frigates of the Royal Navy would have undoubtedly resulted in a much higher kill rate for the close-range air defence systems aboard Royal Navy ships in the Falklands than was in fact obtained.

A more advanced **GWS Mk 27** variant was cancelled in 1987. This would have used an active seeker and a phased-array tracker and would have offered twice the range of the earlier missiles.

SPECIFICATION	
Sea Wolf	(180.4 lb); HE-FRAG warhead
Type: point-defence missile	**Performance:** maximum speed
Dimensions: length 1.9 m (6 ft 2.8 in); diameter 0.3 m (11.8 in); span 0.45 m (1 ft 5.7 in)	Mach 2+; range 6.5 km (4.04 miles) or 10 km (6.2 miles) in vertical-launch form; altitude limits about
Weights: total round 82 kg	4.7-3050 m (15-10,000 ft)

Terrier and Tartar Naval medium-range surface-to-air missiles

The **Terrier** area-defence missile was developed from the technology involved in the Talos missile programme, but preceded the Talos into service. The Terrier was more compact, being small enough for employment on the missile frigates (large destroyers) being built to carry missile systems.

Slow development

From the start of its development in 1949, the Terrier evolved gradually, only one major component at a time being changed to produce new variants. The original Mach 1.8 beam-riding missile was designated **BW-0** (later **RIM-2A**) with a range of 18.5 km (11.5 miles) and altitude limits of 1525-15240 m (5,000-50,000 ft). The next version, the **BW-1** (**RIM-2B**), was a re-engineered BW-0 but had no significant performance improvements in either range or altitude. In 1956 there entered service the **BT-3** (**RIM-2C**) with new tail controls, improved beam-riding guidance and a new motor propellant. The improvements increased the velocity to Mach 3 and the range and maximum altitude limits by 50 per cent. This was rapidly followed by the **BT-3A** (**RIM-2D**) of 1958 with surface-to-surface capability

and the SAM range of 37 km (23 miles). A nuclear version with the 1-kT W45 warhead was also produced alongside this variant and designated **BT-3(N)**, later changed to **RIM-2D(N)**. The last planned variant, the **HT-3** (**RIM-2E**), entered service one year earlier than the BT-3 and introduced continuous-wave semi-active homing, which increased its low-altitude engagement capability and improved the single-shot kill capability figure by more than 30 per cent. The last HT-3s, delivered in the mid-1960s with the **RIM-2F** designation, had a new sustainer and power supply for a range of 74 km (46 miles).

Production ended in 1966 after some 8,000 rounds.

Above: A member of one of the earliest naval SAM generations, the Tartar was supplied to the navies of the US, Australia, France, Italy, Japan, the Netherlands and the Federal Republic of Germany.

Right: The first trials of the AEGIS air-defence system used Tartar and Terrier missiles while the Standard Missile was developed. Here, a Tartar missile is seen as it is launched from the trials ship USS Norton Sound against a Firebee supersonic drone.

In 1952 it was decided to produce a semi-active homing missile to complement larger systems in tackling low-flying targets. The result was the Mach 1.8 **RIM-24A Tartar**, effective at 1.85/13.7 km (1.15/8.5 miles) and 15/16765 m (50/55,000 ft). A product-improved Tartar was soon sought, this **RIM-24B Improved Tartar** entering service in 1963 with the range boosted to 32.5 km (20.2 miles) and the upper altitude limit to 21335 m (70,000 ft). It also had an anti-ship capability. About 6,500 rounds were made, and most countries supplied (Australia, France, Netherlands, Italy, Japan, US and West Germany) later converted to the Standard Missile.

SPECIFICATION	
RIM-2D(N) Terrier	span 1.074 m (3 ft 6¼ in)
Type: medium-range area-defence missile	**Weights:** missile 535 kg (1,180 lb); booster 825.5 kg (1,820 lb); warhead W45 1-kT nuclear
Dimensions: length of missile 4.115 m (13 ft 6 in) and of booster 7.874 m (25 ft 10 in); diameter of missile 0.343 m (1 ft 1½ in) and of booster 0.457 m (1 ft 6 in); missile	**Performance:** maximum speed Mach 3; range 37 km (23 miles); altitude limits 150-24385 m (500-80,000 ft)

SPECIFICATION	
RIM-24B Improved Tartar	**Weights:** total round 594 kg (1,310 lb); warhead HE
Type: medium-range area-defence missile	**Performance:** maximum speed Mach 1.8; range 32.375 km (20.1 miles); altitude limits 15-21335 m (50-70,000 ft)
Dimensions: length 4.72 m (15 ft 6 in); diameter 0.34 m (1ft 1½ in); span 0.61 m (2 ft)	

The Terrier has been replaced by the Standard Missile, but for many years it provided air defence for the US Navy. The RIM-2E, seen during launch from the cruiser USS Josephus Daniels in 1973, had a maximum range in excess of 70 km (43 miles).

Sea Sparrow Naval short-range surface-to-air missile

In the early 1960s the Sparrow air-to-air missile proved to be the best missile to form the basis of the **Basic Point Defense Missile System** (BPDMS) for the US Navy. The first missile used, the **RIM-7E5**, of what has now become a family of **Sea Sparrow** missiles, was derived from the AIM-7E AAM. This was then reconfigured into the **RIM-7H** round and then the **RIM-7F** was used, based on the much improved AIM-7F. The performance of the semi-active radar-homing Sea Sparrow was quite impressive as its engage-

A Sea Sparrow missile is launched from its octuple box launcher aboard the amphibious command ship USS Mount Whitney.

The only missile defence carried by US Navy aircraft-carriers is the Basic Point Defense Missile System, using Sea Sparrow missiles. The system has been in service for some time, as this picture of the USS John F. Kennedy, taken in the Mediterranean, demonstrates.

SPECIFICATION

RIM-7M Sea Sparrow
Type: point-defence SAM
Dimensions: length 3.98 m (13 ft 1 in); diameter 0.203 m (8 in); span 1.02 m (3 ft 4 in)
Weights: total round 228 kg

(503 lb); warhead 40-kg (88-lb) HE fragmentation
Performance: maximum speed Mach 3+; range 22.2 km (13.8 miles); altitude limits 8-15240 m (25-50,000 ft)

ment range was between 14.9 and 22.3 km (9.25 and 13.86 miles) depending upon the target's altitude, which could lie between 30 and 15240 m (100 and 50,000 ft). All versions were, however, considered deficient against low-flying cruise missiles, which had by then become a major threat to US naval forces. In order to rectify this defect, low-altitude radar guidance and fusing capabilities were to be given to RIM-7F Block I missiles to enable them to hit targets below 15 m (50 ft), while Block II missiles were to get enhanced ECCM features. Both fixes were dropped from the programme, however, as the RIM-7F was superseded in production by the **RIM-7M** version of the AIM-7M with a monopulse seeker and all the improvements from the start. The US Navy replaced all earlier Sea Sparrow variants with this missile.

The **NATO Sea Sparrow** system differs from the BPDMS mainly in having fire-control systems that allow completely automatic engagements from target acquisition to missile impact. The missile used is the folding-fin **RIM-7H5** version designed to fit the more compact eight-round launchers that NATO navies use. An **Improved PDMS** was introduced into US Navy service in 1973, and this has a much improved target-acquisition radar and data-handling system.

The latest model is the **Evolved Sea Sparrow** development of the **RIM-7P** for use in the Mk 41 vertical-launch system with a jet vane control unit to vector the missile onto the right trajectory after clearing the ship's superstructure.

RAM Naval short-range SAM

The RAM, or Rolling Airframe Missile, employs components of the Sidewinder AAM and the Stinger portable SAM in addition to a passive radar system.

US Navy interest in a short-range lightweight missile remained strong even after the Phalanx 20-mm close-in weapon system programme began in 1969. After considerable Congressional pressure on the US Navy, West Germany and Denmark stepped in to save the programme by signing memoranda of understanding to develop the **RIM-116A Rolling Airframe Missile**, usually abbreviated to **RAM**, for their frigates and FACs.

The missile's name is derived from the fact that it is rotating as it emerges from the launcher, after which fins are extended. Guidance is entirely passive, and initially uses a two-antenna broad-band radar seeker to point the terminal homing IR seeker head at the target. When this picks up the 'glint' of the target, the radar seeker is turned off as the IR guidance is considered much more accurate, although the current Block I operational missile retains dual-mode seeker capability for maximised interception capabilities. The ship's fire-control system informs the missile's radar interferometer of the incoming missile's active seeker frequency.

First test launched in 1975 by design parent Hughes (now Raytheon), the RAM employs the motor, fuse system and warhead of the Sidewinder AAM, the IR seeker of the Stinger SAM, and the passive radar system described.

The RIM-116A Block 0 and Block I missiles reached initial operational capability in 1993 and 1999 respectively, initially to provide protection for the US Navy's amphibious warfare ships, and are generally launched from a 21-tube system on a Phalanx gun mount, but there is also an 11-tube launcher suitable for installation on smaller vessels.

This is the first test launch of RAM over water, with only the nose of the missile out of the launch box, but with the front fins already deploying.

SPECIFICATION

RIM-116A RAM
Type: point-defence SAM
Dimensions: length 2.82 m (9 ft 3 in); diameter 0.127 m (5 in); span 0.445 m (1 ft 5½ in)
Weights: total round 73.5 kg

(162 lb); warhead 10-kg (22-lb) HE fragmentation
Performance: maximum speed more than Mach 2; range 9.4 km (5.85 miles); altitude limits low to medium

Well on its way, the RAM missile accelerates towards its maximum velocity of Mach 2. The system was designed to complement the Phalanx 20-mm CIWS in providing comprehensive close-in defence against anti-ship missiles.

Standard Shipborne medium-/long-range area-defence SAM series

First run by General Dynamics and now by Raytheon, the Standard Missile effort began in 1963 to create a successor to the RIM-24 Tartar and RIM-2 Terrier SAMs as the **RIM-66 Standard MR** (Medium Range) and **RIM-67 Standard ER** (Extended Range), respectively. These MR and ER versions use the same core missile supplemented, in the ER models, by a booster stage. The first missiles are **SM-1** (Standard Missile 1) weapons. The main advantages of the SM-1 are solid-state electronics and electrically rather than hydraulically powered control surfaces for improved reliability and shorter reaction time. The SM-1 also had a new Mk 1 autopilot adaptable to changes in factors such as velocity and atmospheric pressure.

Flight tests began in 1965, and the **RIM-66A** (**SM-1MR Block I**) entered service in 1967. It had the same dual-thrust rocket motor as the RIM-24 Tartar, a continuous-rod warhead, and a conical-scan radar seeker. Slight improvements led to **Block II**, **III** and **IV** missiles, of which the last was the main production variant with improved ECCM and shorter minimum range.

The **SM-1MR Block V** was designated **RIM-66B** as it

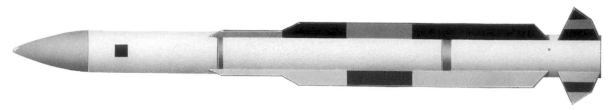

had changes such as a plane-scanning seeker, faster-reacting autopilot, new blast-fragmentation warhead, and new dual-thrust motor, the last increasing range and ceiling by about 45 and 25 per cent respectively. The final **SM-1MR Block VI** was

Above: Although it is part of a line of missiles whose physical form stretches back to the late 1940s, the Standard Missile, in its SM-2 form, is used in the advanced Aegis air-defence system.

Right: Standard Missiles of the SM-2MR type aboard the guided-missile trials ship USS Norton Sound. The SM-2 almost doubles the range of the SM-1 initial model, and the greatly updated and upgraded electronics of the guidance system ensure improved overall performance.

The 'Arleigh Burke'-class guided-missile destroyer USS O'Kane launches an SM-2 version of the Standard Missile family, with the upper part of the missile just evident to the left of the smoke plume. Following in formation are the guided-missile frigate USS Crommelin (right) and the 'Spruance'-class destroyer USS Paul F. Foster (centre). The 'Arleigh Burke' class launch the SM-2MR and SM-2ER from the Mk 41 Vertical Launch System. By the beginning of the 21st century, in excess of 21,000 Standard air-defence missiles of all versions had been built. The weapon also has a secondary anti-ship capability.

An SM-2ER Block IV (RIM-156A) missile is fired from the 'Arleigh Burke'-class guided-missile destroyer USS Higgins in October 2002. In addition to validating the weapon in question, live fire operations give the ship's crew the experience of launching operational weapons and also serve to hone their war-fighting skills.

Above: The 'Belknap'-class cruiser USS Wainwright fires an SM-2ER missile off San Juan. With the aid of its large booster, the extended-range version of the Standard Missile is capable of ranges in the region of 150 km (93 miles), and the improved electronics and guidance enhance the performance considerably.

the **RIM-66E** of 1983 with the **SM-2** monopulse seeker and a new proximity fuse.

The **SM-2** is primarily the SAM element of the Aegis fleet air-defence system. The SM-2 has semi-active radar homing only in the terminal phase, with a new inertial guidance unit and programmable Mk 2 autopilot (with mid-course update facility) to guide it toward the projected intercept point. Not requiring SAR guidance throughout its flight, the **SM-2MR** has an effective intercept range 60 per cent greater than that of the SM-1MR as it flies a more energy-efficient path. Another enhancement is the monopulse terminal seeker. The first of the missiles, in 1978, was the **SM-2MR Block I** for service as the **RIM-66C** and **RIM-66D** on Aegis and non-Aegis ships respectively. The **SM-2MR Block II** of 1983 introduced a new high-velocity fragmentation warhead and, to deal with faster and more agile targets, an improved motor that virtually doubled the range. The **RIM-66G** is the Aegis version, **RIM-66H** is for Aegis ships with the Mk 41 Vertical Launch System (VLS) and **RIM-66J** is for non-Aegis ships. The **SM-2MR Block III** of 1988 introduced an improved proximity fuse and later a combined radar/IR seeker: variants are the **RIM-66K** for non-Aegis ships, **RIM-66L** for Aegis ships and **RIM-66M** for VLS ships.

Long-range versions

The RIM-67 was developed to replace the Terrier long-range SAM. The **SM-1ER** is the **RIM-67A** in blocks essentially identical to those of the SM-1MR except for the replacement of the dual-thrust motor by a sustainer motor supplemented by a booster. The SM-2MR has corresponding **SM-2ER** versions (for non-Aegis ships) known by the designation **RIM-67B**. The **RIM-67C (SM-2ER Block II)** introduced a new booster that almost doubles its range. The **RIM-67D (SM-2ER Block III)** has a new sustainer and improved fuse. Declared operational in 1999, the **RIM-156A (SM-2ER Block IV)** has a new finless booster, designed for vertical launch on Aegis/VLS ships. Two anti-ballistic missile derivatives of the SM-2ER Block IV were intended to arm updated Aegis ships. These were the dual-role **SM-2ER Block IVA (RIM-156B)** lower-tier component and the three-stage **SM-3 (RIM-161A)** upper-tier component, although the first weapon was cancelled in December 2001 after successful flight tests.

An Aries ballistic missile target is seen just after lift-off from the Pacific Missile Range Facility at Barking Sands, Hawaii, on 21 November 2002. Minutes later it was intercepted by a developmental SM-3 launched from the Pearl Harbor-based Aegis cruiser USS Lake Erie. The SM-3 is designed for the exo-atmospheric interception and kinetic destruction of theatre ballistic missiles.

SPECIFICATIONS

RIM-66A (SM-1MR)
Type: shipborne medium-range area-defence SAM
Dimensions: length 4.47 m (14 ft 8 in); diameter 0.343 m (1 ft 1½ in); span 1.07 m (3 ft 6½ in)
Weights: total round 578.8 kg (1,276 lb); warhead 62-kg (137-lb) Mk 51 continuous-rod HE
Performance: maximum speed Mach 3.5; range 32 km (19.9 miles); ceiling 19810 m (65,000 ft)

RIM-66B (SM-1MR)
Type: shipborne medium-range area-defence SAM
Dimensions: length 4.724 m (15 ft 6 in); diameter 0.343 m (1 ft 1½ in); span 1.07 m (3 ft 6½ in)
Weights: total round 621 kg (1,370 lb); warhead Mk 90 blast-fragmentation HE
Performance: maximum speed Mach 3.5; range 46 km (28.6 miles); ceiling 24385 m (80,000 ft)

RIM-66C (SM-2MR)
Type: shipborne medium-range area-defence SAM
Dimensions: length 4.724 m (15 ft 6 in); diameter 0.343 m (1 ft 1½ in); span 1.07 m (3 ft 6½ in)

Weights: total round 626 kg (1,380 lb); warhead 113-kg (250-lb) Mk 115 blast-fragmentation HE
Performance: maximum speed Mach 3.5; range 74 km (46 miles); ceiling 24385+ m (80,000+ ft)

RIM-67A (SM-1ER)
Type: shipborne medium-range area-defence SAM
Dimensions: length 7.976 m (26 ft 2 in); diameter 0.343 m (1 ft 1½ in); booster span 0.457 m (1 ft 6 in)
Weights: total round 1343 kg (2,960 lb); warhead 62-kg (137-lb) Mk 51 continuous-rod HE
Performance: maximum speed Mach 2.5; range 65 km (40.4 miles); ceiling 24385 m (80,000 ft)

RIM-67B (SM-2ER)
Type: shipborne long-range area-defence SAM
Dimensions: length 7.976 m (26 ft 2 in); diameter 0.343 m (1 ft 1½ in); booster span 0.457 m (1 ft 6 in)
Weights: total round 1352 kg (2,980 lb); warhead 113-kg (250-lb) Mk 115 blast-fragmentation HE
Performance: maximum speed Mach 3.5; range 148 km (92 miles); ceiling 30480 m (100,000 ft)

Ikara Anti-submarine missile

The initial design of the all-weather **Ikara** missile was undertaken by the Australian government, but when the Royal Navy expressed an interest in the system the programme became a joint one with British Aerospace to produce the variant known as **GWS Mk 40**. A further version, the **Branik** was developed for the Brazilian navy. This last differed from both the Australian and Royal Navy systems in employing a special-purpose missile tracking and guidance unit (fully integrated into one of the launch platform's two fire-control computers) and also featured a new lightweight semi-automated missile handling system.

Solid-fuel rocket

The Ikara was powered by a solid-fuel combined booster and sustainer rocket, and in all forms was launched on a bearing to bring it to a torpedo payload-dropping position near to the target. Data for the latter's position was supplied either by the launch platform's own sonar or by a remote datalinked source such as another ship or helicopter. The information received was used for a continuous update of the optimum drop zone position on the ship's fire-control computer, which then passed it (in the form of control commands by the ship's radio/radar guidance system) to the missile in flight. Once the Ikara arrived at the target area the torpedo (a lightweight Mk 44 or Mk 46 homing torpedo, semi-enclosed in the missile body) was command-ejected via the communications link. The Ikara body then continued on, clearing the area and crashing, while the torpedo descended by parachute to achieve the best orientation and entry into the water and then began to start its search pattern.

The ship classes fitted with the Ikara variants were the 'Niteroi' ASW frigate version of the Brazilian navy (four units with one launcher and 10 missiles); the 'Perth'-class destroyers (three units

Ikara was a guided missile bearing a homing torpedo, the former flying to the approximate target area before releasing the homing torpedo to begin its search pattern.

each with two launchers and 24 missiles) and 'River'-class frigates (six units each with one launcher and 24 missiles) of the Royal Australian Navy; the sole Type 82 destroyer HMS *Bristol* (which was fitted with one launcher and 20 missiles) and the 'Leander Batch 1'-class frigate conversions (each with one launcher and 14 missiles) of the Royal Navy and the single 'Leander Batch 1'-class conversion HMNZS *Southland* (ex-*Dido*) of the Royal New Zealand

Navy. The Royal Navy put up for disposal another 'Leander Batch 1' unit, HMS *Ajax*, and ultimately removed the Ikara system from its inventory for operational reasons.

Modified version

In contrast the Australians teamed up with the Italians to produce a **Modified Ikara**

missile with folding fins, a box launcher and the guidance system of the Otomat SSM. The Modified Ikara could carry either of the two original torpedoes as its payload, or the Swedish Type 42 series, the Italian A244/S and AS290, and the British Stingray depending upon customer requirements.

Ikara is launched from the Brazilian navy's Mk 10 frigate Defensora. Brazilian Ikaras differ from the original system in employing a special-purpose missile-tracking and guiding unit, fully integrated into one of the two fire-control computers.

Left: Once Ikara was launched, its flight path was controlled from the ship's computer, which calculated the optimum position for the release of the torpedo, a Mk 44 or Mk 46 weapon.

SPECIFICATION	
Ikara	payload
Dimensions: length 3.42 m (11 ft 2½ in); wing span 1.52 m (4 ft 11 in); height 1.57 m (5 ft 2 in)	**Payload:** lightweight ASW homing torpedo (Mk 44 or Mk 46)
Weight: varies according to	**Performance:** maximum speed Mach 0.8; range 24 km (15 miles)

Malafon Anti-submarine missile

The Société Industrielle d'Aviation Latécoère **Malafon** surface-to-subsurface winged missile started development in 1956, and by 1959 a total of 21 test launches had been completed. The first sea launch and guidance test took place in 1962, with full systems evaluation of over 20 launches taking place in 1964. The final operational trials took place in 1965.

ASW weapon

The Malafon was primarily an ASW weapon, but could also be used to attack surface targets if required. Detection and designation for subsurface targets was provided by the ship's

Malafon is a shipborne homing acoustic torpedo delivered to the target area by a command-guided missile. Although primarily intended as an ASW weapon, it could be used to engage surface targets.

sonars, while for surface targets it was by radar. The Malafon was ramp-launched, propulsion for the initial seconds of its flight being provided by two jettisonable solid-fuel boosters. Once these had been discarded the flight was unpowered, the gliding missile being sta-

bilised by an automatic pilot and radio altimeter. Flight control was effected via a command radio link, the missile being tracked with the aid of flares attached to the wingtips. On reaching the drop-zone area, at a distance of some 800 m (875 yards) from the estimated target

position, a parachute was deployed to slow the Malafon. This caused the 533-mm (21-in) L4 acoustic-homing torpedo payload to be ejected into the water to complete the target attack.

Fittings of the Malafon system on French navy ships were made to the

'Tourville' class (three units), 'Suffren' class (two units), 'D'Estrée' class (four units), the *Aconit* and the *La Galissonnière*. In each case the fit comprised one launcher and 13 missiles in a magazine. The last weapons were retired from service in 1997.

Malafon was carried by 11 French vessels, in each case the fit consisting of a single launcher and 13 missiles. The DDG Duquesne carried its Malafon launcher forward of the four MM.40 Exocet launchers and immediately abaft the funnel and mast. The 'Suffren'-class ship lost Malafon capability in 1997.

SPECIFICATION	
Malafon **Dimensions:** length 6.15 m (20 ft 2½ in); wing span 3.3 m (10 ft 10 in); diameter 0.65 m (2 ft 1¾ ft) **Weight:** 1500 kg (3,307 lb)	**Warhead:** L4 acoustic-homing torpedo **Performance:** maximum speed low subsonic; range 13 km (8.1 miles)

Bofors ASW rockets 375-mm rocket-launcher systems

The initial four-tube **Bofors 375-mm** (14.76-in) ASW rocket-launcher system was developed in the early 1950s, and became operational on Swedish navy destroyers in 1955-56. The ship's sonar provides target data for calculating the launcher elevation and bearing for firing. Single or multi-round salvoes can be fired, the ballistic shape of the rockets ensuring a predictable and accurate underwater trajectory. Once empty the launcher is automatically reloaded in three minutes from the magazine located directly beneath it. Three types of rocket can be used, these differing in the types of motor and fuse in order to give different operational characteristics. The

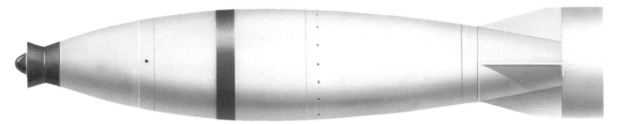

The missiles fired from the Bofors 375-mm ASW launcher system have three different types of motor, giving a variety of ranges. Missile trajectory is flat to produce as short a flight time as possible, thus reducing the chances of successful evasive action by the target submarine.

four-tube launcher is no longer in production, but was used extensively by the navies of Colombia, Japan, Portugal, Sweden, Peru, Turkey and West Germany. France used a six-tube variant built under licence by Creusot-Loire.

During 1969-72 a twin-tube variant, the **SR375**, was developed and was used by Brazil, Egypt, India, Indonesia, Malaysia, Morocco, Nigeria and Spain. The total number of rounds in the twin-tube launcher magazine is 24, while for the four-tube launcher it varies from 36 on most ships to a

maximum of 49 on the two Peruvian destroyer classes bought from the Dutch navy. The Swedish navy used its sole remaining four-tube system on the destroyer *Halland* during the early 1980s when it was involved in hunting suspected Soviet submarine intruders.

Above: *The SR375 twin launcher can fire its missiles either separately or simultaneously, and the ballistic characteristics of the missile ensure the maintenance of an accurate trajectory once underwater.*

Left: *The magazine of the four-tube launcher is located directly underneath, and once available rounds have been expended the launcher is replenished from below.*

SPECIFICATION	
four-tube launcher **Calibre:** 375 mm (14.76 in) **Weight:** 7417 kg (16,352 lb) **Elevation:** +15° to +90°	**two-tube launcher** **Calibre:** 375 mm (14.76 in) **Weight:** 3861 kg (8,512 lb) **Elevation:** 0° to +60°

ROCKET TYPES				
	Weight	**Length**	**HE charge**	**Range**
M/50	250 kg	2/2.05 m	100 kg	355-850 m
	(551 lb)	(6.56/6.73 ft)	(220 lb)	(1,165-2,790 ft)
Erika	250 kg	2/2.05 m	107 kg	655-1635 m
	(551 lb)	(6.56/6.73 ft)	(236 lb)	(2,150-5,365 ft)
Nelli	250 kg	2/2.05 m	80 kg	1580-3625 m
	(551 lb)	(6.56/6.73 ft)	(176 lb)	(5,185-11,895 ft)

Notes:
1. The NV50 and Erika can use the Stidar time and impact fuse.
2. All three can use the Zambo proximity and impact fuse with an influence radius of 15 m (49 ft). Length variation depends on fuse type.

RBU Anti-submarine rocket-launchers

Over the years the USSR developed a number of multi-barrel rocket-launchers under the designation **Raketnaya Bombometnaya Ustaovka (RBU)**, working on the forward-firing 'hedgehog' principle. The rockets are immune to torpedo counter-measures, and under certain circumstances can be used as anti-torpedo weapons if there is enough warning. The rockets are fitted with either contact or magnetic influence fuses. The most widely used version was the fully automatic 250-mm (9.84-in) **RBU-6000**, which entered service in 1960. The 12-barrel launcher is arranged in a horseshoe shape with an automatic fuse-setting system, and the RGB-60 rockets are fired in a paired sequence. The projectile weighs 70 kg (154 lb) overall, and loading is accomplished barrel by barrel with the launcher in the vertical position.

The RBU-6000 was usually fitted in conjunction with the fully automatic six-barrel 300-mm (11.81-in) **RBU-1000** introduced in 1962 but firing a larger rocket with a 55-kg (121-lb) warhead.

Earlier systems of the RBU series included the 1957-vintage automatic 312-mm (12.3-in) 16-barrel **RBU-2500** with manual reloading; the 1958-vintage five-barrel 250-mm **RBU-1200** with manual reloading, automatic elevation but manual training; and the 1962-vintage six-barrel 300-mm **RBU-600** with man-ual reloading. Most systems have three to five complete sets of reload rounds in the ship's magazines, while the rocket types are common to each calibre except that the RBU-1200 fires an earlier type of rocket with a 34-kg (75-lb) HE warhead.

Practically all the Warsaw Pact navies used one or more RBU systems, and Soviet client states also used them widely. The People's Republic of China has taken some of the earlier designs and produced its own variants.

SPECIFICATIONS	
RBU-6000 **Calibre:** 252 mm (9.92 in) **Range:** 6 km (3.73 miles) **Barrel length:** 1.6 m (5 ft 3 in) **Weights:** rocket 70 kg (154 lb); warhead 21 kg (46.3 lb)	**Range:** 1 km (0.62 miles) **Barrel length:** 1.5 m (5 ft) **Weights:** rocket 120 kg (265 lb); warhead 55 kg (121 lb)
RBU-2500 **Calibre:** 312 mm (12.28 in) **Range:** 2.7 km (1.68 miles) **Barrel length:** 1.6 m (5 ft 3 in) **Weights:** rocket 85 kg (187 lb); warhead 26 kg (57 lb)	**RBU-600** **Calibre:** 300 mm (11.81 in) **Range:** 0.6 km (0.37 miles) **Barrel length:** 1.5 m (5 ft) **Weights:** rocket 120 kg (265 lb); warhead 55 kg (121 lb)
RBU-1200 **Calibre:** 252 mm (9.92 in) **Range:** 1.45 km (0.9 miles) **Barrel length:** 1.4 m (4 ft 7 in) **Weights:** rocket 71.5 kg (158 lb); warhead 32 kg (71 lb)	**Miscellaneous data** The RGB-25 rocket fired by the RBU-2500 system is 1.34 m (4 ft 4¾ in) long and has a minimum range of 550 m (605 yards), and the flight time is between 3 and 25 seconds. The rocket sinks at 11 m (36 ft) per second, and the lethal radius is 5 m (16 ft 5 in) after detonation at a depth of between 10 and 320 m (33 and 1,050 ft).
RBU-1000 **Calibre:** 300 mm (11.81 in)	

Above: 'Krivak'-class frigates have considerable anti-submarine potential. Among the weapons carried are two of the ubiquitous 12-barrel RBU-6000 ASW rocket launchers, mounted abreast of each other forward of the main bridge structure.

Right: A 'Petya II'-class light frigate, on station in one of the Soviet navy's frequent forays into the waters around the Philippines, displays its twin 12-barrel RBU-6000 rocket launchers, as well as the desire of Soviet sailors to get in as much sunbathing as possible.

SS-N-14 'Silex' Anti-submarine missile

The **RPK-3 Metel** system, generally known in the West as the **SS-N-14 'Silex'**, is an anti-submarine weapon system that the Soviets carefully convinced the West was an SSM system when its empty launchers were first deployed at sea in 1968. The system uses a missile (several variants) based on the P-120 (SS-N-9 'Siren') anti-ship missile, and initially appeared in two basic forms fired from the KT-100 launcher with Musson command system in the 'Krivak I'-class frigates, and from the KT-106 launcher with the Grom-M command system (also controlling the SA-N-3 SAM system) in the 'Kresta II'- and 'Kara'-class cruisers.

The SS-N-14, seen on a 'Udaloy'-class destroyer, is based on a launcher carrying four missiles each with a solid-propellant rocket motor and payload of one depth bomb or torpedo.

In overall terms, the SS-N-14 is a command-guided and rocket-powered winged missile launched to a point above the target's estimated position, where it releases a parachute-lowered payload (initially a 5-kT nuclear depth bomb or a 457-mm/18-in but later a short 533-mm/21-in homing torpedo). The dual-purpose **URPK-3** missile also carries a warhead in its body so that it can be used as an anti-ship weapon. Against targets in direct-path range, detected and tracked by hull sonars, the missile is commanded to drop its torpedo immediately above the submarine position, but against a more distant target a helicopter is used to key the payload drop command.

Modified versions are the **URPK-5 Rastrub-A** (85RU missile with KT-100U launcher in 'Krivak II'-class frigates from 1980) and **URPK-4 Rastrub-B** (85RU missile with KT-106U launcher and probably the Drakon command system in 'Udaloy'-class destroyers from 1985).

Above: A close-up of the bridge and starboard quadruple missile launcher of the large anti-submarine destroyer Udaloy also shows one of the 'Eye Bowl' fire-control radars associated with the SS-N-14 system (visible atop the bridge immediately above the massive missile containers).

Left: The plethora of weapon and sensor systems common to all Soviet warships is dominated on this 'Krivak'-class frigate (seen in the English Channel) by the massive quadruple bow launcher for four SS-N-14 missiles. This weapon system is conceptually similar to the French Malafon and Australian Ikara systems.

SPECIFICATION	
SS-N-14 'Silex' (85R missile)	**Performance:** speed Mach 0.95;
Dimensions: length 7.2 m (23 ft 7½ in); diameter 0.57 m (1 ft 10½ in); height 1.35 m (4 ft 5 in)	cruising altitude 1,315 ft (400 m); range 50 km (31 miles)
Weight: 4000 kg (8,818 lb)	**Payload:** one 5-kT nuclear depth bomb or 533-mm (21-in) torpedo

SS-N-15/16 'Starfish' & 'Stallion' Anti-submarine missiles

Designed by Novator and accepted for service in 1969, the **RPK-2 Viyoga** system (using the 82R missile fired from 533-mm/21-in torpedo tubes) is an anti-submarine system known in the West as the **SS-N-15 'Starfish'** and launched mainly from submarines. This weapon is in essence a Soviet copy of the US SUBROC, originally armed with a 10/20-kT nuclear depth bomb but later with an alternative in the form of the UMGT or now the APR-2E torpedo. A surface version is fired from 533-mm tubes on the two 'Kirov'-class battle-cruisers and one 'Udaloy II'-class destroyer: after launch, the weapon plunges into the sea, stabilises itself and only then ignites its rocket motor. In its submarine-launched form the weapon can be launched at depths down to 50 m (165 ft), and its minimum range is 10 km (6.2 miles).

A 650-mm (25.6-in) successor to the RPK-2 is deployed in two versions both known in the West as the SS-N-16 'Stallion'. Entering service in 1979, the RPK-6 Vodopod with the 83R missile uses a torpedo warhead, while the RPK-7 Vodopei with the 84R missile presumably uses a nuclear depth bomb warhead. Improved versions are the URPK-6 Vodopod-MK and Vodopei-MK, using the 83RN and 84RN missiles. The associated surface ship systems are Veder (torpedo-armed 86R missile) and the Vspletsk (86R missile probably with a nuclear depth bomb). The RPK-6 may have been the first Soviet 650-mm weapon, and thus responsible for the shift from 533-mm to 650-mm torpedo tubes. The greater size effectively doubles the range possible with the SS-N-15, to some 100-120 km (62.1-74.6 miles). Currently the only warhead is a short 533-mm torpedo, and the only known surface ship application is the frigate *Neustrashimy*.

Above: The 'Alpha' class, the fastest (and probably the most expensive) boats in the world, were known to have been fitted with the SS-N-15 'Starfish' missile.

Left: Believed to have been inspired by the American SUBROC, the SS-N-15 is fitted to Soviet nuclear attack boats and possibly to diesel-powered submarines such as the 'Tango'-class unit seen here.

SPECIFICATION	
SS-N-15 'Starfish'	**SS-N-16 'Stallion'**
Dimensions: length 6.5 m (21 ft 4 in); diameter 533 mm (21 in)	**Dimensions:** length 6.5 m (21 ft 4 in); diameter 650 m (25½ in)
Weight: 1900 kg (4,189 lb)	**Weight:** 2150 kg (4,740 lb)
Performance: speed Mach 1.5; range 45.7 km (28.4 miles)	**Performance:** speed Mach 1.5; range 120 km (74.6 miles)
Payload: 15-kT nuclear depth bomb or 533-mm (21-in) torpedo	**Payload:** 200-kT nuclear depth bomb or 533-mm (21-in) torpedo

SGE-30 Goalkeeper 30-mm close-in weapon system

The **SGE-30 Goalkeeper** naval air-defence system is an autonomous radar-directed short-range weapon designed for fully automatic defence against high-speed missiles and aircraft. Based on the GAU-8/A cannon with an assembly of seven barrels rotating at 4,200 rpm, the weapon was created as a joint venture by the Dutch company Hollandse Signaalapparaten and the US company General Electric (now Thales Nederland and General Dynamics). The Goalkeeper has all its elements on a single mounting.

The Goalkeeper consists of a coherent pulse-Doppler radar which operates in the I-band for track-while-scan target search and acquisition. This is based on an antenna that turns at 60 rpm, and can detect targets at ranges up to 29 km (18 miles). The radar can track 30 targets and assign four targets for engagement.

Once the target has been identified, an Identification Friend or Foe transponder determines whether the target is friendly. If it is an enemy, the target is handed over to the monopulse-Doppler dual-frequency I/K-band tracking and engagement radar, which determines the target's exact altitude and tracks the target as it approaches the ship.

Sea Vulcan

The GAU-8/A Sea Vulcan 30-mm cannon operates on the 'Gatling' principle. The operation of the system is completely automatic, from target detection, through target destruction and termination of the engage-

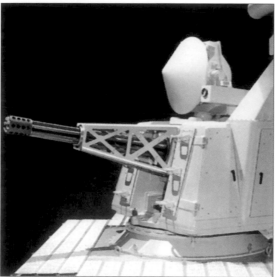

ment, and on to detection of the next target.

Missiles as low as 5 m (16.4 ft) have been shot down, and the system can also be used against diving targets. The Dutch version of the search radar can detect targets which are approaching at up to 30° in elevation. When operating in automatic mode, the system is limited to engaging targets at ranges of between 2 and 7 km (1.2 and 4.3 miles) approaching at speeds over 540 km/h (336 mph).

For multiple attacks the radar has an automatic kill-assessment subsystem to assign target priorities. The MPDS discarding-sabot round has a penetrator of high-density tungsten alloy rather than depleted uranium, and 'softer' targets are tackled with an HEI round: these rounds have muzzle

velocities of 1190 and 1010 m (3,900 and 3,318 ft) per second respectively, and 1,190 rounds are carried in a linkless feed/drum storage system. To replenish this storage/feed arrangement a bulk loading system is employed. The mounting can be traversed through 360° at 100° per second, and the cannon can be elevated between -25° and +85° at 80° per second.

The Goalkeeper entered service in 1980 and is used by the British, Dutch, South Korean and other navies.

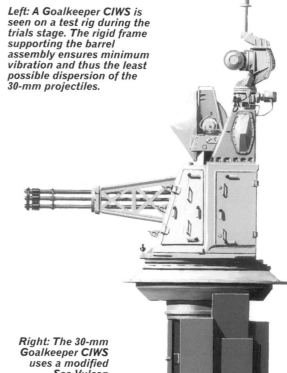

Left: A Goalkeeper CIWS is seen on a test rig during the trials stage. The rigid frame supporting the barrel assembly ensures minimum vibration and thus the least possible dispersion of the 30-mm projectiles.

Right: The 30-mm Goalkeeper CIWS uses a modified Sea Vulcan version of the seven-barrel GAU-8/A Avenger aircraft 'Gatling' gun, with search and tracking/fire-control radars integrated onto the mounting.

The SGE-30 Goalkeeper can engage multiple targets, the system having demonstrated kills of simulated supersonic anti-ship cruise missiles at ranges of 500 and 400 m (1,640 and 1,315 ft) respectively within about one second of switching target.

SPECIFICATION	
SGE-30 Goalkeeper	(2,185 yards)
Calibre: 30 mm (1.18 in)	**Rate of fire:** 4,200 rounds per minute
Number of barrels: seven	
Elevation: -25° to +85°	**Weight:** 9881 kg (21,784 lb) with ammunition
Muzzle velocity: 1010 or 1190 m (3,318 or 3,900 ft) per second	**Number of rounds carried on mounting:** 1,190
Effective range: 2000 m	

Meroka 20-mm close-in weapon system

Developed by CETME and Bazán (the latter now part of the Izar group), the **Meroka** CIWS consists of a turret with two rows each of six 20-mm Oerlikon KAA cannon, a PDS-10 control console which incorporates a digital fire-control computer, a RAN-12/L search and target-designation radar, and an on-mount PVS-2 Sharpshooter monopulse

Doppler tracking radar with low-light thermal-imaging TV camera. The barrels have a combined rate of fire of 9,000 rounds per minute, but only 720 rounds are carried on the mount itself. An additional 240 rounds apiece are carried in each of three external boxes. The normal mode of action is by radar control, but the camera can be used for manual standby

The Spanish light carrier Príncipe de Asturias has four Meroka CIWS mountings, two located forward on flares below the edges of the flight deck, and two aft above the stern.

operations via a monitor unit and controls on the below-deck console. The **Meroka Mod 2B** has a more advanced fire-control processor and an Indra (formerly ENOSA) thermal imager.

Twenty systems were ordered by Spain in place of more expensive foreign

CIWS. The initial allocation for the Meroka system was four weapons systems on Spain's flagship carrier *Príncipe de Asturias*, one system for each of the six 'Santa María'-class frigates and two systems each for the five 'Baleares'-class frigates. Spain's 'Galicia'-

class LPDs and 'Alvaro de Bazán'-class FFGs are each protected by one system. The Spanish navy claims an 87 per cent probability of destroying a missile with a 12-round burst of 0.102-kg (0.225-lb) APDS projectiles.

SPECIFICATION	
Meroka	(2,185 yards)
Calibre: 20 mm (0.78 in)	**Rate of fire:** 9,000 rounds per
Number of barrels: 12	minute
Elevation: -15° to +85°	**Weight:** 4079 kg (8,993 lb)
Muzzle velocity: 1290 m (4,232 ft)	**Number of rounds carried on**
per second with APDS	**mount:** 720 (see text)
Effective range: 2000 m	

Bofors 40L60 and 40L70 40-mm automatic guns

The original 40-mm Bofors L/60 gun was one of the principal air-defence weapons of the US Navy in the Pacific actions of 1941-45. It served well into the 1970s and was last mounted on such vessels as the attack transport USS Sandoval, which is seen shadowed by a Soviet navy minesweeper of the T-143 class.

The original **Bofors 40L60** automatic anti-aircraft gun, so called for its 40-mm calibre and L/60 barrel, was introduced to service in 1936 and is still in service with a number of navies. Such is the durability and capability of the design that this anti-aircraft gun has held enduring appeal for navies across the world. Despite the fact that this 40L60 weapon has been out of production for some years, it could until recent times be found, in reconditioned form, on modest numbers of new-build warships.

Production is now concentrated on the **Bofors 40L70** development introduced in 1948 and offering improved performance through the incorporation of a number of improvements including a longer L/70 barrel. Three basic types of single-barrel mountings for the 40L70 are offered, these differing in the amount of automation provided. Gun control can be either local or remote, the latter using either a below-deck fire-control system or an above-deck optical director.

Proximity fuse

To increase the lethality of the older 40L60, two new types of ammunition have been developed by the parent company as the PFHE (pre-fragmented HE) with a proximity fuse, and the APHC-T (armour-piercing high-capacity with tracer). The 40L70 has its own family of ammunition which includes PFHE, HCHE, HE-T (HE with tracer) and practice types. The pulse-Doppler

radar proximity fuses fitted to the two PFHE round types allows missile targets to be engaged, the 40L60 version having a detonation distance of between 4.5 and 6.5 m (14.76 and 21.33 ft), and the 40L70 round detonating at a distance of between 1 and 7 m (3.28 and 22.97 ft) depending on target size and type.

Otobreda development

The 40L70 is also used in the Breda (now Otobreda) 40-mm one- and two-gun mounts from Italy. These are used by more than 20 navies, including Italy's 'Garibaldi'-class ASW aircraft carrier, 'Vittorio Veneto'-class helicopter cruiser, and 'Lupo'-, 'Artigliere'- and 'Maestrale'-class frigates.

Above: The Otobreda/Bofors 40L70 naval mount with an Otobreda 144-round automatic feed device allows the number of personnel required on-mount to be reduced to two. A third is on standby to reload the feed mechanism during lulls in firing.

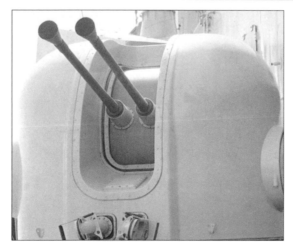

Among the most popular of Bofors-gun mounts are those provided by Otobreda, the 40L70 being used in both single- and twin-gun forms. The so-called Compact twin turret is currently in service or on order for more than 20 navies worldwide.

SPECIFICATIONS	
Bofors 40L60	**Bofors 40L70**
Calibre: 40 mm (1.57 in)	**Calibre:** 40 mm (1.57 in)
Number of barrels: one	**Number of barrels:** one
Elevation: -10° to +80°	**Elevation:** -10° to +90°
Muzzle velocity: 830 m (2,723 ft) per second	**Muzzle velocity:** 1005-1030 m (3,297-3,379 ft) per second
Effective range: 3000 m (3,280 yards)	**Effective range:** 4000 m (4,375 yards)
Rate of fire: 120 rounds per minute	**Rate of fire:** 300 rounds per minute
Weight: varies, but typically between 1200 and 2500 kg (2,646 and 5,511 lb)	**Weight:** (without ammunition) SAK 40L70-350 2890 kg (6,371 lb), SAK 40L70-315 1700 kg (3,748 lb) and SAK 40L70-520 3790 kg (8,355 lb)
Number of rounds carried on mount: varies according to mount type	**Number of rounds carried on mount:** SAK 40L70-350 96, SAK 40L70-315 96 and SAK 40L70-520 144

Naval Gun Types GAM-BO1 and GBM-AO1 20-/25-mm AA guns

The single-barrel 20-mm **GAM-BO1** is a simple unpowered locally-operated mount that uses the Oerlikon-Bührle KAA automatic cannon. It is capable of engaging surface targets out to 2000 m (2,185 yards) and aircraft-sized targets out to 1500 m (1,640 yards). A night sight can be fitted if required. Several navies adopted this weapon, including the Spanish navy's 'Lazaga'- and 'Barceló'-class fast attack missile craft. The Royal Navy's 'Invincible'-class carriers, 'County'-, Type 42 and Type 82 destroyers, and Type 22 Batch 1/2 frigates were each fitted with two, and non-converted 'Leander' Batch 3 frigates carried one apiece. The adoption of the gun by the Royal Navy was as a result of its experiences during the Falklands War.

For increased firepower there is the larger-calibre 25-mm **GBM-AO1**, which is similar in characteristics to the GAM-BO1 system but mounts the 25-mm KBA-C02 cannon with a double belt feed. The engagement

Although a relatively simple weapon, the 20-mm Oerlikon Type GAM-BO1 was chosen by a number of navies for its light weight and robustness. The Royal Navy adopted it in conjunction with twin 30-mm mounts to boost close-range AA defences after the Falklands War.

Above: Similar to the 20-mm weapon, the 25-mm GBM-AO1 fires a heavier shell. Its low weight makes it simple to install aboard vessels down to the smallest FAC, and no electrical power is required for operation.

ranges are the same as those of the 20-mm cannon but the shell is heavier. Several unidentified navies have adopted this weapon.

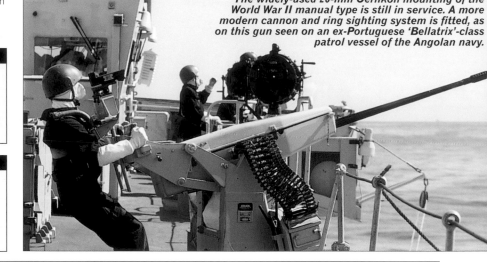

The widely-used 20-mm Oerlikon mounting of the World War II manual type is still in service. A more modern cannon and ring sighting system is fitted, as on this gun seen on an ex-Portuguese 'Bellatrix'-class patrol vessel of the Angolan navy.

SPECIFICATION	
GAM-BO1	
Calibre: 20 mm (0.787 in)	**Effective range:** see text
Number of barrels: one	**Rate of fire:** 600 rpm
Elevation: -15° to +60°	**Weight:** (with ammunition) 500 kg
Muzzle velocity: 1050 m (3,444 ft) per second	(1,102 lb)
	Number of rounds on mount: 200

SPECIFICATION	
GBM-AO1	
Calibre: 25 mm (0.984 in)	**Effective range:** see text
Number of barrels: one	**Rate of fire:** 570 rpm
Elevation: -15° to +50°	**Weight:** (with ammunition) 600 kg
Muzzle velocity: 1100 m (3,609 ft) per second	(1,323 lb)
	Number of rounds on mount: 200

Type GCM-A 30-mm twin AA gun

The Oerlikon-Bührle 30-mm **Type GCM-A** has been produced in three different versions: the **GCM-AO3-1** with an enclosed gunner's position, stabilised control and optional remote control from a fire-control system; the **GCM-AO3-2** which is essentially the same as the GCM-AO3-1 but with an open gunner's position; and the **GCM-AO3-3** without a gunner's position and thus fitted only for remote control. The 30-mm KCB cannon used in the GCM-AO3 is also used in the American twin 30-mm EMERLEC-30 and the British Laurence Scott (Defence Systems) single-barrel LS30B systems.

As a direct result of the lack of close-range air-defence guns during the Falklands War, and to aug-

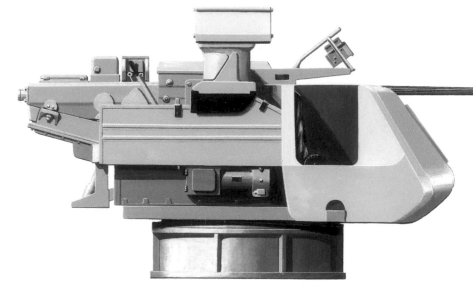

After its experience during the Falklands War, the Royal Navy bought a number of twin 30-mm GCM-A mounts fitted with Ferranti gyroscopic lead-angle computing sights from BMARC Ltd to supplement its existing close-range anti-aircraft armament.

Left: As is common for this type of weapon, the GCM-A has been designed for fitment to small surface vessels. The A03-2, with an open gunner's station, weighs only 2515 kg (5,545 lb) complete, and can be operated both locally and with remote control.

Right: A twin 30-mm Oerlikon mounting is seen with the barrels at full elevation on a Royal Navy Type 42 destroyer. Some of the GCM-A mountings fitted to this class of warship were subsequently replaced by six-barrel 20-mm Phalanx CIWS installations.

ment secondary armament, the Royal Navy purchased a number of licence-built GCM-AO3-2 mounts from the British company BMARC. These were fitted to the sole Type 82 destroyer (HMS *Bristol*), and the 12 Type 42 destroyers remaining after HMS *Sheffield* and *Coventry* had been sunk in the conflict in the South Atlantic. Unfortunately in the case of the Type 42s the ships' boats had to be removed in order to incorporate the two mountings required and prevent top-heaviness.

The muzzle velocity of the 30-mm Type GCM-A is similar to that of the 20-mm Oerlikon weapon that was also selected by the Royal Navy, but the shell of the 30-mm weapon is consider-

ably more powerful, having around three times the muzzle energy and thus offering a greatly increased effective range against aerial threats.

SPECIFICATION	
Type GCM-A	**Rate of fire:** 1,300 rpm
Calibre: 30 mm (1.181 in)	**Weight:** (with ammunition) A03-1
Number of barrels: two	2910 kg (6,415 lb), A03-2 2515 kg
Elevation: -10° to +75°	(5,545 lb) and A03-3 2560 kg
Muzzle velocity: 1080 m (3,543 ft)	(5,644 lb)
per second	**Number of rounds on mount:**
Effective range: 3000 m	A03-1/2 500, and A03-3 640
(3,280 yards)	

Type GDM-A 35-mm twin AA gun

Similar in concept and design to the highly successful Oerlikon twin 35-mm Type GDF land-based anti-aircraft guns, the naval 35-mm **Type GDM-A** is intended primarily for use against air attacks, but if required can also be used to engage surface targets at sea and on land. The stabilised mount is an all-weather system with its electronic control units located below decks. The cannon fitted are of the KDC model, which are fully automatic in operation. The turret has three possible modes of use: fully automatic with control exercised from either a below-decks fire-control

system or an upper-deck optical aiming unit fitted with an auxiliary computer; local operator control with the gunner using a joystick and gyro-stabilised gunsight; and emergency manual control using two hand wheels and the gunsight when power to the mount is cut. Each of the cannons has 56 ready-use rounds of ammunition, with another 224 rounds in total reserve. At least five countries have acquired this turret for their warships, namely Ecuador, Greece, Iran, Libya and Turkey. An Italian version of the 35-mm naval mounting is designated **GDM-C** by Oerlikon.

Above: The original Oerlikon guns were largely used as naval weapons, but the 35-mm KDC cannon used in the GDM-A is derived from a towed weapon developed in the late 1950s. The Italian model, known to Oerlikon as the GDM-C, uses the slightly heavier KDA variant.

Left: Produced as a private venture by OTO-Melara, the twin 35-mm OE/OTO mount uses the Oerlikon KDA 35-mm gun, which is similar to the KDC gun employed in the Swiss company's Type GDM-A system. The Libyan navy bought the OTO-Melara mount for its 'Assad' class of missile corvette.

SPECIFICATION	
Type GDM-A	**Effective range:** 3500 m
Calibre: 35 mm (1.378 in)	(3,830 yards)
Number of barrels: two	**Rate of fire:** 1,100 rpm
Elevation: -15° to +85°	**Weight:** (with ammunition) 6520 kg
Muzzle velocity: 1175 m (3,855 ft)	(14,374 lb)
per second	**Number of rounds on mount:** 336

AK-230, AK-630/M and AK-306 30-mm anti-aircraft guns

The first Soviet 30-mm mount was the **AK-230** L/60 system which entered service in 1960 to replace the elderly 25-mm L/60 twin anti-aircraft gun on new-build major and minor warship classes. The small enclosed turret is usually known by the nickname 'Dalek' because of its physical appearance. The two 30-mm cannon are fully automatic in operation, and the barrels are water-cooled. The theoretical maximum rate of fire for the guns is 1,050 rounds per minute, but the maximum realistic rate to prevent damage is actually in the region of 200-240 rounds per minute. The guns are usually used in conjunction with a 'Drum Tilt' fire-control radar or a remote optical director. On smaller ships the AK-230 also possesses a surface-to-surface role, the maximum effective range being 2600 m (2,845 yards) with a projectile weighing 0.54 kg (1.2 lb). The system has been widely exported to Soviet-supplied states as the gun forms the main armament of the 'Osa'-class missile craft.

To counter the threat of missile attack the Soviets developed the 30-mm weapon further to produce an AO-18 'Gatling' gun version with six 30-mm barrels inside a larger barrel-like cylinder in a similar shaped mount known by the designation **AK-630**. Design of the gun started in 1963, the first prototype was built in 1964 and weapons trials were conducted until 1966. By 1967, the weapon had been accepted for service and two years later production began. The AK-630 is designed to fire at a fast rate as large a number of the 0.54-kg shells as possible, with high-density metal penetrators to destroy cruise missile-sized targets at relatively close range.

Usually mounted in pairs with a 'Bass Tilt' fire-control radar, the AK-630 mount has appeared on the 'Kiev', 'Kynda', 'Udaloy', 'Sovremenny', 'Slava' and 'Kresta II' classes, and has been retrofitted to several older ships. On smaller warships it is usually found as a single mount together with a larger-calibre gun and a fire-control radar. The weapons are belt-fed from a flat magazine in the case of the AK-630, and fed from a drum magazine in the case of the **AK-630M**, a modified version of the original weapon.

AK-630M

The AK-630 and AK-630M weapons are slaved to a fully integrated self-defence system. The collective name of this weapon is the **A-213 Vympel-A**. This system includes the AO-18 six-barrelled gun, a fire-control radar, and optical and TV fire-control systems. A single Vympel system is capable of controlling two 30-mm gun mounts, or a single 30-mm system and one 50-mm weapon.

The gun can hit aerial targets at a range up to 4000 m (4,375 yards), and surface targets up to 5000 m (5,470 yards). The TV sighting system is able to target vessels of torpedo craft size and upwards at ranges of up to 7.5 km (4.6 miles), while aerial targets can be detected at ranges of 7000 m (7,655 yards).

AK-306

In 1983 a decision was taken to modify the AK-630 to the **AK-630M1-2** status. This would have seen the addition of an extra six-barrel mounting, although the idea was later abandoned.

A smaller version of the AK-630 system, dubbed the **AK-306**, was designed for use on lighter vessels such as hovercraft, ekranoplans and fast attack craft. The only differences between the AK-630 and the AK-306 (or **A-219**) are that the latter's automatic firing system is powered electrically rather than by exhaust gases as on the earlier gun, and that the system is designed for use only with an optical fire-control system without any option for radar. This has resulted in a gun less suited for the engagement of aerial targets, and thus of greater utility against surface targets. The AK-306's design began in 1974, and by 1980 the system had been accepted into service.

Right: The Soviet distribution of CIWS mountings was liberal, with vessels such as the nuclear-powered 'Kirov' class equipped with up to eight 30-mm Gatling types, of which the four stern turrets are shown here. The Soviets also developed a high-density penetrator round for the system.

Below: The 30-mm turret for twin automatic cannon was standard fit aboard Soviet light force units, and is shown on the bow of a Soviet navy 'Osa I'-class missile boat. The turret was also exported widely to Soviet allies, satellites and client states.

SPECIFICATIONS	
AK-230	**AK-630**
Calibre: 30 mm	**Calibre:** 30 mm
Number of barrels: two	**Number of barrels:** six
Elevation: 0° to + 85°	**Elevation:** 0° to + 85°
Muzzle velocity: 1000 m (3,281 ft) per second	**Muzzle velocity:** 1000 m (3,281 ft) per second
Effective range: 2500 m (2,735 yards)	**Effective range:** 3000 m (3,280 yards)
Rate of fire: 1,050 rounds per minute	**Rate of fire:** 3,000 rounds per minute

AK-725 57-mm anti-aircraft gun

The oldest of the Soviet navy's 57-mm anti-aircraft guns was the **ZIF-71** single-barrel L/70 mounting which was found on some 'Skory (Mod)' destroyers. This version was followed in the late 1960s by **ZIF-31** and **ZIF-74** twin-barrel versions that were initially associated with a number of the smaller warship classes such as the 'T-58'-class patrol vessels and radar pickets. The final version of the weapon to appear was the **ZIF-75** quadruple mount with the barrels arranged in two superimposed pairs. All three systems can be controlled locally, the twin and quad guns using either 'Hawk Screech' or 'Muff Cob' fire-control radars to obtain target data for below-decks electronics. The gun fires a 2.8-kg (6.2-lb) shell that, in later years, was

Above: The twin 57-mm turret mounted aft on the Soviet 'Grisha III'-class corvette was introduced in the 1960s. Water-cooled, it is a fully automatic system.

Right: 'Kanin'-class units of the Soviet navy had two 57-mm quadruple mountings located forward, and the mountings' guns were supplied with proximity-fused ammunition.

revised with a proximity fuse to increase its lethality against missile targets. The weapons can also be fired in the anti-surface target role, in which the maximum effective range is 8000 m (8,750 yards).

In the early 1960s a new **AK-725** (**ZIF-72**) twin 57-mm L/80 water-cooled DP mount was introduced. This is fully automatic in operation from the below-decks ammunition handling room to the gun mount itself. The fire-control radars used are the 'Muff Cob' or 'Bass Tilt' systems, while the ammunition is of

the same type as that used by the L/70 gun.

However, the weapon's performance was considered to be ineffective against the type of sea-skimming missiles becoming ever more prevalent. In 1987, during a Soviet naval exercise, an inert missile was fired which locked onto the *Musson*, a 'Nanuchka'-class small missile ship. The vessel's AK-725 mount was firing directly up to the point of impact but it was unable to hit the missile, which impacted the ship, killing 39 crew.

SPECIFICATIONS

AK-725	ZIF-75
Calibre: 57 mm (2.24 in)	**Calibre:** 57 mm (2.24 in)
Mounting weight: 14.5 tonnes	**Mounting weight:** 17 tonnes
Number of barrels: two	**Number of barrels:** four
Elevation: -10° to +85°	**Elevation:** -10° to +85°
Muzzle velocity: 1020 m (3,346 ft) per second	**Muzzle velocity:** 1020 m (3,346 ft) per second
Maximum range: 8450 m (9,240 yards)	**Effective range:** 6000 m (6,560 yards)
Rate of fire: 200 rounds per minute	**Rate of fire:** 100 rounds per minute

Seaguard 25-mm close-in weapon system

The **Seaguard** 25-mm naval air-defence complex is a close-in weapon system project between Switzerland, Italy and the UK. It consists of above-decks search and tracker modules, a GBM-B1Z Sea Zenith mount with four 25-mm KBB-RO3/LO4 cannon, and a below-decks ammunition feed and operator's console with the associated electronics. The search module has a G-band

radar, and the tracking module a J-band radar, a FLIR sensor and a laser range-finder.

Cannon-feed

Each of the cannon is independently fed from the below-decks ready-use supply, where sufficient rounds are available to engage 18-20 different targets without reloading. Typical engagement ranges are from

1500 m (1,640 yards) down to 100 m (110 yards) against missiles and out to a maximum of 3500 m (3,830 yards) against aircraft.

Ammunition types fired include an HE incendiary round and an AMDS (Anti-Missile Discarding-Sabot) round. If required, the mount can be elevated to +127° to cover steep-diving targets. The Seaguard system is used by Turkey on its eight 'Barbaros'- and 'Yavuz'-class frigates.

Right: The obvious difference between Seaguard and most other close-in weapon systems is the provision of four barrels independently fed with ammunition, instead of a single rotary cannon. This allows for redundancy in the feed system.

Left: The first navy to adopt the Seaguard 25-mm CIWS was that of Turkey, which has the weapons fitted to its 'Barbaros/Modified Meko 200'- and 'Yavuz/Meko 200'-class guided missile frigates. Ammunition is provided for the engagement of 14 targets without reloading.

SPECIFICATION

Seaguard	
Calibre: 25 mm	**Effective range:** 100-3500 m (110-3,830 yards)
Mounting weight: 7.09 tonnes	**Rate of fire:** 3,400 rounds per minute
Number of barrels: four	
Elevation: -14° to +127°	**Number of rounds carried on mount:** 1,660
Muzzle velocity: 1355 m (4,446 ft) per second	

LS30R and DS30B 30-mm naval gun mounting

In the early 1980s a British company, Laurence Scott (Defence Systems), developed a lightweight naval mounting for the 30-mm Rarden gas-operated cannon designed by the Royal Armament Research and Development Establishment and initially used as the primary armament of a number of British light armoured fighting vehicles. This **LS30R** mounting was power-operated and line-of-sight stabilised, and intended as the primary gun armament of small naval vessels and also as the secondary gun armament of larger vessels such as frigates and even destroyers, with emphasis on the provision of close-in protection against agile surface vessels such as fast attack craft for example.

An extensive series of tests was carried out by the Royal Navy both at sea on board the converted trials frigate HMS *Londonderry*, and on land at the Fraser Gunnery Range at Portsmouth. These trials confirmed the high accuracy of the weapon, which hit a 2-m² (21.5-sq ft) target some 80 per cent of the firing time at ranges between 1000 and 1300 m (1,095 and 1,420 yards) in conditions from good to poor visibility.

If required the mount could be fitted with a predictor, image intensifier, IR camera and/or low-light TV camera for remote firing. The ammunition types fired by the Rarden cannon include HE, APSE and also APDS rounds.

The LS30R was adopted for use on Royal Navy warships as a replacement for older weapons, such as the 20-mm Oerlikon and 40-mm Bofors weapons deemed to lack sufficient capability for continued viability in the conditions prevalent from the mid-1980s.

It was planned that the LS30B would be introduced from 1986, initially on offshore patrol vessels. Early experience confirmed suspicions that had already been voiced, however, about the real value of the 111-kg (245-lb) Rarden L/85 cannon. In its naval form the weapon was effective in terms of its accuracy, range and lethality, but was severely limited in tactical terms by its rate of fire, limited to a cyclic rate of only 90 rounds per minute as a result of the cannon's ammunition of only six rounds, fed in three-round clips.

The mounting had already been considered with revised 30-mm armament, namely the Oerlikon KCB and the Mauser Model F, as the **LS30B** and **LS30F** respectively. The 158-kg (348-lb) Oerlikon L/75 weapon was therefore standardised for what then became the **DS30B** mounting used in conjunction with the Defence Equipment and Systems Mk 5 optronic fire director. The primary advantage of the KCB belt-fed cannon over the Rarden weapon is its cyclic rate of 650 rounds and its 90-round repeat burst capability.

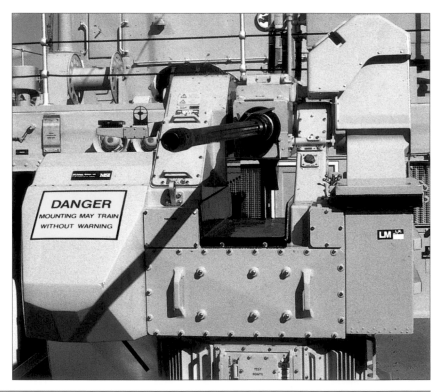

The LS30R's low rate of fire and very limited ammunition supply meant that it had to be aimed with a machine-gun before the main weapon was fired for effect.

The Oerlikon KCB is a more capable weapon than the Rarden cannon in the task of tackling fast-closing targets at shore range, for it has a higher rate of fire and a more extensive range of ammunition types.

SPECIFICATION

DS30B

Calibre: 30 mm	yards) against vessels and 2750 m (3,005 yards) against aircraft
Number of barrels: one	**Rate of fire (cyclic):** 650 rounds per minute
Elevation: -20° to +65°	
Muzzle velocity: 1080-1175 m (3,543-3854 ft) per second	**Weight:** 1200 kg (2,645 lb) with ammunition
Effective range: 10000 m (10,935	**Rounds on mount:** 160

EMERLEC-30 30-mm twin naval gun mounting

Designed and built by the Emerson Electric Company, the **EMERLEC-30** 30-mm twin mounting was originally developed as the **EX-74 Mod 0** for the US Navy to install on the CPIC coastal patrol and interdiction craft, of which only one prototype was ever built. The EX-74 was to have been used in conjunction with the Mk 93 gun fire-control system incorporating the Kollmorgen Mk 35 periscopic director.

Based on two Oerlikon KCB cannon, the EX-74 was

This weapon system could be controlled from the main fire control centre on a ship. However, an air-conditioned cab with night sights was also fitted for the gunner

then developed for export sale as the EMERLEC-30, which has an environmentally controlled cabin for the gunner, day reflex and/or night image-intensifying sights, and an integral below-decks magazine. The

mount can also be operated by remote control from the ship's fire-control system. In emergency an on-mount battery can provide all the power required to operate the guns and fire the full complement of ready-use ammunition carried. Manual gun controls are also fitted as a further back-up.

The mount has been in series production since 1976 and is known to have been bought by the navies of countries such as Colombia, Ecuador, Ethiopia, Greece, Malaysia, Nigeria, the Philippines, South Korea and Taiwan. In most cases the mounting has been installed on missile-armed fast attack craft and large patrol boats. The mounting is highly capable, its fire-control system, high rate of fire and ammunition making it very effective against both aircraft

and light surface vessels.

The mounting is capable of traverse through 360°, and its capabilities are enhanced by its high rates of movement: 90° per second in azimuth and 80° to 85° per second in elevation, both with high acceleration. The two types of ammunition most commonly associated with the EMERLEC-30 mounting's KCB cannon are the HEI, SAPHEI and APDS types. The HEI and SAPHEI rounds each weigh 0.87 kg (30.69 oz) and

fire their 0.46-kg (16.225-oz) projectiles with a muzzle velocity of 1080 m (3,543 ft) per second. The HEI projectile carries 36 g (1.27-oz) of Torpex explosive, while that of the SAPHEI round carries 26 g (0.92 oz) of the same explosive and can penetrate 12 mm (0.47 in) of armour at 1000 m (1,095 yards). The APDS round has a muzzle velocity of 1175 m (3,854 ft) per second.

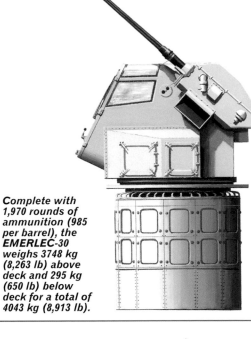

Complete with 1,970 rounds of ammunition (985 per barrel), the EMERLEC-30 weighs 3748 kg (8,263 lb) above deck and 295 kg (650 lb) below deck for a total of 4043 kg (8,913 lb).

SPECIFICATION	
EMERLEC-30	
Calibre: 30 m	yards) against vessels and 2750 m (3,005 yards) against aircraft
Number of barrels: two	**Rate of fire (cyclic):** 1,300 rounds per minute
Elevation: -15° to +80°	
Muzzle velocity: 1080-1175 m (3,543-3,854 ft) per second	**Weight:** 1885 kg (4,156 lb) without ammunition
Effective range: 10000 m (10,935	**Rounds on mount:** 1,970

Phalanx Mk 15 20-mm naval close-in weapon system mounting

A product successively of General Dynamics, Hughes and Raytheon, the **Phalanx Mk 15** close-in weapons system was created for the automatic search and detection, target threat evaluation, tracking and firing against high-performance anti-ship missiles and aircraft as a 'last-ditch' defence. The Phalanx is built around the 20-mm M61A1 six-barrel 'Gatling' gun, and is hydraulically powered. The mount also carries 989 rounds of APDS ammunition firing

depleted uranium projectiles for assured destruction of incoming missiles at short ranges, a radar for target acquisition (top of the mounting) and a radar for target and projectile tracking (front of the mounting).

The system was first fired in prototype seagoing form in 1973, and the baseline **Mk 15 Block 0** entered production late in 1977, the first operational units being installed on the aircraft carriers USS *Enterprise* and *America* during 1980.

The **Mk 15 Block 1** of 1988 switched to pneumatic operation to provide an increase in the maximum firing rate from 3,000 to 4,500 rounds per minute, boosted the ammunition capacity to 1,550 rounds with the option of tungsten rather than DU penetrators, and improved the radar and processing software. The **Mk 15 Block 1A** introduced a high-order processing language. The **Mk 15 Block 1B** of 1999 added a side-mounted integrated FLIR sensor for

better engagement of slow and/or hovering targets, especially under all-weather conditions when there is electronic jamming, and also fires the new Enhanced Lethality Cartridge. Baseline

2C improvements provide an integrated multi-weapon operations capability.

The Phalanx system is widely used by a large number of Western navies.

The Phalanx Mk 15 system is based on autonomous operation once activated. The closed-loop fire-control system tracks the incoming target and outgoing projectiles to ensure that the two coincide in time and space as early as possible and thus well before the missile strikes the ship.

Above: A US Navy Phalanx Mk 15 system opens fire during an exercise at night. The system can hold 989 or, in later models, 1,550 20-mm rounds.

SPECIFICATION	
Phalanx Mk 15 Block 1B	**Effective range:** 1485 m (1,625 yards)
Calibre: 20 mm	
Number of barrels: six	**Rate of fire:** 4,500 rounds per minute
Elevation: -20° to +80°	
Muzzle velocity: 1113 m (3,650 ft) per second	**Weight:** 6169 kg (13,600 lb)
	Rounds on mount: 1,550

Breda Compact Tipo 70 40-mm L/70 twin naval mount

The **Breda Compact Tipo 70** 40-mm L/70 twin naval mount is a joint venture by Breda Meccanica Bresciana and Bofors to produce a system capable of providing an effective point-defence capability against aircraft and anti-ship missiles. The mount is fully automatic in operation, and features a high rate of fire together with a considerable ready-use ammunition supply to the two guns, which are laid by remote controlled high-performance servo units. The mount is available in two versions, the **Tipo A** and **Tipo B** that differ only in weights and the amount of ammunition carried in the turret's magazine (736 rounds in the Tipo A and 444 in the Tipo B). In each variant the magazine itself is divided into two halves, each with a hoist serving one barrel. Three types of 40-mm ammunition are fired: AP Tracer, HE with a direct-action impact fuse, and HE with a proximity

fuse. Both turrets are in production and service with a number of navies round the world, especially as the secondary armament of missile craft.

Dardo

When the mount is coupled to a Selenia RTN-20X I-band fire-control radar with a direct electronic link to the ship's main surveillance radar and fire-control system, the weapon then forms part of the **Dardo** close-in weapon system designed specifically to counter high-speed anti-ship missiles detected only late in their attacks. It does this by utilising the turret's rapid response, high rate of fire and proximity-fused ammunition in order to ensure a kill. The Dardo CIWS is widely fitted in frigate-sized and larger vessels of the Italian navy, and has also been exported to several countries whose navies have bought Italian frigates and missile corvettes.

The Breda Compact Tipo 70 mount is widely used as the secondary gun armament of missile corvettes and the like, providing effective capability against aircraft and missiles, and also against FACs.

SPECIFICATION	
Breda Compact Tipo 70	per second
Calibre: 40 mm	**Effective range:** 3500-4000 m
Number of barrels: two	(3,830-4,375 yards) depending upon
Weight: (with ammunition) Tipo A	target type
7300 kg (16,093 lb) and Tipo B 6300	**Rate of fire:** 600 rounds per
kg (13,889 lb)	minute
Elevation: 0° to + 85°	**Number of rounds carried on**
Muzzle velocity: 1000 m (3,281 ft)	**mount:** see text

Left: Although it lacks any capacity for autonomous operation in the fashion of a true close-in weapons system, the Breda Compact Tipo 70 mount offers the power of two well-proved 40-mm guns firing highly effective ammunition and carried in a mounting with a good ammunition capacity and high rates of traverse and elevation.

Below: On smaller FAC(M)s, the Breda Compact Tipo M can be employed as the forecastle-mounted main gun, its capabilities against surface as well as air targets making it an effective and moderately inexpensive single answer to these dual threats.

Index